Worker Rights and Labor Standards in Asia's Four New Tigers

A Comparative Perspective

Worker Rights and Labor Standards in Asia's Four New Tigers

A Comparative Perspective

Marvin J. Levine
University of Maryland
College Park, Maryland

PLENUM PRESS • NEW YORK AND LONDON

Library of Congress Cataloging-in-Publication Data

Levine, Marvin J., 1930-
    Worker rights and labor standards in Asia's four new tigers : a
comparative perspective / Marvin J. Levine.
        p.   cm.
    Includes bibliographical references and index.
    ISBN 0-306-45477-7
    1. Employee rights--Asia.   2. Industrial relations--Asia.
3. Labor laws and legislation--Asia.   4. Comparative industrial
relations.   I. Title.
HD8653.5.L48   1997
331'.01'1095--dc21   97-8964
                                                               CIP

ISBN 0-306-45477-7

© 1997 Plenum Press, New York
A Division of Plenum Publishing Corporation
233 Spring Street, New York, N. Y. 10013

http:/www.plenum.com

10 9 8 7 6 5 4 3 2 1

Printed in the United States of America

To Dina, Tali, Mark, and Ron

Preface

"From one acorn, a large tree grows." Paraphrasing this time-honored adage, this book developed from small beginnings. My original intent was to develop a journal article dealing with labor relations in the free trade areas of China known as special export zones (SEZs). It soon became evident that little independent labor union activity on the part of Chinese labor organizations was permitted, although foreign joint ventures had unions. My interest was whetted as to the reasons for the almost complete absence of independent Chinese unions and I expanded the investigation of SEZs into an examination of Chinese labor relations in the macro sense.

In the course of studying labor relations in the People's Republic, I ran across a book about Thailand by Robert Muscat which referred to that country as the "fifth tiger." Singapore, Hong Kong, South Korea, and Taiwan are known as the "four tigers" of Asia because of their dramatic economic growth during the past three decades, accompanied originally by restrictions on worker rights and minimal labor standards. I decided to expand what was developing as a book on China into a study covering three other Asian nations that also have experienced heightened economic activity in recent years but at the cost of governmental repression of freedom of association and collective bargaining rights. These three countries are Indonesia, Malaysia, and Thailand, and along with China, I have chosen to refer to them as Asia's "four new tigers." For that matter, in the final analysis, worker rights and labor standards can be subsumed under the general rubric of human rights.

These nations are known as developing countries as against the developed economies of the West, based on levels of economic activity and per capita incomes of the population. I have attempted to explain how worker rights and labor standards have fared against the background of higher growth levels, and whether economic improvements have resulted in political liberalization in these nations. The question is how closely these four countries will follow the Western model or whether they will develop a distinctly Asian paradigm of worker rights and labor standards.

I am grateful to the following persons for their assistance: Dean Miriam Erez of the Israel Institute of Technology for the generous use of research facilities during a recent sabbatical; Lee Preston of the University of Maryland for his incisive comments during the early stages of the book; Arne Kallberg of the University of North Carolina for his thorough review of the manuscript; Alanna Knaus for her invaluable computer assistance; and Barbara Shaw for her timely work on tables and diagrams.

Last but not least, thanks are owed to my editor, Eliot Werner, for his belief in the viability of this endeavor.

Contents

Forced Labor. Unemployment. Unemployment Reduction
Plans. Unemployment Insurance. Social Security Reform.
Pension Developments. State Enterprise Pension Reform.
Health Insurance. Policy Cohesion. Freedom of Association.
The Shenzhen Unions. Unions in Joint Ventures. Future
Prospects.

Proposal. The New Remuneration System. Costs,
Anomalies, and Union Protests. Impact on Grievance
Machinery. Necessity for Review. The Plight of the
Plantation Workers. The Guest Worker Program.
Definitional Exclusion. Wage Levels. Contract Labor.
Foreign Workers. An Evaluation.

PART I

Prologue

CHAPTER 1

Introduction

Four economies in East Asia—the Republic of Korea, Hong Kong, Singapore, and Taiwan (the Republic of China)—exhibited such rapid economic growth during the 1965 to 1990 period that they were termed the "Four Tigers" by many observers. Also close on their heels, the economies of three newly industrializing Asian nations—Indonesia, Malaysia, and Thailand—have grown more than twice as fast as the rest of Asia, roughly three times as fast as Latin America and South Asia, and 25 times faster than Sub-Saharan Africa.[1] However, no assessment of Asian growth and productivity would be complete without including the performance of China, which has achieved annual double-digit growth during the past decade, so much so that 160 million Chinese have emerged from poverty.

These economic success stories have featured high growth rates, substantial reductions in poverty, agricultural transformations, rapid fertility decline, and manufactured export growth policies. Yet, one must inquire about the human capital component involved in these developments, as diagrammed in Figure I-1 where we have developed a descriptive model worker rights/labor standards system, which will measure the level of de jure and/or de facto protection afforded workers in the four countries we will cover. Obviously, this is an ideal system and in a real industrial relations environment one would expect considerable variability from the norms established by an optimum paradigm. A number of questions need to be asked as we follow this line of inquiry. For example, what has been the labor trade-off in terms of the status of worker rights and labor standards in these rapidly developing nations? Are there laws establishing minimum wage and maximum hour requirements for workers? How are female and child labor regulated, if at all? How are union organizing and collective bargaining treated? To what extent does organized labor participate in the political process and are its interests effectively represented? What is the status of occupational safety and health legislation and workers' compensation? Which fringe benefits are defined by statute? Is due process afforded workers whose employment is terminated? Are unemployment benefits available to cushion the shock of economic displacement? Does export-oriented economic policy include the sale of goods produced by forced or prison labor? Will workers receive at least a minimum level of subsistence from publicly mandated pension and retirement plans

3

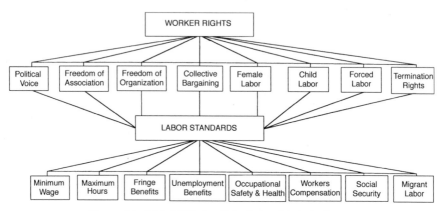

FIGURE I-1. A Model Worker Rights/Labor Standards System

included in social security programs? What safeguards are in place to prevent the exploitation of both domestic and foreign migratory laborers?

Indonesia, with a population approaching 200 million, is the world's most populous Islamic state. Malaysia is the most economically successful Islamic nation. China's 1.25 billion people have only one recognized labor federation (which is government controlled), while Thailand has an independent labor federation and is the only country of the four to be studied that has not experienced colonial status.

In Malaysia, the government has restructured the labor sector to suppress radical activity in an effort to ensure political stability, abolishing trade-based labor unions and promoting the creation of enterprise-based "in-house" labor organizations. In this framework, management and company union representatives are required to jointly formulate and implement work-related policies, following the Japanese model of postwar labor relations. Similarly, labor movements in Thailand and Indonesia, while not being systematically restructured, are nonetheless routinely suppressed at the first sign of radicalism, primarily due to official fear of communism.

No assessment of Asian developments would be complete without consideration of mainland China, in the 1990s Asia's second largest economy after Japan, in terms of total Gross Domestic Product. Despite their pivotal contributions to a burgeoning economy, however, Chinese workers have no legal right to organize independent unions or even to demand safe working conditions. There also is no national minimum wage. In no small part due to these factors, many students shifted their focus from democracy to workers rights after the 1989 Tianenman Square massacre.

We will examine the interplay between these and other significant economic, political and sociological variables. Key issues to be explored will include the following:

1. The arguments that the leaders of China, Indonesia, Malaysia, and Thailand are presenting to counter Western demands for the introduction of minimum labor standards in trade agreements.
2. The inhibiting effects of divergent national values and cultural characteristics on improvements in the status of worker rights and labor standards.
3. The means to provide countries at all stages of development with opportunities for growth that do not depend on abuses of labor standards.
4. The reasons why positive economic developments in China, Indonesia, Malaysia, and Thailand have not produced concomitant improvements in labor conditions.
5. The status of protective labor legislation and its implementation.
6. The type of political regime and the choice of development strategy have important economic consequences for labor.
7. The question as to whether progress toward democratization and human rights is dependent on economic development is complex. In the relationship one has to take into account intervening variables, e.g., the size and character of the middle class, the set of inherited values in a society that affects people's attitudes toward government and liberty, the mechanisms for the distribution of income and wealth.
8. The role that the International Labor Organization (ILO) can play in improving worker rights and labor standards in newly industrializing countries.
9. Politicies and programs to improve working conditions for women and children.

The following synopsis of recent important developments in China, Indonesia, Thailand, and Malaysia will help establish the setting for our investigation of these important topics. An exhaustive literature review determined the paucity of sources dealing with most of the topics covered in the book. Also, due to authoritarian regimes in the four countries, it was not feasible to draw upon governmental sources for information since their biases would prevent the gathering of reliable data. Consequently, I found the Lexis-Nexis database to be invaluable in this respect and utilized sources with higher reliability such as the *Bangkok Post, Business Times* (Malaysia), *Australian Financial Review, Asian Wall Street Journal Weekly, International Herald Tribune*, and *The Straits Times* (Singapore). Wire service reports from the Reuter News Service-Far East and Reuter Textline also were utilized extensively as were State Department Human Rights Reports and Country Reports.

CHINA

The Chinese political system, severely shaken by the prodemocracy protests in 1989, still exists, outliving the communist regimes in the former Soviet Union and Eastern Europe. There has been a significant political transformation since the Mao

Zedong era, although not as drastic as that in the economic system. The main political objective of the country shifted from external revolution to economic development after 1978. The concepts of communism and socialism have undergone fundamental revisions; they were largely stripped of dogmatic ideological elements and became relatively pragmatic. The 14th Party Congress of October 1992, adopted the new concept of "a socialist market economy" and endorsed the pragmatism of Deng Ziaopeng, who claimed to introduce market mechanisms and other capitalist-like economic measures.

The economic reforms began in the rural areas where 800 million Chinese live, emphasizing limited private ownership and Western-style demand–supply variables, and resulted in dramatic increases in per capita income and living standards. Reforms in urban industrial centers stressed the matching of labor demand with supply and attracted high levels of foreign investment in response to the government's export-driven development policy.

These important changes are commonly presented as the product of an ongoing process to develop the institutional and conceptual framework for a socialist commodity economy. At the heart of the rural economic reforms are the contract responsibility systems, which are generally viewed as successful because of the stimulating effect of tying personal incomes directly to output and sales. Recent urban industrial management reforms are based on a comparable assumption that the key to raising labor productivity and improving enterprise efficiency lies in developing contractual relations between the firm and the government and between management and labor. The centerpiece of the urban industrial management reforms is also a set of contract responsibilities that stipulate the rights and responsibilities of each side and tie the personal incomes of managers and employees to both enterprise and personal performance.

As the agricultural economy stagnated at the end of the 1980s, the lessening of government restrictions produced heightened labor mobility, with literally tens of millions of farm workers descending upon urban centers in search of work. Resultant higher levels of unemployment and underemployment have created the potential for social instability in the large cities. Government rhetoric featuring decisions to allow hugely unprofitable state enterprises to slide into bankruptcy has not been matched with meaningful implementation. Policymakers in Beijing are reluctant to impose economic hardship on state employees, fearing that the prospect of economic disequilibrium will jeopardize the perpetuation of Communist Party political control. Double-digit growth rates slowed appreciably in 1995 and 1996, as Beijing stressed deflationary monetary policies.

The labor reform system has been one of the most controversial aspects of the reform efforts. Central to this reform is the idea of abolishing the "iron rice bowl." This means eliminating the system of permanent job tenure and state allocation of jobs. These reform strategies have produced considerable turmoil and instability for China's 150 million industrial workers. Inflation, although reduced substantially in the mid-1990s, threatens to produce the steepest decline in real incomes since the 1989 antigovernment violence. Government at all levels has been unable to indefinitely finance lifetime job security for a bloated, inefficient public sector workforce. Nor can laid-off workers find a softer berth in the private sector, which includes nominal collectives, the hugely successful township and village enterprises, and joint foreign ventures. A reserve army of millions of migrant rural workers flooding into the cities makes it a buyer's market for labor. Employers can afford to be cavalier about wages, working conditions, and occupational health and safety standards in the workplace.

Chinese workers, no longer legally bound to their work units, have experienced the downside of labor reforms, such as an increased incidence of job-related injuries and diseases. Governmental suppression of independent unionism has prevented legitimate representation for China's workers. Moreover, a comprehensive reform of labor laws has not yet resulted in less state repression of efforts at formation of a free labor movement. The central government in Beijing has good reason to be concerned about what it views as a deteriorating situation. Years of rapid economic growth have transformed Chinese society, loosening centralized control over the huge population. For example, in Guangdong, workers angered by dangerous labor conditions have formed more than 800 illegal trade unions and China has witnessed a 50% increase in the number of arbitrated labor disputes, including thousands of strikes and slow-downs. Furthermore, unofficial estimates are that hundreds or thousands more disputes may have flared up without reaching arbitration.

The plight of workers is putting pressure on China's only official labor organization, the All-China Federation of Trade Unions (ACFTU), to help improve factory conditions or risk ceding the role to the still tiny number of labor activists seeking to organize free labor unions. An unauthorized union, the Preparatory Federation for Workers' Rights and Guarantees, continues to issue broadsides and claims credit for wildcat strikes across China, despite unremitting police pressure upon charter members.

For a party that came to power as a peasant-worker movement, labor unrest poses a fundamental challenge to its legitimacy—the last thing the Communist leadership needs on the eve of a potentially wrenching succession crisis as the health of the maximum leader, Deng, rapidly deteriorates. Writing in *Foreign Affairs*, Kenneth Lieberthal paints an ominous picture:

> Large-scale political unrest in China is a possibility. Despite enormous success in achieving rapid economic growth, there are fundamental strains in the society. Inflation, over 20 percent in recent years, is dangerously high, and corruption is widely resented among the populace. Tens of millions of "floaters" have flocked to the major cities, differentiation of wealth is growing, many state enterprise workers fear the effects of further development of the market economy, control over individuals through their work units has eroded, and massive construction projects are displacing hundreds of thousands, causing tensions. If the political succession to Deng Xiaoping does not go smoothly, these underlying pressures may erupt into enormous street demonstrations and protests.[2]

We will discuss developments as China continues to evolve away from the totalitarian model of the Mao era and the authoritarian regime of the Deng period. The question remains whether the drive toward economic decentralization will continue without a reversion to centralized control in the name of preserving societal stability.

Or will China gradually become a "soft authoritarian" regime like Taiwan or South Korea in the early 1980s?

INDONESIA

Indonesia is the largest Muslim country in the world, with nearly 200 million people, and the fourth largest overall. In the mid-nineties there is an abundant supply of inexpensive labor available to employers, although finding skilled and professional staff is extremely problematic. The labor force of 75.5 million is larger than most Asian countries' populations and predictions are that a plentiful supply of unskilled workers will keep wages low for decades to come. The labor pool is growing at about 2.5% annually, with more than 2.3 million young workers entering the job market each year. Although the economy is likely to continue healthy growth in coming years, the workforce will grow even faster. Reliable unemployment statistics are difficult to come by but estimates range as high as 30%, with underemployment hovering around 40%. Over 55% of Indonesia's workers are engaged in some form of agricultural enterprise.

President Suharto is in the fourth decade of his paternalistic dictatorship over the former Dutch colony. Like China, Indonesia has sustained high annual GDP growth rates, ranging from 5.8 to 7.5% since 1988. Unemployment was not considered a serious problem until the mid-1990s. As a concept, its relevance was questioned, especially for the country's large population. The basic assumption has been that, given the poverty in which most people live, the great majority of Indonesians cannot afford to be without a job and will accept any employment regardless of low pay and squalid working conditions.

However, the national economic structure is undergoing rapid changes. These include increased urbanization, the growth of manufacturing, a greater incidence of wage employment, and higher educational attainment. High levels of unemployment and underemployment have emerged as serious national problems. In the absence of a national minimum wage, area wage councils operate under the auspices of the national wage council to establish regional minimum wages. These standards, which vary markedly from one area to another, however, have constantly lagged behind basic needs figures and fallen short of providing a decent standard of living for millions of Indonesians, because local governments have not taken these minimum requirements seriously. For instance, the minimum wage recently in the urban Jakarta region is Rp 2,000 (U.S. $2) daily. The only official national labor federation, the government-organized Serikat Pekerga Seluruh Indonesia (SPSI), has calculated that the basic wage in Jakarta would pay for less than 80% of a worker's minimum physical requirements by the end of the century—but this still will leave Indonesian wages among the lowest in Asia.

Little or no attention was paid to workers' problems in Indonesia until the end of the 1980s, but the Indonesian government's export-led economic boom produced a strong reaction after three or four years. According to the *Far East Economic Review*, quoting Indonesian labor activists, workers are "paid slave wages, are often malnour-ished, have little concept of their legal rights and barely share in the profits they create. An upsurge of strikes, work stoppages, and demonstrations supports the contention that labor unrest is increasing."[3] Statistics on strikes are sketchy, but there has been a marked increase in the number of unauthorized wildcat strikes in recent years. While the government remains committed to improving the lot of workers, Jakarta does not back strike activities.

A direct consequence of the labor unrest has been the emerging strains in Indonesian relations with the United States stemming from Washington's tougher approach on labor issues and human rights. American labor leaders have long been critical of wage levels and working conditions in Indonesia but were unable to attract serious interest under the Reagan and Bush administrations. The Clinton administra-tion warned Jakarta to improve labor conditions if it wished to preserve access to the General System of Preferences (GSP) program of reduced tariffs for exports to the United States.

A key issue in the dispute has been Jakarta's refusal to officially recognize any major labor organization other than the state-dominated SPSI, which is widely regarded as a tame organization and is not recognized by the International Confedera-tion of Free Trade Unions (ICFTU). When the Indonesian Labor Welfare Union (SBSI) attempted to hold what would have been its first national congress, it was banned from doing so by the police. A second development that fueled local criticism (and was subsequently picked up on by a visiting U.S. trade delegation) was the rape and murder of female labor activist Marsinah in May 1993, several days after she had helped organize a demonstration for wage increases at a factory in which she worked in East Java. In November 1994, Muchtar Pakpahan, the leader of SBSI, was jailed for three years for inciting violence, although he was released before his sentence was up.

Indonesia and other Asian countries have been critical of the Western linkage between worker rights and international trade liberalization. They have strongly condemned the Western approach toward the issue of human rights in the developing nations. They contend that the norms and precepts for the observance of human rights vary from society to society and from one period to another within the same society. Their position is that in the developing countries, individual human rights should be balanced with the level of national economic development—otherwise it would damage social stability and economic growth.

As an illustration, the Indonesian policy can be gleaned from the opening speech by President Suharto at the Tenth Non-Aligned Movement Summit held in Jakarta on September 1, 1992. As the new chairperson of the movement, he denounced Western attempts to exploit human rights by linking them to economic aid. He made it clear that the rights of the individual had to be balanced with the rights of the community. "Such a balance is critical," he pointed out, "for its absence can lead to a denial of the rights of the society as a whole and can lead to instability and anarchy."

We shall discuss the influence of a nation's cultural values on worker rights and labor standards. Suharto's comments have a cultural connotation that undoubtedly contributes to the fact that Indonesia does not have a strong labor movement by

Western standards. The labor relations system is based on the national ideology of *Pancasila*, or five principles, as enunciated in the 1945 constitution. The elaboration of Pancasila in the field of industrial relations emphasizes the traditional Indonesian values of harmony, mutual self-help, and consultations leading to consensus. Government, labor, and employers are expected to work harmoniously together to achieve national development, social justice, and an equitable share of economic development.

As with China, the central government recognizes only one union, and although Jakarta has been promoting decentralization allowing independent unions legal affiliation, it remains to be seen whether independent industrial unions will evolve into effective and free labor organizations. In the meantime, only Chinese workers receive less pay than Indonesian laborers.

THAILAND

Over the past 30 years, Thailand has consistently been among the five fastest growing countries in the world. It has an economy in which industry has surpassed agriculture as a proportion of GDP. Since 1965, Thailand's economic growth rate has averaged over 7% annually and its share of world trade and foreign investment continues to grow. Since the 1960s, the government has closely aligned its policies with the needs of foreign investors, especially multinational corporations. This has been in conjunction with the government's absolute control over the labor movement and the organizing activities of Thai workers. Many of the repressive laws introduced in 1960 to curb labor movement organizing are still in existence, and despite the outward appearances of more liberal tendencies from within government circles, security laws—which previously focused on the Communist Party—have been broadened to include "economic offenses" as well. Demonstrations by workers against their employers are quickly put down and news of it suppressed, especially on radio and television stations which are owned either by the government or the army, Privately owned newspapers and magazines have a bit more freedom to report the news.

In common with other Asian nations, Thailand has concentrated on labor-intensive industrialization as the way to economic development. In the 1960s, under a policy of import substitution, there was an attempt to create a Thai manufacturing industry and to raise the level of agricultural production. Economically, import substitution failed as the overall level of imports—machinery, components, and raw materials—actually increased. Despite its failure as a development policy, import substitution had a long-lasting structural effect on the pay and conditions of Thai workers.

In order to maintain the companies' high profit levels, wages were reduced and hours were extended. Trade unions were banned. This was made possible by the authoritarian rule of the military government. All working people suffered severely from the effects of reduced incomes and longer working hours. As wages became lower and lower, more and more women—especially young women—entered the industrial labor force in order to help with the basic family income. Companies also began to realize the advantage in hiring women, who could be paid even less than men.

Although this development policy failed in its objective to create a modern, self-sufficient Thailand, capable of producing a wide range of goods for middle-class consumption, it nevertheless laid the groundwork for a new development strategy that demanded, above all, a low-paid, flexible, and subdued workforce. In the 1970s Thailand shifted its development policies toward promoting exports and actively sought investment by multinational firms. The government offered financial inducements and a skilled and submissive workforce already established in labor-intensive operations. One of the most important of these has been electronics, which characterized the shift in the 1980s away from light manufacturing to the production of high value products for export.[4] The government of Prime Minister Barnhart Silpa-archa is continuing these policies into the mid-1990s.

Influenced strongly by these developments, organized labor in Thailand had been fragmented and disunited even before legislation removed state enterprises from the Labor Relations Act and dissolved unions in that sector in April 1991. Thailand has one of the lowest levels of unionization in Asia with under 3% of the industrial workforce being organized. Furthermore, most of the Thai unions are based in a single business. Until the military takeover in 1991, union strength was concentrated in the state enterprise sector, which, with 167,000 members, accounted for half of total union membership and had most of the largest and strongest unions. Private sector organization progressed only slightly, due to a number of legal and cultural factors militating against further organization in private firms—such as ineffective legal bars to unfair dismissal and traditionally paternalistic relations between employers and their workers.

Before the dissolution of the state enterprise unions, the strongest single labor organization was the State Enterprise Relations Group (SELRG), a loose coalition of 25 state enterprise unions. On November 14, 1991, the SELRG reorganized itself as the State Enterprise Relations Confederation (SERC). After the military government dissolved the SELRG, the following major labor federations competed for leadership of the labor movement: the Thai Trade Union Congress (TTUC); the Labor Congress of Thailand (LCT); the National Congress of Thai Labor (NCTL); and the National Free Labor League (NFLL).

Unity and cohesion among the four key federations remain an elusive goal for Thai unionists. Individual union leaders continue to put their personal goals and aspirations ahead of the movement as a whole. Furthermore, even within some congresses, serious rivalries and factional problems prevent internal unity and agreement. Nonetheless, in 1992, the congresses were able to unite in presenting joint minimum wage demands to the government, countering the National Wage Commission's position that minimum wages should be abolished since market forces would determine a fair daily wage. Predictably, the labor movement opposed the idea while employers tended to support it. Workers cited publicized cases of employment of children under inhumane conditions as evidence of how employers would treat workers if there was no minimum wage. Also, in January 1993, the LCT, TTUC, and several industrial federations set up a committee to look into a merger into a single federation.

The International Labor Organization (ILO) strongly protested the dissolution of state enterprise unions and also decried revisions of local laws that required at least 50% of the workers at a workplace to be involved in any call for a work stoppage, claiming this makes it almost impossible for workers to strike. Weakened by the breakup of the most powerful state enterprise union, organized labor remains fractionalized, with little bargaining power. Also, Thailand's legislature includes few direct representatives of the labor movement.

In reality, individual workers in Thailand rarely have significant bargaining leverage. Those who wish to affiliate with unions may, at least in theory, enhance their bargaining strength. The normative structure for labor–management relations in Thailand is thorough and comprehensive, drawing upon many of the labor law concepts familiar to American employers and unions. In some respects, the Thai Labor Relations Act resembles the U.S. National Labor Relations Act, being comprehensive in coverage, although it exempts farm workers and civil servants. State enterprise workers were covered until specifically exempted in 1991.

A number of factors have contributed to Thailand's traditionally low rate of unionization. Culturally, the Thais are not as adversarial as are their counterparts in many Western countries, particularly the United States. They have been characterized as warm and hospitable, very trusting, and even childlike. Consequently, a Thai employer's relationship with employees tends to be paternalistic and workers usually take management's power for granted. Moreover, neither the rules of labor law nor the government's enforcement of them provide effective barriers to unfair dismissals for union activities. Particularly where employees are unrepresented, they have little bargaining power in an economic climate of rising unemployment and underemployment.

While the present economic outlook remains promising, a number of recent challenges to sustained growth have presented themselves in quite dramatic ways. A wave of strikes and protests against layoffs revealed Thailand's loss of competitiveness as a low labor-cost country and its lack of a trained labor force for more technology-intensive industry. Also, even where unions exist, hard-nosed collective bargaining is rarely practiced. The adversarial system of industrial relations has not developed as yet in Thailand.

MALAYSIA

Malaysia has a moderately broad regime. The government relies on the Malay aristocracy and landowners (who provide support from a portion of the rural mass base), the large number of Chinese business managers (who can deliver portions of the urban base), and a growing multiracial urban professional class. The governing coalition is an attempt to encompass as broad a social spectrum as possible while maintaining Malay political control and a secular state.

In April 1995, the coalition led by Prime Minister Mahathir Mohamad won a landslide in the general election. An important contributor was the swing in the Chinese vote away from the opposition Democratic Action Party (DAP) to the Malaysian Chinese Association (MCA), which supports Dr. Mahathir, indicating that the Chinese in Malaysia have come to accept Malay political dominance.

Malaysia is formally an electoral democracy, although those opposition groups that are tolerated (many are not) are manipulated to ensure the "correct" outcome to elections and other political debates. The government follows thoroughly cooptive policies and generally relies on collaborative and paternalistic mechanisms of control to attain substantial national consensus, although outright coercion is reserved for the rare occasion when the formal tools do not work. Malaysia has constructed a multiethnic ruling coalition of Muslims, Christians, and Hindus that provides broad support from ethnic Malays and at least some support from other ethnic communities. While it is hardly all encompassing—excluding substantial components of the religious and secular Malay community, as well as a good portion of the Chinese community—it is also diverse enough to provide state authorities options to build coalitions in support of their policy preferences with elements of the regime and some outside it. Malaysia is characterized as a state-dominated system, where the administration has considerable flexibility.

In 1995, the Malaysian economy grew by 9.6%, making it the eighth consecutive year in which real GDP grew by more than 8%. Projections for 1996 called for a "cooling off" in the economy, with a growth rate of a mere 8.5%. The government has played down the risks of overheating the economy, pointing to a low 1995 inflation rate of 3.4%. In particular, foreigners are blamed for not appreciating the magnificent achievement inherent in Malaysia's economic growth record.[5]

In the ideal social model, money and freedom are connected. As investment strengthens a country's economy, assuring a more prosperous, stable government, individuals are freed from the preoccupation of poverty and correspondingly gain greater control over their labor. In reality, however, a tension exists between increased economic growth and the protection of workers' rights. Underdeveloped nations seeking to industrialize tend to market the abundance of natural resources in their country, including and often emphasizing the availability of cheap labor. As industrialization benefits these nations, and foreign investors reap profits, workers expect to share proportionately in those gains. The respective governments may thus find themselves caught between the investors they have carefully courted and the workers they govern. At some point these countries will be forced to choose between continued governmental favoritism toward foreign investors and government insistence on minimum health, safety, and wage standards for workers. The former risks the exploitation and distrust of constituents, while the latter risks alienating foreign investors who may move their business elsewhere.

Malaysia is currently torn between promoting foreign investment and developing worker rights. Years after the successful implementation of various incentive plans designed to attract foreign investment, Malaysia's labor force has become increasingly restless. It has become a major concern for investors who were originally attracted to Malaysia, despite its comparatively high wages, because the country has a reputation for peaceful labor relations. The dispute has centered around the right of Malaysian workers to form independent unions. Presently, the right to unionize is limited. There are strict guidelines that govern the circumstances under which the government will recognize a union. Strikes must be approved by a government agency and workers who strike without following the regulations may be dismissed without remuneration.

In recent years, international labor rights organizations have focused international attention on the Malaysian labor policy, accusing the government of suppressing the rights of workers to bargain collectively. Because the situation in Malaysia is similar to other developing countries hoping to attract foreign investment, the manner in which it addresses the labor situation is likely to set an important precedent.

According to the General Agreement on Tariffs and Trade (GATT), Malaysia is the twenty-third largest exporter and the twenty-fourth largest importer, and its position has improved since it first made it to the league of major traders in 1990. The rapid economic growth it has experienced is no mean feat. It outperformed many developed countries and was the fastest growing economy in the region, after China. There can be no doubt of Malaysia's economic success, but what about its protection of worker rights and labor standards? We shall analyze the impact of Malaysian rules and regulations on Malaysian workers, discussing the regulation of labor and the events leading up to the union controversy. We shall also explain the internal and external forces pressuring the government to formulate labor policy and the government response to these forces. The situation for workers and investors is likely to worsen unless a compromise is reached in which investors bear the cost of increased worker freedom.

In the first section of the book, we begin with a discussion of developments in China, notably the political and economic landscape.

Part II

China

Further, the hierarchical regulations governing the enterprise specifically prohibit the union from taking up workers' grievances. This activity is assigned by the central committee to the Party Committee, the "legitimate" line of authority. The expected role of the trade union in China is to provide a political education for the work force and although charged with protecting the workers' interests, to cooperate with management.

J. H. COLL[5]

The People's Republic of China is an immense nation, the third largest land mass in the world behind the former Soviet Union and Canada, with a population approaching 1.3 billion, far and away the most populous country in the world. Its labor force is twice as large as the populations of the United States and Canada combined. Its agricultural labor force is about 100 times as large as its U.S. counterpart. Over 400 million Chinese are under the age of 20. The Chinese aged 15 to 19 (120 million) and aged 20 to 24 (126 million) are now struggling to enter the labor force at a time of dynamic change and shifting ground rules. More than half the population has received only a primary school education.

More than 75% of China's labor force is engaged in agriculture, which accounts for only 20% of China's GNP. There are approximately 150 million urban workers and an additional 110 to 120 million persons employed in township and village enterprises in rural areas. Recognizing an opportunity to broaden its appeal, China's tiny but determined dissident community has seized upon labor issues as a promising new form of agitation. Strikes, all of them illegal, are increasing substantially across the nation. Interestingly, many of these labor disputes are not classic struggles of workers pitted against bosses. Instead, they feature alliances of vested labor and management interests against urgently needed public sector reform. Central authorities, frightened by prospects of mass unemployment and social unrest, have had little choice but to keep bailing out the state enterprises with infusions of working capital.

Although the All-China Federation of Trade Unions (ACFTU) does not function as a labor organization in the conventional sense of the term—its primary role as a governmental adjunct is to enhance productivity—we will examine issues such as the proper role of unions in improving labor market outcomes, equity of incomes, job security, and workplace standards in China. As Figure II-1 demonstrates, China is woefully inadequate in its protection of worker rights and labor standards. The pivotal question becomes whether the transition to a market-driven economy from a centrally planned model will take account of the needs of labor. Or will the drive toward economic decentralization continue without a reversion to centralized control in the name of preserving social order? Governments and workers are adjusting to a changing world, but the legacy of the past can make change difficult or frightening (see Figure II-1).

It should be remembered that China remains a one-party state, ruled by the Chinese Communist Party through a 21-member Politburo and small circle of officially retired but still powerful senior leaders. Almost all top civilian, police, and military positions at the national and regional levels are held by party members. Despite official adherence to Marxism-Leninism, in recent years economic decision making has become less ideological, more decentralized, and increasingly market oriented. Fundamental human rights provided for in the Constitution, including freedom of speech and association, are frequently ignored in practice, and challenges

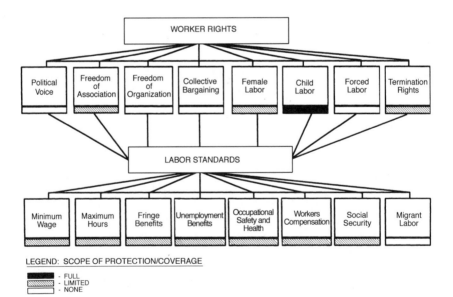

FIGURE II-1. Workers Rights/Labor Standards in China

to the Communist Party's political authority are often dealt with harshly and arbitrarily. The state judicial, procuratorial, and penal systems are poorly monitored due to the absences of adequate legal safeguards or adequate enforcement of existing safeguards for those detained, accused, or imprisoned. Labor activists who promote freedom of workers to join independent labor unions for the purpose of collective representation have been subjected to widespread and well-documented human rights abuses, including torture, forced confessions, and arbitrary detentions.

We will discuss these and other developments in this first section of the book, beginning with an analysis of the political and economic background as it affects worker rights and labor standards in the People's Republic of China.

CHAPTER 2

The Political and
Economic Background

AFTER TIANENMEN SQUARE

Political and economic decisions are inextricably intertwined in most nations, and China is no exception to this general rule. We will now examine significant political and economic developments since the prodemocracy movement was crushed in 1989, in order to determine their actual and potential impact on the labor scene.

The structure of China's political system merits treatment since its parameters indicate whether hopes for political liberalization with concurrent improvements in the status of workers are realistic possibilities in the mid-1990s.

RECENT HISTORICAL OVERVIEW

The People's Republic was established in October 1949 following a civil war in which Chinese Communist forces ousted the Kuomintang (Nationalist) government of Chiang Kai-Shek, which fled to the nearby island of Taiwan. Communist Party (CCP) Chairman Mao Zedong launched the Great Proletarian Cultural Revolution of 1966 that was designed to prevent the establishment of a ruling class over the working peasantry. In 1982, CCP Politburo (Political Bureau) leader Deng Xiapeng purged the party of all left-wing Maoists, installed socialist economic reform policies, and initiated stricter national censorship against Western "bourgeois liberalization." On June 3–4, 1989, the government ordered a crackdown on student-led prodemocracy demonstrators in Beijing's Tianenman Square, who were demanding that Deng and Premier Li Peng resign. Hundreds, possibly thousands, were killed in the incident, while others fled to Hong Kong to escape the subsequent wave of government arrests and executions. In 1993, tension continued to build between China and the international community over Beijing's poor human rights record, and the government pressed to speed up the second phase of Deng's socialist economic program. In June 1994, heightened friction with the United States over Washington's demand that China improve its human rights record was greatly ameliorated by the American decision to renew China's lucrative most favored nation (MFN) trading status with American businesses; a status that had been linked by U.S. leaders to Beijing's improvement of its human rights policies. In the summer of 1995, as this book was being written, U.S.-Sino relations plummeted due to the arrest of the prominent dissident, Harry Wu, who happened to be a U.S. citizen, for alleged theft of state secrets and China's marked displeasure at the visit of the Taiwanese president to Washington at the invitation of the Clinton administration, which succumbed to pressure from the right wing of the Republican-dominated Congress.

STRUCTURE OF GOVERNMENT

China is divided into 22 provinces, five autonomous regions, and three munici- palities. The provinces range from the most populous, Sichuan, with 109 million people, to its vast neighbor Qinghai with just 4.5 million. The most recent adjustment was the 1988 severing of Hainan Island from Guangdong province on the south coast, to become a separate province, as well as a special economic zone (SEZ). Four other SEZs had been established in 1980 on the southern seaboard. The SEZs enjoy considerable financial autonomy, and a more liberal climate for foreign investors, although their role was somewhat undercut by the opening in 1984 of 14 more coastal cities with similar incentives to foreign investment. The autonomous regions have no more autonomy than provinces. The names, however, recognize the prerevolutionary predominance of non-Han (the majority ethnic group) ethnic groups in Guangxi (Zhuang, an ethnic group in southwestern China), Tibet, Xinjiang (Turkic, Uighur Muslims), Inner Mongolia (Mongols) and Ningxia (Chinese, Hui Moslems). The municipalities of Beijing, Shanghai, and Tianjin are provincial-level entities. Below the provincial level, administration is further subdivided into prefectures, counties, and townships, and within cities, into districts. The communes established during the Great Leap Forward of 1958–1959 as the country's basic administrative unit have been disbanded. In some places, however, the communes' subdivisions—"pro- duction brigades" comprising several villages, and "production teams," part of or an entire village—still function within the new framework of contract responsibility systems. By the end of 1991 there were 151 rural prefectures, 187 prefecture-level cities, 289 county-level cities, and 1,894 counties. There were 650 districts—the urban administrative subdivision. The next major administrative change is to be the incorporation of the Special Administrative Regions of Hong Kong, when it reverts from the United Kingdom to Chinese sovereignty in 1997, Macau, to be handed back by Portugal in 1999, and Taiwan, to be "reunified" soon."[1]

China's present Constitution was adopted by the National People's Congress on December 4, 1982. It recognizes the Communist Party as the core leadership of the republic and restores the largely ceremonial post of president as head of state. It abolishes the right to strike and excludes freedom of speech. The Constitution guarantees minority rights, equal pay for equal work, and freedom of worship, and requires family planning and the payment of taxes.

Executive power is vested in the State Council, whose members are appointed by the National People's Congress for terms that run concurrent with Congress. The Council is composed of the president, vice president, premier (state council chairperson), vice premiers, state councillors, and ministers, all of whom are responsible to the National People's Congress. Assisted by the vice president, the president appoints representatives abroad and ratifies treaties. The premier presides over the State Council and administers all national policies with the assistance of the vice premiers and state councilors. Ministers are responsible for matters related to their respective portfolios. The national People's Liberation Army (PLA) also commands substantial political influence under the leadership of the Central Military Commission chairperson.

In theory, the supreme organ of state legislative power is the National People's Congress (NPC). It passes laws and treaties, nominates the executive, and approves the constitution. Its roughly 3000 members are indirectly elected from lower-level People's Congresses every five years. It meets in a plenary session of two to three weeks once a year, usually in March or April. In the interim many of its powers are vested in a Standing Committee, of around 200 members, which drafts laws and handles NPC business when it is not in session. In practice, the NPC has never acted as the true source of power. It has been a rubber stamp, approving decisions made by the Communist Party.

Under Deng a measure of direct electoral democracy has been introduced at the lower-level People's Congresses, at the township (or district) and county levels. There are elections every three years. In theory, any candidate can stand if nominated by ten voters, and there have to be between 30 and 50% more candidates than seats. In practice, however, all candidates are required to support the leading role of the Communist Party.

The highest organ of state administration is the State Council, in effect the cabinet. It composition is decided on by the NPC, acting on recommendation from the Communist Party. It is headed by a prime minister, whose term is in theory concurrent with the five-year life of the NPC. The work of the State Council is presided over by an executive board, usually with about 15 members, comprising the prime minister, his deputies (in 1993 there were four deputy premiers), state councillors, and a secretary-general. Below the State Council come the various ministries and commissions, as well as a number of important state-owned industrial enterprises (see Figure 2-1).[2]

In the past, the NPC's nearly 3,000 delegates met for two weeks each year to rubber-stamp policies that had already been considered by much smaller groups in less public settings. In March 1995, however, China's parliament witnessed unprecedented dissent on votes on two candidates proposed by the government for elevation to the rank of vice prime minister. Wei Bangguo received the support of more than 85% of the 2,752 delegates, but the second candidate, Jiang Chungyun, received only a 63% positive response. Secret balloting resulted in 391 abstentions, while 605 delegates opposed Mr. Jiang, and 10 did not vote at all.

Western politicians would regard these results as a landslide, but in China candidates routinely garner 90% or more of the vote. The target of the dissenters was

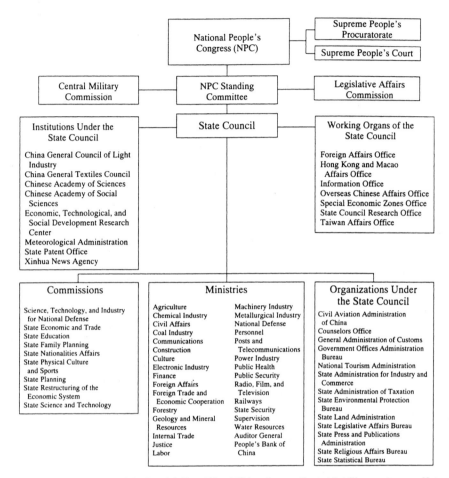

FIGURE 2-1. Government of the People's Republic of China. *Source*: Central Intelligence Agency. *Note*: The Eighth National People's Congress convened March 1993. This chart represents the organization of the Chinese government as of February 1994.

not the candidates but their powerful sponsor, Jiang Zemin, who is a one-man troika, presiding as state president, general secretary of the Communist Party, and chairman of the Central Military Commission. He has been officially designated the "core of the next generation of China's leadership," and while today he is perceived as receiving the polite support of rivals, he is considered vulnerable if, as is considered probable, a period of national instability follows after the demise of his sponsor, the 92-year-old Deng Xiaopeng. He had handpicked the two new vice-ministers, as well as cronies and proteges to top positions in the government, party, and army, to solidify his political base. The lukewarm endorsement of Bangguo and Chungyun was interpreted as equivalent to a vote of no confidence in Mr. Jiang by the National People's Congress.[3]

JUDICIARY

The Supreme People's Court is elected by and responsible to the National People's Congress. It is the highest judicial body and oversees a hierarchy of lower people's courts. Headed by an independent Supreme People's Procuratorate, a parallel system of procuratorate courts ensures the observance of law and the prosecution of criminal cases. It supervises corresponding lower procuratorates at various regional and local levels.

The hierarchy of people's courts, ranging from local people's courts through intermediate and then higher people's courts to the Supreme People's Court, is headed by the Ministry of Justice. The ministry was reestablished in 1979 (it had been abolished in 1959 during Mao's "Great Leap Forward"). Before 1979, arrests and sentences had to be approved by Community Party committees. Although this practice was abolished in 1979, criminal law is still largely applied by the government as a form of public education, with periodic campaigns of mass arrests and executions used to frighten law-breakers.

People's courts, at all levels, deal with criminal, civic, and economic matters in separate tribunals. Local people's mediation committees supplement the work of the courts by dealing with minor criminal offenses and civil disputes, as well as helping implement government policy (such as the one-child per couple policy) at street level.

There is a similar hierarchy of people's procurates, reestablished in 1979 after their abolition in the cultural revolution, extending from the localities to the Supreme People's Procurate. These check up on state officials in the courts and the public security organs to ensure that they are observing the law.

THE STATUS OF INDEPENDENT LABOR UNIONS—CONTROL AND SUPPRESSION

Although economic developments have loosened the Communist Party's grip over ordinary citizens, it has maintained a constant vigil over labor activities. Despite the internationally recognized role of unions to protect workers' rights and interests, Beijing pursues a policy of outlawing all labor organizations outside the auspices of the official All-China Federation of Trade Unions. In 1994 the party began to strengthen party cells in business enterprises in efforts to suffocate the development of autonomous workers' organizations in China. The crackdown on independent workers' unions intensified, with labor activists across the country harassed and arrested by authorities at all levels. The increase in propaganda on party cells in the workplace by the official media was interpreted as a further move to intensify party control over the independent workers' movement. Moreover, the nonstate sector was not exempted from the requirement to set up party cells.

Some 60% of the shareholding enterprises and a total of 900 foreign-funded firms in the Shenzhen Special Economic Zone established party cells. The local newspaper characterized party members in one joint venture in Shenzhen as the "core" of production and management in the enterprise. "The Hong Kong partner is so confident with these party cells ... that it has proposed scrapping the board of directors' decision to have a Hong Kong-appointed deputy general manager to oversee the enterprise," it said. However, the Trade Union Center in Hong Kong cast doubts on the effectiveness of these party cells.[4]

The process by which political control is preserved over trade unions is described in the following terms:

> The standard policy of union leadership appointment (and removal) by party committee or company directors is designed to produce willing shills. Appointment is reward for loyal party service and the appointee is expected to propagandize and certainly not create waves. Recently Party General Secretary Ziyan spoke out and recommended that union leaders be elected. As a result attempts are being made to institute open election of union officials at shop floor levels. Obviously, resistance from the established bureaucracy is formidable and gains are slow.[5]

If the Communist Party is unable by these political means to control labor organizations, President Jiang Zemin has unequivocally stated that "resolute measures used to quell the 1989 protests were necessary to maintain social stability and economic development and will be repeated if the need arises." While student and intellectual activists have been carefully monitored, the major focus of the authorities' recent clampdown has been on workers' organizations. Worker dissatisfaction over rising prices and government corruption was the real force behind the mass protests in Beijing and other major cities in 1989. The government has been determined to prevent labor organizations such as the shortlived Beijing Autonomous Workers' Federation, established by labor activist Han Dongfang in 1989, from gaining a foothold in the factories again.

The authorities have launched a number of preemptive strikes against embryonic labor organizations, detaining more than 100 activists over the past five years. With labor unrest increasing once more in many Chinese cities, efforts have been concentrated on preventing workers' groups from mobilizing a potentially explosive movement which could pose a serious threat to Party rule.

For the Party, social stability must be maintained at all costs. Without stability, the Party argues, there can be no economic development. Throughout Chinese history, the erosion of central authority has signaled the collapse of the dynasty, something which the party leaders are well aware of and perhaps no one more so than Jiang Zemin.[6]

THE FIVE CONFLICT PERIODS

In actuality, Chan has pointed to five episodes during the past 50 years when Chinese workers, sometimes led by official unions, have engaged in forceful political action.[7] The Party has successfully minimized the significance of these events so that the general populace has only a dim recollection of their occurrence. The first conflict occurred soon after liberation when the Communist trade unions lost a power struggle for independence from the Party. The incident was noted only as the culmination of intraparty factionalism. The second conflict broke out in 1956–57 during the Hundred Flowers period and resulted in the imprisonment of workers and union activists and the demise of Lai Ruoyu, the new chairman of the ACFTA, who had led a drive for a more independent federation. The third round of confrontation occurred during the Cultural Revolution (1966–69) and produced widespread violence. It was of wider scope that the 1989 workers' movement, in terms of its duration and the number of workers ultimately jailed or killed. The workers' organizations that arose in 1967 were highly sophisticated and their relative autonomy resembled that of quasi-political parties. However, their activities were completely overshadowed by the publicity generated by the violence of the Red Guards. The fourth period of political confrontation developed when groups of workers massed at Tianenmen Square in 1976 to commemorate Zhou Enlai's death. This event was officially recorded as a popular rebellion against the tyranny of the Gang of Four, without any working class overtones. The fifth cycle of confrontation occurred within the protest movement of 1989, but again the role of workers (and the labor unions) was minimized in the public consciousness due to the inordinate publicity accorded student activities and the government on this occasion labeled worker participants as unemployed vagrants and hooligans.[8]

In the history of sporadic Chinese working class movements in which Communist labor unions participated as allies, questions have been raised as to the similarity of their goals, and whether the unions had ever defended workers' rights vis-à-vis the Party. Obviously, the unions and other cadres, when functioning merely as an arm of enterprise administration, opposed workers' interests in their corrupt, inefficient, and ineffectual activities. However, the bureaucratic organization within the political structure of China's one-party communist state sometimes acted in support of the Party's collective interests and/or its members' individual interests.

ECONOMIC OVERVIEW

The most gratifying result of the comprehensive economic reforms undertaken during the 15 years has been a strong spurt in production, particularly in agriculture in the early 1980s. Industry has also posted major gains, especially in coastal areas near Hong Kong and opposite Taiwan, where foreign investment and modern production methods have helped spur production of both domestic and export goods. Output has risen substantially, particularly in the favored coastal areas. Popular resistance, changes in central policy and loss of authority by rural cadres have weakened China's population control program, which is essential to the nation's long-term economic viability.

The rate of urban unemployment in China has remained at the low level of under 3% in the 1990s, while average real wages are up by 4.5%. The Chinese government has also expanded the range of unemployment insurance and provides a modest level of insurance for retired workers.

Officially, the Communist Party professes its awareness of the need for vigilance and reform. It understands that economic liberalization has raised peoples' expectations and it is trying hard to coopt interests that might otherwise coalesce into rival party centers. It is starting to champion consumer rights, workers' rights against foreign employers, even environmental concerns. It is reconsidering an old idea of developing a more professional civil service.

The Party also has been reassured of its hegemony by its relatively steady relations with the army despite a purge of fractious officers in 1992. Mao once maintained that "the party rules the gun"; in practice, the relationship has proved rather more ambivalent, the two hierarchies being scarcely separable. Every officer of the People's Liberation Army is a party member. Meanwhile, the PLA's budget has been substantially increased, for example, by 25% in 1994. Many of its units are profiting from economic reform by managing private businesses on the side. One estimate is that the PLA now owns about 20,000 commercial companies, half of them in Guangdong.[9]

Since China started economic reforms in 1978, the economy seemed to have established a pattern. Growth would start, accelerate, generate inflation, and once every five years, the authorities would slam on the brakes. Hence, in the summer of 1993, China's economic czar, Zhu Rongji, decided the economy needed cooling, and restraints were applied. Since then, however, the brakes have been released twice and are now being applied for the third time.

At the annual National People's Congress in the spring of 1995, Prime Minister Li Peng acknowledged that "mistakes" made "at all levels" of his government saw inflation in 1994 read 21.7%, the highest level since the Communist takeover in 1949. The unacceptably high rate, according to Li, "aroused great resentment among the masses," and foreshadowed a broad economic retrenchment policy. Consumer price inflation, hitting hard on the average Chinese's purchasing power, saw the prices of many basic goods and grains increase 60% during the year. The economy grew at 11.8% in 1994, compared with the sought-after goal of 9%. Li's comments implied that a timely austerity program could have headed off inflation and brought growth down to a manageable level. He heads the conservative wing of the Party, whose most hard-line members have begun to complain that Deng Xiaoping's economic reforms have created such destructive forces as unemployment, inflation, corruption and vice.[10] During the last round of overheating in the late 1980s, Beijing's tough austerity measures sent growth crashing to 4% from 11% in a matter of months.

By mid-1995, the situation brightened due to governmental efforts to boost the agricultural sector, the main villain in 1994's price rises. Agricultural investment was expected to increase by 20 to 30% in 1995 without any major new price reforms. Both growth and inflation rates decelerated slowly but consistently and the economic consensus was that GDP growth would average 10.2% for the year compared with 11.8% in 1994, while retail prices would gain 14.7%. However, while the macro-economic situation stabilized, inflation still hovered at around 20%.[11]

Predictions were that the very tense political atmosphere in Beijing would not improve until the succession issue was settled for the short term, at which juncture monetary policy would be further tightened, causing the growth rate to fall to 10.2% in

1995 and 9.0% in 1996. Inflation, although slowing would remain well into double digits.

THE STRUCTURE OF EMPLOYMENT

A Chinese worker living in an urban area may be employed in one of the following four forms of business enterprises. There is the one-person or family business and there is the cooperative for working with others; both are almost always labor intensive. Some state enterprises with high labor costs and negative profits have been compulsorily converted to cooperatives to maintain employment. The fourth form is the joint venture with a foreign firm or (in the Special Economic Zones along the coast near Taiwan, Hong Kong, and Macao) the wholly owned foreign firm. A combination of decontrol and the growing openness to foreign trade renders the first two and the fourth responsive to market conditions, but the bulk of nonfarm output is still in the state sector. The key concept in the reform applied to state enterprises is "dual track"; the total productive capacity is no longer committed to the output of a planned target, and capacity above requirements is to be utilized only if a profitable disposal can be foreseen. State enterprises now generate no more than half the total industrial output because township, private, and cooperative industries have grown so fast during the past decade.

China's employment situation is unique and interpretation of the available data is not without problems. The extent of state production in the economy is falling, although it still accounts for 20% of the labor force, and various decentralized agencies are promoting development and employment growth, especially in the coastal regions, often in conjunction with foreign investors. These are generally in the form of township and village enterprises (TVEs) which are believed to have increased their employment from around 30 million in 1980 to nearly 100 million in 1991, constituting some 40% of total industrial employment.

LABOR REFORM-CONTRACT EMPLOYMENT

A new system of contract employment, which had been introduced in the 1980s, threatened the old arrangement which stressed guaranteed lifetime job security for Chinese workers. Nevertheless, the old system was allowed to survive alongside the new, resulting in sharp inequalities between the two categories of workers. Moreover, managers' permanent job tenure remained undisturbed. It was only in 1991 that a "full workforce contract system" went into experimental operation in selected state enter-prises. As the name suggests, the system requires all employees of an enterprise, including senior staff, such as the manager and Party secretary, to sign conditional and renewable contracts with the employers, i.e., the local or central authorities.

After a visit in early 1992 by Deng Xiaoping to booming Shenzen, a special economic zone in South China, his speeches were widely circulated throughout

China, and set off a mood of increasing optimism for the prospects for economic reform. In particular, Chinese reformers renewed efforts at labor reform with a new slogan to "break the three irons and the one big pot." The iron rice bowl, the iron chair, the iron salary, and the one big pot symbolized the major elements of the formerly inflexible labor system, guaranteed lifetime employment, protection from demotion, and minimum salary differentials. A labor work conference in 1991 established a national goal of implementing the labor contract system, stalled during the previous period of retrenchment, in all enterprises within 10 years.[12]

Under the contract system, which was expanded in 1986, initial contracts have a duration of from one to 5 years while long-term contracts of employment run more than 5 years. If a worker remains on a company payroll for at least 10 years, he or she then becomes eligible for an open-ended contract.

While the majority of public comment supports continued reform and increased contacts internationally, dislocation from labor reform is generating debate and some discontent. Workers continue to be concerned with the increased uncertainty of their jobs. Young workers and women are particularly hard hit. Although official unemployment is in the 2 to 3% range, 80% of this figure consists of young people who have never held a permanent job. Women workers suffer not only higher unemployment, but increasingly blatant employment discrimination, as evidenced by greater difficulty in finding work and high unemployment rates.

The government is trying to soften the dislocations caused by reform. For example, a number of ministries—Labor, Personnel, Civil Affairs—are involved in developing a more generalized social welfare system for the country to replace the reliance on work units, which cannot provide services economically, and expanding benefits beyond the state sector.

WAGE REFORMS

Under China's traditional system, workers in state enterprises were paid a fixed wage that increased with length of service, and production bonuses distributed on an "egalitarian basis," regardless of performance. In 1988 a "job-related wage system" was introduced in a few enterprises on an experimental basis. Under this arrangement, the management, in consultation with the trade union committee and the Party committees, set a specific wage level for each position which fluctuated according to the overall performance of the enterprise. In addition to this job-related fluctuating component, the incumbent would receive a fixed component reflecting length of service. A worker or manager moving to another job would be paid a different wage or salary. Nevertheless, a clear link between individual performance and individual pay was still missing.

In order to remedy this deficiency, the central government in 1992 issued a directive giving managers direct control over wages. The immediate aim was to create pay scales that would reward individual effort and skill, instead of seniority and political performance, and thus boost productivity. "What we want is a market mechanism in our labor system—an efficient system in which our labor departments will set only the total payroll and leave recruitment and wage distribution wholly to the firms themselves," explained Vice Labor Minister Zhu Jiazhen.[13]

As part of overall industrial reform aimed at reinvigorating large and medium-sized enterprises after the retrenchment period, firms are being encouraged to reform salary systems by introducing merit raises, piecework systems, merit promotions, and examination and evaluation systems to more clearly link performance and remuneration. Firms also now insist that they will demote incompetent managers, although we have no way of knowing how often this occurs.

Enterprises vary widely in their interest and ability to take advantage of the new emphasis on reform. Some of the most innovative had already reformed their businesses in such imaginative ways that the new policies have little meaning to them. For example, one Beijing factory, already on a piecework system, indicated that the labor contract system would have little impact on their employment practices. Still others manage to implement the letter of the reforms without making any real changes in the workplace culture. For instance, many firms give most workers 10-year renewable contracts and plan to automatically roll the contracts over when they expire.

LABOR FORCE SURPLUS AND UNEMPLOYMENT

The latest statistics saw that China has more women workers, more older and better educated workers, and an increasing number of workers in nonstate businesses. Figures from the state statistics bureau show that China had a total workforce of 602.2 million at end of 1993, an increase of 1.3% over the previous year, outpacing the growth of the country's population. The figures show that, due to development in urban service trades and the adoption of new working techniques, working women accounted for 43.8% of the total labor force, somewhat higher than in previous surveys. Workers between the ages of 25 and 34 accounted for 28% of the total, and those between 35 and 54 accounted for 36%, while the average age of the entire workforce was 36, one year older than in 1990, and five years older than in 1978. As for their schooling, the workforce had received eight years of education on the average, one year more than in 1990, and three years more than in 1978. Meanwhile, some 94% worked in state-owned or collective enterprises, only 6% worked in private or foreign-funded businesses, but this was an increase of 3% over the figure for 1990. Overall, 56.4% worked in agriculture, a drop of 3.6% compared with 1990, and workers in industry and the service trades accounted for 22.4% and 21.2%, respectively. China's rural businesses have absorbed 27.9% of the rural labor force according to the central government.

The supply of workers in China will continue to outstrip demand for a long time to come. The Ministry of Labor predicts that by the year 2000, there will be 68 million people in cities and over 200 million in the rural areas waiting to be placed in jobs. Over 30 million more workers have found employment in cities during the past decade, although despite governmental efforts, a large number of people still are unemployed. State-owned enterprises have been overstaffed with workers, and are in dire need of streamlining. Consequently, they have little latitude for hiring additional workers. Aggregate unemployment reached 5 million at the end of 1994. In the mid-1990s, in the cities, there was a floating population of 50 to 60 million who had come from rural areas, who were part of the surplus labor force in these areas, and Beijing was attempting to place them in their local township enterprises.[14]

As part of the pervasive concern about "social stability," Chinese officials have begun to worry openly about unemployment. The priority is to find jobs for those laid off in the state sector, and to stem the "blind flow" of underemployed farmers pouring into the cities. It will be necessary to create jobs in services, and even abroad to ease the situation. The magnitude of the problem in the countryside was highlighted by a labor ministry official who claimed that 140 million of the 450 million-strong rural workforce were unemployed, while only 200 million had farm jobs, and 110 million worked in rural industrial and service enterprises. The problem appears to be worsening despite the industrial boom. Whereas in the five years from 1984 to 1988 rural enterprises absorbed 12.6 million new workers annually, in the following five-year period the number dropped to 2.6 million, as profits were diverted into plant, equipment, and speculative investments.

The "blind flow" always attracts attention around the Chinese New Year holiday, when migrant laborers swamp the transportation network as they go home for the holidays, and again when they return to work in the large cities, often accompanied by friends or family members seeking employment. Nationally, the number of migrants or floating workers is variously estimated at between 50 and 100 million.[15]

WORKER ATTITUDES

What do Chinese workers think of their present lives? A recent survey conducted among 7,000 of them showed that 67.2% regarded their living standards as having been raised "considerably" or "a little." Twenty percent thought standards had been maintained, while 12.6% felt their living standards had declined. The largest household expenses result from buying food and sending children to school, according to the survey. Most spare time, as described by the majority, is devoted to household chores, watching television, and helping children with their homework, while reading or other recreational activities followed in importance. About 1.8% of the respondents have spare-time jobs. As to their discretionary income, 18.8% indicated they deposit it in banks, and 31% said they are inclined to spend it. The survey revealed that the older the survey subjects, the greater their saving propensity, while younger persons preferred to spend extra funds. The survey was jointly conducted by the Chinese Academy of Social Sciences and the State Statistics Bureau in some 12 cities in four provinces. Most of those who thought their living standards had improved in recent years were leaders of work units, service workers, and some industrial workers and technicians, and most of them were between 26 and 35 years of age. Some 45.3% of the people surveyed attributed the rise in living standards to the "rise in wages and bonuses," 23.5% to "the increase of employment of family members," and 2.4% said it came from " moonlighting." But what caused declines? Forty-eight percent placed the blame on price increases, 19.4% stated they had to spend too much money on gifts, and 13.2% attributed the decline in living standards to declining income levels. Most of those surveyed cited housing and social welfare as the most acute problems at present, and a sizable number hoped for a more varied cultural life. Although the wages of workers and per capita income of the urban residents increased about 10 and 17%, respectively since 1986, still one-third of them considered their living standards had declined. Apart from occupational differences, income inequalities exist, and price increases in recent years have reduced the income gains following reform policies.[16]

INCREASING WORKER DISCONTENT AND UNION IMPOTENCE

As we have seen, the emphasis on economic efficiency has left millions without jobs and produced fears of social instability. Witness the following scenario. Not long ago Xiao Li was a mechanic at a state-owned factory in Beijing which made electronics spare parts. Then the factory cut his salary by 30%. Two months later, it stopped paying him altogether and told him he could stay at home. Since then Xiao Li (not his real name) and most of his former colleagues have received no salary and no welfare or medical benefits, though they still have state-provided housing. "The workers are unhappy, yes. What can we do? We have no alternatives," he says. "Our trade unions cannot represent the workers' interests at all."

For Xiao Li and his friends, this represents a huge departure from the guaranteed cradle-to-grave "iron rice bowl" employment and welfare package that China's workers once relied on. The electronics spare parts factory has virtually stopped production because, like many of China's moribund and inefficient state enterprises, its products could not compete with foreign imports and rival products from modern factories in the south of China. Its workers, although still officially employed by the factory, are eking out a living by hawking goods or repairing bicycles.

The Chinese government is terrified that the existence of millions of people like Xiao is a threat to social stability. China has the world's fastest growing economy but half of the country's state enterprises are losing money. Millions of factory workers are owed wages or are not being paid at all. Safety and working conditions can be abysmal, and strikes and labor disruptions are becoming increasingly common as workers vent their anger.

The overall unemployment figures are hard to establish. Officially, urban unemployment is more than 5 million, as previously noted, but this does not take into account the estimated 30 million who have nothing or little to do at their work units. The rural situation is equally alarming. Over the past five years, estimates are that between 50 and 100 million people have moved from the countryside to urban areas in search of jobs. The majority do find work, often in the coastal development areas or on labor sites in the cities, but unknown millions remain idle in rural areas, or drift around the cities. Li Boyong, the Minister of Labor has admitted that China's employment situation is extremely difficult and the country faces unprecedented challenges in dealing with joblessness.

China's leaders have fresh memories of what happens when popular discontent boils over. While in 1989, ordinary people focused on such everyday problems as inflation and official corruption, now unemployment and workers' rights have become the new stress points. In addition, working conditions in both state and joint ventures can be appalling. In the first 10 months of 1993 there were 65,000 deaths in industrial accidents. Over the same period there were 28,200 cases of industrial fires, killing 1,480 and injuring 51,340. The fact is that health and safety measures are rarely implemented.

In the joint venture and foreign factories in the coastal regions, workers get their wages but complain of "sweatshop" conditions. In the past few years there have been 1,100 labor disputes, strikes and slowdowns in the Shenzhen Special Economic Zone, almost all involving foreign-funded firms.

Strikes in state enterprises tend to be hushed up, but Beijing is more open about disputes in foreign-funded factories. Complaints filter out about conditions in some of the Taiwan and Hong Kong-run export-oriented manufacturing plants in south China, where employees are forced to work huge amounts of overtime to meet orders, locked in their workplaces, and offered scant protection against industrial hazards. In November 1993, a fire at the Hong Kong joint venture Zhili toy factory in Shenzhen killed 84 workers who were locked into their dormitories, invoking images of the scores of women workers killed in the Triangle Shirtwaist factory fire in 1911 in New York City. Six months later the government announced that foreign-funded firms will have to be unionized under the government-run ACFTU. However, it will not permit any independent workers' representation. The Communist Party is wary of a Polish-style Solidarity movement emerging. An anonymous Chinese official even suggested that the presence of the quietly spoken labor activist, Han Dongfang, in Hong Kong was tantamount to turning the colony into "a pioneering battleground for subverting China." He told a local newspaper: "It would be very interesting to know how Britain would react if we were to deploy thousands of IRA in Shenzhen."[17]

OFFICIAL OPTIMISM

Against this sobering background, Beijing issued an optimistic forecast regarding future economic prospects for the average Chinese family. Official circles predicted that ordinary Chinese families will be able to afford cars early in the next century. "China, with its population of about 1.2 billion, is now the world's single largest automobile market," Deputy Director General Lu Chunheng told a Beijing press conference. He believes that rapidly improving living standards should make Chinese-made cars affordable to ordinary citizens by the year 2010. Estimates are that per capita income will continue to grow by 20% a year until the end of the century. Unfortunately, at present cars such as the Santanas produced by a Shanghai joint venture with Volkswagen sell for about 180,000 yuan ($20,690), roughly 18 times the annual salary of the ordinary urban resident. However, the government contends that the continuous expansion of the automobile industry should reduce production costs with a resulting reduction in the prices of Chinese-made vehicles, making them affordable because the average annual per capita income is rising rapidly in China's urban areas. In 1993 it was estimated at 2,337 yuan ($259), nearly 30% more than the previous year.

China now has 116 automakers, more than any other country in the world. However, output is limited because the industry is still developing. China produced 230,000 cars in 1993 and 350,000 were planned for 1994. It aims to expand its manufacturing capacity to 2 million cars in 10 years by developing existing plants and building new ones.[18]

ECONOMIC AND POLITICAL REALITIES

China's economic reformers face daunting challenges. There is much confusion over how to apply the tools of bankruptcy and privatization in China's aged industrial structure. The mass migration, involving tens of millions of people, strains the country's transport system and spotlights the forces at play in China's increasingly chaotic economy. The so-called floating population has provided much of the labor for the country's recent economic boom. It also funnels some of the wealth created on the coasts back to poorer inland areas. But as the tide of unmoored workers continues to swell, it threatens to erode China's social order and could become a destabilizing force in the country. If China's economy slows dramatically, many of these workers would be left with no place to go. The rural areas from which they come already are awash with millions of unemployed individuals.

While the migrant population is not viewed as a cohesive political force, displaced laborers—out of work and far from home—could be candidates for labor organizers or other political movements. More immediately, the migrants compete for resources and jobs that might otherwise go to laid-off workers from state-owned enterprises, a potentially more volatile group.[20]

In the meantime, China's ongoing reform of the labor system, centering on labor, wages, and social insurance, is in place in more than 200 cities and counties nationwide. Some 40% of the country's total workforce is now under a contract system. The framework for a totally new labor system suitable for the nation's socialist market economy should take shape by the year 2000.

Enterprises throughout China have been granted expanded autonomy in hiring people, especially in the distribution of wages. Almost all of the workers employed in recent years have been subjected to contracts, demonstrating that the market mechanism is playing a decisive role in the distribution of wages. In China the idea of freely selecting a job meeting one's own interests and needs is prevailing. A job offered by the government is not now necessarily a life-long endeavor. On the other hand, work units enjoy greater freedom to select their employees. More than 2000 enterprises across China have been singled out as pioneers in reforms which allow them to decide their own wage levels. More than 17,000 job introduction agencies have been established to help the unemployed find gainful employment, and jobs have been found nationally for more than 8 million people annually in recent years. In addition, the country's various labor markets have become the primary vehicle for providing job opportunities for the jobless.

On the political front, the Communist Party's strengthening of party cells in enterprises will further suffocate the development of autonomous workers' organizations in China. The crackdown on independent workers' unions has intensified during the past few years, with labor activists across the country harassed and arrested by authorities at all levels. The recent increase in propaganda on party cells in the workplace by the official media is a further move to expedite party control over the independent workers' movement. These cells can be viewed as a local effort to reassure top party leaders who feared a loosening of controls, in view of recent worker unrest, particularly in the ailing state enterprises.

Since decentralization of authority has made it easier for local officials to negotiate deals with foreign investors, Beijing wants to reassert control by ordering foreign-funded ventures to set up branches of its ACFTU, nicknamed a "yellow union" by critics for its willingness to cooperate docilely with its masters in the central government. Having it in the factories and offices will therefore help Beijing gain influence over management and local government officials. It will not, however, improve the plight of most workers since the trend has been that whenever management negotiates with the ACFTU, the union ends up in total agreement with management.

As Beijing attempts to reassert a measure of control over the entrepreneurial South, the central government also must deal with the deep-rooted labor problems in the industrial North. State enterprises, which dominate the northern economy, employ nearly half of China's urban population, and half of nearly 100,000 state firms are losing money. Official statistics put urban unemployment at 5 million but by other accounts that figure is too low. According to Han Dongfang, the labor activist exiled to Hong Kong, as many as 50 million workers, half the total workforce at state firms, are on the verge of joblessness.

At the moment, Beijing is unwilling to allow many businesses to go bankrupt for fear of social unrest. The government experienced worker anger recently in the northeastern province of Heilongjiang, where some 2 million workers lost their jobs in 1993. More than 100,000 workers took to the streets in the province's two major cities, Harbin and Qiqihaer, to protest pay cuts. China's economic strong man, Vice-Premier Zhu Rongji, visited the province and fired its governor. This action did not deter workers, however, who continue to engage in unpublicized strikes or slowdowns across the country to demand decent wages and better working conditions.

Beijing hopes to create a social welfare system to ease some of the pressure. On July 1, 1994, unemployment insurance became mandatory in the capital city, where labor and management contribute to a fund used to pay off unemployed workers. In other cities, the government is setting up an "unemployment warning line," or an acceptable rate of unemployment. If a locality exceeds that amount, it can use newly formed central and provincial unemployment insurance funds. Beijing also announced a new labor law that was 16 years in the making. Effective January 1, 1995, the law set a minimum age of 16 for workers, a minimum wage, and an average workweek not to exceed more than 44 hours and six days a week.

In this turbulent setting, the government is moving to prevent the rise of a Solidarity-type labor movement by suppressing labor activists.[21] The general perception is that eliminating the iron rice bowl means eliminating, or at least reducing, job security. What is unclear is just how much insecurity is enough to produce the stimulating effect desired. One of the reasons for the confusion lies in the perceived need to communicate different messages to different kinds of workers while trying to make it appear that the policy is being applied in an even-handed way.

There is an acute shortage of skilled labor in China. Highly qualified workers and technical personnel generally welcome the introduction of the labor contract system because it opens a loophole to enable them to win concessions in the form of better wages, working conditions, or fringe benefits such as housing from managements who fear losing scarce human resources in a context of growing competition between companies.

On the other hand, there is an acute surplus of unskilled labor, and those people face a situation where management will be able to demand higher levels of labor intensity and hold down wages simply because of its newly-won power to refuse to renew labor contracts. The decision to fire or lay off workers must be approved by the workers' congress, unlike the decision not to renew a contract. This places workers whose skills are not in short supply in a very vulnerable position, particularly when their contracts are not the product of any sort of collective bargaining, or even individual negotiation for that matter, but simply documents drawn up by management to be signed at the time of hiring.

The expansion of short-term contracting of labor is beginning to have a noticeable impact on employment. On the one hand, a growing proportion of the worrisome millions of unemployed migrants who have become so visible, are contract workers whose contracts have been completed and not renewed. For example, the great majority of 2 million migrants from Sichuan alone were said to be holders of expired labor contracts. In contrast, a new shortage of workers willing to work in foundries, coal mines, and cotton spinning and knitting mills has been attributed to the coupling of unhealthy working conditions with a labor contract system that has eliminated job and wage security.[22]

THREATS TO POLITICAL STABILITY

On the political horizon the death of Deng Xiaoping will mark the end of the domination of China by a generation of leaders hardened by decades of peasant guerrilla warfare. The inevitable transition from a society and an economy run as a series of military campaigns to a more flexible, less orderly regime of decentralized decision-making has, remarkably, already been accomplished, easing the task of transition to Deng's successors. Deng has succeeded in filling the top posts of the Party and the government. There is some prospect of the current leadership holding power for the near future. Nonetheless, political stability cannot be taken for granted beyond that.

Deng has managed to assemble a younger collegial leadership to succeed him and has handed over all his formal positions of authority to them while retaining paramount influence offstage. He has already survived long enough to see the new team cut its teeth on the tricky issues of economic reform, though the more intractable problem of political reform has been postponed indefinitely. This is no mean achievement.

After Deng leaves the scene, the facade of unity may not last long, despite the widespread desire, shared even by many who oppose the government, to avoid turmoil. After the violent events of 1989, which resembled the chaos of the Cultural Revolution period, there is a very basic consensus among the political elite that differences should be muted in order to prevent a breakdown of the political system. While this shared fear will constrain dissent within peaceful limits for some time after Deng dies, there are three reasons for concern about future political stability.

First, there is the lack of a clear successor to Deng. China does not easily submit to rule by coalition. What is hoped for is a strong man to put his imprint on the next few decades. However, no such charismatic leader has yet emerged. President Jiang Zemin, chosen by Deng as the core of the post-Deng leadership group, embodies the most formidable combination of power positions that has appeared in China since Mao Zedong delegated the state presidency to Liu Shaoqui. Liu then combined his role as head of state with those of secretary-general of the Communist Party, the top party post since the position of chairman was abolished after the death of Mao, and that of chairman of the party's central military commission, effectively the head of the armed forces. Jiang, who is not himself a military man, has been bolstering his support in the People's Liberation Army in preparation for the power struggle that could erupt after Deng dies. He is, however, not expected to last long. Regardless of his past achievements in Shanghai and his ability, well-known abroad, to speak foreign languages, he is not greatly respected in China, where he is frequently compared to Hua Guofeng, Mao's immediate successor, who faded into virtual oblivion after presiding over two years of the pre-Deng interregnum. The very quality that makes Jiang the ideal compromise candidate for temporary leadership, his lack of forcefulness, will count against him when the knives are out. The prime minister, Li Peng, has shown extraordinary political agility in retaining his post, a feat achieved by creating his own constituency in the bureaucracy, which is threatened by economic liberalization and pressures for political reform. Moreover, his instinct for holding economic growth at sustainable, relatively slow rates and retaining levers of control over the economy makes him look good when the economy is buffeted by concurrent inflation and unemployment. But in the long term he is incapable of overseeing the transition to a market economy because he has no real understanding of it. For different reasons, other pretenders to the top leadership are unlikely to be able to wield supreme power.

What is likely instead is that the balance of influence will shift between members of the politburo standing committee in response to changes in society and the economy.

The second, and more fundamental, threat to political stability is the development of social tensions generated by the process of economic change initiated by Deng in 1978. There are now numerous groups of malcontents. Much of the rural population, especially in inland areas, has been left behind by economic growth and modernization. Tens of millions of peasants, rendered unemployed or underemployed by the household responsibility system which markedly increased rural production in the early 1980s, are now migrant laborers, poorly paid, with no job security, subject to instant dismissal and expulsion from the cities. Resentment over official corruption, which fueled the Tianenmen protests in 1989, continues to mount—especially among those who are not in a position to share its benefits. The opening of China to foreign culture, which has accompanied its opening to trade and investment, coupled with the spread of mass communications, including satellite television and smuggled videotapes, is making it more difficult for the government to control the flow of information and perceptions of the outside world. The Marxist–Leninist thought of Mao Zedong has collapsed as a belief system, and all the leadership has so far been able to supplant it with is an uninspiring, ideologically vacuous, and contradictory melange of greed and nationalism. There has been a tremendous secularization of popular thinking, with economic ambitions almost entirely displacing political ideals. The apparent languor of the population at large is illusory. Beneath the veneer of conformity lurks deep cynicism and mistrust of those in authority which many people no longer fear to voice quite openly, though not, since 1989, in the media. Added to these tensions is the resurgent nationalism in Tibet and Xinjiang and the reluctance of the provinces to remit tax revenue, and powers, back to the central government.

The third obstacle to stability is the failure to reform the political system. A key tenet of the Deng Xiaping model of reform is that the top leadership should retain a tight hold on political power while decentralizing economic power. This much was clearly established at the beginning of the reform process in 1979, when Beijing's Democracy Wall was closed down and dissenters were arrested for trying to include democracy as the fifth modernization after the four modernizations of agriculture, industry, science and technology, and the military were being promoted by the Deng leadership. In the short to medium term, the maintenance of the Communist Party's monopoly of power is the least complicated method of ensuring the continuity of central government control. Entrepreneurial energies are not diverted into constitutional wrangling and electoral contests because such options are closed. Moreover, the plethora of opportunities for economic and social advancement provided by the mushrooming of enterprises outside the government sector has relieved competitive pressures among the nomenclatura. On the other hand, the political system does not possess the capacity to alleviate the imbalance caused by rapid economic development by redistributing income, as shown by the failure so far to implement tax reform. Nor does it allow for the venting of discontent, which is forced into unofficial channels where it may run out of control. For example, in peasant riots like those witnessed in at least half the provinces in 1993, or in the recent wave of labor disputes.

What legitimacy the government enjoys is purely negative as the people prefer any government to complete chaos. The government cannot claim that it was fairly elected, nor can it claim to continue the revolutionary tradition of the communist victors of the 1946–49 civil war.

Underlying these problems is the fundamental incompatibility of the obsolete Stalinist political framework with the market economy that has been developed as its life support system. Economic liberalization has been chipping away at the foundations of bureaucratic power for some years and whole layers of officialdom are increasingly being exposed as having no rational function. Dispensing with their services by retiring them early would be expensive and would be resisted every step of the way, but retaining them involves prolonging subsidies to inefficient, unprofitable state enterprises.

Another problem, perhaps even more urgent, is labor productivity, or output per worker, which has been calculated as having accounted for less than one-fifth of China's economic growth from 1986–90. Capital investment was the main engine, accounting for about 65% of GDP growth. Although China's capital needs remain great, productivity will have to grow much faster if the recent breakneck economic pace is to be maintained. This means stripping overstaffed state-owned enterprises of excess workers and, possibly, lowering wages.[23]

EFFECTS OF BANKRUPTCY

One recent change could, however, lead to a huge improvement in this state of affairs. China's 10-year-old bankruptcy law has seldom been used. A bankruptcy experiment is taking place in 18 industrial cities, including Shanghai, Tianjin and Harbin. It is backed by 7 billion yuan ($800 million) put into a special bankruptcy fund to cover the resulting losses of the country's banks. The experiments should at last establish proper bankruptcy procedures in China, although the existing bankruptcy law needs revision. That could transform the long-term prospects for the state-owned enterprises that are healthy enough to survive. At the moment, their convalescence is delayed by loss-making competitors. Once these are gone, their progress, and the returns to the foreign investors working with them, should greatly improve.

Even with the new initiative, the reform of China's 100,000 state-owned firms is likely to remain an ad hoc affair, with different things happening in different cities and provinces. The freewheeling southern provinces are certain to prove quicker at exposing public firms to the market than their northern and central neighbors.

China took two decades to establish the agricultural communes that were scrapped in the 1970s. Although some thought that restructuring them would prove almost impossible, it actually took less than three years. The time frame for reorganization of the neolithic state enterprises may also prove to be surprisingly short.[24]

Goh Chok Tong, the Prime Minister of Singapore, offered the following formula for dealing with China.[25] "How does the world deal with a China that is both an opportunity and a challenge?" He maintained that there are two difficult choices.

It can seek to stifle China's growth to preempt a strong China, or it can accept and integrate China into the global system.... Give China time and space to initiate changes and to accept its international responsibilities.... Ultimately, economic progress can produce the desired changes in China better than threats and sanctions. Rising affluence, not government decree, will bid up wages in China and improve the working conditions of its labor force. A country that has a stake in global trade and economic growth will have an interest in upholding international laws and standards.

This forecast may prove too optimistic, but the world will be better off should it prove to be an effective analysis of the present scene. The China that greets the 21st century will be a vastly different entity from the current confused mess that gropes at the complexities of transforming itself into what the ruling Communist Party pragmatically describes as a "socialist market economy."

CHAPTER 3

The Industrial Relations Scene:
The Players, Problems,
and Prospects

Frederick Deyo, in discussing the severity of labor controls Asian governments may impose, states:

> In general, it can be assumed that given the political, administrative, and other costs incurred by imposition of severe labor controls, elite groups will impose only those controls they feel are required in order to establish order or to achieve important political or economic goals ....[1]

Obviously, the elite group in China is the Chinese Communist Party (CCP), which seems determined to maintain a stranglehold over all power bases in the Chinese political and economic system. Consequently, its tentacles extend into the world of work. The only sanctioned labor federation, the ACFTU, merely acts as a "transmission belt," stimulating labor productivity and disseminating the party line.

In this fashion, the CCP is a major player in the industrial relations scene. A party committee keeps watch within every institution of government at every level. This system was copied from the Communist Party of the former Soviet Union, but expanded in translation. Whereas the day-to-day management of state-owned firms in the Soviet Union was usually left to managers, in China each factory was taught to strictly comply with the mandates of its party secretary. Economic reform is supposed to have brought more autonomy for factory managers, but that has not always been readily granted.

Nicholas Kristof and Sheryl Wudunn point at the prospect of enhanced power for labor in their recent book, *China Wakes*. They believe that ideological correctness has all but disappeared in the party and has been replaced by opportunism on the part of Communist leaders. Their analysis then focuses on the potential power of the labor movement:

> Yet today a rival power center may be emerging in China: the industrial labor force. Indeed it may be a charismatic labor leader who presents the greatest challenge to this dynasty. This would be someone like Lech Walesa in Poland, who can mobilize workers to strike and shut

41

down the economy. Intellectuals have been at the vanguard of the democracy movement throughout this century, but one reason they have not succeeded is that there was no broad coalition of workers marching behind them. University students are still a tiny fringe of society, accounting for just one-fifth of one percent of the population, whereas workers total 150 million and dominate the cities.... The workers have enormous leverage because of the possibility of a general strike, and no one was more aware of this than Deng Ziaoping himself. Deng in his private speeches warned about the "Polish disease," and it was the growing participation of workers in the 1989 Tianenman protests that convinced him to send in the tanks.[2]

Just as China's economic boom has brought increased prosperity to millions, so too is life for ordinary Chinese becoming easier and freer. Kenneth Lieberthal is of the opinion that "there has been a substantial evaluation—economic, social and political—that makes the state less intrusive in people's lives."[3]

Indeed, the central judgment that Deng Xiaping made at the end of the 1970s now appears to have been a misguided one. Deng gambled that by opening the door to the outside world, China could absorb foreign investment, trade, and technology while turning aside the cultural and political influences, "or bourgeois liberalization," that would challenge Communist Party rule. Instead, years of double-digit economic growth are transforming Chinese society itself, loosening Beijing's control over 1.2 billion people.

In a Shanghai factory, the subject at mandatory party meetings is bonuses, not politics In coastal cities and interior villages, attendance at underground churches is soaring. Virtually no one accepts the ideology called Communism anymore.

Many of these grassroots changes here alarmed the party leadership, already preparing for an inevitable power struggle after the ailing Deng dies. Their quandary resembles the proverbial Catch-22 solution. Beijing must encourage economic growth to stay in power, but that only increases the potential for greater individual freedom. It is noteworthy that only a few years ago the government could dictate where citizens lived and worked, when they married, and when they could have a child. But today a rising middle class is quietly challenging centralized control.

At this point, it is questionable, however, as to what role another important industrial relations player will assume. This is the All-China Federation of Unions (ACFTU).

THE ACFTU

China has only one labor federation, the ACFTU, which functions on three levels: national, local (provincial, city and county trade unions and union councils) and primary (enterprise level). This is much as it has been since 1949, despite an expansion of union membership as industrial development drew more workers into industry. However, the number of trade union branches increased from 100,000 in 1951–52 to over 540,000 recently. The ACFTU membership grew from only 2.4 million in 1949 to 103 million by 1994; it is distributed among 16 national industrial unions and 8,260 unions with 1.3 million members have been established in foreign-invested enterprise.[4]

The size of the unions varies considerably, from large organizations with 400,000 members to unions with only 3 to 5 members. The 16 national unions are ACFTU affiliates.[5] The giant federation has been described as a national umbrella organization for all of China's unions. Its 100 million-plus membership underlines the potential Chinese organized labor possesses to forcefully represent and protect workers' economic interests.[6] Unfortunately, however, China's trade unions play a significantly different role in the workplace than do Western labor organizations. Chinese unions have been described in this manner:

> Operating unions function on an industrial basis, drawing membership from blue and white collar groups, and on a local and regional basis, paralleling the organization and control of industry. National unions operate vertically along industrial lines, while local, provincial, and regional units operate horizontally to represent the varied unions in the geographic area.... Trade union functions in China follow the pattern of other Communist countries. The unions transmit the party line, encourage production in a variety of organized ways, engage in political and ideological education, oversee safety and sanitation, handle grievances (though not exclusively), and execute numerous welfare and cultural responsibilities (social insurance, spare time education, recreation and so forth).[7]

Ostensibly membership is voluntary, but almost all join as a result of peer and cadre pressure. Revenues are derived from a 0.5% levy on monthly wages and a 2% tax on the enterprise's wage fund.[8]

The ACFTU observed its 70th anniversary in 1995, having been founded in 1925 by the framers of the Chinese Communist Party, and views its role primarily as one of improving labor discipline and increasing production rather than championing the rights of workers, although it generally opposes employee layoffs and has demonstrated some interest in protecting workers' safety and health.

Although nominally an independent organization, the ACFTU is closely controlled by the Communist Party. Union membership is voluntary for individuals, but it is compulsory for each enterprise to have a union. Virtually all state sector workers and nearly 90% of all urban workers belong to ACFTU chapters. If a worker is unemployed, he or she is not considered a union member. Since 1983, the ACFTU constitution has required that any attempt to set up or dissolve a union be endorsed by its membership and approved by higher bodies in the national trade union structure. Thus, workers are allowed to organize worker groups independently, but once they have decided to form a union, they are forced to affiliate with, and accept the leadership of, the ACFTU. For the most part, unions in China maintain: "We must protect the Communist Party and the enterprise's production, for if the river has no water, the tributaries will run dry." The ACFTU increased its efforts in favor of protecting workers' basic wages in layoffs during 1990 and early 1991. With the turn toward reform in late 1991, the AFCTU returned to its emphasis on educating workers about the benefits of reform and promoting productivity. Local unions also perform a variety of social and welfare functions, such as handling disability benefits, and operating clubs, eating facilities, nurseries, and schools.

The ACFTU claims contact with trade unions in over 120 countries or regions and has stated its intention to establish links with foreign unions regardless of whether the foreign union maintains any prior affiliation with the International Confederation of Trade Unions (ICFTU), the World Federation of Trade Unions, or other organizations.

STATE ENTERPRISES

Another important player in China's labor reform efforts is its state enterprises. The transformation of China into a socialist market economy has encountered formidable obstacles. One involves the status of state-owned firms whose management has been reconfigured over the last decade to promote the efficient production of marketable products, in contrast to centrally planned production which previously featured quotas for inferior quality goods produced by workers who received egalitarian wages and benefits not linked to their performance.

In fact, state-owned businesses were considered extensions of government ministries and departments. They received instructions on what and how to produce. So long as managers fulfilled their production quotas, they could consider themselves successful. Chinese enterprises went a step further than those in the former Soviet Union, after which they had been modeled. The large ones became small welfare states providing for their employees and their families, subsidized housing, medical treatment, including hospitalization, kindergarten, primary and secondary schools, shops, restaurants, and even policemen and law courts. The factory director functioned as a mayor, more concerned with the welfare of his flock than company profits or labor productivity.[10]

State enterprises, 10% of which are located in the northeastern region of China, range in size from shops with a handful of workers to giant autoworks, refineries, and steel mills like Anshan Iron and Steel in Liaoning Province, which supports 250,000 workers as well as 250,000 pensioners and dependents.[11]

ENTERPRISE MANAGEMENT REFORM

State enterprises had long been subject to the tutelage of administrative and central government machinery, which sometimes proved a brake on initiative and hampered effective management and production of the enterprise concerned. After lengthy deliberation, a new law was promulgated in 1988 by the Seventh National People's Congress ensuring that both decision making and full accountability rest with the management of the enterprise concerned and are concentrated in the chief manager responsible under what is termed the "management to rest with enterprise" system. This constituted a major departure from the earlier "collective responsibility" philosophy, under which decisions were taken in committees drawn from a wide spectrum of interests. The enterprise director is now, under the law, responsible for "building up a materially developed and culturally and ideologically advanced enterprise." The role of trade unions was to ensure that the interests of the workers were fully safeguarded and that the views of all the workers were properly reflected through the union committee in democratic supervision of enterprise activities.[12]

RESULTS OF REFORM

In the effort to reinvigorate large and medium size enterprises, firms have been encouraged to reform salary systems by introducing merit raises, piecework systems, merit promotions, and examination and evaluation systems to more clearly link performance and remuneration.

Enterprises vary widely in their interest and ability to take advantage of the new emphasis on reform. Some of the more innovative had already reformed their firms in such imaginative ways that the new policies have little meaning to them. For example, one Beijing factory already on a piecework system indicated that the labor contract system would have little impact on their employment practices. Still others manage to implement the letter of the reforms without making any real changes in the workplace culture. Moreover, many firms give most workers 10-year renewable contracts and plan to automatically roll the contracts over when they expire.

Many firms simply keep excess workers on as full-time employees. Estimates for underemployment among urban workers range from 10 to 20%. Still others use layoffs to try to cut their costs. While the number of workers on layoff has decreased significantly from the high in 1990, firms still use the technique of keeping workers "inside the factory, waiting for employment" to hold a line on costs. Since a worker's salary is often 50% subsidies and bonuses, companies can cut costs by reducing the worker's salary to as little as 70% of basic pay while he is "waiting for employment." Significantly, layoffs or other "waiting for employment" programs are determined by seniority. Thus, the impact falls on the young, and not necessarily on the incompetent. Nevertheless, the growing tendency of firms to pay bonuses only when the worker has actually worked gives the worker a powerful incentive to look for work where he or she will actually be employed. Such programs reduce but do not eliminate the problems posed by the inability of companies to fire workers.

While the majority of public comment favors speeding reform and opening to the outside generally, dislocations from labor reform are generating debate and some discontent. Workers continue to be concerned with the increased uncertainty of their jobs. Young workers and women are particularly hard hit. Although official unemployment is minuscule, 80% consists of young people who have never held a permanent job. Women workers suffer not only higher unemployment, but increasingly blatant job discrimination, as evidenced by greater difficulty in finding work.

The Chinese government has made a number of moves to ameliorate the dislocations caused by reform. In particular, a number of ministries—Labor, Personnel, Civil Affairs—are involved in developing a more generalized social welfare system for the country to replace the reliance on work units, which cannot provide services economically, and expanding benefits beyond the state sector. Government officials are investigating how to expand benefits to collectives, foreign-owned, and joint ventures, and how to establish funds at the provincial rather than local level as insurance against bankruptcies.

Both the Labor Ministry and the ACFTU has been very active in job retraining and job creation for displaced and unemployed workers. Efforts have focused on improving skills of older and women workers, who have reportedly been hurt by reform. There are also efforts to encourage young people to obtain more vocational training before entering the job market. These reforms seem to have had an effect on the youth who are far more aware of the need for skills acquisition than they were a decade ago. These initiatives are vital because although the unemployment rate remains astonishingly low at less than 3%, private estimates place the real unemployment rate to be two to four times this level.

THE PACE SLOWS TEMPORARILY

Beginning in 1993, the trend toward bankruptcies of state-owned industries was temporarily interrupted due to political considerations. This last stage of reform requires enormous political will since it threatens the source of much of the Communist Party's power. Party cadres dominate the management of state industries. Tax revenues from state factories sustain the central government and the party in Beijing, providing 65% of traditional tax revenues.

Fortunately for many recently laid-off workers, the private sector is still expanding rapidly enough to employ many of them shed by state industries. The economy is growing more than 10% annually, despite the red ink generated by nearly half of the state enterprises.[13]

THE EFFECTS OF BANKRUPTCY

Bankruptcy poses a serious problem for Chinese decision makers. They realize that a number of state enterprises would be insolvent if they were not being propped up by state loans that they have no ability to repay. The major deterrent to allowing bankruptcies is concern over what to do with workers who will lose their jobs, how to find them new jobs, and stop them from creating unrest.

Another obstacle is pressure on court officials by local officials who want to protect local interests and are reluctant to see local companies fail. Law officers are paid by the local government, making them vulnerable to such pressure. Nevertheless, a revision of the basic bankruptcy law took place in 1995, thus accelerating the pace of closures. The amendment will broaden the types of firms that can go bankrupt, cut the time needed for courts to process applications from the current six months, and remove the need for prior approval by government offices in charge of a state firm or its trade union.

After the brief hiatus in 1993, the number of Chinese firms that went bankrupt in 1994 more than doubled, with projections of 3,000 in 1995 as loss makers were forced to become profitable or go under, and the move to force tottering state-owned firms into bankruptcy won court support in 1994. The increase is a sign that authorities across China were coming to terms with the concept of bankruptcy, a taboo in the days of central planning.[14]

The need for reform is clear, carrying with it the necessity of an expanded unemployment program. The larger question is: who is going to pay for it? To minimize the impact, the first batch of state firms earmarked for bankruptcy would be small firms employing no more than 1,000 workers.[15] The watchword among Chinese bureaucrats trying to solve the unemployment and underemployment problem is "tertiary industry" (the service sector). Policymakers have advocated such initiatives as a steel mill opening a restaurant or a beauty parlor in order to absorb excess labor. Some work units, with excellent political connections, have been able to establish profitable, unrelated businesses, such as international hotels on prime real estate in Beijing and Shanghai. However, such options are not open to the majority of money-losing state companies. For those lacking resources, managerial skill, or political connections, a tertiary enterprise represents just another money-losing operation.

If collectives, joint ventures, and township and village enterprises are able to absorb workers laid off by state enterprises, the adverse employment effect will be considerably lessened. The Chinese leadership still remembers the nightmare of Tianenmen Square, an explosion of anger that had more do with jobs than democracy.

MIGRANT LABOR

Another significant factor affecting economic reform efforts in China is the massive influx of rural Chinese to the cities, estimated to be as many as 100 million people. Known colloquially as the *mang lui* or "blind flow," this migration is changing the face of China. Fifteen years ago, 80% of China's population lived off the land; today 65% does.

This huge army of migrant laborers has been caused by the disintegration of China's strict residence registration system. For the first 30 years of Communist rule, Chinese mainly stayed where they were born, bound by their *hukou*, or residence registration. Controls started to relax in the late 1980s, and peasants traveled to cities in winter when the land was fallow. By the 1990s, millions of peasants moved to the cities year-round. There they earn nearly three times what they could in the country-side, sending much of it home and sometimes supporting entire villages. From now until the end of the century, estimates are that 200 million rural Chinese laborers will be migrating to urban centers in search of employment.[16] In Beijing presently, migrant workers account for 15% of the capital's population, many of them unemployed. The proportion in some southern cities is reported to be 70%. The majority of the "floating population" are unable to find jobs in the industrial sector, most often settling for a small street job in the service sector or a domestic job such as a maid, a restaurant worker, or at best, an unskilled job at one of the several construction sites in the capital, in Shanghai or elsewhere.

Migrants who are able to obtain regular work are more fortunate. Most, however, are regarded as temporary employees and do not enjoy job tenure. Many work under appalling conditions in unsafe and poor working environments and with no protection against unreasonable hours of work. Employer objections to the establishment of trade unions and the lack of organization among migrant workers also mean that they are at the mercy of capitalists and managers.

Even when there are rules and regulations, however, their implementation may not be realized. Official laxity in enforcement is often due to reluctance to upset employers, especially foreign bosses. Meanwhile, violations are overlooked through the bribery of officials.

The government, addressing the issue of migrant labor, conducted a survey of 22 cities and counties in southern China's Sichuan, Yunhan, Guizhou, Hunan provinces and the Yuangxi Zhuon Autonomous Region. More than 50% of the migrant rural laborers settled in township enterprises, while many others found jobs in collectively owned or family-run enterprises. Predictions were that 22 million new workers would come to the five provinces during the 1994 to 2000 period. Combined with the 27 million existing surplus rural laborers, the total number will reach nearly 50 million. Nonagricultural businesses in the surveyed region can employ no more than 17 million, leaving 32 million surplus laborers until the end of the century.

Many rural laborers have little cultural or technical knowledge, handicapping their chances of finding jobs in cities. Illiterate people in Sichuan and Yunnan provinces make up 25% of the total labor force. Less than 20% of migrant workers in the five provinces have received any training. The five provinces have abundant farm products and labor, making it easier for them to develop labor-intensive processing industries that use agricultural products as raw materials. But about 70 to 80% of the migrant laborers have sought work in heavy industries such as mining and metalmaking, resulting in a large amount of dual production and inefficiency.[17]

The situation in the Yangtze River delta region is also fraught with difficulties. Along with Shanghai, the provinces of Jiansu, Anhui, and Zhejiang form a dense market of 193 million people, a population nearly as large as Indonesia's and a consumer base 55% larger than Japan's. This booming delta region's growth has been fueled primarily by its autonomous township and village enterprises (TVES). These dynamic, market-oriented businesses, mostly in light industry, are run by increasingly shrewd entrepreneurs.

However, this rapid growth has brought with it some serious problems. The booming delta region is rapidly becoming China's principal destination for rural migrants seeking jobs. There are an estimated 9 million migrant workers in the delta, largely in the Shanghai–Nanjing corridor. Central government officials estimate labor demand for migrants will grow 10% annually into the next century, meaning that there could be 22 million rural migrants in the Yangtze delta by the year 2005.

Migration already is posing serious challenges to local governments, which must provide housing, infrastructure, security, and social services, including family planning. Until recently, the local governments have not budgeted for these services, and the enormity of the migration in the past five years has caught them unprepared. Granted that the rural population is being freed from the farmland as the country's economy changes rapidly to a market-oriented one, and the migration of surplus rural labor is necessary in a reasonable allocation of human resources, which is conducive to the economic development of China. However, random migration has had negative effects such as increased criminal activity and greater under- and unemployment.[18] Millions, probably hundreds of millions, have been on the move in an attempt to escape what Karl Marx called the "idiocy of rural life."[19]

The floating population has become a major issue in the political and economic life of China, of great concern to the Communist Party and the State Council, which have commented on the need to work out a national policy on the matter, which is currently being handled by local administrations. A party official called local governments and authorities to take "firm and timely measures to enhance the administration of the floating population." His assessment of the problem was that it was necessary to absorb rural surplus laborers through "strengthening comprehensive agricultural development, developing rural industrial enterprises, and speeding up development of towns and small cities."[20]

SUCCESSFUL MEASURES—DEVELOPING TOWNS AND CITIES

The admonition that it will be necessary to develop many more towns and cities to slow the migration of surplus rural labor has met with a response, albeit on a provincial rather than national level. For example, Central China's Hunan Province has accelerated the development of its small towns, which in turn absorb a growing number of surplus rural workers. Over 3,000 rising towns have provided employment for 4 million local farmers. With the development of these small towns, the output value of rural industries and the service sector exceeded that of agriculture for the first time in 1993.

Hunan, a traditional agricultural province with 85% of its population living in rural areas, has a 40% surplus of rural laborers. While stressing the importance of improving rural industrial mix, the province has worked out the strategy of developing small towns to exploit local advantages. It has also encouraged rural and privately owned enterprises to contribute to the development of small towns, and help upgrade local economies in which farmers are playing a key role. Some cities and counties are carrying out pilot reforms in urban residence registration by adopting preferential policies for local farmers to open businesses in towns and get better education for their children.

Meanwhile the province strives to open various channels for the pooling of capital such as the sales of land use rights and introduction of funds from the outside. During the past five years, the province has collected nearly 10 billion yuan (about $1.2 billion) for infrastructure construction in small towns. Yueyang county, which has shifted 80,000 farmers during the past decade, has completed the construction of three towns for business activities, 10 new villages, and five wholesale markets for farmers, whose business volume accounted for 60% of the county's total income. Jinjiang town in Changsha county has formed a dozen industrial zones specializing in casting, tea production, tanning, garment making, timber processing, and some other industries. Now the number of the town's industrial and commercial enterprises has increased from the original 21 to 686; their total income has increased from 5.8 million yuan to 120 million yuan. The town has absorbed a total of 1,800 surplus laborers from its rural areas.

With the rapid development of small towns in the province, many rural surplus workers who went to work in south China's coastal developed areas several years ago now have returned home.[21]

TOWNSHIP AND VILLAGE ENTERPRISES

Multitudes of small enterprises, called TVEs or township companies are dominating China's rapidly growing private sector. Their innovative, flexible, market-driven approach is creating millions of jobs which are necessary to absorb the massive labor redundancies plaguing China's state sector. In 1993, the most recent year for which statistics are available, China had 24.5 million township companies that employed one in five or 120 million of its 602 million labor force. Even more impressive, that year saw them generate 60% of the nation's total industrial output, overtaking the state-owned enterprises for the first time since Mao proclaimed the People's Republic in 1949.

The township company label includes a broad range of company organizations and ownership structures. They may be substantially owned by individuals, partnerships, foreign investors, banks, local governments, or combinations thereof. Their contribution to the problem of migrant labor is that they have been and will continue to be a source for absorbing the growing excess labor force in the rural sector, where there are 450 million agricultural workers, more than half of them classified as surplus. Although surplus rural labor is absorbed into rural industry and the transient work force, the ACFTU's newspaper, the *Workers Daily*, has estimated that by 2000 "latent unemployment" in China's rural areas may reach 310 million.[22] This problem would undoubtedly have been more acute still, had the TVE's not been so successful in soaking up labor. Their proliferation was encouraged by the Communist Party as a buffer between countryside and city that might absorb the shock of population movements. They have done that job well, but they have also proved so profitable that they have drifted almost entirely out of the party's control.

A POLICY SOLUTION

Wong has pointed out the need for a comprehensive policy for solving the migrant labor problem:

So far, the central and local governments have not found a way to manage the migrant challenge. Existing policies and practices are haphazard, piecemeal and uncoordinated. No central agency exists to plan, administer and supervise work relating to the floating population. In the case of Guangdong, we have seen some valuable attempts to grapple with the problems. However, most measures are reactions to contingencies rather than long-term solutions. What's more, migrants are a very mobile group. What happened to Guangdong is now happening to Shanghai and other places undergoing fast economic growth. Unless the right to free movement is curtailed, people will flock to places where opportunities are more abundant. National policies rather than local ones are imperative in dealing with what is after all a national issue.[23]

THE ABSENCE OF COLLECTIVE BARGAINING

This migratory pressure has been the subject of lively discussions between employers and unions. Managers believe that the movement of unskilled labor should be encouraged, to support growth, to hold in check the trend toward increased wages, and to put the required infrastructure in place. The unions denounce the predictable impact that the massive "import" of cheap labor has on prevailing wages and on the right to collective bargaining. However, the trade union response in China differs from countries with a free, independent labor movement. The government-controlled ACFTU thus far has limited itself to several studies of the problem but can only be expected to echo the party line, whatever that may be in the future. The labor body has registered complaints against exploitative wages and unsafe working conditions.

In any event, migrant workers' interests would not be represented if they became trade union members since only permanent workers and contract employees could benefit from Western-style collective bargaining. Rural laborers are hired in both TVEs and state enterprises as "agreement" workers. These agreements are in fact contracts. The only difference is that the employees are legally considered farmers rather than workers and are therefore not entitled to be under the labor contract system. At the same time, wage reform has vastly increased the number of incentives open to workers regardless of whether there is a contract.[24]

WORKERS CONGRESSES—WORKER PARTICIPATION IN DEMOCRATIC MANAGEMENT

The general assembly of workers, known as the worker congress, takes on a number of collective bargaining unit responsibilities that Western-style unions carry out but which the ACFTU is not authorized to perform in the Chinese industrial relations setting. Joan Coll describes the activities of the worker congress:

No longer merely advisory in nature, the Workers Congress has the power 1) to adopt or challenge resolutions submitted by the director on production plans, budgets, etc., 2) decide on the use of funds and resources including allocation of housing, regulation of rewards and punishments, and welfare of workers; 3) approve the structure of management, wage adjustments, and vocational training; and 4) recommend or reject cadre (management) appointments based on previously (centrally) established criteria.[25]

Helburn and Shearer note that other specific functions performed include the examination and approval of union–management "collective contracts" and the examination and approval for trade union fees. It becomes obvious that the worker congress is more powerful than a Chinese trade union because collective contracts in China are not similar to Western collective bargaining agreements but are documents that specify the functions of trade unions.[26]

Workers' congresses are held once or twice a year and attended either by all of an enterprise's employees or by employee representatives, to discuss union plans, the enterprise's budget, factory management, and the distribution of benefits. Since 1989, Chinese union leaders have attempted to make the worker congresses more responsive to the basic welfare concerns of ordinary workers. In spite of the renewed emphasis on party control over the unions in the post-Tianenman period, worker congresses maintained some of their enhanced powers, most notably the right to examine and discuss major decisions affecting the enterprise, including distribution of benefits and wage reform, and the right to remove incompetent managers. The use of these rights varied widely, with many worker congresses continuing to act largely as rubber stamps for deals hammered out among the manager, the union representatives, and the party secretary.

A circular intended to promote democratic management of Beijing companies threatened to punish state-owned enterprise managers who interfered with the operation of worker congresses. It noted that over 95% of state enterprises in Beijing had worker congresses which convened twice a year. Delegates to the congress are elected by secret ballot by the workers, one delegate per 10 workers. However, according to a survey by the Beijing Federation of Trade Unions, only 20% of the city's worker congresses were considered "healthy," 60% "are only marginally operative," while 20% "exist in name but are not functional."[27]

When the congress is not in session, the factory trade union committee acts for the congress. When in session, the workers congress hears and discusses work reports by the factory director or manager in order to supervise the operation of the factory while the director is responsible for production. Significantly, the Communist Party still retains political control since both the congress and the factory director are controlled by the plant party committee (see Figure 3-1).

The chairman of the Beijing Municipal Federation of Trade Unions alleged that the worker congress role was very limited "because factory leadership tended to ignore them." He claimed that "a few had no more than formal existence, and did nothing to encourage workers' initiative."[28] On the other hand, the vice-chairman of the ACFTU praised the role of the worker congress system. He stated that the system is upheld "in China's constitution, the enterprise law, the trade union law and the corporate law." He complained, however, that "in some areas, the democratic involvement mechanism has not been beefed up in line with autonomy rights gained by enterprises." He stressed that state-owned enterprises, state-funded corporations,

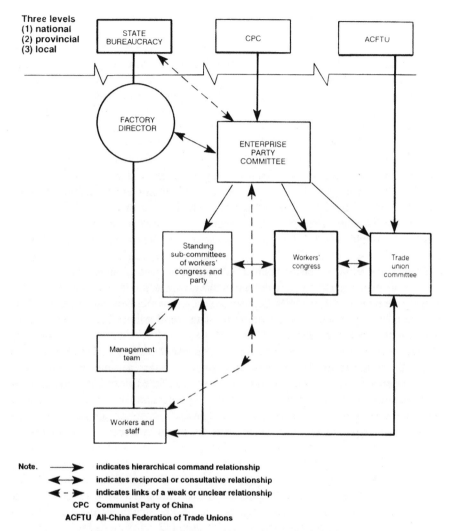

FIGURE 3-1. A simplified diagram of the decision-making structure of a Chinese state enterprise. *Source:* Rothman, M., Briscoe, D.R., & Nacamulli, R.C.D. (Eds.) (1993) *Industrial Relations Around the World: Labor Relations for Multinational Corporations* (p. 90). New York: Walter de Gruyter.

and limited liability companies funded by the state should improve their worker congresses in their adherence to the new corporation and enterprise laws. Corporations should have workers' representatives on their boards of directors and boards of supervisors. Also, workers should account for one-third of the membership of the boards of directors and one-third to one-half of the boards of supervisors membership.[29]

THE MINISTRY OF LABOR (MOL) AND PERSONNEL (MOP)

The Ministry of Labor is a functional body under the State Council responsible for administering work in the field of labor. Since the founding of the People's Republic, the ministry has experienced major changes in its organizational structure. In November 1949, the Central People's Government set up the Ministry of Labor to be in charge of labor administration. In June 1970, it was merged with the State Planning Commission and the State Economic Commission, to become the Labor Bureau within the new State Planning Commission. During reorganization of the State Council in September, 1975, the State General Bureau of Labor was established, directly answerable to the State Council. May 1982 saw the birth of the Ministry of Labor and Personnel, as a result of the merger of the State General Bureau of Labor, State Bureau of Personnel, State Staffing Committee, and Bureau of Scientific and Technical Personnel of the State Council, in accordance with the "Decisions on Schemes to Implement Reforms in the Ministries and Commissions under the State Council," adopted by the Twenty-Third Session of the Standing Committee of the Fifth National People's Congress. Finally, in the light of the scheme to reorganize the offices under the State Council approved by the First Session of the Seventh National People's Congress in April 1988, the Ministry of Labor and Personnel was dissolved and the new Ministry of Labor came into being (see Figure 3-2).

The Ministry of Labor and Ministry of Personnel have areas of responsibility similar in some ways to those of the U.S. Department of Labor and the Office of Personnel Management, respectively. The MOL oversees a nationwide system of labor bureaus at the provincial and local levels. The Ministry of Labor's most important tasks are running the national employment service and social insurance systems. In addition, the MOL helps establish wage policy and set safety standards. The MOL, through its local and provincial offices, maintains labor service centers and sponsors job fairs and labor markets for job seekers.

In tandem with the Ministry of Foreign Affairs, the Ministry of Labor sets China's international labor policies and oversees China's participation in the ILO. The ILO opened its Beijing office in 1985 and runs a number of programs in China, concentrating primarily on worker safety and health. Recent programs have also focused on freedom of association. China has ratified 17 ILO conventions, but has not ratified several key conventions including No. 87 (Freedom of Association), No. 98 (The Right to Organize and Collective Bargaining) and No. 105 (Abolition of Forced Labor).

The Ministry of Personnel oversees the employment of almost all college graduates regardless of type of employment and all "cadres" regardless of educational level. It is in charge of labor and personnel policies for technical and managerial positions in government and the state sector and for all employees of universities and research institutes. Among the college educated, only those in the foreign-invested and private sectors are outside the MOP's purview.

The MOP introduced a new governmental personnel system in 1992 that it hopes

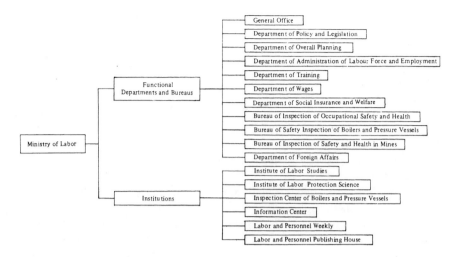

FIGURE 3-2. Organization Chart, Ministry of Labor. *Source*: Labor Administration: Profile on the People's Republic of China, International Labor Organization, 1989.

will allow for selection and promotion on the basis of technical qualifications rather than political acceptability.[30]

LABOR MOBILITY

With reform of the job assignment system, Chinese workers have greater freedom to find their own jobs rather than accept assignments by the government or their school. Companies also have greater freedom in choosing whom to hire. There is no longer a job assignment system for middle and high school graduates. As soon as students are legally eligible for employment (i.e., aged 16 or over) and have completed as much school as they wish, the school issues an employment eligibility certificate. Young people are then free to seek out work in any manner they wish. Local labor bureaus have established labor markets (job fairs) and labor service companies (employment offices) to assist young people and others looking for work in their job searches. Many enterprises also advertise in newspapers and recruit directly from neighborhood or specialized secondary schools.

Labor reform for college graduates has moved much more slowly. While the State Education Commission says it is no longer in the business of making job assignments except for teachers, many tertiary institutions continue to control the job assignment process for their graduates. The amount of control varies widely by the nature of the institution and by province. Graduates of teachers colleges and universities (all of whom receive a free education in return for the commitment to teach) continue to be assigned. Similarly many specialized institutes are run by industrial ministries, which then control their graduates' assignments. For general colleges and universities, most provinces have regulations guaranteeing students a choice in their jobs after graduation. However, interpretation and enforcement of these regulations vary. While Guangdong province appears to apply these strictly across the board, Beijing has allowed its institutions to attempt to direct their graduates to state enterprises rather than joint ventures and foreign company representative offices. Most areas have established Talent Markets (job fairs for skilled labor) to accommodate college graduates and those seeking transfers. Despite the barriers, increasing numbers use these services annually. Others choose to look door-to-door or in newspaper advertisements.

Mobility for those already employed is even more problematic. Without doubt such mobility has increased greatly in the past 15 years, but severe impediments still exist for many if not most workers. A major impediment is structural. Since housing and social insurance are provided by the work unit many of these benefits are not transferable. Social insurance programs are now generally on a city- or county-wide basis, which makes it somewhat easier than in the past to transfer within a single geographic area. Although many housing reform experiments have been started, housing remains the single greatest impediment to transfers.

The single greatest legal barrier to mobility is the requirement that certain workers receive permission from their current employer to transfer. While contract workers are free to transfer at the end of their contractual period, 84% of urban workers are still under the old permanent employment system and need to acquire such permission. In addition all college graduates are considered to be permanently employed "cadres" and require permission. For cadres and skilled workers such permission is often difficult to obtain even if the workplace has a surplus of such employees. Many employers fear that if they let one employee transfer the rest will choose to, and thus they prefer to block all transfers.

Regardless of whether an enterprise is legally allowed to block a transfer, many can effectively do so by refusing to transfer the employee's personnel file (*dang'an*). This file is generally held by enterprise management, except in the case of foreign ventures, when it is often left with the local labor or talent market. No state enterprise or government office can hire without the transfer of the personnel file. Often employees in this position find the only possibility is to quit the previous job and remain unemployed until the previous employer abandons the fight and returns the file to the labor or talent market. Most enterprises seeking to hire transfers report that the current employer can effectively block a transfer for six months or a year, but not forever. The problem for the potential transferee is that by that time the new job may have been filled by someone with a more accommodating previous employer.

Many labor and talent markets have set up arbitration committees to deal with some of these transfer problems. Their efficacy varies, often in the face of the relative power of the two employers. Many foreign-invested firms find they have to pay a "ransom" to the previous employer to achieve the transfer. This "ransom" may be to cover the real costs of the workers' housing and training or it may be in reality a bribe.

In addition, workers transferring from areas with weak social insurance structures to more developed ones (i.e., South China) will need to pay a fee to enter the system. This is generally paid by the new employer.

Residence permits continue to distort mobility. The transient labor population is growing rapidly; nevertheless, most of these workers are at the bottom of the economic heap. To obtain a good job and full benefits a worker needs a residence permit (*hukou*) for his place of employment. Most localities severely ration the number of residence permits they will issue to transferees. Although some areas in South China will pay sufficient premiums to skilled workers to make taking a temporary job without a residence permit attractive for the short-term, in general, urban residents find it undesirable to move without transfer of residence status.

The Labor Ministry has been attempting with limited success to institutionalize labor transfers by creating links between labor bureaus in labor short and surplus provinces. Thus far the problem has escalated far too rapidly for the ministry to control it. Many businesses themselves have chosen to recruit directly from interior provinces rather than waiting for the New Year's crush. In the long run this type of recruiting may have an impact, but it seems likely that for the next few years the annual post-New Year's migration will continue and with it raised hopes and crushed dreams.

CHAPTER 4

The ACFTU, Labor Law, and Labor Reform

Prime Minister Li Peng's 1995 government work report discusses every conceivable topic related to China's drive to establish a socialist market economy. However, there is one notable omission; nowhere to be found are any references to "trade unions" as vehicles which can contribute to the realization of this ambitious objective. The reasons for this omission become clear when the role of labor organizations is examined, and one then realizes why Chinese unions drew so little publicity from a top government official.

THE ALL-CHINA FEDERATION OF TRADE UNIONS (ACFTU)

The All-China Federation of Trade Unions is divided into local chapters at the factory level. As a United Front organization, the federation is controlled by the Communist Party and generally does not assume an adversarial role vis-à-vis management. The unions affiliated with the ACFTU have as their primary functions the transmission of social and political values and the protection of workers' welfare and recreation activities. In general, joint ventures have reported little union interference, although some firms have experienced aggressive activities on the part of labor organizations, including strikes. In many foreign-invested enterprises, unions are responsible for distributing wages, bonuses, housing, and other payments to workers. Union representatives have the right to attend board meetings when labor matters are under discussion and may negotiate with management on behalf of individual workers.

Tian Yukun, chief of ACFTU's Grass-Roots Section, has stated that the federation was composed of 600,000 unions, which have played an important part in the political education of the workforce.[1] They are officially described as the "transmission belt" of party policy; that is, their primary function is to inculcate in workers the virtues of diligence and hard work. Although entrusted with protecting workers' interests in welfare issues, unions are expected to cooperate with management. Nevertheless, prior to the advent of enterprise reform in the early 1980s, when market forces took over as the sole criterion for production planning, the power relationship was not completely one-sided as employers were highly dependent on the unions to elicit extra effort from workers in order to meet production targets at the end of planning periods. Skilled workers, particularly, in the absence of strong financial incentives, had to be coaxed to improvise to keep the often very antiquated machinery of production operating properly.

The recent reorganization of duties and responsibilities for the enterprise has done little to reduce the considerable overlap in the roles of the trade union and the party committee. Both have always been concerned with political education, but in the past the labor organization was ranked lower in the power hierarchy and its functions were more mundane. That is, they were centered on matters of labor productivity and worker morale and welfare, rather than with the interpretation of national policy. With much greater emphasis now being placed on economic efficiency and restrictions on the powers of the party committee, the status of the trade union in the enterprise hierarchy may become more significant. In particular, the reliance presently being placed on the "collective contract" system and on various forms of economic responsibility for individuals, implies a strong "productionist" role for unions.

Nevertheless, this does not mean that the State is introducing an adversarial system of collective bargaining between management and labor since the trade union movement is officially committed to working with management and the party committee to solve problems. The key objective in the Chinese system of employee relations remains to arrive at a consensus that satisfies all concerned parties. Moreover, the trade union is precluded from taking up workers' grievances, for it is the responsibility of the party committee to deal with complaints against management. Only the party secretary has official access to higher authority within the state apparatus, and this is what ultimately counts because it is the state that appoints the factory director who has full responsibility for the enterprise.[2]

Despite the apparent reordering of the role of trade unions, the political risks of promoting increased trade union autonomy was underscored by the purge of the party's general secretary, Zhao Zeying, after the suppression of the pro-democracy movement in 1989. Granted, it may not have been the only thing held against him by the government, but undoubtedly his prounion comments contributed to Zhao's downfall. He addressed the eleventh national congress of the ACFTU in October 1988, attended by more than 15,000 worker delegates from all walks of life. Zhao proselytized the notion that trade unions should be nongovernmental, democratic organizations which needed to introduce competition into their leadership election system. In the past, union leaders were usually appointed or removed by the government or by factory directors. He applauded the ACFTU and local trade unions for the important part they had played in mobilizing all workers behind Deng Xiaoping's economic reforms, but he stated that the trade union's function of safeguarding workers' rights and interests had been previously neglected, and this hampered their development. Zhao said, "We should learn from both the positive and negative lessons of the workers' movement and try to represent and safeguard interests as well as the integrated interests of the nation," referring to problems in economic development.[3]

The Continuation of Party Control

Apparently emboldened by Zhao's remarks, independent labor organizations' activities increased slightly in 1991. There were reports of a number of such organizations, including some modeled after the Polish Solidarity Movement, operating at that time. Because such organizations are outlawed, they must conduct their activities sub rosa, and it is impossible to evaluate the extent or the effect of the government's reported attempts to suppress them.

After the Tianenman protest, China's leaders attributed much of the unrest to "incorrect political thinking" among Chinese workers and students. A move was instituted to improve party discipline and political training in enterprises, and there were a number of reports in 1991 of union officials losing their positions for political reasons. The new union law, introduced at the March 1992 National People's Congress continued to emphasize the union's didactic role and its part in supporting the party and the government.

The 1992 Trade Union Act—Toward Freedom of Association?

The Trade Union Act of 1992 replaced an earlier 1950 statute and presumably took account of the significant changes that had occurred in China during the previous decade. The law accords unions a prominent place in society, and the first words are: "This law is enacted ... to ensure trade unions' position in the country's political, economic, and social life."

Although the tone of the language might be different, some of the aims laid down for Chinese trade unions are, ostensibly, comparable to those of any free trade union movement: "trade unions should safeguard the legal rights and interests of staff members (management) and workers"; trade unions should organize staff members and workers to take part in "democratic management" and supervision of their enterprises. Statements which exhort trade unions to encourage workers to have "lofty ideals, good moral sense, and good education, and maintain good discipline" are, perhaps, less familiar in the language of conflicting interests.

On a more practical plane, the Act states that government at all levels should provide the necessary facilities to enable trade unions to conduct their activities. Union committee members are to receive their wages when meetings are held within working hours. Unions are to be funded by their members, by enterprises, and by local authorities.

There are, however, several vital elements that are missing. There is neither the substantive basis, nor the procedural framework, for wage bargaining, conditions of work, or grievance handling, to equip the unions with any meaningful voice in employment matters. In the words of the Act, unions have nothing more than the right "to *submit suggestions* (emphasis added) ... on working conditions as well as on safety and public health facilities"; "to *suggest solutions* (emphasis added) ... when management has compelled workers to do dangerous work"; or "to *voice their opinions*" (emphasis added) on unfair dismissal. And if an enterprise violates labor law, all the union can do is "look into the matter." Procedures for handling labor disputes are, to all intents and purposes, taken care of in one sentence: "Trade unions take part in enterprises' mediation of labor dispute."

The statute should be taken in context since China introduced it after little more than 10 years of economic liberalization. It may represent a step towards independent trade unions, but it is unlikely that China will rush into allowing the formation of free and independent unions. In the words of the president of the ACFTU, Ni Zhifu, the new Act "embodies the essential features of China's peculiar socialist worker movement."

The Act makes it clear that unions are to be organized "to enable them to serve socialist modernization." In short, they are to be used within the existing structure of socialism in the country, and are intended to strengthen this system. For example, unions are to be organized on the traditional Communist system of "democratic centralism," i.e., one in which power is concentrated at the top of the pyramid.

In this respect, the Act delegates greater power to the apex of the edifice—the government—and major acts by one level can only be passed with the approval of the level above. To quote the Act: "Trade union organizations at a lower level are under the leadership of those at a higher level." Indeed, control now reaches to a lower level than before, for whereas previously only workplaces with more than 200 people could form unions, now those with more than 25 workers can. This change was designed to unionize the 60% of industrial workers employed in urban cooperatives, service establishments, and joint ventures established since reforms began in 1979.

For some, a problem of the law is that the government both owns the enterprises (or at least the majority of them), tells management what to do, and controls the unions. In the words of a maverick labor leader, the new law is "an ACFTU charter tricked out as a statute." He adds "contradictions must be mediated by an impartial— and that means independent—trade union. A government union cannot do the job when the government is the boss."

INTERNATIONAL REACTION

The pyramidal structure of union authority, and the Chinese government's reluctance to permit independent unions in the Western sense of the term, have exposed the government to foreign criticism. Workers' Autonomous Federations (WAFs) were established in 1989, only to be banned after the massacre in Tianenmen Square in June that year. The Chinese maintain that they are illegal organizations because they had not complied with formal registration procedures. However, under

Chinese legislation the application for registration was bound to be rejected, and it was therefore impossible for them to become legal.

The ILO's Committee on Freedom of Association, referring in its 275th Report to Case No. 1500, brought by the International Confederation of Free Trade Unions (ICFTU), stated that the WAF's were pursuing "the normal activities of a workers' organization promoting and defending the interests of its members." On this matter, in its 279th Report, the committee urged the government "to ensure that the right of workers to establish organizations of their own choosing and the right of these organizations to function freely are *recognized in the country's legislation and guaranteed in practice*" (emphasis added).

China has not ratified either the Freedom of Association and Protection of the Right to Organize Convention, 1948 (No. 87), nor the Right to Organize and Collective Bargaining Convention, 1949 (No. 98). But as the committee has pointed out, when a state decides to become a member of the ILO it accepts the fundamental principles of the organization, such as those set out in the constitution and the Declaration of Philadelphia, including those relating to freedom of association. It remains to be seen whether the law will really encourage the formation of free and independent labor unions.[4]

The Revised 1993 Trade Union Law

China's 1982 Constitution provides for "freedom of association," but the guarantee is heavily diluted by references to the interest of the state and the leadership of the Chinese Communist Party. Independent trade unions are illegal. Although union officials recognize that workers' interests may not always coincide with those of the Communist Party, the Union Law passed by the National People's Congress in March 1992, states that the union is a party organ and its primary purpose is to mobilize workers for national development.

The revised 1993 Trade Union Law requires that the establishment of unions at any level be submitted to a higher level trade union organization for approval. The ACFTU is the highest such organization, and it has not approved the establishment of any independent unions. While the foreign press has reported that some exist, because of severe repression they operate only deep within the shadows. The vast majority of workers have no contact with any union other than the ACFTU. There are no provisions allowing for individual workers or unofficial worker organizations to affiliate with international bodies.

The ACFTU's primary attention remains focused on its traditional constituency, state sector employees. The Trade Union Law mandates that workers may decide whether to join the union in their enterprise. By official estimate, 10% of workers in collectively and state-owned enterprises have chosen for their own reasons not to join. There have been no reports of repercussions for workers who have not joined ACFTU unions. Diversification of types of businesses over the last decade of reform has vastly increased the number of workers outside this traditional sphere of the ACFTU. In fact, over half of China's nonagricultural labor force is now largely nonunion and outside the state industrial structure—in collectives, village and township enterprises, private and individual firms, and foreign-invested enterprises. In township and village enterprises, one of the fastest growing sectors of the economy, only one-tenth of 1% of workers are unionized. Unemployed workers are not considered union members.

The ICFTU Complaint

The ICFTU alleged that in May and June 1992, the Public Security Bureau (PSB) secretly arrested activists of the clandestine China Free Trade Union Preparatory Committee and appeared to have dismantled this organization. On May 15th, another clandestine union group, the Free Trade Union of China, issued a manifesto. Preemptive arrests took place just before the June 4th Tiananmen anniversary. These included seven members of the clandestine Liberal Workers Union detained by the PSB to prevent them from circulating commemorative leaflets. Accurate figures on the number of Worker Autonomous Federation detainees still being held after the 1989 events are not available. The ICFTU alleges that hundreds of workers are still being held.

Responding to the ICFTU complaint, the governing body of the ILO in March 1993, requested that the Chinese government should modify "many provisions" of the Trade Union Act that are contrary to the principle of freedom of association, expressed concern at the severity of the sanctions pronounced by the courts against members or leaders of the Workers' Autonomous Federation, and asked that detained workers be released immediately.[5]

Unions in Foreign-Invested Enterprises (FIEs)

Workers in companies with foreign investors are guaranteed the right to form unions, which then must affiliate with the ACFTU. According to national statistics, 30% of foreign-invested firms now have unions. Other official estimates reveal that about 10,000 trade unions with a total of 500,000 members have been established in the nearly 20,000 foreign-funded companies in Guangdong province. However, a 1993 American embassy survey of foreign-invested ventures in Beijing indicated the unionization rate had diminished from 60% in 1991 to 40% in 1993.

The ACFTU intensified its efforts to establish unions in over half of China's foreign-funded firms by the end of 1994. The effort to promote unions in such firms was launched to help resolve labor disputes, most of which occurred in nonunion companies. Ambiguous contracts failing to comply with state labor regulations, unduly long working hours and heavy work loads, low pay and substandard safety conditions, made labor disputes inevitable. The majority of the 250,000 labor disputes and strikes since 1988 have occurred in joint ventures.

An ACFTU official cautioned, "but we do not advocate strikes since they hurt both the factory and the worker." He stated that unions will try to resolve problems before such extreme measures are undertaken. The 1992 labor law stipulated that unions have a seat on the boards of enterprises so they can express workers' complaints and wishes. Trade union priorities were expressed by the same official who said, "our tasks in foreign-funded enterprises are first to implement the open policy, second to safeguard workers' legitimate rights." Evidently the ACFTU policy has been ineffective in preventing the labor disputes in joint ventures and foreign-funded firms that have occurred in recent years.

At the local level, the Beijing Municipal People's Congress Standing Committee passed a resolution providing that foreign funded and private enterprises must support and offer financial assistance to their employees who wish to organize unions within one year after the enterprises open for business. Under this resolution, which took effect in November 1994, trade union representatives were armed with the right to attend board meetings to discuss the enterprise's development plans, production management, as well as employees' rewards, disciplinary measures, salaries, welfare, labor protection, and social insurance.[6]

In Hubei province, the law rate of unionization was cited as the reason behind serious abuses of labor rights in the central region of the province. Of the 1100 foreign-funded enterprises, only 372 had unions. The *Hubei Daily* reported that overtime, dismissal without sufficient reasons, improper implementation of a workers' insurance system, and equal-job/unequal-pay were more significant in foreign-funded enterprises.

"Because of the low rate of unionization, it is difficult to guarantee the lawful rights of workers," the paper said. Huang Yuan, a standing committee member of the Hubei Province Committee, was quoted as saying: "To form a union is an important measure to better handle the various internal relationships in these foreign-funded enterprises."

Labor unionists in Hong Kong suggest that the low rate of unionization in Chinese foreign-funded firms was the result of strong resistance from employers who feared militant labor action would follow.

The coastal Shangdong province had its own set of regulations on employment management in foreign investments approved by the provincial people's congress, and designed to protect the rights of employees as well as employers. There were 14,860 foreign-owned firms employing more than one million workers in Shangdong at the end of June 1994, with the number of labor disputes "soaring."[7]

The New Labor Law

The Standing Committee of the National People's Congress passed the most comprehensive labor law ever enacted in China in July 1994. The statute went into effect January 1, 1995. It includes the provision of a statutory minimum wage, to be set by provincial governments, an eight-hour working day, a minimum of one day's holiday per week, a maximum 44-hour work week (that is, no work on Saturday afternoon) and a minimum working age of 16. Employers will have to provide contracts setting out the full terms of employment, including rates of pay, hours of work, job description, termination of contract, and regulations to be observed. Women workers are to be protected from harsh working conditions and will be entitled to a minimum of 90 days' maternity leave. Employers may not discriminate against workers on grounds of race, nationality (ethnic origin), sex, or religion. The intention of the new law and of the accompanying laws on safety and social insurance which are to follow it is to mollify the increasingly militant workforce and forestall the widespread social unrest that remains the government's greatest fear.

The State Council (cabinet) decreed that trade unions affiliated with the ACFTU were to be established in all foreign-invested businesses by the end of 1994, a year earlier than the ACFTU had stipulated. This measure is aimed at preventing strikes, most of which were taking place in foreign-invested and private enterprises, where there usually are no unions to siphon off dissent.

WAGE GUIDELINES TO BE INSTITUTED

The government also is setting up machinery to establish wage guidelines based on increases in consumer prices and in labor productivity. This resembles a national incomes policy similar to the German model, with the government, employers, and unions jointly determining a maximum rate of wage increase at the beginning of the financial year. The aim is to provide a means of restraining wage increases to maintain the profitability of firms and export competitiveness. At the same time, the new guidelines are intended to ensure that workers are to some extent compensated for the price increases that will follow the removal of the formerly imposed price controls and the gradual removal of consumer subsidies.[8]

With labor-related issues, where much is decided at the local level, the intervention of local labor departments and their willingness to oversee activities of local employers will determine how successfully and widely the new law is enforced. A politburo member commented on the new legislation:

> At present, trade unions at all levels should advance trade union work as a whole and promote reform and construction of themselves by taking advantage of the opportunity created by the implementation of the labor law. Under the condition of developing a socialist market economy, trade unions at all levels must expand their role in protecting the workers' legitimate rights and interests and be good at fully exercising the rights and interests vested in trade unions and workers by the labour law.... Trade unions at all levels should ... make persistent efforts in integrating the party's basic line-that is, taking economic development as the central task with the trade unions' functions in protecting the workers' rights and interests.... It is necessary to subordinate ourselves to and serve the overall interest of reform, development and stability.[9]

These remarks clearly demonstrate the continuation of the party's political influence during the reform effort and the subordinate role to be played by the labor movement. This central fact should not be overlooked. Despite the promulgation of

China's first set of comprehensive labor laws, which guarantee the right to organize unions, independent trade unions and strikes are still prohibited.

Contractual Arrangements in Foreign-Invested Enterprises

Under basic labor regulations, joint ventures may sign a collective labor contract with a local entity such as a trade union, or separate contracts with individual workers. Most joint ventures outside of the special economic zones follow the former practice, establishing one contract to regulate the company's relationship with both its employees and the trade union. However, China's new labor regulations seem to recommend that firms should now sign contracts with individual workers rather than group contracts with the trade union. Under the new rules, these contracts must be approved by the local labor bureau, which then sets up model contracts for use in different industries. Some labor bureaus already provide such model contracts, although the practice is not as yet widespread.

In almost all cases, compensation beyond the basic wage constitutes a very large portion of a venture's labor costs. Local governments also tax firms and workers to support social security and unemployment insurance funds. In general, foreign ventures are free to pay whatever wage rates they want. Chinese income tax laws often make it desirable to provide greater subsidies and services rather than higher wage rates, and these decisions are often taken after observing the local practice.

Termination of Employment

The ability to terminate workers varies widely based on location, type, and size of enterprise. Generally, it is easier to fire workers in the south than in the north, and in smaller enterprises than in larger ones. Terminating individual workers for cause is legally possible throughout China but may require prior notification and consultation with the local union. Large-scale layoffs, especially in North China, can arouse opposition from the local government and from the workers themselves. Where workers are hired by short-term contracts or agreements, it is relatively easy to dismiss them at the end of the contract period.

Worker Rights

The joint venture laws requires joint ventures to allow union recruitment but does not require a joint venture actually to set up the union, as management does in state enterprises. In recent years, most coastal provinces have passed stricter regulations that require unions in all foreign-invested firms. To date most such businesses do not have unions and some, in contravention of Chinese law, have agreements with localities not to establish unions in their enterprises. A dramatic increase in labor disputes in foreign-invested companies in 1993 prompted labor officials to begin drafting industrial relations legislation. At the same time the ACFTU declared its intention to establish unions in 50% of all foreign-funded firms before the end of 1994. It is illegal according to Chinese law to oppose these efforts. However, although China is a signatory to a number of ILO conventions, it has not signed any key ILO conventions on freedom of association or forced labor.

ACFTU OBJECTIVES

The key goals of the All-China Federation of Trade Unions for the near future include wage increases, improved working conditions, and the protection of the interests of Chinese workers in foreign firms. The labor federation set a goal, exceeding its former one, of setting up unions in 80% of all foreign firms in China by the end of 1995.[10] The goal was to unionize all foreign firms in coastal areas and 60% in the interior. At the end of September 1994, the rate of unionization in foreign firms was only 32%. Excluding small businesses, the percentage rose to 53%. Estimates had 100,000 new foreign enterprises starting business in China in 1995.

The Ministry of Foreign Trade and Economic Cooperation requires the establishment of unions as a precondition for the licensing of joint ventures. The Ministry of Labor conducts an annual survey of labor conditions at foreign firms and can direct firms to establish unions. The Communist Party has also instructed its local affiliates to promote the formation of unions at foreign firms. Not all foreign companies have acted quickly to set up unions. For example, one Hong Kong business in Xiamen finally allowed a union to form after eight years of negotiations. At one point, this firm refused to meet with a visiting government delegation. They were finally persuaded to permit a union to form but it took a coordinated effort of the city, the government, and the Communist Party.

ACFTU ACCOMPLISHMENTS

Chinese unions are operating hundreds of facilities offering jobs to unemployed workers as factories are being streamlined for higher productivity. According to ACFTU officials, thousands of people have found new jobs through the help of union job agencies which, unlike other agencies, serve only the needs of the workers. In Harbin, capital of Heilongjiang province, local unions run dozens of "flea markets" to assist workers in financial difficulties. ACFTU cited these examples to show how unions are taking to heart the problems facing those who are paying a price for China's reforms. Chinese workers, the federation claims, have, as a whole, benefited from the reforms. Their monthly cash income has risen by an annual average of 5% since the economic restructuring commenced in 1979. However, many workers face job insecurity and the loss of income now that employers have autonomy in management, employment, and compensation decisions.

The Shanghai Number Three Iron and Steel Mill has trimmed its staff by over 20% during the past three years. In response to the management intention to reduce the number of workers by 5210, the mill's union committee called a special session of the worker congress to discuss and examine the plan. The intention was finalized only after the plan won the approval of the congress. Subsequently, 1500 workers who were laid off were given jobs at service companies jointly established by the management and union. Of the rest of the displaced workers, 137 insisted that they be allowed to continue working at the mill. The union negotiated with mill management and persuaded it to rehire all of the 137 before the end of the year, except those who preferred to find jobs by themselves.

Despite these successful efforts, the ACFTU has admitted that nearly 7 million Chinese workers still live below the poverty line, which means 20 million persons when family members are included. In response to this problem, unions throughout China have set up 400,000 foundations, which offer subsidies to such families or loans to help them start family businesses. These foundations have raised 104 million yuan for this purpose over the past three years. In addition, Chinese unions are running 110,000 companies and using part of the profits to help workers classified as "poverty-stricken." Unions have also organized mutual aid groups that provide insurance against the death or illness of workers' family members. By the end of 1992, 8.7 million workers had been insured after each made a payment of up to 100 yuan.

The ACFTU cited the example of the Kailuan Coal Mines in Hebei province, where the compensation amounts to 10,000 yuan—about three years' wages for an average miner—for a single death. In Shanghai, China's largest industrial city, the municipal government published a decree on the minimum wages set for employees at firms in the city's urban sector. In the absence of a national law on minimum wages, the Shanghai union federation called for local legislation and was successful. In a dozen cities, government raised the subsidies for people below the poverty line at the request of local unions.[11]

Progress in Tianjin

More than 220 trade unions have been set up in 800 foreign-funded enterprises in the development zone of Tianjin, the largest port city in North China, with a membership of nearly 40,000. The development zone views the unions as a major means for protecting the rights and interests of workers and promoting the development of foreign-funded firms. The first trade union in the zone was formed in 1987. During the 1987–95 period, unions mediated 309 labor disputes. The labor organizations attach great importance to the protection of the legal rights and interests of women employees. When a young woman worker surnamed Zhang was fired by her employer after she gave birth, the relevant trade union showed her foreign employer a regulation forbidding such dismissal issued by the State Council, and she was immediately reinstated. Due to such efforts, 20,000 female employees in the development zone enjoy the rights and interests they are entitled to.

According to ACFTU statistics, 17,293 foreign-funded companies established a union in 1994, raising the total number of such enterprises to 32,458, some 68.6% of the total overseas-funded firms in operation in China.[13]

UNIONIZATION OF RURAL WORKERS

The rural-based industrial workforce was 31 million strong in 1986, and now is much larger. Not surprisingly, almost none of these peasant-workers have a union to turn to. As of 1992, only 0.1% of the rural enterprises contained unions. These tend to be the very largest rural factories, representing 3% of the rural-based industrial workers.[14]

NONRECOGNITION AND PARTY CONTROL

There is a very serious obstacle hampering the developing of independent trade unions in China. Existing labor organizations must work under the control of the Communist Party and unions opposed to political control are banned. An ACFTU official stated his opposition to autonomous labor organizations in these terms: "Otherwise, we will miss the correct political orientation of trade union reform and construction leading to great errors."[15] He claimed that during the social turmoil in 1989, most workers had struggled resolutely against the so-called autonomous workers unions' efforts to oppose the party leadership, exposing their true nature to the workers, whom he maintained had been hoodwinked and coerced into joining these organizations.

THE ITF POSITION

The government prohibition of free, independent unions has drawn the attention of the International Transport Workers Federation(ITF), whose Asian affiliates are increasingly establishing contact with Chinese unions despite the fact that the latter are controlled by the government in Beijing. The ITF has adopted a policy that it will not have any formal dealings itself with the state-run Chinese unions, but its affiliates are free to establish bilateral contacts. The ITF does not recognize the ACFTU, nor the Chinese Seamen's Union (CSU) on the grounds that they do not, in the ITF's view, represent the real interest of workers. The CSU claims to have 1.6 million members, making it one of the largest shipping unions, but the ITF pointed out that every seaman in China is enrolled in the CSU without having any say in the matter.

The ITF believes that such contacts are, however, open to exploitation by the

Chinese government and has submitted a complaint against China's abuses of trade union rights to the International Labor Organization.[16]

OBSTACLES TO OVERCOME

Obviously, a country like China with from 380,000 to nearly 600,000 unions (estimates vary) and upwards of 100 million members has a tremendous potential for representing and protecting the economic interests of its workforce. However, this role, which is automatically conferred upon Western unions, has not yet been filled in a significant manner by Chinese unions. In order for Chinese labor organizations to realistically protect workers' rights and influence the development of internationally accepted labor standards, they must deal with five serious problems.

First, there is a paucity of organization at the macrolevel. Most unions are basically local, parochial in their perspectives, lacking unity, and without the regional or national visibility and the communication infrastructure to adequately fulfill their representational responsibility. Unity will not come without the emergence of leadership that will create the national coalitions common in most industrialized nations. Understandably, the Chinese government casts a disapproving eye on such efforts, exposing these leaders to great privation, and pervasive threats of imprisonment and death.

Second, the iron grip of the Communist Party shows no signs of relaxation. Union leadership is appointed and removed by party committee or company directors, producing a horde of fawning sycophants. In fact, eligibility for union leadership is dependent upon loyal party service, with the appointee's role primarily that of an unquestioning party propagandist. Former party General Secretary Zuyin recommended the direct election of union officials at shop floor levels, but, as already noted, his support for the 1989 prodemocracy movement ended his career and concerted resistance since from the established bureaucracy has put this option on hold for the foreseeable future.

Third, the workers themselves have no unity of purpose. The traditional Chinese subservience to strong, centralized control and adherence to socialist doctrine stands in the path of purposeful action. Party cadres constantly bombard workers with the message that Communist education and propaganda are the overreaching objectives of trade unions. Some workers also perceive unions as nothing more than worker welfare agencies. In the last few years, there are indications that the improvement of workers' interests is being increasingly mentioned as the raison d'etre for Chinese labor organizations, but a consensus has not yet coalesced around this issue.

Fourth, corruption is endemic among party cadres who have parlayed political power into material benefits for themselves, their families, and friends without evincing any concern for society's truly needy. Furthermore, those on the party's enemy lists face maltreatment without recourse. Workers are basically helpless to correct these inequities. In this regard, the union leader is also a factory manager who exploits his union position, promoting the enterprise's objectives at the workers' expense.

Fifth, the recent, comprehensive set of labor laws, like their less complete predecessors, appear to protect workers' basic economic interests. It remains to be seen, however, whether they will ever be fully implemented or whether they will suffer the same fate that befell earlier legislative efforts which failed to remedy a host of labor abuses in a meaningful way.

A final important point is that unions in China lack credibility due to the factors just enumerated. Bluntly put, unions have not had the power to force employers to grant workers necessary benefits, and workers are skeptical that labor organizations will ever manage to protect their interests. The scenario remains a bleak one for labor reform as nearly two decades of experimentation with a socialist market economy draw to a close.[17]

EVALUATION OF LABOR REFORM

An ILO survey of China's workforce makes pessimistic reading. Unemployment is rising while efficiency remains at a standstill. More than 10 years after reform of China's employment system began, the country's labor market remains stubbornly rigid and largely unchanged.

The March 1995 survey, which studied the employment conditions of 300 enterprises of varying ownership in Beijing, Shanghai, Guangzhou, Tianjin, and Shenyang, paints a stark picture of mounting unemployment and underemployment. The investigation further concluded that current employment policy is doing little to ameliorate a potentially explosive social situation.

The survey's conclusions reinforce what the China missions of several multi-lateral aid and lending agencies have been saying quietly for some time; that labor reforms to date have done little to improve China's labor efficiency. Labor surpluses in the public sector continue to hover at around 20% of the workforce; public compensation systems do not reward performance; wages are high relative to the cost of capital. According to a recent United Nations report, the cost of urban labor relative to energy costs in China is three times more than in India; the price of labor relative to capital shows a similar disparity.

The principal conclusions of the ILO survey suggest that there are bad times ahead for enterprises of every type in China, be they state-owned firms, joint-stock companies, village and township enterprises, or foreign-invested businesses. Among the key conclusions are:

1.   Labor surpluses will increase. The survey's estimate of the national labor surplus which is defined as the difference between actual and desirable levels of employment, puts the number of "on-leave" and "in-job" redundant workers at 18.4% of China's total workforce. This compares with Chinese government estimates of a 10 to 25% labor surplus and a recent World Bank estimate of 11%. Surplus workers comprised 6.6% of the workforces surveyed in joint ventures, 5.4% in township and village enterprises, 21% in joint stock companies and state-owned

enterprises, and 24.1% in state labor service enterprises, which are collectives set up by state-owned firms to redeploy their surplus workers.

Predictably, labor surplus rates varied significantly across regions; Tianjin managed a phenomenal 34% surplus. By contrast, surplus workers accounted for only 6.6% of the workforce in surveyed companies in Guangzhou. In Beijing, Shanghai, and Shenyang the levels of estimated labor surplus were 13%, 17%, and 19.5%, respectively. More than half of the enterprises surveyed predicted an increase in labor surplus, while only 18% expected a decrease. Of the principal reasons given for labor surpluses, state-owned enterprises emphasized the negative effects of product and market changes on their businesses as well as the responsibility of state enterprises to absorb workers. Joint ventures were more likely to mention technological and organizational changes which, while eventually leading to better efficiency, tend to create surplus labor which is difficult to retrench.

2.   The survey suggests that there has been some decline in employment in China's state sector since 1993. Among state-owned firms surveyed, the total number of employed persons dropped about 3% between 1993 and early 1995. While all other types of enterprises registered employment increases, it was not enough to suggest that nonstate firms would be capable of absorbing the swelling numbers of redundant state employees. Small and medium-sized firms accounted for most new hires; these jobs, however, tend to be the least stable.

3.   State firms still have little control over recruitment policy. Labor market reforms have so far failed to increase state managers' control over recruitment. Among state enterprises surveyed more than 40% of new recruits were assigned by local authorities while another 23% were surplus workers transferred from other enterprises. State enterprises are also pressured to hire special groups of job seekers such as graduates from technical colleges and demobilized soldiers. Two-thirds of workers in state firms were still designated permanent rather than contract staff. Among the various enterprise types, only township and village enterprises and joint ventures relied mainly on the open labor market to hire contract workers.

4.   The social welfare burden adds costs and bureaucracy across the board. Despite government promises to shift the burden of social welfare from enterprises to local government, the survey found that a wide range of nonwage benefits continue to be provided by all types of enterprises. Of the 300 firms surveyed, more than three-quarters provide medical care and food facilities, two-thirds provide housing and training facilities, and at least half provide childcare centers and transportation for workers. Surprisingly, no significant differences were revealed between the state sector and nonstate sector in terms of social welfare provision. Indeed, joint ventures and joint stock companies showed the highest level of benefit provision in the areas of housing, medical care, and training. The majority of enterprises said they were planning to maintain or increase current levels of welfare benefits, especially housing. Almost 30% said they were planning to increase housing facilities in the near term.

5.   Labor bureaus are part of the labor market problem, not the solution. Local labor authorities place the responsibility and financial burden of coping with surplus

labor almost entirely on individual enterprises, a practice deeply resented by enterprise managers. More than 70% of the managers surveyed said that labor market authorities should play a more active role in the redeployment of surplus workers. Only 18.3% of managers reported receiving government help in coping with labor surpluses, with large urban state enterprises as opposed to smaller, nonstate firms being the main beneficiaries. When available, labor bureau assistance to enterprises is rudimentary at best. Assistance such as training of surplus workers, encouragement of self-employment and more flexible or reduced work hours was rarely mentioned by survey respondents. The survey concludes that government employment services have made little impact on the labor market. Only 11% of newly recruited employees came to surveyed enterprises via labor bureaus and less than 1% of all new hires were previously recipients of unemployment benefits. This latter finding suggests that labor market policies to increase the reabsorption of unemployed workers into the workforce have so far been ineffective.

THE ACFTU—REPRESENTATION OR RHETORIC?

As noted above, the vast majority of Chinese workers have no contract with any union except the ACFTU. Officially, the ACFTU's primary goals are improving labor discipline and mobilizing workers to achieve party and government goals. In the reform era these goals have been to increase productivity and encourage participation in and support for reform. In fact, the ACFTU is a deeply conservative organization whose main goal appears to be preservation of as much of the status quo as possible.

The ACFTU and local trade unions have generally shown themselves to be supportive of permanent employment and the type of egalitarianism signified by the "one big pot." The ACFTU's hesitancy toward reform, especially as it adversely affects workers, was demonstrated in a speech by ACFTU President Ni Shifu in December 1992, where he used in an official capacity a turn on the three irons that had become popular with workers, characterizing certain factory managers as having "iron hearts, iron heads, and iron hands." In general, the ACFTU has been reluctant to support layoffs and terminations.

The lack of liaison between the labor ministry and the ACFTU is notorious, and severely limits the ACFTU's influence over labor policy. The ministry has transformed itself from a central planning to a labor service orientation, and is full of fairly eager reformers. The labor organization, however, seems lost in the new vocabulary of reform and unable to make effective policy suggestions that are both economically sensible and sensitive to workers' needs. As a result, the federation is generally ignored in discussions of enterprise reform and its role is limited to running some social services and in theory teaching workers about reform. In practice, it cannot teach workers about a process it does not understand and is left to be occasionally obstructionist and often ineffectual.

One of the most marked failings of the ACFTU has been in organizing new segments of the workforce. Over half the nonagricultural workforce is now outside the state industrial structure, in collectives, village and township enterprises, private and individual firms, and foreign-funded companies. The vast majority of these workers are not members of the ACFTU, and the union has made a negligible effort to organize beyond its state enterprise base.

While a few township and village enterprises have local branches of the ACFTU, many others insist that unions are not possible in TVEs, because the employees continue to be classified as "farmers" rather than "workers." In general, it appears that the few unions formed are in TVEs that have a party secretary (i.e., a Communist Party position) as part of the management. The ACFTU does not appear to actively organize, nor do the workers form the group and then affiliate. Some party secretaries apparently take it upon themselves, as they would in a state enterprise, to establish the union representative position and affiliate with the ACFTU. Whether an enterprise has a party organization depends on the size of the enterprise and when and where it was formed. There do not appear to be any consistent national standards. The result is that most TVEs have no worker representation whatsoever. Some have worker congresses, but these generally meet only once a year.

Most joint and foreign-invested venture employees are also without union representation. An update of the national figures is not available, but the general trend appears to that as the number of foreign-invested ventures has grown the union's ability to organize them has diminished.

The ACFTU's failure to organize stems from a lack of resources and the changing nature of foreign venture hiring. Many of the early joint ventures were formed with an existing state factory. The new venture inherited a state enterprise workforce and with it the already formed union. While this type of joint venture continues to be formed, many joint ventures as well as almost all wholly foreign-owned ventures, hire directly for the new enterprises.

There are some "sweetheart" contracts with local governments, which in contravention of Chinese law guarantee a union-free shop, but these appear to be in a small minority of ventures. In some, generally large, joint ventures, the contract specifies formation of a union. In most cases the ventures take the view that under the Joint Venture Law and other relevant statutes workers have the right to form a union, but management has no obligation to actively encourage union formation. The union would thus need to come in and organize the workers, or workers would need to seek out the union.

The ACFTU simply has no experience in actively organizing unions. As in the case of TVEs the foreign-invested firms that have unions, other than those inherited or by contract, have no active party organization. When one city labor union was asked whether it had any materials or advice to offer workers who wanted to form their own union, they had nothing to offer.

The ACFTU and its local chapters appear to be extremely uncomfortable grappling with the new issues that new ventures create, such as part-time work, distribution of benefits, much larger income differentials, and far greater labor mobility. Many of the workers, generally young and somewhat individualistic, are less likely to join a union unless they believe there are tangible benefits. Because unions at many state enterprises control sizable welfare funds the advantages in the state sector are obvious. In a new venture the advantages are all purely hypothetical.

Nevertheless, because of the Chinese legal structure workers lose some protections by not having a union. One significant loss is protection from unreasonable mandatory overtime demands. Many of the smaller export-processing factories in South China as well as some TVEs routinely demand 12-hour days and some provide Sunday off every other week. When labor bureaus are consulted on these violations their explanation is that these employees are victims of a legal loophole. The law requires the union's consent before any imposition of mandatory overtime. If there is no union the factory management is not required to consult with anyone else. Similarly, a union representative is theoretically the employee's advocate in dismissal and other proceedings. While some union representatives are in the manager's pocket, as noted above, most are averse to firings of any kind and will probably try to protect the worker. Without a union, there is no representative and no arbitration procedure in cases of dismissal.

Thus, while the union, lacking a collective bargaining procedure and dominated by the Communist Party, is not able to serve workers' interests fully, in most cases it can provide some services that workers require. To date, however, it has shown itself unconcerned with the fate of workers in the newly developing portions of the economy and is thus rapidly becoming less relevant to the workforce as a whole.

It is in state enterprises and large collectives that more effectively functioning staff and workers representative councils tend to be found, and in these enterprises the grassroots trade unions are better staffed and organized with greater resources to attend to workers' welfare, and perhaps even to encourage workers' rights. In other words, it is in the state enterprises that the trade unions' dualistic functions could best be developed. At times of tight political control and production mobilization campaigns they may side with the state and management to push through top-down policies. In politically relaxed and economically liberal times, they are given a chance, if they so choose, to transmit grassroots discontent upwards, or even to play an adversarial role against management, of course, within limits. Given the right climate, trade unions can play a crucial role and their allegiance can swing either way or both ways. Such a climate existed in the 1980s but is absent in the 1990s.

CHAPTER 5

The Law, Contracts, Strikes, and Dispute Settlement

Under the policy of economic reform there has been a graduate devolution of production and marketing decisions to individual enterprises. The Law on State-Owned Industrial Enterprises ("Enterprise Law") of 1988 states that the manager, rather than the factory Communist Party Committee, is responsible for day-to-day management of the enterprise. The law speaks in general terms about the "managerial responsibility system," which gives managers ultimate decision-making power over production and management. In practice many factory managers and party secretaries continue to be one and the same person. Other factory managers find it prudent to operate a kind of tripartite system, whereby company policies are thrashed out between factory management, the factory party committee, and worker congress or union representatives. The wisdom of this cooperation is reinforced by the fact that, according to the Enterprise Law, factory managers are subject to removal by the worker congresses for incompetence or malfeasance. Recently, the Chinese press has reported several such removals. Moreover, close working relations are enhanced since, in almost all cases, managers, union officials, and party officials are all members of the party committee.

Enterprises' prerogatives were further codified in the "Regulations on Transforming the Management Mechanisms of State-Owned Industrial Enterprises," issued in July 1992. The regulations state that enterprises are free to hire workers without restriction as to type of recruitment, numbers hired, or contract terms. They are also free to set wages, but wage increases must correlate to productivity increases. Finally, enterprises are free to hire technicians and managers or to develop their own promotion systems to promote management from the ranks of ordinary workers.

Since the beginning of the 1990s the nature of the relationship between labor and management has undergone substantial changes. Traditional labor-management relations, characterized in the past by interactions between the workers and the government in state-owned firms has turned into relations between workers and enterprises and has become increasingly market- and contract-based.

THE COLLECTIVE CONTRACT

China will establish a collective contract system in more businesses of various kinds. The experiment will be first conducted in foreign-funded firms and some state-owned companies. If some enterprises were not qualified to sign comprehensive agreements, they could sign contracts about single issues, such as wages. The collective contracts must provide a clear description of pay, working hours, vacations, etc. The ACFTU has suggested that the duration of contracts should be three years. The enterprise and its trade union, the workers' representative, were to have "consultative meetings" regularly, with the results of consultation to be legally binding and furnished to the workers. Collective contracts of state firms can also include the goals of economic growth and social development as agreed to by the union and management.[1] There are indications that the laws are being enforced. For instance, a cotton mill in Xinxiang city in the province allowed its women employees, who comprise 75% of its total workforce, to avoid night shifts from the seventh month of pregnancy through the first year of lactation.[2]

PRELUDE TO COLLECTIVE BARGAINING

At this point in our discussion, a caveat is in order. Can the above-described collective consultation and contracting system be considered collective bargaining in the Western sense of the term? In the United States, for instance, the scope of topics covered by collective negotiations between management representatives and union representatives acting as agents for workers is very broad, normally including "wages, hours, and working conditions." The answer to the query appears to be that China definitely does not practice Western-style collective bargaining at the present time.

Under a 1988 law and subsequent regulations, Chinese-style collective bargaining was permitted only by workers in private enterprises which at that time employed less than 3% of workers. By 1993 there had been no reports of collective bargaining actually taking place. Most private firms were small and nonunion. At that juncture, the ACFTU had not been granted legal status as a collective bargaining agent. Hence, its role was limited to consultations with management over wages and regulations affecting labor and working conditions, and efforts to serve as a conduit for communicating workers' complaints to the management of firms and municipal labor bureaus.

The new 1995 law is modeled on the conventions of the International Labor Organization and covers promotions, labor contracts, working hours, protection for female and juvenile workers, wages, social insurance, welfare, and labor disputes, among other issues. However, the law fails to maintain collective bargaining, the most common method to settle labor disagreements in other countries, although Chinese unions can sign collective agreements covering wages, hours, breaks and vacations, safety and health, insurance and welfare.

THE LABOR CONTRACT SYSTEM

Introduced in the mid-1980s as a cornerstone of labor reform, the contract employment system was intended to create a labor pool subject to market forces by providing workers with real employment options, which would unleash worker initiative and thereby boost enterprise productivity. Although the number of contract workers in state-owned enterprises increased from 3.5% to almost 10% from 1985–88, their impact on the labor system was not appreciable. The state still controlled contract details and many contract workers were not completely accepted in the workplace due to the temporary nature of their contracts. Furthermore, lower-level bureau and enterprise cadres tended to resist implementation of the system because of its perceived threat to their political power.[3]

China's domestic economic reform program can be summarized in three propositions: private ownership can occupy a useful place in a socialist economy; market forces should be allowed to influence the allocation of goods and the determination of prices; and material incentives should be the principal mechanism for stimulating greater productivity and efficiency. To achieve this reform on the urban economic front, the Chinese government has attempted to decentralize economic decision making down to the enterprise level.[4] In late 1982 and early 1983, they began experimenting with contract labor in state enterprises, and in February 1983, "the Ministry of Labour and Personnel issued a formal circular calling for implementation of the labour contract system."[5] On July 12, 1986, the State Council promulgated the Interim Provisions for the Implementation of the Labor Contract System in State Enterprises.[6]

Within this framework, new industrial workers are employed as "contract system workers" although those previously engaged as permanent workers still enjoy lifelong employment. Contracts must last for at least one year and contain provisions covering production tasks, probation, working conditions, remuneration, labor discipline, and penalties. In addition, the "old-style" temporary workers are also required to sign contracts, but this does not mean that they have been converted into "contract system workers" for the purposes of the new system: they remain temporary workers with benefits different from those accorded to contract system workers. On the other hand, the situation of employment varies from one type of firm to another. In state-owned firms and collectives, there is a mix of permanent workers, contract workers, and temporary workers. In foreign-invested firms, there are contract workers and temporary workers, while in other firms there are only temporary workers. Tables 5-1 and 5-2 show the proportion of contract workers among total employees.[7]

The old permanent employment system has given way to a more flexible contract-based system, under which individual worker performance will be evaluated. In practice, only the very few workers with highly technical skills are able to negotiate effectively on wages and fringe benefit issues. In mid-1995, nearly 150,000 firms had signed labor contracts with 55 million workers, accounting for about 55% of the country's urban labor force. In addition, nearly 100 enterprises have experimented

TABLE 5-1
Contract Workers in 1989 and 1992

Type of	Number (millions)		Percentage of total	
enterprise	1989	1992	1989	1992
SOEs	11.90	20.58	12	19
COEs	2.36	3.99	7	11
FIEs[a]	0.16	0.66	34	—

[a]Includes joint ventures and enterprises owned by overseas Chinese or by other foreigners.
Sources: Calculated from China Labour and Wages Statistical Yearbook, 1990 and Yearbook of Labour Statistics of China, 1993.

with the signing of collective labor contracts. At the end of 1995 more than 80% of the businesses nationwide had established labor contracts in a bid to protect workers' rights and interests.[8] Estimates were that all private firms would have labor contracts in place by the end of 1996.

The contracts are expected to run anywhere from six months to 10 years. In general, workers converted from permanent employment receive long-term contracts to ease the transition. The labor contract normally will tie bonuses to individual, workshop, and enterprise performance. At the end of their contract period, both workers and businesses theoretically have the freedom not to renew the contract. While enterprises' freedom to release workers varies widely by locality and current policy, it is clear that unsatisfied workers can now choose to leave without facing the previous problem of obtaining the work unit's permission, an often impossible task

TABLE 5-2
Contract Workers in SOEs, 1985–92

Year	Number (millions)	Percentage of total employees in enterprise
1985	0.33	3.7
1986	5.24	5.6
1987	7.35	7.6
1988	10.08	10.1
1989	11.90	12.0
1990	13.72	13.3
1991	15.89	14.9
1992	20.58	18.9

Sources: Reproduced from China Labour and Wages Statistics Yearbook, 1990 and Yearbook of Labour Statistics of China, 1993.

for skilled workers. Moreover, the vast majority of cases brought to labor arbitration and mediation involve contract workers, indicating that with a written contract both employer and employee are more clear about the ground rules and more likely to object when their rights are violated.

The national goal announced in October 1991 was to have all permanent workers under the labor contract system by the turn of the millennium. Although the program is now moving rapidly, it is not clear whether the goal will be met. Some of the largest employers in China, especially in heavy industry, have thus far failed to implement the labor contract system even for new hires. Enterprises such as steel mills and petroleum refineries, which invest heavily in their workers' technical training, are extremely reluctant to initiate a program that allows for labor mobility.

The great deficiency of the labor contract system is that it does not allow for collective bargaining. Contracts are negotiated by individuals with their employers. While some highly skilled workers have the bargaining power to influence the shape of the contract, in most cases the contracts are written by management and signed by workers. Moreover, workers are not involved in the transition from permanent employment to the labor contract system. A policy decision is made and workers are handed a finished product. The nature of the contract is nonnegotiable; only salary duration and work requirements are even theoretically negotiable.

RECENT STATUS OF COLLECTIVE BARGAINING

Since the new labor law went into effect the Ministry of Labor has worked on a vast range of supplementary legislation to implement the new statute, including a labor contract law governing the practice and content of both individual and collective labor contracts. Government officials state the labor contract law, the social insurance law, and the safety production law are all priority legislation expected to be approved during the next two years, and collective bargaining is a major plank in the labor reform program. The ACFTU has been impassioned in its support of collective bargaining, calling it the focal point for implementation of the labor law.

The ACFTU, with the assistance of local labor departments, has launched experiments in collective bargaining in several provinces and cities, including Beijing, Shanghai, Tianjin, Fujian, Hunan, Shandong, and Guangdong. Western observers say Beijing and Shanghai labor bureaus appear more cautious in implementing collective bargaining reforms than labor officials in Guangdong and Fujian, where some of China's worst workplace violations have occurred. While the ACFTU stands to gain enormously from the spread of collective bargaining, many of the pilot projects have not fared well to date. Problems plague the implementation of collective negotiation in both state and foreign-owned firms. Major obstacles in state enterprises include the fact that state employees are not convinced of the advantages of collective bargaining. The ACFTU's own research suggests that in well-managed state firms workers and management already enjoy good relations and see little need to bargain collectively. Similarly, in loss-making state enterprises employees are cynical about the value of collective negotiation to extract further wage gains. The perception that local labor departments rather than enterprise management control wage decisions also dampens both parties' enthusiasm for collective bargaining. Second, defining the two sides at the negotiating table is problematic in state enterprises where employers are not always sufficiently separate from workers. Accustomed to living off government handouts, managers at state enterprises tend to accommodate workers' wage demands regardless of profit position. Moreover, union leaders are often selected by enterprise management or government officials rather than by the workers, suggesting they may not always reflect workers' concerns. Third, the ACFTU's knowledge of and experience with collective bargaining varies widely across 30 regional union organizations and 16 affiliated national industrial trade unions. In larger cities, ACFTU offices and labor departments offer sophisticated models of collective contracts to assist local unions in negotiations with employers. In less developed regions, unions struggle with very little guidance or sense of what should be discussed as part of the collective bargaining process. With the assistance of the International Labor Organization and other foreign groups, the ACFTU has launched an education campaign to improve workers' knowledge of collective bargaining and the labor law.

PROBLEMS IN FOREIGN-INVESTED ENTERPRISES

Among foreign-invested enterprises the expansion of collective bargaining practices has proceeded haltingly because of a separate set of obstacles:

Few Firms Have Unions

Under the new labor law, workers in companies without unions can nominate representatives to bargain on behalf of the workers. In reality, though, the operation of a collective contract system is closely linked to the establishment of a union, with the latter usually being a prerequisite for the former. To extend the collective bargaining experiment beyond a handful of high-profit joint ventures such as Beijing Jeep, the ACFTU will have to intensify its unionization campaign.

Lack of Official Support

Some regions and investment zones eager to attract overseas involvements, issue promises of "no social unrest" or antiunion regulations in an effort to convince foreign companies that unions will not be tolerated in their locale. A notice released jointly by six government departments in November 1994 requesting that foreign-owned enterprises speed up the establishment of unions was purposely vague in setting a schedule for the inception of enterprise unions. Even the Ministry of Labor's support for unionization of foreign-invested businesses remains lukewarm, with some factions within the ministry satisfied to see worker representatives rather than official unions undertake the collective bargaining process.

ACFTU Reluctance to Act

On paper, the ACFTU and its local affiliates have substantial rights, including the right to stop production under dangerous circumstances and to be involved in an enterprise's economic decision making. In practice, however, the ACFTU is not confident that government or workers will support the full exercise of these rights. "Before economic reform, the ACFTU didn't even imagine that workers could have rights," said one Western observer.

Presently, ACFTU chapters throughout China are grappling with the question of how far to assume the role of workers' protector. The ACFTU's tendency to bureaucracy has also not helped bolster its image among employers and workers. Local ACFTU chapters with no experience in organizing workers often resort to issuing orders requesting that foreign management establish the union on behalf of the workers—an order which in almost all cases is studiously ignored by the companies in question.[9]

The vice-president of the ACFTU, Li Qisheng, has stated that Chinese law stipulates that workers enjoy collective bargaining power so that, represented by official trade unions, they could participate in the formulation of worker-related company rules. However, international labor unionists claim Chinese workers often have difficulties safeguarding their rights. Although the ACFTU claims to represent most workers, many have quit or given up on it because it fails to offer practical assistance.[10]

THE CONFLICT BETWEEN LAW AND REGULATIONS

A separate set of regulations governing the workplaces of foreign-funded firms went into effect in August 1994, and subsequently was criticized by the foreign legal professions for its conflict with existing protective legislation and regulations. One foreign lawyer described the regulations for labor management in foreign investment enterprises as "a shoddy piece of work which does not match either the spirit or quality of China's Labour Law."[11]

Critics charged that the regulations take away rights previously granted to foreign-invested firms under other joint venture laws and regulations and increase the potential for government interference in the workplace. The regulations also apparently restore the previous separation of foreign-invested from state-owned companies for labor law purposes, a division apparently all but abolished by the 1995 labor law, which was to apply to virtually all Chinese organizations and enterprises. Also, by their very existence, the new foreign-invested enterprise labor organizations endorse different practices for companies with foreign as opposed to wholly domestic ownership. This dual treatment could prove troublesome during China's negotiations to join the WTO because it violates the WTO's principle of equal treatment under the law for all firms regardless of ownership.

While the new regulations aim to unify the previous hodgepodge of laws and regulations governing labor in joint ventures and other kinds of foreign-funded firms, their effect has been to produce confusion rather than clarification. Certain provisions of the labor regulations are at odds with the labor law. Among the areas of conflict are:[12]

Resignation

Article 31 of the labor law guarantees employees the right to resign, subject to 30 days notice. However, the foreign-invested enterprise labor regulations are silent on this issue, which may imply that an employee does not have the right to resign his position for personal reasons.

Termination

The FIE labor regulations allow both employer and employee to terminate employment without notice if the other party fails to perform the labor contract. The regulations, however, fail to spell out clearly what conditions would be defined as "failing to perform the labor contract." The labor law, by contrast, does not mention the failure to perform the contract as a reason for termination.

Union Involvement in Terminations

The new labor law requires a firm's management to consult with the union only where a company is planning to undertake large-scale reductions in personnel. By contrast, the FIE labor regulations specify that in each individual case of termination by notice, the labor union's opinion must be solicited by management.

Other problematic areas of the FIE labor regulations include:

Autonomy in Labor Matters

Both the labor law and the joint venture regulations of 1986 and 1988 refer to the autonomy of foreign-invested companies in recruiting employees. However, the FIE labor regulations state that foreign enterprises should normally recruit their employees from an employment agency recognized by the local labor bureau; they need to obtain consent if they want to recruit employees living elsewhere. By contrast, the 1986 and 1988 regulations provided that no consent or approval is required to employ people directly, regardless of whether they live in the same district or another locale.

Recruiting State Workers

The 1988 joint venture regulations encouraged foreign-invested companies to hire personnel currently employed in state-owned firms, and curtailed the rights of state employers to obstruct such a transfer. The FIE labor regulations do not reiterate the principle, but instead stipulate in Article 5 that foreign-invested firms may not recruit staff and workers who have not been released from previous employment.

Preference for Nationals

Article 6 of the FIE labor regulations requires preference be given to Chinese nationals in recruitment matters, and requires those foreign companies seeking to recruit expatriates to first obtain the approval of local administrative and labor departments. While the requirement that local labor bureaus approve expatriate hires has been in effect since March 1993, it has not been enforced to date. In the future, however, the rule may be more rigorously applied, making it difficult for companies to obtain working visas for expatriates whose hiring has not received proper approval. To avoid disputes, foreign companies are advised to spell out clearly in the joint venture contract and articles of association that certain positions shall or may be filled by expatriates.

Which takes precedence? Government officials have confirmed that where a conflict between the two sets of legislation exists, the Chinese labor law will override the FIE labor regulations. But some foreign lawyers say companies should not rely on this being the case. Instead, where the law is unclear, foreign companies should try to have the local labor bureau verify labor contracts. If the labor bureau has verified the contract, it is unlikely that the relevant provision would be stricken down by a labor arbitration committee in the event of a labor dispute.

PROVISIONS OF THE NEW LABOR LAW

The regulations were designed to facilitate the implementation of China's new comprehensive labor law, because the labor law is aimed to standardize labor relations in an all-around manner and to protect the legitimate rights and interests of both the employee and the employer. The supportive rules and regulations also range widely from special protection of the underaged to specifying length of work day or week. Concerning the wage system, there are regulations on the introduction of the minimum wage and on wage payments. With respect to labor contracts, there are stipulations on the economic compensation incurred by violation as well as by termination of a contract, and on the collective contract.

Since the implementation of the Regulation on Discharging Employees, enterprises have gained the power to dismiss workers. According to this regulation, there are five grounds on which discharging an employee may be justified: breach of labor discipline; bankruptcy of the firm; unsuitability of the worker for the job after a trial period; inability of the worker to resume duties even after medical treatment, following a non-work-related illness or accident; and employee's imprisonment or conviction of a crime.

Job placement agencies will be formed, to fill a vital need in China, which has a surplus labor force of more than 100 million people. The law forbids the employment of workers under the age of 16. The law also guarantees that working people have the right to join trade unions if they want to. Such unions will be independent and watch over workers' interests, while helping to ensure that the enterprise can operate efficiently.

Trade unions have been popular among the state-owned and collectively owned enterprises, and the government has encouraged their establishment. However, a study of 12 provinces and municipalities by the ACFTU showed that only one-third of the 52,340 overseas-funded firms surveyed had set up unions by mid-1994. It turns out that nationwide unionization rates are 40% for nonagricultural workers and 90% for workers in state enterprises and urban collectives.

Laid-off workers are to receive compensation, a provision that is already in place in certain test areas. In Beijing, for instance, if a worker loses his job involuntarily, he is to receive a monthly allowance ranging between 145 to 172 yuan ($16.7 to $20) for as long as 24 months. While levels and methods of payment are to be determined by the employers, monthly cash payments are to be made to unemployed workers.

Minimum wages will be required, with local governments authorized to set minimum payments consistent with regional rates. The work day is to last not more than 8 hours and the work week not more than 44 hours. When overtime work is inevitable, it will be limited to 3 hours daily and 36 hours a month. Workers will receive overtime pay and will have time off on weekends and public holidays. Worker protection and sanitation standards will be required and women workers will receive special protection.

A social insurance fund will also be started, requiring employers to pay social insurance fees. The funds will be distributed to workers when they retire, suffer injuries, become ill, lose their jobs, or give birth.

In case of labor disputes, they will be resolved either by arbitration or in court.

Employers found guilty of violating the labor law will be subject to civil or criminal penalties.

The new law followed years of research and debate. Chinese legislators held heated debates on how to use such a statute to push employers, especially foreign investors, to upgrade working conditions. Currently some foreign-funded companies have especially harsh working conditions.[13]

STRIKES AND WORK STOPPAGES

The right to strike was included in China's 1975 and 1978 constitutions. It was removed from the 1982 constitution on the grounds that the socialist political system had eradicated contradictions between the proletariat and enterprise owners in China. However, the 1992 Union Law, states that if a local union and its safety officers find a workplace to be dangerous and the enterprise does not address the problem, the union "has the right to suggest that the staff or workers withdraw from the sites of danger." Thus, Chinese leaders apparently view strikes as justified only when they respond to problems such as sudden deterioration in safety conditions.

Informal work stoppages and slowdowns to express worker discontent, which are not counted as "official" strikes, nevertheless, are not uncommon, and are tolerated for brief periods as long as vital services and national security industries are not affected. Although there are no known formal regulations regarding strikes in special economic zones, authorities appear slightly more tolerant of strikes in the zones than in the rest of the country.

There have been a number of serious strikes in recent years that have been reported in the local Chinese press and often reported in the Hong Kong newspapers. Strike statistics are not published by the Chinese government and it is not possible to determine the validity of strike numbers reported in the foreign press.

In general, the 1992 Union Law assigned unions the role of mediators or go-betweens with management in the case of work stoppages or slowdowns. Nonetheless, well-documented work stoppages occurred in several locations during 1993, for example. There were two highly visible strikes in Guangdong's Zuhai City, namely a three-day strike over wages at a joint venture electrical components factory. Ministry of Labor officials broke with their past practice of denying the existence of strikes in China by providing details about recent strikes in Tianjin and Xian. Strikes in 11 foreign-funded firms were widely reported in the Chinese press.

One particularly high-profile case involved a foreign-owned footwear factory at which 1200 workers struck over poor working conditions and alleged mistreatment of several of the workers by management. The 11 enterprises mentioned above were held up as examples of the disregard for local regulations by foreigners and indications of the need to establish unions in foreign-invested businesses. The strikes were uniformly resolved in favor of workers, and firms were required to bring facilities up to regulatory standards. Foreign press reports indicated that in 1993 there were 190 strikes and protests across China involving about 50,000 workers. Worker discontent was at its highest level in five years and industry was plagued by a wave of strikes, go-slows, walkouts, and even physical attacks on managers as workers engaged in increasingly militant action to protest against their fate.

Strikes are "inevitable" as China pushes ahead with economic reforms, Labor Minister Li Boyong admitted when the number of labor disputes stood at 3000 in the first three months of 1994 alone. However, while admitting that some disputes had led to actual work stoppages, he stressed that the number was "very small" as most had been settled through arbitration. For that matter, of the 60,000 labor disputes recorded since 1986, most were resolved through conciliation and arbitration, according to the government, which said that the vast majority had occurred in foreign-owned, joint venture, and private firms, although state-owned enterprises have not been spared.

Twenty thousand labor disputes were officially reported in 1994 and one source indicated there have been 250,000 strikes and labor disputes since 1988, a much greater incidence than reported above. Disputes usually center on ambiguous contracts, work hours, low pay, and poor safety conditions, and contracts at many factories which fail to comply with official labor rules.

Worker discontent with high inflation rates and an increase in unofficial labor activism are among the primary reasons for the labor unrest. Another common motive for strikes within domestic companies is to protest layoffs caused by restructuring. Some localities, such as the Dalian Economic and Technological Development Zone, have implemented antistrike regulations requiring all disputes between employers and employees to be mediated by the ACFTU. Under these regulations, the ACFTU must give its permission for workers to organize a strike, and workers have to notify their employers 72 hours before any action was taken. Workers striking without AFCTU authorization would lose the chance to be employed in the development zone again.

Under existing labor law, either workers or employers may bring disputes to the labor dispute mediation committee in their own employing unit. If mediation fails, the workers or employer may bring the dispute to the labor dispute arbitration committee organized by the local labor service bureau (LSB).[14]

It is impossible to determine how many strikes occur in China, much less how many involve local unions. There have been cases of union officials leading strikes and other labor actions, all of which are illegal under Chinese law. In at least one instance union opposition to a reform program that would involve massive layoffs was so strong as to provoke a local reorganization to increase direct party control over the local union's activities. The U.S. counterpart in such a situation would see a national union imposition of a trusteeship over the wayward local. In this example, of course, Communist Party control obviously met with government approval since it is all but impossible to separate party reactions from government-sanctioned policy. The union was put under the direction of the "United Front Department," a Communist Party-affiliated office.[15]

In general, neither side lets labor disputes get so out-of-hand. As noted above, local government officials usually slow down the pace of reform as they sense too much labor dissatisfaction. These changes of policy are generally initiated by the government with no consultation with the local union. The union has only indirect influence, through its willingness to publicly challenge certain labor reforms.

ANTISTRIKE LEGISLATION—A LACK OF UNIFORMITY

The official government and party line on the legal regulation of strike action is that it is necessary due to the adverse effects industrial actions have on society and the economy. Strikes have been compared with nuclear weapons; they should be utilized only as a deterrent and be used as a last resort.

Authorities in the Dalian Development Zone in Liaoning passed an 18-point law severely curtailing workers' rights to strike. Other development zones and special economic zones reportedly also have plans for similar laws. A Dalian union official justified the legislation: "We cannot say that strikes are illegal since there is no law against them. Our stand is that we don't encourage them ... but neither do we oppose them."[16] His opinion was that the law should clearly state the workers' right to strike. But he stressed that there also should be legal restrictions, reflecting a not uncommon ambivalence on the part of Chinese labor leaders.

Dalian's law states that any negotiations between employers and employees can only be conducted through the government-controlled AFCTU, which is not surprising. However, the labor leader maintained there was no need to apply Dalian's practice to Guangdong, since strikes there had been intrafactory without causing adverse effects on affected communities.

The lack of uniformity in antistrike laws is shown by the fact that Qingdao Development Zone, which has no regulations of its own, used the Dalian law to quell a labor dispute at one of its foreign-owned companies.

Strike activity in Dalian declined from 20 in the first half of 1994 to 6 after the above-mentioned law was enacted with the approval of the chairman of the Dalian subsidiary of the ACFTU. The Dalian law was utilized to end a strike in Qingdao where a Korean firm was struck by 4000 workers. The legal department of the ACFTU predicted that the Dalian law was likely to be followed by the rest of China.[17]

DISPUTE SETTLEMENT MECHANISMS

In China, two types of disputes are susceptible to resolution by arbitration and mediation. Article 84 of the new labor law provides that:

> The labor administrative department of the local government may organize various quarters concerned to mediate in the event disputes occur from signing a collective contract and the parties concerned fail to settle the disputes through consultations.

This refers to disputes which occur during the contract negotiation process. Subsequent language of the same article describes the procedures to follow in disputes which arise during the administration of contracts:

> When disputes occur upon carrying out a collective contract and the parties concerned fail to settle the disputes through consultation, they may go to the labor dispute arbitration committee for arbitration; if they disagree with the arbitration ruling, they may file a suit at the people's court within 15 days after being notified of the ruling.

In practice, labor dispute arbitration committees have been required at the provincial, municipal, county, and district levels. Many provinces established arbitration committees in the fall of 1986 as a result of "instructions" sent down from the government. Zhejiang Province established its committee on October 1, 1986 and detailed regulations were formulated in April 1988. These regulations covered "fixed laborers" and contract workers with contracts exceeding one year. All state enterprises that had worker congresses and union committees were required to establish mediation committees. There is no mediation committee requirement for joint ventures, wholly foreign-owned firms, or collectives.

The mediation committee must be composed of at least one worker representative, one union representative, and one administrative representative, and may range in size from three to seven members, but the administrative representatives cannot constitute more than one-third of the committee. If mediation fails, the arbitration committee must conduct an arbitration hearing.

Normally, the dispute resolution process begins with an application to the arbitration committee, which has to first attempt mediation. This approach has a high success rate in the majority of cases; i.e., during the period from the fall of 1986 to September 1987, arbitration committees handled 2,079 cases nationally. Of these cases, 1,930 or 93% were handled through mediation, reflecting China's historic preference for resolution of disputes through mediation.[18] If a decision is reached through mediation, the arbitration committee must prepare a binding agreement to be signed by the parties.

As a practical matter, in Zhejiang Province, the provincial arbitration committee handled few disputes. Most disputes were handled by municipal arbitration committees. The provincial regulations provided that the provincial arbitration committee will handle those cases in which jurisdiction between the city and city-district committee is not clear, as well as cases involving enterprises which operate across provincial boundaries.

Chinese administrative levels are complex. Generally, in each of the 29 provinces, there are cities which are divided into urban and rural districts. Each city's administrative agencies are not defined simply by the geographical limits of the city, and there are no areas in China which are not organized under a city or prefecture.

As the majority of businesses are state run, each enterprise has its connection to state-operated administrative agencies at the corresponding level. It is generally not difficult to determine which labor arbitration committee to proceed to if the enterprise is operated by the state. The situation becomes more problematic if the enterprise is a collective, and substantially more difficult if it is a joint venture or a wholly foreign-owned firm.

Labor arbitration departments in China have three main functions: First, they go to localities to ensure that regulations, disciplines, and contracts in force at the enterprises comply with state laws. This prevents friction between firms and workers. Second, they help set up mediation committees in individual enterprises, and finally, if mediation fails, arbitration committees render a verdict.

A SHORT HISTORY OF LABOR ARBITRATION

The Communist Party has used labor mediation and arbitration to resolve labor disputes since the 1930s, when it instituted rules for mediation and arbitration of such disputes within the area under its control. As the Communists began to consolidate their control at the end of the civil war in 1949, the government established procedures for the resolution of labor disputes through arbitration. These procedures applied to disputes arising in privately held firms, of which there were a substantial number in 1949.

A Labor Bureau was established and organized with divisions at the city, provincial, and national levels. From 1949 to 1955, the Labor Bureau dealt with over 200,000 labor disputes. While the bureau was viewed as playing an important role in resolving labor–management disputes during the early history of the People's Republic, virtually all labor enterprises in China were nationalized after 1956, and the arbitration agency of the Labor Bureau was abolished. Labor disputes between workers and the state were viewed as theoretically impossible and as inconsistent with socialist governance.

The country implemented a single publicly owned economy, under which the jobs of workers and staff members were guaranteed and their wages and salaries, though being divided into several grades, were officially fixed. Few labor disputes occurred, or if they did take place, the government denied their existence.

After the abolition of the arbitration agency, labor disputes were theoretically handled by what was known as the Letter and Visiting Department through an administrative agency, or more frequently, at the enterprise level. However, in practice no predictable procedures for processing labor disputes existed, and no significant efforts were made to institute a uniform procedure for labor dispute resolution. Labor dispute cases were rarely heard, because factory heads and enterprise managers had not been entrusted with the right to fire employees, and they were thought to work and live in "an agreeable socialist family" and "ate out of the same big pot." In China, employees are usually regarded as the property of their work units and some units are reluctant to allow their employees to transfer to other jobs.

China resumed its labor dispute mediation and arbitration system in October 1986, after a period of over 30 years. A dispute settlement procedure has been in effect since 1987. The procedure provides for two levels of arbitration committees and a final appeal to the courts. Of the 50,000 cases brought to arbitration in 1992, most were resolved at the first or second level, with less than 5% reaching the courts. According to Labor Ministry officials, most arbitration cases are filed by contract workers or their employers, an indication that the new contract system provides a clearer set of ground rules which both sides can attempt to enforce.

CAUSES OF INDUSTRIAL UNREST

One of the recent causes of industrial turmoil necessitating more extensive utilization of mediation and arbitration procedures involves a growing tendency on the part of Chinese managers toward the use of Tayloristic management techniques.

Their measures include tightening labor discipline, imposing heavy penalties, raising production norms, and restructuring the reward system. The situation for workers has been aggravated where managers have happened to be tactless, tyrannical, or partial toward certain workers, the changes bureaucratic and unreasonable, and worse yet if the factory director has been blatantly self-serving. The latter half of the 1980s witnessed degenerating labor–management relations, and poor working conditions became one of the main causes of an increasing number of strikes.

The number of labor disputes in China has sharply increased. Labor arbitration committees across the country in 1994 accepted and heard 19,098 cases, up 59% from 1993. The number of disputes taken to labor arbitration in 1993 was 12,358, a record and up from 8150 in 1992.

The marked increase indicates that more employees are resorting to the law to guard their rights and interests. Among the disputes, 17,962 cases, more than 94% of the total, had been settled by the end of 1994. The disputes focused mainly on the employees' minimum wage and welfare. In China's coastal provinces, most labor disputes involved unsafe conditions. In Guangdong province, more than 40% of the labor disputes occurred in overseas-funded enterprises or joint ventures. Most of the disputes ended with employees winning the cases. In a bid to deal with the increasing labor dispute trend and safeguard workers' rights and interests, nearly all the provinces, municipalities, and autonomous regions have set up labor-related supervision institutions.[19] There are 225,000 labor dispute mediation committees in nearly half of the state-owned and collectively run enterprises, with support from the administrative departments and trade unions.[20]

NEXT U.S.–CHINA DISPUTE AREA—LABOR RIGHTS

Labor rights could emerge as the next major issue to strain Sino–U.S. ties now that the United States has delinked human rights and trade by renewing China's most favored nation (MFN) trading status. If Washington were to pressure China to improve labor policies, as it has done with Indonesia and Malaysia, the issue could be even more contentious than MFN.

"U.S. policy moves in mysterious ways … (but) it could happen"; "It is going to raise hackles in China? Absolutely"; these were the comments of an anonymous government official in Washington. Even in 1989, Beijing had not been overly concerned with demonstrations in Tiananmen Square until workers began to join in. After the crackdown, labor activists were often given heavier jail sentences than students. Han Dongfang, the founder of China's first independent trade union, topped Beijing's "most-wanted list" of workers after the crackdown and was jailed for 22 months without trial. After being released to seek medical treatment in the United States, he was expelled from China when he tried to return home, and remains in exile in Hong Kong.

Beijing would see U.S. intervention on labor rights as even more unacceptable than on human rights, especially given rapid social changes. Washington has linked the renewal of certain trade privileges for Indonesia to progress on workers' rights. That stance, along with U.S.-backed efforts to include labor rights in discussions on membership in the WTO, has angered Asian capitals. Whether that policy will be applied to China remains in question. However, after Washington's retreat on MFN, Beijing would be less inclined to take seriously any other protests. Moreover, any row over labor policy would be less likely to spill over into trade relations the way MFN did because a political rather than a trade issue is involved.[21]

CHAPTER 6

Worker Rights Issues

As described in preceding chapters, there is no shortage of labor issues for labor activists or independent unions to pursue in mainland China. In this, the concluding chapter in Part II, we will describe the primary areas of concern involving worker rights and labor standards which have developed as China has experienced close to two decades of economic and labor reform efforts.

WAGES

Before wage reform, workers salaries were set according to a uniform national scale based on seniority and skills. In 1983 there were calls for a radical change in the wage system, which had been established in 1956 and had been encumbered by problems through years of patchwork modifications. Beginning in 1978 businesses expanded their decision-making powers and instituted the economic responsibility and bonus systems. But there were no fundamental changes with regard to the egalitarian wage system, which seriously dampened the enthusiasm of workers for production, obstructed development, and downgraded the political integrity and sense of organization and discipline among workers.

Wage reform has been central to labor reform since the beginning of the reform policy. Early reforms focused on increasing incentives for workers by raising wages and increasing bonuses. However, salary scales, numbers of employees, and even the sizes of bonuses were generally set by the Labor Ministry and its local labor bureaus. The result was that bonuses were essentially group-based, as has been pointed out previously.

In the wake of Deng's trip to the South in 1992, enterprises were given more decision-making autonomy over production and personnel. One of the most significant reforms was to reduce government control over wages in state enterprises. Wages in other types of ventures, for example those that are even joint and foreign-owned are more free, since the government stopped imposing salary caps.

Under the new wage system, pay levels vary according to the type of employment. However, the idea behind the reform is to link wages with enterprise productivity and individual performance. The new wage system, "the structural wage system," has been practiced since 1985. It incorporates a distinct mix of basic wages (traditional standard wages), functional wages (by status or seniority), and floating wages (such as bonuses, which link enterprise and individual performance).

Table 6-1 indicates that wholly foreign-owned firms had the highest wage levels in the second half of the 1980 and collectively owned enterprises (COEs) had the lowest, but that from 1990 to 1992 wages in wholly foreign-owned firms lagged behind those in joint ventures and firms owned by overseas Chinese. Average wages in state-owned enterprises (SOEs) and COEs rose gradually and steadily. However, during periods when the central government implemented tight financial controls and an economic adjustment policy, as in 1988 and 1990, the economic activities of foreign invested enterprises (FIEs) were affected and wages fluctuated.[1]

Following wage reforms, a total wage bill for each collective and state-owned enterprise is set by the Ministry of Labor according to four criteria: (1) As a percentage of profits; (2) as a contract amount with the local labor bureaus; (3) for money-losing businesses, according to a state set amount; and (4) as an enterprise set amount subject to ministry review. Individual firms determine how to divide the total among the workers, a decision usually made by the company managers in consultation with the enterprise party chief and the union representative. Worker congresses are authorized to review plans for wage reforms, although these bodies serve primarily as rubber stamp organizations. Wages are generally equal for the same type of work within firms. Incentives are provided for increased productivity.[2]

THE WAGE SYSTEM

Until 1995, there was no legal minimum wage in China, although under the old system of set salary scales, the bottom of the scale was a de facto minimum wage. In

TABLE 6-1
Average Annual Wages, 1985–92 (in renminibi)

Type of enterprise	1985	1986	1987	1988	1989	1990	1992
SOEs	1213	1414	1546	1853	2055	2284	2878
COEs	967	1092	1207	1426	1557	1681	2109
FIEs							
· Joint ventures	2111	2082	2245	2447	2669	2905	3973
· Enterprises owned by overseas Chinese	2500	1613	1830	2966	2995	3687	4415
· Wholly foreign-owned firms	2144	2380	2826	2012	3567	3411	3616

Sources: Reproduced from *China Labor and Wages Statistics Yearbook, 1990* and *Yearbook of Labour Statistics of China, 1993*.

his report on the 1993 plan, delivered at the National People's Congress in 1993, Vice Premier Zou Jiahua said that as part of the reforms which allow enterprises to decide their own wage distribution, the government would introduce a minimum wage system and methods for regulating and controlling this wage. No time frame was given for when such reforms would be introduced.

Bonuses and subsidies have become integral to the Chinese wage system (see Table 6-2). Salaries tend to be higher in the private and individual sectors of the economy, but workers in these sectors often do not enjoy the benefits provided to workers in urban collectives and state enterprises, in particular subsidized housing and health care. Workers in state enterprises continue to earn more than those in collectives. The exception is in South China where all workers, regardless of the ownership of their place of work, earn considerably more than in the rest of the country.

In most parts of the country employers are making a concerted effort to cut down on the amount of subsidies in the total wage bill. Thus far they have been notably unsuccessful, particularly in the south, where caps on wages made nonmonetary incentives crucial for attracting workers. Current wage reform may reduce the use of subsidies, but it is unlikely to completely eliminate it. The tax system encourages the use of nonmonetary compensation.

In general, foreign ventures are free to pay whatever wage rates they want. Chinese income tax laws often make it desirable to provide greater subsidies and services rather than higher wage rates, and these decisions are often taken after observing local practice. Workers are either paid a salary, hourly wages, or piecework wages. The provision of subsidized services, such as housing and medical care, is very widespread, and compensation beyond the basic wage constitutes a very large portion of a foreign venture's labor expenses. Local governments also tax enterprises and workers to support social security and unemployment insurance funds.

MINIMUM WAGES

For the first time, the new 1995 labor law established a guaranteed minimum wage to be established by individual localities, while the central government was

TABLE 6-2
Components of the Chinese Wage System

	1978	1980	1986	1991
Regular wages	85.0	69.8	56.3	48.6
Piece-rate wages	0.8	3.2	8.7	9.0
Bonuses	2.3	9.1	12.8	17.8
Subsidies	6.5	14.1	18.8	22.1
Other wages	3.4	2.2	1.6	1.7

authorized to implement "macrocontrols" over the "total amount" of wages and salaries. The law does not specify the nature of these controls; whether they mean totals for an individual, an enterprise, or a local jurisdiction. The suspicion is that the central government used the term *controls* to allow it to implement wage freezes as a means to fight inflation, if the need arises in the future. Also, some localities are reportedly considering implementing maximum wage rules.[3]

Soon after the new law become effective, 16 provinces and municipalities were practicing a minimum wage system. Among these, 6 implemented wage minima before 1995, including Beijing, Shanghai, Zhejiang, Fujian, Shandong and Guangdong; 10 started the practice in 1995, including Tianjin, Shanxi, Liaoning, Jilin, Anhui, Hainan, Guizhou, Yunnan, Shaanxi, and Xinjiang. The minimum wage levels vary in different locations because of variable rates of economic development. The highest minimum wage rate is about 320 renminbi in some parts of Guangdong, followed by 280 renminbi in some parts of Hainan and Fujian. The lowest rate is 120 renminbi in some parts of Shanxi. Most of the provinces have two minimum wage levels according to local situations.[4]

Implementation of the minimum wage standard was not uniform. Accordingly, in Beijing in April 1995, at the National Labor Planning and Wage Conference, the Ministry of Labor instructed the provinces, autonomous regions and municipalities to enforce the minimum wage standard by June 30, 1995.[5] Sichuan, the most populous province in China, met this deadline by working out a set of regulations that stipulated the minimum wage payments for workers to be effective on July 1, 1995. The regulations are applicable to enterprises and individually owned firms as well as government departments, social organizations, and others. The minimum wage monthly payments ranged between 125 yuan and 180 yuan (the average monthly wage in China is approximately $44 a month).[6]

East China's Jiangsia province followed suit several days later by introducing minimum wage limits in enterprises in all of its 11 cities, setting three different monthly levels: 210 yuan (about $24), 175 yuan (about $20), and 140 yuan (about $16), respectively.[7]

ENFORCEMENT

Many other provinces and cities failed to meet the January deadline set by the government. A major area of concern is enforcement at the local level. While the efforts of the ACFTU and the Ministry of Labor have been very strong in Beijing, where the minimum wage is 210 yuan (about $24). their ability to ensure that local unions and labor bureaus comply with the new law is limited. The director of the International Labor Organization in China commented:

> Decision-making power is highly centralized and doesn't reach the local level. There's no chain of command between the Ministry of Labor and local labor authorities. The Chinese

labor law covers the basic provisions found in any decent labor law. However, it will take three to five years before the sufficient supplementary regulations necessary for proper implementation are ready.[8]

This means rural and township enterprises as well as smaller joint ventures are likely to escape compliance for some time. Unfortunately, these are the types of businesses where conditions are the worst as the large state enterprises and major foreign companies operating in China have had few problems of non-compliance.

LATE PAYMENT AND FINES

A problem that caused more than 200 riots in 1993 was the nonpayment or late payment of wages to workers who were issued IOUs or scrip in lieu of monetary payments. The situation developed in the early 1990s and became more acute as the number of state firms going bankrupt increased and some enterprises scaled back to partial production. Article 50 of the new labor law covers this contingency by providing that "workers' wages shall be paid monthly in the form of currency and shall not be deducted or unpaid without reason." This is an apparent attempt to prevent cash-strapped firms from paying workers in kind or in promissory notes. Also, the new statute provides that "equal wages shall be paid for equal work."

Article 50 ostensibly will prohibit wage deductions in the form of flagrant fines. The Labor Ministry charged that:

> Many foreign-funded enterprises have very rigid factory regulations. They are ruled by penalty, fines can be imposed on workers under various pretexts and the slightest lowering of vigilance in work on the part of a worker may cost him a fine of a certain amount. Those who take sick leave must pay an amount as a fine, those who take casual leave must pay an amount as a fine and those who refuse to work overtime must pay an amount as a fine too.... In the case of a Chinese staff member working with a foreign-funded enterprise in Fujian, he earned nearly 100 yuan a month but the cumulative amount of fines deducted from his pay for a certain month was as high as 150 yuan or more.

A survey of workers indicated that one-fifth of 2,000 randomly selected respondents were concerned about the failure of employers to pay wages on time. The survey indicated that women workers were being more seriously affected that men, while those in smaller firms were hit harder than their counterparts in medium and large-scale operations. More male workers than females said that a wage problem did not exist. However, 29% of workers from small enterprises, compared with 8% from large companies stated that their work units failed to pay them on a regular basis.[9]

A supplementary Law on Wages (including minimum wages) is to be enacted between 1997 and 2000 to aid in the implementation of the new labor law.[10] The 1995 law imposes penalties for failing to follow wage regulations. Local labor bureaus are authorized to fine, assess damages, or terminate operations, depending on the nature of the violations.[11]

WAGE INCREASES

While inflation has become a problem in recent years, reaching 25% in 1994, wages have more than kept pace with rising living costs. For example, the average per capita wage of Chinese workers had risen to 3,236 yuan in 1993, an increase of 19.4% over the previous year. The wage–inflation margin widened in 1994, as the average annual wage of state employees totaled 4,510 yuan ($535), up 33.8% from 1993. After adjustment for inflation, the average income of Chinese workers increased 7% in 1994. The most recent statistics indicated an inflation-adjusted wage increase of 6% for urban workers in the first quarter of 1995. This sharp rise was attributed to the implementation of minimum wage levels in many areas in 1994 and enterprises' wage adjustment. Also, with continued inflationary pressures, many areas increased employee subsidies.[12]

GUIDELINES

In 1994 the Ministry of Labor formulated a system of guidelines for enterprise wage increases, to be put into effect in the "near future." The system is aimed at ensuring proper wage increases in companies and further strengthening of the government's supervision and macrocontrol over wages. The guidelines will be determined by a tripartite committee composed of representatives from the state's labor departments, trade unions, and associations of entrepreneurs. The guidelines will be based upon annual labor productivity increases and changes in the cost-of-living index for urban residents. Simultaneously, the guidelines will consider multiple factors which have an impact on wages, such as price increases, labor costs, market labor demand–supply variables, and foreign trade trends. The guidelines, which will function in terms of wage increase ranges and absolute increase amounts, will be issued in April of every year, with an effective term of one year. Their objective will be to maintain a rational, coordinated balance between wage increases, economic growth and upward price movements.

THE NINTH FIVE-YEAR PLAN

By the end of the ninth five-year plan (1996–2000), China will institute a wage system in accord with the modern enterprise system, in which the market mechanism will be implemented. State-owned enterprises will then be authorized to decide on their wage scales, while private sector firms will decide their own wage levels mainly through collective consultations and negotiations. The government is expected to work out the national wage guidelines on the basis of GNP, employment, prices, investment, and other norms. All districts, trades, and enterprises in the country will define their wage increase ranges in accordance with these guidelines. The government will then regulate wage growth through economic measures, such as finance, taxation, and interest rates, and legal and administrative measures.

INCOME DISPARITIES

Another development labor activists are aware of is the growing income gap between urban and rural workers. In the mid-1980s, the average urban income was barely double the average rural one. By 1995, city dwellers earned three times as much as those on the land. With double-digit inflation in some Chinese cities, urban wages are rising rapidly but the incomes of many farm families have barely budged. Recent government figures put the average income of urban households at 355 yuan ($42) a month; for rural households the figure is less than 1,000 yuan a year ($125). A geographically immense market, riddled with cultural differences, is thus becoming even more fragmented.[13]

Furthermore, there are also significant income differentials between urban Chinese families which is growing more pronounced. Based on categories devised by the National Statistics Bureau, more than 55% of urban Chinese families are "comfortable," with annual incomes ranging from 10,000 to 30,000 yuan ($1,200 to $3,600) and financial assets equaling 28,000 yuan. The five categories established by the Bureau to estimate income are: poor, adequate food clothing, comfortable, wealthy, and very rich.

Poor families, or those whose annual income falls below 5,000 yuan and whose financial assets total 3,000 yuan, account for 4% of urban Chinese. The second category, with income between 5,000 and 10,000 yuan and financial assets around 9,000 yuan, accounts for 34%. The wealthy group, with annual income between 30,000 and 100,000 yuan and financial assets of 87,000 yuan, account for 6% of urban residents. The top category, with an average annual income of 100,000 yuan and 280,000 yuan of financial assets, accounts for 1% of the total but holds 93 times the financial assets of the poor.[14]

In Guangzhou, where household incomes are among the highest in the country, office workers with good English skills can earn $1200 a month at multinational companies. Such top earners are relatively rare. They form no more than a blip on income distribution graphs. In a 1994 study, Guangzhou was divided into eight income groups. At the top of the range are people whose monthly household income exceeds $363. They make up 15% of the city's population. At the bottom are the 6% whose households earn less than $73. The most typical income range, $145 to $181, encompasses nearly 25% of the city's population (see Figure 6-1).

How far does $181 go? For anyone who needs a telephone, the answer is not very far. In Guangzhou, installing a residential phone line costs $483; just a few years ago it cost half as much. A college education costs from $600 to $800 a year, where not long ago it cost nothing. The welfare state still exists but only barely. It offers assistance to any Guangzhou resident whose income falls below $20 a month. Those with wages

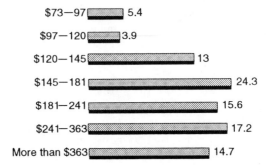

$73—97 ▨ 5.4
$97—120 ▨ 3.9
$120—145 ▨ 13
$145—181 ▨ 24.3
$181—241 ▨ 15.6
$241—363 ▨ 17.2
More than $363 ▨ 14.7

FIGURE 6-1. Monthly income for Guangzhou households in 1994, in U.S. dollars. *Source*: Survey Research Group (China) Ltd.

above this poverty line are left to their own devices. To get by, workers often siphon off supplies and products from their work units to sell on the black market while others hold second jobs. Consequently, the government, which cannot pay a decent wage because of low productivity, goes further into debt as morale and productivity sag further.[15]

THE CADRE SURVEY

These growing income disparities between urban and rural residents and among urban dwellers do not bode well for future social stability. A survey of Communist Party cadres indicated that the majority of the respondents believed that growing income maldistribution in China could lead to the disintegration of the country.

The report found 84% of the cadres believed that the widening income gap could lead to social instability and unrest. When asked to list the three worse effects of growing economic imbalances in China, the cadres listed unfair distribution of wealth, social instability, and disintegration of the country.

The income differentials have reached alarming proportions. For example, the gross domestic product (GDP) in Shanghai relative to that in the impoverished Guizhou Province has risen from 7.4 times in 1991 to 8.4 times in 1992. Guangdong was at least three times wealthier than Guizhou. The income difference was even more pronounced at the county or village level. In Guangdong Province, the GDP of the richest area was 34 times more than Heping County, the poorest county in the province.

China was compared to the former Yugoslavia, where the maximum income disparity before the country disintegrated was only 7.8 times the GDP.[16]

HOURS OF WORK

Another important aspect of the employment relationship involves the block of time an employee is required to devote to his or her occupation or job. The 8-hour day is the most basic right and interest the working class all over the world has struggled to achieve. Chapter IV of the new labor law, Article 36 states: "The state implements a working hours system under which a worker may not work more than eight hours a day or more than 44 hours a week on average." Article 37 follows with this language: "For workers who work on piece-rate wages, employing units shall rationally determine their work quotas and piece-rate standards based on the working hours system provided for in Article 36."

Subsequent provisions detailed vacation, holidays, days off, and overtime provisions were described in Article 41 as follows. Note the limitations:

Article 41. To meet production and operation needs, employing units may extend working hours not more than one hour a day in general after consulting with trade unions and workers. The working hours may be extended by no more than three hours a day in extraordinary circumstances, provided that the health of the workers is ensured. However, the working hours may not be extended for more than a total of 36 hours a month.

Article 42. The extension of working hours shall not be restricted by the provisions of Article 41 of this law under any one of the following circumstances:

(1) When there is threat to workers' lives and health and to the safety of property due to natural disasters, accidents, or other causes which must be urgently handled;

(2) When there is a breakdown of production equipment, communications and transportation lines and public facilities, affecting production and public interests, which requires urgent repair;

(3) Other circumstances provided for by laws and administrative regulations.

Article 44 describes overtime pay requirements and Article 45 deals with paid annual leave:

Article 44. Under any one of the following circumstances, employing units shall pay workers remuneration higher than their normal working hours wages according to the following standards:

(1) For work during extended working hours, remuneration of no less than 150% of the workers' wage shall be disbursed;

(2) For overtime work during the workers' off days when compensation time cannot be arranged, remuneration of no less than 200% of the workers' wage shall be disbursed;

(3) For overtime work during legal holidays, remuneration of no less than 300% of the workers' wage shall be disbursed.

Article 45. The state implements a paid annual leave system. Workers who work continuously for more than a year are entitled to paid annual leave. Specific measures shall be formulated by the State Council.

The above provisions were included in the law due to revelations of many egregious situations caused by patently unreasonable employer work time requirements.

MANY OVERTIME VIOLATIONS

In August 1993, the Guangdong Provincial Labor Bureau carried out a survey among the more than 14,000 staff and workers at 17 foreign-funded enterprises in Shenzhen, Zhuhai and Dongguan. It discovered that working hours at most of these companies were 10 to 12 hours daily, and there were no Sundays or other days off. The Guangdong Provincial Federation of Trade Unions also conducted a survey in 105 foreign-funded firms and discovered that with the exception of seven, in which the workers work three shifts, all the rest asked their employees to work extra hours.

One company even asked workers to work 36 hours at a stretch. Some foreign-invested firms increase workers' labor quotas at will. In a Sino-Japanese joint venture watch company in Zhuhai, the labor quota per worker per shift in the workshop turning out second hands is fixed at 4000 pieces, while the quota set in Japan is only 2,500.

Overtime pay is very little, usually 0.5 to 1.0 yuan per hour. In several foreign joint ventures in Guangdong, the workers have had no holidays for 11 consecutive months. Some foreign businessmen have deliberately set very high production quotas for the workers and have set very low payment for each piece of a product. As a result, the workers are compelled to work long hours, with some fainting at their machines because they could not cope with the excessive workload. Other foreign-funded companies simply ignore the new work hour system which was included in the new labor law.[17]

The workers of the B shift in the assembly workshop of a toy factory in Zhuhai, once worked overtime up to 170 to 192 hours each per month and the highest cumulative overtime work record was 214 hours that month, amounting to about 26 working days.

An electronics company in Qingdao kept its employees on overtime of up to 100 hours a month each on average over more than a year since its opening. A certain knitwear company once forced its workers to work three days and three nights nonstop and, as a result, many workers collapsed at their machines.

The researchers explained the reasons for these extreme overtime violations:

> Let us now review the reward workers gain from overtime work. China's labour policy clearly provides that pay for overtime work, either calculated on a piece or time rate basis, will be 1.5 times the normal rate and work on legal public holidays shall be paid for as double the normal pay. However, in most foreign-funded enterprises, workers do not get their due pay for extraordinarily long overtime work.... Why then is the practice of working overtime still so common? Are workers willing to work overtime? In fact, most wage-earners do not want to work overtime but, rather, they are forced to do so. A knitwear company set a rule: "Anyone who refuses to work overtime is liable to a fine of 25 yuan." So if a worker refuses to work overtime, he will lose three days' wages. Therefore, workers dare not resist the management's order to work overtime although they have a lot of grievances and complaints.[18]

The present law requires that employees who are employed on a piecework basis are also required to adhere to the eight-hour, five-and-one-half day schedule. Some foreign employers get around what amounts to an overtime limitation by never ordering their employees to work overtime, but instead set a higher production quota. More than 200 garment workers in a factory in Tianjin solely funded by the Republic of Korea filed complaints over the high production quotas set by the factory. They said it is impossible to fulfill the quota within eight hours. They had to work overtime. If they failed to meet their quotas, they would not receive their pay for the day's work. Therefore, the workers were forced to continue their work until 8 or 9 o'clock at night, sometimes even later.

In almost all the foreign-invested enterprises, overtime is settled as part of a worker's monthly salary. That is to say, he or she will not be paid if they refuse to work overtime. It is common for workers to be punished for refusal to work overtime.[19] In Fujian, one of the relatively rich provinces, thousands of foreign firms, many of them medium to small Taiwanese companies, employ more than 400,000 thousand Chinese, mostly from other provinces, making such goods as running shoes and plastic toys. An official from the Fujian Labor Bureau commented on the treatment of the workers: "They say they respect human rights, I say what they do is exploitation. If they are sincere about human rights, then they should stop exploiting Chinese workers."[20] He said working hours were "eternally" long. Sixteen hours a day, with overtime pay as low as 50 fens (half a yuan) an hour has become almost the norm among joint ventures in Fujian.

TEMPORARY WORKERS

Another labor issue has developed in the special economic zones, where pay, working conditions, and benefits are closely controlled by the authorities. The competition for jobs is strong, and at least on the surface, labor problems seem few and far between. However, there is an expanding gray area of export processing zones (EPZs), which may include almost any factory or rural cooperative which is manufacturing for export. Here, conditions are often Dickensian and pay unimpressive. Recent research at Hong Kong University also suggests that many workers in these zones may be signing themselves into servitude as "temporary contract workers."

These employees are usually poor women from inland rural areas, often sent at the bidding of family to earn enough money to pay for a brother's education or a relative's house. Most are single, between the ages of 17 and 25. Their residence permits remain with their home village, making them ineligible to be categorized as workers elsewhere and to take advantage of the benefits this would bring.

Working hours for temporary contract workers are generally long, up to 14 hours or more a day, often for months at a time. When an order arrives, the factory frequently will work overnight, seven days a week. There is no sick or maternity leave. Employees who become pregnant or ill are sent home, often without pay. There are no pension payments.[21]

The International Confederation of Free Trade Unions (ICFTU) based in Brussels issued a report in June 1994 alleging that 60% of employees in 20 foreign enterprises worked seven days a week.[22]

The Chinese government, sensitive to the above-described practices, instituted a uniform 44-hour work week effective March 1, 1994, shortening the official 48-hour work week which had been operative since 1949. The order applied to all enterprises and sectors of the economy, including foreign-funded companies. It prohibits employers from making adverse adjustments to workers' functions, benefits, or salaries to compensate for the shorter period of work. The decree allows for a phase-in period or different methods of structuring individual hours under special circumstances. It also states that sectors which already have shortened work days due to particular working conditions, such as the chemical, mining, and textile industries, should try to make appropriate adjustments.

Many government workers will work a five-day week one week and a six-day week the next. Labor officials stated that a 40-hour work week may be possible by the year 2000. The stated intent of the adjustment is to provide workers with more time for study, family activities, and other pursuits, and to increase work efficiency and quality of life. At the same time, due to overall low efficiency in Chinese services and production, the Labor Ministry reported that it would be premature to move to a 40-hour week for the near future.[23]

THE FIVE-DAY WORK WEEK

Surprising many, just 14 months later on May 1, 1995, the government announced a five-day, 40-hour work week throughout industry. Chinese workers will work eight-hour days and five-day weeks according to the state ruling. Experts said that the reduction of working hours is due to China's economic and social development.

Over the past 17 years, the country has had an average economic growth rate of 9% and has seen a great improvement in living standards. A government survey indicated that 80% of the respondents preferred an extra day off without pay to working longer hours for more pay. The new system compares with that in use in many countries. Some 144 countries and regions have adopted it. Economists also viewed the change as a force that will help drive the country's economy. The service industry will be the main beneficiary of the new system; since some one million new jobs are expected to be created in the railway, air transportation, and tourism sectors.

Economists in the industrial sector agreed that the new system is a double-edged sword for industries, in that increased costs for companies are inevitable as the work time decreases with salaries remaining the same. At the same time, however, unemployment can thus be dealt with and economic efficiency in turn will be the only allowable criterion for enterprise development.[24]

In line with the new time arrangement, every Chinese worker is entitled to a two-day weekend every week instead of every other week, as it used to be. The new rule, to be phased in over two years, delivers an effective pay increase to Chinese workers, who will receive the same salary for what amounts to 10% less work. However, it is likely that some employers will simply reorganize their payrolls to handle work requirements with existing workforces rather than hiring extra employees. Many Chinese businesses are vastly overstaffed, by as much as 30% in unprofitable state-owned enterprises. The biggest losers will be the more productive firms, many of which are foreign-funded. Their options will be to hire additional workers or require overtime in order to meet orders.

Foreign-invested companies are being pushed to implement the five-day week immediately. State-owned enterprises can determine their own timetables for introducing the new requirements, affording them a competitive advantage. Foreign investors expressed reservations, but although they complained about temporary difficulties, most felt the overall impact would be marginal.

Wages and labor productivity are comparatively low in China and the widespread belief was that a few lost working hours could be easily absorbed. For that matter, a number of Western multinationals, including U.S. consumer electronics giant Motorola have long been operating a five-day week.

"Good rest ensures good work," stated a manager with Shanghai Volkswagen, another five-day-a-week employer and the most successful joint venture company in China. Other foreign enterprises quickly fell into line with the new legal time requirement.

Chinese labor unions also welcomed the shorter week, claiming it could ease unemployment, officially recorded at 2.9% of the urban workforce in mid-1995. Economists, however, are skeptical, believing that Chinese factories will first dip into their pool of idle workers before hiring new workers to work extra shifts. Also, not every Chinese worker will benefit from the new arrangements, since 70% of the population still live in rural areas where work is a seven-day affair. Contract workers are not covered by the law either.

As for the 260 million primarily urban workers meant to gain from the government's largesse, more leisure time will be a mixed blessing, as there is a dearth of recreational activities in Chinese cities.[25]

WORKING CONDITIONS

Although there have been recent noticeable improvements for Chinese workers in their wages and working hours, much remains to be done in the area of working conditions. Cases of workers' rights violations have been frequent and widespread. The most exploitative kind of management practices are most commonly found in the small- and medium-sized factories that are either collectively or privately owned, in numerous cases by Hong Kong, Taiwanese, or other foreign entrepreneurs.

It was not uncommon as late as 1989 to encounter sweatshops in towns across China, employing 32.5 million people, which at that time constituted approximately one-third of the entire industrial workforce. Conditions in their work environments resembled those of the nineteenth-century Dickensian industrial revolution. Many of the workers were erstwhile peasants (including children) employed on a temporary or seasonal basis. But despite the abysmal labor conditions, these mostly first-generation workers are not likely to be in the vanguard of a rebellious social sector. For them, any nonagricultural job, no matter how exploitative, constitutes a move up the socio-economic ladder.[26] Many of these unskilled, transient laborers are at the bottom of the economic heap, engaged as temporary workers without job tenure, working under appalling conditions, in unsafe and substandard working environments.

INDUSTRIAL ACCIDENTS

The failure to address the needs of workers is often borne out by frequent and serious outbreaks of industrial accidents. It is not difficult to pin down the causes of such debacles, one of which is employer responsibility. Many enterprises where disasters occur are under joint or foreign ownership. The overseas owners concerned are plainly obsessed with maximizing output and cutting costs, to the complete disregard of work safety. Another factor is the absence of laws and regulations on industrial safety. Some investors actually choose to operate in places without stringent rules so that they can get away with flagrant exploitation of their workers. Besides, employer objection to the establishment of trade unions and the lack of organization among migrant workers also mean that they are at the mercy of entrepreneurs and management.

Even if there are rules and regulations, however, their implementation cannot be assumed. Official laxity in enforcement is often caused by reluctance to upset employers, especially foreign bosses. Meanwhile, infringements can also be ignored through bribing officials.[27] On the other hand, working conditions are generally much better in the very large state enterprises, where the bureaucratic structure is well established and management is somewhat more constrained by the rules and regula-tions imposed by the government.

MINE SAFETY

While significant numbers of transients earn reasonable wages in conditions comparable to those in the state sector, some jobs are filled only by transients because permanent workers are unwilling to accept occupational hazards For example, Chi-nese mines are staffed primarily by unqualified temporary workers because the permanent workers refuse to go underground.

In 1993, for the first time, China produced figures on industrial accidents: officially, 15,140 fatalities in 1992. The real figure is probably much greater. Coal ministry statistics reveal that, in mines alone, around 10,000 people a year die in explosions. Government statistics do not help much to clarify the situation. The only categories offered for accidental deaths are "extraordinarily serious," "serious," and "ordinary."[28] Investigations into accidents and disasters often indicate that managers and employers have disregarded safety rules, and local inspection teams are inade-quate or corrupt. On average, nearly 500 people die from industrial accidents in China each week, a dismal record that has attracted condemnation from the ILO and international labor unions.[29]

In November 1994 a labor ministry decree called for better supervision in China's mines. Coal mining deaths rose 73% in the first half of the year. Actual figures were not released, but mine collapses, explosions and other accidents killed more than 9000 miners annually in the early 1990s.[30] Despite official claims that mine safety improved, the situation has actually worsened as the number of private and individually operated coal mines soared. The nonexistence of independent trade unions and the very low social and economic status of Chinese miners, many of them peasants, were the main factors behind their plight. Many have left farms for the mines where there was no awareness of safety and employers placed production as the highest priority. Wang Jiaqi, a dissident in exile in the United States who worked for three years as a coal miner, reported that a coal mine in Tangshan, Hebei province, had dismantled a gas alarm system in the early 1980s because it disrupted production. Coal miners, victims of silicosis, had a 20-year working span before they were forced to retire or transfer to other jobs. In order to fill vacancies, mine bosses would take contract and temporary workers who enjoyed no medical, housing, or retirement protection.

Some were migrant workers from other provinces who work without contracts, have no knowledge of mining, nor are they informed about safety operation. Some only sign an agreement stating that the miner will be compensated if he dies in an accident and on the condition that no lawsuit will be pursued by his family. Furthermore, the compensation following a fatality totaled 20,000 yuan in one case, more than a miner could earn in a lifetime. The solution to this intolerable situation must be raising miners' safety awareness and the creation of free trade unions so that workers can experience genuine collective bargaining power.[31]

THE SHENZHEN SITUATION

The 1993 conflagration in a foreign-funded factory in Shenzhen, in which approximately 100 workers died, shocked the world and focused attention on Shenzhen and nearby areas, where antiquated fire fighting equipment and escape mechanisms have contributed to an alarming rise in fire victims. Dirty, noisy, and poorly illuminated workshops contribute to the safety problem. Frequently, workers' certificates are retained by employers to prevent them from seeking employment elsewhere where conditions may be better.

Workers frequently change their employers due to the poor working conditions. Shenzhen government departments have often received complaints from workers against their employers for illegally detaining their certificates. Some Shenzhen firms have collected the workers' identity certificates and border passes and then locked them in drawers under the pretext of helping them get temporary residence permits. An employer in a garment processing factory in Shenzhen did not apply for temporary residence permits for over 100 workers eight months after collecting their identity certificates and border passes, and refused to return the certificates to the workers, despite repeated demands, using the excuse that the "necessary procedures for applying for temporary residence permits are underway" or that the "certificates were lost in the process." When the department concerned, after receiving the complaints, inquired of the employer about the matter, the latter continued to lie, saying that they "kept" the certificates because the police substation rejected the workers' applications for temporary residence permits. A factory, which specializes in processing supplied materials, set aside the workers' certificates for fear they would seek jobs in other factories, and the employer, when questioned in the department concerned as to the reason, shouted, "If I do not retain their certificates, will my factory not be forced to suspend production if they go over to other factories?"[32]

The need for action is clear. In foreign-funded factories, which employ about 6 million Chinese in the coastal provinces, accidents abound, In some factories, workers are chastised, beaten, strip-searched, and even forbidden to use the bathroom during work hours. At a foreign-owned company in the Fujian province city of Xiamen, 40 workers, or 10% of the workforce, have had their fingers crushed by obsolete machines. According to official reports, there were 45,000 industrial accidents in Guangdong in 1993, claiming more than 8,700 lives.[33]

SAFETY AND HEALTH MEASURES

Another reason for the alarming increase in work-related accidental deaths is the fact that many companies ignore worker safety in the design and construction of their plants, and are unwilling to spend money to protect their workforces. A survey of 329 foreign-funded firms in Xuhui District and Pudong New Area showed that 232, or 70.5% of them, did not consider safety facilities during the design and construction stages.

Other surveys conducted by local labor departments found that most of the local foreign firms were not willing to spend money on safety measures. More than 50% of them did not have safety protection departments and personnel trained in worker safety. Safety training programs were also neglected in many of these companies.[34]

The official government line is that occupational health and safety are constant themes and all work units are required to designate a safety officer. However, safety consciousness and the level of safety remain extremely low. Every year there are thousands of negligence and accident cases involving criminal or civil liability. Most recorded cases in China involve physical injuries caused by machines, or accidents in the transportation or mining industries.

OCCUPATIONAL DISEASES

Chinese epidemiological officials have only recently become aware of the threat to workers from chemicals and are just beginning to monitor such threats. In 1993, the

Zhuhai city public health department conducted a simple survey in seven Taiwan-funded enterprises. The findings indicated that the percentage of benzene, toluene, and xylenol in the air were all 8 to 10 times higher than the respective international standards. The problem was especially severe in such industries as toy making, plastics, shoemaking, fabric printing and dyeing, and chemicals. Incidents of poisoning took place in three foreign-funded toy manufacturing plants, causing 81 casualties, of whom four died and eight were permanently disabled.

A poisoning case which occurred in a garment factory in Dalian City causing 42 casualties was due to the poisonous gas released by the fabric supplied by an overseas customer for processing. In Qinhuangdao City, 12 workers in a Sino-foreign joint venture were poisoned the first day the plant started operations. A monitoring operation conducted by the Dalian City Occupational Research Institute at the workshops of 14 currently operating foreign firms generating occupational hazards revealed that only six enterprises met the public health standards. Shenzhen City has conducted an air pollution survey in 547 firms wholly or in part run by foreign interests and found that only 29.6% of the imported equipment installed at these companies have anti-pollution devices and only 26% of the machines in these firms have gone through pollution tests before being put into operation. Regarding the risks Chinese workers face, the survey finding concluded: "There are still more horrible things. Industrial accidents and occupational diseases are a pair of swords hung over the workers, the former being the hard and overt one and the other being the soft and covert one. They are constantly threatening the workers' lives and impairing their health."[35] The litany of workplace horrors described above occurred despite Article 56 of the new labor law which ostensibly protects workers in the following terms: "Workers have the right to refuse to work at risk when ordered and forced by management personnel of employing units to do so in violation of rules and the right to criticize and sue the management for actions that endanger the safety of their lives and health." Efforts supposedly are being directed by the government to educate all the parties in the Chinese labor–management relationship in all relevant provisions of the new labor law. It remains to be seen how effective these measures will be in informing workers of their rights when many are either illiterate, ignorant, or terrified of offending their employers lest their jobs be placed in jeopardy. Chinese and foreign employers will also have to match rhetoric with deeds to protect workers from exposure to these insidious dangers in the workplace.

THE PLIGHT OF WOMEN WORKERS

In evaluating the status of China's female workers the formal legal protections afforded women have consistently masked reality. For instance, the 1982 Constitution states that "Women in the People's Republic of China enjoy equal rights with men in all spheres of life" and promises, among other things, equal pay for equal work. The 1988 "Women's Protection Law" provides a minimum of three months' maternity leave and additional childcare benefits for women. The regulations, which do not affect rural workers, are designed to provide additional incentives to women workers of childbearing age to abide by family planning policies. However, the expense of these provisions to employers is widely believed to have increased discrimination against female workers. Many employers, who now have new freedom to choose whom to hire, openly advertise for only male workers and will cite the costs of maternity and childcare benefits as a major factor in their choice of employees.

The Chinese government took a major step toward dealing with the ramifications of the Women's Protection Law when the Law on the Protection of Rights and Interests of Women was passed by the March 1992 National People's Congress. The law specifically outlaws discrimination in hiring or firing based on pregnancy, maternity leave, or childcare considerations. While outlawing discrimination in employment, the law leaves open a broad and vague category of "work or physical labor to be suitable to {women}." Promotion of the law by central and local governments began in earnest in 1995 in preparation for the Fourth World Conference on Women, held in Beijing in early September.

A primary reason for drafting the law is to bolster women's equal claim to property in the event of divorce, widowhood, inheritance and in the allotment of farmland by local village authorities, a right until recently has been noted more for its breach than observance. The Women's Law vests the All-China Women's Federation with primary responsibility for protecting women's rights and interests, but also cites trade unions and the Communist Youth League as organizations which, within the scope of their work, should strive to support women's rights. Chapter 4 of the law prohibits certain discriminatory acts on the part of employers and guarantees working women the following rights:

1. Equal rights, with men to work.
2. Equal pay for equal work.
3. Equal access in the allotment of housing and enjoyment of welfare benefits.
4. Equal rights to promotion, rank, evaluation and determination of professional and technological titles.[36]

The law also prohibits dismissal of women for reason of marriage, pregnancy, maternity leave or baby nursing. It requires employers to offer special protection to women during menstruation, pregnancy and the post-natal period.

THE QUANTITATIVE AND QUALITATIVE EVIDENCE

Statistics indicate that despite the impressive set of legal protections and higher labor force participation rates, the quality of employment for women still is inferior to that of men. Approaching five decades after the Communist Party swept to power, Chinese women hold little more than a third of full-time jobs. Women accounted for 37.4% of the total workforce in 1994, up from 35.4% in 1980, according to government figures However, most working women had jobs requiring limited education or technical skills. The service sector was dominated by women.

Official figures indicate that women account for 60% of China's agricultural labor force and that rural men are shifting in ever greater numbers to nonfarm township and village enterprises or out of the countryside altogether. Less than 20% of government officials and office workers were female. The number of women in the workforce had increased 52.5% between 1980 and 1994, while the male workforce grew 46.2%.[37]

China's corporate sector, domestic and foreign, also is not an attractive arena for women. Neglect of women's potential, whether deliberate or inadvertent, remains a defining characteristic of human resource management. Shoddy pay and treatment of women are the inevitable consequence. Chinese women are still mainly involved in nonknowledge and nontechnology intensive sectors. The percentage of women employees in service businesses is higher than males, but employees in other major sectors are mainly male.

While the principle of equal pay for equal work for men and women is basically in place, due to current differences in cultural and professional competence as well as occupational composition, income gaps still exist. According to a 1990 survey, the average monthly income for male and female workers in urban areas were 193.15 yuan ($23) and 149.60 ($18) yuan respectively, with women receiving only 77.4% of men's pay. In rural areas, the average annual incomes for men and women were 1,518 yuan and 1,235 yuan respectively, with women getting 81.4% of the earnings of men.

An inquiry group from the Standing Committee of the National People's Congress inspected hundreds of enterprises across China. The purpose was to uncover foreign-funded and domestic firms that violate women's employment rights. The government appears particularly interested in making examples of overseas-funded companies to appease both domestic and international women's groups, which are scrutinizing China's record on women's rights.

China's reform policies have created higher incomes and better opportunities for its working men and women, but the country's labor market remains massively tilted in men's favor. Indeed, as the government retreats from its traditional role of assigning workers to jobs, it has created new opportunities for employers to discriminate against women when it comes to hiring, dismissal, compensation, and promotion.

The All-China Federation of Trade Unions (ACFTU), the All-China Women's Federation (ACWF), and other groups who have undertaken research in this area suggest that domestic companies are probably the most prominent violators of women's rights. But foreign firms are far from blameless and have contributed to the serious obstacles Chinese women face in the workplace. A 1993 study by the ACFTU estimated that at least 70% of workers laid off from ailing state enterprises are women. A March 1995 survey of 300 enterprises in five different cities undertaken jointly by the Ministry of Labor and the International Labor Organization also found that on average women made up 70% of the workers described by management as surplus in enterprises of varying ownership. Women laid off or deemed surplus labor by their employers fall into three main categories: women with low education or few skills; women of childbearing age; and women over 40 judged to be in poor health.

HOURS VIOLATIONS

Another area of discrimination involves hours of work Companies are mistreating their female employees and violating legal requirements by forcing women to work overtime, failing to execute proper contracts, and breaking rules governing maternity leave. Of 177 foreign-owned, joint venture, or cooperative companies investigated in Shanghai, almost half had not properly implemented laws limiting the working week to 44 hours. Some companies were forcing female employees to work up to 137 extra hours a month. Women's rights and interests were best looked after in joint ventures set up by an established foreign company and in firms where management was dominated by the Chinese side or labor unions were effective in carrying out their protective role.[38]

HOUSING

Article 23 of the Women's Law bars enterprises from discriminating against women in the allocation of housing. But many state enterprises continue to offer housing only to their male workers. Other Chinese work units provide housing to senior female employees only if they are married, a requirement rarely applied to male workers. Joint ventures which vest control of housing policy with their Chinese partners often inadvertently abet this unequal treatment of female workers.

Housing discrimination also takes more subtle forms. Some foreign companies with sizable factory operations avoid building employee housing by intentionally hiring large numbers of young female workers. They assume that these women will be content to live with their families until they are married and allocated a house by their husband's work unit. These firms also tend to assume that women are less likely to organize a union which may demand housing benefits.

Enforcement of laws against housing discrimination has so far fallen between the cracks of China's bureaucracy. Policing workplace violations is the responsibility of local labor bureaus, but housing policy and reform of the traditional housing system rests with the State Commission on Restructuring Economic Systems (SCRES).

OVERT DISCRIMINATION AGAINST NEW GRADUATES

Obtaining employment upon graduation from universities and other educational institutions is a growing challenge for young women. With fewer openings in China's flagging state sector, enterprise managers' prejudice in favor of male graduates is becoming a serious problem. During campus recruitment drives, some employers post signs that say women need not apply. The problem is so serious that some university administrations now require employers to interview one female graduate for every male interviewed. In their defense, employers cite the higher costs of employing women in terms of health insurance coverage and mandated maternity leaves as the major reasons for their reluctance to hire young women. In some cities, local governments are addressing the cost issue by setting up experimental regional maternity leave funds to remove the burden from individual enterprises.

But old-fashioned sexism is also at play, particularly when women are being considered for management or sales positions. With few prospects in the state sector, China's brightest young women are turning to foreign firms in droves, and to those companies' benefit. Men often see joining a state enterprise or the bureaucracy as an easier option for employment. However, for ambitious, talented women the foreign sector is often the only career avenue available.

SLOW-TRACK PROMOTION

Undervaluing female employees' qualifications and ability is not just a state sector phenomenon, it is a China-wide trend. Indeed, many female graduates take such a dim view of their chances in the job market that they apply only for secretarial jobs. Some of the brightest do this by joining the Foreign Enterprise Service Corp (FESCO) as secretaries. As the human resource manager of a major foreign oil company puts it: "We have many female university graduates applying to become secretaries with our company and it is us who have to say to them 'Why not try working in sales or as a management trainee with us.' "[39]

These inequities have developed even though Chinese women workers are better educated than their male counterparts. Thirty-eight percent have completed senior middle school, almost 7% more than in the case of men workers. Women now average 9.4 years of education compared with only 8.7 for men. Yet, despite their higher educational attainment, women are failing to obtain a proportional share of managerial and professional positions.

TOWNSHIP AND VILLAGE ENTERPRISE OPPORTUNITIES

Local labor bureaus, neighborhood party committees, trade unions, and the ACWF are all scrambling to deal with the wide-scale outplacement of women by organizing training and offering job placement services. But with few job openings in the state sector, most female workers, especially semi- and unskilled women, are considered lucky if they can move into lower-paying jobs with township and village enterprises and private firms. For that matter, rural women in China are an important driving force in the development of township enterprises. At present, rural China has more than 100 million workers in township businesses, and 40 million of them are females. The ratio is even greater for women working in the food, clothing, knitwear, and other woven products, toy and electronics factories, as well as traditional handicrafts and service trades.

On the plus side, China's economic reforms have improved the lot of women in rural areas. The rural economic restructuring, conducted since the end of the 1970s, unleashed the immense labor potential of women. Women have become an important and indispensable force in invigorating and promoting the rural economy. Females account for more than half of all workers in agriculture, forestry, animal husbandry, fisheries, and water conservancy. In major cotton-producing areas, the management of cotton fields is mostly undertaken by women. Of the 14 million self-employed rural individuals engaged in commerce and service trades, women account for about one-third. In areas where the commodity economy is relatively developed, rural women engaged in business account for half of farmers who have gone into trade. About 50 to 60% of the total rural output value is generated by women. They have come to dominate the livestock and poultry industries, two of the most common and profitable activities. On average, a woman earns 40% of a household's income, compared with about 25% before the reforms.[40]

RETIREMENT BIAS

China's official retirement age is 55 years for women and 60 years for men, a fact which in itself encourages unequal treatment of the sexes. Moreover, in their efforts to reduce overstaffing, some enterprises are retiring female workers as early as 45. Also, many government organizations have formal policies which preclude women above 50 years of age from being promoted because they are considered too close to retirement. The central government in Beijing says a labor verification system has been established to ensure that female state workers facing early retirement are being treated fairly. But the government also says employment pressures rule out the possibility of raising the retirement age for women to the same level as men in the near term.[41]

ASSESSMENT OF LEGAL PROTECTION FOR WOMEN

While laws exist to protect women, in practice discrimination based on gender has persisted. Reports by women of discrimination, sexual harassment, unfair dismissal, demotion, and wage cuts have continued. Most women employed in industry work in lower skilled and lower paid jobs. Women hold relatively few positions of significant influence within the Communist Party or government structure. Persistent problems have remained with regard to the status of women, who have often been the unintended victims of reforms designed to streamline enterprises and promote greater labor mobility.

It would generally appear that the increase in the quantity of employment opportunities for Chinese women has not been matched by similar positive trends in the quality of employment. On the whole, women workers' rights remain inadequately emphasized, relatively unknown, and insufficiently observed.

CHILD LABOR

Another area where attention has been focused involves the employment of young children. There is no specific prohibition of child labor in China in the new labor law. Two articles, 58 and 64 respectively, provide "special labor protection" to underage workers who are defined as workers who are at least 16 years of age but less than 18. These underage workers are not to be employed in mining or hazardous occupations and other strenuous jobs.

Earlier legislation was specifically addressed to and banned the employment of children. Regulations developed in 1987 prohibit the employment of school age minors who have not completed the compulsory 9 years of education. Statistics on school attendance indicated that approximately 20% of school-age children in the cities and villages do not attend school, and are therefore likely to be working. The number may well be higher in poorer and isolated areas, where child labor in agriculture is assumed to be widespread. In connection with a campaign against vice, there were reports in the press and by public security officials of female minors being sold into prostitution or to factories as laborers.

In April 1991, the State Council issued a regulation reiterating a 1988 Ministry of Labor circular, which provides enforcement provisions to prevent the employment of children under age 16. It imposes heavy fines, withdrawal of business licenses, or jail for employers who hire child laborers. There are some reports of attempts to enforce these regulations in South China, where the problem is assumed to be more acute. Of the child laborers employed outside of agriculture, most are likely to be in the private sector or in small or rural collectives, since the state sector is vastly overstaffed.

School attendance records indicate that the vast majority of elementary school students, aged 7 to 11, are in school, 97.95% in 1992. Education officials attribute the small non-attendance figures to children in remote or isolated areas or handicapped children for whom there are no appropriate facilities or whose parents do not want to send them to school. Attendance drops off somewhat for junior middle school students, aged 12 to 15, and the figure was 79.2% in 1992. This represented a 2% increase in attendance over the previous year.

Dropout rates for lower secondary schools, ages 12 to 15, in several southern provinces exceed 9% while the national average is 2.2%. This suggests the booming economy in that region is enticing more children to leave their studies to find jobs. In poorer, remote areas, child labor in agriculture is widespread.

Provincial education commissions and local labor bureaus have increased their efforts in recent years to eliminate child labor in industry and to enforce mandatory education laws. The result is that most industrial employers attempt to hire workers over the age of 16, of which there is no shortage. In this regard, with the large number of "waiting for employment youth" in their late teens or early twenties, many urban state enterprises refuse for social policy reasons to hire workers below the age of 18. Most independent observers agree with Chinese officials that China's urban child labor problem is relatively minor. No specific Chinese industry is identifiable as a significant violator of child labor regulations.

AGE DISCRIMINATION

An employment issue occupying the other end of the age continuum deals with discrimination directed against older workers, who are finding it increasingly difficult to compete. While no statistics are available, in conversations, many factory managers admit that they use the "labor optimization" procedure, whereby they rationalize job descriptions and eliminate surplus labor, as an opportunity to lay off older workers. Many managers complain that older workers do not have the skills needed. Still others note that many older workers are in poor health. Other than as an experimental program in a few southern counties, China does not have a disability insurance and retirement system. Managers therefore use general layoffs to dismiss such workers.

By all accounts older women are having an especially difficult time. While young women are fairly well educated, older women entered the workforce at a time when discrimination was much more virulent than it is now. They were poorly educated on entry and received almost no opportunities to upgrade their skills thereafter. While managers may want to keep on a certain number of experienced men, most view older women simply as a burden.

For the minority of older women who are well educated or highly skilled the differences in the statutory retirement age especially rankle. Retirement for men is 60, while for women it is 50 in industry and 55 elsewhere. Traditionally many women have desired early retirement to take care of grandchildren, but today women, especially educated women, prefer to make this decision themselves and not be forced out of the workforce before they are ready. However, thus far efforts to equalize the retirement age have been unsuccessful.

Legislation has been proposed to protect the interests of senior workers who have worked for more than 10 consecutive years in an enterprise. They would be allowed to work for the enterprise as long as they choose and not be laid off due to advancing years. In demographic terms, China is witnessing an ever larger portion of its population reaching older age levels. Newspapers commentators have called it the "raging silver wave." People over age 60 made up 8.8% of the population in 1990, but they will grow to 18.8% by 2025. There are 110 million people over 60 today; by 2025 the number of elderly will approach 400 million. That will put pressure on families, companies, and the government, all of whom will have to take care of them. As a result, measures to prolong the productive work life of physically and mentally fit older workers will assume greater importance as the societal burden for their care increases.[42]

FORCED LABOR

"Corrective" labor in Chinese prison or reform camps has been a long-standing practice for reforming prisoners. It has also been an important aspect of China's legal system and judicial policies since the Communist Power assumed power. Although this policy of reform through labor is practiced elsewhere in the world, it recently attracted the attention of some Western countries, leading to heated debate.

While China has generally abandoned its traditional use of massive convict labor for constructing infrastructure projects and public facilities, prisoners are still sometimes "mobilized" to augment public security forces and for public works projects. Imprisonment in China usually entails compulsory labor. As the names imply, forced labor is a cornerstone of the Chinese "Reform through Labor" and "Reeducation through Labor" systems. Almost all persons the courts sentence to prison or forced labor camps, including political prisoners, are required to work, usually for little or no compensation. China also maintains a network of "Reeducation though Labor" camps, whose inmates are sentenced by an administrative process and who also work. Reports from human rights organizations and released prisoners demonstrate that at least some prisoners in pretrial detention are also required to work.

Under the "staying at prison employment" system, some prisoners are denied permission to return to their homes after release and instead are forced to remain and work in the vicinity of the prison. While the Ministry of Justice claims that only 200 to 300 former prisoners are currently held under this system, many outside observers believe that the true number is far higher.

Chinese penal policy emphasizes "reform first, production second," but compulsory labor aims both to rehabilitate prisoners and to help support the facilities. Prisoners in labor reform institutions work a full 8-hour day and must also engage in both ideological and basic literacy and skills training. In addition, in labor reeducation facilities there is a much heavier emphasis on education than on labor.

Working conditions in the penal system's export-oriented light manufacturing factories are similar to those in ordinary factories, but conditions on labor farms and in coal mines are exceedingly harsh and in the mines possibly more dangerous than in ordinary mines. There have been an increasing number of reports that "Reform through Labor" and possibly "Reeducation through Labor" facilities as well, rent prisoners to ordinary factories to work.

The State Council's 1992 White Paper on criminal reform reported that prison labor production for 1990 was valued at $500 million. This figure, which cannot be confirmed, would not include the output from "Reeducation through Labor" facilities. It is acknowledged that Chinese prison labor is used for many types of production: infrastructure (roads); heavy industry (coal, steel); light manufacturing (clothing, shoes, small machine tools); and agriculture (grain, tea, sugar cane). Press reports, the 1990 Chinese Yearbook, and U.S. Customs Service investigations demonstrate that some of these goods are exported.

By the Tariff Act of 1930 the U.S. prohibits imports of goods produced by prison labor. The U.S. Customs Service has issued orders barring a number of products reportedly made by Chinese prisoners from entering the United States and has physically detained a few shipments of such goods. In 1991 the Chinese government published a restatement of its regulations barring the export of prison-made goods. On August 7, 1992 the U.S. and Chinese governments signed a memorandum of understanding on trade in prison labor products, which allows for both sides to exchange information and evidence related to suspected exports of prison labor products from China to the United States and enables U.S. officials to visit suspect facilities.

Under the MOU the Chinese have provided requested investigation reports on 31 suspected facilities. Five facilities investigated by the Chinese were found to have had prisoners engaged in some aspect of export production at some point in time, though not necessarily to the United States; of these, two with export activities at the time of the investigation reportedly received unspecified administrative sanctions. U.S. officials have conducted on-site visits of three suspected facilities and another facility visit has been scheduled. The detention orders on two of the visited facilities were lifted, one in December 1993 and one in January 1994. The other case is still under study.

In January 1995, apparently reflecting increased sensitivity to criticism by human rights organizations, China reported that its numerous and notorious labor camps have disappeared under a new law on prisons, and will be known simply as jails. To conform with a landmark law on prisons passed by the Standing Committee of the National People's Congress, the Justice Ministry will change the names of its "Reform Through Labor" institutions. The title "Reform Through Labor" is no longer being used but the function, nature, and objectives of China's prison management work remain unchanged. Under the new law, no distinction is being made between jails for ordinary prisoners, life prisoners, and prisoners under a two-year suspended death sentence.[43]

At the risk of sounding cynical, this transparent change in nomenclature will not satisfy human rights activists who have been demanding meaningful changes in Chinese forced labor policies. Of course, China has not signed ILO Convention No. 105, which prohibits the use of forced labor for purposes of economic development.[44]

UNEMPLOYMENT

China's economic reform program's near-term development goal is to provide its people with a well-off life by the end of the 20th century, an objective that is not impossible. Its long-term goal is to lift its people's living standards to those of an average developed nation. In this respect, the country's limitless labor supply is actually more of a burden than an asset. China has a labor force of 800 million and this is expected to reach 900 million or 1 billion in the next few decades. Projections estimate that in the next 10 years China will have 210 million rural inhabitants and 68 million urban residents waiting to be employed or reemployed.[45]

Today, the alarm has sounded about worsening unemployment and chronic problems in state industry which is under enormous pressure in the transition to a market economy. Low official unemployment figures vastly understate the extent of the problem as some estimates put urban unemployment at about 20% of the workforce. The huge rural labor surplus numbers between 130 million and 200 million, millions of whom have been seeking employment in the cities, adding to pressures on hard-pressed municipal authorities.[46]

Chinese workers first began to experience the bitter taste of unemployment in the late 1980s, when state-run enterprises began to jettison surplus workers as they began to pay closer attention to efficiency and labor productivity. The number of China's unemployed climbed to 1.87 million in 1994, equal to the reported total for the previous seven years; and the average duration of joblessness increased from four months to half a year. State enterprises across the nation reported 15 million surplus workers, 3 million of whom are staying home for an undefined period of "leave," living on a minimal budget. Approximately 3.58 million workers had to make a living by seeking odd jobs after the factories they worked for closed down or suspended production due to lack of profitability, shortages of raw materials, or other reasons.

UNEMPLOYMENT REDUCTION PLANS

Because of these developments, the Labor Ministry launched a reemployment program on a trial basis in 1994, a plan which sought to create 8 million new jobs for the unemployed over a five-year period. Thirty large cities, including Shanghai, Shenyang, Zingdao, Hangzhou, and Chengdu were chosen as the locales. The project, which involved the combined efforts of government, companies, all levels of society, and workers, emphasized the provision of new jobs for those unemployed for at least six months. The principal measures utilized to reach this goals included providing job market information, technical training courses, providing meetings between employers and employees, and working out preferential policies for potential employees.

Liaoning province, an old industrial base in Northeast China, has 1.6 million underemployed workers in addition to a 110,000-strong jobless population, not to mention a huge number of transient laborers. To meet this challenge, the local government has set up an employment department composed of 15 government offices including labor unions, which found 168,000 jobs for unemployed workers in its first year of operation. Enterprises in the country's leading industrial center of Shanghai laid off 521,000 surplus workers during the 1990 to 1994 period. In 1994, the city assisted 127,000 of those laid off to find new jobs.[47] Also, as mentioned earlier, China shortened the work week by four hours across the country, effective May 1, 1995, in an effort to create more jobs for the unemployed.

Ostensibly designed to improve employee welfare, the new policy will force labor-intensive operations, such as hotels and low-cost manufacturing enterprises to hire more workers or raise efficiency to maintain productivity. Estimates were that for every 10 people hired by a firm, it would have to add an extra person to maintain the output or productivity level as a result of the change in the work week. One hundred fifty million people work at state enterprises and 14 million at foreign-funded firms. Based on state sector employment, the new rule should create employment for approximately 15 million people. Unfortunately, about two-thirds of these state companies are losing money and cannot afford to add more workers. Unemployment could be as high as 10% as many in unprofitable state firms no longer worked although they remained on the payroll and drew a portion of their salaries. China has promised to speed up reform of these loss-making state enterprises but has not been ready to deal with the expected army of unemployed which would result from the necessary bankruptcies and layoffs. A Chinese sociologist called the mass of surplus state workers "the most unstable factor in China."[49]

Unemployment Insurance

To ease the economic adversity caused by layoffs, an unemployment insurance plan announced in February 1995 will pay every dismissed state sector worker 70 to 80% of the national minimum wage for up to two years. Those who fail to find a new job in two years will still be entitled to other welfare benefits. A limited scheme already operates for workers laid off by certain joint ventures or privately run enterprises.[50]

The new unemployment compensation program is an improvement over the old system, which had only a vague definition of the term *employment*. In the past, state sector workers were more likely to be deemed underemployed, as state firms were forbidden to lay off unnecessary employees. Now workers fired by state firms, retired workers, and those who become unemployable due to accidents or illness will be covered.[51]

The scheme's potential cost is huge and the funding requirement would impose a huge burden on the state sector. It is estimated that more than 15% of the mainland's 100,000 state enterprises are heading for bankruptcy simply because their obsolete products are failing to find markets. If SOEs are required to contribute to the new unemployment insurance plan, the questions remain of how much they will have to pay and whether a general standard should applied to all companies, public and private. The government needs to approach these concerns cautiously. Otherwise, the state firms will prefer to keep its surplus workers underemployed, which is less costly than laying them off.

Although the Labor Ministry will bear part of the costs, its share would be minor, leaving the People's Bank of China to bear the lion's share of the financial responsibility. China's central bank has already allocated 7 billion yuan ($HK 6.44 billion) in partial payment of the loans owed by SOEs to other state banks. While funding details remain to be clarified, there is concern at the implications attendant to the closing of inefficient state firms. The success of the state sector restructuring depends very much on whether the workers are psychologically well prepared for the shutdown of their companies. The new plan would not necessarily increase compensation for unemployed workers. In addition, there would be strong resistance to layoffs and closures from the heavy industrial bases of Northern China, such as Liaoning province. In Liaoning, SOEs support more than 70% of the local population of nearly 40 million. The province makes up 10% of the country's state businesses. The key to success lies in the provision of new jobs and a retraining program. Such radical reform carries the potential for social unrest. So the urgency of China's attempts to create a safety net for the unemployed is hardly surprising.[52]

SOCIAL SECURITY REFORM

The unemployment insurance plan just described is only one of the basic components of a comprehensive social security system in China. Reform in the retirement and health insurance programs is another critical priority. As it now stands, the reason why Chinese authorities find it difficult to implement the bankruptcy law, which has been in force several years, is that former employees of shutdown factories are deprived of all social insurance. The economic restructuring process underway has highlighted the need for a parallel overhaul of the existing social security system to make it compatible with and supportive of the economic reforms in progress in order to provide better protection for the entire population.

PENSION DEVELOPMENTS

The existing system is in trouble because it is largely based on, and contributes to, a huge loss-making operation, namely, state enterprises. At present, these enterprises have to pay for most of their workers' housing, health insurance, disability and old-age pension, food allowances and other welfare benefits, in addition to wages. Nearly half of state firms are technically bankrupt, and the government is seriously considering plans to shut them down. This, of course, means that social security in general, and the pension scheme in particular, will eventually have to be financed and administered differently. In October 1991, the State Council adopted a resolution which would pave the way for radical pension plan reform.

China's basic old-age pension program only protects workers feeding from the so-called iron rice bowl, i.e., civil servants and the lifetime employees of state enterprises and large collectives. Yet none of these beneficiaries contribute to the funding of the systems. By contrast, private sector workers and farmers are simply not covered. Moreover, apart from a few experimental plans that cannot be made comprehensive due to a lack of financial resources, the rural population, the majority, has little hope for major improvements in the foreseeable future. The China National Committee on Ageing (SNCA) has proposed that the traditional system of family support for the elderly should be encouraged and institutionalized to provide at least some formal basis for social protection in rural areas. The proposals also envisage the introduction of a rural pension scheme. This would be a historic step of great significance in the social insurance development of China, especially if we consider the fact that the rural population represents 74% of the total population.

The elderly in rural areas have traditionally been dependent on family support to survive. Public assistance, known as the "Five Guarantees" program, in principle provides the indigent elderly with means for food, clothing, housing, medical care, and burial. Since the breakdown of the agricultural communes, the sources of funding for this program have become more precarious than before and currently the average benefit, paid to just under 3 million of the rural elderly, is only about 10% of average rural per capita income.

Active family planning policies and consequent demographic developments will produce a need for enhanced social security support for the rural aged in the future. A rural old-age insurance scheme is therefore being progressively introduced throughout rural China by the Ministry of Civic Affairs. The program now has some 20 million members and went into full operation in 1995.[53]

STATE ENTERPRISE PENSION REFORM

A significant change occurred in 1986 when the government set up a special pension program for state employees hired under a newly created labor contract system. Such workers have to contribute 3% of their wages to a pension fund. Responsibility for administering the program was entrusted to local governments through newly established Social Security Agencies (SSAs) subordinate to the city or county labor departments. In a related experiment, SSAs were also put in charge of a resource pooling of retirement pensions for permanent workers in some cities and counties, the funding being provided by enterprises and local governments.

These developments are examples of the government's efforts to prepare the state sector workforce for a gradual transition to a market-oriented economy. Yet, these measures did little to remedy the basic shortcomings of the existing system which covers only about 20% of the country's population with old-age pension insurance. Additionally, owing to the lack of an independent pension administration, many administrative functions such as collection and distribution are still carried out in isolation by thousands of individual enterprises.

Some of these reforms are addressed, on paper at least, by the State Council Resolution on the Reform of the Pension System for Enterprise Workers. The resolution applies to all state enterprises and, optionally, to urban collective enterprises. It provides for the gradual establishment of a system combining basic pension insurance, enterprise supplementary pension insurance, and savings-based workers' individual pension insurance with a view to sharing the financial burden of pension insurance between the government, enterprises, and workers.

Basic pension funds will be established by the government and administered by the SSAs on behalf of a pension fund commission vested with supervisory powers and set up by each local government authority. Ultimate responsibility for the operation of pension insurance for workers in urban enterprises rests with the Ministry of Labor and the local labor departments. Provincial authorities that have not yet established a pension insurance fund must endeavor to do so by pooling existing city- and county-level funds at the provincial level. After such funds have been established, existing pension funds for permanent workers and contract workers will eventually be merged. Enterprises directly subordinate to central ministries must participate in unified pension fund management at the provincial level, unless they are subject to regulations providing otherwise.

Workers' contributions to the basic pension funds, initially exceeding 3% of standard wages, as has been noted, will be implemented gradually on the basis of wage readjustment. Enterprises, for their part, will be required to make monthly pretax contributions to these funds, assessed as a percentage of their total wage bill. Fines will be imposed for late payment. The contributions of workers and enterprises will be registered separately and transferred to a special interest-earning bank account opened by the SSAs.

The current procedure for paying basic pension benefits to retirees, i.e., through enterprises, will not change for the time being. In the future, however, their pensions will be increased gradually, in proportion to the amount of standard wages (as opposed to "total wages," which includes fringe benefits). More generally, basic pensions will be adjusted in the light of the urban cost-of-living index and wage increases.

Enterprise supplementary pension insurance can be established by any firm for its own workforce, depending on the amount of resources available from the company's material incentive bonuses and welfare funds. The administration of these programs, like that of basic pension insurance, is entrusted to the local SSA. The government will encourage enterprises to set up such supplementary plans. Similarly, it will encourage workers to participate in savings-based individual workers' pension insurance.

The State Council's resolution stipulates that insurance systems will also be gradually established for workers employed in "foreign investment enterprises and privately owned enterprises." Furthermore, separate ministerial regulations on pension reform will be formulated by "government bodies, administrative institutions and rural areas, including township and village enterprises."[54]

HEALTH INSURANCE

In the mid-1990s there are two programs of compulsory health insurance. The first is restricted to government employees, those retired from government service, university students, and demobilized soldiers. In 1991, the number of persons insured by this arrangement was about 28 million. The second plan covers the larger part of the population, i.e., some 112 million people, employees and retirees of state-owned enterprises.

Some state-owned enterprises are now employing contract workers who may be given more restricted coverage while their dependents are not covered at all. Thus, only about 140 million workers enjoy compulsory coverage by a health insurance program.

The main weakness of the existing system, however, is that health care providers are paid on the basis of the number of services rendered. This gives the provider the economic incentive to furnish as many services as possible, particularly those services which yield a substantial profit to the provider. All over the world it has been found that fee-for-service payment leads to the escalation of costs. The inevitable response, in China as elsewhere, has been to make insured persons bear part of the costs which, if carried to lengths which effectively control costs, greatly limits the value of the insurance.

The second main weakness is to make each enterprise bear the costs for its own employees. Given the government's intention to move toward a market economy, in which labor will be mobile, the present arrangements for health care represent a considerable obstacle to achieving that aim. An employee moving from a state-owned enterprise to a cooperative, private company, or joint venture risks losing all rights to health care. Even a move between state-owned firms could be counterproductive because length of service determines the extent to which an employee has to contribute to health costs.

What can be done to remedy these weaknesses of the existing system? Reform proposals envisage urban health insurance entirely financed by the contributions of employers and employees and the copayments of the latter. This would enable resources to be directed toward the rural areas and to assist all those currently without insurance in obtaining the means to acquire it. The innovative approaches used in the experimental implementation of unemployment, pension, and health insurance programs have on the whole led to useful results, although there is now a need to coordinate these experiments in order to ensure the necessary system cohesion.

POLICY COHESION

Reforming pension, unemployment benefit, and health insurance schemes will not, of themselves, resolve the underlying issues of structural adjustment in the economy. The government will have to integrate these elements closely with other reforms, particularly those affecting the labor market.

The era of experimentation should gradually be brought to a close. A representative institutional body should be set up or reactivated to formulate policy guidelines at the national level in the field of social security. It should be matched by corresponding provincial bodies, responsible for translating the national policy at the provincial level and for managing the system of social security. Finally, a single tripartite agency, at the provincial level, should be entrusted with all aspects of the administration of social security, including pensions, unemployment, and other benefits.[55]

FREEDOM OF ASSOCIATION

Obviously, the government-controlled ACFTU will support the social security reform efforts just listed. If China allowed independent trade unions to form and function, they too could play an important role in social insurance efforts, as well as in improving wages, hours, and working conditions for workers, as labor organizations do in the West. On paper at least, the People's Republic seems to guarantee these rights. Articles 7 and 88, respectively, of the new labor law appear to address this issue directly:

> Article 7. Workers have the right to participate in and organize trade unions. Trade unions represent and safeguard workers' legitimate rights and interests and carry out their activities independently according to law."
>
> Article 88. Trade unions at all levels shall, according to the law, safeguard workers' legitimate rights and interests and supervise the way employing units abide by the Labor Law and regulations.

However, the new law does not expand the role of labor unions from that outlined in previous legislation. While workers in all enterprises have the right to organize and participate in labor unions, the law does not mandate the establishment of unions. Those that are created must be organized "in accordance with law," meaning that only government-sanctioned unions are to be permitted.

THE SHENZHEN UNIONS

Having their rights and interests repeatedly encroached upon, workers in Shenzhen and nearby areas set up unions on their own to deal with the unlawful practices of enterprise operators. Initial statistics have indicated that there are currently more than 800 trade unions at various levels. The main task of these labor organizations is to seek a solution for the problem of unequal payments to workers through discussion with employers. Generally speaking, workers are willing to join unions, but they do not do so openly because they are afraid they will be laid off for such activity.

Although these unions play a positive role in safeguarding workers' rights and interests, they have several serious deficiencies. First, the unions are not very well organized and resemble secret societies, which lack a set of management principles and rules, and thus usually act based on feelings and personal loyalty. Second, many unions do not have a well-considered strategy for safeguarding their legitimate rights and interests. Certain of these unions have presented inappropriate demands which are unacceptable to management. Third, their efforts have so far been frustrated both by police repression and workers' passivity and indifference. At one factory, labor activists were well into their standard presentation to the young migrant workers, explaining the benefits a labor union might bring, when they realized the workers had no idea what the term *labor union* meant.[56]

UNIONS IN JOINT VENTURES

Although China is a signatory to a number of ILO conventions, it has not signed any ILO conventions on freedom of association. Consequently, the move underway to require unionization of all joint ventures is unlikely to affect many American, European or Japanese firms. Many of these already have unions for their employees.[57]

Compliance also has been spotty in areas where unions have not made inroads. For example, less than a fifth of foreign firms operating in Fujian had set up unions by the end of 1994.[58] In Sichuan, only 23.4%, or 360 of the province's 2,300 foreign-funded factories had formed unions in 1995. Not only had they resisted union formation, these companies also fired innocent union leaders who were trying to redress problems of work safety, bogus contracts, unjustified salary cuts, and forced overtime.[59]

Statistics show that 81.5% of China's foreign-funded companies opened after 1992, by which time 29,500 unions were established. By the end of 1994, there were 32,000 labor organizations in foreign firms, or 40.6% of the total businesses.[60] The drive to organize these enterprises also received an unexpected setback when the ACFTU formulated a new timetable, scaling back its mandate that all foreign-financed companies set up state-controlled unions by the end of 1994. Under the new rules, 60% of foreign companies outside the bustling coastal region must at least finish preparations for state unions by the deadline and new firms opening anywhere in China must comply within a year of commencing operations. No reason was given for easing what some foreign managers said was an overly ambitious, ill-considered target.

It should be kept in mind that federation unions are carefully controlled tools of Communist Party policy, and guarantee a compliant workforce, whether in state enterprises, private industry, or foreign venturers.[61] The requirement for unionization of all foreign venturers may prove overly ambitious as the ACFTU may not have the resources to visit the thousands of small assembly operations targeted by the drive, since its membership remains highly concentrated in large, state-owned companies.[62]

FUTURE PROSPECTS

An optimistic forecast posits that China's workers will eventually follow South Korea's labor model. Repressed there, too, by a series of military dictatorships, the labor movement fought alongside students and other sectors of society for democracy. The battles were bloody, dividing the nation in the early 1980s. In the end, Koreans won both democracy and a strong, legal trade union movement. In China, today, and for that matter, in the rest of Asia outside Japan, however, workers' rights are still honored mostly in the breach, and labor movements are still struggling for a foothold.

PART III

Indonesia

> The meeting room was hot. Outside there were about 80 pairs of shoes, like the merchandise of a pavement vendor. The door stood open. There was no need to close it against the neighbours: most will never have heard of trade unions. The sounds of children playing and a neighbour's television, broke through the Sunday stillness. The workers listened intently as the union leaders underlined the justness of the struggle: Indonesia ratified the International Labour Organization Convention of 1956, which ensures the right to associate in free trade unions.
>
> Indonesia workers risk freedom for their rights. *Reuter Textline Guardian,* October 14, 1991, 15.

Indonesia has many parallels but also differences that stand out from the People's Republic of China. Both have authoritarian forms of government that brook little dissent and are frequently cited by international human rights organizations for violations of basic human rights. Workers rights are subordinated in export-driven trade policies catering to foreign-investor enterprises intent on maintaining cheap labor costs and compliant trade unions.

In both countries, only one government-controlled labor organization is permitted to function as attempts to stimulate autonomous unionism and Western-style collective bargaining are suppressed and basically neglected, respectively. Unskilled labor is overabundant but shortages of skilled workers are plaguing human resource managers. Labor laws are honored more in the breach than in the observance as both nations fail to match rhetoric with deeds. Labor unrest in the form of strikes and work stoppages has increased substantially with workers protesting against low wages and dangerous working conditions.

Yet labor activists in both countries find it all but impossible to capitalize on growing labor militancy because of governmental duress, including military intervention. Both the Communist Party in the People's Republic and Golkar, a so-called nonpolitical functional group, block progressive legislative initiatives in their allegiance to authoritarian leadership. Potentially destabilizing succession crises loom in both China and Indonesia as Deng Xiaoping slowly fades from the scene and President Suharto's regime is in its fourth decade, both without anointed successors.

Despite these similarities, there are putative distinctions in our binational comparison. To begin with, Indonesia's economic development over the past two decades has been obscured by the dynamism of China's economic advances, particularly during the past half decade. However, Indonesia's economic progress has been at least as remarkable. Its economy has grown steadily from year to year, with GDP growth seldom below 5% or greater than 7%. China's macroeconomic planners would do worse than to study the policies, plans, and programs of their Jakarta counterparts.

The Wild West, anything goes environment of Guangdong Province in China is fueled by seemingly endless hordes of rural migrant workers, with less concern shown for environmental problems and workers' rights than in Indonesia, where a recent package of radical liberalization measures has opened up industries and services to 100% foreign ownership.

The Indonesian marketplace is less fragmented than that of China with more centralized decision making, presenting difficulties for small companies but favorable for larger capital-intensive firms. Corruption is endemic in both nations, coupled with the necessity for the right political or family connections. However, it can be argued that in Indonesia, slow improvement is occurring as corporate and government affairs are subjected to closer public scrutiny while the situation in China continues to deteriorate.

Also, according to World Bank statistics, each Indonesian has a per capita annual income of $2,970 expressed in purchasing power, compared to $1,910 for each Chinese citizen. Moreover, although these countries are plagued by inequality of incomes between the wealthy and poor classes, once again Indonesia is doing better than China, as the lowest 40% of Indonesians receive 19.8% of the national income compared with 17.4% in China. Furthermore, since 1990, China's income distribution has become markedly more skewed by the rapid development of the coastal provinces.

While China emphasizes mass education, public health, and growing urbanization after two generations of "people's" government, its illiteracy rate of 27% exceeds the 22% level in Indonesia. Its higher education enrollment is also much less than Indonesia's, and urbanization is also more widespread in the largest Islamic nation in the world. In fact, the only major social indicator where China is ahead of Indonesia is in life expectancy.

Our worker rights/labor standards model for Indonesia shown below depicts limited coverage or protection in numerous variables but considerably more real progress in these areas than that experienced in China. The circumstances surrounding these results will be more fully explored in the next section.

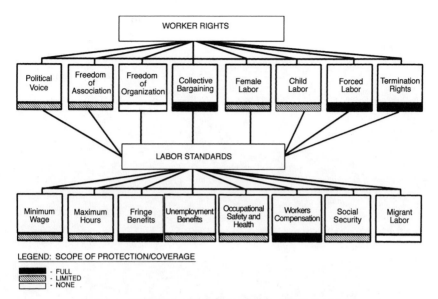

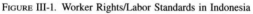

FIGURE III-1. Worker Rights/Labor Standards in Indonesia

CHAPTER 7

A Political, Economic, and Demographic Overview

BASIC DEMOGRAPHIC FEATURES

Indonesia is the fourth largest country in the world, the largest Muslim nation, with an estimated 1994 population of 198,055,000. It is larger than any other nation in Southeast Asia and consists of some 13,700 islands in the Malay Archipelago. The country's only land borders are with Malaysia on the northern part of the island of Borneo and with Papua New Guinea to the east of West New Guinea on the island of New Guinea. The Philippines are located to the northeast, Australia lies to the southeast, and the Indian Ocean lies to the south and southwest. Its land area is 741,053 square miles or about one-fourth the size of the United States.[1]

According to the 1990 census, two-thirds of Indonesia's population lives in rural areas, leaving an urban population of approximately 55.4 million. The population is just about evenly divided between males and females, with slightly less than half the population under 20 years of age. Indonesia's population is spread unevenly throughout the 3,000-mile long archipelago, with 60% living on Java (107.5 million) and 20.3% (36.8 million) on Sumatra, the country's two main islands.

Indonesia's high birth rate and low infant mortality will coincide to generate dramatic change in the age structure and put new pressures on economic development in the next three decades. The World Bank forecasts that Indonesia's population will rise from 198 million in 1995 to 280 million by 2030. A staggering 75% of this increase will be in the working population, aged 20 to 64. It will begin with a rise in the younger workforce, aged 20 to 24, in the next few years and be followed by an explosion between 2000 and 2005 in the population aged 25 to 34.[2]

Indonesia's labor force is estimated to number nearly 80 million. During the 1990 to 1995 period, the population grew at a rate of 1.8% annually. By the period 2015 to 2020, that rate is expected to drop to 1.7%. However, the working age population is expected to continue to increase at a rate higher than overall population growth for sometime into the future. During the 1980 to 1995 period, the working age population grew at a rate of 2.9% and is expected to drop to only 1.98% in the 2015 to 2020 time frame. This means there will be 2.5 million new workers entering the labor force annually. As some demographers have projected, Indonesia's population growth rate will reach replacement level in 2000 to 2005 and then fall below that level. Then the earliest the country can expect to see a reduction in the absolute number of its population is the year 2085.

Demographic imbalances are being created by the economic development process itself, and in particular, by the rapid pace of industrialization, because most of the new industrial plants are located in the vicinity of major urban centers, especially on Java. As more agricultural land is converted to industrial, residential, and recreational uses on Java and Bali, and employment opportunities shift from the rural areas to the suburban industrial areas, the process of rural–urban migration is also gathering pace, with the growth of the urban population thus exceeding the rate of overall population growth. The strain on the urban infrastructure is becoming severe. Although the government has begun to attempt to curb this flow since 1993–94, inter alia by imposing restrictions on the conversion of fertile agricultural land to nonagricultural uses, these measures are likely to have only a modest impact as long as the gap between rural and urban income and employment opportunities continues to grow.[3]

HISTORICAL OVERVIEW

The Republic of Indonesia proclaimed its independence from the Netherlands on August 17, 1945, although the Netherlands did not formally transfer sovereignty to the new state until December 27, 1949. Dr. Sukarno, a leader in the struggle for independence, was elected president at that time and served as head of state until March 1967.

The first 15 years of Indonesia's history as a sovereign state were marked by political instability and economic decline. The liberal democratic republic established in 1950 was characterized by revolving-door cabinets, regional revolts, and economic mismanagement. The situation was exacerbated after 1959, when the president, Dr. Sukarno, dissolved the elected House of Representatives and replaced it with a Provisional People's Consultative Assembly comprising members of nationalist, religious, and Communist groups, all of whom were presidential appointees. This era of "guided democracy" was a period of political turmoil during which economic prudence was often eclipsed by revolutionary zeal in domestic policy making, and confrontations with the Netherlands and Malaysia were the prime feature of foreign policy. It culminated in September 1965 in an abortive coup d'etat led by a group of army officers in which the Indonesian Communist Party (Partai Komunis Indonesia, PKI), said to have been supported by Chinese arms and money, was allegedly involved.

The September 1965 coup marked the end of the "Old Order," as the period of Dr. Sukarno's presidency later came to be known. It was crushed by the army with much bloodshed, during which as many as 750,000 alleged members of the PKI and its affiliated organizations were killed. In March 1966 the "New Order" was established when the executive power of government was transferred to Major General Suharto. He became acting president in March 1967, and has been elected for five further five-year terms in 1973, 1978, 1983–88, and 1993. After nearly 30 years in office, however, President Suharto's government now faces an impending need to ensure a smooth political succession, and a gradual and controlled handover of authority to the younger generation is already in progress in the armed forces and at some levels of government.

Effective political power rests with the military establishment aided by Golkar, a government-sponsored coalition of "nonparty" functional groups. Since the 1960s, the republic's territorial boundaries have been extended. On May 1, 1963, Indonesia was granted sovereignty over Dutch New Guinea (Irian Java), which was officially incorporated into the country in September 1969 after the controversial implementation of an "act of free choice" to determine whether the territory's population wished to remain in Indonesia. In 1975–76 Indonesia invaded and annexed the former Portuguese colony of East Timor, which was formally integrated into the republic in July 1976 as the nation's twenty-seventh province.

However, resistance to Indonesian rule by rebel guerrilla groups has resulted in continued fighting between government and insurgent forces on the island, and in 1993 the United Nations still did not recognize Indonesia's claim to the territory. Finally, Indonesia's long-standing claim to sovereignty over the seas separating its many islands was accorded international recognition in April 1982, following the eleventh session of the United Nations International Convention on the Law of the Sea. This more than doubled the country's total area and permitted Indonesia to declare the archipelagic seas an exclusive zone in October 1983.[4]

THE CONSTITUTION

Indonesia is governed under a constitution drawn up in 1945 in the wake of the proclamation of independence. It is based on the five principles of monotheism, humanitarianism, Indonesian unity, representative democracy by consensus, and social justice embodied in the state ideology, Pancasila. Originally perceived as a temporary document, this constitution is relatively brief and consists only of a preamble, 37 articles, four transitional clauses, and two additional provisions. Although replaced by a federal constitution at the time of the transfer of sovereignty in 1949 and by a liberal democratic constitution in 1950, the 1945 constitution was reinstated in 1959 by President Sukarno as a basis for the system of guided democracy. It has remained in force since then, and was taken over by the New Order government established by President Suharto in the mid-1960s.

It has been permanently adopted by the People's Consultative Assembly and was supplemented by the General Elections Law of 1969. The 1945 Constitution establishes a strong presidential form of government with a highly centralized administrative structure. The preamble condemns all forms of colonialism and enshrines the Pancasila, or guiding principles of Indonesian government.

The Constitution provides Parliament with a mechanism to call the president to account in extraordinary circumstances. The 1945 constitution provides for six principal organs of state:

1. People's Consultative Assembly (MPR)
2. Presidency and vice-presidency
3. House of Representatives (DPR)
4. Supreme Advisory Council
5. State Audit Board
6. Supreme Court.

Of these, the most important political institutions are the DPR, the MPR, and the presidency. The DPR consists of 500 members, of which 400 are elected under a system of proportional representation every five years and the rest are appointed from within the ranks of the armed forces, whose members are not permitted to participate in the elections. The MPR is the highest authority of state and consists of 1,000 members, comprising the 500 members of the DPR as well as a further 500 members appointed by the government from the political parties in proportion to the results of the general elections as well as representatives from the military and the provinces. This body meets in ordinary session every five years, normally in the year after the general elections, when its principal functions are to sanction the guidelines of state policy and elect the president and vice-president for the next five years. It last convened in March 1993, when it reelected President Suharto. The presidency is the highest executive office of state and also has great legislative powers since presidential decrees and presidential decisions have the same legal force as laws enacted by the DPR. The president also selects a cabinet of ministers, who are not members of the DPR but are chosen from all walks of life. Draft legislation prepared by these ministers is, however, submitted to the DPR for approval and enactment. Presidential powers encompass a variety of independent executive and administrative duties, including the selection of a cabinet, which is responsible to the president, and the appointment of the Supreme Advisory Council, which is consulted on important state matters.

After winning independence from the Dutch, Indonesia attempted a multiparty system of government between 1950 and 1959. But the "Period of Liberal Democracy" was so chaotic that many Indonesians still refuse to use the word *liberal*, even in the context of economics or business. The charismatic President Sukarno tried to rule using what he called "guided democracy," which has been described as a mix between populism, paternalism, and the Javanese tendency toward benevolent absolutism.

Indonesia has been a top-down, authoritarian society. Under the New Order, the political system was restructured. Political parties were neutralized ideologically and were run along the lines of interest groups or "functional" groups, as they are known in Indonesia. In 1973, President Sukarno's government further simplified Indonesian politics by encouraging the fusion of nine parties into two, the United Development Party (PPP), which grouped the Islamic parties and Indonesian Democratic Party (PDI), which amalgamated the nationalist and Christian parties. The move was aimed at reducing conflict between rival parties. Golkar is the third, and largest, political party, although, with bitter memories of the fifties and sixties, Golkar members prefer the term *functional group*.[5]

INTERNATIONAL RELATIONS

After President Suharto took charge, Indonesia's foreign policy underwent a transformation. President Sukarno's ambitious quest for recognition as a revolutionary leader of the Third World, which had led him to pursue a prominent and frequently anti-Western role on the world stage, was abandoned and replaced by a more pragmatic and low-key approach stressing stability in Indonesia's international relations to enable the country to concentrate on domestic economic development. While adhering firmly to the principle of military nonalignment, Indonesia therefore has been drawn increasingly close to the West during the past two decades, and enjoys generally good relations with most Western countries, although these relations have suffered setbacks as a result of trade disputes.

THE SIXTH TERM

President Suharto's reelection to a sixth five-year term in March 1993 was a foregone conclusion. For one thing, he appoints 60% of the 1000 member People's Consultative Assembly that elects the president. For another, no one seriously challenged his right to the presidency. Suharto has hinted at gradual political reform in his new term, but not at the cost of political instability. Minimal changes might include reducing the number of government positions reserved for the military and allowing the two officially recognized opposition parties to operate in rural villages. Fundamental reforms, such as more power sharing between the president and the MPR, are unlikely. During the 1994–98 term, Suharto will prepare for an eventual succession, although it is not certain he will be ready to step down even in 1998. When it comes, succession could be traumatic, as Indonesia has no modern history of smooth political transition. Suharto is likely to start making known whom he prefers to succeed him several years before the election to allow time to build consensus support.[6]

THE PARLIAMENT

The 500-member House of Representatives exercises legislative authority. Of its 500 members, 400 are directly elected and 100 are appointed by the president. The House of Representatives meets at least once a year. All laws must be approved by it, but the president has an absolute veto. While he or she may enact ordinances during times of emergency, they must be either ratified by the House during its next session or voided. According to the constitution, the highest authority in the state rests with the People's Consultative Assembly, composed of 500 House members and 500 other seats allocated to regional delegates, representatives of political organizations, and members of Golkar. All decisions are made unanimously, in accord with the constitutionally mandated principle of government by consensus.

The Parliament considers bills presented to it by government departments and agencies but does not draft laws on its own, although it has the constitutional right to do so. The government seeks to resolve potential parliamentary concerns before bills are officially presented. Parliament makes technical and occasionally substantive alterations to bills it reviews. Through consultations and hearing with ministers and other executive branch officials, press statements, and field trips, Parliament is contributing more actively than before to the content and execution of government policy. This was especially true in 1991, when debates over "openness," press control, land tenure, travel restrictions, and the role of Parliament itself were given wide publicity. Nonetheless, Parliament remains clearly subordinate to the executive branch. The ruling Golkar party, which is based on the military, the bureaucracy, and business and rural support, saw its popularity fall to 68% in the 1992 parliamentary elections, down from 73% in 1987. It more likely than not will be loath to allow much political reform in the interim until the next parliamentary elections in 1997.

Critics contend that, although it has a mandate to do so, Parliament has never passed or even contemplated legislation of its own. Instead, the 10 to 15 bills it considers each year are all drawn up by government ministries and passed on through the legal affairs bureau of the State Secretariat. The bureau acts in a coordinating role, liaising with other affected government agencies. Some bills can take up to six months to enact, depending on their complexity.[7]

LOCAL GOVERNMENT

The 27 Indonesian provinces have assemblies forming the apex of a three-tier system of local government that also includes regency and village assemblies. The central government appoints provincial governors and regents from among nominees proposed by the regional and regency legislatures.[8]

THE JUDICIARY

The judicial system consists of the Supreme Court, high courts in the major cities, and district courts. The courts administer three kinds of civil law: Shari'a (Islamic law); a civil code based on Roman law for Europeans; and a combination of the Code of Commerce and the Civil Code for other Asian groups, such as ethnic Chinese and Indians. Steps are being taken to codify these statutes, but the work has not yet been completed. The same criminal law applies to all ethnic and religious groups.

Unfortunately, the judiciary is not independent. The Supreme Court does not have the right of judicial review over laws passed by Parliament. Although since 1985 the Supreme Court has had the power to review ministerial decrees and regulations, the court has not yet used this power. Chief Justice Purweto Gandasubrata in early 1993 laid out the procedures under which limited judicial review cases could be brought to the court, a move that was hailed as a significant step toward greater judicial independence. While judges receive guidance from the Supreme Court on legal matters, they are civil servants employed by the executive branch which controls their assignments, pay, and promotion. They are subject to considerable pressure from military and other governmental authorities. Such control often determines the outcome of a case. The Chief Judge of the State Administrative Court in Medan, for example, issued a restraining order in January 1993 against the military commander in Medan after the commander intervened in the leadership struggle of the Batak Protestant Church. The commander then publicly criticized the judge, whose home was vandalized shortly after he handed down his decision. A few days later the judge was suddenly told he had been assigned to attend a two-week legal workshop far from Medan. While he was gone, his deputy took over the case, and vacated the restraining order.[9]

Without a system of judicial review, there can be no judicial or legal warranty, and this would encourage the abuse of power that occurs when the executive, rather than the judiciary, interprets and thus ensures the enforcement of a law or regulation of its own making. This is what happens in Indonesia when the government bans the mass media by revoking publishing licenses. The 1994 case of the three weekly news magazines was one of a series of press bans by the New Order government over the years. The crucial point is that banning the mass media by withdrawing publishing licenses without resort to the courts, which would provide a means of self-defense, is against the principle of the rule of law. As such, it represents an abuse of power and a serious violation of human rights as contained in the 1945 constitution.

Surprisingly, also in 1994, the judiciary began to demonstrate unexpected independence. In an act of defiance, the Supreme Court ruled in May that nine people found guilty in June 1994 of brutally murdering the labor activist, Marsinah, in May 1993, had been wrongfully convicted. This appeared to confirm a widely held belief that the nine defendants, who included the owner and several senior managers of the firm in which Marsinah worked, had been framed by the security forces, who are thought to have committed the crime themselves. In the wake of this development, the authorities have reopened the Marsinah case and have pledged to conduct the new investigation in a scrupulously transparent manner. This was followed by reports that military police officers had begun to question a number of soldiers at a military installation where, it is alleged by human rights activists, Marsinah was tortured and killed by troops called into the factory compound to break up the strike in which she was involved.

Also, a large number of labor activists detained in connection with the upsurge of labor unrest in late 1993 and early 1994 were released. The most celebrated of these cases concerned Muchtar Pakpahan, the founder and national chairman of the un-authorized independent Indonesia Welfare Labor Union (SBSI), who was released in late May 1995 after having been sentenced to a three-year prison term in November 1994, which was subsequently increased to four years in January 1995. While no reasons were given for the early releases in most of the cases, official reports stressed that Mr. Pakpahan's release was only temporary, and was based on a legal technicality related to a pending appeal of his case in the Supreme Court. Depending upon the court's verdict, he could be detained again.

While the early release of Pakpahan and his colleagues may well be justified by reference to legal technicalities, there are strong indications to suggest that they also reflect, at least in part, a response to external pressure on the government to improve its observance of human and workers' rights. The pressure has been applied particularly forcefully by the United States, which has been threatening since 1993 to withdraw Indonesia's trade privileges under the Generalized System of Preferences (GSP) unless significant improvements are made on labor rights. In April 1995, the U.S. Assistant Secretary of State John Shattuck, visited Indonesia for 10 days. Pressure has also been applied by the ILO and the World Bank, both of which issued strong statements urging the Indonesian government to improve labor conditions. Official spokesmen have vehemently denied succumbing to these pressures, and in the wake of Mr. Shattuck's visit, lashed out at the United States for its "stubborn" insistence on promoting labor rights. However, it may be more than a coincidence that the release of the labor activists took place only a few weeks before the expected arrival of a fact-finding mission from the U.S. trade representative to review the GSP issue, and before the annual meeting of the ILO, at which the Indonesian government was expecting to face strong criticism.[10]

POLITICAL PARTIES

Before the establishment of the New Order, Indonesia had a plethora of political parties representing all conceivable shades of political opinion. The PKI, which at the time was the second-largest Communist party in Asia after that of China, was banned in March 1966 because of its alleged involvement in the coup attempt of September 1965. Arguing further that the multiplicity of political parties had been a principal cause for the political instability of the New Order period, the government initiated a merger of the seven remaining parties in 1973. Thus, today only two such parties remain, as noted previously.

Political parties are not permitted to establish permanent organizations in rural areas, where they are only allowed to campaign prior to elections. Under 1985 legislation, moreover, both parties, and indeed all other mass organizations, must acknowledge the state philosophy as their sole ideological foundation, thereby precluding the possibility of a loyal opposition, which is regarded as irreconcilable with the consensus-based system of Pancasila democracy stipulated by the 1945 constitution. Golkar, on the other hand, is not officially regarded as a political party and is therefore not subject to the strictures imposed on political parties.

Three organizations participate in the general elections to the DPR and Golkar has won substantial overall majorities in the last five polls, with overall majorities of about 60 to 75%. The president has the right to dissolve any party whose policies are not compatible with state goals or whose membership does not encompass one-quarter of the country's population. Golkar, though technically not a political party, is the dominant political organization.[11]

Only three political organizations are allowed by law. The PDI and PPI are not considered opposition parties and seldom espouse policies much different from those of the government. The leaders of these organizations are approved, if not chosen, by the government, and their activities are closely scrutinized and often guided by government authorities. Golkar maintains close institutional links with the armed forces and KORPRI, the nonunion association to which all civil servants automatically belong. Civil servants may join either of the political parties with official permission, but most are members of Golkar. Former members of the PKI and some other banned parties may not run for office or be active politically.

The Democracy Forum is a small prodemocracy group formed in April 1991. The League for the Restoration of Democracy, also formed in 1991, is a more radical prodemocracy group led by the president of the trade union, Solidarity, which is not recognized by the government. The Forum for the Purification of People's Sovereignty was created in August 1991 by leading dissident General Hartono Resko Dharsono. Other illegal groups include the Communist Party of Indonesia, Petition 50, a group of dissident political activists and army officers formed in 1980, and a number of regional insurgent groups.[12]

OTHER POLITICAL FORCES

Beyond the political parties and Golkar, the most important political forces in Indonesia are the military, the Muslim community, and a growing class of well-connected businessmen. The military has always been regarded as playing an important role in maintaining Indonesia's political stability, and a number of retired military officers hold important posts in the cabinet, MPR, DPR, and other political institutions. The Muslim community is an important force simply by virtue of its size, with some 85% of Indonesia's population adhering at least nominally to Islam. While maintaining its commitment to a secular state structure and responding forcefully to challenges from the relatively small minority of Muslim extremists, the government has therefore been careful to maintain good relations with organizations representing the vast majority of politically moderate Muslims. These are being cultivated by a group of civilian politicians centered around the influential Minister of State for Research and Technology, B. J. Habibie, who see them as a political counterweight to the military in the struggle for succession that is expected to follow President Suharto's eventual departure from the political scene. The large business groups, finally, consist primarily of ethnic Chinese entrepreneurs, many of whom owe at least their initial successes to politically powerful Indonesian patrons, and to relatives and associates of senior government officials, including several children of President Suharto himself. While they do not play a direct or formal role in politics, their influence is usually sufficient strong to ensure that the government does not take any political decisions detrimental to their interests.[13]

The government shows no hesitation in using force to thwart any threat against the state. Political turmoil was limited to a few incidents prior to 1993. The most serious was the November 1991 killing of about 50 people in Dili, East Timor, who were protesting against the rule of the area by Indonesian security forces. After Suharto won reelection in March 1993, the number of strikes by dissident labor unions escalated sharply, and culminated in the massive riots in Medan in April 1994.

The government controls political activity. It has restructured the political parties, set regulations for elections, depoliticized university and religious life, set up classes in the harmonizing values of the state ideology of Pancasila, introduced public criminal trials, and controlled the news media. An army structure reaching down to the village level ensures security against any rural insurgency, at least on Java.[14]

INCREASED POLITICAL CONTROL

The process of tightening political control began in mid-1994, when three major publications were banned, and has been continuing. All important social and political institutions, included the DPR, the political parties, and mass organizations, the press, the military, the labor movement, and human rights groups have been subjected to official repression during the last two years. This reflected a growing concern among the ruling elite over a possible erosion of political stability at a time when the established order has undergone gradual but significant changes. President Suharto's advancing age is giving rise to growing speculation about the impending political transition and provoking a great deal of jockeying for position.

1994—A YEAR OF LABOR TURMOIL

Although the grip on the country of the military and the governing Golkar party remain as firm as ever, President Suharto himself is looking increasingly beleaguered. Thus far, the support of the military appears to be solid. However, if the various eruptions of civil unrest continue, there is the possibility that the military–Golkar hierarchy might feel compelled to encourage Suharto's early retirement, with his designated successor and vice-president, General Try Sutrisno, moving smoothly into place until his election to the presidency can be arranged.

At it is, President Suharto is under fire from workers, striking for better pay and conditions; the press, whose attempts to investigate corruption at the top have been met with the closure of offending publications; and in East Timor, where continuing peaceful demonstrations against Indonesia's illegal occupation are a source of irritating international embarrassment for the regime.

Indonesia saw an explosion in worker discontent in 1994. In February, a one-hour general strike brought 250,000 workers to the streets in protest against low wages and lack of union representation. With threats from the United States in particular, to suspend Indonesia's trading privileges under the Generalized System of Preferences (GSP) unless reforms were instituted in the labor market, the government raised the minimum wage by 27%, repealed the decree that allowed the armed forces to intervene in labor disputes, and allowed the setting up of independent trade unions.

Up until that time only one union was allowed, the All-Indonesian Workers' Union (SPSI), which is government-controlled.[15]

In Indonesia, unfortunately, passing laws and implementing them are two very different things. On the one hand the government went out of its way to obstruct the formation of independent trade unions and on the other took no action to enforce the payment by employers of the new minimum wage. Thus, one would-be independent trade union, the Union for Workers' Prosperity (SBSI), has twice been refused registration by the government and is therefore an illegal organization. Meanwhile, the refusal of employers to pay the minimum wage generated a strike in the north Sumatran town of Medan, the country's fourth largest industrial center, in April 1994. With an estimated 50,000 workers in the streets, the demonstrations rapidly turned into a full-scale riot against both the government and the, largely ethnic Chinese, employers. At least three people were killed and the army had to be called in to restore order.

Nevertheless, the massive military crackdown in Medan and the arrest of union leaders did not calm the situation. The SBSI continues to operate from its Jakarta offices in defiance of the government, organizing illegal union meetings. The union is now entrenched in the myriad of businesses in the capital's industrial suburbs. The union has estimated unemployment in Jakarta at 800,000, with underemployment boosting that figure to around 2 million. As a result, employment is highly insecure and the daily wage paid is still frequently below the minimum IR3,800 ($1.60) per day. Then, just as the government was preparing to host the Asian Pacific Economic Conference (APEC), 4,000 workers at an Adidas shoe factory near the capital went on strike in the largest work stoppage in the country since the debacle in Medan the previous April.[16]

DISCRIMINATION BANNED—OR IS IT?

Indonesians exhibit considerable tolerance for ethnic, racial, and major religious differences, with the important exception of official and informal discrimination against ethnic Chinese. Since 1959, noncitizen ethnic Chinese have been denied the right to run businesses in rural Indonesia. Regulations prohibit the operation of all-Chinese schools for ethnic Chinese citizens, formation of exclusively Chinese cultural groups or trade associations, and public display of Chinese characters. Chinese-language publications, with the exception of one officially sanctioned newspaper, can neither be imported nor produced domestically. Private instruction in Chinese is discouraged but takes place to a limited extent. No laws prohibit speaking Chinese, but the government emphasizes learning and using the national language, Bahasa Indonesia.

Many people of Chinese ancestry have nonetheless been successful in business and the professions, and the enforcement of restrictions is often haphazard. Some ethnic Chinese have enjoyed particular government favor. Social and religious groups exist which are, in effect, all-Chinese and not proscribed. Jakarta authorities have ended the practice of marking local identification cards to indicate Chinese ethnicity. However, 1991 saw an increase in anti-Chinese feeling in many quarters of Indonesian society, particularly against the affluent Chinese.

Under the law, and as President Suharto and other officials periodically affirm, women are equal to and have the same rights, obligations, and opportunities as men. Some Indonesian women enjoy a high degree of economic and social freedom and occupy important midlevel positions in the civil service, educational institutions, labor organizations, the military, the professions, and private business. Although women constitute one-quarter of the civil service, they occupy only a small fraction of the service's top positions. Women make up about 40% of the overall labor force, with the majority in the rural sector. Despite legal guarantees of equal treatment, women seldom receive equal pay for equal work and disproportionately experience illiteracy, poor health, and poor nutrition. Traditional attitudes which limit women's aspirations, activities, and status undercut state policy in some areas. Several voluntary, private groups work actively to advance women's legal, economic, social, and political rights and acknowledge some success in gaining official cognizance of their concerns.[17]

A FEMALE CHALLENGER

Ironically, a woman may create problems for the present Indonesian regime. Megawati Sukarnoputri, the daughter of the late president and founder of modern Indonesia, is the leader of the Indonesian Democratic Party (PDI), who withstood a challenge to her party leadership in 1995. She leads a simple life, in contrast to Sukarno's several children, who have enriched themselves in business due to their connections, has the support of Indonesia's poor, and has potential support among its disaffected middle class in her demands for greater democracy. Hence, her presence has infused the 1997 elections with a degree of uncertainty, in that, if truly free, the plebiscite might result in significant gains for the PDI, particularly in the industrial heartland of east Java.[18]

THE INDONESIAN ECONOMIC LANDSCAPE

Between 1965 to 1990, the Asian economies grew faster than any other region of the world, led by Japan and the high-flying Four Tigers (Hong Kong, Singapore, Taiwan, and Korea), but with the newly industrializing nations of Thailand, Malaysia, and Indonesia making rapid gains.

In Indonesia, there is an unrivalled wealth of natural resources that support an economy which over the past two decades has demonstrated a remarkable capacity for rapid and sustainable growth.[19] Indonesia's economy has been growing at an average rate of 6.8% a year over the past 25 years. Much of this growth stems from the sale of oil and gas, of which Indonesia is a leading producer. Falling oil prices have taken their toll recently. Indonesia's budget for the fiscal year 1993–94 recorded a deficit for the first time in 27 years.

Fifteen years ago, Indonesia was almost closed to outsiders. Since then, the government has been systematically dismantling a strict and complex maze of regulations to encourage more foreign companies to invest. Indonesia's large, modestly priced workforce has attracted growing numbers of foreign investors over the past decade. Singapore has been the country's top investor, with investments totaling $679.3 million. Hong Kong and Japan rank second and third, respectively.

Economic growth in the next five years is projected to be over 6% with more than 10% annual growth in the industrial sector. Industrial export growth should grow at 17.5% annually. All this will help create employment opportunities for the estimated 2.5 million young people who join the labor force every year.

Industrial priorities for the next five-year plan are clear. Indonesia intends to develop industries with high technology content to give more added value to its primary products and to absorb its large labor force, since unemployment is a serious issue. Some sources estimate that 38% of the population is not gainfully employed. The government is focusing on national manpower planning, reforming training policy and programs, and setting up a national productivity center. There is also a possibility of exporting some of Indonesia's excess manpower to neighboring countries.

Cheap labor is readily available, but skilled workers are scarce. More than 30% of the workers in the government-controlled union earn less than 40 cents per day. Many laborers in Central and East Java are reported to earn only about $6 per month. The minister of manpower determines the minimum wage for the private sector, but companies are free to pay more. Wages are especially low in heavily populated rural areas. Productivity often matches the low wages and complaints of widespread neglect of minimal safety conditions by employers are frequent.

Wages are higher in Jakarta and in remote areas where labor is scarce and demand is high, but even in Jakarta some workers in the textile and food industries earn only 50 cents per day. Wages generally range from the legal minimum of $1 per day for a laborer to $257 a month for good clerical personnel. Highly qualified local workers command higher salaries.[20]

The vast majority of the labor force is engaged in agriculture, which is, however, characterized by a high degree of underemployment. The government's development plans envisaged most of the increase in the labor force being absorbed into the manufacturing sector, which accounted for 12.4% of the additional employment opportunities created between 1980 and 1990. The service sector and the public service have also been important sources of employment for new entrants into the labor force during this period. The state sector which, in addition to the military, comprises central, provincial, and local government institutions, as well as state agencies and public corporations, has in fact been one of the fastest growing employers. Latest available data indicate that the number of civil servants almost doubled during 1982–92, from 2.05 to 3.95 million.

The Indonesian government regards the provision of adequate employment opportunities for the country's rapidly growing labor force as one of its prime economic policy objectives. It has for some time given a strong preference to development projects with a high potential for generating employment, and has also sought to enforce shortened shifts and minimal wage increases. In spite of these measures, figures indicate that the number of registered job seekers has risen dramatically in recent years; for example, from some 855,300 in the 1988–89 fiscal year to more than 2 million in 1992–93.[21]

In the longer term, creating jobs for the country's relatively young population will pose a continuing challenge for economic policymakers. Estimates are that creating jobs for new labor force entrants will require annual GDP growth of 5% or better for the foreseeable future. Another challenge will be completing and consolidating deregulation reform. Entrenched interests and restrictive regulations in certain sectors continue to pose obstacles to increasing the flexibility and efficiency of the economy. The overall rate of GDP growth is forecast to average more than 7% per year in 1995–99.

While the long-term growth figures have been impressive, they have been accompanied by persistent problems with inflation. For instance, 1994 data showed an increase in the composite consumer price index for 27 provincial capitals amounted to 9.6%, higher than the 9.2 mark for 1993. This was well above the 5% target set by the government. This fairly high rate of inflation was attributed to a number of causes, including the strong growth of demand, a high rate of credit expansion, an increase in the administered price for electricity and supply disruptions for such important products as rice and cement.

Until 1998 high growth in domestic demand, the government's unwillingness to restrain monetary growth too forcefully for fear of triggering a recession, the persistence of relatively high import prices, and the government's continuing efforts to roll back various price distortions, not the least of which involves the reduction of its own numerous subsidies, will all help to keep inflation fairly high. Consequently, projections anticipate only a gradual reduction in the inflation rate to 7.5% by 1998.[22]

THE "BERKELEY MAFIA"

President Suharto has presided over 29 years of economic development, some of which we have just detailed, and, of course, authoritarian politics. As an important player in his regime during this period, the military has seen its influence reduced recently as responsibility for policy making has been handed over to technocrats. This is particularly visible in the management of the economy, where the "Berkeley Mafia," who are mainly graduates of the University of California, have been entrusted with wide-reaching deregulations in the financial sector and major industrial reforms.

Despite being authoritarian, the New Order government has recognized that running the economy requires greater sophistication, and a more technocratic orientation with more qualified professionals in government. On economic policy the government is split between two groups, known as the "technocrats" and the "technologists." The former seek to pursue a policy of economic liberalization aimed at promoting the growth of a market-oriented economy with a strong private sector. The latter seek to develop Indonesia into a center of high-technology manufacturing through active government intervention and support.

Suharto's unexpected replacement in March 1993 of his senior economic officials, who had been Western-trained and who had maintained close relations with the International Monetary Fund and the World Bank, did not result in the deterioration of the business environment or in a decline in Indonesia's interest in attracting private foreign investment. Suharto continues to stress the proposition that in order to advance economic development, it is necessary to continue the deregulation process and to stimulate private foreign investment.

State-owned business enterprises officially number 214; unofficial estimates suggest that the actual number of such firms may be double that figure. Their economic performance is so poor that government economists have frequently advised selling them to private business. Widespread opposition, however, to full-scale privatization has developed from powerful bureaucratic profiteers and from economic nationalists, making such a move unlikely. In addition, the deep involvement of the Suharto family in state enterprises also hinders such a move.[23]

WORKER RIGHTS ISSUES

As a result of the labor unrest which erupted in April 1994 and continued to simmer for the following six months, the government has become extremely sensitive to the issues of pay and working conditions, especially in the rapidly growing manufacturing sector, on which Indonesia is coming to depend as the source of a growing proportion of its nonoil/gas exports. This sensitivity has been enhanced, moreover, by strong external pressures for an improvement in workers' rights, which may gain momentum if, as expected, the issue is taken up by the newly established World Trade Organization.

Responding to these pressures, the government twice initiated an increase in the statutory minimum wage during 1994–95, and announced its intention to review it every year. On April 1, 1995, the minimum wage was raised by between 10 and 35% in 19 provinces; the minimum wage in Jakarta was increased by 21%. Although many firms already pay more than the basic minimum wage, the next few years will almost inevitably witness more rapid wage growth. This could seriously undermine the government's economic development strategy, and attempts undoubtedly will be made to restrict wage increases to the growth of productivity or to offset the effects of domestic inflation on workers' living standards, even though the government has declared that its main criterion for determining minimum wages will be a minimum physical need standard established for each province of the country.

Low-cost, unskilled labor is plentiful. Despite some public sympathy, trade unions exert little influence; strikes are illegal unless lengthy procedures have been completed. When strikes do occur, the government calls for negotiations and a resolution in the spirit of Pancasila. Such appeals usually succeed because of the underlying threat of force. Foreign workers can be employed only under clearly defined conditions, but because of the need for foreign investment, restrictions have been eased for exporters. Workers are carefully policed, and extraordinary measures are taken to ensure a peaceful workforce and a hospitable climate for investment.

The low cost of labor, along with the large, docile, and skilled labor force, is a major attraction for investors from the United States, Japan, South Korea, Taiwan, and Hong Kong, who manufacture and export shoes, textiles, and electronics to world markets. Despite regular complaints in the media about dangerous labor conditions and pervasive violations of minimum wage regulations, the government will probably not allow laborers to organize so effectively on behalf of higher wages that they discourage foreign investment. It will probably adjust the minimum wage modestly and incrementally. This conclusion, however, could become invalid if the government bows to U.S. pressure on workers' rights. The probability is that labor is likely to be less docile in future years.[24]

ACCOMPLISHMENTS AND FUTURE PLANS

From its seat in Jakarta, the capital city with a population approaching 10 million, the Indonesian government rules a country that is divided into 300 distinct language groups. The government's main challenge has been to meld the country into a cohesive whole. The introduction of Indonesian as a common language did much to achieve this. Strong central government was also a major force, as is the increasing prosperity of the people themselves.

Indonesian's population is 88% Muslim but religious tolerance is part of official government policy. In 1970, 60% of the population lived below the poverty level, and Indonesia's main concern was producing enough food for its people. Today, Indonesia is a net exporter of food, the poverty level is down to 14%, and the industrial sector outperforms agriculture. Per capita gross domestic product is expected to rise to $1,007 by 1999 from $676 in the mid-1990s, and real GDP should increase to $157 billion from $129 billion. Indonesia's economy has been built up through a series of five-year plans. By focusing on high-value-added industries, Indonesia hopes by the year 2019 to nearly quadruple its per capita income, from the present $676 to $2,631.[25]

By then it plans to have moved tens of thousands more people off densely packed Java to outer islands. Indonesian officials hope this "transmigration" policy, which already has relocated some 3 million people since the early 1980s, will help integrate the 300 ethnic groups who make Indonesia an anthropologist's dream but a politician's nightmare.

The government revealed its clearest vision of the next century's economy when the planning authority, Bappenas, for the first time set long-term numerical targets in 1994. One goal is to raise Indonesia's long-term sustainable growth rate to an annual 8.7% by 2019, from the present 6.8%. By then, the population is expected to hit 258 million, with 39% living in cities, versus today's 34%. The workforce is expected to swell from 80 million to 148 million. President Suharto recently predicted that by 2019, Indonesia's per capita income will reach the level of newly industrialized countries and the country will emerge as "a strong industrial and commercial nation."[26]

AN EMERGING MIDDLE CLASS?

Once viewed as the country least likely to succeed, with a 1969 per capita income of $70 (half of Bangladesh's) and 60% of its population below the poverty line, its economic transformation has been acknowledged in the World Bank's well-documented study, "The East Asian Economic Miracle." Said the bank: "If the momentum of development can be maintained, Indonesia can realistically expect to be a solid, middle-income country with a per capita income of $1,000" by the turn of the century. Adds Nicholas Hope, director of the World Bank's Jakarta mission: "In terms of macroeconomic development, Indonesia is a role model for the developing world."

Indonesia has begun to create an increasingly visible and affluent middle class. Some 40 million Indonesians already earn more than $1,630 annually. By the year 2000, it is estimated that 10.5% of the population, up from the present 3%, will earn more than $3,600 per year. Tax collection is increasing, indicating greater wealth. But despite all this new wealth, the challenge is enormous: Indonesia, with a combined unemployment and underemployment of nearly 40%, must create 2.5 million new jobs each year in an increasingly competitive environment for attracting foreign investment.

To accomplish all that, however, Indonesia may have to rely less on one Dutch legacy that has made many businessmen rich: monopolies. Says Salim Said, chairman of the Jakarta Arts Council: "After 26 years of Suharto we haven't really produced a real middle class; we have produced conglomerates. The government has produced a small amount of rich who have good links with the government."[27] It remains to be seen whether this group of acquisitive people will decide that political liberalization should follow economic development.

A COMPETITIVE WAGE ADVANTAGE

Indonesia's competitive advantage in Asia is pronounced. Its wages in some industries are lower than China's, and the World Bank estimates that its productivity is higher. Indonesian wages, at 30 cents an hour, are one-third of Thai or Malaysian wages, and one-tenth of those in South Korea. But low wages hide the problems of disguised unemployment and political pressure. Casting a pall over many of its admirable ambitions, however, is the country's sorry human rights record. Indonesia also has advanced the least of any major Asian nation, with the possible exception of China, toward participatory democracy.

LABOR FORCE TRENDS AND REQUIREMENTS

The shift in Indonesia's age profile and a rising participation rate, as economic growth encourages new labor force entrants, both account for the rapid growth in the size of the labor force. Moreover, as a result of interisland and rural–urban migratory flows, a substantial proportion of this additional labor force will congregate in the urban centers of the "inner" islands in search of employment in industry, commerce, or public administration. This steady flow of new entrants to the labor force will provide the economy with abundant supplies of unskilled labor, and ensure that labor costs remain relatively low even though greater efforts will have to be made to ensure that wage rates meet at least the minimum basic needs of industrial employees.

Although strong economic growth should enable the vast majority of the new entrants to find suitable employment, many will have to join the already large urban service sector. Although it possesses a high absorptive capacity and thus enables its members to eke out a livelihood, this sector is marked by a low productivity level, and does not therefore offer a long-term solution to the pressures of rapid population growth. That still lies in the creation of high productivity industrial jobs through high levels of investment in appropriate industries.

In spite of the extensive investment by both the public and the private sectors in educational and training facilities, the available supply of skilled manpower, especially at the technical and managerial levels, remains inadequate to meet the demands of the rapidly growing economy. Although the government is interested in ensuring that priority is given to the employment of local staff wherever possible, it will almost certainly permit the increased employment of expatriate personnel in sectors experiencing particularly acute shortages. However, these permits will continue to be issued for limited periods only, and will in most cases continue to be conditional upon the training of local employees by the expatriates.[28]

NEAR TERM OUTLOOK

Although it normally remains as a background factor, religion has historically been an important political issue in Indonesia and played a significant part in several of the regional rebellions of the 1950s. The government's secularism has frequently provoked Muslim resentment, which is kept under control by a combination of suppression and co-option.[28]

Despite a veneer of democracy (elections and three political parties), Indonesia has an autocratic system of government that accords great power to the president who has direct legislative powers. The state ideology of Pancasila does not recognize the Western concept of a loyal opposition, and the military justifies its role in political and social issues, including an automatic unelected presence in national and local parliaments, through a "dual function" concept, giving it special civic rights and responsibilities in addition to its defense and security roles.

Indonesia is relatively stable because the Suharto government tolerates little opposition to its policies and has used military force to stamp out dissent. Memories of the bloody anti-Communist purges in 1965–66 encourage Indonesians to prize stability, even at the cost of freedom of expression. A growing pattern of religious and ethnic violence elsewhere in the world also strengthens popular support for the military's role in binding together the diverse faiths and cultures in this vast archipelago.

Although rising living standards have helped win popular support for the Suharto government, tactics such as manipulated elections of village captains and increased censorship of the mass media, have sparked restlessness for a greater measure of democracy. The government's success at raising educational levels has also created a more critical populace. Public acceptance of corruption is also wearing thin as a result of high-profile banking scandals and government campaigns against siphoning off aid to the poor.

The government faces virtually no risk of losing power in the near future. Two political parties are allowed to compete against government-backed Golkar, but they are kept on a short leash. They cannot, for example, organize support outside urban centers except at election time. These alternative parties are also weakened by political infighting and military allegations of Communist links.

Although still widely respected, President Suharto has lost some of his popular support because of an inability to control the extensive business activities of his relatives and other associates. The president keeps returning to the big question of succession without adding much to an opaque statement about serving out his current term which ends in 1998, while remaining noncommittal about whether he would seek another one. He will be 77 years old by then. The front runners at this stage are vice-president Try Sutrisno and the civilian minister for research and technology, B. J. Habibie. The latest dark horse to emerge is Finance Minister Mar'ie Muhammad.

In contrast to its restrictive political system, Indonesia has an increasingly deregulated and dynamic economy which has produced significant material gains for a wide segment of Indonesian society. Indonesia nevertheless remains a poor country. Agriculture and extractive industries, especially oil and gas, remain important sectors of the economy, but a broad and expanding manufacturing sector accounts for a growing percentage of exports. Corruption and influence peddling are endemic and continue to distort the economy.

STRIKES AND WORKER RIGHTS

Despite official suppression, the number of strikes reached an unprecedented level in 1994, although they have since declined due to a government crackdown on unions and enforcement of minimum wage increases. However, labor turmoil could erupt again as many employers have stirred worker anger by raising wages but reducing benefits.

Moreover, growing external pressures for improved workers' rights have manifested themselves in recent years. While the government has responded with some measures, including minimum wage increases, the repeal of a controversial decree permitting the military to break up labor disputes, and a restructuring of the official labor union, SPSI, this has not silenced its critics either inside or outside Indonesia. There have been continued complaints of official harassment of an independent and hitherto not officially recognized union established in 1992, SBSI, which has become increasingly active in recent months and begun to attract a considerable membership.

Consequently, the government faces a serious dilemma. While it is keen to avoid both destabilizing labor unrest within Indonesia and a damaging trade dispute with the United States, it recognizes that much of the industrial investment that has occurred in recent years has been in labor-intensive industries, which have only been attracted to Indonesia by low labor costs and tight controls on union activism.

Growing income disparities and a widening income gap between regions all point toward a turbulent era. Indonesia's notoriously low wages and lack of workers' freedom have given labor groups and protectionist U.S. lobbies ample ammunition. The government has promised to prosecute companies which refuse to pay workers the minimum wage and stated that labor organizations other than the All-Indonesian Labor Union will be allowed to engage in collective bargaining.[31]

On the economic front, inflation is not receding to single digits. The inflationary pressures stem from, among other things, privatization and rapid urbanization while unemployment refuses to decline. Still, if these challenges can be met, the Indonesian economy could well be one of the fastest growing countries in Asia during the remainder of the 1990s. As Indonesia marches into the next century, however, the challenges will be different. As it prospers, it will have to deal with new views and problems as diverse as its ethnic mix.[32]

CHAPTER 8

Unions, Employers, and Labor Market Developments

All relationships in Indonesia, interpersonal and institutional, are guided by the national ideology of Pancasila, which as we have seen emphasizes harmony, mutual self-help, and consensus decision making. Pancasila also theoretically applies to industrial relations in that government, labor, and management are expected to work cooperatively to achieve overall national development goals, including the establishment of social justice and an equitable apportionment of the fruits of economic progress.

The settlement of all labor problems through consensus and in an amicable manner is stressed, along with the notion that workers should behave loyally toward their employers. Meanwhile, employers are to treat workers as dignified human beings, not merely as factors of production. This industrial relations system is also intended to protect the right of labor to properly carry out its functions. Unfortunately, while considerable lip service is given to Pancasila, the increasing frequency of labor disputes in recent years indicates that the national ideology has yet to be operationalized in the interaction between labor and management.

While state enterprises are not allowed to unionize, private sector workers, including those in export processing zones, are free to form worker associations or company-level unions. However, as the following comment by the deputy secretary-general of the All-Indonesia Workers' Union (SPSI) indicates, management in Indonesia retains the upper hand in its dealings with trade unions:

> Thus because Pancasila Industrial Relations favours consultation between employer and employees, instead of strikes and lockouts, employers still play a dominant role in stipulating wages, social benefits and other workers' welfare. This means that most benefits still go to employers, even though gains should be distributed proportionately to all factors of production.[1]

BACKGROUND

Literally speaking, Indonesia was forced to start from scratch in the field of labor relations. In the decade and a half after World War II, Indonesian labor organizations came under Communist Party control in the prelude to the abortive coup in 1965 and were subsequently obliterated along with their Communist leadership. Henceforth, the Indonesian government has always sought to exercise close control over the country's organized labor force.[2]

The All-Indonesian Labor Federation (FBSI) was officially established on February 20, 1973, as a result of a merger of all unions which existed in Indonesia at that time. As a federation, FBSI consisted of 21 industrial unions organized in 26 out of 27 provinces. In the second congress of FBSI in 1985, attended by the 20 industrial unions and the 26 provincial unions, it was decided to convert the federation into a unitary form of organization and to change its name to the All-Indonesian Workers' Union (SPSI). As a result, the 21 industrial unions were reorganized into nine industrial departments (Fig. 8-1).

Only registered unions, company level or national, can negotiate binding labor agreements with employers. Company-level unions may not form larger organizations or affiliate with a national union other than the SPSI. To become a national union, a workers' organization must meet specific requirements for recognition. A national union must be recognized before it is permitted to bargain with employers or represent workers before Department of Manpower dispute settlement panels. To be recognized a union must first be registered with the Department of Home Affairs as a "mass organization." It must also meet specific organizational requirements to obtain Department of Manpower recognition.

Civil servants are not permitted to join unions and must belong to KOPRI, a nonunion association whose control development council is chaired by the Minister of Home Affairs. Teachers must belong to the Teachers' Association (PGRI). While technically classed as a union (its status was changed from an association similar to KORPRI in April 1990), the PGRI has continued to function more as a welfare organization and does not appear to have engaged in trade union activities.

State enterprise employees, defined to include those working in firms in which the state has a 5% holding or greater, usually are required to join KORPRI, but a small number of state enterprises have SPSI units.

INDEPENDENT UNION STATUS

A free trade union, Solidarity (Setiakawon) emerged in 1991. Although it is not officially permitted under the government's one union policy, it has not been banned outright. However, intelligence agencies have maintained a close watch on its activities, and in 1991 its secretary-general was held incommunicado for four days while agents tried to coerce his signature to a statement promising Solidarity would not strike.

At its first national congress on December 16, 1990, it called for an increase in the minimum daily wage to $3.00 from its level of $1.10 to $1.50 in Jakarta and less elsewhere. In 1991 Solidarity reported an informal membership of up to 25,000 in the

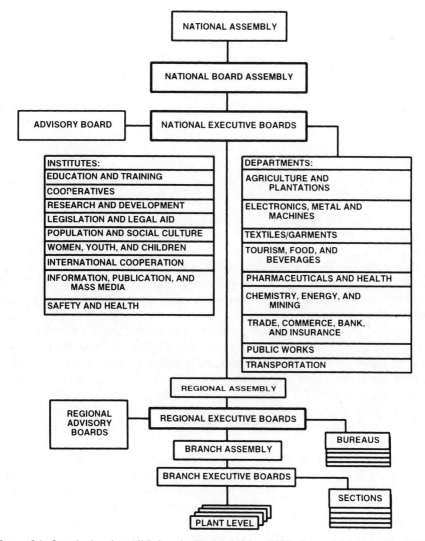

FIGURE 8-1. Organization chart All-Indonesian Workers' Union (SPSI). *Source*: Muinuddin Khan (Ed.). *Labour Administration: Profile on Indonesia* (ILO: Bangkok, Thailand, 1989), p. 32.

garment, textile, food and beverage, repair shops, chemical, rubber and leather industries, mainly in the Jakarta area. It also initiated protest demonstrations by low-paid industrial workers in front of the Department of Manpower in Jakara, and intends to carry on its organizing work and to investigate the wages and conditions of workers at major exporting companies. On this basis, it hopes to attract international attention to present inequities and to win international support for trade union rights in Indonesia.

With the government refusing to recognize this union, and threatening to have it banned, its prospects of achieving its goals are highly uncertain. It may be rescued by external pressure, however. The International Conference of Free Trade Unions (ICFTU) has lodged a formal complaint with the ILO accusing Indonesia of violating trade union rights, and the American Federation of Labor-Congress of Industrial Organizations (AFL-CIO) has petitioned the U.S. government to withdraw the trade privileges accorded to Indonesia under the Generalized System of Preferences (GSP) until such rights are granted.[3]

THE SBSI AND ITS SUPPRESSION

The Indonesian Workers' Welfare Union (SBSI) was established as an alternative to the government-controlled SPSI in May, 1992, at a meeting in Bandung. It claims to have 97 units and 250,000 members. On October 28, 1992, police and the military halted an SBSI meeting, for which a permit had not been requested. The union's leader and several officials were detained overnight by the police, questioned, and then released, and the SBSI's leader was detained again by the police the next day and released early in the morning.

On June 19, 1993, police halted a seminar on freedom of association being held in SBSI's offices while an ILO official was present. On July 28, 1993, the police and military prevented the SBSI from holding its first congress because the government had not granted the union's request for a permit for the meeting. Until August 1993, the military kept the SBSI's office under surveillance.

The SBSI has twice, on October 28, 1992 and August 10, 1993 attempted to register with the Department of Home Affairs as a social organization, a prerequisite for registration as a union. In the first instance, no action was taken on the union's application and in the second an official of the Department of Home Affairs refused to accept the SBSI's documentation. Registration under the "Ormas law" governing large social organizations is required for all such organizations to function legally.

Although the Ormas law does not specify a requirement for approval from other government bodies, a spokesman for the Department of Home Affairs stated that his department could not accept the SBSI's registration without a positive recommendation from the Department of Manpower. In line with its policy that only unions organized "by and for workers" can be recognized, the Department of Manpower has refused to recommend the registration of the SBSI as a social organization under the Ormas law on the grounds that its founders were not workers, but human rights activists and lawyers. According to the SBSI, only two members of its executive board are lawyers and the rest are workers, including some who are ex-SPSI officials. The government contends that if the SBSI reconstitutes itself as a nongovernmental organization, it would be registered under the Ormas law. The SBSI, however, has refused to accept this offer.

The February 11th Strike

In February 1994, the SBSI attempted to conduct a national strike. It requested all of its members and sympathizers to cease work for one hour on February 11th. The principal demand behind the strike was the new regulation on company unions which named the SPSI as the only legal national union in Indonesia. The SBSI claimed that 250,000 workers participated in the strike. Other observers believe this figure considerably overstated the participation in the strike. Two days prior to the strike the head of the SBSI and 16 other officials or members were detained by the police. The SBSI president was released after being held and questioned for three days.[4]

The Merger Suggestion

In June 1994, the National Human Rights Commission called on the Indonesian government to recognize SBSI in the interests of workers' rights, or allow its merger with the officially approved SPSI federation so that the "struggle for workers' rights" would be more effective. Shortly thereafter, SBSI officials made several visits to the headquarters of the commission, complaining that their leaders and officials were being harassed. Yet the commission merger proposal was interpreted as indicating that the government might have been moving to take a conciliatory tone toward SBSI.

Legislators and activists alike acknowledged that the SBSI's ability to draw at least 250,000 members and mount a series of strikes across the nation demonstrated that it had the makings of an effective labor organization. The SPSI, by contrast, was criticized for its weakness and inability to champion workers' interests. Despite its long history and status as the only recognized workers' federation, it has been able to count only a little over 2 million of Indonesia's 80-million strong workforce as members.

The SBSI's chairman, Mr. Muchtar Pakpahan, stated that he had been approached by government representatives, including those from the military, to consider the idea of a merger, and a similar suggestion had been proferred by visiting executives of the ICFTU. Also, an executive committee member of the SPSI was quoted as saying that the federation would not object to taking on individuals from the SBSI as members. Individuals would be allowed to join the SPSI but not under the SBSI banner, because the organization was not recognized by the government. Activists involved in the SBSI would also have to prove that they came from workers' organizations and not from nongovernmental organizations if they intended to join SPSI.[5]

The travails of the SBSI since its founding have occurred despite the fact that Indonesia has ratified the ILO Convention which ensures the right to associate in free trade unions. The union has a presence in plastics, steel, garments, and food processing in the Jakarta industrial suburbs of Bekasi and Tangerang.[6]

OTHER LABOR ORGANIZATIONS

In terms of actual union strength, labor activists claim that there are really three labor unions in Indonesia. Aside from the SBSI, the other two are the SPSI and the Free Labor Association (SBM). Union leaders also allege that while they remain unrecognized by the government, the civil servants' union and the teachers' association previously mentioned receive government support. Only the state-sponsored SPSI is recognized by the government, which maintains that any problems relating to the country's workforce should be mediated by a representative of the Department of Labor. A legal aid official observed: "The government still persists in perceiving labor unions as security risks detrimental to development programs."[7] Apparently freedom of association is perceived differently by the government and private organizations.

PGRI

On April 5, 1990 the Indonesian Teachers' Association (PGRI) was officially recognized as a trade union, bringing to two the number of registered unions in Indonesia. Since receiving official recognition, the PGRI has not made any noticeable changes in its structure or programs. It has a membership of 1.3 million and representation in all 27 provinces, 307 municipalities, 3500 districts and 62,800 counties.

SPSI

The SPSI organizes "workers" rather than "laborers," and according to government figures, as of September 1993, it had 9,601 work site units. There were 37,334 companies registered with the government with 25 or more employees. Thus, 25.72% of the firms most easily organized under government regulations have SPSI units, and of these businesses, 83.97% have collective labor agreements.

Workers are no longer required to obtain employers' consent before setting up an SPSI factory unit. They simply notify their employer and proceed if they do not receive a response within two weeks. Only about half of the factory-level SPSI units have collective bargaining agreements. The union recognition requirement has also been eased. An organization must maintain union offices in at least 5 of the country's 27 provinces, branch offices in at least 25 districts, and 100 plant-level units. In practice, however, there is no evidence that the Indonesian government intends to relinquish its one-union rule.

There have been organizational changes affecting the SPSI. In September 1993 the SPSI began changing from a unitary to a federative structure, registering 12 of its industrial sectors as separate unions. In 1994 the government also permitted the formation of individual plant-level unions with the power to negotiate collective bargaining agreements. However, these plant-level units are forbidden from affiliating, or even soliciting advice from any national union other than the SPSI, whose officials claim they have limited power because many enterprises still do not allow SPSI units to form within their organizations. This contention appears credible in light of the fact that of the 7464 companies in Jakarta, only 21.8% have unions, and only 9.5% have active unions.[8]

SPSI claims it has 3 million members, although only about 900,000 actually pay dues. For approximately the last 20 years, all dues collected through the checkoff have been sent by the employer to the Department of Manpower, which then distributes the funds to the unions. Both SPSI and Department of Manpower officials say this system was implemented at the request of the SPSI because the SPSI was administratively incapable of collecting dues from all parts of the country.

SPSI critics have charged that it is not independent and its leader is a senior member of Golkar, the ruling party, and that he and two other senior SPSI officials are members of Parliament representing Golkar. For that matter, only five members of Parliament represent labor organizations.

A number of provincial level SPSI officials are also members of their regional parliaments and are affiliated with Golkar. At all levels, some SPSI officials are also public employees. The head of the SPSI Pharmacy sector union has complained that 60% of the officials in his organization were civil servants. A number of SPSI officials are also former military officers with no prior union experience. The result of this situation is that, at a minimum, the SPSI is ineffective in representing the interests of its members. One SPSI official from Central Java estimated that just 60% of the SPSI factory-level units in Central Java consistently meet expectations of their members. He reportedly asserted that many SPSI officials are influenced by management and that the settlement of disputes is not subject to membership approval. Strike reports indicate almost without exception, that factory SPSI units were not involved and, in some cases, attempted to prevent workers from taking industrial action of any kind.

In May 1993, in anticipation of the decentralization of the SPSI, members of the union's executive council were given positions as deputy chairmen in one of the SPSI's industrial sectors. The SPSI held its National Leadership Meeting in Bandung from November 23rd through the 26th, 1992. At that time, it approved the general principle of decentralization. In October 1993, the Minister of Manpower formally approved the decentralization of the SPSI and awarded certificates of registration as independent unions to 12 of the SPSI's industrial sectors. As of the beginning of 1994, none of the sectors had held a national conference to elect its leaders or draft constitutions. These unions were still operating with leaders appointed during the period when the sectors were components of the SPSI and under basically similar constitutions which were given to them at the time of their registration as unions.[9]

Seafarers' Union (KPI)

During the November 1990 restructuring of the SPSI, the KPI or Seafarers' Union was made one of the 12 sectors. Because of its past autonomous stature, this shift in position initially created alarm, which was soon diminished by assurances that KPI would continue to function as a autonomous unit along with the other sectors. KPI provides a variety of services for its members and their families, such as scholarships for families of deceased members, educational programs for crew members of tourist ships, and medical services. It also operates two cooperative stores.

It has a total membership of approximately 21,363 and has collective bargaining agreements with 71 foreign shipping companies and 12 national companies. The KPI reported that in 1990 basic salaries for its members rose as much as 10% because of its collective bargaining efforts. The KPI is active in the ITF affiliated Asian Seafarers' Union and in November 1990 hosted the Asian Seafarers' Union summit meeting. A number of other organizations operate as quasi-trade unions. One of the more active ones is INKOPAR.

WORKERS COOPERATIVE MOVEMENT (INKOPKAR)

INKOPKAR is a coordinating network of over 1,700 cooperatives with a membership of over 2 million. Its main function is to strengthen the institutional capacity of cooperatives. Most of the members are from the industrial sector. The rest are from the financial and service sectors. The ILO assists INKOPAR with membership monitoring, consultation services, and management training. INKOPKAR has provided assistance to dock workers to open their own shops in the service sector, and also conducts local leadership training courses and national level seminars.

COLLECTIVE BARGAINING REQUIREMENTS

Indonesian employers and unions do engage in collective bargaining, which usually takes place at the plant level and covers wages, fringe benefits, and working conditions. Agreements are in force for a maximum of two years, with a possible extension of one year. The government requires that firms with more than 25 employees issue lists of their work regulations, including details of wages, proposed pay increases, fringe benefits, and protection for labor. Biannual approval of these regulations is contingent upon the presence of a union.

The company regulations must be approved in advance by the Department of Manpower. Any union at the plant level must be accepted as an SPSI affiliate in order to get government recognition, and the government urges employers to promote the formation of such unions at their plants. A union may be recognized in any plant where 25 or more of the employees desire one. Once 25 employees have joined an SPSI union, the employer is obligated to bargain with the union. A majority of the workers in a firm must vote to establish the union.

The movement toward an organized national labor union is slow because the labor force has little experience with unions. The unions themselves have not developed adequate dues-collecting systems, are short of money and lack trained organizers and leaders. In addition, unlike their Western counterparts, they are culturally indisposed to direct confrontation with management.

The government tries to present an evenhanded approach to labor and management, but in the current economic climate it has been squarely in management's corner, and any increase in strike activity is unlikely to be tolerated.

Employers' Organizations

As the structure of Indonesian unions has evolved, employers have also developed their own employers' organizations. The membership of an employers' organization may consist of individual employers, enterprises, or regional or industry associations, or all of these. Private firms which are members generally tend to consist of large and medium-sized companies. Many small companies tend not to be members mainly because they do not find any particular need for labor relations-related services.

In the past many employers' organizations have been engaged in the core activity of industrial relations services which have taken the form of advisory services on labor issues, collective bargaining with trade unions, and settlement of labor disputes, making representations to the government on labor policy, and participating in tripartite institutions such as minimum wage-fixing bodies. Over a period of time this labor relations role has increasingly been transformed into a preventive one; that is, one of creating a climate and structure to promote better relations through settlement, negotiations, and avoidance of disputes.

Within the past decade or so, some employers' organizations have, with the ILO's support, commenced, and in some cases increased, activities in human resource management training, supervisory development and training, occupational safety and health, improved productivity, population control, and family welfare programs, etc. At the national level, employers' organizations have increased their capacity to participate in policy formulation by taking a more active role in influencing labor legislation and policy, promoting deregulation and policies which favor business growth.

APINDO (see Fig. 8-2) is the officially recognized organization authorized to speak for employers on matters relating to labor–management relations and similar socioeconomic subjects. It has been given authority by KADIN, the Indonesian Chamber of Commerce, to represent employers in industrial relations matters and manpower issues. It is the only recognized employer organization to represent the employers in dealings with the Ministry of Manpower. APINDO represents Indonesian employers in the ILO and international matters. It also provides representation for employers in the various tripartite bodies dealing with wages, productivity, and health and safety, which are central to the Indonesian concept of industrial relations. Companies seeking approval of company labor regulations or collective labor agreements from the Department of Manpower are required to join APINDO.[10]

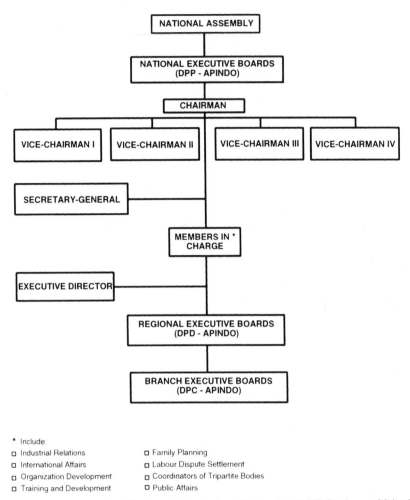

* Include
  □ Industrial Relations   □ Family Planning
  □ International Affairs   □ Labour Dispute Settlement
  □ Organization Development   □ Coordinators of Tripartite Bodies
  □ Training and Development   □ Public Affairs

FIGURE 8-2. Organization chart Employers' Association of Indonesia (APINDO). *Source*: Muinuddin Khan (Ed.). *Labour Administration: Profile on Indonesia* (ILO: Bangkok, Thailand, 1989), p. 70.

The need for industrial peace and harmony, always a core factor in achieving economic and social progress, has increased in importance, since it is viewed as a precondition to restructuring, privatization, and productivity growth. Developing sound labor relations systems and practices through promoting dialogue and communication, consultation and dispute avoidance, and settlement mechanisms in addition to developing tripartism, negotiating skills, innovative or new pay and compensation systems, are all important preoccupations of Indonesian employers' organizations.[11]

EMPLOYERS AND THE MINIMUM WAGE

APINDO has stated that its member employers are likely to switch to capital-intensive operations if demands for higher wages lead to strikes and are not matched by higher productivity. Companies would consider moving away from labor-intensive operations and opt for automation, even though costs would be high, to help avoid strikes and industrial disputes. Indonesia could lose its competitive edge if domestic wages continue to rise.

Indonesia introduced a minimum wage requirement early in 1994, and in September of that year made it compulsory for employers to pay a one-month bonus to workers for a religious festival. Under the minimum wage rule, workers in Jakarta were to receive at least RP 3,800 ($1.80) per day. However, before the regulation could be implemented in Medan, workers unhappy with the amount, took to the streets in one of the worst labor riots in recent years.

The head of the Employers' Association of Indonesia charged:

> We had agreed to implement the minimum wage rule in Medan. But the workers' union leaders wanted to us pay double the amount stipulated by the government. We don't want to have the lowest paid workers in the world. But union officials should not make exorbitant demands. If firms close down or go bankrupt, the workers will also be losers.[12]

He claimed the minimum wages being paid by the private sector would cover 98% of a person's basic needs and that any move to increase wages would have to be discussed by the tripartite committee comprising the government, employers, and workers.

Indonesia for many years has used cheap labor to lure foreign investment into a country where 27 million people live in poverty. Earlier in 1994, the Indonesian government rejected a request by the employers' association to delay the implementation of the new minimum wage. APINDO claimed its employers should be given at least a three-month notice to allow them to adjust to the minimum wage levels. APINDO asked the government for the suspension of the decree, arguing that companies needed time to recalculate all production costs, while other smaller firms, due to their financial position, could not pay the new minimum wage level.

The government rejected this request, stating that none of the companies belonging to the employers' association submitted applications to the Manpower Ministry, as required, to postpone the application of the new wage minima. The manpower minister noted that inadequate wages were one of the three main causes of strikes in Indonesia; the other two were unfavorable working conditions and opposition to union formation by certain companies. In 1993 there were 185 strikes involving 103,490 workers. The minister reminded management that there are no regulations or laws which prohibited workers from engaging in work stoppages to win their demands.[13]

Interestingly, several months later, APINDO's president criticized the government for paying many civil servants less than the minimum wages private firms had been ordered to pay their employees. He said:

Government is not practising what it preaches. Graduates are paid as much as errand boys in
the private sector. It is ironic that the government tells us to raise minimum wages but the
government itself pays starting salaries below the minimum physical requirement levels.[16]

The minimum physical requirement of RP 4,600 ($2.10) is the government-set
amount needed by a worker for his expenses for a day in Jakarta. It is marginally
lower in other parts of Indonesia, where there is a lower cost of living.

Private sector minimum wages in Jakarta and West Java were to increase by 21%
to RP 4,600 on April 1, 1994, the date set each year for minimum wage adjustments.
The minimum wage for 1995–96 in 19 other provinces averaged less than $2 per day
after the increases, which ranged from 10 to 35%.

APINDO's president maintained that despite the April wage increase, Indonesian workers were still among the lowest paid in Southeast Asia, despite the fact that
the country's wages only constituted "an average 15 percentage of the total cost of
production."[15]

LABOR FORCE TRENDS

Unions and employers in Indonesia deal with workers from different perspectives, the former interested in providing them with material benefits and employment
security, the latter concerned with the need to fill job vacancies with productive
personnel. Hence, labor force trends are of interest to both parties in the labor–
management relationship.[16]

The number of jobs that have been created and future employment projections
influence the organizing and recruitment strategies of unions and companies, respectively. The age, gender distribution, education, and industrial composition of the labor
force are important factors in these considerations. For example, there are more male
than female industrial workers (55 to 45%), although women are a growing presence,
concentrated mainly in the electronics and clothing industries.[17]

A 1991 population survey estimated the working age population, defined as
individuals ten years and older, at 138,843,849. Of this total, almost 80 million were
economically active, comprising the labor force, indicating a labor force participation
rate of 57.58%. Unemployment was estimated at 2.64%. A person was considered to
be working if he or she worked at least one hour during the week of the survey. Of the
working age population not economically active, i.e., not in the labor force, 28.38
million were attending school, 21.23 million were engaged in housekeeping, and 9.28
million fell into a residual category, "others" (see Table 8-1).

Of the approximately 80 million person workforce, about 25 million are in the
government and state sectors, the armed forces, and private businesses. Unfortunately, more than 50 million persons have been labeled as "unproductive" workers.
They are engaged in the informal or nonindustrialized sector, known as the service
sector in Western countries. This includes cottage industries but also a large number
of people who do things such as selling food and newspapers in the streets simply to
survive.[18]

TABLE 8-1
Projections for Working
Age Population, Individuals
10 Years and Older (000)

Age cohort	1990	1993	1998
10–14	21,482	23,174	23,259
15–19	18,297	18,645	20,015
20–24	16,128	17,649	20,628
25–34	28,869	30,775	34,271
35–44	19,266	22,159	26,456
45–54	14,253	14,319	16,646
55–64	9,358	9,938	11,294
65 +	6,756	6,910	8,598
TOTAL	135,040	143,569	161,165

Source: Department of Manpower, Office of
Manpower Information and Planning, Jakarta,
Republic of Indonesia.

During the Indonesian government's fifth five-year development plan (Repelita V), 1988–93, the Department of Manpower estimated that 10,650,00 jobs would be created while the labor force was expected to grow by 10,754,000 persons. (Actual figures for this period are not yet available.) For the next five year plan, 1993–98, the department expected the labor force to grow by 11,155,000 individuals and envisioned the creation of nearly 10.5 million employment opportunities (see Table 8-2).

Table 8-3, based on Department of Manpower figures, shows the estimated number of jobs created during Repelita V, and the expected growth in Repelita VI by

TABLE 8-2
Labor Force Projection (000)

Age cohort	1990	1993	1998
10–14	2,237	2,364	2,196
15–19	7,698	7,667	8,024
20–24	9,784	11,031	12,972
25–34	20,415	22,311	24,795
35–44	14,540	17,164	20,488
45–54	10,529	10,816	12,494
55–64	5,598	6,546	7,454
65 +	2,715	2,717	3,347
TOTAL	73,914	80,615	91,770

Source: Department of Manpower, Office
of Manpower Information and Planning,
Jakarta, Republic of Indonesia.

TABLE 8-3
Employment Increase by Sector (000)

Sector	Repelita V	% of new jobs	Repelita VI	% of new jobs
Agriculture	4,220	39.6	3,569	34.0
Mining	114	1.0	182	1.7
Manufacturing	1,570	14.7	1,920	18.3
Electricity	25	0.2	42	0.4
Construction	584	5.5	696	6.6
Trade	2,326	21.8	2,052	19.6
Transportation	568	5.3	626	6.0
Finance	99	0.9	217	2.1
Service	1,144	10.7	1,168	11.1
Total[a]	10,650	99.7	10,472	99.8

[a]Percentage totals less than 100 due to rounding.
Source: Department of Manpower, Office of Manpower Information and Planning, Jakarta, Republic of Indonesia.

sector. While manufacturing has increased in relative importance as the source of jobs for the expanding labor force, agriculture still absorbs the greatest absolute number of new labor force entrants.[19]

UNEMPLOYMENT

Unemployment, for the most part, has not been considered a significant problem for Indonesia. As a concept some economists consider it of questionable relevance, especially for the country's large rural population. The basic assumption underlying this argument is that, given the poverty in which most people live, the greatest majority of Indonesians cannot afford to be without a job and will accept any employment regardless of how low the pay. The only people who can afford to be unemployed, and be selective about which jobs they take, are the country's well-off minority, Unemployment data is consistent with this thesis.

However, with the changing structure of the economy, including increased urbanization and the growth of manufacturing and other components of the formal sector, and concomitant changes in the labor force such as increased wage employment and higher levels of education, unemployment is becoming a meaningful problem.

Like most labor force statistics, unemployment figures must be used with caution. Table 8-4 shows unemployment estimates from a variety of sources. The Supas is an intercensual survey conducted in the middle of the 10-year interval between censuses. The Sakernas is a labor force survey. Because of the variability in unemployment estimates, and comparability problems between various sources,

TABLE 8-4
Unemployment Rates (%), Various Sources

Source	Male			Female		
	Urban	Rural	Total	Urban	Rural	Total
1971 Census	5.0	1.9	2.4	4.5	1.4	1.8
1976 Supas	5.4	1.2	1.9	5.9	1.5	2.0
1976 Sakernas	6.9	1.9	2.7	5.1	1.1	1.6
(Sept.–Dec.)						
1978 Sakernas	7.0	2.1	2.9	3.8	1.4	1.8
1980 Census	2.7	1.0	1.4	3.0	2.2	2.3
1990 Census	5.6	1.7	2.8	7.6	2.6	3.9

Source: Manpower and Employment Situation in Indonesia, 1992,
Ministry of Manpower, Jakarta, Republic of Indonesia, p. 65.

comparison between the 1980 and 1990 censuses provides the most reliable picture of unemployment trends. Tables 8-4, 8-5, and 8-6 compare unemployment rates by age groups, gender, and urban/rural residence. The preceding two tables show a clear trend in unemployment, with comparatively high rates of joblessness among the young, school leaving age groups. In urban areas, the unemployment rate for both men and women under 25 years of age is very high and close to three times the 1980 levels. While unemployment for these age groups in rural areas was not as severe, it still showed a significant increase over the levels recorded in 1980. With the increasing use of technology in agriculture, rural areas are likely to see further increases in unemployment. For example, the increased use of herbicides will result in more rural female unemployment because weeding is traditionally a woman's task. Some of

TABLE 8-5
Unemployment Rates for Males
by Age and Residence 1980 and 1990

Age groups	Urban		Rural		Total	
	1980	1990	1980	1990	1980	1990
10–14	6.0	25.7	2.4	7.0	2.6	9.0
15–19	8.3	18.7	2.7	5.6	3.5	8.2
20–24	6.8	16.1	1.9	4.0	3.1	8.0
25–29	2.3	5.6	0.9	1.2	1.3	2.7
30–34	1.0	1.6	0.6	0.6	0.7	0.9
35–44	0.8	1.1	0.5	0.3	0.6	0.6
45 +	1.0	1.1	0.5	0.4	0.6	0.6

Source: Manpower and Employment Situation in Indonesia, 1991,
Ministry of Manpower, Jakarta, Republic of Indonesia, p. 65.

TABLE 8-6
Unemployment Rates for Females
by Age and Residence, 1980 and 1990

Age groups	Urban		Rural		Total	
	1980	1990	1980	1990	1980	1990
10–14	4.7	17.7	3.8	7.9	3.9	9.5
15–19	5.7	15.1	3.8	7.7	4.1	9.9
20–24	6.5	17.5	3.0	5.9	3.8	10.0
25–29	2.6	7.8	2.1	2.0	2.2	3.7
30–34	1.5	2.2	1.7	1.0	1.7	1.3
35–44	0.9	1.1	1.5	0.8	1.4	0.9
45 +	0.8	1.0	1.3	0.8	1.2	0.8

Source: Manpower and Employment Situation in Indonesia, 1991,
Ministry of Manpower, Jakarta, Republic of Indonesia, p. 65.

these unemployed will undoubtedly also migrate to urban areas in search of work, causing a consequent increase in unemployment there as well.

SIGNIFICANCE OF EDUCATION

The labor force, employed and unemployed individuals, from the perspective of educational attainment, shows a similar structural trend during the last decade. The only segment of the labor force for which unemployment decreased was those without education, according to Table 8-7. While the data in Table 8-8 should be taken as more indicative than precise, it nevertheless reveals a significant change in the educational structure of the labor force. The number of workers who have not completed primary school (those with no education and some primary schooling) has been sharply reduced, from 67.2 to 45.5%. At the same time this group has gone from comprising 53% of the unemployed to only 28.6%, again a significant reduction.

The statistics for those with a high school education or better have also shown a marked change, but not necessarily a desired one in terms of unemployment. In 1980 this group comprised 6.4% of the employed population, a figure which increased to 14% in 1990. However, as a percentage of the unemployed population, it was 15.1% in 1980 but expanded to 41.9% in 1990.

The latter figure is especially significant in light of the frequent reports of shortages of skilled labor, especially technicians, middle level managers, and supervisors and professionals, such as engineers and accountants. While a certain amount of unemployment in this category can be attributed to those educated individuals from well-off families who can afford the luxury of waiting for the job they desire, it could also indicate a serious mismatch between training and education and the needs of

TABLE 8-7
Unemployment Rates (%)
by Educational Level, 1980 and 1990

Educational level	(%) 1980	(%) 1990
No education	1.3	0.9
Some primary school	1.3	1.6
Primary school	1.8	2.5
Junior high school	2.8	5.4
Senior high school/diploma I/II	4.1	9.3
Academy/diploma III	2.0	6.5
University	1.5	8.6
Total	1.7	3.2

Source: Manpower and Employment Situation in Indonesia, 1992, Ministry of Manpower, Jakarta, Republic of Indonesia, p. 67.

businesses, substantiating the complaints of businessmen that workers with academic credentials all too often do not have the right or adequate skills. The educational level of the workforce remains relatively low with about 60 million, or 75% having completed only primary school or less. Roughly 9.5 million labor force participants have completed high school, either general or vocational high school, while only 750,000 members of the labor force, or 0.9%, have a university education.

Statistics published in the latest World Bank report on Indonesia reveal the

TABLE 8-8
Distribution of Employed and Unemployed Population
by Educational Level, 1980 and 1990

	Employment (%)		Unemployment (%)	
Educational level	1980	1990	1980	1990
No education	29.6	17.4	22.5	14.9
Some primary school	37.6	28.1	30.5	13.7
Primary school	21.2	31.5	22.9	24.3
Junior high school	5.1	9.0	8.9	15.2
Senior high school/diploma I/II	5.6	12.0	14.3	37.0
Academy/diploma III	0.4	0.8	0.5	1.6
University	0.4	1.2	0.3	3.3
Total	100	100	100	100

Source: Manpower and Employment Situation in Indonesia, 1992, Ministry of Manpower, Jakarta, Republic of Indonesia, p. 68.

national scope of the education gap. Only 9% of children from families in the poorest one-tenth of the population attend junior high school, compared to 76% of children belonging to the wealthiest 10%. In the case of senior high school, the gap widens to 2% and 69%. In the greatest display of inequality, less than 1% of the bottom half of the population attend universities or colleges, compared to 27% for the top one-tenth.[20]

Educational attainment levels also are important because they influence the skill composition of the labor force. In Indonesia, this is reflected in the present severe shortage of skilled personnel of all types which will continue to be a serious problem for foreign firms investing in the country. The government has in principle allocated a high priority to human resource development, particularly with respect to the needs of technology and industry. Unfortunately, it has yet to formulate a clear policy or program for their development. The teaching profession, from primary school to university, continues to be woefully underpaid and poorly trained and there is no significant government program for assisting students to study overseas.

WOMEN WORKERS

According to analyses of census figures, 37.8% of the Indonesian labor force in 1988 was female, and the proportion was expected to rise to 40.2% over the next decade. Agriculture is still the largest source of employment for women, but the proportion of the female labor force employed in this sector fell from 63.3% in 1971 to 53.7% in 1985, largely as a result of changes in harvesting technology. On the other hand, women's employment in industry and services increased over the same period. In particular, the 1970s saw a considerable rise in the employment of young women in urban manufacturing. Currently, over 2 million Indonesian women work in industry.

More than being just a special category of workers, women *are* the workforce in many enterprises. They comprise 47% of the total workforce in manufacturing and dominate certain industries such as tobacco, textiles, and food and beverage processing. As in other East and Southeast Asian countries, the preference for employing women in certain sectors has been attributed to employers' beliefs that they are more dexterous, more patient, less assertive, and more deferential to authority.

While women and men have equal rights and protection under the law, the society is largely patriarchal and hierarchical, and traditional attitudes toward women still influence many aspects of life. A recent resurgence in the faith and practice of Islam in Indonesia has been credited with strengthening the perceived primary roles of women as wives and mothers. Although the government actively promotes greater participation of women in the economy, it explains that "women's role should be in agreement with their responsibilities and duties to create a healthy, happy and contented family." The official vision of men and women as separate but equal partners in national development has yet to become a reality, for women are subject to discrimination in both employment opportunities and pay.

UNDEREMPLOYMENT

The usual definition for underemployment in Indonesia is working one or more hours but less than 35 hours a week. The extent to which underemployment is a problem in terms of individuals, however, is not clear. For instance, multiple job holding is common and some of the responses given by individuals to surveys may relate to their primary job only. In some sectors, notably agriculture, work is seasonal. In agriculture as well, many workers work shorter hours by choice. Finally, some researchers note a difference in the results of village studies and national surveys, with the former reporting lower levels of underemployment than the latter. However, the high level of underemployment is indicative of the lower productivity which is still pervasive in the economy as a whole.

Comparing underemployment in 1980 and 1990, there appears to have been only a marginal increase in the number of those working less than 35 hours, from 36.9 to 38.6%. There was also very little change in the number of individuals working less than 25 hours, serious underemployment, from 22.7 to 22.5%. The data show that women are more likely to be underemployed, with 52.8% of women workers working less than 35 hours in 1990 compared to 30.7% for males. A similar situation obtains for those working less than 25 hours a week: 34.5% of female workers as opposed to 15.8% of male workers. The 1990 figures differ little from those for 1980. As Table 8-9 shows, the highest rates of underemployment for both sexes occurred in agriculture and registered a significant increase in 1990. This increase could be the result of a number of factors including respondents' increasing off-farm employment, but reporting only farm hours worked, an increased number of people performing the same amount of work ("agricultural involution"), and increased use of mechanical farm implements.

For men, after agriculture, the next highest levels of underemployment are those in the trade and service sectors, 22.3 and 23.3%, respectively. These apparent high levels may result from the fact that these two areas are important as sources of secondary data. These are also sectors in which the service sector is dominant. The levels of underemployment for women are also high in these sectors, again the result of women's high degree of representation in service sector activities. The underemployment figures, however, may overstate the extent of the problem. Table 8-10 shows that many people are satisfied with the hours they are working. Also, numbers of people working 35 or more hours are seeking additional work. Of those individuals working between 35 and 44 hours, 8.4% desire additional work. Of people working between 45 and 59 hours, 7.4% want to work more. There even appears to be a significant number of people working 60 or more hours a week, 5.4%, who desire more work. Overall, 8.1% of those employed seek further work. More of these individuals are in rural areas (10.9% of males and 7.03% of females, although employed want to work more) than in urban settings (5.3% of males and 3.15% of females).

These figures raise the question of the efficacy for Indonesia of the conventional

TABLE 8-9

Distribution (%) of Working Population by Hours Worked
According to Industry and Sex, 1980 and 1990

	1980	1990	1980	1990	1980	1990
	Agriculture		Manufacturing		Construction	
Males						
<25	22.4	22.9	10.1	8.3	7.0	6.9
25–34	16.6	20.0	7.5	7.5	5.5	5.9
35–39	54.5	53.7	65.8	70.4	68.8	72.9
>60 +	6.5	3.4	16.6	13.8	18.7	14.3
All Hours	100	100	100	100	100	100
Females						
<25	42.6	46.5	27.4	25.1	14.2	19.6
25–34	19.6	22.1	13.6	14.4	9.7	9.3
35–39	35.5	30.3	49.3	52.0	61.5	62.8
60 +	2.3	1.1	9.7	8.5	14.6	18.3
All Hours	100	100	100	100	100	100
Both Sexes						
<25	28.7	30.6	17.7	15.6	7.0	7.2
25–34	17.5	20.7	10.1	10.5	5.6	6.0
35–39	48.7	45.5	58.6	62.4	68.7	72.6
60 +	5.1	3.2	13.6	11.5	18.7	14.2
All Hours	100	100	100	100	100	100

	Trade		Transportation		Services		All Other Industries	
Males								
<25	14.0	21.1	7.5	7.8	10.2	9.1	17.4	15.8
25–34	9.1	10.2	5.3	7.2	10.8	14.2	13.0	14.9
35–39	50.8	53.2	49.8	52.9	64.8	66.0	57.3	58.3
60 +	26.1	24.5	37.4	32.1	14.2	10.7	12.3	11.0
All Hours	100	100	100	100	100	100	100	100
Females								
<25	24.0	22.1	9.0	9.9	20.3	18.3	34.0	34.5
25–34	13.3	14.2	6.1	5.0	13.0	16.6	16.6	18.3
35–39	41.6	42.7	67.8	73.8	44.1	45.2	39.8	38.2
60 +	21.1	21.0	17.1	11.3	22.6	19.9	9.6	9.0
All Hours	100	100	100	100	100	100	100	100
Both Sexes								
<25	18.7	17.0	7.5	7.9	13.3	12.6	22.7	22.5
25–34	11.1	12.2	5.4	7.2	11.4	15.1	14.2	16.1
35–39	46.4	48.0	50.0	53.2	58.4	58.2	51.7	51.1
60 +	23.8	22.8	37.1	31.7	16.9	14.1	11.4	10.3
All Hours	100	100	100	100	100	100	100	100

In contrast to men, underemployment in manfacturing was high for women, 39.5%,
although it declined slightly from its 1980 rate of 41.0%. Information is not available for the
40–50 age group.

Source: Manpower and Employment Situation in Indonesia, 1992, The Ministry of Manpower, Jakarta, Republic of Indonesia, p. 71.

Table 8-10
Percent Underemployed Looking for Work
or Reasons for Not Seeking More Work, 1990

Hours worked	Seeking work	Feel not needed	Lost hope	In search	House keeping	Not capable	Other	Total
0	09.1	26.5	1.1	03.1	38.8	4.6	16.6	99.8
1–9	08.4	33.2	1.7	15.7	31.8	2.1	06.8	99.7
10–24	09.3	48.5	1.5	07.1	27.5	0.7	05.0	99.6
25–34	10.2	65.2	1.7	00.9	17.2	0.1	15.1	100.4

Note: Totals do not equal 100 due to rounding
Source: Penduduk Indonesia 1990, Table Pendahuluan Hasil Sub-Sampel, Seri: S.1, Table 28.9.

concept of underemployment. With even "fully employed" persons seeking more work, the problem seems not to be jobs per se, but jobs which provide sufficient income. This view is reinforced by the figures on second jobs. According to the 1990 census, 5.81% of the labor force had a second job. In urban areas this was less common, with 2.19% of males holding a second job and 1.05% of females. In rural areas, the figure is considerable higher: 8.75% for men and 4.73% for women. Using the figures for those seeking more work and those already holding a second job, bearing in mind that the two categories could overlap, may give a very approximate indicator of the extent to which adequate jobs are not available. This rough indicator for rural males is 19.65%. Twenty percent of rural males are seeking more work and, importantly, more income.[21]

INFORMAL SECTOR

The informal sector in Indonesia is significant, with some estimates placing two thirds of the labor force in the sector. There is no precise definition of the informal sector, but the Central Bureau of Statistics uses employment status to differentiate between formal and informal sectors. Of the five statuses by which the bureau classifies working individuals, three are considered to be in the informal sector: self-employed, self-employed assisted by family member or temporary help, and unpaid family worker. The other two statuses, employer and employees, are considered to be part of the formal sector. The manner of defining who is in the informal sector has a number of obvious problems, especially its inappropriateness to agriculture, and, concomitantly, to rural areas. It is most relevant to secondary and tertiary sectors and to urban areas.

Considerable emphasis is being placed on the informal sector which together with the agricultural sector employ over 75% of the workforce. Normally this term refers to commercial operations that are not registered with the government, are difficult for government to tax or control, and do not use formal banking or financial services. In general the informal sector consists of poor people who provide goods and services to other poor people, such as sidewalk vendors, water sellers, plastic, paper, and metal recyclers, and pedicab drivers. Since 1987, the Department of Manpower has had a very active program, funded with assistance from the World Bank, to develop the informal sector. APINDO has been requested by the ILO to draw up a proposal for activities in this sector. Also, government programs have been instituted to provide protection and incentives to what are generally economically weak enterprises, through a system of tariff regulations and small-scale credit schemes.

Quickly surveying the two preceding tables by key sectors, it is interesting to note that even though the concept of the informal sector used here is of limited value in enumerating the rural informal sector, nevertheless agriculture in both the formal and informal sectors grew at about the same rate. This, however, may have been the result of better counting in 1990 of women who perform agricultural work on farms compared with 1980. Agriculture also has the second highest percentage of informal sector workers, 82.31% or approximately 30 million out of 36 million. The sector also created the most jobs, in absolute terms, in the 10-year intercensual period, nearly 8 million.

In manufacturing the trend is clearly away from the informal sector, with the figures validating the highly visible growth of large scale manufacturing in the Jakarta region and other urban centers. During the period between 1980 and 1990, the manufacturing workforce nearly doubled, with the informal sector growing by 21.6% and the formal sector by 155.2%.

TABLE 8-11
Change (%) in Informal Sector Employment by
Employment Status and Main Industry, 1980–90

Sector	Self-employed	Self-employed +	Family worker	Informal sector
Agriculture	−11.05	35.35	59.79	29.34
Mining	−87.18	−49.03	20.52	−54.60
Manufacturing	−6.40	−6.49	122.86	−21.55
Electricity	1.40	4.23	−79.56	−7.75
Construction	48.30	51.20	−5.82	45.02
Trade	44.40	66.74	79.42	55.97
Transport	128.07	59.24	−10.73	107.57
Bank & finance	5.32	−37.08	−24.34	−14.34
Other services	−14.55	−31.64	−42.66	−23.58
Total	8.41	−33.16	55.06	58.97

Source: Manpower and Employment Situation in Indonesia, 1992, Ministry of Manpower, Jakarta, Republic of Indonesia, p. 77.

TABLE 8-12
Change (%) in Formal Sector
Employment by Employment Status
and Main Industry, 1980–90

Sector	Employer	Employee	Formal sector
Agriculture	77.33	27.95	30.96
Mining	31.87	407.40	383.70
Manufacturing	−11.08	165.60	155.16
Electricity	39.00	120.86	118.59
Construction	41.03	112.35	106.93
Trade	102.09	153.10	145.80
Transport	−93.15	84.94	70.53
Bank & finance	53.35	158.51	155.65
Other services	−39.19	62.83	58.43
Total	19.52	79.39	75.78

Source: Manpower and Employment Situation in Indo-nesia, 1992, Ministry of Manpower, Jakarta, Republic of Indonesia, p. 77.

Testifying to the building boom in the late 1980s, the construction sector in the formal sector grew at twice the average rate for the informal sector. Construction employment in the informal sector also grew, albeit at a somewhat slower growth rate.

With the exception of agriculture, only in the transportation sector did informal growth outpace the formal sector's employment expansion. This is likely the result of Indonesia's reliance on human or motor powered pedicabs and the use of motor bikes to carry single persons and sometimes whole families from one place to another. Even minibuses and modified vans used for public transportation are often organized on an informal basis.

The trade sector is primarily informal, with only 15% of jobs in the formal sector. Additionally, after agriculture, it is the second largest sector in terms of employment, providing jobs for 10.75 million workers. Employment in the informal sector grew between 1980 and 1990 by 56% and even more rapidly in the formal sector, by 145.8%. The overall rate of job growth was 62.7%.

EMPLOYMENT OF EXPATRIATES

As Tables 8-13 and 8-14 indicate, the rapid growth of the Indonesian economy in recent years, combined with the shortage of managerial, professional, and skilled workers has necessitated the use of expatriate labor. There was a doubling of new expatriate workers between 1988 and 1991, with half of the expatriates employed in managerial or professional positions. In 1984, less than a third of expatriate workers

Table 8-13
Work Permits Issued to Foreign Residents, 1984–91

Type	1984	1985	1986	1987	1988	1989	1990	1991
New	6,597	7,691	7,628	7,508	6,124	8,119	9,290	16,049
Extension	1,030	10,779	11,372	11,321	6,561	11,278	11,242	11,620
Job change	439	233	211	324	223	226	229	255
Total	18,066	18,703	19,211	19,153	12,908	19,623	20,761	27,924

Source: Manpower and Employment Situation in Indonesia, 1992, The Ministry of Manpower, Jakarta, Republic of Indonesia, p. 124.

were employed in similar jobs. By 1991 the number of technicians had also doubled while numbers of foremen and operators had declined significantly.

Expatriate employment is governed by Minister of Manpower Regulation 4 of 1984, which specifies the types of firms that may hire expatriates, and requires plans for training Indonesians. The regulation also outlines the application procedure and approval process for work permits. Fewer restrictions exist for the employment of foreigners in export marketing and tourism jobs.

Recognizing the generally low level of skills in the labor force, the foreign investment law allows employment of expatriates, but only in positions that Indonesians cannot fill, and only if regular and systematic training is provided in order to allow Indonesians to replace expatriates.

In 1992 the government ruled that all companies employing expatriates must pay a tax per foreign employee of $100 a month. In August 1994 the minister of information announced that this charge would be scrapped, at least in the case of positions for which no suitably qualified Indonesians were available. To date, however, the levy has continued to be collected. A scandal emerged late in the year when it was revealed that a major business group, Sinar Mas, had imported more than 700

Table 8-14
Expatriate Workers by Type of Work (%),
1984–91

	1984	1986	1988	1990	1991
Managers	13.9	13.0	24.1	14.1	12.6
Professional	17.8	21.3	40.0	30.6	42.8
Technicians	11.1	14.3	7.4	15.6	21.2
Foremen	45.1	41.1	24.4	32.8	10.0
Operations	12.2	10.3	4.2	6.9	13.5
Total	100.0	100.0	100.0	100.0	100.0

Source: Manpower and Employment Situation of Indonesia, 1992, The Ministry of Manpower, Jakarta, Republic of Indonesia, p. 124.

Chinese workers to construct a series of small power plants. The publicity led to increased official scrutiny of the use of expatriate workers, and immigration authorities have in some cases conducted inspections of residential areas and workplaces to check on the credentials of foreign workers. Nonetheless, many expatriates manage to work for limited periods with no more than a tourist visa; for example, in the booming fields of advertising and television. In early 1994, protests erupted in Surabaya when it was discovered that many English teachers were taking advantage of tourist visas.[23]

LABOR EXPORTATION

The surplus of unskilled workers discussed earlier has necessitated consideration of another important policy option, that of exportation of Indonesian workers to other countries in need of unskilled labor. Indonesian workers have been mainly sent to the Middle East, Malaysia, and Singapore through the intercountry recruitment branch (AKAN) of the Department of Manpower, which has stated that the sending abroad of workers would continue and efforts would be made to increase the number. Approximately 300,000 were sent overseas during the last five-year development period. Estimates are that over 500,000 will be sent over the next five years.

In order to prevent the exploitation of Indonesians working abroad, the government intensified efforts to provide protection for the over 100,000 Indonesians working in the Persian Gulf region, particularly in Saudi Arabia. Besides assuring that all workers going abroad to work were enrolled in the social insurance program (ASTEK), more responsibility was placed on the shoulders of the Indonesian labor attaches located in the region. During the Gulf War the government sent a special intergovernmental team to the region to monitor the situation of the Indonesian workers and to provide assistance and information regarding developments in the area.

AN ASSESSMENT

Indonesia illustrates why free trade requires an open society. Suharto, the former general turned president, has ruled Indonesia with an iron hand since the late 1960s and forbids dissent at all levels. His military has brutally crushed political movements opposed to his dictatorial rule.

Struggling to live with a minimum wage of $2 a day, Indonesian workers have tried to develop an active labor and human rights movement. But with the president and the military behind them, Indonesian employers do not take protest lightly. The army is routinely deployed to break up strikes.[24] Workers also lament that sweatshoplike conditions remain in some factories and that employers have taken away allowances to compensate for the increase in the minimum wage. Above all, the workers say the increase in the daily minimum wage has helped little because of increasing inflation.

Indonesian businessmen, however, maintain that workers are being paid enough. Their point of view is that the government has set the minimum wage. If employers pay that amount, there should be no disagreements voiced by labor. Employers believe that the skill level of Indonesian workers should also be considered, and most are unskilled. They are very concerned that Indonesia's industries remain competitive in the global economy.

Not cowed by management, labor activists feel Indonesian workers, largely unaware of their rights, continue to be exploited by their employers. Even the law offers little recourse. Poorly paid labor inspectors and police often turn to corruption and collude with employers to keep workers in check.

In many respects, the Medan riots were the product of the successful economic strategy pursued by the Suharto regime in recent years and aimed at transforming this once agrarian economy into a manufacturing center. Because of the abundance of cheap labor, the government has been able to present the country as a haven for cost-conscious manufacturing companies, inducing them to relocate their operations to Indonesia. The economic strategy has attracted billions of dollars in foreign investment and helped keep annual average economic growth rates at about 7%. But the policy, which has greatly enriched some, has also bred misery for others. Crippling poverty forces Indonesia's unskilled labor force to take whatever employment is available in order to survive. With nearly 2.5 million new job entrants into the labor force each year, workers cling to their jobs, no matter how harsh the conditions.

Today, although it has the legal right to organize in any enterprise with more than 25 workers, the only officially recognized labor union, the All Indonesian Workers' Union (SPSI), has been hindered in its organizing efforts at a large number of firms by employers' resistance, government failure to enforce the law, and its own limitations. In the midst of these developments, it is difficult to estimate how collective bargaining will fare in the latter half of the 1990s. As in the past, even today collective bargaining does not enjoy the popularity it has in industrialized market economies in the West except in countries such as Japan, Australia, New Zealand, and Singapore. One reason for this is that the level of unionization in Indonesia is low and there is a definite movement toward plant-level negotiation which is undermining traditional collective bargaining at the national or industry-wide level.

There has recently been a sharp increase in labor unrest in the industrial sector as workers have begun to organize and demand improved wages and working conditions. These demands have been reinforced by growing external pressures for improved workers' rights, with the U.S. government in particular having threatened to withdraw the trade privileges granted to Indonesia under the Generalized System of Preferences (GSP). While the government has responded with some measures, including an increase in the minimum wage, the repeal of a controversial decree permitting the military to break up labor disputes, and a restructuring of the official labor federation (SPSI), this has not silenced its critics either inside or outside Indonesia.

There have been continued complaints of official harassment of an independent and hitherto not officially recognized, labor union established in 1992, (SBSI), which has become increasingly active and begun to attract a considerable membership. The Indonesian government faces a serious dilemma. While it is anxious to avoid both destabilizing labor turmoil within Indonesia and a damaging trade dispute with the United States, it recognizes that much of the industrial investment that has taken place in recent years has been in labor-intensive industries, which have only been attracted by low labor costs and tight controls on labor activism. Many of these firms operate at comparatively low productivity levels and may well lose their competitiveness if labor costs are increased. Resolving this problem is one of the most important challenges facing the government. "The Indonesian economy has benefitted from the exploitation of the workers. But this can't continue because it will become an explosive social issue," say Abdul Hakim, a lawyer and a workers rights advocate.[25]

Additionally, labor market conditions have recently become more of an issue in Indonesia. Despite the rapid economic growth over the past several years, high underemployment remains a major problem because of the rapid annual growth in the labor force. Over the next five years almost 91.5 million workers are forecast to enter the labor force; however, according to the new Five-Year Development Plan, only about 90.7 million new jobs will be generated. As a result, the underemployment rate is likely to remain near 38% of the labor force.

Moreover, in the event of an economic downturn, industrial relations could turn violent should factories start laying off workers. Here is where liberalization of the existing labor legislation to allow genuinely independent unions to negotiate on behalf of their members would be a salutary development. Such unions would have an interest not only in improving their members' pay and working conditions but also in protecting their members' jobs. Any genuine risk of plants becoming uncompetitive to the point of closure because of unrealistic demands by workers could cause these demands to be moderated by the unions representing the workers.

Chapter 9

The Legal Framework

As with other nations, Indonesia has enacted a set of laws that regulate the activities of individual employees, unions, and employers in the labor relations arena. However, unlike China, which now has a comprehensive statute governing all aspects of the employment relationship, Indonesia has a number of laws and regulations which establish the legal framework for labor–management dealings.

Proceeding from the premise that wages do not account for an enterprise's total labor costs, an extensive body of labor law and regulations provides workers with vacation pay, maternity leave, public holidays, overtime and sick pay, severance and service pay, etc. Workers also receive transportation and food allowances and holiday bonuses. Workers in more modern facilities receive health benefits, social security contributions, and free meals.

Minimum Wages

In the absence of a national minimum wage, minimum wages are established by regional wage councils working under the supervision of the National Wage Council. This is a quadripartite body consisting of representatives from labor, management, government, and universities. It also establishes a basic needs figure for each of the 27 provinces, a monetary amount considered sufficient to enable a single worker or family to meet the basic needs of nutrition, clothing, and shelter. The minimum wage rates constantly lag far behind the basic needs figures and fall short of providing a decent standard of living.

Observance of minimum wage and other laws regulating benefits and labor standards varies from sector to sector and from region to region. Employer violations of these guarantees are considered to be fairly common and often the subject of strikes and employee protests. Government supervision and enforcement have been weak or nonexistent, even though the government has issued regulations calling for periodic inspections and providing for fines or imprisonment for employers who do not comply.[1]

The government reviews the minimum wage annually and readjusts it in line with the minimum physical need standard for each province. Both the absolute levels and the proposed rates of increase of these minimum wages vary from province to province. For Indonesians working abroad the government has set the minimum monthly wage at $400. The monthly minimum wage for unskilled workers such as domestic help has been set at $250. The Ministry of Manpower in cooperation with the Association of Manpower Suppliers established these new minimum wage levels to improve worker welfare.[2]

RECENT WAGE DEVELOPMENTS

In the wake of growing labor unrest Jakara is taking measures to improve the labor market environment, including increases in minimum wage levels and improving the enforcement of the minimum wage regulations. In 1994, there was a sharp decline in the number and duration of strikes as more companies were forced to comply with the wage regulations.

The minimum wage levels were adjusted upward on April 1, 1995 across the nation within a range of 10 to 35%. In the industrial zones around Jakarta, the minimum daily wage rose 21% from $1.73 to $2.07. The lowest rates are in Yogyakarta and Sulawesi, where the rate was set at only $1.29 on a daily basis. Also on the same date, a new law was enacted that increased the penalties for firms that fail to comply with the regulations.

Despite these increases in the minimum wage levels, Indonesia will still remain highly competitive in terms of labor costs. The average cost of labor in the manufacturing sector recently was $2.25 per day, compared to $4.32 per day in China. The only other country in the region with wage levels close to those in Indonesia is Vietnam, where the minimum wage rate for foreign firms is about $2 per day.[3]

It also bears noting that generally, basic wage levels are far from the whole story in calculating labor costs. Indonesian fixed wage workers customarily receive transportation and other allowances in cash or kind, or both, as well as holiday bonuses. Fringe benefits and daily allowances can double labor costs at the low end of the labor scale and have a significant impact at the higher end. Companies are free to determine the wages and salaries of employees beyond the minimum wage. Usually the larger, more profitable domestic and foreign companies pay their workers salaries which are above the minimum wage. Wages vary significantly according to industry and location within Indonesia. Wages in the oil industry are much higher than in the agricultural estates, and wages in urban Jakarta are much higher than in rural Java.

The following basic monthly wages provide a rough estimate of what a typical joint venture manufacturing company would pay nonsupervisory workers: welder $75 to $200 (RP 174,225 to RP 464,600); assembler $40 to $125 (RP 92,920 to RP 290,375); security guard $75 to $100 (RP 174,225 to RP 232,300); material handler $35 to $75 (RP 81,305 to RP 174,225); accounting clerk $100 to $300 (RP 232,300 to RP 696,900); typist $125 to $200 (RP 290,375 to RP 464,600); and bilingual secretary $750 to $1000 (RP 742,250 to RP 2,323,000).

ENFORCEMENT

In terms of what Jakarta does to enforce the laws and regulations, employers who are not in compliance by reneging on minimum wages, welfare, and other benefits to workers are placed on a manpower ministry blacklist, which is then distributed to ministries and provincial governors and monitored by the authorities. The ministry tells these agencies to consider denying services or loans to noncomplying firms. A company that violates regulations three times is put on the blacklist. A leading cause of strikes in Indonesia has been the failure of employers to observe the labor regulations, particularly regarding minimum wages.

Workers have been urged to come forward and inform either the local manpower offices or their local representative of the All Indonesian Workers' Union (SPSI) if their employers were violating the law. The SPSI's Secretary-General Bomer Pasaribu announced that his organization was ready to help the government implement its plan to blacklist offending companies.

Employers were also warned that unspecified sanctions would be applied against firms that continued to mismanage employees, disregard workers' rights, and allow resentment to boil over into unrest which could have political consequences. This appeared to be an indirect reference to the Medan riots when labor turmoil sparked rioting which caused the death of a Chinese businessman, damaged property, and scared off foreign investors for a time.

The blacklist is the latest threat by the government as it moves to get employers to acknowledge their obligations and foster a climate of peaceful industrial relations in the country. Jakarta has already urged the courts to impose jail terms on errant employers rather than fines, the maximum of which is a mere RP 100,000 ($65).

In their approach to improved enforcement, the government also formed an integrated team to enforce the laws and regulations in Jakarta and its surrounding areas. The team, whose members are from the ministries of manpower, industry, the attorney general's office, and the Jakarta military command, was formed in the region to enhance compliance efforts. The area, a home to approximately 65,000 companies, is quite prone to unrest sparked by labor disputes between management and workers. Most past labor conflict occurred in labor-intensive companies and those which had relocated to Indonesia from South Korea, Japan and Taiwan. The basic cause of the disputes, as elsewhere in Indonesia, involved management infringement of minimum wage requirements.[5]

As an indication of its seriousness of purpose in enforcement efforts, the Ministry of Manpower released figures showing that it took 202 companies to court for their labor law violations during the 1994–95 fiscal year. Of the offenders, 48 had already been punished by local courts. The types of violations included noncompliance with the regional minimum wage, workers' social security benefits, overtime, occupational safety and health, and hours of work. The manpower ministry also informed other agencies, such as the Ministry of Industry, the Ministry of Trade, banks, and provincial governors of the nature of the violations and the action that had been taken to spur compliance.[6]

EXEMPTION REQUESTS

Despite the government blacklist threat, in July 1995 it was announced that a total of 82 Indonesian companies nationwide had applied to the manpower ministry for exemptions from the new minimum wage levels. The majority of the 157,819 firms registered with the ministry complied immediately with the wage increases but 82 applied for exemption for various reasons, mostly financial difficulties. A more disquieting fact was noncompliance by 59 companies, who totally ignored the minimum wage requirements. Their cases were processed for possible prosecution. If found guilty by the court, these employers could be liable to fines of between RP 25,000 ($11) and RP 300,000 ($137), and/or, between six months and one year imprisonment.[7]

EMPLOYER–EMPLOYEE INCOME DIFFERENTIALS

The Indonesian government soon after the announcement of its enforcement efforts, revealed that there is a striking disparity in incomes of workers compared to those of their employers. Some 70% of Indonesian workers are paid wages that are barely enough for their basic needs while their bosses earn up to 200 times more. Mr. Soewarto, the Director-General of Industrial Relations, stated the following: "Salaries given to the boards of directors and managers are 40 to 200 times higher than wages received by common workers." He said employers should realize that wide income disparities may spark social unrest. The income gap has never been higher than 15 times in either Japan or neighboring countries.[8]

That Indonesia is one of Asia's lowest wage countries is evidenced by the fact that, on average, an employer can hire seven or eight workers in Indonesia or Vietnam with what he or she is required to pay a Singapore worker.

Indonesia has set itself the target of quadrupling real per capita income over the next 25 years. This means achieving an income of $2,600 by the year 2018. To achieve this target, Indonesia must move away from being a country that is largely agriculture-based to one dominated by industry and services.[9] With average minimum wage levels hovering near the $2 level nationwide, this appears to be an extremely ambitious objective.

FRINGE BENEFITS

Fringe benefits constitute a significant part of the cost of labor to employers, averaging about 30 to 50% of the base salary for most workers but it may be substantially higher for lower-paid personnel. In Indonesia, the only fringes stipulated by law are two weeks of annual vacations, national holidays, sick leave and maternity leave with pay, severance compensation and, upon termination or retirement, long-service pay. Most firms routinely provide an additional bonus of one month's base salary or more to employees each year.

The Department of Religious Affairs decrees official holidays on an annual basis. Thirteen days of public holidays are recognized in Indonesia. Legislation determines the annual leave period. Employees are entitled to a maximum leave of 12 working days with full wages after 12 months' continuous service, and this is forfeited unless taken within six months of being earned. Other fringe benefits are determined through individual negotiation or collective bargaining. These usually include family and cost-of-living allowances, free medical, and sometimes dental, care for the worker and his or her family, extra rice allowances for the worker's family (in addition to any ration the worker receives as part of his or her base wage), housing and transportation, or allowances in lieu thereof, and work clothes. Many firms have pension plans.

To avoid administrative red tape, many foreign investors pay higher cash wages in an attempt to avoid payment in kind completely and to minimize major fringe benefit costs, such as housing and transportation. Top personnel frequently enjoy additional benefits, including paid home and local leave, housing and company cars. The Minister of Women's Affairs, Mien Sugandhik, has recently advocated extended maternity leave from three to four months to allow a longer nursing period for mothers, in line with World Health Organization recommendations. However, critics object that the extended leave would discourage employers from hiring women. Also, employees expect to receive an additional bonus of one month's base salary or more prior to the Lebaran holiday, and may resort to strike action if it is not forthcoming from management. (Lebaran is a 2-day Moslem holiday usually observed in March to mark the end of Ramadan, the month of fasting in February.)

In practice, it turns out that employers often apply much higher standards. In the financial sector, for example, salaries have risen rapidly over the past few years, and personnel piracy has become commonplace. For health care, employers contribute 6% for married employees and 3% for single workers, although the salary used for determining contributions is limed to 1 million rupiah per month. Benefits include outpatient treatment, inpatient treatment for seven days in the hospital, pregnancy and maternity care, diagnostic support, emergency treatment, and special services such as glasses, prostheses, and hearing aids. When a company provides more generous health insurance than that offered by the government, it is allowed to withdraw from the state health-care program.[10]

HOURS OF WORK

Labor legislation provides for a 7-hour working day, with a maximum work week of 44 hours. In practice, the week is usually 37 to 40 hours. After 4 hours of work, there must be a break of at least 30 minutes. Shift work is allowed. Overtime must be compensated at an extra 50% of the normal hourly wage for the first hour and an extra 100% after that, with double pay for Sundays and holidays for the first 7 hours and triple pay thereafter. Compulsory overtime is common for factory workers, particularly among those who live in company dormitories.

Normal office hours for white collar workers are from 8:00 A.M. to 4:00 P.M., with a one-hour break, from Monday to Friday and 8:00 A.M. to 1:00 P.M. on Saturday. A work week of five eight-hour days has become increasingly common. Regulations allow employers to deviate from the normal work hours upon request to the Minister of Manpower with the agreement of the employees.

HEALTH AND SAFETY

Companies in Indonesia are expected to maintain facilities to ensure the health and safety of their employees and to increase the efficiency and productivity of their labor force. The Safety Act of 1970 requires employers to provide protection against fires, industrial accidents, and defective building structures. Company owners and workers alike have been warned by the Department of Industrial Relations that they face court actions if they are found to be ignoring work safety requirements.

In the more profitable and largely Western-operated oil sector, safety and health programs function reasonably well. However, safety and health programs in the country's over 100,000 large firms in the nonoil sector are still hampered by the limited number of qualified inspectors from the Ministry of Manpower. Less than 1,300 inspectors have nationwide responsibility. Other problems include the delays in establishing the required plant safety committees, the need for more and better training of government inspectors and plant safety personnel, and the lack of worker appreciation for sound health and safety practices.

A National Health and Safety Council, an advisory body established under the auspices of the manpower ministry, was created in 1990 to oversee the enforcement efforts of over 6,000 company safety committees. Workers are obligated to report hazardous working conditions, and employers are prevented by law from retaliating against those who do, but in practice enforcement is weak.[11]

TERMINATION OF EMPLOYMENT

The manner in which an employee is separated from his or her job is regulated by law in Indonesia. Because of high unemployment, the government makes it extremely difficult for employers to discharge workers. There are many legal restraints on firing a worker who has been employed continuously for at least three months. Even if a production cutback is necessary or the worker is found to be unfit, he or she may not be discharged without the approval of the Department of Manpower, which requires that an agreement on severance pay be reached between employer and worker.

Termination payments usually amount to one month's wages for each year of service up to the first four years of employment, plus one month's wages for each subsequent five years of service, up to a maximum payment equivalent to nine months wages. In the event that management and the employee cannot agree on a specific arrangement and reach a deadlock, a tripartite regional labor disputes board renders an award. Appeals can be taken to the tripartite Central Labor Disputes Board (P4P), whose decision is final. Even when a company closes due to bankruptcy or other economic reasons, severance pay is required although in practice it often is not paid.

Many employers considering applicants for clerical positions and higher find it imperative to make clear in writing that the first few weeks of employment are on a trial basis only, thus avoiding the complications that can arise if an applicant does not fit the job. Indonesian law allows for a three-month probationary period at the beginning of employment. In any event, to avoid difficulties in firing workers, companies often pressure them to resign, offering severance pay well above the minimum legal requirements.

In the public sector, the law of termination favors the employee. In termination cases the parties must try to privately resolve the case before the employer may seek a mandatory dismissal permit from the regional disputes committee. Termination of more than 10 workers is considered a mass termination and requires permission from the central disputes committee. Generally, permits will not be granted in connection with union activity, the employee's religious beliefs, or other proscribed reasons.[12]

A cultural factor also enters the picture in termination decisions. Even when management is contemplating the removal of an employee for substandard performance, the decision often follows careful deliberations because the company is considered to be an extended family. Hence, terminating workers rather than reassigning them to other tasks, does not fit well into such relationships.

CHILD LABOR

An employment area that continues to be a major problem in Indonesia concerns the utilization of child labor. The government acknowledges that there is a class of children under 14 years of age who, for socioeconomic reasons, must work, and notes that the child labor laws, which provide detailed safeguards, have not been fully enforced.

Employers are supposed to report in detail on every child employed, and the Ministry of Manpower is authorized to carry out periodic inspections. Employers not complying with the law and regulations are legally subject to fines of $65 and/or up to three months in jail for each infraction, but the government still relies on persuasion and teaching employers rather than penalizing them. The Manpower Ministry admits that employer compliance with regulations is inadequate, with less than 50% of companies employing children having registered, and that it still lacks enough qualified inspectors to carry out inspections. Observers claim that more than 2 million children under the age of 14 are working half- to full-time, mostly in family-run businesses in the informal sector and at agricultural sites, where enforcement is difficult. Efforts to control child labor focus primarily on instituting educational programs for working children.

Special protections exist for children aged 7 to 14 and such employment must be with the permission of the child's parent or guardian. Employers are required to ensure that these children have access to a junior high school education within the framework of the compulsory schooling law. The Department of Manpower conducts periodic inspections and can impose sanctions for violations. Dangerous work and night work are specifically forbidden. Work is limited to four hours daily at the prevailing wage rate.[13]

FORCED LABOR

Compulsory or forced labor is prohibited by law. However, in 1990 credible reports asserted that military and civilian officials in Irian Java cooperated with Jakarta-based timber companies to compel Asmat tribespeople to cut down trees and transport them downstream to waiting ships, and the government resettlement program raised serious questions of informed consent. There were also documented reports of labor contractors in Jakarta selling girls as domestic servants or to brothels near plantations, and of men sold as agricultural workers. The government response was that it was investigating the allegations but the results of its inquiry were not revealed either in 1990 or 1991.

RETIREMENT PROGRAMS

The provision of adequate income during the retirement period of life is an important concern in Indonesia, as in all nations, and the scope and type of private and public pension programs therefore is an important aspect of national policy. In this regard, there are 521 licensed pension funds, consisting of 508 employer-managed funds and 13 independent pension plans. In terms of ownership, 107 of these were state pension funds and 417 private pension funds.

Most of these funds are small, with only 5% of Indonesian citizens registered in such arrangements. The total assets of all funds amount to about $9 billion, the largest being state enterprise pension funds, TASPEN, for civil servants, and ASTEK, for noncivil servants. Both are administered as limited liability companies. As with insurance funds, Indonesian pension funds are not permitted to invest abroad.

The great majority of pension funds are owned and operated by foundations, under a legal structure derived from 19th century Dutch commercial law. These foundations were tax exempt until the beginning of 1995, when new legislation was introduced. Before then, neither audits nor financial statements were required. As a result, little information about the disposition of pension funds was publicly available. Exceptions are the civil service and armed forces pension funds, which operate as limited liability enterprises.

Earlier, a regulatory framework for the operation of pension funds was established through a 1992 statute permitting the establishment of two types of pension funds: employer-managed and independent. Employer-managed pension funds may invest in securities to a maximum of 10% of every issuance of each security. Investment in money-market securities is not to exceed 10% of total pension fund assets, while investments in time deposits and certificates of deposit may be placed only with a bank that is neither the founder nor affiliated with the founder of the pension fund. The 1992 law requires any company that has promised retirement benefits to set up a pension fund registered with the Ministry of Finance.

The significance of pension arrangements, of course, increases as a nation's population ages. In Indonesia, an increase in life expectancy to around 65 to 68 years suggests fairly rapid growth in the 65-plus age group. It has been suggested that in countries where family and village ties are much more important than in developed countries, the social burden of an aging population should not increase significantly Furthermore, as nutrition and health services continue to improve, increases in life expectancy are expected to continue as well, with a growing proportion of the population reaching retirement age. This is unlikely to create much extra demand for social services as long as the tradition of caring for the aged within family units remains constant. However, should the extended family structure, so familiar in Asia, give way to the nuclear family, as has been the case in many Western nations, private resources for caring for retired and aged persons may not be sufficient, and public responsibility for such care may be necessitated.[14]

SOCIAL SECURITY

When various forms of economic deprivation are encountered in Western societies, a social security safety net is in place in most of them to provide at least a subsistence level of existence. Indonesia is derelict in this area, for it does not have a comprehensive social security system. The culture of this island nation dictates that employers are expected to adopt a paternal role and are responsible for the health and well-being of employees and their families. Unemployment and sickness benefits do not exist at the national level. There is, however, the government social insurance program known as ASTEK, which went into effect in 1978 and is mandatory for any privately owned domestic or foreign enterprise, public undertakings (PERUM), state operating companies (PERSERO), or any other state-owned firms with more than 10 workers or a monthly payroll exceeding RP 1 million. In an attempt to bring more workers under the umbrella of ASTEK, this standard is periodically revised downward.

In 1990 ASTEK, formerly a state-owned limited public corporation (PERUM) was converted into a state-operating company. The government felt this new status which allowed the firm to make profits, invest, and act more in a commercial manner would increase its effectiveness and efficiency.

For some time ASTEK has experimented with several other programs. A voluntary workers' health insurance program was initiated in 1985 and is in place in 19 cities. At the end of 1990 a total of 594 firms employing 145,000 workers had subscribed to the program.

There is an accident insurance program, with premiums for accident insurance amounting to 0.24–1.74% of wages, depending on the industry. A worker who suffers an industrial injury is entitled to be reimbursed for transportation costs to the hospital and for first aid, outpatient charges, rehabilitation expenses, temporary disability, partial or permanent disability, and, in the worst case, death. In the event of injury, a worker receives 100% of his or her salary for the first 120 days and 50% thereafter. The plan pays 100% of medical costs at hospitals or public health centers.

Life insurance coverage is also available, with premiums that employers pay amounting to 0.3% of wages and benefits up to 700,000 rupiah per worker.

For the retirement scheme, the employer contributes 3.7% of wages and the employee contributes 2%. If the participant dies prior to retirement for any reason except an occupational accident, beneficiaries may claim a life insurance benefit and a burial allowance.

The All Indonesian Workers' Union (SPSI) has criticized the government for failing to make social security provisions mandatory and for falling below the level of social security legislation in neighboring countries.[15]

FREEDOM OF ASSOCIATION REQUIREMENTS

A much prized worker right is being allowed to join a labor organization of one's choosing without government restrictions. As noted previously, Indonesian workers rights in this respect are limited since the only recognized labor organization is SPSI. Private sector employees, including those in export-processing zones, are free to form or join SPSI local unions without previous authorization, but in order to bargain on behalf of its members, a union must meet the requirements for legal recognition and register with the Ministry of Manpower. The SPSI claims to have about 10,000 local plant-level units.

Unions draw up their own constitutions and rules and elect their representatives while under close government scrutiny and subject to government approval prior to registration. Less than 6% of the estimated 80 million-strong labor force is organized.

Government approval is required for meetings held outside union headquarters and this permission is routinely given. A union may be dissolved if the government believes it is acting against Pancasila. There are no laws or regulations spelling out the procedures for dissolution, and there have been no reported cases of union dissolution. The SPSI is free to maintain contacts with international labor organizations.[16]

REGULATORY CHANGES

During 1992 and early 1993, the government made two significant changes in the regulatory environment for unions. The first change in October 1992 repealed the regulation which dealt with a "Manual for the Establishment, Maintaining Relationship and Development of a Labor Union within the Company," and substituted it with a regulation which provided for a replacement "Manual on the Formation and Establishment of Worker Unions in Companies." The second change in February 1993 repealed the regulation on "Labor Organization's Registration," and replaced it with a rule "Concerning Registration of Worker Organizations."

The two regulatory changes were made to accommodate the planned formation of independent sectoral unions and restructuring of the SPSI. From a legalistic perspective, the most significant reason for the rescission of the 1986 manual was that it defined a union as a component of the SPSI. This provision would have been inconsistent with the establishment of independent industrial unions envisioned in the restructuring plan for the SPSI. According to senior SPSI leaders, there were two other serious deficiencies to the Manual. It required workers to consult with management prior to the formation of a company-level union and it specified criteria for election to union office. In reality the requirement for consultation was interpreted as necessitating employer agreement to the setting up of a company union, which was often not granted, while the criteria were used by employers to influence if not determine the selection of union officials. Employers would claim only they had sufficient knowledge of the educational background and abilities of workers to ensure the Manual's criteria were met. Because of this, many current SPSI factory units are led by individuals selected by employers and who have little credibility with their units' members.

The new guidelines eliminate the reference to the SPSI in the definition of a union, instead defining a union as "a workers' organization based on the type of work and which possess management structures at the company, branch, area, and national levels." Consultation with management is no longer required; management must only be informed of the workers' decision to form a union and the workers may proceed if they hear nothing from management after 14 days. Finally, the criteria for election to union office have been reduced. The guidelines require union officials to have been employed by the company for one year, or less if the company has not been in operation for a year, and "have a good work record consistent with the specification of the union."

The guidelines, however, continue to establish structural parameters for unions. Unions must be industrial, based on the "type of work," and they must have a hierarchical structure with components at the work site, branch, district, and national levels.

The 1987 regulation on union registration imposed significant organizational prerequisites on unions in order to receive recognition from the Department of Manpower. In order to be recognized, a union was required to have branches in at least 20 provinces, 100 districts, and 1000 companies. These requirements effectively imposed an almost insuperable obstacle to the formation of new unions. The new regulation considerably reduces these requirements. It requires, as a condition for recognition, that a union possess 100 work site branches, 25 district organizations, and at least five regional organization. For workers confined to only a single or a few geographic areas because of the nature of the work, e.g., mining, a union must have at least 10,000 members to obtain recognition. However, although these requirements are less onerous than those promulgated in 1987, they still are in conflict with freedom of association standards as interpreted by the International Labor Organization. In addition, another 1993 regulation requires that a union be set up "by and for workers." The Department of Manpower interprets this clause to deny recognition to groups in which it considers nonworkers, such as lawyers or human rights activists, are involved as organizers.

Despite the apparent easing of the regulations on union registration, there is, de facto, a single union system. It is the government's stated policy to seek to improve the effectiveness of the recognized SPSI unions rather than ease the process for the formation of alternative organizations. The only unions recognized by the Department of Manpower are those which previously constituted the SPSI's industrial sectors. The Minister of Manpower has stated that any unions which form in the future should affiliate with the SPSI federation and that the government will not recognize any unions outside the federation.

In January 1994, the government made two further regulatory changes. The first established the right of workers to form company unions. In addition to establishing company unions, this regulation reverts to the old practice of defining a union as the SPSI. The second replaced three previous ministerial decisions relating to settling labor disputes. The principal result of the new regulation was to take off the books a clause which suggested that local Department of Manpower officials, when confronted with a labor dispute, coordinate with the local security forces. This clause was often used to justify calling in the armed forces whenever there was a strike. The effect of this change in terms of military involvement remains to be seen. In a speech to the annual SPSI national leadership meeting in December 1993, the Commander-in-Chief of the Indonesian armed forces noted that the role of the military in labor matters is controlled by a 1990 regulation which permits the military and its intelligence services to become involved in labor issues at any stage in the issues' development.

THE RIGHT TO ORGANIZE AND BARGAIN COLLECTIVELY

Collective bargaining is provided for by law, but only registered trade unions can engage in it. The Ministry of Manpower supports the collective bargaining concept as an instrument of industrial relations in accordance with Pancasila. The overwhelming majority of the SPSI's collective bargaining agreements are negotiated and concluded bilaterally with employers. Once notified that 25 employees have joined a registered union, the employer is under an obligation to bargain. As a transitional stage to encourage collective bargaining, regulations require that every company which has 25 or more workers must issue company regulations defining the terms and conditions of employment. Before a company can register or renew its company regulations, it must demonstrate that it has consulted with a committee consisting of employer and employee representatives, in the absence of a union.

The degree to which these agreements are freely negotiated between unions and management without government interference varies. By regulation, negotiations are to be concluded within 30 days. If not, the matter is submitted to the Ministry of Manpower for mediation and arbitration. In practice, most negotiations are concluded within the 30-day period. Agreements are for two years and can be extended for an additional year.

Negotiations usually take place at the plant level among management, government representatives, and workers and cover wages, fringe benefits, and working conditions. The government requires that firms with more than 25 employees issue company regulations, including details of wages, proposed pay increases, fringe benefits, and protection for labor. Revised labor agreements are then filed with the appropriate office of the Ministry of Manpower.

The Department of Manpower and the SPSI agree that only about half of the claimed 10,000 company units have collective bargaining agreements and both have expressed disappointment over the slow progress being made in increasing the number of collective agreements, company regulations, and SPSI units. The major contributing factors, they recognize, are the lack of worker familiarity with trade union practices, employer resistance, employee apathy, and employee fear of possible employer retaliation.

Regulations expressly forbid employers from prejudging or harassing employees because of union membership, and employees have been urged to report harassment to the government. The SPSI claims that some employers discriminate against its members and those wishing to form SPSI units.

If collective bargaining agreements cannot be reached through negotiation, workers are allowed to strike. In practice, however, there has never been a "legal" strike in Indonesia. Workers assume that demands for consensus settlement of a dispute will leave them with few real gains. They also run the risk of dismissal if plans to strike are discovered in advance.

Indonesia has for many years been the subject of complaints in the ILO regarding the ban on organizing public sector unions, insufficient protection against antiunion discrimination, restrictions on the registration of trade unions and collective bargaining, and the exercise of the right to strike. At present, Indonesian law still does not conform with the requirements of ILO Convention 98, which Indonesia has ratified, and which guarantees the right to organize and bargain collectively.[17]

THE RIGHT TO STRIKE AND DISPUTE SETTLEMENT

In August 1990 Indonesia repealed a controversial 1963 presidential decree which prohibited strikes and lockouts in vital industries, services, and enterprises. The decree, although reportedly never implemented, was theoretically applicable to about 170,000 persons. The press, however, treated the announcement as a government endorsement of the right to strike, coming as it did in the midst of extensive coverage of work stoppages and strikes. Workers, in general, influenced by the reporting, took this development as a sign that they now had a right to strike, though this has always been the case for the majority of Indonesian workers.

Before a strike can occur in the private sector, the law requires intensive mediation by the Ministry of Manpower and prior notice regarding intentions to strike or lockout. Because of these requirements, most disputes are settled through deliberation and consensus. Most strikes are brief, spontaneous and nonviolent. The SPSI's Executive Board believes that strikes almost never serve the interests of workers who are as poor and hard pressed by unemployment as those in Indonesia. It also strongly agrees with the government that strikes disrupt harmony and social cooperation, basic Indonesian values which are also essential to national development.

The SPSI company units tend to take the opposite view and often, without consultation with the SPSI Executive Board, encourage concerted activity. Public employees do not have a right to strike. The central board of KORPRI and its secretariats at all provincial levels have established the Employee Relations Bureau, which is responsible for settling labor disputes. By law, a separate disputes resolution and appeals process exists for civil servants in the event of a labor dispute.[18]

Many strikes and protests take place in support of fired union officials. Charges of antiunion discrimination are handled by the administrative tribunals. Many union members believe that the tribunals generally side with the employer. Because of this perceived partiality, many workers reject or avoid the process and present their disputes before the Parliament and other agencies.

It turns out that in practice there are no clear, established procedures regarding the settlement of disputes although a system of compulsory arbitration is usually applied in labor disputes if mediation proves to be unsuccessful.[19] The government is reviewing Indonesia's labor legislation, most of which dates to the 1950s. The current major legislation deals with industrial safety (a 1951 law); industrial relations (1954/1978); labor disputes (1951); severance conditions and payments (1964/1978); the employment of foreigners (1958); wages (1981); and social security and insurance (1992). The government issued a number of new regulations in 1993 and 1994 that expanded or modified these labor laws.[20]

RIGHTS AND STANDARDS—THE REALITY

Table 9-1 presents a breakdown of items commonly included under labor standards. Those labeled "basic rights" include standards where a global consensus seems to have been attained and which are thus amenable to international monitoring. The final category, civil rights, encompasses standards which have also come to be accepted as consensual by democratic nations. While agreement on the latter is less broad, it is sufficiently widespread to justify requiring governments, especially those which claim to be democratic, to observe them.

The intermediate categories, survival and security rights, depend for their implementation on local conditions and do not lend themselves readily to fixed international standards. They are best left to bargaining between workers, employers, and governments, once basic and civil rights have been fully implemented. Negative consequences associated with premature importation of labor standards to developing

TABLE 9-1
Types of Labor Standards

Type	Examples
I. Basic rights	Right against use of child labor
	Right against involuntary servitude
	Right against physical coercion
II. Survival rights	Right to a living wage
	Right to accident compensation
	Right to a limited work week
III. Security rights	Right against arbitrary dismissal
	Right to retirement compensation
	Right to survivors' compensation
IV. Civic rights	Right to free expression
	Right to collective representation
	Right to free expression of grievances

Source: Alejandro Portes (1990). "When more can be less, labor standards, development and the informal economy." In Labor Standards and Development in the Global Economy. Stephen Herzenberg and Jorge F. Perez-Lopez (Eds.). Washington, DC: U.S. Department of Labor.

countries such as Indonesia have involved primarily these intermediate categories, and not those which could plausibly form part of an internationally accepted package of labor rights.

Of the two middle categories, it is the implementation of extensive job security, rather than the existence of a minimum wage or other survival rights, which have created the greater resistance. Hence, apart from basic and civil rights which may become amenable to internationally enforceable standards, the implementation of others also require fine tuning, lest they act as a brake on economic growth or on the extension of minimal protection to the greatest number of people. There is reason to doubt the popular dictum that developing nations function best when wages are allowed to sink to their "natural" levels. Firms that rely on very cheap labor lack incentives to innovate technologically and their workers lack the motivation to remain with a particular firm or collaborate with management in increasing its efficiency. Their paltry wages also add insignificantly to domestic demand.

It is therefore necessary to ask what labor standards can be applied that combine effective protection for the greatest number with the implementation of successful plans for national development. The question suggests part of the answer, namely the need to fine tune the application of labor standards to local conditions, rather than opt for either their wholesale rejection or acceptance.

Chapter 10

Labor Disputes and International Pressures

Significant developments in Indonesian industrial relations in the 1990s have been discussed in preceding chapters. Strikes, repression of independent unions and labor activists, the role of the military in labor disputes, the threatened suspension of trading privileges, and concerns expressed by international organizations have drawn our attention earlier in summary form. In this chapter the importance of these events will be explored in greater detail to determine their impact on worker rights and labor standards.

Strikes and Their Aftermath—1991–94

In Indonesia, while Pancasila principles call for labor–management differences to be settled by consensus, all organized workers with the exception of civil servants, have a legal right to strike. However, before a strike can occur in the private sector, the law requires intensive mediation by the Ministry of Manpower and prior notice regarding the intent to strike. Most disputes are settled through negotiation and consensus, due in part at least to fear of police and employer retaliation. In 1991 there was a significant increase in the number of strikes, in some cases triggering the intervention of the military or police who were called to the strike locations. The nature of military and police involvement at work stoppage sites was varied. Most often the security forces limited themselves to protecting property and preventing violence, although there were reports of conscious attempts to intimidate strikers. Their mere presence no doubt had a dampening effect on the willingness of workers to pursue strike or other protest activity.

During 1992 and through 1993, the number of strikes continued to increase. The majority of strikes were caused by worker demands for minimum wages. However, other prominent demands included the formation of SPSI units, compliance with regulations relating to overtime payments, maternity and menstrual leave, and, during the Muslim holiday of Labaran, the traditional bonus tendered at this time. In a statement to the DPR, the lower house of the Indonesian legislature, the head of the

SPSI claimed that in Java alone there were 344 strikes in 1992 and 343 in 1993. He attributed previous lower government figures to the fact there are insufficient Department of Manpower offices to keep track of all the work stoppages in the country. The head of the Tripartite Commission for East Java, a government industrial relations advisory body with members from employers, the SPSI, and government, stated that in 1993 in the province of East Java there were 183 cases of strikes involving the loss of 645,000 work hours. During the first two months of 1994, the Jakarta region alone was hit by a wave of strikes, precipitated primarily by the failure of firms to pay the new minimum wage. Although no official figures were available, it is likely the number of strikes nationwide during this period approached 150.

The government's reaction to the increasing frequency of strikes was mixed. Initially, in 1992, the then Minister of Labor, Cosmas Batubara, indicated that the government understood the reasons for the industrial actions since the demands of workers were "normative," meaning the demands were aimed to obtain rights to which they were legally entitled, such as the minimum wage. Later in the year, especially in the fourth quarter of 1992, government statements suggested the involvement of "third parties" in the strikes and the possible involvement of foreign parties. Several government spokesman referred to the existence of a "dalang," the puppeteer in the traditional Javanese shadow play, who they alleged was manipulating workers, especially in the large Jakarta industrial suburb of Tangerang.

Many strikes occur suddenly and without prior attempts to resolve problems and may not be included in official statistics. There were a few reports of employer retaliation against strike leaders, but this seemed to be the exception rather than the rule. Most strikes were settled relatively quickly and all the workers returned to their jobs. Strike outcomes varied: In some cases employers quickly complied with worker demands that salaries be increased to the legal minimum wage. Others were less successful, with workers returning to work with only partial gains or none at all.

Since the April 1994 Medan riots, the minimum wage is more generally paid but there have been dozens of small strikes and there is still no credible channel to resolve labor disputes. As a 22-year-old worker at a shrimp exporter said, "We need to strike to get anything." She is paid the minimum wage, and spends about half for rent and food. She has only contempt for the only recognized union, the SPSI: "They work for the company, not the laborers."[1]

According to Table 10-1, Indonesia over the five-year period of 1990–94, recorded 905 strikes involving nearly 480,000 workers. The figures indicate that the work stoppages caused a loss of over 3 million production hours. The government laid the blame at the feet of the management of those enterprises that had failed to accommodate their workers' rights in regard to minimum wages, leave, and social security allowances.

An interesting disparity developed between government strike data and the figures furnished by SPSI during the 1992–94 period. The union figures were double those revealed by the government. Two possible interpretations are suggested to explain the differences: Either the government deliberately understated the incidence of strikes to minimize their significance, or the lone state-controlled labor organiza-

TABLE 10-1
Indonesian Strike Figures, 1990–94

	Strikes reported by Ministry of Manpower	SPSI[b]
1990	61	na
1991	130	na
1992	251	344
1993	185	343
1994	278	1,130
	Workers involved[a]	Work hours lost[a]
1990	31,234	262,014
1991	64,530	582,477
1992	143,000	1,019,654
1993	103,490	966,931
1994	136,699	226,940

Source: [a]Ministry of Manpower, Jakarta, Indonesia; and SPSI.[b]

tion was directed to inflate the figures to create the perception of a semblance of independence from government control.

The heightened incidence of labor disputes apparently did not impress the Indonesian ambassador to Australia when he declared that the right to strike was a reform Indonesia would never consider:

> This is really the worst-case scenario for us. Based on Indonesian cultural traditions, the right to strike is false. I do not see why there is a need to strike when the government is on the side of the laborers. Right now, the priority for Indonesia is to increase its exports. This is a matter of life and death for us.[3]

On several occasions in 1991, the Minister of Manpower said the strikes were the result of workers' increasing awareness of their legal rights. During the first 11 months of that year, there were 112 officially recorded work stoppages. Most of these were unauthorized wildcat strikes, and so technically illegal, but there were no reports of strike leaders or workers being prosecuted for conducting them.

The largest strike, involving approximately 12,000 workers engaged in the manufacture of automobile tires in the industrial area west of Jakarta, prompted the Minister of Political Affairs and Security to charge that "would-be heroes" and other unnamed parties were behind this and other strikes.[3]

A February strike by employees of a Korean shoe manufacturer was unusual, because it was permitted by the government. The workers were on a solid legal footing since they had walked out in protest at not being paid the legal minimum wage.[4] Seventy-six percent of strikes in 1991 were over wages and another 8% over the right to form unions. Interestingly, most were in industries with above-average earnings, reflecting new demands by younger and better educated Indonesian workers.[5]

In another labor dispute, approximately 3,000 workers from three textile factories in Tangerang, West Java, went on strike to demand higher pay and better allowances. Some 1,000 of the strikers went to the Tangerang Regional Council to complain about low daily salaries, daily transport allowances, and annual bonuses, as well as poor quality daily meals. The factories only paid the workers RP 100 ($0.04) daily transport allowance, RP 3,000 ($1.40) annual bonus, and RP 500 ($0.25) for daily meals. The workers complained that these payments were too low to meet their demands. The striking workers also alleged that the factories charged them for treatment from company doctors and refused to cover their medical expenses if they sought help from other physicians. The strikers prepared to negotiate their demands with company executives, but management refused. Then the angry strikers began to damage factory equipment, including windows and doors.

After the Manpower Ministry stipulated a minimum salary of RP 2,600 ($1.20) per day beginning September 1, 1992, these factories raised the daily salary in line with the ministry's decree, but cut down the operational allowance. By so doing, the actual income of the workers remained the same, not showing any improvement. After the change in payment, an official from the manpower office said the companies had not violated the regulation on minimum payment. In the strikes, workers in the three textile factories refused to allow the companies' labor unions to become involved in the negotiations, accusing them of defending the companies' interests, not those of the workers. Tangerang is a recently opened special economic area with most factories being joint ventures or export-oriented enterprises, and is regarded as a very strike-prone region.[6]

In another incident, also in Tangerang, 1,000 angry workers demanding better working conditions set fire to several buildings and cars at a South Korean footwear factory. The striking workers were angry because they were receiving only RP 2,100 ($1.02) for a 10-hour workday when Indonesian labor law stipulated a 7-hour workday. Workers complained of being forced to work 10-hour days for the minimum wage of RP 2,100.

Responding to these worker concerns, in July 1992 the government effectively raised the minimum wage in Jakarta and surrounding areas from RP 2,100 per day to RP 2,600 per day. However, reports indicated that worker demonstrations increased fourfold in the week following the wage increase, in part due to the hesitancy of employers to adopt the new minimum wage rules.

In late September, 5,000 factory workers at a South Korean factory which produced sports shoes in Serang, West Java, staged demonstrations that led to rioting and the destruction of company property. The strikers reported they were angered when the company failed to provide transportation and other allowances to the company's employees.

The largest strike occurred in October and involved about 8,000 workers at five garment factories in Tangerang when workers walked off their jobs to force the company to meet the government's new minimum wage guidelines. Managers defended their actions, saying they needed more time to meet company owners to discuss the new wage guidelines and their implementation. The government faulted employers for failing to speedily raise the workers' wages to comply with the new wage standards. The labor minister pointed out that companies were implementing wage increases once labor demonstrations threatened to halve factory production. He contended companies could minimize worker walkouts by acting quickly to raise the level of workers' payments. A lack of better defined labor guidelines for the implementation of worker wages and clear-cut methods for evaluating management compliance led to abuses by some firms. However, stiff competition from other Asian countries in the race to attract foreign investment encouraged the Indonesian government to maintain a cheap labor force as an incentive to investors to locate their production facilities in Indonesia.[7]

As strikes in industrial areas increased, workers went so far as to approach the Indonesian parliament for help. In one instance, more than 200 workers employed at a factory owned by Manpower Minister Abdul Latief complained to parliament members that the company had violated wage agreements, intimidated union organizers, and refused to allow them to form a union branch. Latief later said that the management of the company would settle the dispute in a fair and peaceful manner.

Newspaper editorials criticized the army, which sometimes intervened and broke up demonstrations by workers on the grounds that they were disturbing security.[8] Most of the more than 300 strikes in Indonesia in 1992 occurred at South Korean firms, followed by Japanese and Taiwanese companies. Most strikes were in the garment and textile industries. The shoe manufacturing industry came second, followed by the electronics industry. In 1992 a total of 152 strikes broke out in industrial areas in West Java, 108 in East Java, 58 in Jakarta, and 21 in Central Java.[9]

Executives at PT Kahatex, a shoe and textile factory in Bandung, 80 miles southeast of Jakarta, said 2000 strikers went back to work after two days of violent protest in which cars were burned and offices ransacked. It was the most violent of a strike wave hitting major cities during a one-week period. They were the latest of some 185 strikes in the November 1993 to January 1994 period. "I am surprised it has been so intensive. But it's logical when you think about it. Firms have been slow to implement the minimum wage, while awareness among workers of the government legislation has been growing," stated Chris Manning, an Australian labor economist.[10] The leaders of a three-day strike at Hong Kong bank branches in Jakarta in January 1994 said they were confident that the Indonesian government would pressure the bank's management into meeting a demand that the bank pay the employees' income taxes. If the demand was met, it would represent an increase of 15 to 25% in the employees' base pay. In return for the bank's concession, strikers would drop three demands: a 6% increase in base pay; better retirement benefits; and the inclusion in annual bonuses of a medical allowance which would be a fixed sum paid annually regardless of whether or not employees required treatment. The bank offered a 3.5% increase in basic pay in addition to a cost-of-living allowance, inflation adjustment, and merit increase. As a result of the strike, one of the bank's two branches in Jakarta was closed.[11]

THE MEDAN RIOTS

In what were the worst outbreaks of labor unrest, protesters ran riot through factories in Medan, a northwestern Indonesia industrial center, in mid-April 1994, tearing apart a doll clothes factory and wrecking cars in the sixth day of labor-related protests. Labor activists said two of their leaders had been arrested and their branches across Indonesia were warned against launching sympathy strikes. "Many of our branch leaders were approached by soldiers making threats and frightening them into not taking part in actions, particularly in the Jakarta area," said one unionist at the independent Indonesia Labor Welfare Union, or SBSI.[12] The SBSI organized Medan's initial strike.

After an uneasy calm in the wake of the riots, in which at least one person was killed and more than 100 people arrested, violence flared again in Medan and its outlying industrial districts. Several factories in Tanjung Morawa, southeast of Medan, were badly damaged after unknown groups of youths climbed fences and gates to attack factories which had resumed production. A doll clothes factory was gutted while a motorcycle spare parts manufacturer was also damaged; elsewhere, cars were destroyed. Labor activists claimed 10,000 workers and 20 factories in the industrial district north of Medan remained on strike, while witnesses said that some protestors appeared to be intimidating those who returned to work.

A total of 101 people were arrested following the protest in Medan but some of them were released later. Police and soldiers remained on alert in the industrial areas because workers refused to return to work. Mass protests then began with workers demanding higher wages and an investigation into the unexplained death of a colleague in a similar demonstration in early March.

The Medan outbreak quickly turned into an antiethnic Chinese protest and one member of that community was clubbed to death after he allegedly rejected demands to pay the legal minimum wage to workers in his factory.

Ethnic Chinese, comprising some 3% of Indonesia's population, are often the focus of resentment by the Muslim majority because of their perceived economic prowess.

In mid-October 1994, a new upsurge of labor unrest embarrassed the Suharto regime as it prepared to host November's Asian Pacific Economic Conference (APEC). A strike by 4,000 workers began at an Adidas shoe factory near Jakarta, while the head of SBSI was sentenced to eight months' jail for "incitement." The Adidas strike was the largest work stoppage since 50,000 workers demonstrated in April in Medan, the country's third largest city.[13]

Overall, for 1994, strikes in Indonesia more than doubled in number, to 1130 cases because companies failed to meet standard working conditions such as payment of the minimum wage. An SPSI official said the number of strikes rose 260%

compared with 312 labor disputes in 1993. He claimed the upsurge in strike actions across the archipelago was caused by employers failing to pay not only the minimum wage but overtime and holiday pay to workers. The average minimum wage at that time was less than RP 4200 ($2) per day.[14]

The minimum wage was substantially increased in April 1995. This did not affect most Western companies, which paid more than the minimum requirement and were thus not affected. However, many local firms paid below the minimum level or cut workers' benefits. The 1994 strike totals set a record and labor strife was predicted to continue in 1995.[15] This prediction proved erroneous since work stoppages lessened noticeably, at least in the first quarter of that year.

THE SCENE IN 1995

The change to a comparatively more peaceful industrial relations situation in 1995 was brought about principally by a no-nonsense attitude on the part of the government, which stepped up policing and warned employers of stricter penalties in the offing should they fail to comply with obligations to pay new wage rates and provide welfare and other worker benefits. The 1994 incidents, in fact, provided the authorities with greater leverage on a number of fronts.

No less a person than President Suharto warned employers of the need to conform to legal requirements. He pointed to the strikes and the Medan riots as examples of what could happen should employers fail to comply.[16] However, there were a number of labor disputes that occurred in 1995. For example, approximately 6,000 workers at a garment factory in a village near Jakarta rallied in protest, demanding better employment conditions. Workers at the Great River Company walked 4 kilometers from their factory in Nangewer in Bogor Regency to the regional House of Representative building. However, dozens of riot police stopped the workers, mostly women, before they could enter the gate of the building. The situation became heated when several female workers managed to break through the police barricade.

Police immediately arrested 13 workers, two of them women. There was no information as to where the arrested workers were taken. The female workers demanded that their employer grant their rights of work leave during menstruation and an annual paid holiday, as stipulated by Indonesian labor law. According to the law, every female employee of either private or state firms has the right to take two days of leave during monthly menstruation. The law also states every worker should be granted 12 paid holidays annually for those who have worked less than three years, and at least one month of paid holidays per year for employees who have worked at a company for more than three years. The factory where the unrest occurred is owned by a daughter of President Suharto.[17]

Several weeks later, a group of Indonesian workers staged what appeared to be the first successful strike against the ban on beards. Some 2,000 workers at the Hintex textile factory, 110 miles southeast of Jakarta, went on strike following the introduction of a ban on male moustaches and beards. After less than a day off work, the company rescinded its order.[18]

AN EARLY WARNING—THE IGGI COMPLAINT

The labor turmoil described above did not go unnoticed on the world scene as the international community noted the developments in Indonesia. International attention was particularly focused on the absence of free, independent labor organizations as Western nations spoke out about the labor abuses in Indonesia and encouraged the Suharto regime to allow freedom of association.

Specifically, a group that had lent Jakarta $4.6 billion in 1991 noted its displeasure at events in the island nation. Johannes Pronk, chairman of the Inter-Governmental Group on Indonesia, which groups rich countries and institutions offering Jakarta cheap loans each year, said IGGI members should support unions in Indonesia as they do at home: "The only solution is to have stronger labour unions which are free labour unions, not controlled labour unions."[19]

The Indonesian government position was that the SPSI was all the country needed, although workers who called the group toothless said they did not like the fact that its leadership is dominated by former military officers. The government refused to recognize the Solidarity Free Trade Union established in 1990. Solidarity activists were arrested following marches to Parliament by workers complaining their employers abused labor regulations. International labor activists entered the fray, claiming that industrial nations anxious to secure major communications and other contracts in Indonesia's dynamic economy more or less ignored labor abuses like pitiful wages, forced overtime, and illegal child labor. Some of the worst offenders are Asian-owned factories which publicized low labor costs in order to secure lucrative contracts from major U.S. shoe makers like Nike or Reebok, according to the activists. In addition to multilateral institutions, the 21-member IGGI is dominated by Japan, Western European nations, and the United States.

THE GENERALIZED SYSTEM OF PREFERENCES (GSP)

An example of international pressure directed against Indonesian labor practices involves what is known as the generalized system of preferences (GSP) program of the United States, under which qualifying developing nations may export specific categories of goods duty free to the United States. In 1984, Congress added new mandatory eligibility criteria for beneficiary countries, including performance standards in the area of internationally recognized worker rights. The amendment authorized the President of the United States to withhold preferences from any country deemed not to be "taking steps" to observe internationally recognized worker rights. The worker rights specified in the law are based on widely subscribed ILO conventions and cover five broad areas:

1. The right of association;
2. The right to organize and to bargain collectively;
3. The prohibition of forced labor;
4. Minimum age for employment of children; and
5. Acceptable conditions of work with respect to minimum wages, hours of work, and occupational health and safety.

A review process is used to determine foreign nations' qualifications for preferential access to the American market. The GSP aid program allows certain goods from developing countries to enter the United States with zero tariffs, as though they were made domestically by American workers, in order to assist workers in some of the poorest countries on earth. The standard to be used in assessing a country's performance is a relative one and should be commensurate with the country's stage of development. Developing countries are not expected to demonstrate the level of labor standards prevailing in the United States and other highly industrialized nations.

INDONESIAN GSP PARTICIPATION

Indonesia has participated in the GSP program since its inception in 1976. In 1992, approximately 14.8% of Indonesia's exports to the United States entered duty free under the GSP program. Normal duties, that would be payable if the country or products did not qualify for GSP on the major tariff categories utilized by Indonesia, range from 2.8 to 11%, with most products falling in the 3 to 7% range.

In terms of value, in 1992 Indonesia exported to the United States $1.151 billion worth of goods that are on the list of GSP-eligible products, but only $643 million worth of Indonesian goods entered the United States duty free under the program. Of the remaining $508 million, competitive need limits restrictions prevented $302 million worth of goods, mainly plywood, from entering duty free under GSP. "Administrative" duty was paid on the remaining $206 million worth of GSP-eligible products because the Indonesian exporters and/or U.S. importers did not complete the administrative requirements for these goods to enter under the program. In recent years, the share of GSP exports as a percentage of total Indonesian exports to the United States has grown. Table 10-2 depicts this trend.

INDONESIA AND PAST GSP REVIEWS

Indonesia has been the subject of petitions related to worker rights provisions of the GSP legislation in previous years. In June 1987, the American Federation of Labor-Congress of Industrial Organizations (AFL-CIO) filed a petition alleging that Indonesia was failing to observe internationally recognized worker rights. In April 1988, the president determined, after careful review, that Indonesia was taking steps to provide worker rights. In June 1988 the AFL-CIO filed a similar petition, which was

TABLE 10-2
Indonesia's Utilization of GSP, 1987–93

Year	Total exports (millions of U.S. $)	Duty free under GSP (millions of U.S. $)	GSP exports as % of total	% failed to utilize[a]
1987				
1988	3,719	49	1.5	n/a
1989	3,494	87	2.8	5
1990	3,542	148	4.2	n/a
1991	3,343	216	6.5	n/a
1992	3,238	276	8.5	11
Jan.–June	4,332	643	14.8	18
1993	2,427	417	17.0	13

[a]Percentage of products in GSP-eligible categories, but exporter and/or importer failed to apply for GSP duty-free status.
Source: Penduduk Indonesia, 1994.

rejected on the grounds that the petition failed to provide substantial new information that demonstrated another review was warranted.

In June 1989, another petition was filed by the AFL-CIO. A finding that Indonesia was taking steps toward internationally accepted standards of worker rights was announced in April 1990, and Indonesia did not lose GSP privileges.[20] In June 1992, two petitions were filed with the GSP subcommittee seeking the withdrawal of GSP benefits from Indonesia. The petitions were submitted by Asia Watch and by the International Labor Rights Education and Research Fund. Both organizations challenged Indonesia's worker rights performance in each of the five areas provided under the law. While alleging the Indonesian government's failure in all five worker rights areas, both petitioners emphasized as most serious the government's alleged refusal to allow workers to form unions of their own choosing (freedom of association) and the involvement of the military in strikes. The principal specific allegations contained in the 1992 petitions are that the Indonesian government prevents the formation of non-SPSI unions by imposing unrealistic organizational prerequisites on new unions for recognition; that the SPSI is closely tied to the government and Golkar, and is therefore not independent; and that the military is involved to a significant extent in labor issues that do not threaten the national security; including harassing union organizers, detaining workers who strike and labor activists, and becoming involved in labor negotiations.

Other charges in the petitions include the systematic failure or inability of the government to enforce minimal labor standards, such as minimum wages, safety and health regulations, and the prohibition against child labor. The Indonesian government in a lengthy response to the two petitions denied the allegations and asserted that the labor rights situation in Indonesia conforms to international standards.

On June 25, 1993, the U.S. Trade Representative announced that the review of Indonesia would be continued for an additional eight months. In the public statement explaining the decision, the GSP subcommittee noted that it identified "possible worker rights problems in all five worker rights categories listed in the GSP statute...." It also observed that "the Government has indicated an interest in amending certain of its laws and practices to bring them into closer compliance with international norms." Given the positive interest shown by the government, especially its willingness to invite an ILO team to Indonesia to advise on the implementation of ILO standards, "the Subcommittee recommended that the review of Indonesian worker rights laws and practices be extended until February 15, 1994, in order to monitor developments in all areas of concern, and to provide the Government with an opportunity to incorporate ILO advice regarding its labor laws and practices."[21]

The U.S. Trade Representative decided in February to extend the review six more months to give Indonesia more time to make adjustments. Meanwhile, the local press maintained pressure on the government by highlighting the case of a murdered labor activist from East Java and chronicling the troubles of an independent labor organization, the Indonesian Workers' Welfare Union (SBSI).[22] After an April 1995 visit, John Shattuck, the U.S. Assistant Secretary of State for Human Rights said he had learned more about Indonesian restrictions on labor activities: "We recognize the government's efforts to ensure that the minimum wage is paid. But it is also important to guarantee that workers have freedom of association to organize and bargain collectively, and that the activities of worker organizations be free from military intervention."[23] These comments prompted an Indonesian official to remark that Washington was being stubborn in continuing to criticize Indonesia's labor record. The Director-General of Manpower Supervision and Industrial Relations, a Mr. Suwarto, stated there was no need for anyone to worry about Indonesian workers' right to freedom of association because it was enshrined in the country's constitution. Referring to the sole union movement sanctioned by the government, he stated: "Workers are free to set up local labor unions at their respective companies without an application to join the All-Indonesian Workers Union (SPSI)."[24] He noted that the government did not recognize the independent Indonesia Welfare Labor Union (SBSI) "since it was set up by politicians intent only on controlling the workers through the union." The SBSI was crippled by the jailing of many of its leaders after protests in the north Sumatran city of Medan turned violent.

On whether Shattuck's impression could affect the extension of U.S. trade privileges under the GSP, Suwarto said it was United States' "full and undisputed" right whether to extend it or not. He was quoted as saying:

On the other hand, the U.S. government should understand that the Indonesian government has been improving labor conditions not because it so desperately wants to retain the GSP facility but because it has all along intended to improve workers' welfare.[25]

The United States has postponed indefinitely a decision on extending GSP. The administration's basic options are to find the Indonesians guilty, to exonerate them, or to keep the case pending and watch further developments. On the merits, there is no question that labor rights are suppressed in Indonesia. As in most human rights matters, however, the decision in this case will be based on a judgment about the trend.

PRESSURE FROM THE ICFTU

Other expressions of displeasure with Indonesia's worker rights record came from the international union federation, the International Confederation of Free Trade Unions (ICFTU), against what it called increasing military pressure on independent Indonesian unionists following worker protests.

Enzo Friso, General-Secretary of the ICFTU, complained of harassment of his own representatives and called on President Suharto to end the intimidation of workers and trade unionists:

> In view of the brutal deterioration of the social climate in Indonesia, the ICFTU ... urges you to instruct appropriate authorities to cease forthwith any and all measures aimed at preventing Indonesian workers to organize independently of civilian and military authorities.[26]

The SBSI said it helped organize the Medan rallies which called for increases in the minimum wage and better working conditions but denied involvement in subsequent riots. The military blamed it for the violence and accused it of Communist links and inciting racism.

The ICFTU, in Indonesia to consider applications for membership by the SBSI and its government-approved rival, the SPSI, said its mission members witnessed a military raid on an SBSI office and were themselves questioned by police. The Brussels-based ICFTU, representing approximately 120 million workers in 124 countries, previously protested several incidents of alleged harassment of SBSI members. The Indonesian government rejected the ICFTU charges and maintained that the protests were no longer a labor issue.

Manpower Minister Abdul Latief said Indonesia was actively promoting labor rights: "Until now the government never pressured workers. It has even promoted their rights. It is clear that the manpower ministry will be in the front line of promoting worker rights."[27]

Indonesian police questioned the four-man ICFTU delegation, which had members from Japan, India, and Belgium, but did not disrupt talks with the SBSI. Latief reiterated the government's position that it does not recognize the SBSI as a union. But he stated that the Medan riots had removed the issue from his ministry's authority. Another official said that Indonesia would not give in to foreign pressure over labor or other issues.

THE ARREST OF MUCHTAR PAKPAHAN

In August 1994, ICFTU General-Secretary Friso sent another letter to President Suharto in which he declared:

> The ICFTU is indeed alarmed at the continuing harassment of SBSI activists at the factory level and the continuing trials of SBSI leaders in Medan. The ICFTU calls on your government to cease harassment and repression of SBSI activists, to lift the threat of banning this organization and to ensure the release of Mr. Muchtar Pakpahan and other

> leaders of this trade union body. Once more we have to protest at this excessive response of your country's security apparatus to the well-founded demands of Indonesian workers....[28]

The ICFTU also urged "member organizations in all five continents" to campaign to free detained independent trade unionists in Indonesia. Indonesia then sought to clarify Pakpahan's arrest, claiming he was detained because authorities needed more information.[29]

The Australian Council of Trade Unions (ACTU) also condemned the arrest of Muchtar Pakpahan, contending that Australia should follow the lead of the United States in linking trade issues in Asia to labor rights. Martin Ferguson, ACTU President, said he was more supportive of the approach taken by U.S. President Bill Clinton, rather than the soft touch approach of the Australian government.[30]

In September 1994, Amnesty International accused Indonesia of using detention and jail to silence advocates of workers' rights. In addition, the ICFTU issued another lengthy report, accusing Indonesia of systematically crushing workers' rights: "Evidence suggests authorities were intent from the start on making the workers' strike and demonstrations degenerate into open confrontation, in an effort to crush all attempts at independent union organizing and in effect to destroy a nascent, nationwide trade union organization."[31] The ICFTU, which grew increasingly vocal in its attacks on Indonesia, catalogued what it said were other instances of official harassment and intimidation of SBSI members since the union's founding in April 1992. It said such tactics included the use of military force, arbitrary arrest, and provocation, and called on Jakarta to release all SBSI members, recognize the union, and lift all restrictions on workers' rights to organize.

THE EUROPEAN UNION LETTER

Several months later, the European Union President adopted the following position:

> The EU has noted with concern the conviction and sentencing of Mr. Muchtar Pakpahan, the leader of the trade union SBSI. The EU recalls that, by virtue of Indonesia's membership in the ILO, it has undertaken to give effect to the principles laid down in the ILO charter. Workers and employers, without distinction whatsoever, shall have the right to establish and, subject only to the rules of the organization concerned, to join organizations of their own choosing without previous authorization. Workers' and employers' organizations shall have the right to draw up their constitutions and rules, to elect their representatives in full freedom to organize their administration and activities and to formulate their programmes. The public authorities shall refrain from any interference which would restrict this right or impede the lawful exercise thereof. Workers' and employers' organizations shall not be liable to be dissolved or suspended by administrative authority. The EU appeals to the Indonesian authorities to refrain from any restrictions of these rights and to take further steps toward establishing a general climate including the freedom of expression in which labour organizations can work freely and independently.[32]

Responding to reports that the SBSI deputy chairman, Soniman Lafau, had been arrested again in Medan, within days of being released from jail, for carrying a calendar produced by the union, the ICFTU claimed that Lafau had been tortured during a previous spell in military custody: "His renewed arrest—on grounds hitherto unknown to the ICFTU—as well as the very real prospect of repeated torture is a cause for utmost concern to the ICFTU and the entire international trade union movement."[33]

THE ILO COMPLAINT

In April 1995, the Committee on Freedom of Association of the International Labor Organization accused Indonesia of the murder and abuse of trade unionists. The Governing Body of the ILO called on Indonesia to investigate abuses of union members and officials and punish those responsible and "enforce respect for fundamental workers' rights." The committee itself acted on charges from world union bodies citing "murder, disappearance, arrest of trade union leaders and workers as well as persistent and continuous violations of trade union rights in Indonesia."[34]

ILO officials hoped that the threat of publicity by the agency founded in 1919 under the old League of Nations, and the oldest in the United Nations system, would make hard-line governments more careful in their handling of labor issues.

While 60 SBSI union activists remained in prison in Indonesia, Muchtar Pakpahan, who had been sentenced to a three-year jail term in November 1994 on charges of inciting workers to riot in Medan the previous April, and whose sentence was increased to four years in January 1995, was unexpectedly released from prison in May 1995. The Indonesian Supreme Court evidently freed him on a technicality and it was unclear whether the high court could still send him back to jail.

The ICFTU immediately welcomed his release and its secretary-general stated:

> This is wonderful news, both for Pakpahan and trade unionism. Pakpahan was unjustly arrested and sentenced by a government which could brook no opposition. His imprisonment provoked foreign condemnation and effectively caused his union, SBSI, the first labor body to seriously challenge the government of President Suharto, to disband.[35]

THE ROLE OF THE MILITARY—THE MARSINAH CASE

The involvement of the Indonesian military in social unrest is based on a long-time involvement in the nation's affairs. For the past 30 years, the Indonesian Armed Forces (ABRI) have played the central role in the government of that country. As the generator of the revolution against the Dutch and the spearhead of independence in 1945, ABRI has traditionally viewed itself as the dominant force in Indonesian political life.

The military has a dual function, known as "dwi fungsi." In other words, ABRI has both a defense security role and the function of promoting social stability and development. One-fifth of the seats in the Indonesian Parliament are reserved for the armed forces. President Suharto, of course, is a retired army general, and ABRI figures, retired and serving, are prominent in the country's cabinet. Until quite recently, provincial governors were almost entirely selected from the military. The role of the ABRI, whether as defender of peace and security or as a sociopolitical force, is still considered the determining factor in the existence of the country and its people.[36] Recently there have been efforts by certain government circles to remove industrial relations from overt military influence. This process began under Cosmas Batubara, who held the manpower portfolio from 1988 to 1993, after replacing the hard-line former security chief, Admiral Sudomo. Yet it would be difficult to argue that the military's influence has been markedly diminished; the death of a trade union activist is tragic testimony of that, but it has declined under Batubara and Latief.

An Australian union official described the ongoing power struggle in these terms:

> While the military argues that industrial relations is primarily a matter of public security and therefore within its responsibility, the opposing view is that it is a vital element of economic policy and therefore falls within the civil responsibilities and thus the purview of the economic ministries. The views of the economic ministries have prevailed and have gained the support of President Suharto with the established areas of responsibility of the military continually being eroded, usually as the military's inability to deal with changes in society are dramatically and sometimes tragically exposed.[37]

Hence, a potentially explosive issue facing Suharto and ABRI is the manner in which the military handles the growing protests and confrontational tactics of independent labor unions, students, and nongovernment organizations (NGOs). The military is reluctant to repeat the use of lethal force in suppressing civil disturbances, and such requests of the ABRI could strain the relationship between the military and Suharto.

Police and the military in a number of instances have been present in significant numbers during strikes, even when there has been no destruction of property or other violence. Military officers occasionally have been reported present during negotiations between workers and management. Their presence has been described as intimidating by plant level union officials.

The government revoked a law allowing the army to intervene in labor disputes at the behest of employers. However, Foreign Minister Ali Alatas, in claiming that because the labor relations climate had improved considerably in the last few years, argued that the military would still play a significant role in developments: "The military will continue to be a security force if things get out of hand. The last thing we would like to see is a labour dispute degenerating into conflict. For a developing country, all our assets are very valuable. We cannot afford to have factories burned down."[38]

The issue of the military's role in labor disputes was highlighted in May 1993, when a 24-year-old labor activist, Marsinah, was murdered in East Java shortly after leading a labor action at the factory where she worked. Evidence was introduced at a court hearing that two military officers were present when she was abducted the day after a strike at the factory. It is not unusual in Indonesia for employers to pay the police or military to settle labor disputes.

Six months later, in January 1994, the New York-based human rights group, Asia Watch, claimed that the military was continuing to intervene in industrial disputes despite the revocation that month of a decree authorizing its involvement. In its report Asia Watch challenged recent reforms in Indonesia's labor law as inadequate and said police and military harassment of independent trade unions continued. It said 11 members of SBSI were fired from a company in south Sumatra in early January after announcing their union membership to management. Four were interrogated by police and ordered to quit the union. Lawyers were quoted as stating that despite the revocation of the decree allowing military intervention in industrial disputes, soldiers interfered in a strike in Tangerang just one day after the decree's repeal.[39]

The Manpower Minister, Abdul Latief, angrily denied this claim, saying that it remained the military's legal obligation to balance economic and political development with stability.[40]

The military switched its tactics in September 1994, by harassing two leading Indonesian dissidents, a human rights lawyer and labor activist. One, a senior member of SBSI, said that his Jakarta home had been surrounded for two days by intelligence officers; the other, the executive director of the Legal Aid Foundation (LBH), said he had been questioned at his Jakarta home over a two-day period.[41]

Finally, in mid-1995, the military said no proof had been introduced linking them in the brutal rape-murder of labor activist Marsinah two years earlier. Marsinah is viewed by labor activists as a martyr for Indonesia's labor movement.[42]

POTENTIAL OUTCOMES

In Indonesia, economic development has been used to enhance the legitimacy of authoritarian governments. As in China, rapid growth has led to intensified repression to head off demands for political liberalization. These events have occurred because the Asian concept of human rights stresses economic development over political rights and collective duties over individual freedom.

The government of Indonesia is clearly not in compliance with international worker rights standards. It is a military regime with one of the world's worst worker rights records. Independent trade unions are not allowed, and the right to strike is restricted. Union activists are intimidated and harassed by government representatives, and although the military was ordered to refrain from intervening in labor disputes, this decree has been violated on numerous occasions.

As a result of the labor unrest which erupted in April 1994, and continued to simmer for the following six months, the Indonesian government has become extremely sensitive to the issues of pay and working conditions, especially in the rapidly growing manufacturing sector on which Indonesia is coming to depend as the source of a growing proportion of its nonoil and gas exports. This sensitivity has been enhanced, moreover, by strong external pressures for an improvement in workers' rights, which may gain momentum if, as expected, the issue is taken up by the WTO.

Responding to these pressures, the government has initiated several increases in the statutory minimum wage recently, and announced its intention to review it annually. Although many firms already pay more than the basic minimum wage, the next few years will almost inevitably witness more rapid wage growth. This could seriously undermine the government's economic development strategy, which is based on the expansion of low-cost, labor-intensive, export-oriented manufacturing activities. This scenario therefore assumes that attempts will be made to restrict wage increases to the growth of productivity or to offset the effects of domestic inflation on workers' living standards, even though the government has declared that its main criterion for determining minimum wages will be a minimum physical need standard established for each province of the country.

Although industrial reforms are occurring, Indonesia remains under political pressure, especially from the United States, because of the slow pace of change. In part, the concerns voiced in the U.S. Congress over Indonesia's industrial relations are motivated by protectionist sentiment. But impurity of motive does not deny the labor abuses that occur, nor the economic impact trade sanctions would have on Indonesia. As such, this pressure is "encouraging" Indonesia to adopt more enlightened labor policies. It is possible to argue that the serious outbreak of labor unrest in 1994 would not have occurred if employers had met workers' demands and complied with minimum wage enforcement requirements. Indeed, if SPSI had articulated those demands, it would have increased its appeal to workers and perhaps helped in keeping the protests peaceful by neutralizing the appeal of SBSI, which is not state controlled. However, the problem is that minimum wages, like much else in the paraphernalia of trade union rights, work well when the labor situation is tight. In fact, in such a situation, there is little need to mandate wages because demand itself will drive them up to realistic market levels.

In contrast, unemployment in Indonesia stands at a massive 38% if the numbers of the underemployed, those who work less than 35 hours a week, are included in labor force statistics. So severe is the situation that the country needs to grow by 6 to 7% a year, a handsome figure by Western standards, merely to absorb the several million job seekers entering the employment market annually.

Undoubtedly, disparities in worker rights and labor standards clearly affect international trade and investment choices. But do high standards and strong enforcement of worker rights act as a drag on trade and investment, slowing global economic development? Or do they enhance mass purchasing power and political stability, thus promoting development?

From the standpoint of international investors seeking to maximize profits, strong worker protections curb the most efficient use of labor and create disincentives to invest. Minimum wage requirements, child labor laws, occupational safety and health standards, job security rules, union organizing rights, and collective bargaining obligations all interfere, to a greater or lesser degree, with pure market forces. They impose costs on companies trying to compete in the global economy. From the investor's standpoint, these costs could be minimized or avoided in countries with lower standards or less stringent enforcement of labor rights and labor standards. Such countries become tempting targets for new investment aimed at cost-saving systems, as both China and Indonesia have in recent years.

For that matter, in trying to attract the foreign capital necessary to fuel growth, Indonesia is facing growing challenges from countries such as China and Vietnam, which have no minimum wages or independent trade unions seeking to achieve this objective. However, wages are not the only factor in attracting investments. If labor activism grows to the point where it drives off present employers to other countries, to say nothing of prospective investors, it is difficult to see how Indonesian workers can benefit from the actions of hard line labor unions. Ultimately, of course, workers will see which demands are excessive and which are sustainable, and they will support the unions, whether government-sponsored or independent, which not only make demands but also have the means of realizing them.

Secretary of Labor Robert Reich addressed these concerns in his keynote address to a symposium on international labor standards and global economic integration:

> As our policy on international labor standards takes shape, I predict that it will have strong roots in our broader policies on human rights. Some labor practices simply place countries outside the community of civilized nations. How can these core labor standards be defined? Here, we will surely rely in part on international convocations, notably the International Labor Organization.... Work done by the ILO and other international organizations, on human rights generally and labor rights in particular, provide a solid foundation for our efforts to develop lists of proscribed practices. Any such list will certainly include goods produced by prison or slave labor. Some forms of child labor—such as work by very young children—will also be found to violate universal norms, even in the poorest countries. Nor is poverty a valid pretext for repressively restricting freedom of association and organization.
>
> Beyond a short list of core labor standards, judgments must become more nuanced. How, if at all, are we to respond to the developing country that allows fourteen-year-olds to work with no limitations or special protections? What of countries where wages are a small fraction of the levels prevailing in the developed world, or where pension and health benefits are alien concepts? What stance should we take towards countries where workplace health and safety conditions are better than barbarous, but still much worse than anything that American or European laws would permit?
>
> It is inappropriate to dictate uniform levels of working hours, minimum wages, benefits, or health and safety standards. The developing countries' insistence that they must grow richer in order to afford American or European labor standards—and that they must trade if they are to grow richer—is essentially correct. Yet this observation contains within it an implicit acknowledgement that standards should not be static, that a country's ability to offer its citizens better working lives rises with development, and that international expectations may properly rise as well. Workers' rights may soon become the biggest human rights issue in Asia.... [43]

Part IV

Thailand

Just as the enclosure of the Thai commons has forced people off their ancestral lands, the industrial growth areas have acted as magnets, pulling uprooted populations to Bangkok's industrial sites where wages average Baht 1,706 per month, or approximately $18.50 per week, and the workweek averages 54 hours. Despite what is, by Western standards, an extremely low wage, the 12-to-1 income differential between industry and agriculture insures that the massive rural-to-urban migration in Thailand will continue. Yet, agriculture still accounts for over two-thirds of employment, illustrating the economic, geographic, and social dualism prevalent in modern Thailand. While Bangkok's industrial economy remains heavily integrated into transnational financial and production structures, the rural provinces continue to suffer.

P. Macek[1]

Thailand is approximately one-third the size of Indonesia, with a population of approximately 60 million, and primarily Buddhist in religious orientation—unlike its Muslim neighbor to the east, Malaysia. Thailand is a constitutional monarchy. Never colonized by a foreign power, Thailand has modernized without much of the political and social trauma experienced in other developing countries. Since 1932 when the absolute monarchy was overthrown, Thai politics on the national level has been dominated by a series of coup-prone military governments. Nevertheless, with a largely homogeneous population, a solid agricultural base, an extensive apolitical bureaucracy, and a well-respected and unifying monarchy, Thai society has enjoyed remarkable stability for several decades. The Thai people tend not to be ideological; a 20-year rural Communist insurgency ended in the early 1980s primarily because of a cut-off in foreign support. Thailand is currently governed by a coalition government, elected in July 1995, led by Prime Minister Banharn Silapa-archa, leader of the Chart Thai (CT) party. The July 2 general election saw the return of traditional politics as the low-key and legalistic parliamentarian Chuan Leekphai was brushed aside by the energetic and unabashedly provincial Banharn. It also marked the return of many of the "devil" politicians, who supported the military junta that unleashed the army on civilian demonstrators in Bangkok during May 1992, and the eclipse of the "angels," led by Chuan, who opposed them. Banharn persuaded six other parties to join him to form a coalition government, as indicated in Table IV-1. (In November 1996, a new coalition government was formed, led by General Chavalit Yongchaïyut of the New Aspiration Party.)

Thailand generally has a good record on human rights. There are not known to be political prisoners and there has been a remarkable tendency to forgive even those who have launched political coups. There are some strange anomalies in the policy on social rights. Some of the minority peoples have yet to secure citizenship, although there has recently been some progress on this issue. An element of xenophobia is apparent in the legal position on foreign ownership of national assets, and Thai women married to foreigners are deprived of the right to own property. Perhaps Thailand's least enviable reputation is its record on labor rights: child labor is widespread and recent legislation banned trade unions in the public sector. Although it is officially illegal, a blind eye is turned to the widespread incidence of prostitution, which is still important for the country's tourism trade.

Organized labor in Thailand was fragmented and fractionalized even before government legislation removed state enterprises from the Labor Relations Act and dissolved unions in this sector in April 1991. Thailand has one of the lowest levels of unionization in the region, with under 3% of the pre-April 1991 industrial workforce organized into unions. Until the military takeover in 1992, union strength was

TABLE IV-1
General Election Results, July 2, 1995

Party	Seats won, 1992	Seats won, 1995
Chart Thai[a]	77	92
Democrats	79	86
New Aspiration[a]	51	57
Chart Pattana	60	53
Palang Dharma[a]	47	23
Social Action[a]	22	22
Nam Thai[a]	n/a	18
Prachakorn Thai[a]	3	18
Seritham	8	11
Solidarity	8	8
Muan Chon[a]	4	3
Total	359	391

[a]Members of the new coalition.
Source: Press reports (Ministry of Information, Bangkok, Thailand).

concentrated in the state enterprise sector, which accounted for over half of total union membership and most of the largest and strongest unions. Private sector organization progressed only slightly, due to a number of legal and cultural factors that militate against further organization in private firms, such as ineffective legal bars to unfair dismissal and traditionally paternalistic relations between employers and their employees

Since the mid 1970s, Thailand has shifted away from the import-substitution strategy it had adopted in the late 1950s and moved toward an export orientation. The external factors for policy reform were the inflow of international capital and the relocation of light industries into the country. The internal factors were pressure from the local business sector, liberal technocrats, and foreign advisors advocating a more liberal development strategy. In Thailand the political context of economic policy was different from that of other Asian nations, such as the Republic of Korea, Taiwan, Hong Kong, and Singapore, where economic development occurred under authoritarian political systems. Thai political circumstances were more liberal. Thai elites since the mid-1970s have been a heterogeneous group, comprising the military–bureaucratic alliance and businessmen competing and negotiating with each other. With rapid, export-led growth in recent years, Thailand is poised to become one of the newest Asian tigers. These developments have contributed to many shortcomings in the worker rights/labor standards model for Thailand, as Figure IV-1 demonstrates.

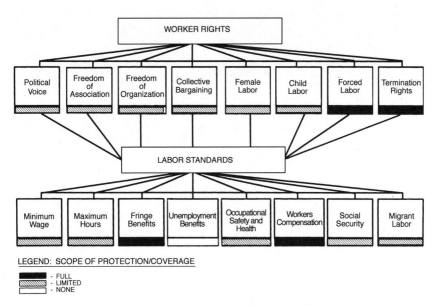

FIGURE IV-1. Worker Rights/Labor Standards in Thailand

CHAPTER 11

The Institutional Background

Thailand has seen at least 22 military coups or coup attempts since absolute monarchy ended in 1932. However, in the July 2, 1995 election, for the first time in many years there was no military intervention and the voting took place against the backdrop of a booming economy that has created an expanding urban middle class. While the population is still predominantly rural, where political life is dominated by money and patronage, urban voters are demanding competent managers who can find solutions to such problems as Bangkok's nightmarish traffic.[1]

THE GOVERNMENT

Historically known as Siam, Thailand was an absolute monarchy under the Rama dynasty until the army seized power in 1932, setting a precedent for a series of military regimes until August 1988, when General Chatchai Choonhaven was appointed prime minister from among democratically elected members of the lower House of Representatives. In February 1991, Chatchai was ousted in a popular and bloodless coup led by supreme military commander General Sunthorn Kongsompong, whose newly created National Peacekeeping Council subsequently dissolved the entire government, abolished the 1978 constitution, and appointed former diplomat Anand Panyarachun to serve as interim prime minister of a new military-run caretaker government. In March 1992, powerful army leader General Suchinda Kraprayoon was appointed rather than elected to replace Anand, causing massive popular uprisings that led to landmark constitutional amendments in May 1992 to reduce military involvement in the government. Following September 1992 general elections, a democratic coalition emerged to capture an effective lower house majority, with Democrat Party leader Chuan Leekpai elected as the nation's first nonwealth, non-military leader in 60 years. Leekpai was forced to dissolve parliament on May 19, 1995, following a land scandal involving wealthy members of his Democratic Party. They were accused of awarding themselves valuable government-owned real estate under a land reform program meant to benefit the poor.[2] The elections in July, 1995 saw a businessman and veteran politician, Banharn Silapa-archa replace Leekpai as prime minister (see Table IV-1).

THE CONSTITUTION

The original 1978 constitution was abolished following the February 1991 military coup, after which the National Peacekeeping Council adopted a new constitution on December 9, 1991 that reinstated an appointed prime minister, cabinet, and a bicameral legislature. It also maintained the political power of the military. In response to massive public pressure, the constitution was amended on May 25, 1992 to reduce military participation in the government by requiring the prime minister to be an elected official.

The present constitution is a slightly amended version of that drawn up by a subcommittee of the National Legislative Assembly which had been appointed by the generals of the NPC in 1991. It derives a good many of its provisions from previous constitutions, although in its original form it sought to offer greater power to the military-dominated Senate. The constitution provides for two houses of parliament, an elected House of Representatives of 360 members and an appointed Senate of 270 members. Among the amendments that were passed following the prodemocracy demonstrations of May 1992, is a provision that the prime minister should be an elected member of parliament, while the speaker of the House of Representatives is president of parliament and responsible for nominating the prime minister for royal approval. Members of Parliament (MPs) are elected on the basis of one- to three-member constituencies and all adults at least 20 years of age are eligible to vote. In January 1995, a number of constitutional amendments were passed in a joint session of the Thai parliament. The amendments, designed to strengthen democracy, stipulate that cabinet ministers may not hold state concessions which confer monopoly power. The voting age was reduced from 20 to 18; the number of lower house MPs is to be determined by a ratio of MPs to people; the number of appointed senators in the upper house was cut to two-thirds of the lower house MPs; and an independent electoral commission was established.

The measures are intended to strengthen democratic institutions and provide greater protection for civil rights. There is no guarantee that the amendments will be followed in practice. But their wording is strong, particularly in the area of civil rights. Now a suspect will be considered innocent until proven guilty, bail requests must be processed quickly, and bail amounts must be reasonable. On freedom of speech and the press, the amendments provide that publications can be closed down only by court order. One amendment declares that men and women are equal by law.

While democracy advocates welcomed new provisions on civil liberties and national elections, they noted that the constitution fails to curb the power of the appointed Senate and contains only watered-down measures on local democracy. They are also uncertain about how the new measures will be carried out. Their caution may be warranted. Thailand, after all, has had 15 constitutions since absolute monarchy ended in 1932. The latest measures revise a constitution put in place by the so-called National Peacekeeping Council, the military junta that overthrew the government of Prime Minister Chatichai Choonhaven in February 1991. Moreover, several of the measures will depend on subsequent legislation to flesh out their meanings. The article calling for an administrative court, for instance, does not say how much power it will have to overrule decisions of government bureaucracies. Also, the power of the Senate, which is composed mainly of people nominated by the leaders of the 1991 coup, is left intact. Proposals to reduce the number of senators, or to create an elected Senate, never made it into the final amendments. While senators are supposed to refrain from politics, many sided with the parliamentary opposition in an attempt to bring down Mr. Chuan's government in December 1994.[3] The amendments had the support of all but nine of the 360 MPs and 270 appointed senators, including many senior army officers. They ended months of political maneuvering that at one point threatened to topple the two-year-old coalition government.[4]

THE EVOLUTION OF EXECUTIVE POWER

The rivalry between Great Britain and France in the region ensured that Thailand maintained its political independence into the modern era, albeit within boundaries reduced by French encroachment in Laos and Cambodia and British influence in the Malay states. Although it retained its political independence, Thailand was in effect colonized in economic terms, especially by the British, who directly or indirectly controlled the exploitation of and trade in the four major commodities, rice, rubber, tin, and teak, which dominated the country's economy from around the middle of the nineteenth century. Despite the reforming monarchies of Mongkut (1851–68) and Chulalongkorn (1868–1910), the economic penetration of the country by the West provoked increasing political conflict between the established monarchical order and new groups in society, and in 1932 the absolute monarch was overthrown in favor of a constitutional monarchy which continues up to the present time.

Nevertheless, it is a particular feature of Thailand that the monarchy has continued to play an important role in the country's affairs, acting as a stabilizing influence at times of political instability and, even in the last decade, the royal family has used its influence in support of the incumbent government to foil at least one attempted coup. The present king, Bhumibol Adulyade, is the ninth monarch of the 200-year-old Chakri dynasty and is universally respected. However, he celebrated his 68th birthday in December 1995 and, although recent worries about his health have subsided, there are still some doubts about the future of the monarchy.

Since 1932 the monarchy has not played a direct role in Thailand's government. The country has instead been predominantly ruled by a succession of military governments, with strong leaders acting very much as autocrats and deriving their legitimacy from the monarchy. Brief periods of civilian government have been characterized by factionalism among competing interest groups, precipitating further army takeovers designed to restore stability. Changes of government by coup d'etat have been numerous, although they are usually bloodless. Throughout the period the civilian bureaucracy has lent an element of stability to the system.

Socioeconomic pressures in the course of the rapid economic growth over the last 30 years have begun to change this general pattern. In 1973 the last of the true military strongmen was removed in an uprising largely engineered by university students, and, although the military regained power by a bloody coup in 1976, military leaders since that time have realized the need to obtain wider civilian support for their governments. General Prem Tinsulanon, the prime minister from 1980 to 1988, accepted the post at the request of civilian politicians to serve as a respected figure who could maintain a balance between the various competing factions. This period saw the emergence of a partial democracy, in which Prem's nominees took the positions of real power in government, but he bowed to pressures for a more overtly democratic government after the general election of 1988 by stepping down in favor of a coalition led by a retired major general, Chartchai Choonhavan, the country's first elected prime minister in 12 years.

While this smooth transition of power appeared to indicate a steady maturing of Thai democracy, factionalism and overt corruption in the civilian government led to another military coup in February 1991. In an attempt to give themselves respectability in the face of foreign criticism, the generals of the National Peacekeeping Council appointed an interim government of respected technocrats led by Anand Panyarachun, a former diplomat and businessman. It ruled until elections in March 1992.

The King is the head of state and serves as symbol of national identity and unity. The King must approve all cabinet appointments and exercises a great deal of political influence despite his constitutionally limited powers. Supreme administrative authority is vested in the prime minister, who appoints and heads a 23-member cabinet. Under the May 1992 constitutional amendments, the prime minister must be chosen from among members of the elected lower house. Cabinet ministers exercise limited powers within their assigned portfolios and are responsible to the prime minister. The defense minister is considered the second highest ranking member of the government.[5]

Thailand is politically stable, despite frequent elections and a recent coup-studded political history. While the political culture may be less defined than in the West, Thailand's structure as a democratic monarchy is unchallenged. Reverence for the King gives him power beyond his constitutional mandate, providing a valve should politically driven events get out of hand. With no shortage of contenders for the premiership, Thailand faces no succession problems, unlike Indonesia and Malaysia. Also, a tendency to appoint technocrats to key cabinet positions has ensured sound and consistent policymaking. A favorable legacy of frequent political changes is that the bureaucracy can ensure day-to-day business is not disrupted.

The 1992 constitutional amendments gave the House of Representatives extended powers, while decreasing the powers of the traditionally military-dominated Senate. The speaker of the lower house is elected from among its members and, under the amended constitution, serves as president of the entire National Assembly, which convenes twice each year.[6]

Prior to the 1991 coup, labor had no explicit representation in the House of Representatives. However, the appointed Senate had four members from the trade union movement. After the coup, the ruling National Peacekeeping Council appointed four labor leaders to the National Legislative Assembly.

THE JUDICIARY

Supreme judicial authority is vested in the Sarn Dika, or Supreme Court, which serves as the final court of appeal for criminal, bankruptcy, labor, and civil cases. Supreme court rulings require a quorum of three judges. The intermediate Sarn Uthorn, or Court of Appeals, reviews cases forwarded from independent regional, provincial, and district courts of original jurisdiction.

There is a national system of labor courts, which is empowered under Thai law to mediate labor disputes. These courts are used frequently to mediate individual grievances between employers and employees. Associate judges of the labor courts are chosen from both labor and management in annual elections for two-year terms.

LOCAL GOVERNMENT

The nation is divided into 73 administrative provinces, including the metropolis of Greater Bangkok. The interior ministry appoints provincial governors and district officers. There are municipal assemblies in the major cities and elected village leaders exercise limited authority in rural areas. Thailand is a unitary state and administrative power lies firmly with the central government. Over 100 cities and municipalities form the only effective tier of local government, but, apart from the Bangkok Metropolitan Administration, few have an adequate tax base, depending instead on grants from the central government. Provincial administration is handled by representatives of the central government ministries and, although there are elected provincial councils, effective power in the provinces is vested in the bureaucracy.[7]

POLITICAL FORCES

Founded in 1946, the Democrat Party is the nation's oldest political organization. It is a center-right group that traditionally supports the monarch and was part of the Chatchai government until 1990, when it went into opposition to protest the allegedly corrupt administration.

Established in 1988, Righteous Force, also known as the Power of Virtue Party, is led by former Bangkok Governor Chamlong Srimuang. Chamlong was instrumental in leading massive antimilitary protests in May 1992 that led to historic constitutional amendments later that month.

The New Aspiration Party (NAP) was formed in 1990 by controversial army leader and former Chatchai administration Defense Minister Chavalit Yongchaiyut.

The 300,000 members of NAP strongly opposed the February 1991 coup and considers itself an anticorruption organization.

Formed in 1989, Solidarity consists of dissidents from the Social Action Party (SAP) and the Democrat Party. It joined Chatchai's restructured administration in December 1990 in an effort to stave off the government's imminent collapse after the then-ruling three-party coalition of the Democrat Party, Mass Party (Muan Chon) and SAP withdrew from the administration.

Founded in 1974, the Social Action Party is an offshoot of the Democrat Party, although slightly more conservative. It joined the Democrat Party in withdrawing from the Chatchai government in December 1990, but joined the Suchinda regime in April, 1992. The SAP left the promilitary alignment in June 1992.

Founded in 1981, Chart Thai (Thai Nation) is a right-wing party that served as the core of the Chatchai government. Its active membership includes a substantial number of military figures. In July 1995, in the general election, Chart Thai finished at the head of a crowded pack, winning 92 seats in parliament, and its leader Banharn, as prime minister, formed a seven-party coalition.

The Muan Chon (Mass) Party was founded in 1985 by government dissidents and opposition members. It withdrew from the Chatchai coalition in 1990.

Prachakorn Thai (Thai Citizens) is a right-wing promonarchy party that entered the restructured Chatchai government in 1990.

The Chart Pattana (National Development) Party was founded in July 1992 by Chatchai after he returned from political exile. Other political parties holding lower house seats are the Rashadorn (Citizen) Party, and the Seri Tham (Virtuous Freedom) Party.

Elections since 1979 have generally resulted in the representation of a large number of parties in the parliament, of which none has ever been near achieving a parliamentary majority. Ideological predilections remain relatively unimportant in the Thai political context, the parties being largely centered around a few leading individuals representing particular interest groups in business and commerce. These figures and their backers spend considerable sums in seeking the election of their followers in the hope that significant representation can ensure a place in government. To share in government is more important than ideological compatibility, and personality clashes among leaders of different parties and even within parties can lead to changes in the coalition structure over the life of a government.

None of Thailand's handful of labor congresses has explicit ties to political parties. The Labor Relations Act of 1975 encourages this policy by exempting union officials from prosecution in pursuing the interests of their followers "provided that the activity does not involve politics." The purpose of this stipulation is to allow strikes for economic reasons, while prohibiting strikes for political reasons, as is common in many countries. In 1990 some members of the Electricity Generating Authority of Thailand (EGAT) union organized a would-be Labor Party, called the "Siam People Party." The EGAT leadership was not involved in this development. The party has yet to make itself a significant force on the Thai political scene.

Extraparliamentary opposition in Thailand is limited. At the height of the Vietnam War the country was harassed by the externally supported Communist Party of Thailand (CPT). The CPT's numbers grew in the aftermath of the 1976 coup, which was among the bloodiest in Thai history and which briefly brought to power a very repressive right-wing government. However, disputes over ideology and declining assistance from Laos and Vietnam created internal dissention in the CPT, which has ceased to be a significant political force over the past decade.

Muslim separatist activity in the South now poses a greater threat to the generally peaceful atmosphere of the country. Since mid-1993 political rivalries in the South over influence within the Muslim community have provoked a degree of civil unrest.

THE MILITARY INFLUENCE

Traditionally, despite the instability of its support in the lower house, a government can rely on the appointed Senate, which has been dominated by the military and reflects the important role of the armed forces in national affairs. Any prime minister must still be acceptable to the military leadership, although the armed forces have taken a much more hands-off attitude since the events of May 1992. Despite this, some elements of the military would like to see the armed forces play an even more influential role, similar to that of their Indonesian counterparts with their self-proclaimed "dual function" combining national security and economic modernization functions.

Democracy is firmly established as an ideology in Thailand, according to one member of parliament, but it has yet to be accepted as an effective mechanism of government. There is no doubting the popular enthusiasm for it, at least as a process. However, the parties and candidates function within boundaries set by the military, which continues to wield a powerful influence in the country's political and economic life. Although some politicians claim the risk of direct army intervention is diminishing in line with the country's economic and social development, none would be so rash as to forecast the day when a prime minister could be chosen without the support of the military.[8]

Yet, in September 1992, prodemocracy protests brought down a government controlled by the Thai military and in the election in July 1995, the military, a traditional power broker in Thai politics, played no visible role in the election campaign.[9] However, a former general was appointed as prime minister in November 1996 to head a coalition government.

INTERNATIONAL RELATIONS AND DEFENSE

The armed forces' influence in Thai society is out of all proportion to their numerical strength. The standing army numbers no more than 190,000 men, of whom 80,000 are conscripts, while the navy and air force are considerably smaller, 62,000 and 43,000 respectively. Nor is the military's equipment the most modern, despite an extensive reequipment program which has regularly absorbed over 20% of the annual military budget in recent years. Most of Thailand's military equipment comes from the United States, although there have been purchases of British and Chinese equipment in recent years.

The armed forces reequipment drive was a reflection of Thailand's position in the front line of the ideological contest in Southeast Asia. The accession to power of Communist governments, in the three countries of Indochina after 1975, followed in 1979 by the Vietnamese occupation of Cambodia, brought Communism to Thailand's eastern borders. Thailand and Vietnam have historically been competitors for influence in Laos and Cambodia, and this rivalry had been given an extra dimension by ideology. Thailand, as a staunch ally of the United States, committed its troops to fight in Vietnam, allowed its territory to be used by the U.S. air force at the height of the war, and more or less openly supported the guerrilla resistance in Cambodia, both by giving refuge to the guerrillas and by turning a blind eye to the channeling of arms to them. The Thai military's apparent continued assistance to the Khmer Rouge has provoked international criticism since the establishment of the new Cambodian government in 1993.[10]

Thailand's relations with other countries are generally friendly. Although recent events in Myanmar have created some tensions as students and other opponents of the regime have sought refuge in Thailand, relations in general are amicable. Furthermore, there is now extensive dialogue with China. Nevertheless, Thailand remains a staunch ally of the West, and although there are no longer U.S. airbases on Thai soil, the armed forces still conduct joint exercises with American troops on land and with naval units at sea.[11]

THE EDUCATIONAL AND SKILL CRISIS

On the domestic front, Thailand's educational system has actually served the country quite well. Primary education in Thailand has been almost universal since 1980 and literacy levels are above the regional average. Equipped with a basic education, Thai workers have proved adept at on-the-job training. But, according to Chalongphob Sussangkarn, a Thai economist, this situation is changing rapidly as the economy develops. Many larger firms, he says, now require workers to have at least secondary education. Yet only 33% of Thai children go on to secondary education.[12]

The primary obstacle to broader educational opportunity for Thai children is the serious problem of child labor, when the youth leave school at early ages to join the labor force. They then are consigned to lives of menial labor in the absence of the requisite education necessary for meaningful, productive lives.

Another problem area confronting Thai labor in the 1990s is the transition from labor-intensive industry to capital-intensive operations with attendant higher skill and educational requirements. The problem has intensified over the past 30 years that the country has relied so heavily on cheap labor for Bangkok and nearby provinces. The fact of the matter is that Thailand can no longer rely on cheap, unskilled labor for its competitive advantage in the global economy. The only alternative is to develop a skilled workforce to produce quality goods to compete on the world market.

Despite rapid growth in the industrial and service sectors, the Thai economy and the Thai workforce remain traditional to a large degree. In 1994, 57% of those employed still engaged in agriculture, either on a part-time or full-time basis. It is common for rural laborers to take jobs off the farm during slack periods in the planting and harvest cycle, or to carry on small businesses in addition to farm work. Agricultural productivity in the northeast region, where a third of the Thai population lives, is marginal. As a consequence, there is a constant flow of generally low-skilled, poorly educated rural Thai seeking work in Bangkok and the more industrialized regions, both as seasonal workers and on a permanent basis. They have provided the main workforce for Thailand's low-wage based rapid industrialization. However, as the Thai minimum wage climbs, lower wage economies in Vietnam, China, and Indonesia increasingly draw low-wage export industries out of Thailand. Much of the Thai workforce is poorly equipped to handle the increasingly sophisticated work in the higher value-added industries that remain.

Over 80% of Thailand's total workforce has only primary education or less. In other newly industrialized economies in the region, typically no more than 40% of workers have so little formal schooling. Thailand's education system is still geared toward the needs of a largely agrarian, traditional economy and society. The government has made expansion of education a priority and is sponsoring legislation to extend compulsory education to nine years. In the mid-1990s postprimary education is available to over 90% of students. At the beginning of the decade, barely half went on for more education after 6th grade. Unfortunately, the present 6.5% unemployment rate for high school graduates is higher than the 3.5% and 4.6% levels for secondary school and primary school graduates. This stems from an education system which is trying to provide students with an academic-oriented curriculum, not one that serves the students' immediate vocational needs.[13]

BUREAUCRATIC INTERVENTION

The government bureaucracy also hinders educational development. A Northern provincial education officer said:

> Education does not respond to the real needs of people. Education is a top-down approach where people at the center design everything for people on the periphery. The more people learn in the school system, the more they lose their self-confidence. If the curriculum does not respond to the needs of the people, we still cannot solve the problem of the human "green harvest." The human "green harvest" is a complicated problem. It is not only poverty which pushes young girls into the commercial sex business. Many other factors are involved. Pouring more money in without proper direction and controls will cause more problems and cannot solve the problem of child prostitution.[14]

In 1993 the government announced plans for a human resources center to supply six key industries, agriculture, textiles, metals, electronics, computer components, and petrochemicals. A proposal was also made for a resource fund with initial backing of Baht (Bt) 2 billion, but its establishment was stalled. Other measures considered included tax exemptions on training expenses for private companies. The government spent Bt124 billion on education in 1994 and planned to increase spending by 10%, to Bt137 billion, in 1995.

The shortage of experienced employees, especially in middle ranks, led to systematic raiding for multinational corporations from the public sector and academia. In 1994 the government lifted a salary limit which had been in effect for state enterprises, to allow them to compete against private firms. One agency, the Electricity Generating Authority of Thailand, reported losing 1000 engineers over the years to the private sector. Companies offered stock options and other incentives to keep staff, but competition promises to become even more cutthroat, especially in expanding sectors such as finance and telecommunications. The Federation of Thai Industries petitioned the government for tax incentives in late 1994 to help pay for manpower development, and several leading Japanese firms announced plans for expanded in-house training programs.[15]

EXPATRIATE RECRUITMENT

Foreigners are increasingly being targeted to fill the gap in professional employment. The number of trained expatriates allowed to work in Thailand rose sharply, from 4,266 in 1982 to more than 13,000 in 1993. However, bureaucratic red tape, corruption, and inefficiency show no signs of diminishing. Although the government has made an effort to streamline procedures to enable foreigners to work and do business in Thailand, bureaucratic procedures continue to undermine any real progress. Bribes are in some cases built into the customs clearance process to bypass other voluminous regulatory procedures. Annual applications for work permits and visas, each issued by different government ministries, are time consuming since neither process is automated, and both are very costly.[16]

Despite legal constraints, authorities largely turn a blind eye to the growing contingent of illegal workers from neighboring countries prepared to work for a fraction of the minimum wage.

AN ECONOMIC OVERVIEW

Thailand's economic development policies are based on a competitive, export-oriented philosophy. Its economy is in transition, from an agricultural economy to a more open and broadly based one with a large manufacturing sector. Although official data indicates the majority of the Thai labor force remains engaged in agricultural production, the manufacturing, wholesale and retail trade, service, and other industries now account for almost two-thirds of the gross domestic product in value terms.

Thailand's remarkable economic development in recent years is largely attributable to a strong consensus among successive governments that a free market orientation is the best basis for policy. Building on a base of strong agricultural production, the Royal Thai government has encouraged diversification toward export-oriented light industries and tourism, and strongly encouraged foreign investment. As a result, the Thai economy has been one of the fastest growing in the world. Since 1965 growth has averaged over 7% annually and nearly 10% annually from 1987 to 1993. Thailand's expanding economy, rising real wages, and the relative passivity of the workforce also contribute to general calm and harmony in industrial relations. Strikes are relatively uncommon, with only 14 official strikes recorded in 1993.

Driven by strong exports and robust domestic spending, the Thai economy expanded 8.5% in real terms in 1994, an even more rapid pace than the 8.2% recorded in 1993. Inflation in 1994 edged up to 5%, led by rising agricultural prices and an average countrywide minimum wage rate increase of 6.9%. Unemployment in 1994 was 3.4%. The International Monetary Fund forecast that the Thai economy would average annual growth of 7.6% between 1995 and 2002, ranking it eighth among the world's fastest growing economies. The 1995 growth rate alone was predicted to be 8.6%.[17]

Thailand's political instability has only a marginal effect on the country's economy. This is because it has an independent central bank and an economy run largely by technocrats. Nevertheless, the relative political stability of the 1980s allowed rapid economic development. Over the past decade, the economy has moved from a predominantly agricultural base toward greater dependence on manufacturing and services for economic growth. Yet, rubber, grains, and sugar are still Thailand's largest exports and the country remains Asia's premier food producer, with more than half of its population employed in the farming sector.

LABOR FORCE COMPOSITION

The Thai labor force totals nearly 35 million out of total population of 59.1 million, according to government estimates. The Ministry of Labor defines the workforce as all Thai nationals 13 years old and over who are actively seeking work. Approximately 12 million Thai students over 13 years of age, housewives, and retired or disabled persons, are considered outside the workforce.

Thailand claims one of the highest female labor force participation rates in the world, over 75%, but two-thirds of working women, particularly in the agricultural sector, fall into the category of unpaid family worker. As the current minimum age for employment is 13, the Thai workforce includes many who are below the minimum age for work, which is 14 years in developing countries, and 15 years in developed countries, as set by the International Labor Organization. Many other children work illegally, largely in the informal sector.

The participation of women in the labor force has always been high, at nearly half of the total. They have been a major factor in the development of household agriculture and industry, and increasingly also in the public sector and private business. Women face few formal legal barriers to full equality with men, with the 1976 Civil and Commercial Code Amendment stipulating equal legal rights for men and women. Moreover, labor laws require that women be given equal pay for work of equal value. Yet indicators suggest that Thai women face some serious obstacles as a result of social and economic factors. Unemployment rates for women are higher than for men. Women are constrained from participation in formal education by such factors as economic hardship, which keeps them on the farm or sends them quickly into wage employment, often to Bangkok as bonded sex-industry labor, and traditional attitudes toward women's role in the family. Thai women are also underrepresented in local and national levels of politics and administration.

The most serious child labor problem is not underage workers, but abuse of child laborers otherwise working legally. Thai law stipulates that workers under the age of 18 can only work with the permission of the government, in daylight hours, for limited hours per week, and in nonhazardous situations. Violation of these restrictions is all too common in small enterprises and in the informal sector, beyond the reach of effective government intervention.[18]

Public sector employment accounts for over a quarter of all salaried employment, and about 6% of the labor force as a whole. There are over 1 million civil servants in Thailand and an additional 250,000 working in state enterprises. Growth in public sector employment has stagnated since the 1970s. The government is now facing a brain drain as many of the best-trained civil servants leave for the private sector. Better pay and faster promotion are the main incentives. Traditional prestige associated with civil service jobs is waning in the face of more lucrative employment opportunities created by a rapidly growing modern economy.

Thailand's labor force is growing by a nominal 2% a year, with industry expanding by 6.3% in 1993. However, there is enormous hidden seasonal employment, especially among the 62% of the population involved in agriculture; thus real labor growth may be closer to 5%. Unemployment has declined gradually since 1987 and underemployment, though still substantial, is shrinking also.

Unskilled labor can be recruited at the factory gate and semiskilled and skilled workers are recruited by advertisement. An increasing number of recruitment agencies and headhunters serve the executive market.

SKILL SHORTAGES

Thailand has promoted itself as a base for industry requiring low-cost but relatively skilled labor. However, in the past several years, it has begun to lose its competitive advantage to Vietnam, Indonesia, and China, especially in the textiles and footwear sectors. Efforts to steer the country toward high value-added production have been impeded by Thailand's lack of highly skilled labor. Key developing sectors, such as the petrochemical and electronics industries, are experiencing severe labor shortages, and firms are finding it increasingly necessary to provide retraining and on-the-job training in order to fill essential positions. Recruitment and retention of talent in management and in the financial sector are increasingly competitive. Turnover of employees in service industries such as hotels and banks was as high as 20% in 1993–94.

Also, the effort to address the shortage of skilled labor appears to be a case of too little, too late. The post-elementary school dropout rate is 50%. Secondary school enrollment, currently only 30% of eligible students, is the lowest among countries belonging to the Association of Southeast Asian Nations (ASEAN). Although Thai universities and colleges now graduate some 140,000 students annually, a fivefold increase over a decade ago, the graduates' skills are often inappropriate. Fewer than 20% of degrees awarded are in the area of science and technology, and only 8% of the 30,000 registered lawyers are qualified in specialist business fields. Thai universities are turning out roughly 5,000 engineers each year, but the country needs about four times that many. Such a shortage limits how quickly and efficiently Thailand can absorb new technologies.

Another important statistic is the secondary school dropout rate of 50%, which means the share of the workforce with only primary education or less will still be 75% by 2000.

Based on these developments, even under the best of circumstances, it would take Thailand 15 more years to achieve the technological capability that South Korea presently possesses.[19]

INCOME INEQUALITY

Another serious problem facing Thai policymakers is the uneven distribution of economic growth. Urban areas have experienced the most rapid growth, while about 12 million Thais, mostly rural dwellers, live in poverty. The government has sought to shift development away from Bangkok to other parts of the country, as reflected in its efforts to transform the southern Thai peninsula into a regional transportation center.

However, the government has yet to deal effectively with large and widening income gaps in the country. The average income in Bangkok is 10 times that of many of the poorer provinces, and the benefits of Thailand's economic growth are increasingly concentrated among the wealthiest 20% of the population. Thailand has one of the most unequal patterns of income distribution in the world and the gaps are continuing to widen. According to the World Bank's 1994 World Development Report, the richest 10% of the population took 35% of the income. The poorest 20% received only 6%. Outside of Latin America and Africa, only Malaysia has a more skewed distribution of income; GDP per capita averaged $1,929 in 1994.

Government figures also estimate that between one-quarter and one-fifth of the population is living below the poverty line of Bt 20,750 ($830) a year for a rural family of two adults and three children, or Bt 31,620 ($1265) a year for an urban family. Nevertheless, important gains have been made since 1960 in the areas of health and nutrition, as reflected in indicators such as the crude death rate, the infant mortality rate, life expectancy at birth, and malnutrition. Major regional imbalances remain, however, and AIDS has emerged as a serious problem.[20]

WAGES AND PRICES

The growing labor force and unemployment served to restrict upward pressure on wage rates in Thailand until recent years. Basic minimum wage legislation is in force, but until 1989 levels had been held fairly stable for some years in recognition of the plentiful supply of unskilled and semiskilled labor. In any case, such rates are relatively easily circumvented by manufacturers, particularly in the more informal sectors of industry. Here, indeed, the use of cheap female and even child labor is not uncommon, and rates are substantially below the minimum. Even in government, salaries for the lowest paid employees remain below the minimum despite recent increases. Taking into account rising inflation, and wishing to win political support from organized labor, the Chartchai government raised the minimum wage rate four times during its tenure, effecting a 37% increase between 1989 and 1991. Since April 1994, the minimum wage in Bangkok, its surrounding provinces, and Phuket has been Bt135 ($5.40) per day. A graduated rate is in force elsewhere in the country where lower rates prevail to encourage investors to establish factories in the countryside and in recognition of lower living costs outside of Bangkok. According to the Ministry of the Interior, less than 2% of the Thai nonagricultural labor force is unionized.

INFLATION

Until 1988 the contribution of inflationary pressures to demand for higher wages was relatively weak. The consumer price index for 1985–88 showed an average annual increase of just 2.7% and only in 1988 did food prices exceed their 1983 levels. Such low inflation marked a major reversal of the trends of the late 1970s, when rapid credit expansion to support the extraordinary growth of finance and security firms, large public sector deficits, the rising prices of imported goods, and the need to adjust utility tariffs sharply upwards had caused the rate of inflation to increase sharply. Rapid economic growth brought an upturn in inflation after 1988, with rate in 1988–90 averaging 5% annually. In 1992, despite the political crisis in May, inflation fell to 4.1% that year and 3.3% in 1993, although in 1994 inflation rose again, to average 5%. These figures brought this comment from Raymond Eaton, chairman of Export Development Trading Corporation, Ltd: "The growth rate that Thailand has continued to achieve is the envy of many countries. When you take into account that inflation runs about five percent, the overall situation is very positive."[21]

THE ROLE OF THE GOVERNMENT

The Thai government owns or controls a substantial portion of the economy. It owns and operates the postal service, telephone, telegraph, radio, and television communications, the railroads, ports, and an airline. Government monopolies also exist in the tobacco industry and in the manufacture of playing cards. Manufacturing industries in which the government participates or has interests include glass, rubber, canned fish products, automobile batteries, petroleum, and petroleum refining.

Other fields controlled by the government through direct participation or special arrangement, including concessions to private operators and licensing, include the mining and exploitation of minerals, the production and distribution of electricity, the water supply, passenger transport other than the government-owned railroad, banking, and insurance, including life insurance. In 1989, the Thai government placed a logging ban on all government-owned lands. Due to the fact that no private individual or company owns any forested area of any significant size, the ban effectively prohibits logging in all remaining forests.[22]

ETHNICITY AND RELIGION

Roughly 85% of the people are of Thai ethnic origin and another 12% are of Chinese descent. The remaining 3% consist of Malays, concentrated in southern Thailand along the Malaysian border, and hill people, who are found along the borders of Burma and Laos.

Most Thai are Buddhists, generally religious in their own lives and tolerant of foreigners of other faiths. No important religious taboos affect their trade. The country and its people are mixtures of old and new, conservative and progressive.

THE INDUSTRIAL RELATIONS SETTING

After coming to power in August 1988, Prime Minister Chatichai Choonhaven sought to cultivate close links with organized labor in an effort to build consensus and create a dialogue on contentious issues, such as wages and salaries, social security, privatization, exploitation of temporary workers, child labor, and industrial health and safety. He had an open door policy with labor leaders. Unlike most of his predecessors he made a point of attending May 1 Labor Day celebrations.

However, the Chatichai government's honeymoon with the labor movement was over by the beginning of 1990. A number of controversial issues eroded labor's support for Chatichai. He continued the previous government's policy of favoring the privatization of Thailand's state enterprises in order to obtain private equity capital while maintaining a cap on foreign borrowing. In addition, some of his promises, such as the creation of a labor ministry, never came to fruition. Throughout the latter part of 1990 and the first two months of 1991, Chatichai was under fire for not supporting organized labor's demand for a countrywide minimum wage of about Bt 112.5 ($4.50) a day.

The military coup of February 23, 1991, which overthrew Chatichai, impacted negatively on the labor movement. The ruling National Peacekeeping Council immediately banned strikes and protests under martial law, which lasted until May. In addition, the NPC brought the minimum wage controversy to a halt by decreeing that the $4.00 rate would stand. Most importantly, in April the NPC-selected National Legislative Assembly voted overwhelmingly to remove the state enterprises from the Labor Relations Act of 1975 and dissolve the unions in the sector. Employees were instead given the right to form "associations." These associations were more limited in scope than unions. A number of international labor organizations condemned this action.

General calm has prevailed in Thai industrial relations. Except for a disruption of port services in early 1990, there has been little major labor unrest. In the private sector, strikes and other unrest are rare.[23]

THE MINISTRY OF LABOR

The Labor Ministry, known officially as the Ministry of Labor and Social Welfare, was created in September 1993. Its functions were previously performed by various departments in the Ministry of Interior, which in one form or another existed as far back as the 1930s. The creation of this cabinet-level department gives the labor constituency a greater and more independent institutional presence in the government.[24]

The new ministry set forth its priorities as follows:

1. Development of labor skills to be the best in the region.
2. Promotion of job creation and an increase in incomes.
3. Building of a welfare base and social solidarity.
4. Laying the groundwork for a ministry that is "of the people and for the people."

Under the direction of the minister and the permanent secretary, the ministry is divided into five departments:

The Department of Employment Services

This department issues licenses for employment agencies, maintains registries of available workers, and provides job placement and counseling services. It is also responsible for overseeing Thai labor abroad, including the issuance of licenses for firms recruiting labor for work in foreign countries. The Department's Alien Occupation Division provides work permits for expatriate workers.

The Department of Public Welfare

This department provides direct assistance to disadvantaged groups such as the elderly, the disabled, victims of disasters, and other groups, and provides occupational therapy for the disabled.

The Department of Skill Development

This department provides preemployment and on-the-job training for several thousand persons each year. It develops skill standards and training programs as well as criteria for the training of instructors.

The Department of Labor Protection and Welfare

This department is responsible for the inspection of workplaces to assure that the relevant labor protection and occupational safety standards are adhered to. It also promotes labor relations and helps resolve labor disputes. The department is responsible for labor data collection and analysis regarding labor protection and industrial relations and the development of appropriate labor regulations.

The Office of Social Security

The social security office administers the workman's compensation fund, which provides financial compensation for injury, sickness, disability or death on the job. It is also responsible for the gradual implementation of the social security system, now limited to injury and sickness or death off the job and maternity benefits. In the future, the system is to include family allowances, old age pensions, and unemployment benefits.[25]

THE SOCIAL SECURITY SYSTEM

Thailand's social security system is relatively new and the scope of coverage is still limited. The system has been criticized for delays in making payments for claims and paying too little to beneficiaries, given that the fund has a large and growing surplus.

Following unsuccessful attempts to establish a social insurance system dating back to 1954, the government in 1990 passed the Social Security Act. The system exists separately from the workers compensation fund. The social security system's coverage is now limited to employees of medium and large scale firms. It is funded by payments by employees, employers, and the government each equal to 1.5% of employee wages. As of the end of 1994, about 5 million employees and over 65,000 companies were covered. Government workers, including those in state enterprises, and employees at foreign embassies and international organizations are not included in the system, but usually have comparable or superior benefit packages. Registered small firms are eventually to be brought into the system. Still outside of the program altogether are millions of Thai agricultural workers as well as workers laboring in the informal sector in firms, usually small, beyond the effective reach of government.

In 1994, the parliament passed an amendment to the Social Security Act of 1990. The 1994 amendments, which went into effect in April 1995, gave insured persons better compensation packages and spelled out more clearly eligibility under the system. Disabled persons previously compensated for only 15 years will, under the amended law, be compensated for life. Compensation for income lost through maternity leave will be 50% of normal pay for a period of 90 days leave. The duration under the 1990 statute was for 60 days.

The government is studying how best to fund the social security system as it seeks to extend coverage to include old age pensions and family allowances, which is scheduled to come into effect in 1996, and unemployment compensation. Unfortunately, the system administrator and the social security office in the ministry of labor still lack sufficient personnel with actuarial skills and a computer system to maintain database resources that are essential if the system is to be efficient and effective in the long term.[26]

LABOR AND POLITICAL ACTION

The Labor Relations Act was written in 1975 when a serious Communist insurgency was still underway and labor unions were believed susceptible to subversive influences. It prohibits unions and labor congresses from having explicit ties to political parties. Nevertheless, annual May Day celebrations demonstrate the potential for political organization. In the annual event, tens of thousands of workers and onlookers parade through Bangkok's busy streets and congregate with impressive organization in a large park area in front of the royal palace. The prime minister, labor minister, and labor leaders address the crowd. The activities are a mixture of politics and fun. Rousing speeches are followed by an afternoon of organized sports competitions and entertainment.

The Labor Relations Act encourages the separation between labor and politics by exempting union officials from prosecution in pursuing the interests of their followers, "provided that the activity does not involve politics." The purpose of this stipulation is to allow strikes for economic reasons, while barring strikes for political reasons.

Today, few political office holders have labor backgrounds. Four senators are members of state enterprise labor associations but do not have close ties to or the support of the most active labor organizations. In early 1994, a member of a state enterprise association was elected to the Bangkok city council. In Bangkok, where most state enterprise association members live, the potential for a unified labor voting block is greater than upcountry because most members of organized labor groups have residences registered in the capital, qualifying them to vote, and vote buying by the well-heeled traditional political parties is less pronounced in urban areas than in the provinces. Nevertheless, there are no dynamic labor leaders with significant public stature on the political landscape and there is no movement on the horizon to organize labor into a cohesive voting block.

None of the political parties consistently take up labor causes. The New Aspiration Party comes the closest to supporting labor because of party leader Chavalit Yongchaiyut's efforts to build a populist image. Chavalit was appointed the first labor minister when the ministry was formed. He turned over the portfolio to Paithoon Kaewthong in January 1994. Late in that year, however, the New Aspiration Party left the government for reasons unrelated to labor issues. The present minister, Somphong Amonvivat, is a businessman turned MP with no labor background. There are sympathetic individual politicians with whom labor leaders work on various issues, but among the labor rank and file there is a widespread perception that there is no party or other politically powerful entity which supports them.

Developing a political constituency for labor is particularly difficult because the hundreds of thousands of factory workers in the Bangkok area, who conceivably could become a powerful voting force, maintain their legal residence and voting rights in their home villages upcountry. The trip home on voting day is expensive and inconvenient for most workers, and even when they do vote they are likely to do so on the basis of local village issues. Nongovernmental organization efforts to persuade workers to change their legal residence to the area in which they work have had only limited success.[27]

TWO SCENARIOS: POWER AND IMPOTENCE

The differing outcomes of two major strikes in 1993 demonstrate the potential for union advocacy in industrial relations and the obstacles that have yet to be overcome. In June the Thai Durable Textile Company announced layoffs of over 300 workers in a move to increase efficiency. As those identified to be let go were largely workers with many years of service, including six prominent union leaders, the union cried foul and called a strike. The union position was supported by the government, which intervened to force the company to reconsider its position. The company then sought to achieve the desired reduction in the workforce by offering a generous severance offer for those who would voluntarily leave their jobs, and nearly 400 workers did so. A separate lawsuit filed by the company against the six work council members was later dropped, and all the union leaders were reinstated in their positions.

The relative powerlessness of the union effort in another labor dispute, the Thai Pattraporn strike, however, contrasts sharply with the favorable result in the Thai Durable situation. In October 1992, the union at Thai Pattraporn called a strike after both negotiations and mediation failed to resolve a dispute over wages and benefits.

The strike lasted nearly a year before the government called on both parties to return to work in July 1993. Rather than complying, the company announced a lockout. The government responded by invoking, for the first time, Article 35 of the Labor Relations Act, forcing the company to end the lockout. The company complied, but rather than submit to binding arbitration, soon declared bankruptcy and dismissed nearly 700 workers.[28]

THAI OVERSEAS WORKERS

Failing to secure employment in Thailand, hundreds of thousands of skilled and semiskilled Thais work abroad. These workers sent an estimated $1.3 billion in 1994 to their families back home. At the end of 1994, the labor ministry reported that over 440,000 Thais were working overseas.

There has been a major geographical shift in Thai overseas labor over the past several years. In the late 1980s, more than half of the Thai labor abroad was in Saudi Arabia. After the murder of three Saudi diplomats in 1990, more than 100,000 Thai left Saudi Arabia as the Saudi restricted visas in retaliation for the still unsolved murder cases. The decline was more than overcome by dramatic increases in the number of Thais working in Japan and Taiwan. Although the government has long managed an overseas job placement program, much of the recruiting and placement of Thai laborers was done by private individuals. Despite governmental efforts to better protect workers, abuses of Thai workers abroad continue, particularly those working illegally in debt bondage under the control of the Yakuza, or underworld, in Japan.

In an effort to avoid such exploitation, the parliament passed an amendment to the Employment Service and Protection of Job Seekers Act which took effect September 1994. Placement procedures are now tightly controlled. Job procurement contracts and skill tests must be monitored by the labor ministry. Placement agencies are required to provide Thai embassies and labor attaches abroad with full lists of names of workers brought into the foreign country. These job agencies must also guarantee bank funds or return tickets for workers placed abroad. Placement firms breaching employment contracts face the prospect of being blacklisted.

FOREIGN WORKERS IN THAILAND

However, despite the large numbers of Thais working overseas, Thailand is probably a net importer of labor. There are an estimated 520,000 illegal migrant workers, primarily Burmese, employed in Thailand. Also, the number of illegal immigrants from Cambodia, Laos, Bangladesh, Nepal, India, and Sri Lanka is increasing. In addition, about 150,000 expatriates work in Thailand with official permits.

The rising cost of Thai labor and labor shortages in certain industries have created a demand for cross-border migrant workers. They usually work in menial and often dangerous jobs at below the minimum wage aboard fishing trawlers or as farm hands and construction laborers. These migrants are concentrated in the five provinces bordering Myanmar (Burma), but are increasingly found in rubber plantations and construction sites throughout the country. The government is considering a relaxation of immigration laws in an effort to regulate migrant workers, but there is still concern about the security and social welfare implications of keeping large numbers of foreign nationals in Thailand indefinitely.[29]

ANALYSIS

Thailand is a relatively stable developing country which has been enjoying rapid, export-led economic growth for several years. However, one problem that has surfaced is large and growing income disparities. Another area of concern involves the Thai workforce, 75% of whom have no more than an elementary school education and therefore lack the skills and training necessary to fill higher-rated jobs. The government must devise policies and programs to improve the skill levels and extend educational opportunities, particularly to end the exploitation of child labor.

Thailand's labor situation is characterized by a two-tiered market between Bangkok and the rural areas of the country. After more than a decade of rapid economic growth, Thailand now has a shortage of labor around the industrial hub of Bangkok. The supply of labor, however, is still plentiful in the other major urban centers and the cost of labor outside of Bangkok is likewise significantly cheaper than in the region of the capital city. The lower cost of labor, together with the more plentiful labor supply, therefore, is encouraging many labor-intensive industries to relocate to the less developed regions of the country even though, at the same time, Thailand is well on its way to shifting from labor-intensive firms to medium and high technology operations.

In the midst of these developments, labor unions have not yet been established as a vital force in Thai society, economy, or politics. The traditional Thai passivity, avoidance of confrontation, employer paternalism, and the relative newness of the Thai industrial sector contribute to the current low levels of union organization. Workers in the state enterprises are more highly organized and more influential than their private sector counterparts. However, their influence was weakened in 1991 when state enterprise unions were disbanded and replaced by weaker employee associations.

Furthermore, unity and cohesion among the labor federations or congresses remains an elusive goal for Thai unionists. Individual union leaders are often accused of putting their personal goals and aspirations ahead of the movement as a whole. Even within some congresses, serious rivalries and factional problems prevent internal unity and agreement.

Labor-management relations in Thailand, while not overly acrimonious, are not well developed. There have been no major strikes recently, but many increasingly bitter labor disputes have occurred. Cultural factors and management disdain for organized labor have suppressed the development of sophisticated labor leaders in many sectors. Rather than engage in serious negotiations, management is increasingly utilizing selective lockouts targeted at labor leaders and unions often respond with wildcat work stoppages.

Despite the gradual development of democracy and the presence of democratically elected governments, labor has little influence in politics. No political parties espouse labor causes. Although migrant industrial workers are concentrated in the Bangkok area, they can only vote in their widely dispersed upcountry home villages. Moreover, unions are still forbidden from engaging in most political activities. Several hundred thousand semiskilled Thai workers who might be politically active have gone to work abroad and a comparable number of Burmese, Laotians, and Chinese now working in Thailand have no legal standing.

Although Thailand has long been noted for its tranquil industrial relations and the lack of organization and militancy of its private sector unions, this situation may change over the next decade. In the past, labor militancy in Bangkok's factories was held in check because most of the workers were temporary migrants from the rural hinterland, staying at most one or two years. Thus, there was little incentive to join unions or demand better pay and conditions. In recent times, however, the rural migrants have been staying several years and comprise an attractive target for union organization.

The concentration of foreign investment in large industrial estates in which tens of thousands of workers are employed has also increased the interaction and communication among the workforce, facilitating union organization. As individual firms grow in size the traditional patron–client relationship between factory owner and employees will be more difficult to maintain. Additionally, the increasing number of 100% foreign-owned manufacturing companies increases the likelihood of cultural misunderstanding between managers and workers, acting as a further impetus to unionization. More strikes are likely due to widespread lack of adherence to minimum wage levels; many employers pay less than the minimum wage.

In a general sense, standards of living for workers in Thailand have shown improvement. However, with greater competition from other countries in the region, there is growing pressure on management to keep labor costs down. Consequently, labor faces increasing social and political problems caused by a weak labor movement and a rapid transformation from a traditional to an industrial economy.

CHAPTER 12

The Labor Law Framework

LABOR LAW AND PRACTICE

In Thailand labor rights and relations are governed primarily by the Labor Relations Act of 1975. Not included under the purview of the Act are agricultural workers, civil servants, and employees of state enterprises. A separate statute, the State Enterprise Labor Relations Act (SELRA), passed in 1991, governs labor in the state firms.

The Labor Relations Act provides legal status to labor unions and sets forth how unions are to be organized and run. Each labor organization must have a constitution and set of bylaws defining membership and privileges. Union officials must be full-time employees. The law permits unions in similar occupations or industries to affiliate into national organizations. As few as 10 employees who either work for the same employer or who have the same line of work may apply to form a union. Membership is restricted to Thai nationals. The Act also provides a series of labor protections. The maximum workweek is 48 hours in industry and 54 hours in commerce. In addition, a rest period of at least 1 hour every 5 hours is mandated. Beyond these hours, employers must pay an overtime premium of time-and-a-half with double pay for holiday and Sunday work. In 1993, the government required that employees must agree to work overtime, except in certain sectors, such as the hotel industry, where the business is a 24-hour operation. In such cases, overtime is limited to 24 hours per week. Employees are entitled to at least 13 paid holidays and up to 30 days of paid sick leave a year, and a vacation of at least 6 days.

There is a national minimum wage structure. As of April 1994, the minimum wage in Bangkok and the surrounding provinces of Nonthaburi, Samut Prakan, Pathum Thani, Samut Sakom, and Nakorn Pathom, and Phuket was Bt 132 ($5.25) per day. In Chonburi, Saraburi, Nakom Rachasima, Chiang Mai, Ranong, and Phangaa the minimum was Bt 116 ($4.62). In all other provinces the rate was Bt 108 ($4.30).

The Labor Relations Act requires employers to have written contracts with their employees specifying separation procedures, grievance procedures, and other rules. Firms must file a record of their rules with the Ministry of Labor. Employers are forbidden from firing workers for union membership or participating in legitimate union activities, or from obstructing legitimate union activities. However, there are no similar protections for those seeking to form unions. Upon proper application to management, union leaders are allowed time off with pay to attend to union business. Workers covered by the law have the right to strike and may not be discharged or coerced for participating in a walkout. However, Thai courts have ruled that strikers may not picket in large numbers, block entrances, seek a boycott of the employer's products, or publish statements against the company. They may only withhold labor. Strikes or lockouts are illegal unless there has been an attempt to negotiate, and the union notifies the government mediator of the intent to strike.

In practice, knowledge of and adherence to labor laws and regulations diminishes with the size and sophistication of the firms involved. Large companies, especially those with Japanese, American, or European investment, generally adhere to labor law. Smaller firms, especially those in the large informal sector, are often not in compliance. Neither labor ministry nor industry ministry inspectors are particularly effective in assuring proper construction and safety standards in the workplace. Appeals for "cooperation" from employers are far more common than fines or shutdowns. Minimum wage standards are widely ignored outside of Bangkok, especially in smaller companies. Dismissal of union activists is also common, and government support for such dismissed unionists is weak. The usual sanction imposed by the labor court is payment of a few months back pay, and the workers are usually not reinstated. Part of the difficulty in enforcing labor regulations is that workers themselves, including many in unions, are not familiar with their rights and the regulations governing industrial relations.

Employers are traditionally paternalistic, valuing worker loyalty and obeisance over ability or productivity. Most establishments have no operational grievance procedures. When there is a labor dispute, workers will often engage in a wildcat strike or walkout, which is usually resolved quickly after a labor ministry official comes in to mediate. State enterprises were removed from the purview of the Labor Relations Act in 1991 and placed under the SELRA. While most labor regulations still apply to state enterprise workers, the SELRA imposed some significant restrictions. Unions were banned, and more circumscribed employee "associations" were allowed instead.[1]

Associations cannot conduct effective work stoppages because strikes of state enterprises were always illegal, but the state enterprise unions had gotten around that by calling extraordinary general meetings on workdays. The SELRA limited such meetings to weekends and holidays. Also, associations were restricted in their contacts with labor congresses and, under Announcement 54, promulgated shortly after the SELRA in 1991, association members can act as advisers to private sector unions only with the permission of the government.[2] This last point is significant because public enterprise unions have historically been much better organized and more sophisticated than those in the private sector. Limiting their association has been seen as an attempt to weaken the labor movement generally. However, in December 1994, the Chuan government approved a redrafted SELRA in cooperation with state enterprise labor leaders which effectively restored the rights state enterprise workers enjoyed prior to 1991.[3]

SPECIFIC LEGISLATIVE COVERAGE

Most Thai labor legislation falls under the civil and commercial code, which governs contracts on the hiring of services, the Labor Relations Act of 1975, and the Social Security Act of 1990. In addition, a series of ministerial and revolutionary decrees dating from the 1970 apply to certain aspects of labor, e.g., the National Executive Council Decree 103, which reserves specific occupations for Thai nationals. Regulations are enforced by the Ministry of Labor and Social Welfare with the help of the ministries in charge of the interior, industry, and public health.

Thai law does not specifically ban discrimination in employment. The Alien Business Law bars foreign nationals from a range of professions.[4]

SELRA AMENDMENTS

State enterprise employees lost the two basic rights of collective bargaining and the freedom to form trade unions under the 1991 legislation, but they regained most of their former rights under 1994 amendments, as noted above. Approved in response to American threats of trade retaliation, the amendments permit one trade union for each state enterprise, with a requirement that 25% of the total workforce become members. Collective bargaining has also been revived, but not the right to strike.

In a compromise to legislators who feared a return to strong-arm industrial action by state enterprises, activity relations committees set up in 1991 were retained but with a revised format. The committees will continue to hear employee complaints, but the new trade unions will in the future represent the workforce.

Thailand's labor movement was substantially weakened by the three-year ban, spanning the 1991–93 period, on state enterprise unions, which were the country's strongest and included more than half of its unionized workers. Private sector unions are mostly limited to single plants or companies, the most active of which are in banking. Only the textile industry is organized as such. Unions are loosely affiliated through one of the eight labor congresses, but moves began in August 1994 to merge them into a single confederation in order to improve labor bargaining power.

STRIKES AND LOCKOUTS

Thai law allows lockouts and strikes in private industry provided certain procedures are followed. However, it is highly unusual for private sector industrial employees to use the strike weapon. Where strikes have occurred, they generally have been because of employee dissatisfaction over poor wages and benefits. A requirement for 50% of private sector workers to support a strike means that all-out stoppages are kept to a minimum. Action is also prohibited until the workforce has gone through the wage bargaining process with management, and unlawful strikes can result in dismissal.

There were more than 200 recorded labor disputes in 1994, but fewer than two dozen resulted in stoppages. An upturn in export sales and the relocation of factories to the provinces reduced labor tension over mechanization, which first came to a head in 1993. Manufacturers are increasingly moving to low wage areas rather than reducing manpower, though this sometimes provokes friction. For example, about 1,000 employees of the Taiwan-owned Ji-Hou Industrial Computer Components factory in Laem Chabang went on strike in late 1994 after claiming they were not being paid the minimum wage. The dispute ended in a new working agreement between management and the employees and did not require arbitration.[5]

The Labor Relations Act of 1975 established procedures for settling labor disputes by a conciliation officers, arbitrator, and labor relations committees and established rules to govern the conduct of strikes and lockouts. However, disputes are often resolved on an ad hoc basis, with intervention by the Labor Department of the Ministry of Interior and/or the Office of the Prime Minister.

EMPLOYMENT CONTRACTS

The 1975 labor law makes contracts mandatory for all companies with 20 or more employees. Labor contracts must specify employment conditions, working days, hours, wages, benefits, termination conditions, complaint procedures, and provisions for amending contracts. Agreements are annual, subject to extension for up to three years by mutual agreement. Employees must select negotiating representatives. In the event of failure to reach an agreement, a government conciliator may be appointed.

The law contains directives to employers and employees requiring that mutually agreed upon contracts must be registered with the Labor Department. When an employer or group of workers desires to change or amend its employment contract, it must submit a written demand for discussion and negotiation to the opposite party. If a bargaining impasse or deadlock develops a conciliation officer from the Labor Department utilizes mediation. If a settlement cannot be reached within five days, however, an arbitrator may be appointed to resolve the dispute, and the arbitrator's decision is final.[6]

Most firms have no operational grievance procedures. Although the government has required large firms to have formal grievance procedures since 1965, traditional subordinate attitudes prevail. State enterprises have developed grievance procedures using grievance committees since Thai workers are more willing to voice complaints through committees than to do so on an individual basis.

UNIONS AND ASSOCIATIONS

The 1975 labor statute regulates the establishment of unions and employer associations. In general, the same procedures apply to both. They must be licensed and registered with the Central Employees' Union and Employers' Association, Registration Office of the Department of Labor, in order to operate.

The private sector labor relations climate is generally peaceful with relatively infrequent strikes. Since a period of social unrest in the mid-1970s, Thailand has averaged fewer than 10 strikes a year.

Many small industries are family owned and operated, but independent employers are a small minority in Thai industry, with many large industries owned or controlled by the government. Employer or manager associations are not widely established.

Antiunion employers will sometimes fire entire union executive committees and the labor court where the complaint is submitted may only require management to pay the discharged employees, at most, a few month's back pay without reinstatement.

In reality, individual employees in Thailand rarely have significant bargaining power. Those who wish to affiliate with unions may, at least in theory, enhance their bargaining strength. The normative structure for labor–management relations in Thailand is thorough and comprehensive, drawing upon many of the labor law concepts familiar to American employers and unions. In some respects, the 1975 law resembles the U.S. National Labor Relations Act in its breadth of coverage.

TRIPARTITE DISPUTE SETTLEMENT

A number of tripartite bodies promote peaceful industrial relations in Thailand. The National Labor Development Advisory Board (NLDAB) provides a forum to discuss labor problems and to recommend appropriate policies. The body has 20 members, 10 drawn from the government, and 5 each from management and labor. Other major tripartite bodies are the Labor Relations Committee (LRC) and a national system of labor courts. Both of these institutions are authorized under Thai law to mediate labor disputes. The older body, the LRC, deals primarily with serious disputes which threaten national economic security, while the labor courts are used frequently to mediate individual grievances between employers and workers. Associate judges of the labor court are chosen from both labor and management in annual elections for terms of two years.

Labor courts were established in 1980 to handle labor disputes. The courts rule on contractual complaints brought by employees against management. The complaints mostly involve severance, overtime, or holiday pay. Court proceedings are informal, with lawyers acting as advisers rather than advocates. The main advantages of the courts are low costs and prompt hearings. Appeals made be taken on points of law to the Dika (Supreme Court).

In 1993 the government formed a labor panel to resolve broader disputes as part of a reorganization that created separate labor and social welfare ministries. The panel includes representatives of employers, employees, and the government and is aimed at addressing grievances before they affect a company's production. Foreign businesspeople have suggested that the Board of Investment (BOI) step in to mediate labor disputes involving foreign firms. The BOI is considering introducing a mediation system, but it has yet to develop a concrete plan.[7]

TERMINATION OF EMPLOYMENT

Employers in the United States are accustomed to exercising broad discretion in the hiring and firing of workers. The situation is totally different in Thailand, where special national statutory limitations and protections apply to individual employment contracts. The Thailand Civil and Commercial Code governs "hire of services" of workers. Among other things, the statute specifically limits the causes for which an employer may terminate an employee's contract.

The rules for dismissal and severance pay have been in force since 1974. Employees may be dismissed without severance pay only if they are temporary workers, have failed to attend work for three consecutive days without reasonable cause, have been negligent or dishonest, have caused intentional damage, or have breached regulations. It is normal for employers to issue warning letters to employees for a first offense in order to build up evidence in case the eventual dismissal is referred to the labor court.

Regular employees are otherwise entitled to severance pay upon dismissal according to the length of the worker's employment; one month's pay for dismissal after less than one year's employment; three months' pay for one to three years' employment; and six months' pay beyond three years. In the case of fixed term contracts, severance pay may not be claimed upon completion, though termination before the completion date may entitle the employee to payment of all compensation due under the contract up to its completion. Unless otherwise provided in an employment contract, retirement can give rise to entitlement to severance pay, even though a provident fund or other retirement benefits may also be payable.[8]

PART-TIME AND TEMPORARY HELP

Thai labor law permits the use of part-time employment, and this has a strong appeal for both local and foreign firms because of the absence of binding regulations. Temporary or part-time workers do not qualify for holiday pay, medical care, or pension rights, though overtime may still be paid in some circumstances. As compensation for the loss of fringe benefits, however, temporary office workers often demand higher wages. Many workers from the provinces prefer such flexible terms because of the need to return home on short notice to help with the annual rice harvest. Export industries such as garments are particularly dependent upon a transient workforce.[9]

WAGES, SALARIES, AND FRINGE BENEFITS

The minimum wage is normally revised annually and has climbed by 12 to 15% each year since 1990. It applies to all occupations except agriculture, forestry and fisheries, and domestic services. The minimum does not apply during an employee's probationary period. Some officials have been pushing for the abolition of the minimum wage, believing market forces would determine a fair daily wage.

Monthly salaries in multinational corporations are generally higher than those in purely Thai companies, in the range of Bt 6,000 to 7,000 ($240 to $280) for semiskilled workers and Bt 9,000 to 10,000 ($360 to $400) for skilled workers. Graduates from overseas colleges can command even better terms. On a monthly basis, lower-level office workers receive Bt 5,000 to 7,000 ($200 to $250), and experienced midlevel employees receive Bt 12,000 to 20,000 ($480 to $800). Executive secretaries receive Bt 25,000 to 30,000 ($1,000 to $1,200), midlevel managers Bt 35,000 to 60,000 ($1,400 to $2,400) and senior managers Bt 50,000 to 140,000 ($2,000 to $5,600). Multinational employees are also more likely to receive a full range of benefits. In view of the high tax rates, senior managers are more attracted by fringe benefits than by salaries.

Few fringe benefits are compulsory, though there are legal provisions for paid holidays, sick leave, maternity leave, injury benefits, termination benefits and other basic benefits under the Social Security Act. Major companies also normally provide health care and accident insurance for employees. In some cases, this is extended to the workers' families as well.

A workers' compensation fund is compulsory for all firms with 20 or more workers. In addition, employers and employees may contribute to provident and superannuation funds. Employer contributions to registered funds are tax deductible and the taxable allowance was substantially increased in 1994.

Further tax incentives are being considered to encourage participation in provident funds, including deductions of 5% of a company's net profit. Maximum and minimum contributions are stipulated, and funds must be deposited with government approved financial institutions. In 1994 the government approved a central provident fund for public employees, who will be required to contribute 3% of their wages. Membership will be compulsory for new employees but not for existing staff, who may continue using a pension plan; the two will eventually be combined.

Personal loans are frequently offered by financial institutions, but this is unusual for other organizations. Annual bonuses range from a low of 19% to a high of 80% of base salary, with the average at about 40%. A typical bonus is one to three months pay at the end of the year, the first month being treated as a normal benefit and additional months depending on the performance of the firm, department, or individual. In some competitive sectors of the employment market, such as finance, bonuses can be much larger, sometimes exceeding a year's salary, owing to efforts to retain and recruit employees.[10]

HOURS OF WORK

Commercial workers in retail trade were required to work a 54-hour week until 1994, when a limit of 48 hours was imposed for all such workers. The factory workweek of 48 hours was reduced to 42 hours at facilities deemed injurious to health or safety. The 1994 changes, which amended labor protections laws dating from 1972, also ruled that workers could not be forced to work overtime, could not work overtime for more than four hours daily, and could not work overtime for five consecutive days.

Compensation for overtime work is discretionary and more widespread in foreign-run firms than local companies. It is normally calculated at 150% of the standard rate, rising to 200% for regular hours on public holidays and 300% for work performed on rest days or overtime on public holidays. Directors and managers do not normally receive overtime pay unless it is specifically provided for in their employment contracts.[11]

If a business has to shut down temporarily, the workers are legally entitled to receive 50% of their monthly salary until work resumes. If the business must close indefinitely, prior notice must be given to the workers. Also, employees cannot take leave for personal business for more than three days a year.[12]

SHIFTS

Working hours of both government and private sectors should be divided into two shifts to relieve traffic congestion during Bangkok's rush hours, with the first working shift starting from 7:00 A.M. to 2:00 P.M. and the second shift from 2:00 P.M. to 8:00 P.M. Employees working the first shift should be those responsible for coordinating their work with people while staff whose duties concerned internal affairs of their organizations should work during the second shift. If these proposals advanced by the communications deputy minister are accepted, the number of vehicles during Bangkok's rush hours would be reduced by about 30%.[13]

HEALTH AND SAFETY

Normally, during every Labor Day celebration, Thai unions emphasize the issue of safety and health in the workplace. This was especially timely in the 1994 situation due to the tragic Kader toy factory fire, where almost 200 workers died. Also, the disclosure that workers at the Lamphun industrial estate were dying because of exposure to toxic chemicals indicated that a large number of Thai workers were working in dangerous conditions.

The labor coalition set up a working group to campaign for the safety of all Thai workers and petitioned the government to commemorate May 10th, the day of the Kader tragedy, as a National Safety Day for workers. To become more effective in safeguarding workers' lives, a tripartite committee comprised of government officials, employers, and workers was recommended, and it would have the authority to inspect factories which were reported to pose potential dangers and health risks.

The Labor Protection and Welfare Department is in the process of proposing higher penalties for violators of safety measures. Today, they are subjected to up to six months' imprisonment or a fine of up to Bt 20,000 ($800), or both. Labor Department officials publicly admit that small firms continue to egregiously violate Thai labor and worker safety laws. In the Bangkok area 200 inspectors are responsible for tens of thousands of companies. The fact is that many small enterprises and factories do not even bother to register, and thus usually escape monitoring by government officials. These firms are especially likely to ignore the labor laws, since their unorganized employees are seldom aware of their rights.

As an example of the scope of noncompliance, in the first nine months of 1990, labor officials found 20,306 out of 29,474 workplaces inspected to be in violation of labor law in some fashion. However, only 594 violated the law seriously enough to receive warnings. The Department of Labor prosecuted 15 of the violators. In addition, 56,500 workers received compensation for on-the-job injuries during this period (439 workers died in job-related accidents). The Factory Control Department of the Ministry of Industry also administers labor laws. The department inspects factories, and has the right to withhold licenses if worker safety standards are not met.[14]

FEMALE AND CHILD LABOR

The Thai government raised the minimum age for child labor from 12 to 13 in January 1990. The Department of Labor is considering raising the age to 15, but has set no timetable for doing so. The law covers children in nonagricultural occupations, with exceptions allowed for family employment and newspaper or flower vendors. Legislation also prohibits the hiring of children between the ages of 13 and 15 in hazardous occupations, in jobs injurious to their morals, and in night work.

Nevertheless, the Department of Labor still lacks inspector manpower and abuses still abound. For example, responsible estimates of the number of girls under 16 participating in the sex trade, many against their will, have ranged from 30,000 to 200,000.

The labor law protects female workers, mandating, for example, limits to the weights they can be required to lift. Females under 18 may not engage in night work, nor in hazardous occupations in manufacturing, construction, or mining. Women are allowed 60 days maternity leave, of which 30 days is paid if employment has been for more than 6 months. The law mandates equal pay for equal work. In April 1993, the interior ministry forwarded to the cabinet two proposals which sought to give female workers the right to 90-day maternity leave with full pay. The first proposal would pay female employees for 45 days of the 90-day leave period, while the second proposal would amend the Social Security Act to provide females with payment for the remaining 45 days coming from the social security fund. The government response was to suggest that 75 days would be paid for out of the 90-day leave period.[15]

THE PROVIDENT FUND

The Provident Fund was created in 1984 to authorize the establishment of private voluntary pension funds that provide benefits to participating employees upon their resignation or retirement. Employers and employees jointly contribute to such funds at various rates determined by individual companies. Unfortunately, most employees are not covered by provident funds, particularly the lower-paid workers who are the most vulnerable to loss of income.

In 1989, plans setting out the creation of a new social security program were drafted and presented to the cabinet with the realization that it would take from five to seven years to implement the plans. The slow movement by the government on the social security system infuriated labor leaders, and some advisors within the government complained that there had been no movement on social security reform for more than three decades. The battle for the implementation of such a program will continue to be a difficult one for the trade unions, since a majority of Thai politicians are also employers and do not wish to cut their profits to support such a system.[16]

As indicated, the scheme is to be phased in over a period of approximately six years. During the first phase, coverage will be restricted to the provision of health care, sickness benefits, disability pensions, maternity benefits (for up to two births), and funeral grants. Coverage will also be limited to workers in establishments which have 20 or more workers. After three years, the timetable calls for the extension of the program to cover firms with 10 or more employees. In the fourth year, people who are self-employed or who have independent jobs may voluntarily join the plan. Civil servants, apart from temporary public sector employees, are not covered because they already enjoy a wide range of benefits.

In the longer term, programs covering retirement, family welfare, and unemployment will follow. The legislation specifically allows flexibility for the government to decide when the country will be ready to meet the financial demands of a retirement program. Once all of the programs are operating, it is expected that the level of contributions to the Social Security Fund will increase to 9.5% of employees' salaries.[17]

SOCIAL SECURITY CONTROVERSY

Controversy has surrounded the program since the passage of the law. Questions have been raised about the fairness of the legislation, particularly concerning contributions from employees of firms already providing generous benefits. Others, including the Director General of the Social Security Office, have expressed doubts about the viability of the program itself as it now stands. Also, labor's support for the law has not been unanimous. Many state enterprise unionists demanded that they be exempted from contributing to the system because the benefits they already receive gratis are superior to those afforded by social security.

The EGAT union, one of Thailand's largest and best organized, even held a protest rally of 3,000 members a few weeks after passage of the act to demand complete exemption. The State Enterprise Labor Relations Group (SELRG), to which the EGAT union belongs, did not support this demonstration. State enterprise workers eventually received partial exemption from contributions. Subsequently, shortly after the dissolution of unions in the public sector, the government proposed a complete exemption.

On the employer's side, many objected to the fact that the law only allowed for whole or partial exemption for employees already on the job when the law was passed. New job entrants had to contribute to the program. Employers felt that this would create two classes of employees, and would cause dissension in their companies.

The most important question concerning the viability of the social security program was whether the Social Security Fund would have sufficient money to cover costs or the government would need to provide significant additional outlays to keep it solvent. Fears were also expressed that the exclusion of more than 200,000 state enterprise workers from the system would cost the Fund at least $10 million annually.

RECENT AMENDMENTS

The reservations expressed about the implementation and viability of the social security system have not all been justified due to subsequent changes in the law. For instance, more generous benefits are now available to workers as the amended Social Welfare Act has finally taken effect. The original statute, passed in 1990, awarded unrealistically low benefits when the cost of living was taken into account. The amended law took effect on March 30, 1995 and increases the grant for a deceased worker from Bt 13,500 ($540) to Bt 20,000 ($800). A disabled worker will receive permanent compensation worth half of his or her wage, instead of 50% of the wage for a period of 15 years. Under the revised law, a grant will also be provided for the funeral of an insured worker who dies during his or her disability, while the dead worker's descendant could also receive a certain grant, the amount of which depended on the duration of the decedent's contribution to the Social Welfare Fund.

In addition, an insured female worker will receive Bt 4,000 ($160) for a pregnancy, instead of Bt 3,000 ($120). She will also be entitled to a further 45 days wage payment after giving birth. In other words, a pregnant worker will from now on be eligible to claim, after giving birth, 90 days compensation to match her 90-day maternity leave.

The number of workers receiving benefits from the Social Welfare Office has gradually increased over the four years since the enactment of legislation, and in 1994 alone served as many as 371,999 workers. An informed source also indicated that the Social Welfare Fund has accumulated over Bt 20 billion ($800 million). However, this amount will still be inadequate to cover the aged, who would only become eligible for benefits after 1998. This costly coverage would require funding in the amount of Bt 100 billion ($3,200,000,000) to sustain the solvency of the Social Welfare Fund, which could easily collapse as has been the case in other countries when funding deficiencies occurred.[18] Table 12-1 indicates the status of recent social security coverage in Thailand.

A FINAL CAVEAT

Although large multinational companies sometimes draw harsh criticism in Thailand, they are often among the country's better employers, according to Preecha Seemeesap, General-Secretary of the International Metalworkers Federation-Thai Council in Bangkok, who states that, "They comply with labor laws, and offer good pay and pension funds."[19]

As noted earlier, the owners of small firms are the most common abusers of labor laws and most of the hardship and privation falls on Thailand's 3.5 million women factory workers. Thailand has about 250,000 factories, of which about 60% pay less than the minimum daily wage, which recently stood at $5 or Bt 125. The violations often take place where workers are uneducated or where competition for jobs is keen. The problem is more acute outside Bangkok, especially in the country's northern region.

Furthermore, legislative accountability to the Thai public apparently is not emphasized, in terms of the manner in which laws are formulated and implemented. Robert Muscat criticizes the way in which these processes are carried out:

> Most Thai legislation is very brief, limited to granting specified ministries or departments within ministries, broadly worded empowerment, Legislation typically contains no instructions as to when, where, or to what extent the powers granted must or must not be exercised. The departments are thereby given wide discretion to apply the law as the bureaucracy sees fit. Normally, no processes of public or parliamentary review, or limitations on regulatory discretion, are included in the empowerments. Cabinet approval of regulations is normally

TABLE 12-1
Social Security Coverage

Year	No. of enterprises	No. of the insured (million)	No. of beneficiaries (million)	Amount paid (million baht)
1991	30,255	2.9	0.6	773.7
1992	30,949	3.9	2.1	2,102.8
1993	55,623	4.6	3.2	2,644.4
1994	65,510	5.0	4.2	3,234.9

Source: Department of Labor, Bangkok, Thailand.

required, but in practice cabinet members seldom object to a regulation tabled by an issuing minister for formal approval; to do so would invite retaliation when an objecting member tabled his own regulations at some future date. Past practice is no guarantee of how any law might be implemented by a future department head.... Past applications (e.g., regarding tax liabilities) can be reversed in retroactive administrative determinations. Few laws contain mechanisms for controlling abuse of discretionary powers.... New laws frequently contradict old ones without cancelling the latter, while the absence of codification can leave it unclear to administrators and the public whether all the laws, or the current law, applying to individual cases has been identified.... Unfortunately, adjudication does not serve well as a clarifying process; courts are not bound by precedent decisions in similar cases.[20]

CHAPTER 13

Labor–Management Relations

In Thailand unions under the Labor Relations Act of 1975, the basic statute dealing with labor–management relations, are divided into three levels: trade unions, workers' federations, and workers' congresses. Prior to the 1991 coup, at the federation level, unions had a significant degree of leverage with the government, especially during periods of political certainty. In terms of issues directly affecting workers, the key issue was the minimum wage. Beyond this, organized labor activity was directed at promoting the interests of powerful groups supporting their interests. State enterprise unions wielded a strong influence on management and the government, forcing it to abandon its privatization policy. They were also able to influence transfers and appointments of key managers.[1]

While at the plant or company level management held the upper hand over labor organizations as far as the power balance, the large labor federations were able to influence the government on policy issues such as the minimum wage and privatization. Unions were restricted to single provinces and industries. The most powerful unions were those in the state enterprises. Unions in the private sector were generally limited to single factories and companies. The government did not act to guarantee the right to organize unions in the private sector, and in most instances organizational efforts were stymied before gaining momentum.[2]

State workers were deprived of the right to set up unions by a regulation issued by the National Legislative Assembly appointed by the now defunct National Peacekeeping Council in 1991. The law prevented employees of state enterprises, which mostly operate public utilities, from engaging in strikes under the pretext of holding a general assembly of labor unions to press the government to respond to their demands. However, Thai labor leaders viewed the change of government following the coup as having a largely negative impact on the labor movement. In particular, the dissolution of state enterprise unions had a detrimental impact on Thai unionism. The state unions were larger, better organized, and had far more influence than their private sector counterpart, and often provided needed funds and expertise to them.[3]

THE EFFECTS ON NEGOTIATION OF THE 1991 LEGISLATION

The provisions of the 1991 provisions passed by the National Peacekeeping Council left the option open for state enterprise administrators to decide whether or not to enter discussions with their employees. Thus it was easy for them to ignore an essential ingredient of the union–management relationship; that of negotiation. While the Labor Relations Act of 1975 applied until 1991, administrators in each state enterprise regularly met labor leaders.[4] Some managers even had weekly lunch or dinner appointments with union officials, who needed only to phone directly to the administration office and ask for an appointment.[5]

After the events of 1991, many state enterprise managers required a formal letter in advance from the union leaders requesting a meeting before an appointment could be set up. For that matter, during the 1991–93 period in some state enterprises, union and management officials never met or communicated in any way. Certain administrators adopted an attitude of superiority toward their labor counterparts, acting as if they were bureaucrats.

Another negative development for labor involved the mysterious disappearance in February 1991 of Thanong Phoarn, the former president of the Labor Congress of Thailand. His absence contributed to the lack of strong leadership in private sector unions. Since his disappearance after the 1991 coup by the National Peacekeeping Council, unity among private sector unions substantially deteriorated. The banning of state unions also caused private labor organizations to lose significant support in their efforts at negotiation with Thai management. The Labor Congress had in the past taken employers to court in efforts to promote workers' rights, but such litigation stopped after 1991 as the new laws allowed broad interpretations of employers' rights to dismiss workers. Under the 1991 conditions, loss of trust in an employee or a low profit margin were enough reason to fire workers without additional proof.

THE 1994 DRAFT LEGISLATION

The new legislation drafted in the fall of 1994 developed at least in part due to criticism by international labor organizations and the U.S. threat to withdraw the Generalized System of Preferences trade privileges if the 1991 laws were not amended. Still, the draft did not mention the right to strike for state employees, although it does allow them to hold extraordinary meetings, with the addition of a provision that the date of the first meetings be set by the administrator. Had the Leekpai government remained in power, the passage of the bill was assured because it was in part proposed by his administration and based on a previous promise made to the labor movement. But the waters were muddied by the July 1995 election of Banharn, a promanagement businessman, whose labor sentiments were unclear.[6]

STRIKES

Under the new legal framework, state enterprise employees cannot strike and before private sector workers can engage in concerted action, 50% of the employees must vote to back a work stoppage. Action is also prohibited until the union negotiators have gone through the negotiation process with management, and unlawful strikes can result in the dismissal of the strikers.[4] Strike activity has greatly diminished, particularly during the 1985–91 period as shown in Table 13-1.

THE IMPACT OF THE LABOR COURT

It has been noted that contractual disputes submitted to labor courts receive prompt hearings and are inexpensive, and these courts have increasingly played a significant role in dispute settlement. For several reasons, however, the courts appar-

TABLE 13-1
Number Labor Disputes and Strikes
in Thailand, 1973–91

Years	Labor disputes	Strikes	Workers involved
1973	577	501	177,887
1974	477	357	105,883
1975	460	241	94,747
1976	340	133	65,342
1977	61	7	4,868
1978	156	21	6,842
1979	205	64	16,203
1980	174	18	3,230
1981	206	54	22,008
1982	376	22	7,061
1983	229	28	10,532
1984	86	17	6,742
1985	220	4	648
1986	168	6	5,191
1987	145	4	1,092
1988	120	5	1,444
1989	85	6	2,678
1990	127	7	2,519
1991 (Jan.–Nov.)	130	6	n.a.

Source: Labor Studies and Planning Division, Department of Labor, Bangkok, Thailand.

ently have a negative impact on the Thai labor movement. For one thing, competition among the national labor congresses for positions of associate judge has become pronounced. This occurs because such a position offers worker representatives both material benefits, in terms of per diem, travel fees, and accommodation allowances, and higher social status since an associate judge is appointed by Royal command and can apply for a Royal decoration. Second, in theory, trade unions enjoy the right to elect their own representatives but in practice self-determination is not fully utilized; rather the lists of candidates are determined by the leaders of the labor congresses who, in turn lobby for acceptance by trade unions. Third, such practice leads to allegations of favoritism and corruption in the labor congresses as well as a loss of confidence among the rank and file in their national leaders and, to some extent, in the institution of tripartism.[7]

THE STATE ENTERPRISE LABOR RELATIONS COMMITTEE

In August 1995, the Thai cabinet approved the draft bill on state enterprise labor relations as proposed by the Ministry of Labor and Social Welfare. The draft bill called for the formation of the State Enterprise Labor Relations Committee, replacing the State Enterprise Relations Committee. The new committee is made up of five representatives each from the government, employers, and employees. Another five qualified persons will be appointed as advisers to the committee but will have no rights to vote in any meeting of the committee.

This committee is authorized to handle labor disputes. Under the proposed law, not less than 10 state enterprise labor unions can form a state enterprise labor federation. The federation can also become a member of a private sector labor congress. However, each state enterprise is allowed to have only one union.[8]

UNION STRUCTURE AND MEMBERSHIP

The Department of Labor and Welfare Protection has noted that nearly 6.5 million people are currently employed in private firms outside the agricultural sector, but union membership comprises a mere 3.3%. Given the total workforce of 250,000 in the state enterprises, 84% are said to belong to an association.

While the numbers of unions are growing rapidly, a slow rate of expansion of members per union in Thailand reflects a lack of awareness by Thai workers of worker rights, educational standards, a mistrust they may have of the power of unions, and the fear of losing their jobs.[9]

Thai labor laws allow the formation of unions with as few as 10 members, which has led to considerable fractionalization at the local union and confederation level. A group of 15 unions, without regard to membership, can set up a national labor congress. As a consequence, more than one union is often established in an enterprise. For instance, there were 22 unions in 1990 in the Bangkok Mass Transport Organization. The textile unions set up two competing textile and garment federations. Table 13-2 shows that in 1994 each of a total of 545 unions had an average of only 70 worker members. Moreover, out of the total number of unions, only 399 or 61% were affiliated to six national centers. That means that, out of the total of 147,500 organized workers, about 67%, or 98,825 were members of the national labor congresses. Among the six national congresses only the LCT and the TTUC have from 5,000 to 45,000 worker members. The NCTL and the NFLUC have 10,000 to 30,000 worker members while the other two congresses, the NLC and the TCIL, have less than 10,000 members.

This picture is a good reflection of the fragmentation of the union movement and its low organizational strength and bargaining power. Moreover, there are claims that the law promotes the existence of company unions beholden to management. Unionists have charged that their efforts are undermined by unsupportive government policies, a lack of protection against antiunion discrimination, and the widespread use of temporary workers and the ease with which in-house unions are organized. Collective bargaining, in practice, is limited to benefits and working conditions but not salaries or wages.

There are no reliable data on union membership. While the labor ministry keeps records on unions and union members, unions claim to represent more workers than the ministry reports, but cannot produce hard numbers. Ministry records as of 1993 showed that 750 unions registered with a combined membership of 195,000. In addition, there are 28 state enterprise employee associations with a reported membership of over 210,000. There were eight labor federations in 1994 competing for membership and leadership of the labor movement. Keep in mind also that not all unions are members of a labor congress.

The disparity between government statistics and union membership claims is illustrated by this example. The Labor Congress of Thailand reports 86 unions with 132,000 members, but ministry records show only 75 unions with 39,000 members.

TABLE 13-2
Data on Organized Labor

Congress Member	Members	Unions, 1994
Labor Congress of Thailand (LCT)	75	39,000
National Congress of Thai Labor (NCTL)	164	29,000
Thai Trade Union Congress (TTUC)	148	43,000
National Congress of Private Empl. of Thai. (NPET)	20	6,100
Confederation of Thai Labor (CTL)	42	6,700
National Free Labor Union Congress (NFLUC)	41	10,400
The Council of Industrial Labor (TCIL)	19	5,600
National Labor Congress (NLC)	36	7,700
Total	545	147,500

Note: Not all unions have membership in a Congress.
Source: Ministry of Labor, Bangkok, Thailand.

Part of the discrepancy is that not all workers represented by a union actually pay dues. According to ministry data, the number of unions and members rose slightly from 839 to 888 and 231,000 to 243,000 respectively between 1993 and 1994. This small increase refers to the net of new unions registered and old unions which were administratively dissolved by the labor ministry because they were inactive for two years. One union official contended that: "There are some 200,000 factories or more so far, but only 814 labour unions exist."[10] Over half of the workforce is employed in the unorganized agricultural sector. Barely 3% of the total workforce, though nearly 11% of industrial workers, is organized. Cultural traditions and unfamiliarity with the concept of industrial relations are often cited as the reasons for these low rates of labor organization.

FIRM SIZE

It is also noteworthy that in the Thai pattern of industrialization the small-scale enterprises of 1 to 99 employees, outnumber larger ones. This prevents a large concentration of wage earners, which is seen as a prerequisite for proletarianization and unionization. Table 13-3 demonstrates that in 1989 there were 158,263 establishments, or 97.5% of the total of all nonagricultural enterprises, which hired less than 100 workers. Employees in these firms accounted for about 45% of the total of 3 million employees. In the tertiary sector, almost all establishments were small scale and hired about a half of all people employed in this sector. Such a pattern of employment indicates the spatial and organizational dispersion of the workforce in the tertiary sector. In manufacturing, large scale enterprises, over 300 workers, accounted for 1.6%, 854 companies, but engaged 47.8%, 718,424 workers, of all manufacturing employees. This is significant in that workers in large manufacturing establishment have more opportunity than those in agriculture and services to become permanent workers and thus have greater potential to be unionized.[12]

WILDCAT STRIKES AND SELECTIVE LOCKOUTS

Unions in Thailand are facing employers who are becoming more organized. Traditionally, there was little cooperation among businessmen. But by the end of 1994, 107 employee associations had been formed along with three employer federations. In the Thai environment, when labor problems arise labor leaders, sometimes ad hoc, often turn to wildcat actions, such as staging organized sick leave, prework/postwork rallies, and walkouts and protests at the labor ministry to attract attention to their case. Thai employers have responded to these pressures with an increasingly popular new tactic: the selective lockout. In the selective lockout, union leaders, labor activists, and their supporters are kept out of the workplace while work continues with nonunion workers and new hires. The tactic has predictably dampened enthusiasm for union participation, but is increasing frustration among those who feel unjustly

TABLE 13-3

Number of Establishments and Employees by Size of Establishment
and Industry in Whole Country, 1989

Sector Size of establishment	Total		Manufacturing		Tertiary		Mining	
	Establish.	Employees	Establish.	Employees	Establish.	Employees	Establish.	Employees
1–99 persons	158,263	1,320,012	51,111	510,172	106,159	788,694	993	21,146
	(97.5)	(44.6)	(95.3)	(33.9)	(98.5)	(55.3)	(95.9)	(65.5)
100–299 persons	2,849	464,835	1,657	274,703	1,159	185,205	33	4,927
	(1.7)	(15.7)	(3.1)	(18.3)	(1.1)	(13.0)	(3.2)	(15.3)
300+ persons	1,283	1,177,178	854	718,424	419	452,537	10	6,217
	(0.8)	(39.7)	(1.6)	(47.8)	(0.4)	(31.7)	(0.9)	(19.3)
Total	162,395	2,962,025	53,622	1,503,299	107,737	1,426,436	1,036	32,290
	(100)	(100)	(100)	(100)	(100)	(100)	(100)	(100)

Source: Labor Studies and Planning Division, Department of Labor, Bangkok, Thailand.

treated. In the absence of constructive dialogue between labor and management, more radical and widespread labor actions are likely as the economy continues to experience rapid structural adjustment.

An example of management's aggressive posture was seen in a situation where the labor ministry ordered a firm which makes copper wires to reinstate its workers after the firm shut down its factory on January 4, 1995 and locked out its employees who had been demonstrating for better pay and welfare benefits for six weeks.

It was the first time such an order had been issued by the government under the mandate of Article 35 of the Labor Relations Act. The directive told Siam Electric Industries in Samut Prakarn province to reemploy its workers at current rates of pay and to set up a labor relations committee to settle dispute. The workers' original demand was for, among other things, an additional monthly cost-of-living allowance of Bt 300 ($12), an increase in the "diligence" allowance, and a four-month year end bonus.

Management's reply to this was to propose on December 23rd that the Bt 500 ($20) monthly allowance already paid to workers and the Bt 350 ($14) diligence allowance be scrapped altogether.

When on January 4th the management shut down the factory, employing 356 workers, 150 of them staged a protest in front of the labor and social welfare ministry. Also, 300 workers assembled in front of the Japanese Embassy and burned in effigy two Japanese employers and three Thai managers.

The labor ministry tried in vain to settle the conflict. Eventually, the labor minister decided to issue the order, because the company's management did not send its representatives for negotiations and it was feared that the workers would move on to protest at other important locations.[13]

ALLEGATIONS OF EMPLOYER WRONGDOING

In early 1995, labor union representatives submitted a letter outlining labor disputes which have involved employer violations of the 1975 Labor Relations Act and which may escalate into major problems in the future. One claim was that employers had exploited loopholes in the law to fire labor leaders who demanded fair treatment. Major problems that had occurred and remained unsolved involve the following firms in Parthum Thani and nearby provinces:

1. Par Garment Company's request for the Central Labor Court to dismiss labor leaders and the company's female workers, members of the union, citing physical violence.
2. The change in employment conditions at Siam Synthetic and Fibre Company, resulting in some workers being required to work on Sundays.
3. The termination of employment for the founders of Central Food Production Company's labor union.
4. The Chaiseri Metal and Rubber Company's failure to comply with an agreement on employment conditions and the labor protection law.

5. A physical attack against female workers by Japanese employers at Furu-kawa (Thailand) Company in Saraburi.
6. The Pathum Thani Gunny Bag Company's failure to offer compensation to workers who refused to move to a new company site in Nakhon Pathom.
7. The Marco Industry Company's failure to comply with agreed working conditions and salaries.
8. The Inchapte Manufacturing Company's failure to pay overtime to workers.
9. The Able Auto Parts Industry Company's termination of labor leaders and 15 workers.
10. Unfair treatment of labor leaders at the Siam Stars Company.

The Thai government is authorized to restrict private sector strikes that would "affect national security or cause severe negative repercussions for the population at large," although this provision is seldom invoked. Labor law also forbids strikes in "essential services," which are defined much more broadly than the ILO criteria for such services.[14]

Intensive state promotion of tripartism in industrial relations in the past two decades resulted in a decline in labor disputes and work stoppages. Many of the labor disputes were settled either by the Labor Relations Committee or through labor courts. From 1976 to 1983 workers' complaints of unfair labor practices on the part of employers were submitted to the Labor Relations Committee. But after labor courts were established labor disputes have been increasingly resolved through this means.

That industrial conflict rarely led to strikes and demonstrations seems to benefit the government, with respect to political stability and relative autonomy in policy development, more than workers in the form of fair wages, working conditions, and welfare. The growth rate in the 1980s was relatively high but real wages determined by the National Wage Committee hardly changed. Moreover, this committee did not play a significant role in improving the enforcement of minimum wage rates. Further-more, the Labor Relations Committee has not acted in a meaningful way in protecting the right of workers to organize unions.[15]

THE CONSEQUENCES OF MECHANIZATION—
THE THAI KRIANG STRIKE

Another major crisis confronting Thai labor in the 1990s is the transition from labor-intensive to capital-intensive industry, which was symbolized by the plight of the Thai Kriang textile workers.

During the past three decades Thailand has relied heavily on cheap labor for factories in Bangkok and nearby provinces, especially in Samut Prakan where Thai Kriang is one of thousands of factories. The situation worsened when the management fired several hundred workers, particularly senior personnel who had been employed at the firm for more than 20 years, in the process of modernizing operations through the introduction of new weaving machinery. The technology requires more highly skilled employees and is more efficient, thus requiring fewer workers. The management claimed that an unwillingness on their part to modernize would endanger their competitive position in the world market. They contended that it would be better to sacrifice a few workers so that the remainder could preserve their jobs. The workers, however, resented the summary dismissals, even though the employer had agreed to compensate the workers according to the law. They argued that the employers wanted to cut costs by dismissing long-term, loyal workers who earned high wages. They rejected the employers reason that the terminated employees were unable to master the required new skills.

The dispute ended in a compromise when management agreed to lay off fewer workers, while the labor and welfare ministry promised to secure alternative employment for the dismissed workers. The strike lasted more than 15 days and ended when management agreed to negotiate with workers regarding their demands for improvements in working conditions, including the demand that the company abide by official annual minimum wage adjustments.[16]

ORGANIZING AND BARGAINING RIGHTS

The labor law, as we have seen, recognizes the right of private sector workers to organize and bargain collectively and defines the mechanism for such negotiations and for government-assisted conciliation and arbitration in dispute cases. In practice, genuine collective bargaining probably occurs only in 10 to 20% of all workplaces and in most instances continues to be characterized by autocratic attitudes on the part of Thai employers. Collective bargaining is permitted in all but state-owned firms; agricultural workers and civil servants also are not permitted to engage in bilateral negotiations.

Since government programs for improving the income and welfare of workers to keep pace with increasing living costs are still limited, with some weaknesses, Thai workers have therefore concentrated their attention on demands for wage increases. At the national level they have submitted, every year, a demand for minimum wage increases. The national tripartite Wage Committee does not take the initiative in this situation since it will call for a meeting only after the workers present their wage demands, which has become a singularly dramatic issue among union members. At the enterprise level, the workers submit wage demands directly to the management. However, regular wage negotiations between labor and management have not been institutionalized at a broader level and are not even accepted in many companies.

In reality, Thai workers lack bargaining power and are deprived of the right to determine their own economic destiny since management has total authority, especially in nonunion firms where workers attempting to organize unions are often forced to resign or face immediate dismissal. Also, due to the lack of legal enforcement, there is an increasing tendency on the part of employers to exploit their workers, which negatively impacts on their minimum wage, end-of-the-year bonus and other fringe benefits.[17]

With rapid growth in the industrial sector in recent years and greater exposure to union organization and practices in developed countries, industrial relations in Thailand are slowly being modernized. Owners of larger firms are realizing that the needs and aspirations of workers cannot be met by traditional paternalism and are now hiring human resource managers to deal with their employees. Nevertheless, even where unions exist, traditional collective bargaining is rarely practiced since the adversarial system of industrial relations has not yet made its appearance in Thailand.[18]

UNION LEADERSHIP PROBLEMS

A serious problem confronting Thai labor unions is the lack of leadership and solidarity plaguing their efforts at successful negotiations with employers. The fact that there are as many as eight labor congresses indicates that none of the labor leaders are outstanding enough to gain recognition from others. More importantly, it appears that some of the congresses have no real intention of vigorously represent the economic interests of their membership but have been established by individuals who are more interested in advancing their own personal interests rather than those of their constituents.

In late 1993 five of the eight groups tried to form a front to create more bargaining power. However, the plan collapsed due to conflicts between two major congresses over the nomination of associate judges to the Central Labor Court. In this regard, infighting among union officials for roles in national tripartite agencies is considered to be the main factor which has weakened the Thai labor movement during a crucial period when a strong labor movement is of vital importance for rapidly growing economic and social development. Rivalry among labor leaders would be a serious obstacle to effective labor representation in the development process.

Along with labor court appointments, labor leaders are competing for positions on tripartite bodies such as the wage and consultative committees for labor development. The working mechanisms of these tripartite entities are usually quite complicated, making it difficult for foreign organizations involved in labor matters to understand the real reasons and motives for the union rivalries which have prevented labor unity in Thailand. Union officials have even fought among themselves for nomination to be Thailand's representatives at the annual International Labor Organization meeting in Geneva and for a larger share of funding support from the government to organize May Day celebrations in Bangkok. These negative developments far outweigh efforts by labor leaders to promote unity by meeting with workers in various industrial estates to persuade them to form unions and join labor councils.

Unfortunately, another problem that negatively impacts upon the public perception of union leaders is the legacy of corruption among public sector labor officials who were exploited by the military, politicians, or employers for their own purposes, but private sector unions generally operate independently of the government and other outside organizations. Unions are free to associate internationally with other labor organizations, and they maintain a wide variety of such affiliations.

While violence directed against Thai labor leaders is rare, the 1991 mysterious disappearance of outspoken labor leader Thanong Poarn remains unsolved. Most observers believe Thanong was kidnapped and killed because of his criticism of the military coup in February 1991.[19]

SUBCONTRACTING

Another problem area for Thai labor involves the efforts by Thai employers to reduce labor costs by subcontracting part of their production to smaller companies. The cost savings result in lower wages and limited or virtually no benefits for employees. Subcontracting is common in export-oriented sectors such as the food and beverage industry, oil production, and the clothing and handicraft industries.

Workers affected by subcontracting are disadvantaged with regard to both their income and employment prospects. They work long hours, sometimes 13 to 14 hours daily, on piecework assignments, and are usually unskilled, or semiskilled personnel. Management also usually does not comply with labor laws or minimum wage requirements. Often, work is done without formal contract arrangements between the primary employer and the subcontractor or between the subcontractor and the workers. Employee benefits such as holidays and sick leave are unilaterally determined by the employer.

Other negative consequences also affect Thai workers under these arrangements. For one thing, many are so absorbed in meeting production requirements that they lack a basic awareness of existing labor legislation and their rights. Also, they do not have time to participate in organizational activity and, concurrently, unions have shown little or no interest in penetrating this subsector. A further deleterious effect of the subcontracting mode of employment is its undermining of the growth of union membership and wages in the organized sector.[20]

TEMPORARY EMPLOYMENT

Another management tactic to cut labor costs involves the use of temporary workers in every aspect of the production process. In general, they have to do the same job as the permanent workers but receive lower levels of remuneration and less legal protection. This is short-term employment used only as a mechanism to reduce production costs. The more generous the wages and greater the benefits an employer provides to a permanent employee, the more that can be saved by hiring a temporary one. Short-term employment also operates efficiently in increasing the length of the work day. Many local firms were able to depress wages below the minimum, but this is becoming more difficult. In the past companies were allowed to employ temporary workers at below the minimum wage without other benefits; these workers were dismissed and then rehired at the end of each "probationary" period. This practice has been declared illegal, and now firms must pay all benefits to all workers from the day

they are hired. Decree Number 11 promulgated in 1989 also shortened the probationary period from 180 to 120 days.[21]

However, unions still face a number of problems. A serious one is that the law
does not prohibit the use of casual, seasonal, and project workers. A survey of
temporary employment after the enforcement of Decree Number 11 indicated that
many employers refused to transfer the temporary workers to the regular payroll. This
was the case, for instance, for 630 employees of the CEI company in Prapradaeng and
the nearby area, 600 employees of the Sammit Motors Company in Omno-Omyai, 150
employees of the PTL Industrial Company in the Rangsit area, and 2,500 employees
of the Piyawat Industry Company in Bangkok. It was found that 11,700 workers, or
11.6% of the total of 101,200 employees surveyed in industry and the hotel business in
Bangkok and nearby areas, were still hired on short-term contracts. Many employers
argued that casual workers were necessary since the assignments were project work.
But in fact short-term workers were to work side by side with permanent employees
on the production line. Only in a few firms did the trade unions succeed in having
management conform to the decree.

It was also revealed that many employers persisted in efforts to evade the law.
For instance, workers were hired for two to three months or 105-day contracts. In this
case they received no benefits when the contracts expired. But after their expiration
the contracts were usually extended. In some firms, workers were told to resign after
the probationary period and were told to reapply for the same job.

Another weakness of Decree Number 11 is that subcontract workers and piece-
rate employees are not protected, though unions strongly recommended safeguards.
The unionists realized that subcontracting directly weakens the union's bargaining
power. The case of the Thai Asahi Company is quite remarkable. After Decree
Number 11, the trade union asked the company to transfer 200 short-term employees
to permanent status. The company later introduced subcontracting on a large scale.
Such tactics effectively threatened the power of the unions.[22]

CONCLUSIONS

In Thailand, tensions are gradually increasing between labor and management in
many low-wage industries because of fundamental changes in the structure of the
economy. Faced with growing competition from emerging lower cost countries in the
region, many firms operating in Thailand face three alternatives: (1) Move production
out of the country; (2) Increase the proportion of the work done in lower-cost
subcontracting arrangements, often with small firms in the service sector which do not
adhere to labor laws; and/or (3) reduce costs through mechanization. Each of these
threatens worker employment and/or wages and benefits in the firms involved. In
actuality, the long-term solution to the dilemma posed by rising wages is to improve
the education and skill base of the workforce, enabling workers to fill higher value-
added, and higher paying, jobs. In the short run, labor–management relations are
increasingly strained.

So far as skill development is concerned, the Thai government should encourage management and unions to cooperate in establishing skill training and retraining programs. A program of this type could begin in some establishments, where the relationship between the management and the unions is well established and harmonious.

On the conflict horizon, there have been no major public attention-grabbing strikes recently. However, the seeming calm does not reflect a smoothly running industrial relations system because of traditional deference to seniors and a cultural aversion to conflict. Thai workers are slow to organize. While U.S., Japanese, and European multinationals operating in the country generally seek to avoid labor problems by maintaining satisfactory wages and working conditions, many other firms view profit-making as largely a function of minimizing labor costs. When conditions are such that workers try to organize, the typical management response is to fire the principal activists. The labor law currently does not protect workers from dismissal for organizing activities prior to the establishment of a union. Over time, the reluctance of workers to organize and management removal of would-be labor leaders have led to lower levels of labor organization, generally inexperienced labor leadership, and little real collective bargaining.

The Seventh Plan (1992–96) of the government emphasized the need for attaining numerous human resource development objectives. These include the above-mentioned skills improvement programs, the promotion of health and safety programs, stressing comprehensive employment opportunities, raising the incomes of female employees, and improvements in working conditions for women and child workers. All of these goals could be facilitated through more effective levels of unionization and if both management and labor recognized the value of meaningful, bilateral collective bargaining.

Presently, private sector unions are in great need of basic training in union administration, collective bargaining, and industrial relations. In addition, union leaders need advanced training in labor economics and socioeconomic development processes, in order to have a better understanding of the dynamic changes taking place in Thailand, and to be able to participate more efficiently in collective bargaining, as well as to help create better industrial relations within enterprises.

Thai employers too need a better understanding of how stable industrial relations can contribute to enhanced productivity, especially employers in the small- and medium-scale firms and foreign investors. Training for employers may reduce the extent of employers' evasion of the law and help strengthen the bipartite system at the enterprise level. A likely side effect is a decline in interventions in workers' organizations by third parties.

Through such strategies it is likely that industrial peace could be achieved, together with a more equitable sharing in the fruits of economic growth.

CHAPTER 14

Worker Rights Issues

A number of issues involving the interests of Thai unions and workers have been noted in previous chapters. The determination of compensation, primarily the minimum wage, factors affecting female and child labor, concern for workplace health and safety, and union opposition to privatization of state enterprises were discussed earlier and will be examined in depth in this chapter to provide a clearer perspective on these important developments in Thai industrial relations.

THE MINIMUM WAGE, 1995

The 1975 Labor Relations Act guarantees an annual adjustment in the basic unskilled wage by a committee comprised of representatives of employees, employers, and the government. The determination of the minimum wage turns out to be one of the most, if not the most, controversial topics this tripartite group assembles to resolve each year. The acrimony that ensues stems from the fact that the wage level agreed to by the tripartite wage committee simply is not adequate to support an urban worker and his family. Combined with extended family member financial contributions, the minimum wage provides the basis for a marginally adequate overall standard of living. However, more than half of Thai workers living in the countryside receive less than the minimum wage, especially in the provinces. Unskilled migrant workers who pour into Bangkok from the poorer rural areas, as well as illegal aliens, often work for less than the minimum wage.[1]

NATIONAL WAGE COMMITTEE HEARING

The debate in 1995 over how much to raise the minimum wage was more drawn out than in previous years as the tripartite committee struggled to deal with labor's initial demand that the wage be raised 15%. Labor's demand was prompted by the 14.5% hike granted to the civil service in October, 1994, and by a general perception that workers' standard of living is stagnating in light of rising costs and that they are not getting their fair share of the country's rapidly increasing prosperity. Employers argued that Thailand's already relatively high wages are driving many industries into lower cost neighboring countries. Academics wondered out loud whether the current system, in place since 1972, of having a three-party committee set minimum wages needed overhaul.

The government responded to the controversy by holding an unprecedented public hearing on the issue to allow the different sides to air their views. At the hearing on May 24, 1995, the government outlined the issues it wished to consider:

1. How many people should the minimum wage be designed to support? There is disagreement over whether it should support only the worker or a family of three.
2. Does it make sense to delineate the minimum wage by province, or should it be done according to industry or skill level?
3. Is the tripartite committee the best vehicle to determine the minimum wage, or would some automatic adjustment mechanism work better to avoid public controversy each year?

Various experts were asked to speak before the floor was opened to the public. The proceedings were also broadcast live by radio and listeners were invited to call in with their questions and comments. The views expressed ranged from assertions that without strong government intervention workers will be exploited, to pleas from workers for more income to help them meet rising living costs.

The holding of public hearings to deal with difficult or controversial, but generally nonpolitical, public issues is a significant new trend in Thailand's democratic development. In earlier years, the making of public policy rarely involved input from outside the government, except for small circles of selected advisors. Labor ministry organizers even coined a new term, *choengprachaaphijarn*, meaning in the manner of public deliberation, as they felt there was no appropriate existing word for such an event.

Shortly after the public hearing, the tripartite wage committee announced the new minimum wage scale and the controversy subsided. The ideas for reexamining the minimum wage have now been examined publicly. Whether any of them will be seriously considered or implemented will depend on the priority given to the issue by the labor minister in the new government formed after the July 2, 1995 election. It remains to be seen if the Banharn administration will act on recommendations to adjust wages by industry, set up an automatic adjustment mechanism, or other suggested reforms.[2]

THE EMPLOYER PROPOSAL

Earlier the Thai employers' association had asked the labor and social welfare minister to reduce the minimum wage in remote provinces to prevent investors from leaving Thailand. An employers' delegation proposed that the wage of workers in remote and border provinces, as well as those in areas where agricultural pursuits are impossible, be reduced 15 to 40% lower than urban minimum wages so that investors could distribute job opportunities among rural residents. The management representatives claimed that the gradual increase in wages has already resulted in the closure of a dozen garment and shoe manufacturing factories, leading to nationwide layoffs of nearly 12,000 workers and to the relocation of investment to nearby countries. The government representative indicated these ideas would receive consideration when the policy of income distribution was formulated.

The representatives of the employers' association also proposed that the labor and social welfare ministry try to persuade about 20 million agricultural laborers to shift to industries to raise their incomes. In response, the ministry urged the employers' association to bring in high technology to manufacturing to improve product quality to match international competition.[3]

The employers also indicated their desire to see the minimum wage imposed once a year to avoid uncertainty in companies' annual budgeting plans. They maintained that whenever the minimum wage was to be imposed, the prices of goods and commodities increased in advance, while the companies were forced to adjust their annual budget to keep pace with the new minimum wage.[4]

The Labor Congress of Thailand (LCT) strongly opposed the employers' proposal to set up exclusive wage zones whereby workers would be paid substantially less than the minimum daily wage in urban centers. They also disputed as irrational the management claim that the lower wage rate would help promote foreign investment in Thailand.[5]

OPINION OF LABOR EXPERTS

The LCT position was supported by Thai labor experts who lent their full support for increases in the minimum wage as necessary to maintain the living standards of the underprivileged and unskilled labor. They said that minimum wage increases, which are invariably opposed by employers, should not have any serious consequences since Thailand always boasts about its projected eight percent economic growth rate.

The minimum wage involves about 2 million unskilled workers at industrial sites throughout Thailand and should be no cause for concern, particularly since the country is experiencing an economic prosperity period. A ministerial adviser with expertise in labor affairs opined that it was not fair to discuss the issue on purely economic grounds because the minimum wage was basically meant to guarantee that the unskilled and underprivileged people could live like human beings. He believes that small annual increases in the minimum wage are not going to enrich employees but will enable them to survive. Also, it is not right to blame minimum wage increases for the rising cost of consumer goods while the government still fails to deal with monopolistic pricing conditions in Thailand.

THE LABOR POSITION

Five labor congresses, the Thai Trade Unions Congress, Labor Congress of Thailand, National Private Employees Congress of Thailand, National Free Labor

Unions Congress, and Thailand Congress of Industrial Labor, pushed for an increase in the 1995 minimum wage from Bt 125 ($5.00) to at least Bt 135 ($5.40), but feared the government and employer's representatives on the tripartite wage committee would not meet the employees' demand.[6]

Some employers, including the Employers' Confederation of Thailand threatened to relocate their investments to Indochina states or China, citing a surge in labor costs in Thailand.

A congress vice-president indicated the congresses would not call a general strike or make any massive move on the issue until May Day, which might see a large rally of workers either outside Government House in Bangkok or at the ministry of labor and social welfare. In previous years, thousands of workers gathered at Sanam Luang public grounds on May 1 to listen to speeches, attend ceremonies, and entertain themselves.

The state enterprise employees' organization supported the private sector workers' call for the minimum wage increase, claiming that a Bt 3 ($.13) increase, which had been predicted as a compromise, would be an insult, like no increase at all when inflation was taken into account.[7]

Occasionally, workers will actively protest the failure of employers to observe legal minimum wage requirements. In one instance the management at Wiwat Cold Storage Company allegedly violated the law. Consequently, employees blocked a road in front of the Songkhla provincial labor office, demanding a wage increase. The company agreed to pay them Bt 108 ($4.32) a day as required by the law and promised not to retaliate against the workers who staged the protest claiming that the company paid wages below the legal minimum. The employees contended they were usually paid Bt 88 ($3.52) for eight working hours and not paid at all if they worked half a day. They said that when they ceased work on holidays, their pay would be reduced.[8]

A REEVALUATION

A recent *Bangkok Post* editorial raised several interesting suggestions for improving the process of minimum wage determination. It characterized the debate that occurred in "this annual horse-trading process" as one where management opposed the figure set by the National Wage Committee, "as too much and employees lament that it is too little...." The writer recommended ways to improve the process, noting substantial noncompliance by employers and the reasons therefore:

> This charade has been conducted annually since the basic minimum wage was introduced for the first time in 1973 at the rate of 12 baht per day. To date there have been at least 20 alterations in the basic wage. But despite all the rhetoric, it is largely an exercise confined to paper. A survey conducted after the minimum wage law was introduced showed that at least 40 percent of employers were ignoring it. Later surveys have indicated this figure to be as high as 76 percent.
>
> The main objection of employers lies in the controversial ruling that employers should not count welfare or fringe benefits as part of the minimum wage. They also bemoan the fact that the annual adjustment of basic wages creates a ripple effect requiring an annual

adjustment for skilled workers as well, although the basic minimum wage is only intended to protect unskilled workers entering the labor market.

A 1990 survey by labor welfare specialists at Thammasat University showed that workers earning the minimum wage used to pay the following expenses:

Food, clothing and housing 66 percent;
Tobacco and alcoholic drink 11 percent;
Transportation and child's tuition 7 percent each;
Medical fees 1 percent;
Entertainment 2 percent;
Other expenses 6 percent.

In real terms those workers in Bangkok earning the minimum wage were in trouble because expenses outnumbered earnings by 593 baht. Larger wage increases are not a permanent solution. They tend automatically to increase the spending and inflationary curve. Likewise, exhortations to be thrifty and frugal do not always fall on fertile ground, human nature being what it is. Fortunately, there are other ways to improve the quality of a worker's life and this is where employment benefits come in. Or would if the Wage Committee would remove its blinkers.

The basic difference between a wage and employee welfare is that a wage depends largely on performance, experience, education and the nature of work. Employee benefits, on the other hand, are offered on the basis of employment in a government or private sector organization to help increase the quality of life of all employees, regardless of particular skills. These generally provide for conditions of well-being, good health and hygiene as well as safety and company-assisted provident funds designed to provide long-term financial security and housing loans.

When the time comes around for ritual haggling early next year it would be more sensible if the Wage Committee concentrated less on arguing over a few baht, which is determined more by market forces than decree anyway, and more on extending employee benefits. Employers should realize that such benefits tend to be cheaper by economy of scale because of the large number of workers they are extended to. Some kinds of welfare can also give the worker access to services or activities which he or she could not otherwise possibly have access to and, in the bargain, help ease financial problems.

Another major factor that should be taken into consideration is that these benefits are extended to a worker's family as well, especially recreational programmes and medical insurance.

There was a time when welfare or benefits were regarded by employers purely as a tool with which to build loyalty and commitment. In fact these are by-products. Employer benefits should be directed solely at enhancing the well-being of a worker and his or her family.[9]

The writer recommended that the authorities act to accept index-linking to the consumer price index as the natural formula for increases in the minimum wage. Also, the government was admonished to pay a great deal more attention to instituting and enforcing comprehensive welfare benefits which promote the physical and mental well-being of the workforce. Whether such constructive criticism will be positively considered in the future by labor, employer, and government wage-setting personnel is an open question.

OTHER WAGE PRESSURES

While unskilled workers are the group most affected by changes in the minimum wage, unions have also been demanding and achieving substantial wage gains for other segments of their membership. Recently, workers possessing higher skill levels have done especially well. For example, in January 1995, the workers at the Phoenix Pulp and Paper Company in Khon Kaen demanded a 27% wage increase. The management would only agree to a 21% increase. About 200 workers, mostly union members, had been protesting since December, accusing the management of ignoring their demand for higher pay and better welfare. The workers initially demanded an 80% increase but later lowered it to 27% in early January.

A rally was held in front of the firm's administration building during which the management was criticized for its failure to settle the dispute and for its alleged favoritism toward overseas employees. About 200 workers took turns attacking management, but there was no work stoppage. Union representatives claimed the company had never tried to solve the problem and insisted on its offer of a 21% wage increase despite the workers' easing their demand from 80% to only 27%. They said the 20% raise would only benefit technicians and foremen who were mostly for-eigners. The 21% increase was to offered in three phases: 7% after negotiation, 8% for an annual increase, and 6% or Bt 50 ($2.00) according to seniority.

The union representatives stated that the workers would soon set the date for a work stoppage and might move into the town of Khon Kaen to stage the protest. "Facts will also be revealed on that day how the company has destroyed the environment and oppressed local workers," was one union official's pointed comment.[10]

Joint Venture Labor Problems

Increasing labor costs have also placed Japanese joint ventures in jeopardy. So many Japanese manufacturers have rushed to set up plants in the same industrial parks at the same time that the supply of skilled labor is falling behind demand. This is happening despite wage increases exceeding 10% a year. One Japanese manager lamented that cheap labor was the reason to come to Thailand in the first place but with increasingly high labor costs, there was little reason to stay there.

The labor predicament faced by Siam Asahi Technoglass Company is typical. The joint venture between Asahi Glass Company and the Siam Cement Group has 700 employees making television parts about 90 miles outside Bangkok. The company plans to add another press, expanding production capacity by 50%. For this, it will need 200 to 300 additional workers.

In the past few years, 60 foreign firms, many of which are Japanese, have moved into Laem Chabang Industrial Estate where Siam Asahi is located, and the estate continues to expand. The adjoining Bangpakong Industrial Park has attracted more than 20 Japanese firms. When Nippondenso Company and others complete their factories in the area, there will suddenly be tens of thousands of new jobs, many of them for engineers and white collar workers. Since only about 10,000 new technicians graduate from Thai schools each year, it is definitely a seller's market.

At all of the Japanese firms operating in Thailand the lack of engineers, accountants, and middle managers is becoming a serious problem. The dilemma is not just finding workers but keeping up with their pay increases. The average 18-year-old's monthly pay has risen from Bt 3,000 ($120) in 1990 to Bt 5,000 ($200) in 1995, over 10% annually.

Some companies are raising the salaries of white collar workers two or three times per year. Others may promise particularly valuable employees the use of company cars, sometimes even with drivers. With workers demanding large pay raises, labor–management relations also have deteriorated in some locations.

Scouting of experienced workers is also increasing. In fact, some firms are thinking of providing housing in order to entice bright students from outside the Bangkok region. The number of graduates has to be increased quickly and more training centers set up to meet this rapidly rising demand. Japanese employers have been urged to take steps to alleviate the problem, as the labor shortage is squeezing Thai businesses as well.

In response to these labor supply pressurers, Keidanren, the leading Japanese business organization, in 1992 provided 800 million yen ($8.33 million) in seed funding for the establishment of the International Institute of Technology at Thammasat University. In 1995, the institute will add information technology and mechanical engineering departments. Asahi Glass is considering funding special graduate courses at Chulalongkorn University in glass manufacturing technology. Nevertheless, a source at one Japanese subsidiary in Bangpakong Industrial Park warned that if the situation continued, they would have to automate jobs such as packing and inspection, the way it was done in Japan.[11]

THE STATE ENTERPRISE EMPLOYEE CONTROVERSY

Earlier a wage controversy erupted involving public sector workers and the government. The State Enterprise Relations Group (SERG) called on the prime minister to review the cabinet decision for the finance and labor ministries to review the state enterprise employees' pay scale. The group believed the resolution was illegal. The cabinet had agreed that state enterprise workers should receive a pay increase but it wanted to review the scale to ensure the average increase was kept to a 15% maximum and the allocation for this purpose was not to exceed 14.3% of the previous allocation. The SERG proposed an average pay increase of 15.64% and claimed that the cabinet resolution violated Article 11 of the State Enterprise Employees Relations Act of 1991, which stated that the State Enterprise Relations Committee is empowered to work out a suitable pay scale for state enterprise employees. The group maintained that the cabinet is authorized only to order a review of the pay scale, not to set a limit on the increase, as suggested by the finance ministry, which is a member of the State Enterprise Relations Committee, a tripartite body composed of representatives from the finance and labor ministries, state enterprises, and employees. Despite dissatisfaction with the cabinet resolution, neither a work stoppage nor a slowdown was threatened.

Labor Minister Phaithoon Kaeothong said the State Enterprise Relations Committee must look at the actual increase in the allocation to see if it was too high compared to that of government officials:

> If the State Enterprise Relations Group is still unhappy, it could seek a ruling from the Juridical Council. They should not resort to using mob rule instead of the law.... We will look through the pay scale rejected by the Cabinet and will base our work on the basis that the average pay increase does not exceed 15 percent while the additional allocation needed must not be more than 14.3 percent.

REPERCUSSIONS

The debate between employers and employees over the minimum wage brings annual acrimony to the deliberations of the tripartite wage committee and raises basic questions about social stability, regional inequities, and economic competitiveness in Thai society. As wages have risen in Thailand and the opportunities for investment in lower-wage areas such as China and Vietnam have expanded, the arguments have become more pointed as labor fights for its "share of the pie" and employers struggle to keep labor-intensive operations in Thailand competitive.

In the past several years, increases in the minimum wage have greatly exceeded the inflation rate, bringing a general rise in the standard of living for workers receiving the minimum rate and for those whose wages are informally linked to the minimum wage. At the same time, wages for the well-educated and highly skilled have outpaced increases in the minimum wage, causing the proportion of Thai GDP that goes to unskilled lower income groups to continue to fall.

Disparities between Bangkok and the rest of the country are also great. The average monthly wage in Bangkok is two to three times the average wages in the provinces where a large labor supply and traditional paternalism favor high employment over high wages. Large variances in wage rates will continue to fuel migration to Bangkok and surrounding areas, despite a higher cost of living and, in many ways, a lower quality of life in the capital.

The inability of labor, particularly unskilled labor, to share more of the benefits of Thailand's rapid economic growth is in part due to the failure to develop a strong political constituency for labor. A more important cause, however, is the fundamentally low level of education and skills among the workforce which retard the ability of many workers to perform higher skill, and higher wage, jobs in an increasingly competitive international environment.

WORKPLACE SAFETY AND HEALTH

Another area of concern for labor activists concerns working conditions in Thailand, which vary widely. In medium-sized and large factories, government health and safety standards are often maintained, but lax enforcement of safety standards is common elsewhere. In the large informal sector, the health and safety environment is substandard.

The government designated 1994 the "Year of Workplace Safety" and initiated a variety of programs to deal with continuing problems. Employers are able to ignore safety regulations in part because nonunionized workers often do not understand safety and health standards and do not report violations. When 188 workers lost their lives in the May 1993 Kader Toy Factory fire near Bangkok, the government brought suit against eight persons, including the managing director. The case commenced in June 1994 and was expected to be lengthy. In 1994, a court found a factory manager and three directors (two of whom are Taiwanese) as well as the company, guilty of failure to provide adequate safety and neglect of duty in allowing illegal, substandard construction at the factory.

Unfortunately, there is no law affording job protection to employees who remove themselves from dangerous work situations and then suffer retaliation from management because they have left their work locations. The ministry of labor promulgates health and safety regulations regarding conditions of work and labor inspectors are responsible for enforcement of health and safety requirements; the strictest penalty is six months in jail.

THE KADER FIRE

The danger to worker's lives was epitomized by the tragic Kader factory inferno. This incident clearly reflected the lack of honest concern for safety standards, and the inability of safety inspectors to compel employers to abide by safety regulations. It was the worst fire in Thailand's history, sweeping through the Kader doll factory in Nakhon Pathom Province on May 10, 1993. It completely destroyed the Kader complex, killing 188 workers and injuring more than 300 others.

Investigations revealed that the building was not structurally sound. The managers had not installed fire alarms or any other emergency precautions. They had also failed to provide accessible fire escapes, as these were locked on the pretext of preventing theft by workers. The fire began while about 1,800 employees were working inside. Most of them jumped to safety from the factory's side doors and windows as the fire engulfed the first floor, sweeping quickly through the factory complex. Minutes after the blaze started, three of the four factory buildings collapsed, killing many workers struggling to get out.

Labor groups complained that the factory was not equipped with proper fire alarms and emergency exits. Some overhead walkways between the buildings were allegedly locked to prevent workers from taking rest breaks during their work shifts. One foreign labor expert claimed that a preliminary government inquiry into the conflagration was completed but it "danced around the real causes" of the disaster, and that "a full accounting has never been published." An engineer familiar with the case revealed that highly flammable materials were stored on the ground and second floors of the factory complex while hundreds of employees, most of them young women, worked on the upper two floors. Kader paid out Bt 19.4 million ($800,000) in compensation to the families of those killed and the injured.[13]

HIGH ACCIDENT RATES

Fortunately, there have been no recurrences of disasters like the Kader incident since 1993. Nevertheless, workplace accident rates in Thailand are alarmingly high and constantly increasing. According to the compensation records of the labor ministry's Office of Social Security, job-related injury claims now average 40 per year for every 1,000 industrial workers. In 1994, 186,053 workers filed claims for job-related injury or illness, up from 155,884 in 1993. This figure understates the total number of injuries as the government only processes claims from registered firms with 10 or more employees. Such firms employ only 13% of the total workforce. In 1994, 863 workers died in job-related accidents, down from a high of 1,023 in 1993, the year of the Kader disaster. In 1993, the government spent Bt 921 million to compensate workers for industrial injuries while in the preceding year Bt 953 million was spent to pay 131,800 employees for their work-connected injuries.

Spurred by the Kader tragedy, labor offices around the country sponsored a variety of safety fairs, promotions, and seminars, and beefed up inspections. The ministry sought, with some success in large and medium-sized factories in and around Bangkok, to ensure that every workplace has a designated and trained safety officer. The law requires every firm with 100 workers or more to employ a full-time safety inspector, and the government is drafting a new law to tighten safety standards in factories. The bill would empower the labor minister to order factory closures for egregious safety violations. As a stopgap measure, the government is seeking the industry ministry's cooperation in not renewing operating permits or issuing expansion permits for companies whose factories do not meet safety standards. Also, low interest loans will be provided for small firms to upgrade safety measures. The labor ministry is studying the possibility of hiring private companies with the machinery and chemicals experts to handle the inspection of factories to ensure they provide safe working conditions.[14]

OCCUPATIONAL HEALTH PROBLEMS

Aside from food canning and tobacco drying, manufacturing in Northern Thailand was once limited to small arts and crafts workshops. Such products are still central to the northern economy, and the handicraft factories are important tourist destinations. However, the opening of the Northern Region Industrial Estate in 1986 introduced a wide variety of export-oriented manufacturing to Northern Thailand, including high-tech products. Currently, only 61 factories operate in the industrial estate, employing 16,000 workers. Nevertheless, if Lamphun is able to solve its shipping problems, there is no railroad loading dock in the town, to develop a hazardous waste disposal system, and to effectively counter rumors of insufficient safety controls in the workplace, the estate could become a major contributor to the northern economy.

Government promotion of these estates resulted from the belief that the workers would enjoy higher wages and better working conditions, as the estates would be characterized by modern facilities including water, electricity, telephones, and waste treatment plants. The recent case, however, of the Lamphun industrial estates, where 13 workers died suddenly in the spring of 1994 from exposure to as yet unidentified toxic chemicals, illustrates that safety standards and working conditions in factories inside the estates are not necessarily guaranteed.

After five years of planning, the Northern Region Industrial Estate (NRIE), initially intended to promote agriculture affiliated industry, was a failure until new industries, including electric and electronic industries, were persuaded to locate in Lamphun. The NRIE's water supply, primarily from the Kuang river, is pumped and stored in a 500,000 cubic meter reservoir. Complemented by underground water pumped by the estate, the water is filtered at a plant with a daily capacity of 7,000 cubic meters and then distributed to each factory in the estate.

It is noteworthy that more than half of the factories in the estate involve electronic know-how from Japan, and the electronics industry is growing rapidly and has a production capacity of millions of pieces annually. However, according to the Thailand Development Research Institute (TDRI), electronics firms are among the five industries expelling the most toxic waste into the environment. Production line workers in these factories are unknowingly exposed to invisible risks such as lead vapor, mercury vapor, and other deadly vaporizing substances.

The TDRI report also indicated that the Industrial Estate Authority of Thailand focused their environmental efforts on the treatment of waste water. As a result, neither waste disposal facilities nor air pollution controls were to be found in any given industrial estate. Worse still, the Industrial Works Department is not authorized to inspect factories under the authority of the Industrial Estate Authority of Thailand.

The Lamphun case is an example of the consequences of policy incompatibility. At the national level, rural industry is being intensively promoted by tempting offers of tax exemptions and other export promotion measures. The government has made it clear that the electronic component industry is to be included as one of the most important northern industries. In addition to being an export-oriented industry that yields huge profits for the country, the electronics industry has created jobs, generated income, and upgraded living standards for northern residents. Unfortunately, such a one-sided focus on economic growth will inevitably result in additional industrial accidents in the future.

At an international level, the NRIE and the destiny of Lamphun residents is directly related to the globalization attempts of many industries. From Japan, investors leave to find sources of cheaper labor and countries where they can export pollution to. They set up production bases in foreign countries, such as Thailand, to produce components which are later exported back to Japan for assembly. Northern

Thailand is among the more attractive locations in which more operations will likely be relocated.

Lamphun still has not heard any plausible answers as to what has polluted its Kuang River, why its children are dying, and whether their drinking water is free of heavy metals from factories. Labor activists believe the deaths of the 13 workers resulted from heavy metal contamination during their work while officials claimed they died of AIDS.[16]

The Investigation

After attending a meeting of the House Committee on the Environment, which discussed the deaths of the 13 Lamphun workers, Dr. Oraphan Methadilokkul, a specialist in the field of occupational disease, indicated that the legislators promised to aggressively promote a proposal to deal with the problem of occupational and environmental diseases. She expressed confidence that the committee would try its best to push the proposal through for the House to consider during the debate on the 1995 fiscal budget draft.

At the committee meeting, Dr. Oraphan presented her proposal to solve the occupational and environmental disease problem in the Northern Industrial Estate which required a Bt 430 million budget to implement. The proposal mainly focused on the establishment of an Occupational and Environmental Medicine Institute as the center of cooperation among the agencies concerned to cope with the problem throughout Thailand. A member of the house committee pointed out that the Labor Department and Labor and Public Welfare Ministry should be allowed to inspect the toxic substance level inside factories to make sure that working conditions met safety standards. From past experience, the Pollution Control Department's inspection team was not permitted to check the environment inside factories. Meanwhile another committee member argued that the governor of the Northern Industrial Estate should be the individual held responsible for the Lamphun deaths because he had failed to perform his duty.

The committee resolved to travel to the Lamphun Industrial Estate to observe the situation before reaching any conclusions on the issue, while deciding that the industrial estate should be prohibited from hiring private companies to move the toxic waste out of the estate because of the threat of damage to nearby areas.[17]

Meanwhile, Dr. Oraphan, who is the president of the Occupational and Environment Medicine Association of Thailand called on the public health ministry to set up occupational health and environment centers to investigate the cause of illnesses among workers at the Lamphun Industrial Estate. She also stated publicly that the labor and social welfare ministry should establish a center to explain workers' rights and benefits to those working in the Northern Region Industrial Estate so they can protect themselves. The doctor also forwarded letters to the health minister and House Committee on the Environment, Health, and Labor and Social Welfare urging them to investigate the mysterious death of the workers in Lamphun: "I am confident that if the public health ministry sends medical experts from various fields to the NRIE in Lamphun, they will be able to diagnose the cause of illness—and death—among the workers. There are now over 20 workers receiving medical treatment."[18]

THE GOVERNMENT'S RETALIATORY RESPONSE

For her efforts to solve these occupational disease problems in Lamphun, Dr. Oraphan was threatened with disciplinary action after speaking to the media about the deaths and illnesses affecting workers there. A senior public health ministry official said the Legal Affairs Division would launch an investigation into her actions. He said the investigation was ordered after Dr. Oraphan, a civil servant with the public health ministry, criticized the findings of an investigation undertaken by the ministry into the deaths and illnesses of the estate workers. The Civil Service Code bars government officials with positions less than director from giving interviews.

Soon thereafter, on May 26, 1994, a labor and social welfare ministry committee, citing Revolutionary Announcement Number 103, ordered Dr. Oraphan to reveal any information she had about the workers at the estate. The notice was issued after information she had provided conflicted with that of a committee set up by the public health ministry. The ministry committee concluded the 13 workers had died of AIDS and other diseases unconnected with their work. Dr. Oraphan, an expert in occupational medicine, criticized the findings and work procedures of the committee.

Meanwhile, a new committee investigating the Lamphun deaths and illnesses reported after its first meeting that it would complete its findings within six months. It said nothing could be done immediately because the committee has to study the epidemiological causes of the illnesses and deaths. It indicated that northern health organizations, including Lamphun Provincial Hospital and McCormick Hospital in Chiang Mai, would continue to provide health care for workers in the North. It was also announced that about 300 women workers in the northern region had submitted a petition to the public health minister asking him to take immediate action concerning the Lamphun case.[19]

In another interesting development, the advisory chairman of another committee campaigning for good health and safety at work criticized Labor and Social Welfare Minister Paithoon Kaewthong for acting slowly in improving the health and safety of workers despite agreeing in March, 1994, that these measures were necessary and had to be urgently undertaken.

Boonthian Khamchu complained that the labor and social welfare ministry had agreed earlier with his committee's call for labor authorities to accelerate factory inspections, appoint a working group to oversee health and safety at work, provide workers with the right to elect their own work safety promotion officials, and to protect and compensate workers suffering work-related illnesses.[20]

POSITIVE CONSEQUENCES

The negative publicity stemming from the Lamphun case and government obfuscation and delay concerning remedial measures, ultimately triggered specific governmental efforts to address health concerns in the workplace. In March 1995, plans were announced to list standard workplace health concerns to prevent their proliferation. All industrial workers would have to undergo regular health checkups within three months. The workers would be tested to monitor the level of toxic substances in their bloodstream that could be caused by the work environment. Workers were assured the results of the health tests would be kept confidential and could not be used as an excuse to dismiss them, and their blood would not be tested for HIV/AIDS because this was contrary to government policy.

The listing of the criteria was to assist doctors in evaluating the cause of illnesses and help disputes among physicians who might differ as to the cause of industrial illnesses when examining the same person. This would also help workers claim health costs under the social security program. Of course, scientific evidence approved by the Public Health Ministry's medical services department would be required to support claims.

Workers at Lamphun faced problems claiming compensation for work-related illnesses due to a lack of information on occupational health issues. The Lamphun Provincial Health Office and Medical Sciences Department was to draft a list of occupational health problems suffered by industrial workers. It was reported that there was an urgent need for the government to list occupational health problems because public health ministry regulations concerning control of the work environment had proved ineffective. Since the authority to implement the law was left to provincial health officials, the law was not being seriously enforced.[21]

THE WORKMEN'S COMPENSATION ACT OF 1994

In the legislative realm, the parliament passed the Workmen's Compensation Act of 1994 to provide assistance to workers disabled by work-related injuries and illnesses. Under the law, worker benefits and eligibility are clearly spelled out. One provision of the statute allows the labor ministry to earmark up to 22% of the compensation fund's yield for funding of workplace safety promotion and prevention. The law replaced 1972 decrees protecting the rights of employees who are unable to work due to workplace-related accidents or diseases. A 20-year fund serves as a cumulative welfare fund, made up of contributions from employees and employers. The fund has reserves of Bt 5 billion ($200 million) and provides for a payment equal to 10 times a year's salary at the minimum wage in the event of death, replacing a previous maximum payment of three times one year's wages up to Bt 10,000 ($400). The deceased employee's spouse is entitled to 60% of the worker's last salary for five years. In case of disability, compensation to a maximum of Bt 30,000 ($1200) will be paid annually for 15 years, up from the previous ten years. Administered by the Labor

Department, the law also requires a minimum level of on-site facilities, including a fully equipped dispensary and medical staff for firms with 200 or more workers, and sets aside about 20% of accrued interest from the 1972 fund to improve on-site safety. It also governs medical and maternity leave. Employers with at least 20 employees are required to contribute 0.2 to 2% of total wages to the compensation fund. This was extended to firms with ten employees in 1996.

EFFORTS, PROBLEMS, AND PROSPECTS

The Thai government claims to have responded to health and safety concerns, especially in the aftermath of the Kader disaster, by beefing up the safety inspection corps, and the Ministry of Labor has made safety one of its top priorities. In provincial offices throughout the country, additional personnel have been trained to perform safety inspections, historically a neglected area because inspectors tended to shy away from the confrontation that such inspections inevitably involve. Also, regulations regarding safety at construction sites, in dealing with boilers, and with lethal chemicals, have been strengthened and now require companies to have a fire safety plan. Despite these efforts, continuing high industrial accident rates and highly publicized claims of industrial poisoning keep the controversy over workplace safety in the limelight.

In the final analysis, however, the fact is that both laws and enforcement in the field of safety and health have been found to be inadequate. Few laws require safety and equipment standards in the workplace, and even those laws are frequently flouted by employers. Due to a shortage of inspectors and money, the Thai government cannot effectively monitor the situation, and relies largely on voluntary compliance. Successive governments have failed to learn the lessons of other nations and prevent tragedies such as the Kader and Lamphun cases. Other disasters could occur at a large department store, a shopping center, or an electronics factory, even though there are plenty of examples in other countries that demonstrate how accidents can be prevented.

The Kader and Lamphun tragedies were not simply a question of worker rights, but about safety, dilatory bureaucratic practices, and improper inspection methods. The government has the choice to implement stringent inspection regulations or to be relaxed about inspections while imposing heavy penalties on those responsible when things go wrong. But successive governments have done neither.

CHILD LABOR—AN OVERVIEW

Child labor is the most persistent problem in Thailand, where the use and abuse of child labor extends beyond the arena of prostitution. The present law allows a child to work once the child has reached the age of 13. In practice, children younger than 13 are commonly employed in "sweatshop" industries that require long hours but without major physical exertion. Most common are the candy wrapping, paper cup, artificial flowers, and bread factories. It is believed that employers prefer child labor due to the meager wages and the children's obedience.[22]

In mid-June 1988, the cabinet approved a Ministry of Interior proposal to raise the legal age for child labor from 12 to 13. The Ministry, of which the Department of Labor was a part at that time, examined the possibility of making 15 the minimum age and of establishing minimum wage scales for working children. In 1995, the minimum age was still 13.

The problem arose due to the increasing number of children in rural families who, due to economic circumstances, were having to help support their families or were being left to fend for themselves.[23] One of the most vocal critics of child labor practices in Thailand has been the American AFL-CIO, which has supported petitions against Thailand under U.S. trade law. However, the U.S. government has declined to interrupt Thailand's eligibility for U.S. import preferences, noting the progress it is making in improving child labor protection.

Problems develop because, while the legal minimum age for employment is 13, most children complete compulsory education at age 12. The law permits the employment of children between the ages of 13 and 15 only in "light work," where the lifting of heavy loads and exposure to toxic materials or dangerous equipment or situations is restricted. The employment of children at night, 10:00 P.M. to 6:00 A.M., is prohibited. The government estimates there are 100,000 children between the ages of 13 and 15 in the labor force, but the actual number is probably much higher.

PROHIBITION OF FORCED OR COMPULSORY LABOR

For several years, the ILO has cited Thailand for violations of Convention 29 on Forced Labor. The primary focus of the ILO criticism is forced child labor, especially child prostitution. Since the ILO raised these concerns, the Thai government has cooperated in setting up important institutional links, particularly with the International Program on the Elimination of Child Labor, to help improve this situation.[24]

The magnitude of the problem became evident in November 1991, when the authorities discovered and shut down a slave labor factory in Bangkok, prompting then Prime Minister Anand Panyarachun to order a review of child labor laws, including penalties, in an effort to eliminate such sweatshops. The police raided the paper cup plant which was cruelly exploiting 32 boys, aged 13 to 17. Some had been sent to the factory by job agencies which faced legal action, including the possible revocation of their operating licenses. The boys were forced to work 16 hours a day without a holiday and were paid only Bt 20 daily (less than $1). They also had been badly beaten. Their employer and his girl friend were charged with assault, illegal detention, and deprivation of freedom, cheating laborers, violating the labor law, and providing shelter for illegal aliens, five of whom were Laotians. The employer was also ordered to promptly pay the children overdue wages and overtime. Six of the rescued boys required hospitalization for their injuries and 22 were placed in the care of the Children's Rights Protection Center. Nine of the children were also to undergo additional physical examinations.

The Prime Minister ordered the Labor Department to determine if more shops used slave labor and to consider imposing heavier penalties for such offenses, if justified following an official investigation. The center asked the government to find suitable jobs for the children after occupational training on a voluntary basis. The children's parents were asked to come to Bangkok to claim compensation from the employer and to decide what to do with their children. Ironically, most of the children said although they wanted to go home they preferred to get a job first, the very reason they came to Bangkok and were lured to work in the factory.[25]

A COMPLEX ISSUE

Thai policies on child labor protection remain unchanged, but the problem has become more complicated since the economy is no longer seen as the only factor bringing children into the labor market. Changing social values and a lack of governmental effort are also considered important contributors to the problem. The government has no clear information and statistics with which to identify the precise number of children involved, where they are, and what they are doing, and this information is vital for long-term planning. Current government surveys are only conducted every four or five years making them out of touch with recent changes.

A positive trend is that more children are remaining in the school system, which implies that there will be less children who have to work. However, this may not be a harbinger of things to come because in industrialized societies, men who work can feed their families, but in Thai society the minimum wage covers only the person who works. This has an impact on the number of child workers in the labor force as parental wages are insufficient to support entire families. Consequently, many young children are forced to enter the labor market to respond to their families' needs. Furthermore, as long as the industrial sector has to compete in both local and world markets, child labor will be one of the investment costs employers will attempt to control. The complexity of the problem is demonstrated by the attitude of families, the job-seeking process, workplace conditions, low wages, and problems of child laborers themselves.

Families and children are developing new attitudes toward work and education. Earlier, only those with no other option had to work. Now, however, there are more and more children and families who see that children have the choice of earning money sooner because of the many employment opportunities provided by the labor market. There has also been an occupational shift of the younger generation from agricultural to nonagricultural occupations.

A survey conducted by the Foundation for Children's Development showed that 28.7% of child laborers came to work because their parents wanted them to earn a living. Some of them, as young as 13, had to shoulder the burden of supporting their families. The survey indicated that 60% of the children had to work more than eight hours daily. In the service sector workers normally have to work longer hours even though the law dictates a work day of no more than eight hours. Children learn about job opportunities through posters and job brokers at main bus and train stations.

An impressive level of income for labor also does not necessarily mean a better living for child laborers. The survey revealed that 6.1% of child workers still have a salary lower than Bt 1,000 ($40) monthly, while 28.24% of them have an average income ranging from Bt 2,500 ($100) to Bt 3,000 ($120) per month ($100–120). They still have to pay more for day-to-day expenses, which raises the issue of whether the government has any mechanism to control the price of necessary commodities which have been rising sharply.

When children incur illnesses caused by hazardous work materials, this problem is not easily perceived because the toxins accumulate inside their bodies and it is difficult to claim compensation from companies or factories for these types of health problems which appear to be invisible.

Children also have encountered difficulties carrying on their lives in new environments. Teen marriage, drug addiction, and crime among child laborers might not be different from that experienced by other teenagers. However, they may suffer more due to the lack of basic institutional support from their families and communities since many live long distances from their homes and parents.

In one case, a 16-year-old girl had four abortions. In another, a 12-year-old boy was rescued by the foundation because his family did not want him back home. They only desired compensation for the loss of his fingers while he was working. Undoubtedly, it is hard to understand why families which are supposed to be support systems for children, refuse their own members.

What appeared to be significant government actions occurred when the cabinet approved 27 measures in 1988 and 15 more in 1993. These measures addressed the fundamental problems of children's rights, debureaucratization, prevention and protection, participation, and the relationship between all of these variables. Yet the problem of the policy has been one of implementation, the policies are still vague, there still is no clear action plan, and no concrete measures have been taken to implement them. As the manager of the Foundation for Children's Development said: "It [the government] should be seeking and identifying problems and needs of children in the workplace, rather than waiting for the problem to come to them."[26]

CHILD PROSTITUTION

The child labor problem may trouble the Thai economy, but child prostitution is more dangerous. Child prostitution in rural areas reflects the dark side of development that comes with unbalanced economic growth. The problem is shaking Thai society to its roots.

Thailand's five-year economic and social development plans, begun in 1961 and now in their seventh version, have caused economic inequality through industrialization, which has in turn spurred the growth in the sex trade among low income people.

As the sexual service industry has expanded, so too has the demand for its services. Not surprisingly its tentacles have reached the remotest villages.

Estimates place 200,000 to 250,000 child prostitutes in Thailand. For years people have been opting for "tok khiew," a Thai phrase meaning green harvest but increasingly used to describe a promise to sell daughters as young as 12 or 13 into the city flesh trade. The government is trying to stop the practice by providing scholarships for girls so they can continue their secondary education. For those who don't pass into the secondary grades, the government is setting up makeshift vocational training schools. However, the plan has made little headway and even teachers in the North are expecting the flesh trade to continue to "harvest" several thousand teenage girls sold by their parents each year.

It is believed girls who go on to secondary school have more chance of staying away from prostitution. One of the efforts being made by nongovernmental organizations to draw the private sector into promoting rural development, apart from stemming overall job migration to Bangkok and other urban areas, is to enlist its aid to keep girls in school.

But poverty alone is not the cause of child prostitution. The root cause of the tok khiew problem in the northern provinces lies in the loss of values, the consumer demand, and the breakdown of families and communities. Consumer demand began growing in poor villages well before the widespread urbanization of the provinces. The return of former prostitutes, labor migration, and huge rural buying power caused by increased income sent back from children who worked as prostitutes abroad, all made rural consumer demand far larger than most people would have guessed.

Many parents have been spoiled by easy money from brokers. Local people always try to obtain television sets, stereos, cars, and modern houses no matter what they have to sacrifice in the process. Girls in the north have been exploited by society, by irresponsible adults, and the people they trust, including their own parents. Some parents sell their daughters into the flesh trade and some girls are willing to go as a token of gratitude to their parents, who feel no guilt when they sell their daughters because of the absence of old values. Materialism has slowly overcome them. The process to spoil people is very complex and has slowly been absorbed into northern communities for many decades.

Even monks and teachers are influenced and lured by consumerism. Some teachers become brokers, urging parents to sell their children. Teachers praise old students who donate money to schools even though the money comes from prostitution. By the same token, monks honor prostitutes who donate money to the temple in the annual kathin ceremony. Parents also honor their children who go into the sex trade and treat them as "very important persons."

In terms of what is being done to end this unseemly trade, there is the Thor Phan Project, which is nongovernmental and supports the government's commitment to ending prostitution by providing educational opportunities for young women in the Chiang Kham district, Phayao. The project identifies girls who are at risk of being sold into prostitution, some of whom may be as young as 10. The project is able to keep 60 girls in school in the district.

Generally, the situation has improved since the government declared its policy to end child prostitution. Fewer children are being sold into prostitution, but many villages in the northern provinces face a new threat, AIDS. Chandra of the Thor Phan Project has the responsibility to help relatives of the AIDS victims. She says:

> AIDS is threatening the area. There are about three or four AIDS victims every month in Tambon Nam Waen. I am afraid that in the next decade, I will have no time to do anything except go to funerals.[27]

AIDS AND CHILDREN

Children are particular victims of the global AIDS epidemic and there are indications that the demand for child prostitutes may be growing as patrons believe that older prostitutes are more likely to be infected with HIV. Also, there is a small, but rapidly growing, number of babies born to HIV-infected mothers. Approximately 30% of these children will be infected and die within a few years. Those who are not infected themselves will be orphaned while still in childhood, and are often discriminated against as an extension of the social stigma directed against their parents. Although the government claims to be committed to eliminating child prostitution, it has failed to enforce the current limited laws against it. In 1994, the government established a special police task force to suppress child prostitution, and the cabinet approved draft legislation that would revise the Criminal Code to toughen the laws regarding abuse of children under 18 years of age. Reliable nongovernmental organizations report that police, however, are unwilling to raid a brothel that has child prostitutes unless the NGO can provide the children's names, due to the problem of false identity cards with incorrect birth years. The police then will only remove those children named before the raid. Compounding the problem, there are no reliable statistics on the number of children involved in the sex industry, only estimates as described above.

REMEDIAL EFFORTS

The use of child labor in Thailand continues to draw attention, both from international organizations, including the ILO, and in the local press. There are no good data on the actual number of child laborers but their existence in Thailand is widely acknowledged both in and out of government. Part of the difficulty in finding a solution to the problem is that child workers are scattered throughout the economy, primarily in the informal sector. There are no major industries that are characterized by child labor, rather, children in small numbers often work in restaurants, gas stations, and small light manufacturing enterprises. There are also sporadic revelations of illegal, forced labor of children in sweatshops wrapping candy or making paper cups, and in brothels.

The labor ministry has increased the number of inspectors specifically responsible for child labor issues, although not all these officers are engaged in full-time inspection work. Enforcement of child labor laws continues to be inadequate with the inclination when dealing with violators being to negotiate promises of better future behavior, rather than seeking prosecution and punishment. This tendency toward leniency undercuts government efforts to strengthen child labor laws and increased penalties for violations. In addition, the labor ministry has set up child labor committees in each province to encourage continuing education for children or to help arrange the legal employment of children with reputable firms.

Nongovernmental organizations have also been active in fighting child labor, utilizing a variety of different approaches, including teaching school children about labor laws and the dangers of debt servitude. There are outreach programs to parents, many of whom in poorer districts encourage their children to leave school and begin working as soon as possible in order to help support the family. Unfortunately, most of these efforts are localized with limited impact on the overall situation.

WOMEN IN THE LABOR FORCE

In Thailand, women have traditionally worked side by side with their men as unpaid family labor in the rice fields and other activities related to agriculture but the agricultural sector is declining in terms of both GDP and employment, as women and men join the new industrial labor force (see Table 14-1). If Thai statistics did not include women working on the family farm, in keeping with the practice of most developing countries, the female participation rate would appear decidedly lower. This is demonstrated by the fact that while only 50% of the adult women in the Bangkok metropolitan area work, 77% of those in rural areas of the Northeast work. Among rural Northeastern women, aged 30 to 34, the rate raises to 92%. Female labor force participation has always been high and stable. Women comprise half of the Thai population and 45% of the employed Thais.

FEMALE LABOR PROBLEMS

Currently, Thai women are shifting from providing unpaid work within the family to serving as paid workers in urban labor markets. The shift is motivated primarily by women's needs to earn supplementary income for their families. In spite of their increasing role in the economy, Thai women still face many problems. These include limited job opportunities, a lack of job security, work discrimination, fewer chances for promotion, and family disharmony. Family responsibilities are not shared equally or adequately by men. Although some families can afford housemaids or part-time helpers, most cannot. However, women use other backup support, such as delegating some household responsibilities to their children. Social values and gender

TABLE 14-1
Employed Women and Men by Economic Branch, 1980 and 1991
(in thousands)

Economic branch	1980		1991	
	Men (%)	Women (%)	Men (%)	Women (%)
Agriculture[a]	8,048 (67.8)	7,893 (74.1)	10,089 (59.9)	8,687 (60.8)
Manufacturing	1,036 (8.7)	752 (7.1)	1,717 (10.2)	1,747 (12.2)
Commerce	881 (7.4)	1,034 (9.7)	1,648 (9.8)	1,828 (12.8)
Services	1,017 (8.6)	869 (8.2)	1,515 (8.9)	1,710 (11.9)
Other[b]	882 (7.4)	107 (1.0)	1,879 (11.2)	311 (2.2)
Total	11,866 (100)	10,657 (100)	16,850 (100)	14,287 (100)

[a]Agriculture, forestry, hunting, and fishing;
[b]Mining and quarrying; construction, repair, and demolition; electricity, gas, water, and
sanitary services; transport, storage, and communication; activities inadequately described.
Source: National Statistical Office, *Labour Force Survey*, 1980 and 1991, Round 1,
Bangkok, Thailand.

role expectations that require women to take charge of the household remain strong, and most women accept them without either questioning them or demanding change.

Employers prefer unmarried women, especially for routine blue-collar jobs in which manual dexterity is needed and low wages are paid. They justify reserving better-paying jobs for men by claiming that women are neither as physically suited for such employment nor as geographically mobile. In times of economic recession, employers usually lay off women first, claiming that men are breadwinners and therefore should continue to hold a job. Employers pay women less than men for work of the same nature and quality. Additionally, given the dual responsibilities in the home and workplace, women employees often lack adequate time to supplement their work with additional study and training. They consequently have little chance to move up the career ladder.

CULTURAL AND SOCIAL ATTITUDES

Thai women are still expected to be supportive of men, dependent on them, and subservient to them, and to yield to the wishes of others as well as to care for others' needs before their own. Many employers believe that women employees are more obedient, less rebellious, and willing to work for less pay than men. They regard men as having higher social status and greater authority. Men traditionally gained power through the monkhood, political positions, the military, and high government service, all of which have been closed to women. However, the growing importance of education and wealth as avenues of status attainment is improving women's ability to compete with men on a more equal basis.[28]

WOMEN IN MANUFACTURING EMPLOYMENT

In Thailand the role of women in the manufacturing sector is quite remarkable. Although the total number of male and female wage workers in this sector is markedly different, women predominate in export industries. In 7 out of 10 important export industries women constitute more than 80% of the workforce. Such industries include integrated circuit boards and electronic parts, garments and textiles, food, jewelry and precious stones, leatherware and footwear, and cotton yarn fiber. These industries brought in Bt 260 billion in export earnings in 1989. A large number of women were engaged in the urban and rural informal sector as subcontract workers in weaving, artificial flower making, wood carving, umbrellas, and food processing. Female employment is favored in such industries as textiles, electronics, handicrafts, and food and beverages since they require only a low skilled workforce. Moreover, women are seen as easily trainable and docile. Some may claim that these women are unskilled and the value of their contribution cannot be compared with higher rated jobs. But it is quite obvious that in the last decade women workers have made significant contributions to the country's economic growth.

Although women workers produce high value-added components, they are less protected than men. A survey on problems of female employment at the enterprise level revealed that women were usually employed on a daily basis and as piece-rate workers while men in the same industries were hired on a monthly and daily basis. Women were also paid less than male colleagues in the same firm even though both contributed equally to the total production.

Ominously, female workers are exposed to a variety of occupational health risks, for instance, strain in food processing industries and eye concentration in electronics establishments. Research into workers' health in 433 textile firms in Samutprakan, one of the country's largest industrial zones, showed that the majority of workers are exposed to working conditions that cause lung diseases and hearing problems.

LEGISLATIVE PROTECTION

The Thai constitution states that all people are equal before the law, a provision that has been used to repeal several laws discriminating against women. Although the Women Lawyers' Association has actively worked to bring about legal reform, some laws still do not grant women equality, such as those barring women from certain civil service positions and from entering the military and police academies. The Civil Service Act of 1934 provides that the head of a department may promulgate a ministerial regulation prohibiting women from doing certain jobs if the nature of the work is considered unsuitable for them.

Government regulations require employers to pay the same wages and benefits for similar work regardless of sex. However, two-thirds of female workers do not earn the minimum wage, and there is a significant gap between average salaries earned by men and women as a result of the concentration of women in traditionally lower paying jobs.[29]

POSITIVE LEGAL DEVELOPMENTS

In 1990 the cabinet approved a foreign ministry proposal that Thailand withdraw two of its reservations to the ILO's Convention on the Elimination of All Forms of Discrimination Against Women. The government had entered the reservations on clauses providing for equal opportunities for women in the same types of jobs, and for equality of women in the area of signing contracts. Thai labor law forbids women to undertake certain hazardous occupations, such as mining and transporting explosives. The government did not announce when the law would be amended to suit the ILO convention.

Nongovernmental organizations (NGOs) concerned with the status of women have pressed the government to abolish discriminatory practices within the civil service. Constitutional amendments passed in early 1995 included a new provision, Article 24, stipulating the equality of men and women. It remains to be seen if it will be implemented.

THE PROSTITUTION PROBLEM

Prostitution, although illegal, flourishes in Thailand and is deeply ingrained societally. Estimates of the number of women engaged in prostitution vary widely because of temporary sex workers and the migratory nature of prostitution. However, reliable NGO statistics generally discount the government's claim that there are 70,000 prostitutes in Thailand; most estimate the number closer to 250,000.

Prostitution exposes women to a number of human rights abuses, as well as a high risk of contracting AIDS. Some women are forced into prostitution, although the number of such cases is unknown. Human rights monitors believe that the majority who engage in prostitution are not kept under physical restraint, but they note that many women become indebted to brothel owners for large sums. It is common for brothel procurers to advance parents a substantial sum against their daughter's future earnings, often without the consent of the young woman involved. The women are then obligated to work in a brothel for a fixed period of time in order to pay back the loan.

In the past several years, there has been an increase in the number of women entering Thailand from neighboring countries to work as prostitutes, and there have been continuing credible reports of corrupt police involvement in illegal trafficking schemes. Incidents of coerced prostitution most commonly involve women from hill tribes or neighboring countries. Brothel operators reportedly favor such women because they are cheaper to procure and their inability to speak Thai makes them easier to control. Sometimes lured with promises of jobs as waitresses or domestics, these women are then often threatened with physical abuse by brothel operators if they refuse to work as prostitutes. Because they are considered illegal immigrants, such women have no right to legal counsel or health care if arrested.

The government has set up vocational training and education programs to combat the lure of prostitution, but despite occasional high profile raids on brothels, it has failed effectively to enforce laws against prostitution, and in many cases, brothels pay off local government representatives and police. There are credible reports of instances in which corrupt police drove Burmese women across the border sometimes in police vehicles and delivered them directly to brothels.

Under the current Penal Code, prostitutes are considered criminals, whereas brothel owners, procurers, and clients are not subject to criminal statutes. In May 1994, the cabinet approved draft legislation that would further criminalize those involved in the trafficking of women and children for the purpose of prostitution or slave labor. While clients of child prostitutes would be subject to criminal prosecution under the legislation, it still would not criminalize the clients of adult prostitutes. Draft legislation was scheduled for parliamentary debate in May 1995.[30] Draft legislation was approved in August, 1995 by the Thai cabinet and sent to the parliament for approval.

The pervasiveness of the problem was driven home by an editorial writer at the *Bangkok Post*, whose comments indicated the difficult nature of the problem:

> The simple fact remains that the huge sex trade at home is still intact. Outsiders will continue to be shocked and prostitution will continue to be seen—albeit narrowly—as a domestic moral problem. Bangkok will continue to be described as an easy sex haven in the western media in forms ranging from sensational tabloids to such officially-recognized information sources as dictionaries, other printed matter, television and computer data.... The deep-rooted sexism that endorses the exploitation of women and the preoccupation with face and image explains why the government's anti-prostitution policies fail to extend beyond token lip service. With its widespread flesh trade, Thailand is fighting a losing image battle against the international media and information technology. But unless Thailand tackles its own sex industry and supporting cultural values, it is Thai women and children who will end up the real losers.[31]

UNION IMPOTENCE

Thailand's labor unions have contributed little to the solutions to women's problems. Although women workers comprise about half of all wage employees and even more than 80% of workers in seven leading export industries, they are under-represented in Thai unions. They have no executive authority and no channel through which to express their problems. Unions usually focus on male workers' problems.

While the unions fought for leave for male workers to enter the monkhood temporarily, as is the custom, typical women's problems of child care, housework, nutrition, and maternity leave are not on the agenda of problems to be tackled by the unions. A factor discouraging women's participation in unions is that women generally have lower educational attainment than men. Thai cultural habits also treat women as only adjuncts to men. Women workers, therefore, have had less opportunity to use their organizing skills, or to plan and participate in developing projects.

Female workers in some industries, for example textiles and garments, are well organized. But the majority in other manufacturing industries and in services lack opportunities. Female trade unionists also do not seem to be equal partners of males in unions. When women join the unions' activities, they tend to let men take the lead. In many textile unions a male worker is often elected as chairman although most of the membership is female. Fewer women obtain leading positions in the national congress. So long as the unions are male-dominated organizations, it is most likely that women workers will continue to be a vulnerable group and specific problems related to female employment will not be tackled.[32]

PRIVATIZATION

Another area of concern expressed by Thai labor organizations concerns the privatization of public sector activities. In most countries transportation and communication industries have been traditionally financed and managed by the state. However, there is now a growing tendency for governments to consider privatizing these debt-encumbered and often inefficient public enterprises.

In its Sixth Plan (1987–91) the Thai government identified the need to increase public sector savings and enhance the quality of infrastructural services by improving the efficiency of state enterprises. One of its medium-term policy objectives is to reduce government intervention and encourage private sector participation in industries hitherto reserved for the state. However, as the government tries to put into effect its privatization timetable it has come up against protests from powerful labor unions as well as the management of public utilities. The government's proposals to privatize many financially languishing state enterprises have become a controversial issue.[33]

The privatization of public sector enterprises is an issue with significant political implications. The principal concern behind the government's privatization efforts is the increasing need for investment in Thailand's inadequate infrastructure, including roads, rails, ports, power, telephones, water, and air transportation. Privatization has been resisted by state enterprise management, organized labor in the state enterprises, and the Thai military forces. The State Enterprises Labor Relations Group spearheaded labor's opposition, which stems primarily from fear of losing benefits and job security.

In the past, Thailand has taken a piecemeal approach to privatization, using means that might not be considered real privatization measures elsewhere. While the government has disposed of a few enterprises conventionally, by sale or closure, the companies involved were minor, a marble factory, a jute mill, and several provincial trading companies. It has not actively pursued the transfer of ownership of the larger operations. There are a number of reasons for this, mostly political. In addition to the public policies regarding provision and pricing of goods and services, other aspects of domestic politics have worked against the transfer of ownership:

1. State enterprise workers are better paid and receive more generous benefit packages than regular civil servants and staff level workers in the private sector. So labor groups have been opposed to institutional changes.
2. Managers regard ownership transfer as career threatening, so management has opposed change.
3. Even the military is not eager to see enterprises sold. After all, what would retired military officers do if they could not become part of state enterprise management?
4. Some of the government agencies that supervise the state enterprises are reluctant to lose the opportunities for privilege and patronage that the system provides, and they oppose change.

Politics notwithstanding, just the sheer size of large enterprises and the large number of employees involved would make it difficult to sell them outright.[34]

THE 1990 PORT STRIKES

The major turning point against privatization came in early 1990, when the port unions successfully protested against the privatization of the Laem Chabang port, some 78 miles southeast of Bangkok. Laem Chabang is one of the new deep water harbors being constructed in a bid to reduce growing congestion, delays, and rising costs of cargo handling services. Plans to privatize this Bt 3 billion ($120 million) facility provoked industrial unrest among port unions earlier in August 1989, when a 36-hour strike cost the government an estimated Bt 22 million ($880,000) in lost revenue.

When it was subsequently decided to bring the Port Authority under the jurisdiction of the newly established National Port Administration Board and to make this board responsible for the operations of three major ports, unions as well as port authorities saw the move as a way of undermining their efforts to keep Laem Chabang out of private hands.

On January 30, 1990, 6,200 dockworkers at Klong Toey Port stopped work to protest against the government's plans. Since public sector strikes are illegal under Thai law, the stoppage was called an "extraordinary meeting." The four day "meeting" crippled operations at Klong Toey, where on one day, there were reportedly 52 ships waiting idly in port, either to be offloaded or to set sail. It was estimated that those delays cost an average $8,000 per day for each vessel. Exporters, importers, and shipping companies incurred considerable losses. Workers were not paid for those days on which they stopped work.

The six port unions refused the government's offer to allow the Port Authority of Thailand to operate one of the four berths at Laem Chabang and to let it bid along with private companies for management of the others. The union Secretary-General Somachi Maksamphan reportedly argued that the Authority should be given a five-year period in which to run all the berths, which should be turned over to the private sector only if they failed to make a profit. Another demand was that the same rules governing pay and working conditions for public sector dockworkers must apply to those in the new facilities. This was a controversial matter given severe criticism about the productivity of port workers and prevailing conditions in the ports.

After four days, senior Thai army officials responded to a request from the unions to act as mediator. The strike ended with an agreement that workers would return to work and negotiations on the issue of privatizing the new port would be resumed. Both parties were faced with the difficult task of reconciling the government's determination to privatize the new port with union demands that Laem Chabang and Kong Toey must remain public entities.

In March 1990, the Chatichai government backed down, and eventually agreed to allow two of Laem Chabangs four wharfs to remain in public hands. Some unions continued to make difficulties for the government throughout 1990 by leveling accusations about the validity of the bids from the company which won the right to manage the two private wharfs. Other port unions backed the choice, reflecting the fractionalization common in Thailand's labor movement. This and other continuing antiprivatization actions, especially from unions of the Telephone Organization of Thailand, the Communications Authority of Thailand, and the Electricity Generating Authority of Thailand helped create strong sentiments against state enterprise unions among officials, the military, and the general public and undoubtedly contributed to their dissolution in 1991.

MIXED RESULTS

In the face of pressure from public sector unions, only a handful of state enterprises have actually been sold. Even in these the government usually retained at least 70% equity, the minimum required to permit state loan guarantees. Management and labor resistance to privatization is likely to be reinforced since state enterprises have regained the right to set up trade unions. Thus far the most popular forms of privatization have been (1) listings of small stakes in state enterprises on the Stock Exchange of Thailand, and (2) farming out of activities under the jurisdiction of state firms to the private sector. Examples of the former include stakes in Krung Thai Bank, Thai Airways International, and the Petroleum Authority of Thailand Exploration & Production. Examples of the latter include a 30-year concession awarded to TelecomAsia to install and operate 2 million telephone lines in Bangkok, and a 30-year contract won by the Shinawatra Group to operate Thailand's first satellite.[35]

THE CHALLENGE OF PRIVATIZATION

Many of Thailand's key industries, particularly in its infrastructure, remain in the hands of the state. The long-espoused effort to privatize state enterprises is controversial with regard to the development of organized labor in Thailand. The level of labor organization and sophistication in state enterprises is generally far more advanced than in the private sector and worker compensation packages are more generous than in most companies. However, it is perceived that the existence of strong labor organizations in the state enterprises makes them less attractive to potential investors.

Thai state enterprises play a vital role in the Thai economy. Totaling over 60 in number, state enterprises are given monopolistic rights to provide most public utilities and are involved in a variety of other activities from cigarette manufacturing to zoo maintenance. With the economy growing at close to double digit figures annually during the 1987–94 period, and with a policy consensus that the government role in the economy should be limited, the public sector has failed to keep up with the demand for basic infrastructure services. Required infrastructure investment is estimated at a staggering $12 billion a year over the next five years, yet the government has capped annual public external borrowings at $3.4 billion, forcing private sector involvement to provide the infrastructure necessary for the economy to continue to grow.

State enterprise labor associations and management as well view privatization as a threat to the pay and benefit packages they feel they have worked hard to negotiate over the years. Wary of direct confrontation with labor, the government has adopted a privatization strategy that begins with very limited share divestiture in the state enterprises and allows some private sector concessions to provide services. While this approach has satisfied state enterprise labor groups thus far, many observers believe it prolongs inefficient provision of services and cannot keep pace with demand. The issue promises to remain controversial. The move toward privatization, however slow, is inexorable, and state enterprise labor leaders view it as a significant long-term challenge.

Chapter 15

International Developments

Worker rights advocates in labor unions, human rights groups, and other nongovernmental organizations (NGOs) have played an increasingly important role in promoting internationally established fair labor standards as a factor in international trade. Particularly in the United States, recent developments have widened the scope for action on labor rights in a transnational economy. Advocates of international fair labor standards have challenged the traditional right of countries to address their labor laws and labor relations as solely internal matters. They have sought to constrain the right of multinational corporations to implement labor policies based solely upon the laws of each nation where they operate, especially where laws are designed to repress rather than protect workers, and provide a competitive edge in international trade.

In Thailand, developments involving worker rights and labor standards have not occurred in a vacuum. Child and female labor, worker health and safety, and state enterprise employee organizing and bargaining rights have drawn international attention. In this chapter, we will examine the nature of international concerns which have been directed toward deficiencies in these important areas in Thailand.

Minimum International Labor Standards

In 1984, a working group of the Netherlands National Advisory Council for Development Cooperation drafted a report on minimum international labor standards. The report considered the desirability of incorporating certain minimum international labor standards into international agreements on economic cooperation and trade policy that involve developing countries. After reviewing the various arguments for and against such incorporation, the report found that the debate remains inconclusive. However, supporters and opponents both agreed on the need to fight protectionism and promote improved working conditions in developing countries. Therefore, an effort was made to identify a number of labor standards whose violation or nonapplication would strongly imply that the basic need for freely chosen work in humane conditions could not be satisfied; it is those standards that ought to be applied in all countries and all economic sectors.

By applying three different types of criteria, social, legal, and economic, to existing ILO conventions, the so-called minimum package of international labor standards was identified. This package consists of the following standards: freedom of association (No. 87), the right to engage in collective bargaining (No. 98), equal remuneration (No. 100), abolition of forced labor (No. 105), prohibition of discrimination (No. 111), full employment policy (No. 122), and minimum age (No. 138).

The report then observed that, under certain conditions, the effectiveness of these standards can be enhanced by including a provision concerning their observance in international agreements involving developing countries.[1]

ILO CONVENTIONS

The ILO is the principal multilateral body devoted to labor rights and labor standards. While its conventions and recommendations reflect consensus among government, employer, and trade union representatives to annual ILO conferences, the ILO has no power to enforce the standards that it sets, although the ILO conventions are broadly accepted standards which, when ratified by a country, create theoretically binding obligations. Unfortunately, the ILO's efforts to ensure compliance by signatory nations are hindered by an absence of effective enforcement mechanisms.[2]

THE ROLE OF THE UNITED STATES

The United States has recognized the importance of labor rights by linking them to preferential treatment for developing countries in trade programs. Labor rights provisions in U.S. trade laws specify five internationally recognized worker rights whose observance conditions a country's beneficiary trade status with the United States:

1. The right of association;
2. The right to organize and bargain collectively;
3. A prohibition on the use of any form of forced or compulsory labor;
4. A minimum age for the employment of children;
5. Acceptable conditions of work with respect to minimum wages, hours of work, and occupational safety and health.

The rationales for these American legislative initiatives have ranged from genuine concern for the welfare of overseas workers to protecting U.S. industry from unfair competition due to substandard labor conditions abroad.

ARGUMENTS PRO AND CON

The United States' position is that countries which trade with it and deny basic labor rights to their citizens are engaging in unfair competition. Labor rights advocates argue that countries and corporations can gain a competitive advantage by employing "social dumping" tactics, such as banning strikes or independent union organizing, holding wages below a genuinely fair return on the workers' productivity, or permitting forced labor or child labor.[3]

On the other hand, opponents of international fair labor standards contend that each nation has the sovereign right to order its labor relations in accordance with domestic economic policies and development strategies. Most labor laws reflect this domestic approach. United States domestic regulations and laws, for example, regulate union organizing, collective bargaining, and other features of labor-management relations, and also set wage and hour levels, occupational safety and health rules, and other minimum workplace standards.[4] As the United States has applied worker rights provisions of its trade laws to other countries, some leaders in those countries have responded with charges that the United States acts hypocritically. They further contend that the American government fails to ratify most of the ILO Conventions and is itself guilty of widespread labor rights violations.[5]

The United States has ratified eleven of 174 ILO Conventions, seven of them relating to conditions in the maritime industry. Of the rest, one ratification concerned approval of ILO constitutional changes. The other three are of wider significance: Convention No. 144 on Tripartite consultations, committing to government-business-labor consultation on labor affairs was ratified in 1988; No. 160 on Labor Statistics, standardizing statistical reporting requirements and measurement methods was ratified in 1991; and most significantly, No. 105 on forced labor was ratified in 1991. United States multinational corporations acceded to ratification of Convention No. 105, given the universality of strictures against forced labor, but strongly resisted U.S. ratification of ILO Conventions favorable to trade unions, such as freedom of association and collective bargaining rights.[6] In this regard, the International Confederation of Free Trade Unions cited the United States as one of 87 countries violating fundamental trade union rights as recognized by the ILO Conventions in its "Annual Survey of Violations of Trade Union Rights."[7]

A problem labor rights advocates in the United States and allied organizations abroad attempting to establish international fair labor standards encounter traditional notions of sovereignty in formulating national labor policies and development strategies. In the same way that entrenched sovereignty principles gradually yielded to international human rights claims after World War II, sovereignty is now being challenged by claims of international labor rights in the field of employment standards and industrial relations.[8]

CHILD AND FORCED LABOR IN THAILAND

A tactic that may affect investment and directly provide a country with a competitive advantage in international trade is the exploitation of workers. For example, the ILO determined that the exploitative use of child labor was a growing factor in world trade, and several media reports in recent years have substantiated these accusations. The use of children younger than age 13 to produce clothing, hand-woven carpets, and other products in India, Pakistan, Bangladesh, and other Asian countries has provoked legislation in Congress to outlaw the importation of goods produced in this manner into the United States. Also, there have been moves to persuade people not to buy products from countries that use child labor. One of the countries routinely accused of this is Thailand.

The campaign in Europe and the U.S. concerning child labor seems to be in favor of nontariff barriers to imports from Thailand. One of the most vocal critics of child labor practices in Thailand has been the American AFL-CIO, which has supported petitions against Thailand under the U.S. trade law. However, the U.S. government has declined to interrupt Thailand's eligibility for U.S. import preferences, noting the progress Thailand is making in improving child labor protection.

For several years the ILO has criticized Thailand for child labor practices in violation of Convention 29 on forced labor. Missions of ILO experts have visited Thailand and determined that steady, but not rapid, progress was being made. The Thai government admitted that serious problems of child labor abuse continue. In its 1994 observation, the ILO exhorted Thailand to move beyond good intentions, to establish a comprehensive legal framework to attack the problem, to strengthen effective law enforcement, and to set up a viable rehabilitation system.

POSITIVE MEASURES

The Thai labor and social welfare ministry, in 1995, began to implement an urgent program aimed at improving the living conditions of workers and their families nationwide and the cabinet approved measures to solve the child labor problem at its roots.[9] Parents in remote areas will be educated to understand child labor problems. Training courses for work skills and job placement will be introduced. Officials from the Labor Protection and Welfare and Public Welfare departments were given six months to develop the program, which will cover two projects. The first will provide job training to children lacking educational opportunities to prevent them from entering into prostitution or becoming street children or criminals. Children under 15 will be sent to designated factories for further training. The labor ministry will later find employers for them when they reach the legal working age and also look at ways to raise an education fund for those children wishing to continue their studies. The second project will focus on increasing the general knowledge and vocational skills of laborers so they can better protect their rights. Businesses will be asked to allow their workers to attend classes after work. The classes would be held at the workplace about three days a week.

Other measures the government is taking include asking for cooperation from labor unions to monitor the abuse of child labor in industry, requesting the Employment Department to provide information on which industrial plants employ child labor, and offering rewards to those who inform the authorities of incidents of child abuse or child detention.

The ILO has allocated $800,000 to several Thai agencies to support a range of projects on child labor in Thailand. The Non-Formal Education Department has received funds to deal with working children in urban areas. The Labor and Social Welfare Department has received a grant for preventing child labor. The Education Center for Daughters and the Community is working on protecting and developing the work of girls in the northern provinces. The Children's Development Fund is also dealing with the problem of child labor in its project while the Foundation for a Better Life for Children has received a grant for a mobile car project for children of construction workers.[10]

While advocates believe that Thailand ought to conform with international labor standards, they also feel that the Thai law should be such that, if possible, children who work should be covered by the Social Security Act that requires employers and the government to contribute to a social welfare fund for workers aged not less than 15 years. Unfortunately, many Thai child laborers are younger than 15 and thus are not protected under social security. Thai children and the elderly were to come under social security in 1996 but the government has further deferred these dates, posing a major obstacle in the path of improving the lives of children. In the final analysis the Thai government, together with the unions and employers' federations should do everything that is feasible for the welfare of Thailand's workers, women and children included. No amount of export potential or financial backing should stand in the way of the enforcement of standards essential to the well-being of Thai workers.[11]

THE ICFTU SANCTIONS

As previously noted, in 1991 the Thai government passed a law disbanding state enterprise unions and prohibiting strikes and other industrial action by state enterprise employees. The reaction of the international community was strongly negative. The International Confederation of Free Trade Unions charged that the April, 1991 actions violated basic human rights and threatened to impose trade sanctions against Thailand. The sanctions were contained in a resolution adopted by the ICFTU executive board which asked affiliated organizations to determine what measures could be taken to withhold or withdraw trade and other advantages from Thailand while it violated basic human freedoms. It called for its affiliates to make every effort, jointly with the ICFTU and the Asian and Pacific Regional Organization (APRO) and the International Trade Secretariat, to put pressure on Thailand by all possible means and to help the Thai trade union movement, in terms of organization, through education programs and other ways, in its struggle for full recovery of union rights and to consolidate. In the meantime, it urged the government to withdraw the antilabor measures immediately and to refrain from any action that would further damage labor relations in Thailand.

The board also voiced "profound" concern over the mysterious disappearance of Thanong Poarn, president of the Labor Congress of Thailand, and expressed its dissatisfaction with the Thai authorities' explanation about labor problems in Thailand given to the ILO meeting in Geneva in June 1991. At the ILO conference, the complaint against Thailand was voiced on behalf of the "Common Front" of international organizations of public service trade unions. In addition to the dissolution of state enterprise unions and the ban against state employee strikes, claims were made that the new labor associations were not allowed to select their own leaders because the law limited their rights to hold office. Also, it was alleged that assets of the old unions could be stolen by the government and turned over to the Red Cross, and that unions in the state sector were forbidden to associate with one another in federations. The Thai delegation defended its government's position, claiming Prime Minister Anand Panyarachun's administration was fully committed to the basic rights of workers regarding freedom of association and their right of collective bargaining.[12]

U.S. TRADE THREATS

In 1993, two years later, the Thai government was trying to persuade the United States of the adequacy of its labor standards. American labor unions leveled accusations that Thailand fails to protect worker rights which threatened to end Thailand's status under the U.S. duty-free concessions program known as the Generalized System of Preferences (GSP). Three issues, child labor laws, worker safety, and the State Enterprises Labor Relations Act, were in dispute.

The Thai government's response was that while progress was being made on child labor and worker safety, further amendments would be needed to the Act to bring it into line with ILO standards. The government had already indicated it would amend the Act.

On December 15th, 1993 the Office of the U.S. Trade Representative was due to announce the result of an investigation into complaints lodged against Thailand by the AFL-CIO, the largest umbrella labor organization in the United States. The AFL-CIO wanted Washington to drop Thailand from the import-duty exemption program. They cited as reasons the National Peacekeeping Council's Announcement No. 54 on certification requirements for union advisors; the Interior Ministry's requirement that any union convention must have the ministry's approval; and the State Enterprise Employee Relations Law. The AFL-CIO saw these as attempts by the Thai government to undermine and destroy the country's labor movement and workers' rights to organize themselves for collective bargaining. The Thai government was hopeful that Washington would postpone its threatened action until it saw what progress Thailand was making in pushing the SELRA amendments through parliament.

On child labor, Thailand extended the minimum education period from 6 years to 9 in order to discourage children from entering the labor force. It also raised the minimum age of child labor from 12 years to 13 and planned to raise it again to 15.

WORKER SAFETY AND THE SELRA

The tragic fire in March 1993, at the Kader doll factory, in which more than 180 workers perished, brought worker safety into sharp focus. The U.S. demanded that Thailand punish those who caused the fire and toughen laws to protect workers on the job. Thailand said those responsible for the fire had been punished and that safety measures had been devised to prevent a repetition of such fires.

Concerning the State Enterprises Labor Relations Act, draft amendments were to be submitted to the cabinet in preparation for introduction in parliament. The law complies with most ILO standards, but it allowed only one union to be established at each state enterprise; the U.S. preferred a more wide-open system. The Thai government said amendments were drafted after consultation with Thai labor unions but the U.S. wanted further proof that such consultations took place. Also, Washington remained concerned about draft amendments that prohibit state enterprise unions from striking. Thailand countered that the law allows unions to call meetings without notifying employers in advance, which was tantamount to a strike.

The remaining American concern centered on a clause that seemed to bar consultants of state enterprise unions from being consultants for private sector unions. The consultants also were required to register with the Labor and Social Welfare Ministry and seven already had done so.[13]

THE SELRA AMENDMENTS

The ILO also condemned the action against the public sector unions. When the Chuan government came to power in 1992, it promised to restore basic worker rights in the state enterprises. After much internal wrangling, dissolution of the state enterprise unions was popular with the public and with business, so the government decided to revise, rather than repeal, the SELRA. Preparation of the necessary legislation proved laborious, and a bill was finally approved by the cabinet in December 1993, prior to a deadline set by the U.S. Trade Representative in its review of the AFL-CIO GSP petition.

In 1994, the SELRA legislation progressed slowly. It passed a first reading in parliament in September 1994 and was turned over to scrutiny committee, a standard legislative practice, for review before presentation again to parliament for a second and third final reading. The 29-person scrutiny committee was chaired by the minister of labor and included members of parliament, government officials, and state enterprise labor leaders. As of March 1995, labor and government representatives on the committee had not yet reached agreement on draft language. Nevertheless, the government assured the U.S. Embassy and visiting USTR officials that it would be high on the legislative agenda when parliament began its next session in May. This action was sufficient for the U.S. Trade Representative in December 1995 to postpone revocation of Thailand's GSP privileges to allow the parliament to pass the legislation. The legislation was enacted and a new version of the SELRA essentially restored all the rights workers in state enterprises enjoyed prior to 1991, with the exception of the right to strike.

LINKAGE OF WORKER RIGHTS WITH INTERNATIONAL TRADE

Internationally, Thailand is still likely to face unease over child labor, an issue developed countries will raise to pressure Third World nations through the World

Trade Organization (WTO). In the latest attempt, the United States and France almost delayed the signing of the Uruguay Round of GATT in April 1994, in an effort to place labor standards formally on the agenda of the WTO. They failed, but in a compromise it was agreed labor standards could be discussed in the preparatory committee for the WTO.

Although the threat from the WTO is unclear, that from the United States seems clearer. In 1994 the Harkin Bill, also known as the Child Labor Deterrence Act was not passed by Congress. The Republican-controlled Congress has not considered it since and prospects for its future passage appear dim. The bill classifies children under 15 as child labor while Thai law allows children between 13 and 18 to work legally. According to the Thai government, the number of child workers varies greatly. However, the ILO puts the number at four million with 600,000 between the ages of 13 and 14.

The Harkin Act would affect 19 developing countries including Thailand. Groups in the United States and Europe want further market openings to developing countries to be made conditional on those countries accepting minimum labor standards. Imports from countries that use child labor, slave or prison labor, or which deny workers the right to form trade unions and bargain collectively, they argue, should be banned. The motive, presumably, is to improve the lot of poor workers in the Third World. But many developing countries suspect, however, that it is really a pretext for protectionism; an attempt by rich countries to deny them the benefit of their advantage in cheap labor.[14]

THE ASEAN POSITION

The Association of Southeast Asian Nations (ASEAN) has expressed concern over attempts by Western industrial nations to link workers' rights with the WTO. A final draft joint communique adopted by ASEAN foreign ministers said such issues should be handled only by the ILO which should support flexible and fair implementation of labor standards considering the needs of developing countries. The document said the linking of workers' rights, labor standards, and environmental issues to trade could become a new pretext for protectionism and could undermine the progress achieved so far in the liberalization of world trade. It also reiterated the grave concern expressed by ASEAN labor ministers that attempts by some developed countries to introduce social clauses into international trade agreements would restrict market access and adversely affect employment opportunities of workers in developing countries. Further, it stated that ASEAN foreign ministers have given full support to Singapore's bid to host the first ministerial conference of the WTO, which was held in Singapore in December, 1996.[15]

At a meeting in Bangkok, regional human rights activists were given a cold reception by Thai government officials when they tried in July 1994, to submit their recommendations to the ASEAN foreign ministers. The representatives of the Southeast Asian Nongovernmental Organizations forum on human rights and development were barred from meeting with the foreign ministers and had to submit their statement to the press.

The forum noted that the ASEAN foreign ministers had expressed serious concern that linking workers' rights, labor standards, and environmental issues with trade could become a new pretext for protectionism. The forum decided existing national institutions failed to promote and protect human rights as well as could be expected and their performance had not met the critical criteria for independence and effectiveness.[16]

Thai opposition to Western efforts to link trade with human rights continued when foreign minister Prasong Soonsiri denounced attempts of Western industrialized nations to link workers' rights with trade as a new form of protectionism. He cited two major developments as cause for serious concern; one is the attempt to introduce social clauses into international agreements as a condition for market access; the other is the effort to impose rigid labor standards. He commented:

> To transplant Western standards to a country in total disregard of its own cultural and social norms would not only jeopardize its economic competitiveness and achievement, but also result in adverse consequences to [the] political and social stability of that country.[17]

THE ILO REPORT—A WELCOME SURPRISE

The developing nations of the world received support from an unexpected source in March 1995, when an ILO World Employment report dismissed the claim by industrialized countries that cheaper imports from developing nations and the relocation of factories there have resulted in their loss of jobs. The report claimed that all nations receive mutual benefits from globalization of trade. The European Union and the United States claim that low wages and low costs in the Third World have given these countries an unfair competitive edge.

The report cautioned against adoption of defensive strategies such as protectionism and warned that these moves are likely to involve a tradeoff in terms of greater inequality. Industrialized nations are increasingly apprehensive that globalization of trade has led to job losses as their unemployment rates climb. Unemployment in the developed countries is now around 10%, with the European Community experiencing the unprecedented high level of 12%. The report, referring to the concern expressed by developed nations, cautioned:

> Such alarm is in fact unwarranted. It is based on the flawed assumption that trade and investment flows are essentially a zero-sum game. The evidence that there are considerable mutual benefits for both industrialized and developing countries is typically overlooked. For example, trade between the industrialized countries and the newly industrializing countries—the main source of import penetration—has been in balance. Alarmist views on the job-destroying effects of imports from, and the relocation, to developing countries are often heard. In reality, exports from industrialized countries to the newly industrializing countries have grown as fast as imports from these countries. Far from being a one-way process of exporting jobs to low-wage countries, foreign direct investment in fact generates significant benefits to the capital-exporting country.... Employment problems are the result

of social choice: commissions or omissions in economic and social policies and shortcomings in institutional arrangements.[18]

THE APPLICABILITY OF GSP TO THAILAND

The Generalized System of Preferences (GSP) scheme evolved under the auspices of the United Nations Conference on Trade and Development, with the first programs being implemented in 1971. Generalized System of Preferences provides for preferential tariff treatment for developing country exports of manufactured and semi-manufactured goods to increase export earnings of developing countries, to promote industrialization, and to accelerate economic growth.

Given that Thai exporters gain from GSP programs, but abstaining from an examination of the quantity or quality of these gains, it is worth examining the likelihood that GSP be withdrawn from Thailand. According to statistical data provided by the United States Trade Representative, in 1993 Thailand was the third largest beneficiary of the U.S. GSP program, behind Malaysia and Mexico. In that year, Thailand exported $2,143,279,761 worth of duty-free goods to the United States and a total of $3,280,204,761 worth of GSP-eligible products to the United States. Since Thailand is such a significant beneficiary of the U.S. GSP program, Thai trade practices, and Thai GSP benefits receive greater scrutiny than they otherwise might. In Washington's view, a number of issues, including Thailand's rapid rate of development and the absence of adequate worker rights laws threaten the gains received under the GSP arrangement.

Thailand eventually may graduate from the GSP process. If Thailand's economy continues to grow and if the Clinton Administration significantly lowers the per capita GNP criteria, the Thai economy could reach the per capita GNP limit sooner than anticipated. The monetary value of Thailand's GSP benefits is diminishing, due to the U.S. withdrawal of benefits for intellectual property rights violations and the continuing decrease in Most Favored Nation (MFN) tariff rates. Thailand's greatest current concerns with the GSP benefits are changes to the GSP program under renewal legislation and the resolution of intellectual property issues, which it is hoped would lead to the reinstatement of previous benefits.

While GSP ineligibility does not appear imminent, it may be useful to weigh the costs and benefits to Thailand of maintaining its GSP status. Clearly, Thai exporters gain from the duty free benefits, since Thai exports totaled more than $2 billion in 1993. However, GSP does not operate without costs for Thailand. It involves adhering to international standards, as interpreted by the United States, in areas such as worker rights, intellectual property rights, and potentially in the realms of services and environmental protection. On the other hand, the development of these standards, painful as they may be, are all part of the economic development process. Since it is unlikely that the United States would completely withdraw GSP benefits in the near term, it is up to Thailand to determine if the costs of the program outweigh its benefits.[19]

THAI OVERSEAS WORKERS

While the issues of worker rights and labor standards in Thailand prompted international scrutiny via GSP applicability, overseas markets for Thai workers have always been important. Income from foreign employment has been the country's second largest nonmerchandise source of foreign exchange in recent years, exceeded only by tourism.

Thai workers have a good reputation as being relatively trouble free and quick to learn. Compared to Philippine and many South Asian workers, Thai workers do not have strong English language skills, but many Thais work in the construction industry where foreign language skills are not essential. About 60% of Thais employed abroad are skilled or semiskilled workers, and hundreds of thousands have left Thailand for foreign employment opportunities. Annual remittances totaled $1.25 billion in 1993.

A CHRONOLOGY OF FOREIGN EXPERIENCE—THE MIDDLE EAST

On January 1, 1989, an estimated 201,500 Thais were working in the Middle East and 66,000 in East Asia. In the late 1980s, more than half of Thai labor abroad was in Saudi Arabia. The murders in Bangkok in February 1990, of three Saudi diplomats responsible for visa issuance severely strained relations between the kingdoms of Thailand and Saudi Arabia and caused a major geographical shift in Thai overseas labor. More than 100,000 Thais left Saudi Arabia as the Saudis restricted visas in retaliation for the still unsolved murder cases. The Thais preferred to resign their positions rather than completely forego home leave due to the difficulty of getting reentry visas. Consequently, at the end of 1990, an estimated 165,000 Thais worked abroad, 36% or 49,400 in the Middle East and 64%, or 115,600 in ASEAN countries. Following the onset of the Gulf War in late January, 1991, the number of Thai workers in the Middle East and East Asia declined by almost 40% from 231,300 in the region at the end of 1990 (see Tables 15-1 and 15-2).

With the end of the war, the Thai government hoped to significantly expand the number of Thais working in the Middle East, particularly Saudi Arabia and Kuwait. Over 200,000 workers had registered with the Department of Labor by the end of April 1991 to work in the region. To assure quality control of exported workers, the Department of Overseas Labor tested those claiming technical skills, such as electricians and plumbers, to determine there bona fides. In addition, the Department of Labor provided short refresher courses to bring the weak skills of some technicians up to par. The Department planned to supply lists of registered workers to private employment brokers on the strict understanding that they charge their clients no more than one month's salary for their services. Officials hoped to resolve visa issuance problems with Saudi Arabia. Moreover, the Thai government considered sending a mission to the United States and the United Kingdom to talk to companies, which obtained contracts to rebuild Kuwait, about the advantages of Thai labor.

In November 1992, Foreign Minister Prasong Soonsri vowed to seek a normal-

TABLE 15-1
Thai Overseas Workers
(end of 1990)

Location	No. of workers
Middle East	
Saudi Arabia	120,000
Libya	25,000
Bahrain	5,500
Qatar	3,000
United Arab Emirates	2,000
Israel	2,000
Others	300
Subtotal	154,800
East Asia	
Singapore	30,000
Brunei	11,000
Malaysia	10,000
Hong Kong	9,500
Japan	4,000
Others	12,000
Subtotal	46,500
Total	231,300

Note: These figures do not include Thais who work abroad illegally.
Source: Department of Labor.

ization of relations with Saudi Arabia. In January 1993, Interior Minister Chavalit Yongchaiyudh set up a senior level committee headed by the Interior Ministry's deputy permanent secretary to monitor ongoing police investigations of the murders of the Saudi diplomats.

The decline in Thai workers in the Middle East has been more than overcome by dramatic increases in the numbers working in Japan and Taiwan. In a two-year period, as a result, the number of Thais working in foreign countries more than doubled (see Tables 15-3 and 15-4). At the end of 1994, there were nearly a half million Thai foreign laborers.

CORRUPTION PROBLEMS

Although the Thai government has long managed an overseas job placement program, much of the recruiting and placement of Thai workers has been done by private individuals. In the past, this industry was unregulated, resulting in widespread abuses of workers. Unscrupulous individuals have exploited the desire of Thais to

TABLE 15-2
Thai Overseas Workers
(end of 1991)

Location	No. of workers
Middle East	
Saudi Arabia	30,000
Libya	18,000
Kuwait	2,800
Israel	2,300
Qatar	2,000
Bahrain	1,600
United Arab Emirates	1,500
Others	2,000
Subtotal	60,200
East Asia	
Singapore	27,000
Japan	25,000
Hong Kong	15,500
Brunei	11,000
Malaysia	10,000
Taiwan	7,000
Others	10,000
Subtotal	105,500
Total	165,700

This figure does not include illegal
Thai workers: an estimated 10,000 in
Taiwan, 26,000 in Malaysia, and
30,000 in Japan.
Source: Department of Labor.

work overseas. The primary abuses were misrepresentation of the type of overseas
employment being offered, excessive fees, and simple theft of deposit monies.

To deal with these problems, the government now requires job placement
agencies to place a bank guarantee of Bt 5 million ($200,000) for each worker or
deposit return tickets for the workers placed abroad by the Department of Labor. Any
placement firms breaching employment contracts are blacklisted. The government is
also attempting to set up a central "labor export center," under which the fees and
quotas of job placement agencies would be regulated.

Fraudulent job brokers contribute to the growing problem of illegal Thai workers
in Asian countries. Many of these individuals originally arrived in these countries
with bogus contracts. After they discovered that the jobs they had expected did not
exist, they stayed on to earn whatever living they could. For example, some returnees
from the Gulf ended up paying as much as Bt 280 ($7,000) to phony placement
agencies for jobs in Taiwan and Japan. In addition, many Thais have gone to "training

TABLE 15-3
Thai Overseas Workers
(end of 1993)

Location	No. of workers
Middle East	
Bahrain	3,500
Israel	3,500
Kuwait	3,000
Libya	20,000
Qatar	3,000
Saudi Arabia	15,000
United Arab Emirates	2,500
Others	4,000
Subtotal	54,500
East Asia	
Brunei	21,000
Hong Kong	25,000
Japan	100,000
Malaysia	30,000
Singapore	50,000
Taiwan	80,000
Others	10,000
Subtotal	316,000
Total	370,500

This figure does not include Thais
who work abroad illegally.
Source: Department of Labor,

programs" only to find themselves performing manual labor in factories.[20] The Thai government, after these disclosures, warned job seekers that they could lose hard-earned cash if they applied for jobs in Europe and the United States through employment agencies, a number of which have been offering such jobs without permission from the Labor Department. Some job seekers were duped and lost all their money. One employment agent arrested by the police charged applicants Bt 120,000 ($4800) each for a nonexistent job in Sweden. The government warned individuals that there is no need for immigrant workers either in Europe or the United States. There are now 280 registered employment agencies involved in sending Thai workers abroad.

PROBLEMS IN JAPAN

There is a problem in Japan, with about 70,000 to 80,000 Thais working legally or illegally facing hardship since 2,000 foreign workers, including Thais, have been

TABLE 15-4
Thai Overseas Workers
(end of 1994)

Saudi Arabia	20,000
Qatar	3,200
Bahrain	3,500
United Arab Emirates	2,500
Kuwait	3,000
Israel	7,000
Malaysia	38,000
Singapore	50,000
Brunei	25,000
Hong Kong	26,000
Japan	80,000
Taiwan	150,000
Libya	17,000
Others	15,500
Total	440,700

This figure does not include Thais
who worked abroad illegally.
Source: Department of Labor.

detained for overstaying their visas. The Thais waited for the Thai embassy in Tokyo to issue temporary travel documents to enable them to return to Thailand. Many Thais were found to have used fake passports to get jobs and others were detained to work illegally by Japanese gangsters. A small number of Thais were forced to work as prostitutes and committed suicide. Three officials from the Public Welfare Department were sent to Japan to study the problems and work out solutions and the government warned Thais desiring employment in Japan that the Japanese government would only employ foreigners with experience in 13 fields, such as education, art, journalism, business, law, medical services, research, and engineering.[21]

About 30 Thais who went to work in Japan died in 1994 from illness or suicide according to the Thai Embassy in Tokyo. Most of the dead people had paid brokers from Bt 90,000 to 200,000 to get jobs in Japan, but found either no jobs available or only jobs that Japanese did not want to perform themselves. The Thais had to work as illegal immigrants and they were not protected by Japan's labor laws.[22] In addition, in early 1995 Japanese television aired a report describing the life of Thai service girls and boys in entertainment places in Tokyo and Osaka. It described most of the workers as having been illegally brought to Japan by sex agencies with money as the prime motivation. The Thais found the pay satisfactory, although very low compared with that of legal foreign workers. But they told of empty and meaningless lives. They could not walk around the cities as they feared being caught by the authorities. The program urged the inclusion of more Thai officials in nongovernmental organizations in Japan and other Asian countries to help ease problems Thai workers faced overseas.[23]

The Situation in Taiwan

In recent years, Taiwan has emerged as a very attractive location for Thai workers. Compared to their counterparts working in the Middle East, workers in Taiwan are getting higher pay and better working conditions. On average, each worker is sending home some Bt 15,000 ($600) a month. However, all Thai workers in Taiwan are considered as illegal foreigners by the Taiwanese government. They are allowed to work there and Taipei turns a blind eye to them because there is a serious shortage of labor in Taiwan, especially for 14 important projects scheduled for completion by 1997.

Taiwan's foreign worker policy is not to accept foreign workers in order to protect the job rights of local Taiwanese workers. However, under circumstances whereby a local worker can easily earn more than $7,500 a year, it appears that Taiwanese workers are reluctant to undertake dirty or dangerous jobs which has caused delays in several projects. Facing pressures from the private sector, the Taiwanese government has agreed in principle to allow foreign construction workers to come to Taiwan for these projects. Foreign workers can only work on the construction project for which they have been employed. Once the project is completed, they have to leave and return to their home countries.

It is difficult to estimate the number of illegal foreign workers because most of them are listed as tourists. However, the number of overstayers in Taiwan are 100,000 and about 11,000 were deported. Illegal foreign workers are roughly estimated at 44,000 with most of them working in the manufacturing, construction, and service fields.

In December 1992, the Deputy Minister of the Interior responsible for overseas job placement ordered the licenses of 24 Thai agencies revoked for overcharging Thai workers seeking to go to Taiwan. The companies had exceeded the legal limitation of a fee of one month's pay. The workers in Taiwan complained of paying commissions of $1,600 to $2,800 for jobs paying $520 a month. Subsequently, the Thai government official charged that the agencies had put out a $120,000 contract on his life, and were telephoning death threats to his home. Later in the month, the official met with the Taiwanese representative to Thailand and they agreed to consider setting up a joint Thai–Taiwanese committee to oversee bilateral labor problems. In February 1993, the interior ministry issued regulations fixing the maximum brokerage fee at $1,520.

The problem of corrupt job placement remained a troublesome one more than a year later when in March 1994, Taiwan charged that a great number of Thais were working illegally in Taiwan, and the 10,000 Thais there illegally were charged exorbitant fees by Thai employment agencies. The government reported that Taipei might stop importing Thai workers unless Bangkok stemmed the flow of illegal workers and cracked down on the employment agencies.[24] Most of the estimated

100,000 foreigners working in Taiwan illegally are also Thais. Of the Thais there legally, most are believed to have paid the equivalent of three months wages to an employment agency to get their jobs. The Thai government claimed it was trying hard to end the flood of illegal Thai workers going to Taiwan in a bid to improve labor relations between the two nations.[25]

The Council of Labor Affairs in Taiwan issued an ultimatum for a possible freeze on allowing Thai workers in to Taiwan and demanded a goodwill response before the end of March 1994, concerning remedial measures on the excessive recruiting fees, up to six months of wages, Thai workers were charged by intermediary employment agencies in Thailand. The CLA said it planned to stop future arrivals of Thai workers if no effective actions were taken. It also demanded that the Thai government establish a special fund for low interest loans to Thai workers so they would not have to sell their homes or properties in order to come to Taiwan to work. Stricter screenings of the background of applicants by Thai authorities was also demanded by the CLA.

In 1994, Thai workers accounted for approximately 80% of the 180,000 approved foreign workers brought into the country. They earned an estimated $500 million a year in Taiwan. In order not to affect local employers in case the threatened freeze is implemented, the CLA allowed Thai workers already working or already granted entry permits to stay in Thailand after their employment contracts expired.[26]

Another problem of enforcing job placement agency fees was revealed when the Director-General of the Thai Employment Service Department, Sinchai Rientrakul, came under investigation for alleged mismanagement and failure to control his subordinates. Mr. Sinchai was charged with failure to take legal action against nine employment agencies which overcharged workers who applied to work in Taiwan. The Labor Ministry had decreed that Thai workers could not be charged more than Bt 38,000 per head and began an investigation into Sinchai's activities. Sinchai said he was ready to testify but that legal action could not be taken against the nine employment agencies because of insufficient evidence. He said the charges against him were disturbing and claimed his "straightforward" working style might have blocked the vested interests of certain people.[27]

The Bt 38,000 fee for each worker included a Bt 25,000 marketing fee and the first month's salary of workers which average Bt 13,000. The fees excluded passport and visa fees, medical checkup costs, and airfares which must be borne by the workers. The Thai government alleged that most job placement firms were charging each worker between Bt 70,000 and 100,000 for a job in Taiwan. Because a large number of Thai wanted to work in Taiwan, the employment agencies had to outbid one another in order to get contracts. The placement companies might pay Bt 40,000 to get a job contract.

To prevent fierce competition, all 174 employment agencies were to form a club and employment contracts would be shared on a proportional basis with the labor and social welfare ministry closely supervising the club. An informed source in the Thai Labor Promotion Committee said he doubted small employment agencies would be given a fair share of the job quota. He said large companies would take most, and the best quotas and they would soon squeeze their small competitors out of the business. A committee formed by employment agencies sought an increase in the service charge beyond Bt 38,000 set by the government, and wanted the minimum charge set at Bt 50,000.[28]

Yet another issue that surfaced between Thailand and Taiwan involved the minimum wage for Thai workers in Taiwan. In late February 1992, the Overseas Employment Promotion Committee of the Department of Labor set a new minimum wage rate for Thai workers abroad, with rates varying according to country and job. In Taiwan the minimum wage was to be from $580 to $800 a month. In March of that year Taiwanese authorities demanded that the Thai government rescind this policy or face a ban on Thais working on the island. The Taiwanese asserted that once a work contract was signed, agreed-upon pay levels should not be changed. Bowing to the demand, the Thai ministry of interior lowered the minimum wage by 5 to 10%. However, Taiwanese authorities rejected this downward adjustment and instituted the ban. Finally, after negotiations between the governments, Taipei announced in May that it was rescinding the ban on Thai workers, after the Thais agreed not to demand that Thai workers receive more than the legal minimum wage in Taiwan.

THE BRUNEI SITUATION

Thai government officials in charge of regulating job placement agencies were accused of demanding under-the-table payments from the agencies in exchange for permits to export Thai workers to Brunei. Employment service firms that failed to pay the illegal fees would be denied a certificate from the labor office in Brunei, meaning that they could not send workers to the oil-rich state even though they had won contracts to export Thai labor there.

The under-the-table payments were just the first of a number of other tricks employed by unscrupulous labor officials to force independent job placement agencies to come under their controlled pool of recruitment companies. One of the tricks was to encourage Thai workers sent by the independent agencies to file false written complaints with authorities that they were overcharged by the agencies. In such a case, the agencies concerned were warned and risked the prospect of having their licenses revoked. If the companies did not want a bad record or risk the prospect of losing business, they would have to make the illegal payments.

Another trick was to encourage Thai workers to complaint that they were not paid by their employers in Brunei for two or three months. Here, the job placement agency concerned would be held responsible and the complaint would be passed on to the Office of the Permanent Secretary in Bangkok by the labor office in Brunei. Then the job agencies would be forced to pay the amount supposedly owed to the Thai workers if they did not want to receive a warning from the Labor and Social Welfare Ministry. The amount extorted would be split among the dishonest officials. Further, if the job agencies tried to find out from the employers if wages were not paid to the Thai workers as alleged, they might have their licenses revoked, in effect causing them more trouble than if they had just paid the extra money.

However, the dirtiest trick employed by the corrupt officials who appeared to work as a team was to instigate Thai workers to quit their jobs and apply for new jobs offered by other job agencies working in collaboration with the corrupt officials. In this scenario, the officials would receive shares from overhead fees to be charged on the workers by the new job agency. In addition, they would also receive fees from the companies which took over the job quota left by workers who quit. The Thai government denied the allegations that labor officials who oversee the export of Thai workers abroad were involved in the alleged corrupt activities.[29]

SINGAPORE

An unusual health problem afflicted Thai workers in Singapore when 73 Thais were reported to have died of Sudden Unexplained Nocturnal Death Syndrome (SUNDS), a major cause of deaths among Thai workers. Most of the workers died within two to four months of arriving in the republic. Alarmed at this development, the Public Health Ministry decided to set up public health offices in countries where there are many Thai workers to provide counseling and medical care. Eligibility for social security payments for Thai laborers in hospitals in Singapore, Saudi Arabia, and Brunei was also approved.

The Mahidol University's public health faculty offered their opinion that genetic factors were involved the death of workers since eight people who died previously had lost family members to the same cause. The academic entity claimed research showed an abnormality of the X chromosome related to genetic factors was the cause of SUNDS and other factors causing the illness among Thai workers in Singapore were stress, excessive work, and the use of drugs. Most Thai workers abroad suffer stress because their employers expect them to work longer and harder than anticipated.[30]

Several years earlier, in 1990, the Thai Deputy Interior Minister sharply criticized the Thai ambassador to Singapore after the latter's comments that the minister had taken improper steps in solving the problem of Thai workers' poor living conditions and poor pay. The minister lashed out at the ambassador:

> I don't like his diplomatic way of working from behind a glass of champagne at social functions. He is the kind of person whose feet do not touch the ground. Probably he wants to be posted to a bigger country so that he can attend more functions with a lot of champagne... I could not stand seeing 30,000 workers being used as slaves.... The ambassador said the Philippines had asked for a bigger wage for its workers. Why didn't the ambassador do likewise?[31]

The ambassador responded, claiming that when 9,300 workers were sent home in 1989, he had gone to see the workers leave by train and boat on many occasions. He also said when the Thai Public Health Minister visited Singapore, he accompanied him to work sites every day. He also maintained that the Thai Labor Department should file complaints about Thai workers' welfare through Singapore's Labor Ministry and not through the media.

The president of the Thai Job Placement Association also criticized Minister

Vatona's proposal that all Thai workers in Singapore should be sent back to Thailand, commenting that Vatona probably wanted to be seen as a hero on the basis of such a remark. The minister denied the allegation, contending that he never stated he would prohibit job placement agencies from sending workers to Singapore. His account was that he only proposed that the export of workers be forbidden because if Thailand becomes more highly developed there would be jobs for all Thai workers at home. Mr. Vatona also vowed support only for good job placement agencies. He added, "As for the bad ones that cheat, I will get rid of them."[31]

HONG KONG

A problem of poor working conditions was revealed in Hong Kong when Thai maids working there claimed abuses by their employers and drew the support of four labor rights groups, which urged the Thai government to fund the operations of an emergency home in Hong Kong to help Thai maids abused or dismissed by their employers. They also proposed that the Ministry of Labor and Social Welfare should be the sole authority in sending Thai maids to work in Hong Kong. The proposals were submitted to the government by representatives of the Asian Migrants Center, the Domestic Helpers Union, the Friends of Thais in Hong Kong, and Friends of Thai Women in Asia. The ministry responded that it had accumulated about Bt 100 million from contributions collected from each worker traveling abroad and this would be used to set up a separate emergency home in Hong Kong. The same contribution would be collected from job placement agencies.

The labor groups pointed out that a large number of Thai maids were abused, beaten up, or fired by their employers. An emergency facility was set up by the Friends of Thais in Hong Kong to aid these women in distress. The home had been operating for two years but was short of funds. The organization asked the government for financial support and also said that the maids had been charged Bt 30,000 to 50,000 ($720–1200) each for a job in Hong Kong by employment service firms. Worse still, the maids were not given any proper training and many of them had their employment contracts ignored by employers because they did not understand the working conditions and terms in the contracts. The four groups suggested that the ministry should assume control of the labor export service to Hong Kong to solve the problem of overcharging and training for workers. It turned out that although there was a Thai law on employment service fees, some officials deliberately failed to enforce the statute. The government stated that all Thais working abroad would be required to complete a training program organized by the Employment Service Department.[32]

ILLEGAL ALIENS

It turns out that Thailand has its own illegal alien problem. Police arrested over 3,000 undocumented workers in 1990, most from Burma and Laos. About 9,000 expatriates work in Thailand with official permits. However, some of those arrested were overseas Chinese and Europeans who overstayed their visitor visas.

Thai employers violating work permit laws face penalties of up to three years in prison and/or a fine of up to $2,400. On several occasions, Thai labor officials threatened to launch a campaign against illegal Taiwanese workers in reprisal for a crackdown on Thai illegals in Taiwan.

Local textile and garment manufacturers urged the Thai government to allow them to hire more foreign workers to ease higher production costs, especially those from Laos, Cambodia and Vietnam. They said the imported workers could offset higher local wages caused by the recently adjusted minimum wages and help lower the industry's overall costs. Importing unskilled workers from abroad would also benefit the government by increasing income tax revenues and ameliorating the problem of illegal workers.[33]

Government figures showed that at the beginning of 1995, more than 520,000 immigrants were working illegally in Thailand, especially in border areas. This nearly matched the 470,000 Thai workers employed overseas. The migrant workers include 334,000 Burmese, 100,000 Chinese, 10,000 Indochinese, and 81,000 from other Asian countries such as Bangladesh, Pakistan, and India. These workers, particularly from Burma, have been the primary labor force in border provinces for nearly a decade.

Provincial industrialists favor these migrant workers because they are more willing to do hard work than their Thai counterparts. They endure bad working conditions and work longer hours than permitted by law. More importantly, they do not demand free health care, welfare benefits, or high pay. They are also quite docile and obedient and make few demands on employers.

The fact is that they have no other choice but to be obedient or they would lose their jobs, be fined, jailed, or deported. In a way, these illegal workers fulfill the need for unskilled labor in the provinces since rural Thais in increasing numbers are leaving their homes to work in the industrial sector where the minimum wage, compared to rural pay rates, is high. The shortage of unskilled Thai labor is compounded also by the departure of Thai workers to foreign countries.

Despite the optimism displayed by local businessmen, state agencies in charge of national security view the illegal labor negatively, as a threat to national security. Indeed, there have been cases where illegal immigrants have organized criminal gangs to pursue illegal activities. Burmese illegals, in particular, have taken part in smuggling goods and used their Thai bases to rebel against the Rangoon government. In recent years, the activities of these immigrants have soured the relations between Thailand and its neighbors.

This is the reason why Thailand has adopted a policy of trying to send these people back into their home countries, which is not an easy task because of long borders and the need for 24-hour surveillance. The truth is that illegal immigrants continue to sneak into Thailand and easily find work. In certain areas, migrant workers from Burma work during the day and return home in the evening. The Thai government is concerned that the situation will deteriorate to the level of slave trade since influential gangs have smuggled in men to work as "slaves" or women to work as prostitutes. Bangkok and provincial police regularly capture girls said to have been hired or forced from Burma and Southern China.

The immigration authorities do not consider it a serious problem for poor immigrants to work honestly as laborers or prostitutes, but are bothered by the prospects of forced labor or forced prostitution. One answer to the situation would be legalization, based not only on the economic interests on the part of employers alone but also on humanitarian considerations and labor justice. Employment authorities are trying to treat lawful migrant workers fairly but find it impossible to protect illegal migrants.

In recent years, given the "hide and seek" game played by the authorities, employers and workers, a migrant might receive only Bt 20 or 30 ($.80–1.20) a day or only meals and shelter in exchange for their labor. Relaxation of laws on the employment of unlawful migrants has occurred in five provinces: Chiang Rai, Mae Hong Son, Tak, Kanchanaburi and Ranong. During the fall of 1994, employment offices in the five provinces surveyed businesses hiring illegal immigrants and registered the workers. There were a total of about 100,000 Burmese illegal migrants working for Thais in businesses including fisheries, charcoal-burning, construction, and farms and food shops. Administrative authorities in the provinces issued ID cards for the migrants. The Employment Department provided them with documents to certify their employment. The cards are valid for five years. Under the program, every employer must deposit Bt 50,000 for each migrant worker with the department. The requirement is to ensure that the employers are responsible for the whereabouts of their workers. Without permission, the migrants are not allowed to leave the district in which they work.

Unfortunately, Thai employers did not respond in good faith. They did not tell the authorities the truth about the number of their migrant workers because they did not want to deposit huge sums. As a result, the real figure might be double or triple the official tally.

Employment of migrant labor has become a problem because the labor employment law enacted in 1917 is obsolete, not reflecting present-day realities. Each year Thailand brought in 10,000 to 11,000 people to work mostly in office management positions or as specialists such as engineers. The law does not allow employment of foreigners for 34 occupations, mostly unskilled positions, which are reserved for Thais. In the past, Thailand had no shortage of workers but the situation has changed greatly and now the country is short of unskilled labor. Obviously, the law should be amended, but there are potentially both positive and negative repercussions.

If Thailand imports unskilled workers, their Thai counterparts will be disadvantaged, with less power to bargain for higher wages. The number of unemployed, unskilled Thais may increase in the long run or else they will continue to earn low wages. Imports or unskilled labor could produce social and political problems and an increase in crime. The government would have to spend more on public utilities to meet the demands of imported workers but imported unskilled labor could fill jobs Thais no longer wanted. Cheap labor could bring down production costs, benefitting buyers of goods. Also, imported unskilled workers would spend money in Thailand and indirectly create more jobs for skilled Thai workers.

PART V

Malaysia

Almost without exception, traditional union tactics of organizing, bargaining, and striking have important effects on trade and investment. Korean workers, after decades of suppression by military governments, countered the suppression with a broad movement of strikes in the 1980s and organizing campaigns that transformed Korea's export base. This movement forced sharp salary increases and challenged management's autocratic control of the workplace. Companies retaliated by moving operations to Thailand, Malaysia, Central America, and other lower-cost export processing areas. As turmoil continued to jeopardize the stability desired by international investors, the Korean government responding by launching new crackdowns on organized labor. Like Korea, the Malaysian government intervened by prohibiting independent, freely-chosen unions in the growing semiconductor industry. This measure created investment problems in Malaysia and placed the government in a precarious situation. If Malaysia continued to prohibit the formation of national unions, the United States considered imposing trade sanctions for labor rights violations. If Malaysia lifted the ban on genuine unions, United States-based multinational companies threatened to leave. Political reform and union tactics presented governments with difficult questions on how to address labor rights in the context of international trade.

L. COMPA[1]

Malaysia has placed third or fourth in recent ratings of national competitiveness indicated in world competitiveness rankings but twenty-third in the "people" area. This highlights its quandary in attempting to reconcile worker rights and labor standards with a rapidly growing economy. The Malaysian government has followed a policy of union suppression to keep labor costs down and facilitate its export-driven economic development strategy.

The government of Dr. Mahathir Mohamed is concerned that wage increases not motivated by productivity gains will have adverse implications for the Malaysian economy as well as workers' livelihoods. In fact, a serious shortage of labor has been partly attributed to reduced productivity and rising labor costs. The need to shift from labor-intensive to capital-intensive industries has been emphasized, as in the case of Thailand, to overcome the current shortage of workers. The human resources minister has stressed the need for a flexi-wage system, which was proposed by the Malaysian Employers Federation (MEF) some years ago, to be restudied. The federation's proposed system, based on Singapore's wage system, was rejected by Malaysian unions and thus was shelved until Datuk Lim Ah Lek raised the matter again.

The government was in favor of the flexi-wage concept but unions had rejected it, favoring a system that ensured fairness and employment security. They harbored doubts that workers would be evaluated objectively by their employers under such an agreement, which labor believed would turn out instead to be subjective and open to abuse.

The flexi-wage dispute illustrated the distrust that has developed between Malaysian labor organizations and the government of that nation. A similar lack of confidence in the intentions of the other side also characterizes the relationship between organized labor and Malaysian employers. For example, private sector unions also criticized the Malaysian Employers Federation for proposing that the government introduce new guidelines on wage increases, saying that the federation's suggestion is a selfish move to suppress workers' wages. The Malaysian Trades Union Congress (MTUC) and the Malaysian Labour Organization (MLO), the country's two main labor bodies for private sector unions, both voiced strong opposition to the suggestion. They contended that the proposed guidelines are unnecessary since the existing ones based on the Consumer Price Index in accordance with the 1982 Industrial Court award are sufficient.

Prime Minister Mohamed maintains that the best way to solve problems that develop between labor and management is through negotiations, with both sides willing to compromise. On its face, this appears to be an enlightened view of labor–management relations since confrontations do not help solve problems but provide a temporary respite even if it be in favor of the momentarily stronger party. Yet negotiations are not immune to economic conditions that are likely to dictate the final outcome in the absence of statutory provisions which stipulate minimum require-ments.

However, in Malaysia only weak in-house unions are permitted in the burgeon-ing electronics industry. The prime minister expressed a preference for this type of union representation when he stated as far back as March 1983 in the *New Straits Times*: "There is need for Malaysia to look into a new concept like in-house unions that have been used successfully by the Japanese who have easily beaten the West which practices an old system of trade unionism."

Unions in Malaysia—as the example in electronics demonstrates—do not have the freedom to determine their own organizational structures, nor can they operate freely without government intervention. Amendments to labor laws, the Trade Unions Ordinance of 1959 and the Industrial Relations Act of 1967, have increased the powers of labor ministry officials to suspend unions, forbid strikes, unilaterally intervene in any labor conflict, invalidate strike ballots, and regulate relations with international labor bodies, as well as prohibit high-ranking union leaders and their organizations from engaging in political activity. As is the case in China, Indonesia, and Thailand, these restrictions are reflected in the limited scope of protection and coverage afforded worker rights and labor standards in Malaysia, as shown in Figure V-1.

We will examine these and other issues in Malaysian industrial relations in Part V, drawing parallels and distinctions with the other three new Asian tigers.

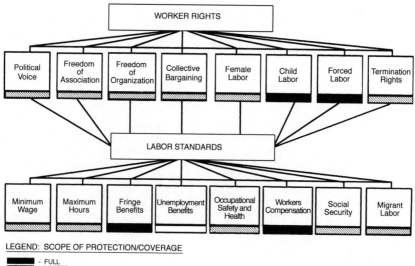

FIGURE V–1. Worker Rights/Labor Standards in Malaysia

CHAPTER 16

Political Events, Economic Facts, and Demographic Variables

THE POLITICAL STRUCTURE

Malaysia is a federation, a democracy, and a constitutional monarchy, but one in which power is strongly centralized. Opposition parties have more scope for gaining power than those in neighboring Asian countries; they can, for example, win control of state governments, but the ruling Barisan Nasional (National Front) coalition tends to counter this by cutting funding to states which vote against it. It also strictly controls the press.

Thirteen states make up the Malaysian federation, which has a parliamentary system of government based on periodic multiparty elections. The ruling National Front coalition has held power since 1957. There is political competition within the United Malays National Organization (UMNO), the major partner in the coalition, and opposition parties actively contest elections, currently controlling two state governments. By law Malaysians have the right to change their government through the electoral process. Malaysian elections are procedurally free and fair, with votes recorded accurately. However, election irregularities detract from the overall fairness of the process. Legal restrictions on campaigning and government influence over the media contributes to UMNO's continuing political dominance. National elections, required at least every five years, have been held regularly since independence in 1957. Through UMNO, Malays dominate the ruling coalition of 14 ethnic-based parties that has controlled parliament since independence. Within UNNO there is active political debate.

In April 1995, the coalition government led by Dr. Mohamed won the most recent election, with 64% of the votes and 84% of the seats in parliament. The National Front won 161 of the newly expanded 192-member parliament. Heavily gerrymandered constituencies ensure that Malay-speaking people, the basis of the National Front's support, form a majority in most places. The government-controlled news media rarely covered the opposition, and party leaders used state resources in their campaigns.

THE LEGISLATURE

The national legislature has two houses, the Senate which has 68 members, 42 of whom are appointed by the king, and the House of Representatives, with 192 directly elected members. The former has a six-year term of office and the latter, five years. There are 13 state governments, each of which has its own constitution. The king is elected by a conference of hereditary rulers from nine states. Malays fill 8 of the 25 cabinet posts.[1]

THE JUDICIARY

The judicial system is based on English common law. Judicial review of legislative acts is conducted by the Supreme Court at the request of the supreme head of the federation. Malaysia has not accepted compulsory jurisdiction of the International Court of Justice.

The public and the legal community have long regarded the Malaysian judiciary as committed to the rule of law. The judicial system traditionally exhibited a high degree of independence, seldom hesitating to rule against the government in criminal, civil, or occasionally even politically sensitive cases. For example, the Supreme Court ruled in February 1988 that the dominant party in the government coalition was illegally constituted. However, the government's dismissal of the Supreme Court Lord President and two other justices in 1988, along with a constitutional amendment and legislation restricting judicial review, resulted in less judicial independence and stronger executive influence over the judiciary in politically sensitive cases. These developments created the possibility that Malaysians who might otherwise seek legal remedies against government actions would be reluctant to do so. The 1988 changes have also resulted in less willingness by the courts to challenge the government's legal interpretations in politically sensitive cases.

The government, following criticism of some of its policies by the Malaysian Bar Council, attempted to gain greater control over the Council in 1991 and early 1992. Although there was concern that the Bar Council's freedom of expression and independence were being threatened, government criticism of the Council has since ebbed.[2]

RECENT HISTORY

In 1957 Malaysia gained its independence from Great Britain, having been returned to British rule at the end of the Second World War. While the cultural diversity arising from the presence of the various ethnic groups has been a source of strength, in terms of human resources and skills, it has laid the foundation for racial problems. In the wake of the 1969 general elections, there was a serious outbreak of rioting, primarily between the Malays and the Chinese. In the early years of indepen-

dence the Malays dominated the political system, while the Chinese had dispropor-
tionate economic power. Chinese economic power has been eroded since the New
Economic Policy (NEP) was introduced in the wake of the 1969 riots with a view to
redistributing wealth in favor of the bumiputera, indigenous, mainly Malay, population.

The Federation of Malaysia was established in 1963. Initially it contained the
11 states of Peninsular Malaysia, Singapore and the states of Sabah and Sarawak
situated some 318 miles across the South China Sea, but Singapore withdrew from the
federation in 1965. The early years of independence were fraught with problems,
including the final stages of a civil war, referred to as "the emergency" which pitted
the mainly Chinese Malayan Communist Party (MCP) against the government,
uncertainties over relations with neighboring countries and interethnic friction. Although the racial tension of the early years of independence has largely been contained, ethnic difference remains the single most important aspect of politics, and the
mitigation of inequality between ethnic groups is the prime goal of the present
government.

A multiracial coalition, known since 1969 as the National Front, has governed
Malaysia since 1957. There are currently nine parties in the ruling coalition. The
United Malays National Organization (UMNO), representing the largest ethnic
group, the Malays, as the largest party in the coalition has headed each government
since independence. The other main parties in the coalition are: the Malaysian
Chinese Association (MCA); the Malaysian Indian Congress (MIC); the Gerakan;
and the Parti Pesaka Bumiputera Bersatu (PPBB), the dominant party in Sarawak.[3]

THE CONSTITUTION

Malaysia is a constitutional monarchy. The head of state, the Yang di-Pertuan
Agong, the king, is elected for a five-year period by the Conference of Rulers, which
consists of the nine ruling sultans in Peninsular Malaysia from the states of Perlis,
Kedah, Perakk, Selangor, Negeri Sembilan, Johor, Pahang, Terengganu and Kelantan.
The four states of Melaka, Penang, Sabah, and Sarawak which do not have sultans,
each has a head of state appointed for a term of four years by the king. Malaysia has a
constitution which sets out both the individual rights of citizens and the basis on
which the federation is formed. To amend the constitution, a two-thirds majority is
required in parliament.

The Malays and other indigenous peoples comprising 59% of the population are
given special rights under Article 153 of the constitution, which includes the reservation of quotas for employment in the federal public service and armed forces and for
business permits or licenses and scholarships. In addition, the reservation of land for
exclusive use by Malays is assured under Article 89. Following the 1969 race riots, the
constitution was amended in 1971 to forbid any further questioning of these special
provisions. The constitution was promulgated on August 31, 1957, a national holiday.
National Day is celebrated on each August 31st to mark this occasion. The constitu-

tion was amended on September 16, 1963 to mark Malaysia's transition into a federation.

THE RIGHT OF ASSOCIATION

Specific statutes limit the right of association, such as the Societies Act of 1966, under which any association of seven or more members must register with the government as a society, thereby including labor unions. The government may refuse to register a new society or may impose conditions when allowing a society to register. The government also has the power to revoke the registration of an existing society for violations of the act, a power it has selectively enforced against political opposition groups.[4]

POLITICAL FORCES

Established in 1946, UMNO has remained the dominant political party in the government, enjoying wide grass roots support among the Malays, with 1.7 millon members in 1991. It currently has the largest number of seats, 71, in parliament. Previously limited to Malays only, it initiated a membership drive in 1992 to recruit *bumiputeras*, a broader term used to include both Malays and the other indigenous peoples such as the Ibans of Sarawak and the Kedazans of Sabah.

Because of its dominance the president of UMNO is also the country's prime minister. At the top of the UMNO official hierarchy is the Supreme Council. At its general assembly in November 1991, the party's constitution was amended to allow the president to appoint 10 members, previously 7, to the Supreme Council. To further strengthen his position Prime Minister Mohamed introduced a series of legislative amendments which tilted the power balance in favor of the executive branch. The Official Secrets Act, the Police Act, which regulates public meetings, the Printing Presses and Publications Act, covering the media, the Internal Security Act (ISA), first introduced by the British as a method of containing the Communist insurgency, and the Societies Act, which governs the formation of political parties and other societies, were all tightened. A constitutional amendment redefined the position of the judiciary, making it more difficult for judges to take independent action.

In January 1989, Dr. Mahathir underwent triple bypass heart surgery and did not return to work until that April. Recognizing the serious opposition to him from within the Malay community, the prime minister spent 1989 consolidating his position. He spoke anew of the need for Malay unity and also released the remainder of the prisoners held since the 1987 clampdown, including the Democratic Action Party (DAP) leader Lim Kit Siang.

Until the race riots in 1969, MCA was the only party of the Chinese community. Since then, its claim to be the sole representative of Chinese interests has been challenged by a number of other parties, all of which are avowedly multiracial in nature. The two major ones are Gerakan, a Penang-based party which is also a member of the National Front, and the DAP, which is the largest opposition party. The DAP has repeatedly claimed it is undermined by government harassment, and several of its leaders have been detained for periods under the Internal Security Act. In the 1990 election the DAP, benefiting from Chinese disillusionment with the limited role of the MCA in the coalition, won 20 seats, against only 18 for the MCA, and remained the largest opposition party. The racial polarization implicit in the voting was viewed as a worrisome trend.

The other significant ethnic minority group in the country, the Indians, are represented by the Malaysian Indian Congress (MIC) whose leader is Samy Vellu. The MIC draws strong support from its community despite charges of lack of accountability in the handling of the party's funds. In 1991 Vellu was investigated by the Anti-Corruption Agency for alleged irregularities in the sale of shares in the privatized state telecommunications enterprise.

SUCCESSION SPECULATION

On the issue of leadership, there is much speculation as to when Mahathir Mohamed will step down. In office since 1981, Dr. Mohamed is the country's longest serving prime minister. He has said he has no intention of leaving office until after 2000, despite suffering from health problems. Recent news stories alleging there is a rift between Dr. Mahathir and his deputy prime minister and expected successor, Anwar Ibrahim, are probably exaggerated, but the prime minister appears annoyed and worried by the ambitions of the younger politicians who support Mr. Anwar.[5]

MONEY POLITICS

Mainly a facet of party leadership elections, money politics does not directly impinge upon foreign business. If there is a connection to business, it is with local companies backing certain candidates in the hope of future political access. Foreign firms are advised to stay out of Malaysian politics altogether.[6]

UNIONS AND POLITICS

Trade unions are not a potent force in Malaysian politics. Existing legislation tightly restricts union activities and it is estimated that only 15% of the total labor force is unionized. There are three federations of unions in the country, the largest being the Malaysian Trade Union Congress (MTUC), with over 500,000 members, followed by CUEPACS, the civil service labor group, and the Malaysian Labor Organization (MLO), which was established in 1989. There has been controversy over a government ruling that permits only in-house, enterprise-based, unions to be formed among electronic workers. The MTUC's attempts to challenge this ruling have won the backing of international labor organizations.

Unions may organize workplaces, bargain collectively with an employer, form federations, and join international organizations. The Trade Unions Act's definition of a trade union restricts it to representing workers in a "particular trade, occupation, or industry or within any similar trades, occupations, or industries." The Director-General of Trade Unions has considerable latitude in deciding whether or not to register a trade union in Malaysia. The Director-General also has the power, under certain circumstances, to withdraw the registration of a union. A union for which registration has been refused, withdrawn, or canceled is considered an unlawful association. While strikes are legal and do occasionally occur, critics claim that this right in practice is restricted.[7]

Unions have long been active in Malaysian politics, although their impact on electoral results has generally been minimal. The desirability of political activism by labor continues to be the subject of heated debate among workers and trade unionists. An MTUC faction favoring a less political role for the organization won a significant victory in 1992 elections.

GOVERNMENT–LABOR RELATIONS

Relations between the Malaysian government and the MTUC have never been warm, but there have been periods of close cooperation and less overt antagonism, although relations in recent years have been strained. The government has criticized the MTUC's position on a number of labor issues, including the congress's stand on several U.S.–GSP worker rights petitions since 1988 and the positions MTUC has taken on ILO issues. Government spokespersons have accused the congress of being duped by foreign labor organizations, alleging these organizations seek to have Malaysia's trade privileges removed to the detriment of Malaysian workers.

In this regard, Human Resources Minister Datuk Lim Ah Lek criticized local union officials who turn to foreigners for help in solving their labor disputes. He charged that recently a trend had developed among union leaders in seeking the assistance from foreign union leaders to settle industrial problems within Malaysia: "We have the evidence in the form of a letter to prove that the local union leaders are requesting the foreign trade union leaders to interfere in our workers' disputes."[8] He said the ministry discovered that a union sent a letter to an international trade secretariat requesting assistance to solve a workers' dispute involving a locally based international petroleum company.

Lim chastised the Malaysian unionists, stating they should stop consulting foreigners to solve local problems with which outsiders were unfamiliar. He added that a solution could be found if efforts were undertaken to settle the issue through union discussion with management, and that the unionists were abdicating their leadership roles by seeking outside aid before trying to settle labor problems themselves. As a last resort, the matter could be brought to the attention of the Industrial

Court. Also, prior government intervention had been successful in resolving 93% of Malaysian labor disputes.

A DEMAGOGIC APPEAL

Prime Minister Mohamed also blamed outsiders and the international media for their sinister efforts to undermine Malaysia. He claimed that the control and influence of international media is in the hands of a small group of unnamed Western capitalists. Mohamed cautioned:

> The rakyat (parliament) should pay serious attention to this development. The media, especially television, have a very strong and powerful influence. The Western individuals controlling the media can also influence our thoughts, attitudes and culture. If we are not careful, we, too, can be influenced to destroy ourselves.[9]

The Prime Minister said that his observations were based on solid information and after close study of the situation. He said direct colonization may have ended but the attitude and intentions of the colonial masters are still evident. He warned they would do it again if given the opportunity.

Mohamed attributed Malaysia's successes to the country's system of administration based on parliamentary democracy and constitutional monarchy. He warned that the country's success has led others in the developed West to be envious. As a developing country, Malaysia has no capital, technology, big internal market or high management expertise, according to the Malaysian leader. The country only has a relatively low cost of living which has enabled it to provide competitive wages. His criticisms became more concrete when he indirectly alluded to Western efforts to link trade with workers' rights:

> If the developed countries can incite our workers to demand very high wages through industrial action, then we will lose our only advantage, that is, our competitive edge. That is why they have been trying to pressure us into liberalizing our labour policies so that our trade unions can act as militantly as theirs. The government sympathizes with workers, but this sympathy needs to be treated carefully. Workers will enjoy better wages when the country's economy keeps expanding. Today's wages are better than before, and there is no need for any form of industrial action.[9]

In an interesting contrast to Mohamed's pointed remarks, several months later Malaysia's Deputy Prime Minister Datuk Anwar Ibrahim sounded the very model of moderation in sharply challenging the widespread Asian preoccupation with economic progress at all costs, seemingly contradicting his prime minister. He mentioned that economic progress in Asia would only be meaningful if it led to improvements in social and civil conditions. His comments illustrated the emergence of a new and distinctive type of Asian moderation and marked a significant moderation of the "Asian model" of economic development. Many Asian leaders, including the Chinese leadership in its dispute with the United States over human rights, have justified a degree of political repression in the name of social stability and economic progress. Ibrahim counseled:

We are dealing not just with percentages and factories, but with human beings.... Empower-
ment of ordinary citizens does not necessarily result in political indiscipline.... As it stands,
there is not one prisoner of conscience in Malaysia. I take pride in that because Malaysia is
unique in this capacity in the region.[10]

Datuk Anwar's relative political liberalization is based on and qualified by the
sustained economic growth of the Malaysian economy. Malaysia has had seven
consecutive years of growth greater than 8% annually. On social issues he argued that
the United States, which is leading Western efforts to improve Asian human rights and
labor conditions, had taken 100 years after the Declaration of Independence to abolish
slavery. It took another century to remove racial discrimination in education. Part of
his agenda for political change appears to be a speedier reform of Malaysia's Internal
Security Act. As a leader of a radical Islamic youth organization in the 1970s, Ibrahim
was himself detained under the Act, on the grounds of having incited racial tensions.
He confirmed that the statute would have to be reviewed.

Based on these comments of Malaysia's top two government leaders, a mixed set
of signals has been recently emanating from Kuala Lumpur. Dr. Mohamed's statements seem based on domestic political considerations in their nationalistic tone
while, in sharp contrast, his heir apparent's remarks sounded measured and reasonable. Perhaps they augur important changes in Malaysia's political landscape.

THE ECONOMIC PICTURE

In terms of economic structure, Malaysia has a relatively open, market-oriented
economy. Since independence in 1957, the Malaysian economy has shown sustained
growth and has diversified away from the twin pillars of the colonial economy, tin
and rubber. Real gross domestic product (GDP) growth averaging 6 to 8% from 1964
to 1994 has been accompanied by the development of new crops such as palm oil
and cocoa and the expansion of the petroleum sector. In 1985–86 the collapse of
commodity prices led to Malaysia's worst recession since independence with real
GDP growth near zero and nominal gross national product (GNP) falling 11%. Since
then, the economy has rebounded, led by strong growth in manufactured goods
exports.

The government plays a large role in the Malaysian economy, both as a producer
of goods and services and as a regulator. The government or government-owned
entities dominate a number of sectors, particularly plantations and banking. Through
the National Equity Corporation, the government has equity stakes, generally of a
minority nature, in a wide range of domestic companies. In all, government-
controlled entities may account for one-third of the economy. These entities are rarely
monopolies and they are one player, albeit generally the largest, player among several
competitors in a given sector. Since 1986 the government has begun to privatize
several entities, including telecommunications, ports, a major highway, and the
national electricity board.

Malaysia encourages direct foreign investment, particularly in export-oriented manufacturing. Multinational corporations control a substantial share of the manufacturing sector. U.S. and Japanese firms dominate the production of electronic components, consumer electronics, and electrical goods. Malaysia is the world's third largest producer of integrated circuits. Foreign investors also play an important role in petroleum, textiles, vehicle assembly, steel, cement, rubber products, and electrical machinery.

Economic development is the highest priority of the Mahathir administration and is considered the primary determinant of national progress and prestige. In 1990, Prime Minister Mohamed outlined a 30-year strategic development plan known as Vision 2020, which has the ambitious goal of transforming Malaysia into a fully developed society by the year 2020. Its concept of development embraces not only the conventional economic sphere but also encompasses political, social, moral, and psychological dimensions.[11]

Finance Minister and Deputy Prime Minister Anwar Ibrahim's budget presentation in October 1994 estimated annual growth at 8.5%, the seventh straight year in which economic growth exceeded 8%. Per capita income has increased to RM 8,856 ($3,406). There were only 2.9% unemployed in the country, inflation was kept at 3.7%, and the poverty rate continued to decline, to 8.8%.

Even more to the point for Malaysia's efforts to become an industrial nation networked into the global economy, the manufacturing's share of GDP was expected to rise from 30.1% in 1993 to 31.5%. Manufactured exports were expected to increase by 28%, raising their earnings to 77.5% of total export earnings compared to 74% in 1993. During that year the country became the nineteenth largest trading nation in the world and ranked seventeenth in competitiveness, third among the non-OECD nations. The economy, therefore, continued to develop in strength in 1994, and ranked among the best in the world in terms of growth rates, poverty eradication, employment, and inflation levels.[12]

AN ECONOMIC SUCCESS MODEL

Malaysia is being used as a model for study by the Pacific Basin Economic Council (PBEC). It has already been the subject of a case study by the Harvard Business School. Whether the path followed by Malaysia in its development process can be emulated and adopted by other developing countries is an oft-asked question. Malaysia has come a long way from being a major producer and exporter of primary commodities such as rubber and tin. Today it is among the world's largest traders. It is the twenty-third largest exporter and twenty-fourth largest importer and its position has improved since it first made the league of major traders in 1990. It has outperformed many developed countries and is the fastest growing economy in the region. It is perhaps the only country in the world with full employment and continues to attract foreign investments both in the manufacturing sector and in the capital market. Unlike many other developing countries, Malaysia, as a result of prudent and pragmatic policies, avoided getting into deep debt.[13]

The Labor Force and Employment

Government estimates placed total employment at the end of 1993 at 7.4 million. The labor force grew by an estimated 3.5% from 1992 to 7.6 million, resulting in a decrease in unemployment from 3.7% to 3.0%. Employment in the manufacturing sector continued to grow, with total employment up 6.3% in 1993 after an increase of 9.3% in 1992. Malaysia's robust economy has allowed the government to relax a civil service hiring freeze introduced in 1985, but public sector employment will continue to decline because of increased automation and the privatization of former government entities.

Labor Shortages

As just mentioned, the official unemployment rate was 3.0% at the end of 1993. Unlike the United States, Malaysia includes discouraged workers in the labor force; a discouraged worker is someone who is employable but has ceased actively seeking work. The effect of this is to inflate the unemployment rate. Manufacturers report an increasing shortage of unskilled labor and concerns about rising labor costs. Some Malaysian economists have argued that Malaysia is already at or near full employment, and that attempts to reduce the unemployment rate, e.g., by encouraging new foreign investment, are inflationary. Others have argued that this wage pressure is mitigated by the availability of unskilled laborers coming from the rural areas, particularly the plantations, with these rural jobs being increasingly filled by guest workers or illegal migrants from neighboring countries. Estimates are that Malaysia will require a total of 700,000 workers during the period between 1990 and 1998. The semiskilled sector will require the largest number of workers, estimated at about 361,000, or 52% of total workers required during the period. This information was contained in a survey report on prospective employment conducted by the research and planning division of the human resources ministry. Apart from semiskilled workers, demand for unskilled workers is seen at 205,000 or 29% of the workers required and craft skills needed are set at 46,800 workers. Based on the studies and surveys conducted by the ministry, it has been found that there are still shortages in the supply of engineers, engineering assistants, technicians, supervisors, and general foremen and clerks. Other shortages in the manufacturing sector included sewing machine operators, oxy-cutting and sewing shearing operators, knitting machine operators, quality inspectors, production operators, and electronic equipment assemblers.

The survey findings in the construction sector showed that shortages in general workers, carpenters, plasterers, bar tenders, bricklayers, masons, and cement workers are now largely filled by foreign workers. The report also said the unemployment rate was expected to decline to 2.8% in the following year. The current labor shortage is likely to persist in view of the higher employment growth that is anticipated as the sustained growth rate is expected to continue providing employment opportunities.[14]

The government has taken a number of steps to alleviate the labor shortage. The policy on employment of immigrants has been liberalized. Efforts have been made to increase the labor force participation rate of women. The government has also allocated funds under the current five-year plan to build five new training institutes and the curriculum of government schools has been reviewed to meet the manpower needs of Malaysia's industrialized economy, Private sector training centers are also being promoted.

WOMEN IN THE WORKFORCE

Women account for 35% of the workforce in Malaysia and 46.5% of working age women are in the labor force. The female share of employment is proportionate to its overall share of the workforce in the professional and technical fields. However, female workers comprise a higher percentage of clerical, agricultural, services, and semiskilled manufacturing jobs and a lower percentage of administrative, managerial, and transport sector jobs than male workers. Women are particularly important in the electronics industry where they make up about 90% of assembly line workers. They also account for more than 70% of the employment in the textile industry. In the public sector, although women make up 31% of the professional and managerial category, they are mostly in the teaching and nursing professions.

Legislation concerning work conditions applies equally to men and women, but there are special provisions for women workers in the Employment Act of 1955. Women are also entitled to 60 full days paid maternity leave, 42 days for government employees, and dismissals by employers during this period are unlawful. There is no legislation for equal pay between men and women but to a large extent women are accorded similar pay for similar work. However, a substantial overall wage gap still exists between men and women due in part to the fact that many women are relatively new entrants and therefore underrepresented in managerial and supervisory positions.

FOREIGN WORKERS

There are estimates of up to one million foreign workers in Malaysia, many of them illegal, who work in low skill jobs in the plantation and construction sectors. Although some illegal workers ultimately are able to regularize their immigration status, others depart voluntarily after a few months, while some are formally deported as illegal migrants. In 1992 the government conducted a registration program designed to regularize the immigration status of illegal workers. After the registration period ended, however, the government launched combined police and military operations to enforce immigration and passport laws. By April 1993, 50,000 illegal immigrants had returned voluntarily to their countries of origin, while 40,000 others had been arrested and repatriated. In 1993, at least 3,000 people deemed to be illegal foreign workers were detained. There have been some credible reports of inadequate rations in the temporary camps which housed them.[15]

Demographic Variables

Malaysia's annual population growth rate was estimated at 2.28% in 1994 and decreased from the 1980–91 period when the population grew at an average annual rate of 2.54%. The population in 1994 was estimated at more than 19 million, and was made up of diverse ethnic groups: Malay and other indigenous peoples at 59%, Chinese 32%, and Indian 9%. The growth rate has been projected to remain constant.

At 54 people per square kilometer, Malaysia is relatively underpopulated when compared with other Asian countries. The population is located mainly in cities on the west coast of Peninsular Malaysia, especially the Klang River valley area, including the capital, Kuala Lumpur, which is Malaysia's largest industrial center. Malaysia has also experienced significant industrial growth in Penang in the northwest and in Johor, near Singapore.[16]

Ethnic Problems—The NEP and NDP Solutions

Malaysia's unique ethnic composition has influenced government economic policy. The New Economic Policy (NEP) was adopted in 1971, as part of the response to the 1969 race riots, to ameliorate the economic plight of the numerically superior Malays and to eradicate poverty irrespective of race. To this end bumiputeras, or native Malays, were to increase their ownership in the corporate sector to 30% by 1990, with other Malaysians holding 40% and the stake of foreigners falling to 30%. The NEP has been the cornerstone of government development policy since 1971, supported by increases in spending on basic services and education and the setting up of trust agencies to finance bumiputera enterprises. In the Second Outline Perspective Plan (OPP2) and the Sixth Malaysia Plan (6MP), both published in 1991, the government revealed that the NEP equity target had not been met by 1990 (see Table 16-1).

Following the expiration of the NEP in 1990 the government introduced the New Development Policy (NDP) in 1991 as the framework for economic policy between 1991 and 2000. While still upholding the NEP's twin objectives of poverty eradication and ethnic redistribution of wealth, NDP places greater emphasis on redistribution through rapid growth rather than outright favoritism. Notwithstanding these changes in priorities, there are still ethnic quotas in business, industry and education.[17]

Changes in Employment Structure

In terms of the changing employment structure of Malaysia, the impact of the NEP upon bumiputera participation in the country's rapidly growing industrial sector

TABLE 16-1
NEP Targets and Achievements, 1971–90

Sector	1970	1990 target	1990 achievement
A: Bumiputera employment (in percentages)			
Primary	66.2	37.4	36.7
Secondary	12.1	26.8	27.2
Tertiary	21.7	35.8	36.1
B: Shares of corporate equity (in percentages)			
Bumiputera	2.4	30.0	20.3
Chinese/Indian	32.3	40.0	46.2
Foreign	63.3	30.0	25.1
Nominee companies	2.0	—	8.4

Source: Government of Malaysia, Second Outline Perspective Plan, p. 49.

has been clearly apparent. A major structural shift has occurred with the percentage of the Malay workforce engaged in agriculture and forestry declining from 66.2% in 1970 to 29% in 1990; with mining and manufacturing up from 12.1% to 30.5% and services from 21.7% to 40.5% over the same period. The nonbumiputera workforce also experienced a similar transformation, albeit less dramatically, but the emphasis placed upon new employment within the production and transportation sectors, together with clerical and related services, has resulted in a participation rate of Malay employment much more in accord with the national profile. Particularly associated with the shift from agriculture into manufacturing has been the increased participation of Malay females within the urban labor force. The rise of such employment, characterized by the young women recruited into the electronics industry, has altered traditional family and community bonds and has accelerated rural–urban migration among young Malays. In terms of both restructuring employment and increasing Malay participation in business through shareholding, the impact of the NEP has been considerable.[18]

CONTINUING ETHNIC FRICTIONS

The government programs just described are commendable in their attempts to defuse ethnic rivalries. However, tensions among the ethnic groups have increased and social interaction appears to have declined. Both the Chinese and the Indian communities resent the methods by which the government attempted to bring Malays into the economic sector. Government decisions in 1987 about the administration of Chinese schools precipitated serious unrest that, in turn, led to an invocation of the Internal Security Act. Leaders of both the Chinese and Malay communities were arrested, purportedly to end racial unrest by detaining those responsible for endangering the peace and security of the country. Most have since been released, many on the condition that they refrain from political activity. Serious dissension continues over Chinese education, however, and significant amounts of Chinese capital and expertise have left the country.

An additional area of instability developed as Chinese voters have become increasingly disenchanted with the policies of the ruling National Front. Prime Minister Mohamed questioned the loyalty of Chinese during the 1990 parliamentary campaign in order to rally votes for his party. However, since that election he has attempted to bolster the confidence of the Chinese community, calling on its members in August 1992 to participate in joint ventures with Malays.

Malays also remain discontented with the economic dominance of the Chinese. Despite the improvements in Malay living standards, economic disparity between Malays and Chinese still exist. This situation has prompted the growing expression of Malay nationalism and caused disarray within and between the two ethnic communities. Moreover, Chinese leaders have expressed concern over their collective future because of the relative decline of the Chinese population. Population projections indicate that the Malay population will grow relative to the Chinese, who will drop from the current 32% of the population to 20% by the year 2040.

A PROGNOSIS

Malaysia is likely to remain as one of Asia's most stable countries; there are virtually no external threats and few serious domestic ones. Ethnic and religious tensions, though still simmering in certain regions, are now outweighed by intercommunal harmony in most areas of Malaysian society. The main risks to the current government come from opposition parties in the states of Kelantan, Penang, and Trengganu in Peninsular Malaysia, and Sabah in Borneo. The position of the National Front coalition government, dominated by the Mahathir-led UMNO, is very secure at the federal level and in most states. It has been in power since independence and won the most seats in parliament in the 1995 general election.

Nevertheless, rapid and sustained growth has caused various problems. Full employment has meant a tight market for both skilled and unskilled labor, despite the presence of nearly a million foreign workers. Understandably, such a large number of foreigners among an indigenous labor force of about 7.8 million, while of critical importance to sustained growth, has created social and political tensions in some areas. The tight labor market is expected to persist as new jobs continue to outstrip the number of new entrants into the workforce. The government continued to address the need for an adequate supply of increasingly better trained and skilled manpower for an industrializing economy. The allocation of 20.6% of the 1995 budget for education and training is the largest ever and reflects the importance the government attaches to this sphere. Potentially thorny political problems lurk in this field, however, as the rapidly developing economy makes greater demands for technology proficiency while the bumiputera community continues to lag behind in educational attainment.

There is a lack of data on progress regarding more equitable distribution of income, another fundamental objective of the National Development Policy. Data on reducing income disparities between the various ethnic groups is also lacking. It would not be surprising, however, if advances in the latter area slowed during the mid-1990s, compared to the 1970s and early 1980s. Since then more emphasis has been placed upon sustaining sound economic growth and fostering a more self-reliant and resourceful bumiputera community.

As for the contribution of Malaysian labor and management to the nation's seemingly inexorable progression toward the fulfillment of Vision 2020, they have been asked to make sacrifices and compromises to create an industrial environment that can facilitate the nation's development. The government has indicated that it will continue to evaluate present labor laws and enact new ones to provide more material benefits, safety, health and social guarantees to workers. Employers are also being encouraged to offer benefits or facilities that exceed the statutory minima. Union leaders have complained about a lack of urgency in dealing with problems, issues, and policies affecting labor, which has asked for fuller participation in the political process. It remains to be seen if Malaysia's economic progress will be translated into tangible benefits for its working class.[19]

CHAPTER 17

The Law and the Reality

THE STATUTORY FRAMEWORK

Malaysia's basic labor laws include the Employment Act (1955), the Trade Unions Act (1959), the Industrial Relations Act (1967), the Employees' Social Security Act (1969), and the Employees' Provident Fund Act (1991). The Employment Act of 1955 covers those private sector workers engaged in manual labor, and those, regardless of occupation, earning less than M$1250 a month. The employment of workers not covered by the employment act is regulated by common law usage and by the terms of employment contracts. The act limits hours of work and overtime, provides for a minimum number of annual holidays, and deals generally with working conditions. The Employment Regulations of 1980, also known as Termination and Layoff Benefits, which fall under the employment act, stipulate compensation levels for employees who are laid off.

The 1959 Trade Unions Act confines membership in trade unions to employees within a particular trade, occupation, or industry. The statute requires all unions to be registered with the director-general for trade unions. Under this law, any union organizing a strike must first obtain the consent of at least two-thirds of its membership by secret ballot.

The 1967 Industrial Relations Act regulates the settlement of disputes among employers, employees and their trade unions. Collective bargaining is regulated by Part IV of this law. The 1991 Employees' Provident Fund Act requires employers and employees to contribute to a national provident fund. Employers' contributions are tax deductible.

The Employees' Social Security Act of 1969 protects employees with monthly wages of RM$2,000 or less against the contingencies of industrial accidents, diseases, permanent disability that prevents them from working, and death. As mentioned earlier, amendments to these laws have increased the power of the government to suspend unions, prohibit strikes, unilaterally intervene in any labor dispute, nullify strike ballots, and regulate relations with international labor organizations, as well as prohibiting union officials and unions from engaging in political activity.[1]

THE RIGHT OF ASSOCIATION

By law workers have the right to engage in trade union activity, and tens of thousands of workers in both the public and private sectors are trade union members; there are at least 28 national unions. Within certain limitations, unions may organize workplaces, bargain collectively with employers, and form federations.

The Industrial Relations Act prohibits interference with, restraint, or coercion of workers in the exercise of the right to form trade unions or participation in lawful union activities. The Trade Unions Act, administered by the Director-General of Trade Unions (DGTU), formulates rules for the organization of unions, recognition of unions in the workplace, the content of union constitutions, election of officers, and financial reporting. The law's definition of trade union, however, restricts a union to representing workers in a "particular establishment, trade, occupation, or industry or within any similar trades, occupations, or industries." contrary to International Labor Organization guidelines.[2]

Malaysian employers can no longer drag their feet in recognizing unions under an amendment to the Industrial Relations Act of 1967. Under the amendment, any notice from the Industrial Relations Department (IRD) in the human resources ministry that authorizes workers to form a trade union must be taken as automatic recognition to the union The proposed union then will be automatically recognized whether or not the company responds or complies with the IRD's notice.

Under normal practice, a union will apply for recognition from the firm when the members it represents in the company exceeds 50% of the total number of workers in the same trade or occupation. Recognition will give the union the right to represent members in collective bargaining, among other things. With the amendment, employers can no longer make excuses or delay in recognizing the union, as has been their reaction in many complaint cases reported to the government. Normally, problems between employers and workers surfaced when the workers presented demands for union recognition. They included disagreements over the counting of secret ballots among workers, overt opposition to the union itself, and arguments over the eligibility of workers.[3]

THE DGTU'S AUTHORITY

The Director-General of Trade Unions may refuse to register a trade union and, in some circumstances, may also withdraw the registration of a trade union. When registration has been refused, withdrawn, or canceled, a trade union becomes an illegal association. Nationwide congresses of trade unions from different industries are required by law to register as societies under the Societies Act rather than as trade unions under the Trade Unions Act. During 1993, acting on complaints by private individuals alleging electoral and constitutional irregularities, the Registrar of Societies required both major trade union congresses, the MTUC and the MLO, to show cause why they should not be deregistered. In their answers, both groups admitted not having followed their own constitutional procedures and agreed to correct the irregularities. Having done so, both bodies retained their registration. In 1994, 517 organizations were deregistered and 1272 organizations were registered as labor organizations. Of those deregistered, 375 organizations failed to submit their annual statements, 13 committed registration offenses, 111 did not exist, and 20 dissolved voluntarily.

ORGANIZATIONAL RESTRICTIONS

Malaysian government policy discourages the formation of national unions. The government advocates a social compact where in each sector, government, management, and workers are part of a comprehensive effort to create jobs, train workers, improve productivity and profitability, and ultimately provide the resources necessary to fund human resource development and a national social safety net. The government has used its power to prevent the Electrical Industry Workers Union, an MTUC affiliate, from organizing national unions in the American and Japanese-dominated electronics industry on the grounds that electrical industry employees and electronics industry workers are not "similar" as required by the Trade Union Act. The government permits only "in-house unions" in the electronics industry. Six such unions have been registered, of which four were recognized by the companies involved, and two had negotiated collective bargaining agreements.

All of the members of one of these unions were dismissed in 1990 following reorganization of its American-owned company's structure. The union charged the company with union-busting and wrongful dismissal. The case was filed in September 1990; an appeal was taken to the Supreme Court, which ruled in favor of management. Malaysia's restrictions on freedom of association in the electronics industry have been the subject of repeated complaints by international labor organizations.

Malaysian labor unions maintain independence both from the government and from political parties, but individual union members may belong to political parties. Although union officers are forbidden to hold principal offices in political parties, individual trade union leaders have served and currently serve in parliament as opposition politicians. Although strikes are legal, the right to strike is severely restricted in practice. Malaysian law contains a list of "essential" services in which unions must give advance notice of any industrial action. The list includes sectors not normally deemed "essential" under ILO definitions. By law federations of trade unions may represent only a single trade or industry or similar trades or industries. Only three national labor federations are currently registered: one for public servants, one for teachers, and one consisting of state-based textile and garment workers unions.[4]

SIGNIFICANT AMENDMENTS

Amendments to the Industrial Relations Act include two controversial clauses. One rules out legal representation for nonunion employees during conciliation negotiations. Unionized workers lost their right to representation during the conciliation process in 1980. Unions argue this will disadvantage their members in, for example, dismissal proceedings; the objective is to keep lawyers out of the process, thus substantially increasing the chances of amicable settlement. Another change empowers the labor minister to designate any industry as an "essential service," as mentioned above. Industrial unrest in such a sector is much more strictly controlled. Despite governmental assurances that it will wield its new power judiciously, some firms may be tempted to pressure authorities to be classified as essential.

Adjustments to the labor law must be able to influence collective bargaining agreements if they are to produce any positive impact on foreign investment. It is the institutionalized habit of three-year collective bargaining agreements, according to employers, that has left Malaysia unable to respond quickly to changes in economic fortune. The Trade Unions Act amendments, minus encouragement for in-house, as opposed to industry-wide unions, management further complains, will have little positive impact on the business environment. The director-general, previously registrar, of trade unions is authorized to refuse to register a union if one already exists, a move that will help minimize the number of organizations employers must deal with.

Also, the Trade Unions Act of 1959 will be amended to make union leaders more accountable for the way they manage union finances and to check mismanagement of workers' funds since there has been an increase in the number of cases of financial irregularities committed by union officials. For example, there have been cases of union leaders submitting expense claims to their organizations for overseas trips when these trips had already been sponsored by the government or international labor organizations. The Malaysian government received reports from union employees, clerks, secretaries, and typists concerning these malpractices. In addition, the government received reports that some union employees were victimized for revealing this wrongdoing.

The MTUC expressed its disappointment that in drafting these amendments, the labor ministry did not seek input from unions. The Secretary-General of MTUC G. Rajasekaran complained:

> The minister talks about tripartism, yet when there are amendments affecting trade unions, there are no discussions at all with the unions.... If there is any abuse of power by union leaders, present laws are more than adequate for the authorities to take action.[5]

His comments revealed his opinion that there was no need for the amendments since the statute already confers substantial authority to act, should abuses occur, on the minister, the director-general, and his subordinate officials. The hope was expressed that the amendments would not curb the growth and activity of unions which were alleged to be in a "deplorable" state of affairs.

The most significant changes to the Employment Act, which covers minimum standards for private sector employment terms, relate to wage definitions, overtime rates, and payment in lieu of leave. "Wages" now will exclude all bonuses, thereby reducing the base for calculating overtime and employees' provident fund contributions. However, productivity incentives still count as compensation, disappointing proponents of a Singapore-style move toward greater pay flexibility.

Malaysia's existing overtime wage rates were unrealistically high, but they have been reduced from triple to double the daily wage, and from 4.5 to 3 times on public holidays. In both instances, overtime payments will fall by as much as 30%. Hotels and other enterprises compelled to offer 24-hour service will be the beneficiary of these wage cuts.

It is unclear whether wage and overtime savings will be offset by plans to expand the Employment Act's coverage. The law formerly covered all manual workers, irrespective of earnings, but it applied to skilled workers only if they earned less than RM$1,000 monthly ($371.75). The amendments extended coverage to another 50,000 workers who earn RM$1,250 ($464.68) or less. This development could increase labor costs and cause inefficiencies: Factory supervisors, entitled to overtime payments because they earn below RM$1,250, would have a vested interest in continuing plant operations.

In late 1994, amendments were proposed that would introduce elements of flexi-wage and flexi-time to promote recruitment of part-time workers and lure women back into the workforce. The Malaysian Employers Federation and the Malaysian Labor Organization said they would support the changes if they resulted in higher productivity and persuaded housewives to enter the labor market. However, the MLO indicated its confusion as to what was actually meant by flexi-time and flexi-wages, and that it would seek clarification from the National Labor Advisory Council (NLAC), which is Malaysia's most prominent forum for discussion of labor issues.

The MEF, however, had submitted its own memorandum on changes to the 1955 law, but said none of what was announced were its proposals. The minister of human resources stated the Act would be amended to encourage more women to work part-time, make working hours and wages more flexible, and remove rigidities as well as bureaucratic rules and procedures in employment. Asked to elaborate on these points, the minister said the amendments he had in mind were actually more comprehensive, covering various aspects of the Act. Calls for amendments to the Employment Act go back to 1990 when estate workers staged a week-long nationwide strike to protest against the number of unpaid working days.[6]

Another change empowers the labor minister to designate industries as essential to the national interest, and therefore tighten control over potential labor unrest. For example, the storing and bulking of commodities is designated as an essential service under the amendment. Services such as banks, the electricity board, the fire service, ports, and airports are classified as "essential," and their unions are required to give three weeks notice of any industrial action.[7]

The Industrial Court's jurisdiction also will be broadened, and another clause contains restrictions on strikes and lockouts in essential services.[8]

THE RIGHT TO ORGANIZE AND BARGAIN COLLECTIVELY

Malaysian workers have the legal right to organize and bargain collectively, and collective bargaining is widespread in those sectors where labor is organized. About

860,000 workers are covered by collective bargaining agreements, representing some 12% of the total labor force.

Designed to curb strikes, amendments in 1980 to the Industrial Relations Act contain provisions that the MTUC believes erode the basic rights of workers, restrict union activities, and result in government and employer interference in the internal administration of unions. Despite subsequent amendments, the MTUC charged that the labor law does not meet ILO standards. Many union leaders also believe that the creation of the industrial court further weakened their collective bargaining rights. Malaysian law prohibits antiunion discrimination by employers against union members and organizers. Complaints of discrimination may be filed with the human resources ministry or the industrial court. When conciliation efforts by the ministry fail, critics note that the industrial court is slow in adjudicating worker complaints.

FREE TRADE ZONE COVERAGE

Companies in free trade zones (FTZs) must observe labor standards identical to those elsewhere in Malaysia. Many workers at FTZ are organized, especially in the textile and electrical products sectors. Workers in FTZ companies in the electronics sector are limited by government policy to forming in-house unions. During 1993, amendments to the Industrial Relations Act removed previous restrictions on concluding collective agreements about terms and conditions of employment in "pioneer industries." Workers in industries granted pioneer status may now negotiate collective agreements on all issues permitted to workers in other industries. The government took these measures in part to respond to ILO criticism of its previous policy with respect to pioneer industries, where the industries were allowed to remain union-free for five years. However, the ILO continues to object to other legal restrictions on collective bargaining.

THE ELECTRONICS INDUSTRY SITUATION

Fifteen American electronic components manufacturers operate 19 plants in Malaysia, employing more than 37,000 Malaysian workers. None of the American-owned firms is unionized. There is no legal prohibition against organizing unions in the electronics industry and workers at some non-American companies, mainly outside the components industry, are represented either by the Electrical Industry Workers Union (EIWU), other unions, or inhouse unions. Malaysian labor law, as already mentioned, limits a union to organizing workers in a single industry or in related industries. The Director General of Trade Unions has to date interpreted this law to preclude the EIWU from organizing electronic component workers.

In September 1988, the labor minister announced that the government would permit electronic component workers to unionize. The National Electronics Industry Workers Union (NEW) was formed, but has been denied registration as a trade union on the grounds that it is seeking to represent workers in both the electronics and electrical industries. The union denied that it represented workers in the electrical industry but its appeal to the labor ministry was rejected. The previous labor minister's policy was that only inhouse unions would be permitted in the electronics industry. The legal basis for such a restriction remains unclear.[9]

DISPUTE SETTLEMENT

In Malaysia, as in other nations, labor disputes cannot always be totally avoided and bilateral negotiations are on occasion likely to fail, with the result that third party intervention is required if labor and management are not to harden their positions and put on a show of strength. Recognizing the potential for disputes, the Industrial Relations Act of 1967 seeks to provide opportunities for compromise and reconciliation so that confrontations will be minimized. Failing this, labor disputes can be resolved by impartial third parties.

Consistent with this declared aim, the Act provides for conciliation whenever there is actual or potential labor conflict. Where a dispute cannot be resolved by the parties themselves, it may be reported to the human resources ministry either by an employer or a union representing workers. The government agency is then required to take such steps as may be necessary for promoting an expeditious settlement. In the public interest, the ministry can intervene to seek to promote a settlement even if the matter has not been submitted to it.

A labor dispute is defined in Section 2 as "any dispute between employers and workmen, or between workmen and workmen, or between employers and employers, which is connected with the employment or non-employment or the terms of employment or the conditions of work of any person." In the Malaysian system, when bargaining efforts fail, the government plays an active role in promoting conciliation and arbitration. Either the union or management may request conciliation by the Industrial Relations Department, which is part of the human resources ministry. Conciliation applies not only to collective agreement disputes between unions and employers, but also to such issues as unfair dismissal whether the employee belongs to a union or not, nonpayment of contractual wages, and so forth. Most disputes are resolved at this conciliation stage. Table 17-1 shows the number and disposition of the disputes of which the ministry was notified during the 1988–92 period. If conciliation and direct negotiations between the employer and the union or individual employee fail to resolve the issue, the human resources minister may refer the case to the Industrial Court. Most cases the ministry refers to the Court deal with dismissals of nonunion workers. The parties themselves may also apply directly to the Court, generally in cases involving noncompliance with or interpretation of a previous award involving a collective agreement. In addition to handling cases concerning terms and

TABLE 17-1
Disputes Reported to Ministry of Human Resources

	1988	1989	1990	1991	1992
Number of disputes reported during the year	988	688	572	502	551
Carry-over disputes from previous year	365	531	625	231	208
Total cases	1,353	1,219	1,197	733	759
Disposed of:					
Conciliation	591	433	454	466	590
Refer to industrial court	98	104	72	56	36
Not referred to industrial court on minister's decision	N/A	N/A	N/A	3	7
Carried over	531	625	671	208	126

Source: Ministry of Human Resources, Kuala Lumpur, Malaysia.

conditions of employment or unfair dismissal, the Industrial Court serves as an arbitration panel to resolve deadlocks in collective agreement negotiations.

THE INDUSTRIAL COURT PROCEEDINGS

If conciliation fails to achieve a settlement, the minister of human resources has the power to refer the dispute to the Industrial Court. Strikes or lockouts are prohibited while the dispute is before the tribunal, so the result, in effect, amounts to compulsory arbitration.

The Industrial Court hears a case as a panel consisting of a chairperson and one member each from lists representing employers and workers. The lists have been established in consultation with the Malaysian Trade Union Congress and the Malaysian Employers Federation. The chairperson is either the President of the Industrial Court or one of the chairs appointed to increase the number of panels. The panel will hear the dispute and render an award, which is binding on both parties. In the case of a collective agreement, the Court may issue a ruling on any aspect of the agreement still in dispute. The union is barred from any industrial action with respect to any aspect of an Industrial Court award. The following table summarizes the Industrial Court's caseload in selected years from 1980 to 1992.

Even nonunion workers are not outside the scope of the Act in terms of opportunities for negotiation and reconciliation. The Industrial Relations statute allows any employee who is not a union member and feels that he or she has been dismissed without just cause to file a complaint to be reinstated. Here again the Director-General is required to promote an expeditious settlement. If there is no resolution of the claim then the outcome is reported to the human resources minister

TABLE 17-2
Industrial Court's Caseload

	1980	1988	1989	1990	1991	1992
Referred by the minister:						
Terms and conditions (inclu. collect. agree.)	25	69	54	44	56	37
Dismissal (union member)	44	35	35	41	1	–
Dismissal (non-union)	63	112	78	151	363	298
Direct referral:						
Amended to a collect. agree.	4	0	2	1	4	2
Interpretation of a collect. agree.	7	7	3	14	37	52
Noncompliance with award	6	36	28	7	53	51
Noncompliance with collect. agree.	15	51	42	63	60	53
Leave to appeal to high court	0	17	3	16	7	10
Total	164	164	345	337	581	503

Source: Ministry of Human Resources, Kuala Lumpur, Malaysia.

who may refer the case to the Industrial Court for a ruling. Sometimes the Director-General of Trade Unions refuses to do so, which can be the cause of much dissatisfaction for the affected worker.

STRIKE PROCEDURES

The law prohibits employers from retaliation against a worker for participating in the lawful activities of a labor union. Therefore, where a strike is legal, these provisions would bar management retribution against strikers and union leaders. However, there have been no reports of such cases alleging employers' actions against strikers, so it is impossible to assess the effectiveness of government enforcement.

Before a strike can be authorized, the law requires a union to obtain the consent of a two-thirds majority of the membership via secret ballot. The Director-General of Trade Unions must be given 14 days notice of the ballot, and strike action may not be taken until 7 days after the notification. The time lapse is to enable the Industrial Relations Department of the labor ministry to intervene and encourage an amicable settlement.[11]

WAGES AND WAGE COUNCILS

Disagreements over wages can cause labor disputes, although in Malaysia wages are determined to a large extent by market forces. The country has no national minimum wage legislation but minimum wages are assigned by law to the catering and hotel industries, retail clerks, cinema workers, and to cargo handlers. Private sector wages are determined through collective bargaining or individual contracts. Wage levels in the private sector have increased steadily. In addition to economic forces, the upward revision of public sector salaries has encouraged private sector increases. Hourly wages are below levels prevailing in industrialized countries, but higher than those of neighboring states, except Singapore.

Under the Wage Councils Act, a minimum wage can be established in industries where the government deems it necessary, such as those mentioned above. Under the statute, workers in an industry who believe they need the protection of a minimum wage can ask for the establishment of a wage council. The council, a tripartite body, composed of labor, management, and government representatives, then meets to set a minimum wage for the industry. One assumption of this system is that workers in industries where unionization is widespread can bargain for wages directly with employers and do not need the protection of a minimum wage.

In most industries tight labor markets and rising wages in general have meant that workers have seen little need for the establishment of wage councils. Minimum monthly wages for workers are in the RM$188 to 242 ($70–90) range in urban areas and 10 to 15% lower for rural areas. All in all, approximately 140,000 workers are covered by these wage councils, where minimum wages have not been revised for over a decade. While the last wage council was established in 1949, several wage councils met in 1991.

The government has proposed the establishment of a national wages council to set suggested wage levels by industry. The purpose of the council would be to try to restrain the rise in wages in Malaysia. Trade union officials oppose the formation of the council, stating that it interferes with their right to bargain collectively. Prevailing wages, even in the sectors covered by wage councils, are higher than the minimum wages set by the wage councils and do provide an adequate living for most workers.

In practice, the minimum monthly wage for unskilled labor in the greater Kuala Lumpur area is RM$376 ($140) a month. In the government's pay schedule, the lowest monthly salary of RM$350 ($130), plus a civil service allowance of RM$70 ($26). Average wages for semiskilled production workers range from RM$753 to 968 ($280–360) a month, with many skilled workers making more than RM$1075 ($400) monthly. An official survey of industry reported that in 1993 average national earnings of workers rose 9.0% compared with 8.0% in 1992. Collective agreements in the manufacturing sector provided for an average increase in base pay of 12.2% in 1993. Collective agreements generally run the statutory minimum of three years.[12]

BONUSES

It is customary in Malaysia for employees to receive an annual bonus equivalent to one to two months salary. Bonus payments by employers are tax deductible as a company expense for up to two months wages or RM2150 ($800) per employee per year, whichever is greater.[13]

HOURS OF WORK

Under the Employment Act of 1955, working hours may not exceed 8 hours per day or a 44-hour work week of 5½ days. In practice, the working week is usually 37 to 40 hours. After four hours of work, there must be a break of at least 30 minutes. An increasing share of private sector employers have shifted to the 5½ day/44-hour week or a 5-day/40-hour week. Union leaders estimate that a quarter of private sector workers are now on a five-day work week. Shift work is allowed.

Overtime must be compensated at an extra 50% of the normal hourly wage for the first hour and an extra 100% after that, with double pay for Sundays and holidays for the first seven hours and triple pay thereafter. Forced overtime is common for factory workers, particularly among those who live in company dormitories. Overtime is limited to 64 hours in any one month period.

Normal office hours for white collar workers are 8:00 A.M. to 4:00 P.M. with a one hour break from Monday to Friday and 8:00 A.M. to 1:00 P.M. on Saturday. A working week of five eight-hour days has become increasingly common.

The human resources ministry enforces these standards, but a shortage of inspectors prevents strict enforcement.[14]

FRINGE BENEFITS

Statutory minimum nonwage benefits are set under the Employment Act of 1955, which applies to all workers earning less than $500 a month, and the Employment Regulation of 1980, also known as Termination and Layoff Benefits. Fringe benefits normally amount to 20 to 30% of base wages. Holiday and annual leave provisions vary widely among industries. Ten paid holidays yearly are mandatory nationwide; the particular days vary by region but usually include at least three national and state holidays as well as four to six national and religious days, such as Chinese New Year, Mohammed's birthday, Christmas, the Hindu Deepavali festival, and the Buddhist Wisak Day.

Employees with less than two years service are entitled to eight days paid leave each year. Employees with service of at least two but less than five years are entitled to 12 days of annual leave, and those employed for five years or more are eligible for 16 days leave. In practice, most employees receive around 14 days paid vacation per year, and executives expect three weeks of annual vacation.

Under the statute, an employee is entitled to 14 days of annual sick leave if employed less than two years, 18 days for two to five years, and 22 days after five years. If hospitalization is necessary, paid medical leave is extended to a total of 60 days. Most companies supply some free medical facilities. Certain categories of female workers are guaranteed 60 days of paid maternity leave at a minimum of $2.50 a day, plus an optional 90 days unpaid maternity leave. Companies sometimes offer free or subsidized medical care and occasionally transportation, depending on location, even though the government has acted to tax fringe benefits more rigorously. On industrial estates, companies usually provide free accommodations, most with free medical attention, electric power, and piped-in water, for about three-quarters of the laborers.

Employee share option schemes are gaining popularity among some of the larger companies in Malaysia. These plans usually invite specific workers to purchase shares at a predetermined rate, adding an incentive to the overall employment package without affecting the firm's cash flow. Companies that have implemented such arrangements include Jack Chia Enterprises Malaysia, Sime Darby, the New Straits Times (Malaysia), Innovest, Menang Corporation, the United Malacca Rubber Estates and Metroplex.

A controversy erupted involving employee share option schemes (ESOS) when the government disclosed that National Union of Telekom Employees (NUTE) had not been given the opportunity to participate in this arrangement. It turned out that the Telekom Malaysia executive chairman and executive director had been allocated options of 300 lots and 200 lots, respectively. Acting Human Resources Minister Lee indicated that the Cabinet was informed of these developments and that a more detailed written report showing how much was given to management under this plan would be forthcoming. The government, Lee stated, was very concerned and sympathetic to the problems of Telekom workers:

> Does it make sense that the poor fellow who earns between RM 500 and RM 600 a month, and who has to work under dangerous conditions, such as crawling into underground tunnels or climbing telephone poles, risking death should he fall, cannot benefit under ESOS? ESOS is unfair to the 20,000 or so workers ... whose numbers are actually quite substantial. At Rashid Hussain, even its drivers are entitled to the company's option scheme. To my understanding the acronym for ESOS is the Employee Share Option Scheme. It is not Executive Share Option Scheme.[15]

Lee said the government took the view that all future share option schemes must consider the interest of all workers. Not just the executives should have the opportunity to purchase securities. With regard to the previous ESOS plan which was unfair to employees, however, he said it was too late to do anything as the options already had been exercised, making it impossible to confiscate the shares.

Marriage leave is also provided by most companies and ranges from two to three days. However, some 10% of the firms believe it is unnecessary to grant their employees this benefit.

Generally, management provides the basic requirements of sick leave, hospitalization leave, and maternity leave as stipulated by the 1955 Employment Act, but not more. Yet some 20% of the companies grant maternity leave to all their female employees irrespective of the number of surviving children. Paternity leave is granted by more than 70% of the enterprises to their employees and it ranges from one to two days.

In the case of the death of an immediate member of an employee's family, almost all companies grant compassionate leave of between two and three days. Other common types of leave include examination and study leave (60%), and prolonged illness leave (70%). Meanwhile, employees in about 12% of the surveyed firms receive no pay on public holidays. About one-third of the companies still encourage their womenfolk to retire early, placing the retirement age for female employees at 50 years and male employees at 55 years.[16]

Termination or layoff benefits are equal to 10 days wages per year of service for less than two years service, 15 days wages per year for two to five years service, or 20 days wages per year for more than five years' service. The government has been concerned about the fate of workers in firms that go bankrupt. Frequently these workers do not receive the statutory benefits due to laid off workers. The government consequently has proposed the establishment of a fund to compensate these employees which would be called the Wages and Benefits Protection Fund to help workers recover their wages and other benefits. Proceeds would come from levies imposed on employers following a sliding scale arrangement, with larger firms eligible for larger assessments. Predictably, while unions support the plan, the Malaysian Employers Federation has expressed its opposition.[17]

THE MEF SURVEY

Visitors to Malaysia are struck by the traffic congestion, particularly in the Bangkok area. It is little wonder that roads are congested since car loans are the most common type of loans provided by companies as part of employees' fringe benefits. According to the findings of a fringe benefits survey conducted by the Malaysian Employers Federation, companies generally provide car loans to their employees at a subsidized interest rate of 4 to 6%. The easily available car loans and the attractive interest rate, compared with the average 8% interest rate imposed by financial institutions, must surely be one of the main reasons for the growing number of cars on the road.

The MEF survey, which studied over 60 types of fringe benefits for executives and nonexecutives, covered more than 290 member firms and over 120,000 local employees. Some 59% of the companies are in the manufacturing sector. In most companies, nonexecutive employees lose out on personal safety, health, and medical benefits. Personal accident insurance is extended by 91% of the companies to their executives compared with 77% of the firms who provide this benefit to their nonexecutives. The survey also showed that 49% of the companies cover the medical bills of their executives' dependents while 16% extended this benefit to their nonexecutives' dependents. Dental benefits are still not widely available; the survey indicated that it is being offered by only 34 and 27% of the companies to their executives and nonexecutives, respectively. It was found that annual leave entitlement offered ranged from 14 to 25 days for executives and 10 to 21 days for nonexecutive employees.[18]

OCCUPATIONAL SAFETY AND HEALTH

In 1994 Malaysia enacted a new Occupational Safety and Health Act (OSHA), which replaced the Factories and Machinery Act of 1967. The OSHA covers all sectors of the economy, except the maritime sector and the military. The Act established a National Occupational Safety and Health Council composed of workers, employers, and government representatives, to set policy and coordinate occupational safety and health measures. The law requires employers to identify risks and take precautions, including providing safety training to workers, and compels companies having more than 40 workers to establish joint management-employee safety committees. The statute requires workers to use safety equipment and to cooperate with employers to create a safe, healthy workplace. There are currently no specific statutory or regulatory provisions which create a positive right for a worker to remove himself or herself from dangerous workplace conditions without arbitrary dismissal. Employers or employees violating the law are subject to substantial fines or imprisonment for up to five years. Minimum standards for occupational safety and health are patterned after British law and enforced by a unit of the Ministry of Human Resources.[19]

The need for the law was strongly supported by government statistics indicating that industrial accidents in Malaysia rose sharply, by 45%, from 88,117 in 1988 to 128,621 in 1993. Although deaths caused by industrial accidents declined by 9.2% from 802 in 1988 to 728 in 1993, the amount of compensation that the Social Security Organization (SOCSO) had to pay to claimants more than doubled in 1993, with claimants receiving some RM 163.9 million ($60 million) compared with RM 63.3 million ($23.5 million) in 1988.

The International Labor Organization had come up with more ominous statistics. A 1992 study revealed that Malaysia lost some RM 4 billion ($1.5 billion) a year from lost production, profits, taxes, welfare, wages, and tangible costs, including a 20% loss in the health budget due to industrial accidents. Estimates were that it would take about five years for Malaysia to significantly reduce the industrial accident rate to the levels achieved by developed nations.

In view of this, the government has granted greater enforcement powers to the director-general of the Occupational Health and Safety Department to monitor the safety of workplaces and help reduce the spate of industrial accidents. Those who violate the laws will be prosecuted, with employers subject to fines up to RM 50,000 ($18,580) and five years imprisonment for failure to upgrade the work environment to a safer level as required after a series of warnings and a notice for improvement by the director-general. The human resources ministry has also enlisted the aid of the housing and local government ministry, utilizing the latter agency's health inspectors to help cover the services sector. Under the act, all workplaces with more than 40 employees are covered, except the armed forces and shipping employees.[20]

The ILO, in its 1992 World Labor Report, indicated that the most productive and efficient companies usually have the best safety records. These productive firms have learned to view industrial accidents as an opportunity to review their working practices to eliminate the potential for a recurrence of the mishaps. Some companies even use the level of industrial accidents as a measure of efficient management.

Commenting on the report, a Malaysian executive said enlightened investors realize that allowing industrial accidents to occur only perpetuates an outdated concept in worker protection and plays to the inefficient production methods of many Western nations:

Industrial safety is an issue that, when implemented properly, will give Asian nations and especially Malaysia a competitive edge over Western economies and at the same time ensure that our workers have safe working conditions without the so-called extra cost of safety.[21]

Safety performance undoubtedly is closely linked to management competence. There is simply no magic answer except hard work and total commitment by everyone to attain high safety standards. Safety indicators include the amount of time workers and management spend discussing safety, the effectiveness of the organization's two-way communication system, and the companies' effective housekeeping of work sites and use of suitable personal protective equipment. As a first step toward success, management must draw up a safety plan based on achievements of measurable objectives. The plan must be followed up with constant monitoring of safety performance. In drafting this safety program, each company must thoroughly assess the possible hazards to the health and safety of its employees.

FORCED LABOR

In theory, certain Malaysian laws allow the use of imprisonment with compulsory labor as a punishment for persons expressing views opposed to the established order or who participate in strikes. The government maintains that the constitutional prohibition of forced or compulsory labor renders these laws without effect. In practice, there is no evidence that forced or compulsory labor occurs in Malaysia, for either Malaysian or foreign workers.[22]

CHILD LABOR

The Children and Young Persons Employment Act of 1966 prohibits the employment of children younger than the age of 14. The law permits some exceptions, such as light work in a family enterprise, work in public entertainment, work performed for the government in a school or training institution, or work as an approved enterprise. In no case may children work more than 6 hours a day, more than 6 days per week, or at night. Ministry of Human Resources inspectors enforce these legal provisions. However, according to credible reports, the government still needs to take further steps to regulate child labor. There is no evidence that child labor is used in industries that export to the United States.[23]

SOCIAL SECURITY

The Social Security Organization (SOCSO) provides workers' compensation and disability and survivor benefits under the Employee's Social Security Act of 1969. All employees earning less than R$2,000 per month, at firms with more than five workers, must be insured under SOCSO's Employment Injury Insurance and Invalidity Pension programs. Under a new government initiative, those who earn more than RM2,000 ($744) a month may opt to join. Employers and workers share the cost of the program.

The Employment Injury Insurance Scheme provides medical and disability benefits, and benefits for job-related injuries or diseases. Benefits for temporary disability run at 80% of the employee's daily wage, while those for permanent disability are 90% of the daily wage. In the event of the beneficiary's death, a widow or widower dependent on the beneficiary for support will receive a pension equal to 60% of the primary beneficiary's benefit, until he or she remarries. Children receive a benefit equal to 40% of the primary benefit until age 20 or marriage. Benefits are payable for life in the case of a handicapped child. Benefits can also be paid to the dependent parents or siblings of a covered employee.

The Invalidity Pension Scheme provides benefits for nonemployment-related total or partial disability. The program also provides funeral, rehabilitation, and survivor benefits. Permanent disability benefits are equal to 50–65% of monthly pay, depending on length of coverage. If a covered worker dies, the primary benefit is payable to any survivors under the same formula as for the Employment Injury Insurance Scheme. As of 1994, a total of 6,584,277 workers were covered by SOCSO, which had reserves totaling RM3.6 billion. In 1991, SOCSO coverage was expanded to include workers' commuting time to and from work.[24]

THE EMPLOYEE PROVIDENT FUND

The 1991 Employees Provident Fund Act provides for a compulsory contributory retirement fund that is payable in full when they reach age 55. All employers and employees are required to contribute to the fund, at the rates of 12 and 10%, respectively, of the employee's monthly wages. Expatriates and domestic servants are exempted. Firms that set up their own pension programs in addition to the above can seek tax exemption.

EPF is fully funded with contributions and accrued interest credited to the individual's account. The amount contributed becomes available in a lump sum at the retirement age of 55 if the contributor becomes disabled and permanently leaves Malaysia and Singapore.

Under 1991 amendments, members may withdraw up to 40% of the price of a low cost house or the entire amount of their savings, whichever is lower, subject to a maximum of RM10,000 ($3718). For other housing, members may withdraw up to 20% of the price of the house, subject to a ceiling of 45% of their savings or RM40,000 ($14,870). New benefits were also introduced to enable mentally and phys-ically disabled members to receive a lump sum payment in addition to their savings.

At the end of 1993, EPF's total membership was 6.94 million, not all of whom are currently employed and making contributions, and the fund's assets were RM71.2 billion. Most of the fund, 52.6%, is held in federal government securities. Members receive a dividend of 8.0% on the accumulated sum in their accounts. Separate programs for teachers, estate employees, and armed forces personnel cover 1,562,000 persons and had assets of RM2.8 billion at the end of 1993.[25]

GOVERNMENT PENSION PROGRAM

The Government Pension Scheme provides pensions to civil servants who retire by age 55, retire on medical grounds, or are required by the government to retire. Civil servants may also be entitled to a disability allowance if they retire because of a service-connected disability. Widows and minor children are also eligible for a derivative pension if the employee dies in service or after retirement. The pension plan is noncontributory, and all pension payments are charged to the general revenue of the federal government.[26]

MANDATORY RETIREMENT

The human resources minister has indicated that the private sector can raise the retirement age to 60 years and beyond as it need not follow the mandatory retirement age of 55 years in the public sector. The private sector is free to decide, without the consent of the government, if an extension of the retirement age is necessary. In fact, some firms are already doing this in response to the tight labor situation, among them Petronas and Esso. The possibility of increasing the retirement age has received approval from both trade unions and employers' organizations.

The minister declined to comment on the retirement age of public sector workers, believing this is a matter that should be handled by the Public Services Department.[27]

DISMISSAL AND TERMINATION

There are legal protections for Malaysian workers who are dismissed or termi- nated from their jobs. In present times, with a serious shortage in many occupations, a primary concern of management is finding qualified workers rather than laying off those currently on the payroll. However, occasions do arise when an employee's services are no longer necessary. At this point the departure or parting becomes significant. If the worker resigns in accordance with contractual provisions or on that basis accepts termination, no difficulty arises. However, the employer must be careful when the employee is "dismissed" which would mean that the worker receives compensation whatever is due him or her up to the point of dismissal, and also in cases where the employee's services are terminated by the receipt of notice or offer of salary in lieu of notice, but the employee challenges the employer's action.

In the latter eventuality, it is necessary to examine the question whether the employer has a right to bring the employer–employee relationship to an end. The words *dismissal* and *termination* denote two different situations. *Dismissal* implies and involves some wrongful act or conduct on the part of the worker which entitles the employer to terminate the relationship immediately. On the other hand *termination* refers to the relationship being brought to an end in the manner contractually agreed to. While termination can be the act of either party, dismissal is always the unilateral act of the employer.

An employer always has the right to dismiss an employee who is guilty of misconduct. It is an accepted fact that there must be discipline within an enterprise to promote orderly conduct. As such when employment is accepted, the employee agrees to be subject to the authority of the employer and the discipline of the undertaking. Any other position would threaten the basis of the employer–employee relationship.

The essence of misconduct is that the act must be intentional and the doer/ employee aware of the harm caused. Furthermore, it must be reckless, and the employee not care if this action is injurious or likely to be injurious to the interest or reputation of the employer. But not all misconduct justifies immediate and summary dismissal. Major misconduct such as fighting, assault, insubordination, staging an alleged strike would justify dismissal, while lesser isolated acts or omissions such as tardiness or eating during working hours may not. While misconduct of a sufficiently gross nature is the traditional common law basis for dismissal, the Industrial Relations Act of 1967 adopts a slightly different stance. In dealing with labor disputes, it apparently attempts to provide security of tenure for workers. It does so by providing in section 20 that a worker who "considers that he has been dismissed without just cause or excuse by the Employer may make representation to the Director General to be reinstated...." This would seem to and does in fact rule out "Contractual Termination." The wording used would seem to suggest that misconduct would come within the meaning of "just cause or excuse." So might other factors and considerations.

While the employee may in the eyes of the employer be guilty of misconduct, following the proper preliminary steps is absolutely essential. Failure to do so may seriously jeopardize the employer's position. If an employer fails to take the preliminary steps which the law regards as essential, he has no power to dismiss and any purported dismissal may be nullified. While this view may be regarded on occasion as being extreme, its importance cannot be disregarded. The need for an inquiry before a decision is made to dismiss a worker cannot be taken lightly. The 1955 Employment Act in Section 14(1) requires that any dismissal be "after due inquiry." However, the act is silent in giving any direction as to the form of the "due inquiry" envisaged.

A ruling by the Industrial Court provides guidance as to the meaning of "due inquiry." In *Local Government Board v. Arlidge*, Lord Shaw of Dunfermline commented that the employer "must do its best to act justly and to reach just ends by just means. If a statute prescribes the means it must employ them. If it is left without express guidance it must still act honestly and by honest means."

Looking at the words "due inquiry" in Section 14(1) of the Employment Act, the industrial court in Industrial Award No. 23 of 1971 went on to comment that the kind of action contemplated was a "bona fide investigation of the facts by the Management into an alleged complaint before dismissing" the delinquent worker.

Thus it behooves employers to ensure than an employee against whom dismissal is considered be clearly told what the complaint is and given the best possible opportunity to defend himself. The greater the formality, the better, to ensure that a serious inquiry has been conducted.[28]

In a way the legal provisions that exist have blurred the distinction between "termination" and "dismissal." This is because originally termination referred to the process of bringing the contract of employment to an end in a manner agreed to by the parties. Dismissal, however, referred to the employer's unilateral right to bring the contract to an end summarily on account of misconduct or other omission or short-coming on the part of the employee. The situation created by the Industrial Relations Act with regard to "dismissal" has important lessons for both the employer and employee. The latter should feel comforted by the protection that the act gives, which is neither absolute or unqualified. On the other hand, the employer must always remember that while the right to bring an end to his relationship with employees is always there, it must be exercised for good reasons and sincere motives and with fairness to the worker.

The employee who wishes to assert his or her rights under the act must present a claim within 60 days of dismissal. If there is a failure to do so, the worker's rights under the Industrial Relations Act are forfeited. The industrial court has the power to reinstate the worker, and if this happens the worker ends up with back pay retroactive to the date of dismissal, covering the period until reinstatement. Moreover, if the court finds that given the circumstances and the prevailing atmosphere it is not desirable to reinstate the employee, it may instead order payment of compensation while ruling that the dismissal was wrongful. The industrial court is charged with reaching a decision that takes into account the public interest, the financial implications, and the effect of the award, along with the economic conditions in the country. These considerations may not be so relevant where an individual is instituting an action for dismissal without just cause, but the court nevertheless is required to act according to equity, good conscience and the merits of the case.[28]

THE MEF POSITION

Employers, when deciding whether to terminate an employee, must ask themselves this question: "Does the work performed by the employee continue to exist after the termination of his employment?" If the work continues to exist, then there are simply no grounds for termination, according to the Malaysian Employers Federation. Quoting industrial court award no. 255/93 between Behn Meyer Company and claimant P. Perjaya Sundram, the MEF said if the job of the terminated worker still exists, it will be impossible to establish genuine termination in the court of law. Moreover, if the worker concerned does not accept layoff, and vacancies suitable to his capacity occur subsequently, then the worker should be offered reemployment. The MEF also urged its members not to breach any expressed terms of employment in a service contract, such as giving insufficient termination notice.

In the case referred to by the MEF, the facts showed that the claimant commenced employment with Behn Meyer as a clerk, and at the time of his dismissal, held the job of a credit control officer. The company had contended that Perjaya Sundram was one of the 67 workers who had to be terminated as a result of it ceasing to be an agent for BASF products. Behn Meyer maintained that the claimant's dismissal was a bona fide termination and was not motivated by any ulterior motives. Termination benefits totaling RM26,023 ($9,674) were offered to the claimant but he refused to accept the sum. The company argued that the claimant and 66 of his coworkers were not terminated due to discrimination. Their retrenchment was a genuine business requirement, costing the company some RM1.3 million ($483,271). Meanwhile, counsel for the claimant argued that the dismissal was totally without just cause or excuse. The claimant's last assignment in the company was to assist in the collection of excess debts. It was argued that debt collection is an ongoing process and there was no evidence that this work had ceased. The industrial court found Behn Meyer had breached the code of conduct for industrial harmony. It held that Perjaya Sundram's termination was not a bona fide exercise and was tainted by an unfair labor practice.

The MEF, as a central organization for employers, is a signatory to this code of conduct. Although the code is not a piece of legislation, it imposes moral obligations on employers, trade unions, and workers.[29]

A problem can arise if a business is sold through intermediaries as a guise to avoid the payment of termination benefits. The human resources ministry is planning to deal with this contingency by proposing amendments to the Industrial Relations Act to protect workers from such underhanded tactics.[30] The cabinet agreed that such amendments are necessary to ensure that workers are not shortchanged when the company they work for is sold. For example, an owner who realizes he has to pay substantial benefits if he sells his firm may first sign an agreement with another firm to handle the company operations for a certain number of years. Before the period expires, however, the owner may sell the company. In that case, the owner is free of any liability, as the responsibility of paying termination benefits falls on the intermediary firm running the operations at the time of the sale. If the intermediary firm is a reputable company with sound finances, then there is no problem in paying the workers. But if the firm is a front set up just to help the owner avoid paying termination costs, then the workers will end up without any money. The present law does not say that the original owner should be liable. Instead, the firm operating the company at the time is responsible for the payments. But in the case of a "two-dollar company," the workers' rights are not protected.

The idea to amend that Act followed the sale of the former Merlin Hotel in Kuala Lumpur in the early 1990s. Its owner, Faber Merlin Bhd. signed an agreement with Kuala Reman Estates Bhd. to run the hotel for three years. Before the term expired, however, the hotel was sold to Ampang Hotel Bhd. As a result, some of the termination benefits were not paid to the workers. The affected employees sued Kuala

Reman, but the company did not have the money to pay the benefits. This did not necessarily mean that Faber Merlin was trying to avoid termination benefits or if Kuala was a two-dollar company set up for that purpose. Nevertheless, the amendments will ensure that workers are not short-changed by irresponsible owners when the company they work for is sold.[31]

Employers have also been put on notice by the labor department that regular employees are not to be dismissed and replaced by foreign workers willing to work for less. The government is investigating a situation at Wembly Rubber Products to determine if 62 technicians, engineers, and local workers were laid off in order to hire foreign workers. The factory employs 2,900 workers, 700 of whom are foreigners.

The plant's human resource manager denied the charge and said the technicians, who were paid between RM450 ($167) and RM650 ($242) monthly, were terminated because recently purchased production machines required less manpower. Meanwhile, 700 workers from Bangladesh, who earn RM 250 a month, were put in the production department which is experiencing a labor shortage. The HR manager indicated the discharged employees could not be transferred to production because they were overqualified for the jobs.[32]

In another case, Carnaudmetalbox Malaysia, the largest can manufacturer in the northern part of Malaysia, was expected to compromise with the Metal Industry Employees' Union (MIEU) in their demand for more generous dismissal benefits for 88 workers let go following the closure of its Prai plant. The company, a subsidiary of the Anglo-French multinational, closed the Prai plant 10 months after its acquisition. It denied the union charge that the closure of the Prai plant was motivated by asset-stripping and was to pave the way for cheaper imports from another of its plants in Thailand.[33]

LABOR LAW REVIEW REQUEST

In October 1993, the Malaysian Employers Federation proposed that government undertake a comprehensive and systematic review of laws and strategies relating to labor and employment. It said principal legislation such as the Employment Act, the Industrial Relations Act, and the Trade Unions Act, as well as human resource strategies, needed reassessment to increase productivity and make Thailand more competitive. It also stressed that the aim of modern labor laws should go beyond the colonial approach that the only function of government is as protector of labor, adding that other aspects of legislation seemed to support the view that the economy was still largely dependent on rubber and tin. The MEF's newsletter said:

> We think the principal legislation as well as laws governing the provident fund and social security need to be assessed fully so that no impediments remain. There is little in the Employment Act that encourages labor toward higher productivity or ensures higher monetary rewards are given to the more efficient.[34]

In this regard, the MEF urged the government to tighten the Industrial Relations Act to lessen the occurrence of illegal wildcat strikes. It also called on the authorities to reevaluate the progress of the Sixth Development Plan strategies in the human resources area, especially in increasing labor productivity, and the need for more efficient labor markets, improved education, and the need for a more effective system of wage adjustment at a time when the labor shortage problem has become more acute.

The government apparently agreed with the management proposal, for in April 1994, a tripartite committee, comprised of representatives from the human resources ministry, the MEF, and three national labor congresses, was established to review all of the 19 labor laws dealing with employment, industrial relations and workers' welfare in Malaysia. Many of the laws were considered outdated and there was a need for further review and amendment. Previous reviews of labor legislation had been conducted on an ad hoc basis.[35]

CONCLUSIONS

Although independent unions may form in Malaysia, a strong case can be made for the proposition that the present statutory framework serves to limit their effectiveness in representing and protecting the economic interests of their membership. These arguments can be made:

1.   A legislative mandate gives the government wide discretion in the registration or deregistration of unions. The use or abuse of such governmental authority has served the government's objective of limiting union power. In addition, unions are prohibited from using funds for political action, a limitation not imposed on Malaysian employers.

2.   A union's most formidable weapon, the strike, has been substantially impaired by law. The government may order what amounts to compulsory arbitration of labor disputes before the Industrial Court. Also, 1980 amendments to the Industrial Relations Act imposed a two-thirds majority requirement in strike votes and a 7-day cooling off period prior to any strike action. Furthermore, during this period, the labor minister can refer disputes to the industrial court for arbitration, making strikes illegal. Sympathy and political strikes are also outlawed.

3.   Laws have also encouraged foreign investments in the export industry by imposing restraints on the labor movement. The scope of collective bargaining in so-called "pioneer industries" is restricted by the requirement of government approval for conditions more favorable than those in the 1955 Employment Act. Moreover, unions cannot bargain over promotion, hiring, dismissal, and related personnel policies in pioneer industries, which were promised five years of union-free operations by the government, which could guarantee this commitment by refusing to register unions during that time period.

4.   In the 1980s, the Malaysian government sought to emulate the Japanese model by expressing its preferences for enterprise or in-house unions, and attempted to limit unionism in the foreign-dominated electronics industry by law and policies which engendered considerable international criticism.

Although Malaysia's consistently high economic growth has placed it in the category of an upper-income developing nation, its concurrent labor policy has become more repressive rather than less restrictive. The independent Malaysian Trade Union Congress, during this period, has gained the support of international labor organizations in its efforts toward the legitimization and implementation of policies supporting the protection of worker rights and the optimization of labor standards.[36]

CHAPTER 18

Labor Relations: Structure, Process, and Practice

UNION STRUCTURE AND MEMBERSHIP

As of 1992, there were 519 individual labor unions in Malaysia with 694,365 registered members, an increase of 7,486 over 1991. These are the most recent figures available. Since unions are not allowed to organize workers in industries outside their primary one, Malaysian private sector unions are organized on industry or company lines. It is not uncommon for more than one union to be represented in a single employer, with the different unions representing different types of employers. The limitation on forming unions that cover more than one industry does not comply with international labor standards which state that workers should be able to establish and join organizations of their choosing without prior authorization.

Most unions are in peninsular Malaysia: Sabah and Sarawak have practically no unions. The majority of the more than 500 unions are in-house unions; the remainder are national unions such as the Plantations Workers' Union, the National Union of Bank Employees, and the Transport Workers Union (see Table 18-1). Current Malaysian law allows only in-house unions, not those organized in an industry-wide, national, or statewide basis. The few existing general unions were formed decades ago, prior to this limitation, although selective permission is still sometimes granted for industry-wide unions.

Individual in-house unions may apply to form a federation of trade unions or become affiliated with the Malaysian Trade Unions Congress. The country's three umbrella labor organizations include about 220 trade unions representing roughly 10% of the workforce. The Congress of Unions of Employees in the Public and Civil Service (CUEPACS) is registered under the Trade Unions Act of 1959, while the Malaysian Trade Union Congress (MTUC) and the Malaysian Labor Organization (MLO) come under the Societies Act.

Unions are generally nonpolitical and are organized along industrial rather than craft lines. Nearly half of the unions are in the private sector. Malaysian unions tend to be well organized and are inspected regularly to ensure compliance with the law.

TABLE 18-1
Membership in Major Malaysian Labor Unions
(Affiliation, if any, in parentheses)

Name of union	1980	1991	1992
1. National Union of Plantation Workers (MTUC)	115,746	77,653	61,432
2. National Union of the Teaching Profession (CUEPACS)	23,947	39,474	49,473
3. National Union of Bank Employees	11,241	20,824	24,709
4. The Amalgamated National Union of Local Authorities Employees, Peninsular Malaysia (CUEPACS)	12,680	20,699	20,789
5. National Union of Telecoms Employees (MTUC)	8,840	18,663	16,417
6. Malay Teachers Union, West Malaysia	N/A	17,459	18,985
7. Electrical Industry Workers Union (MTUC)	5,171	15,307	17,856
8. National Union of Commercial Workers	15,065	2,504	11,661
9. Transport Workers Union, Peninsular Malaysia (MTUC)	8,503	10,775	10,375
10. National Energy Board Employees Union (MTUC, CUEPACS)	7,536	10,456	10,063
11. National Union of College-Trained Teachers	N/A	9,282	11,060
12. National Union of Hotel, Bar and Restaurant Workers (MTUC)	N/A	9,948	5,981
13. Non-Metallic Mineral Product Manufacturing Employees Union (MTUC)	N/A	8,734	10,083
14. Wood Product Manufacturing Employees Union	N/A	8,655	12,000
15. National Union of Petroleum and Chemical Industry Workers	8,408	8,039	9,975
16. Armed Forces Workers Union (CUEPACS)	6,873	7,988	7,837
17. Metal Industry Employees Union (MTUC)	6,993	7,908	10,083
18. Malayan Technical Services Union (CUEPACS)	6,463	6,794	7,144
19. National Union of Employees in Rubber Manufacturing Products		6,744	6,145
20. Amalgamated Union of Employees in Government Clerical and Allied Services—AUEGCAS (CUEPACS, MTUC)	N/A	6,733	6,514
21. Food Manufacturing Industry Employees	N/A	6,490	7,046
22. National Union of P.W.D. Employees		5,966	5,944
23. Medical and Health Services Employees Union (MTUC)	N/A	5,655	5,800
24. FELDA Employees Union (MTUC)	N/A	5,619	6,530
25. Penang and Province Wellesley Textile and Clothing Industry Union (MTUC)	6,333	5,439	4,734
26. National Education Institution Employees Union		5,358	5,066
27. Malaysia Airline System Union		5,179	7,509
28. Tenaga Junior Officers Union		5,000	5,023

Source: Ministry of Human Resources, Kuala Lumpur, Malaysia.

In addition, unions are often drawn along ethnic lines, with Chinese and Indians predominating.

DECLINING MEMBERSHIP

After growing steadily up to 1983, trade union membership stagnated from 1983 to 1987. There was a net gain of nearly 11,000 membership in 1988, when approximately 18% of wage earners were in 418 registered labor organizations with a membership of 612,000. The Malaysian Trade Union Congress, a prominent union coordinating body, has advocated the creation of a labor-oriented political party. That possibility is still under study, but for the present the organization is usually associated with the opposition Democratic Action Party (DAP).[1]

Union membership failed to match the growth in employment in the 1980s, resulting in a drop in the level of unionization to 9.1% compared with 11.3% in 1985. The decline in the membership in the National Union of Plantation Workers (NUPW) from 120,000 in 1980 to only 61,423 in 1992 offset gains made by other unions. The NUPW is by far the largest Malaysian union, accounting for about 9% of all organized workers. The NUPW leaders attribute the union's falling membership to the use of contract and undocumented workers who do not join the union, and the conversion of rubber estates to palm oil which is less labor-intensive. Another factor is reduced rubber estate employment due to the conversion of rubber estates near urban areas into housing developments. Other unions have grown or shrunk with the fortunes of the industries they cover. Growing numbers of illegal workers also serve to weaken the position of unions, especially in the plantations.

Federations of unions set up under the Trade Unions Act are restricted to one industry in the same fashion that local unions are. Broader-based labor bodies like the MTUC and the MLO, registered as societies, are technically regarded as societies whose membership consists of trade unions. By law, societies of trade unions have the same rights as regular labor unions. The federation of public sector unions, CUEPACS, is made up of teachers unions and state-based textile and garment worker unions. Unions can belong to only one labor center, but many CUIEPACS-federated unions are members of the MTUC. One CUEPACS affiliate is a member of the MLO.

THE THREE FEDERATIONS

Unions are required to register, as noted above, and are closely watched to minimize the escalation of labor disputes. While legislations has curbed union activism, Malay membership is increasing, an indication of the increasing participation of bumiputera ("sons of the soil") workers in the industrial sector. A total of 138 unions with approximately 500,000 members were affiliated with the MTUC, the largest federation, in 1994. The CUEPACS groups together totaled about 89 unions with approximately 75,000 members employed by the federal and state governments and the statutory bodies. Twenty-two unions in the civil service applied to join CUEPACS, which amended its constitution to permit affiliation by these unions in 1991. These moves opened the door to some 80 unions representing about 200,000 workers to join CUEPACS.

In 1989, disillusionment with the national union leadership of the MTUC prompted several large unions, led by the National Union of Bank Employees, to organize a rival labor federation, the Malaysian Labor Organization. In a response to the criticism that the MTUC is overly politicized, the MLO constitution stipulates that office holders cannot hold a position in any political party, although MLO members may join any political party. Fifteen unions with a total membership of 142,000 joined the MLO.[2]

The MLO membership consists of the National Union of Bank Employees, the UAB Executive Staff Union, the National Union of Newspaper Workers, the Council for Subordinate Grades, the Non-Metallic Mineral Products Manufacturing Employees Union, the National Union of Petroleum and Chemical Industry Workers, the HSBC Officers Union, the MISC Employees Union, the All-Malaysian Estates Staff Union, the National Union of Tobacco Workers, the Sabah Banking Employees Union, the National Union of College Trained Teachers, and the Rediffusion Workers Union.[3]

UNION RIVALRY

Frequent disagreements among Malaysia's three labor federations have contributed to an image of divisiveness, disarray, and inept leadership. For example, in July 1990, the MLO notified the International Confederation of Free Trade Unions (ICFTU) of its existence as the country's second labor federation. Apparently, the MLO intended to affiliate with the ICFTU and stand as a rival to the MTUC with the world labor organization, although the MLO's secretary general stated there were no definite plans to seek ICFTU affiliation but rather to grow in strength and establish itself as a national labor body. The MTUC responded to these developments by stating that it would not tolerate the formation of another federation and would protest the affiliation of any other Malaysian labor organization with the ICFTU.[4]

Not unexpectedly, relations between the MTUC and the MLO have remained strained. The MTUC leadership criticized the MLO for splitting the labor movement, accusing the rival federation of being government-sponsored. Despite the opposition of the MTUC, the MLO was invited to join the National Labor Advisory Council (NLAC). The NLAC is a tripartite, labor, government, and management group set up to advise the Malaysian minister of human resources on labor policy. The government also named the MLO as an advisor on the Malaysian delegation to the ILO conference in Geneva in 1992. Four MTUC officials have traditionally served on the board of the Employee Provident Fund (EPF), but the government chose to reappoint only two of the MTUC's four representatives, appointing two MLO representatives to fill the remaining vacancies.[5]

Later, in 1994, the MTUC protested the government's decision to appoint CUEPACS as Malaysia's worker delegate to the annual ILO conference in Geneva in July of that year; CUEPACS was selected since the MTUC had been the worker delegate in 1993. The two federations were taking turns as Malaysia's delegate, but the MTUC complained that this arrangement was no longer valid. The third national union federation also asked to be considered as a delegate.

In announcing the CUEPACS selection as the worker delegate, the human resources minister said its appointment was based on the rotation system as practiced since 1980, and that the views of both the MTUC and CUEPACS had been taken into consideration. The ILO annual conference hosts government, employer and union representatives from more than 150 countries to discuss issues affecting the working world.[6]

Still unconvinced, MTUC president Zainal Rampak stressed the point that the labor congress is Malaysia's largest union center and should be given precedence over CUEPACS and the MLO.[7] The matter was finally resolved when the credentials committee of the ILO retained CUEPACS as Malaysia's worker delegate because the MTUC had "acquiesced" to the rotation system practiced by the two since 1982, when the decision to alternate the appointment of the Malaysian worker delegate was agreed upon by MTUC and CUEPACS following a 1982 meeting in Geneva. Following the agreement, the rotation system was adhered to by both congresses, although the MTUC challenged the appointment of CUEPACS in 1984 and 1992. On both occasions, the MTUC subsequently withdrew its objection. Regarding the 1994 conference, the MTUC proceeded with its objection and filed the complaint with the credentials committee, stating that the worker delegate should be represented by the most representative labor organization.[8]

As with Thailand, Malaysian union officials appear preoccupied with their own personal goals and ambitions, rather than evincing a whole-hearted commitment to the organizations they head. This perception was further strengthened by internecine bickering between the MTUC and CUEPACS which continued after the CUEPACS selection as the worker delegate. The MTUC objected to the choice, alleging that his organization "is not happy with the way CUEPACS representatives have been performing in past ILO conferences."[9] However, there was not unanimity with this characterization among other MTUC officials, who privately accused some of MTUC's past leaders of "sleeping on the job" during ILO conferences or making countless trips to Geneva only for holidays. Unfortunately overlooked during these acrimonious exchanges is Malaysia's interest in the ILO and the consideration of important trade and labor issues of considerable importance to Malaysia's labor movement.[10]

Earlier, the MTUC had complained that the manner in which its delegates were appointed to the Social Security Organization (SOCSO) was unfair since the government had not first solicited the opinion of the MTUC before the selections while the MLO had been invited to nominate its representatives.[11]

Government Regulation

In Malaysia, the Minister of Labor and Manpower is authorized to suspend a trade union for six months upon a finding that the union is being used for political purposes or has acted in ways prejudicial to national security and public order. The government has shown unusual determination in resisting demands for wage increases by CUEPACS, the public service employees' union. Its efforts to maintain salaries at their present levels have provoked considerable criticism from CUEPACS and other labor organizations. In this respect, the government and CUEPACS have been at odds over the authority of the Departmental Joint Council (DJC) to determine federal wages. The government, through the Public Services Department, contends that the DJC affects only state and local workers, not federal employees. Further complicating relations is a decision by the national labor federation, the Malaysian Trade Union Congress, to boycott the National Labor Advisory Council, which attempts to reconcile labor–management relations, in retaliation for a government bill that would allow company unions.[12]

The MTUC publicized plans to reorganize divisions which were not active and set up divisions in states which still do not have any, apart from attracting more unions to become affiliates. The federation expressed concern over the failure of the government to allow independent unions in the electronics industry. Its president, Zainal Rampak asserted, "We will also pay attention to the desire of electronics workers to set up a National Union of Electronics Workers of their choice in line with Article 10 of the Federal Constitution."[13]

An MTUC About Face

In most instances, Malaysian unions act responsibly in their dealings with the government and management. The limits of responsible conduct may have been reached, however, when in 1994 the MTUC promised the government that it was dropping its confrontational approach in government–union relations. It also reversed its previous opposition to in-house unions in the electronics industry. Mr Zainal stated:

> People want us to be less confrontational; well, we are going to give it to them. This year, we will be more consultative in everything we do, in the hope that this will lead to better things for workers.... You cannot expect us to make the change if the employers and the Government—our partners in development—do not change as well. The MTUC cannot be expected to avoid confrontation if, say, there are parties who continue to deny workers better benefits even during the current boom times.[14]

The MTUC embarked on a drive to increase its membership as well as to improve its services to affiliates. Even here, the congress has decided to do the unprecedented— place special emphasis on in-house unions whereas in the past it has been known to greatly oppose this concept. The MTUC had been adamant about employees in the electronics industry being represented by a national union instead of enterprise unions. Now it will not oppose electronics workers forming in-house unions if that is their wish.

This policy reversal was sure to raise eyebrows among those opposing in-house unions generally as the weakest form of labor representation, and to wonder whether the MTUC was more interested in a positive public image than effective labor leadership. The government also expressed its reservations when the MTUC went even further and said that it might not raise the electronics workers issue at International Labor Organization conferences. Human Resource Minister Datuk Lim Ah Led speculated:

> After what they have done in the past—trying to remove Malaysia's Generalized System of Preferences (GSP) status granted by the U.S., and trying to get the Government to be expelled from the ILO—we have to remain cautious with this overture.[15]

The MLO was not as charitable in its interpretation of this unexpected policy change by the MTUC, indicating their belief that MTUC leaders had compromised their principles in an expedient fashion simply because they wanted the government to select the MTUC as the workers' delegate to the next ILO conference.

The government also criticized the MTUC for reneging on its promise to be less confrontational when it refused to accept its own leaders after they were nominated by the government to the National Labor Advisory Council. The human resources minister said this demonstrated that the congress looked down on the capability of its affiliates and instead should respect his ministry's nominees from its own ranks. The MTUC had stated it intended to boycott NLAC meetings in protest against the human resource minister's decision to reject five nominations made by the MTUC. The minister had replaced the five with his own nominees.

The human resources minister countered by maintaining that the government cannot accept nominations by any workers' organizations when there are more capable leaders who have shown their dedication in contributing toward labor development. He stated that sometimes the government had to use its prerogatives to nominate representatives for the workers' organizations in the NLAC.[16]

NEED FOR TRIPARTISM

Since government, management, and labor interests are represented in labor relations issues, cooperation among the three parties is essential for the satisfactory resolution of problem areas. As noted above, the MTUC has complained about the manner in which the government selected representatives to the NLAC. The Human

Resources Ministry, sensitive to these complaints, has emphasized the need for objective tripartism. It warned that selfishness on the part of either the government, employers, or workers could spell the end of the tripartite approach to handling labor issues in Malaysia. Minister Lim stated his concerns: "The three parties must practice mutual trust, respect, and cooperation in carrying out their various responsibilities."[17] He also argued that if any one of three interest groups is concerned about its own benefit at the expense of the other two, then the tripartite practice would fail. He commended the maturity of both employers and workers in understanding and meeting their responsibilities which ensured that tripartism would continue.

The friction between the government and the MTUC continued in 1994 when the labor congress said it wanted section 9 of the new Occupational Safety and Health Act of 1993 to be amended or repealed. The section grants the Human Resources Minister discretionary authority in appointing members of the National Council for Occupational Safety and Health, the body that draws up policies and programs to implement the new law.

The threat to the continued viability of tripartism comes from the fractiousness of the MTUC because of its rivalry with the MLO and CUEPACS, as has been pointed out previously. The government also apparently fails to understand that its policies of wage restraint and close monitoring of union activities engenders hostility on the part of workers and the institutions that represent them.[18]

AN IN-HOUSE UNION CHRONOLOGY

What many union leaders see as official encouragement of company unions has long been a contentious issue in Malaysia. The MTUC has reversed its position and the government also has not been consistent in its stance toward these weak enterprise labor organizations. The following chronology is instructive in this regard:

In 1987 the NLAC discussed for six months proposed labor law changes aimed at encouraging the formation of in-house labor unions. Although the sessions were described as acrimonious, amendments were scheduled to be presented to parliament in June of that year. Then proposals were introduced to give every new company a one-year period with no union activity allowed. Thereafter, workers could choose between forming an in-house union or affiliating with a national union, with the law clearly spelling out the terms and procedures to minimize conflicts with national labor organizations. As is now the case, an in-house union could not be registered if workers in a plant already were organized under the national union rubric.

In 1989, the government told the electronics industry that only in-house unions would be tolerated, closing the door on electronics workers' moves to form a statewide union. It appeared that Kuala Lumpur was determined to keep the country's unions weak, and ensure the continued presence of foreign investors. The government strengthened the ability of the Director-General of Trade Unions to veto registration of trade unions. He then used the new powers to reject a bid to organize a National

Union of Electronics Workers (NUEW). Its advocates took their case to the Supreme Court. However, the government stopped short of amending the Trade Union Act to facilitate in-house, as opposed to industry-wide unions.

Then, in December 1990, the government lifted a ban on the unionization of the electronics industry, a move affecting an estimated 85,000 workers. In response to foreign investors' protests, Kuala Lumpur modified its decision requiring that the electronics unions be organized on an in-house rather than an industry-wide basis.[19]

As of December 31, 1992, 336 in-house unions represented 285,805 workers, up significantly from 306 in-house unions representing 268,623 workers in 1991. Most in-house unions started in public sector companies, although the privatization of the telecommunications department and other government services moved a number of in-house unions into the private sector. The government, and particularly the prime minister, saw in-house unions as creating a better industrial relations climate between employers and workers, in part because one union would represent all workers in a firm. The leaders of the national unions see them as weakening their own unions and reducing the protection union membership affords a worker. Table 18-2 indicates that in-house unions are primarily a feature of the public sector, including statutory bodies and local government. In the private sector, in-house unions represent 16.6% of organized workers.[20]

TABLE 18-2
In-House Unions in Malaysia

	1982	1988	1990	1991	1992
Public sector					
In-House Unions	133	136	170	174	177
Membership	130,235	139,997	180,896	191,150	172,890
Total Union Membership	300,704	299,156	305,151	314,338	306,719
% in In-House Unions	43.3	46.5	59.3	60.8	56.4
Private sector					
In-House Unions	36	88	113	132	159
Membership	20,127	61,203	67,674	77,473	112,915
Total Union Members	310,780	317,761	333,017	344,318	373,288
% in In-House Unions	6.5	19.3	20.3	22.5	30.2
Total					
In-House Unions	169	244	283	306	336
Membership	150,362	200,200	248,570	268,623	285,805
Total Union Membership of both Public and Private Sectors	612,218	617,501	638,168	658,656	680,007
% in In-House Unions	24.6	32.4	39.0	40.8	42.0

Source: Ministry of Human Resources, Kuala Lumpur, Malaysia.

COLLECTIVE BARGAINING

Legislation in Malaysia sanctions collective bargaining, which can be defined as employees in a single establishment, several establishments with the same owner, specific enterprises, or an entire industry or occupational group, which negotiates terms and conditions of employment with labor organizations. Private sector wages are determined through collective bargaining or individual contracts. Wage levels in the private sector have increased steadily although labor contracts are not in common use, partly because Malaysian law, especially the Industrial Relations Act, effectively restricts collective bargaining rights because of compulsory arbitration of labor disputes.[21]

In 1987, the government told unions it was considering a three-year wage freeze in the public and private sectors, which was later implemented in the public sector. The Labor Ministry maintained it was not realistic for unions to press for the renewal of collective bargaining every three years. At that time civil service unions rejected government proposals to freeze wage increases or adjustments for public sector employees. In fact, thousands of workers supported a nationwide picket organized by the MTUC to protest against these proposed cost-cutting measures.

Even without government intervention, the rate of wage increases had begun to decelerate on its own. Much collective bargaining centers around the Consumer Price Index, which had risen by only 3.9% in 1984, 0.3% in 1985, and 0.7% in 1986. Collective agreements concluded in 1986 provided for average wage hikes of 8.8%, compared with 15% in the two previous years.[22]

The largest U.S. investment in Malaysia is in the petroleum sector. Exxon has two subsidiaries operating in Malaysia. Esso Production Malaysia Incorporated (EPMI), which is 100% owned by Exxon, handles offshore oil and gas production. Esso Malaysia, which is 65% owned by Exxon and 35% by a range of Malaysian individuals and institutions, refines and markets oil products in Malaysia. Bargainable employees at both companies are represented by the National Union of Petroleum and Chemical Industry Workers (NUPCIW), which has negotiated collective agreements with management. Some EPMI employees have broken away from the NUPCIW and formed a separate in-house union. Pay and benefits at both firms are well above the Malaysian norm.[23]

THE INDUSTRIAL MASTER PLAN

The government has developed an industrial master plan with the objective of restraining wage increases to 3% for 10 years while increasing productivity by 10% annually. In 1990, however, in the first year of the plan, wage increases were estimated at 5 to 10%, versus productivity growth of about 4%.

Because of the official policy requiring preference for Malays, considerable competition has developed among employers for the few qualified Malay managers and technicians available. As a result, premiums of as much as 25 to 40% of the average pay scale are sometimes offered to lure qualified bumiputeras to new positions.

There are no nationwide or industrywide standards for fixing wage rates, nor is there a legal minimum rate. Where unions represent industries or establishments, wages are settled through collective bargaining. In 1992, in peninsular Malaysia, a total of 334 collective wage accords involving 72,200 workers were concluded, compared with 384 agreements involving 78,900 workers in 1991. Roughly 70% of these agreements were for workers within the manufacturing and commercial sectors. Public sector wage increases are reviewed only once every three years.[24]

THE BANKING AGREEMENT

As an example of collective bargaining which produced tangible results, the Malaysian Commercial Bank Association (MCBA) and the Association of Bank Officers Peninsular Malaysia (ABOM) signed a new collective agreement in 1994 bringing a salary increase of about 13% for some 3,000 officers in 15 banks in the country. The increase of between RM 120 ($44.60) and RM 350 ($130.11) retroactive to January 1, 1994 involved an additional total expenditure of RM 15 million ($5,576,208) for the banks, and was expected to be extended to thousands of officers of similar status in the financial institutions as, traditionally, their terms of service are based on the MCBA–ABOM collective agreement.

The 13% increase which matched the consumer price index cost-of-living figure, was the highest ever secured by ABOM. The previous agreement, handed down by the Industrial Court for the 1991–93 period, ranged between 11 and 12%. The lowest increase was in 1988, only about 3%. In what was described as "the best deal ever," the MCBA also agreed to a 1% increase in the employers' contribution to the Employees Provident Fund, increasing it to 16%, 4% above the statutory rate of 12%. The workers' contribution remained at 10%. Employees working on the rest day will be paid RM 35 for the first three-and-a-half hours and RM 70 for any work in excess of that duration, but not exceeding seven hours. The allowance for shift work was also increased. The banks also agreed to increase the insurance coverage for employees from RM 100,000 ($37,175) to RM 110,000 ($40,892). Medical benefits for family members were also raised to RM 600 and covered disabled children above the age of 18 years who are not gainfully employed. The MCBA also agreed to include a new provision granting union representatives a voice on matters related to safety and health at the workplace.[25]

COLLECTIVE BARGAINING ARGUMENTS

As far back as 1980, private sector workers and their unions asked for the renegotiation of labor contracts and sought wage adjustments at least equivalent to the increases granted to nearly three-quarters of a million government workers. The

Malaysian Employers Association disagreed with this demand, stating that labor contracts negotiated during the previous 18 months should remain in force. Contracts due for renewal in less than six months could have a "voluntary and temporary" wage adjustment appended but any such benefit would have to be reconsidered when the contract was renegotiated.

Adding more weight to the pressure for higher pay scales, the MTUC and other major labor organizations cited government-directed price increases in gasoline, sugar, cooking gas, and many other essential commodities. Union spokesman further cited a 6.6% rise in the consumer price index and an inflation rate as high as 10% as justification for their demands. Foremost, however, remained the contention that the hefty civil service pay increases granted by the government would contribute to immediate increases in inflation, creating a disparity between private and public sector earnings, a disparity that would only widen until the next contract renewal.

In response, the MEF stated that its detailed analysis of the government's revised pay scales compared to collective agreements, revealed that except for certain starting wages in the lower categories, most private sector salaries for similar jobs were still higher than public sector compensation scales. The MEF claim was not accepted by the MTUC, who argued that the difference, if any, was small at the lower pay scales and disparities probably would continue to exist as they had in the past. Heavy pressure was placed on the government by the MTUC, one of the most assertive of the Malaysian labor congresses, to convene the National Joint Labor Advisory Council to discuss wage adjustments.[26]

DISPUTE SETTLEMENT

The Industrial Relations Act of 1967 governs the settlement of disputes between employers and workers and the exercise of trade union rights. In 1980, it was amended to confer more power upon the government to deal with disruptive strikes. These amendments were criticized by local labor organizations and the ILO since strikes are discouraged by a system of controls which promote settlement through negotiation or arbitration by the Industrial Court. While strikes are legal and do occasionally occur, critics claim that this right is restricted in practice. As Table 18-3 shows, strikes are relatively few in Malaysia and generally of short duration.

What is termed Malaysia's crisis management approach to solving industrial disputes has reduced the number of days lost to strikes by more than 90%. Under the policy, which allows government officials to intervene and mediate in disputes, there has been a noticeable improvement in the time taken to resolve disputes. In 1990, for instance, 47% of Malaysia's 17 strikes were resolved within two days, but by 1992, 12 out of the 17 strikes (71%) had been resolved within the same period.

There were fewer than 20 strikes in 1984 and 1985, 23 strikes in 1986, and only 13 strikes in 1987.[26] The low level of strike activity continued during the 1988–92 period. Most of the disputes involved plantation workers and occurred during wage negotiations. For example, the largest number of strikes in 1991 occurred in the plantation

TABLE 18-3
Strikes in Malaysia, 1987–92

	1987	1988	1989	1990	1991	1992	Total
No. of strikes	13	9	17	17	23	17	106
Mandays lost	11,035	5,784	N/A	301,978	23,448	16,200	358,445
Workers involved	3,178	2,192	4,761	98,510	4,207	6,110	118,958

Source: Ministry of Human Resources.

sector, 18 involving 1,920 workers; there were two involving 1,753 workers in the manufacturing sector. In 1992, 11 of the 17 labor disputes were in the agricultural sector and five in manufacturing, resulting in an aggregate of 16,200 worker days lost. This represented a decline in strike activity from 1991, although the number of workers involved increased from 4,207 to 6,110.[27]

The Malaysian government, responding to criticism of its dispute settlement procedures, has stated that critics failed to emphasize the fact that a majority of the cases referred to the industrial court were often settled through the intervention of the Labor Ministry and its Industrial Relations Department. It claimed that its records demonstrate that 80 to 85% of the cases are solved through the intervention of the Industrial Relations Department, and this fact is not appreciated.[28]

Nevertheless, production can be interrupted when unionized workers have grievances and when collective negotiations are unsuccessful and reach an impasse. For instance, in August 1993, more than 100 bank officers drew up picket lines outside the Menara Maybank in Kuala Lumpur, after their association and the bank failed to reach agreement on a new collective agreement. The picket line was formed during lunch break after the deadlock in negotiations.[29]

Another dispute broke out in January 1994, when Shell Oil workers threatened to enlist the aid of foreign labor organizations in their dispute with Shell over the suspension of three union officials. The Shell Employees Union threatened to seek the assistance of the ICFTU and the International Chemical Employees Federation if Shell Malaysia failed to resolve the issue. The union directed its 700 members to work-to-rule as a protest against the suspension from work of three of its leaders. It also threatened to boycott Shell products and social activities. The union, an affiliate of the MTUC, took these actions in protest against the refusal of the management to discuss the September 1993 suspensions. The union also demanded the management withdraw show-cause letters to its president and assistant secretary, or: "failing which, we will seek the assistance of the ICFTU, ICET and the MTUC to boycott Shell products."[30] The MTUC also warned Shell management not to take things for granted or treat the union's demand lightly. In its response, Shell claimed its management always was willing to talk to the union leadership provided the workers were represented by union officials who were current company employees. Shell also claimed it had called several meetings with the union which failed to materialize.[30]

In another situation, union members petitioned the Industrial Relations Department, alleging that management had engaged in illegal practices regarding union security and employee compensation. The National Union of Employees in Companies Manufacturing Rubber Products (NUECMRP) submitted a report to London concerning a dispute at LRC Malaysia, a rubber glove manufacturing company in Kulim, Kedah.

The union was asked by the department to submit the report on allegations related to harassment, victimization, and provocation, including threats of dismissals raised by LRC Malaysia employees. LRC Malaysia management was also asked to submit its version of events to the department at the same time. The NUECMRP officers met department officials in a bid to resolve the dispute which had arisen over what the union claimed to be an unjustified contractual agreement on workers' annual pay increments. LRC Malaysia allegedly repatriated its profits to settle debts incurred by its overseas parent company, London International Group (LIG), instead of paying its workers. However, LRC Malaysia then offered an increment of 5% to its management staff, which the NUECMRP described as violating the Industrial Relations Act.

The union's report raised, among other things, the dismissal of five workers, including four union work site committee leaders, the alleged harassment and victimization of workers, alleged intimidation of workers into offering false testimonies, and barring union officials from representing workers at domestic inquiries. The dispute has wide-ranging repercussions, requiring government intervention to safeguard the interests of Malaysian workers employed by a foreign multinational company.

Approximately 600 workers, who were union members, picketed outside the company premises in Kulim for two months after the company refused to pay them their contractual increments due on January 1st. Following the government's intervention in the matter, the workers stopped picketing on June 8th. The dispute dealing with the contract was scheduled for an Industrial Relations Court hearing in September. The union urged the authorities to take immediate measures to prevent foreign multinations from repatriating profits earned by their local subsidiaries to ensure the fair distribution of profits to Malaysian workers.[31]

In the summer of 1994, the MTUC said the ILO would scrutinize Malaysian labor practices at its annual conference in Geneva. An ILO committee was scheduled to investigate complaints raised against Malaysia relating to restrictions placed on unions' monitoring of employers' hiring and firing practices and the denial of collective bargaining rights for civil servants, which were withdrawn by the government as far back as 1979.[32]

A POSITIVE SCENARIO

One year before, in 1993, despite the numerous labor disputes just detailed, industrial harmony seemed to prevail in Malaysia. Like preceding years, there were no major strikes nor pickets, as trade unions and the workers they represented joined hands with industry to strengthen the economy's resilience in the face of a global slowdown.

For Western investors, this achievement, understandably, was even harder to comprehend or imagine. Industrial disputes are the norm in the West, whatever the inconvenience to the public or the economy. In France, farmers' associations possess the power to even prevent the government from making a decision that affects national and world trade. In the United Kingdom, the sacking of a security guard, whether justified or otherwise, can reach a point where public transportation throughout the nation came to a standstill, which is what occurred in the middle of 1992.

On the union front, three labor congresses, the MTUC, the MLO, and CUEPACS, continued to coexist in peace. At the international level, Malaysia is now represented at both union and employer levels in the ILO's decision-making governing body. Throughout 1993, the only major snag in the labor scene was when the election of the MTUC, held in December 1992, was nullified by the Registrar of Societies. As a result, the MTUC and its 100-odd affiliates were preoccupied for most of the year preparing for reelections.[33]

AN EVALUATION OF EVENTS

Of the countries surveyed, the industrial relations scene is most similar in Malaysia and Thailand. Malaysia's labor movement faces some of the same difficulties which confront that of Thailand but there are significant differences as well. Both countries have independent unions which are supposed to legally function free of management interference. Yet, employers in Thailand and Malaysia penalize pro-union workers through wrongful termination and harassment. There is government intervention; some would call it interference, in labor–management relations in Malaysia through industrial court action in labor disputes which amounts to compulsory arbitration, basically nullifying effective strike action. In both nations, strike activity is legally restricted. Also, unions display little militancy and are plagued by internecine rivalries and complaints that labor leaders are more interested in official perquisites than effective constituent representation. Labor movements in both countries apparently value a nonconfrontational mode in dealings with employers and the government.

While Thai union membership is the lowest of the four countries, Malaysian union membership has been gradually increasing in contrast to Thai stagnation. Malaysian workers enjoy higher wages than their Thai counterparts as labor costs have risen sharply due a serious shortage of skilled workers in a booming economy. Both governments actively promote export-driven economies which seek to restrain labor costs and prevent industrial conflict from driving off foreign investment. Malaysia has reached full employment but Thailand is experiencing considerable underemployment. Both nations have serious shortages of skilled workers.

Prime Minister Mohamed has maintained that there is no shortcut for both entrepreneurs and workers to get rich. He argues that picketing and threats may succeed in achieving higher wages and other rewards but a country that achieves notoriety through extensive labor unrest will not attract foreign investment, resulting in rising unemployment. The Malaysian leader has stated that if wages are raised without corresponding increases in productivity, working hours will be reduced and industrial actions will occur with increasing frequency. The result will be increasing costs and a decline in national competitiveness. He notes that, according to the 1993 World Competitiveness Report, Malaysia is the fourth most competitive among industrializing nations.

Mohamed justifies his country's economic development approach and labor policies in this manner:

> The fact is that industrial peace and high productivity are more effective and lasting in raising workers' wages than other dated means such as industrial action. Wage increases in this manner do not cause inflation. Therefore, additional income means higher purchasing power. If the increase in wages is due to threat, without any rise in productivity, then inflation will happen.[34]

Malaysia no longer has a general comparative advantage in labor costs. Countries like Thailand, Sri Lanka, and India have lower wage levels for skilled workers, while Korea and Taiwan have comparable wage levels and higher productivity. Export competitiveness is an integral part of the administration's new strategy to ease the country's debt-service burden.

If Malaysian workers are receiving a fair share of the profits attained by Malaysian business enterprises, if labor standards meet international expectations, and if their rights to freedom of association and meaningful collective bargaining are protected, then the government is functioning as a credible democracy. However, the facts demonstrate that there is still considerable room for improvement in these areas. The government appears determined to keep unions weak as the membership rate fluctuates between 9 and 12%, and the perpetuation of in-house unions in the electronics industry is sufficient proof that worker rights and labor standards in Malaysia still fall considerably short of international expectations.

CHAPTER 19

Unresolved Issues

In the preceding chapter we discussed the Malaysian government's encouragement of in-house unions. This policy is an example of a union regulatory system aimed at reducing whatever bargaining power workers may have with management. The in-house or enterprise union model is currently the norm in the electronics industry, one of the problem areas examined in this chapter, along with the plight of plantation workers, the flexi-wage proposal linking pay with productivity, the new remuneration system of compensation for public sector employees, and problems created by the large influx of foreign workers.

UNIONS IN ELECTRONICS

The second largest concentration of American investment in Malaysia, after petroleum, is the electronics sector, especially the manufacture of components, such as semiconductor chips and various discrete devices. None of the 15 American electronics plants, employing more than 37,000 Malaysian workers, is unionized. There is no legal prohibition against organizing unions in the electronics industry and workers at some non-American firms, mainly not in the components industry, are represented either by the Electrical Industry Workers Union (EIWU), other unions, or in-house unions.

THE HISTORY OF LABOR RELATIONS

Malaysia had a long-standing de facto ban on unions in the electronics sector. The EIWU originally attempted to organize workers in the semiconductor factories in the 1970s. The Registrar of Trade Unions, now the Director-General of Trade Unions, ruled that these companies were in the electronics industry, not the electrical industry, and could not be organized by the EIWU. Subsequently, several unsuccessful efforts were made to form a national union in the electronics sector, which accounted for 34% of the jobs created in Malaysia between 1981 and 1983.[1]

The government restrictions on union activity preclude workers from negotiating reasonable wages for their services. Electronics assembly line workers, for example, are paid the lowest wages in the manufacturing industry, even though their work earns the greatest export profits.

The proposed formation of a national union for electronics workers is a long-standing issue and has been taken up by both local and international trade union leaders, during which the Malaysian government was repeatedly accused of denying the right of its workers to unionize. The ban on unions was a major factor in the 1988 AFL-CIO petition requesting suspension of Malaysian's GSP privileges. In mitigation, the Malaysian government pleaded that, as a developing nation, Malaysia was unable to conform to all ILO standards immediately. However it pledged that adherence to worker rights standards would be improved in stages. On that basis, Malaysia was retained on the United State's GSP list. In 1988, Malaysia exported $634 million worth of goods to the United States.

In December 1990, the government decided to lift the ban on unionizing the electronics industry, surprising and angering industry executives, while union officials welcomed the decision, saying they wanted to move quickly to enlist the workers in the industry and to secure new collective bargaining agreements. Most electronics manufacturers were attracted to Malaysia because it had tax-free pioneer status, low cost labor, and a union-free industrial climate.[2]

Concerted union organizing drives soon followed, aimed at signing up the thousands of workers in the sector. At the same time, employers' associations questioned whether the unions would be of any benefit to employees and spoke about reevaluating their investment policy. The industry had flourished in part because of an initial 15-year ban on unions, coupled with tax holidays and the ability to secure 100% foreign ownership.[3]

The National Electronics Workers Union was established earlier in October 1988 to represent the industry's workers. The Malaysian Trades Union Congress sued the Malaysian government in an attempt to have the new union officially recognized. The MTUC argued that the Trade Union Act provided the right to form national, as opposed to in-house or company unions.[4] By 1990 workers were protesting against the government restrictions on labor unions.

Standing for hours in factory production lines, often forced to work overtime and on public holidays, Malaysian workers produce a myriad of electronic components. Mostly women, the 130,000 workers in the electronics sector are the driving force behind Prime Minister Mahathir Mohamed's industrialization policy. In rural areas, starting pay for electronics workers was as low as RM178 ($66) per month, compared to RM215 to RM269 ($80 to 100) in urban areas. Annual increments were unilaterally decided by management and were known to be as low as RM178 (15 cents) per month in some companies. In comparison, electrical workers, members of the EIWU, started with a minimum RM323 ($120) with an automatic 10% annual increase.

THE HARRIS AND HITACHI CASES

Dissatisfaction with this state of affairs flared when 1,000 workers of the Hitachi Consumer Products Company at Bangi, 12 miles south of Kuala Lumpur, staged an illegal strike in June 1990, to protest the management's refusal to allow them to join the national Electrical Industry Workers Union. In an unprecedented move, and with the tacit approval of the government, Hitachi fired all of the workers in the largest mass termination in the country over a labor dispute. Under the law, only unionized workers are allowed to strike and only after giving advance notice to management and the government. The government justified its distinction, maintaining that it did not recognize national union membership for workers from companies which produce components or part of and not the whole finished product, as was the case with Hitachi. Despite repeated protests from union leaders, the government stood firm on its decision, saying it would jeopardize the national economy if national unions were permitted, because foreign electronics firms came to Malaysia due to low labor costs.

This policy invited a storm of international criticism. American and international labor organizations accused Malaysia of violating labor rights and petitioned Washington to withdraw Malaysia's special trading status with the United States. Similar petitions two years earlier made the Malaysian authorities lift a 17-year ban on unions in electronics and allowed in-house unions to organize. Six in-house unions formed and were registered in the electronics sector. Two were recognized as sole collective bargaining agents. One was disbanded by its members.

However, these development only further fueled the controversy because the Harris Solid State Workers Union was Malaysia's most famous electronics labor organization. Formed following the government's decision to register in-house electronics unions, this union was viewed by many as a test case for the government's new policy. The union campaign to force recognition by Harris was long and bitter, with both management and the union accusing each other of unfair tactics, and with both sides accusing the government of favoring the other. After the union demonstrated that a majority of Harris Solid State employees belonged to the union, it was recognized as an in-house union for 2,500 workers in January 1989. However, protests and allegations of union suppression flared when almost all of the workers were moved to a nonunion sister company, leaving behind only 25 workers, the union leaders.

Then in May 1990, the Harris strike hit the front pages of local newspapers when the workers refused a management offer to form an in-house union because the single example in an American company had proved unworkable.[5] The Harris Corporation claimed two of its three Malaysian companies were merged into a third, Harris Advanced Technology; the other two concerns, Harris Solid State and Harris Semiconductor were closed, and 21 union activists lost their jobs.[6]

By 1992 the Malaysian government still refused to bow to international and local pressures to allow the country's electronics workers to form a national union. The International Metalworkers' Federation claimed that electronics workers were suffering as a result. It alleged that the multinationals paid good salaries to managers and made large profits, but the rewards were not equitably passed on down the ranks. In fact, the general terms and conditions of employment for electronic workers in Malaysia were far poorer than those of their counterparts in Taiwan, Korea, or Singapore. The purchasing power of an electronics workers in Malaysia was less than half that of a Singapore employee performing the same job. And it was considerably lower than in Korea and Taiwan. Often managers used very autocratic and highly sexist practices. Women, for example were dismissed on becoming pregnant with no appeal procedures.

Harris Semiconductor faced charges in the industrial court for the dismissal of the 21 members of its in-house union after the union members refused to recognize the new company that was formed after Harris merged with its Solid State subsidiary. Harris had also ignored a government order to recognize the union. Seemingly unaffected by the Harris developments, multinationals like Motorola, Advanced Micro Devices, Wang, Sony, Sanyo, NEC, Robert Bosch, Siemens, and Thomson all operated in Malaysia, although it was not known which opposed unions.

The government resisted the international pressures to force them to accept national unions, claiming investors would be frightened off and workers would be able to hold their management to ransom. The International Metalworkers Federation (IMF) agreed with the government fear that foreign investors would be discouraged if the government changed its unyielding opposition to national labor organizations. Moreover, the MTUC threatened to pressure foreign firms, contending that there are national electronics unions in other countries and Malaysia should be no exception.

Malaysia also came under fierce pressure from the United Nations to change its position vis-à-vis the ban on national unions. At the ILO meeting in Geneva in May 1992, Malaysia was told to reconsider its positions and bring its law into line with ILO conventions. Other Third World nations, including Congo, Ecuador, Pakistan, and Uganda expressed their anger that Malaysia should be allowed to flout international laws to attract foreign investors.

Presently, it is unclear whether the electronics multinationals will be forced to conform in Malaysia. The issue has caused the government considerable embarrassment in the United Nations. But as one observer commented: "The UN cannot send in paratroopers over this. And there are no union enforcement battalions."[7]

Claims and Counterclaims

According to the government, electronics workers are said to be the highest paid in the country. This finding by the Department of Statistics (DOS) has been used as ammunition by the government which argued that the prohibition of an industry-based electronics union has little to do with promoting the welfare of these workers. In what it claimed to be the most authoritative findings on wages up to that date the DOS reported that in 1991 the monthly average income of electronics workers was between RM50 ($18.60) and RM250 ($93) higher than earnings in the electrical, plastics, textiles, wood and rubber products sectors. With the exception of workers in the petroleum and gas sectors, the monthly income of electronics workers was the highest, at RM721 ($268), followed by the furniture and textiles sector with respective incomes of RM659 ($245) and RM643 ($239). At the bottom were workers in timber mills who received only RM482 ($179) per month; workers paid at a daily rate received an even lower income. Nonetheless, there were likely to be some flaws in these comparisons since different skills and hours worked were not taken into consideration.

However, the unions disagreed with these figures, particularly unions in the manufacturing sector. In particular the Electrical Industry Workers Union and the Metal Industry Employees Union argued that the reported wage levels in the electronics sector was an overestimate because it was based on wages for both executive and nonexecutive employees. This criticism may, however, not be valid since it is likely that the same method of computation was used for all sectors so that there would be a similar bias for all sectors, assuming that the ratio of executive to nonexecutive employees was the same.

To dispel the charge that electronics workers were being manipulated in the absence of a national union, the Manpower Department of the Human Resources Ministry announced that it would conduct periodic surveys to compare salaries, fringe benefits, and allowances received by electronics workers with those received in sectors represented by national unions. Citing similar findings to the DOS, the department also said that unlike workers in other sectors, family members of electronics workers enjoy free first class hospitalization benefits. While intended to support the view that the policy of only allowing in-house unions in the electronics sector does not diminish welfare, this argument sparked demands from the Metal Industry Employees Union that their employers should provide better medical and hospitalization benefits.[8]

By the spring of 1993, labor shortages strengthened the hand of Malaysian workers, leading to a noticeable increase in union activity, especially in electronics. As the movement to unionize the electronics industry at the national level gained momentum, more in-house unions appeared as management efforts to resist the creation of a national electronics union received government support and were likely to succeed. That summer the government stated it had no objection against the Malaysian Trades Union Congress raising the unionization issue in electronics at the ILO conference in June as long as it did not "collaborate" with international organizations. The Human Resources minister stated: "They must, however, not involve the IMF, the International Confederation of Free Trade Unions and the American Federation of Labor and Congress of Industrial Organizations."[9]

The minister said the economic well-being and massive flow of investment into Malaysia did not depend on whether or not there was a national union in its industries. He added that the investments were the result of political stability, government open policy on investment, and the attitude of Malaysian workers who were so quick and eager to learn. On the MTUC's mission to secure a decision among ILO conference delegates for a policy to protect workers in the developing countries against multinational corporations, Minister Lim said: "I do not think that workers in this country are exploited. If people think that the Government will allow employers to exploit Malaysians ... they must be out of their minds.... We have a duty to workers here who are also voters."[10]

At the previous ILO conference, the MTUC had collaborated with the International Metalworkers Federation on a campaign to suspend Malaysia from the ILO in protest against Malaysia's policy to allow only in-house unions in the country. Minister Lim also issued a veiled warning against comments the MTUC president Zainal might make at the ILO conference, indicating that Zainal's statements would be monitored by the government. However, he declined to elaborate on the measures that would be taken against Zainal should he distort facts. He added that the government had a right to explain to workers whenever facts were distorted.

AN INTERNATIONAL COMPARISON

The Malaysian government continued its campaign to justify in-house unions, claiming that there is not one single union of electronics workers in any of the industrialized Group of Seven (G-7) countries. In fact, the Human Resources Ministry claimed, according to one of its studies, that union memberships in these countries, as a percentage of the total workforce, are declining. The study, which examined the union situation in the United States, Japan, Great Britain, France, Germany, Italy, and Canada, found that electronics workers in these countries are represented only by in-house unions or national unions of electrical/metal workers. The study also found that the electronics industry is the least unionized in the world largely because it provides better services and working environments to its workers, even without the unions demanding them. For example, electronics workers in Malaysia have been among the top earners in the manufacturing sector for more than two decades, according to the human resources minister, who added that the 16 U.S. electronics firms operating in Malaysia are ranked among the world's top 500 corporations and operate in a union-free environment.

Based on these findings, the government opined that the centralization of collective agreements at the national level may not be suitable for future expansion of the industry. Minister Lim commented:

> Future expansion of the industry depends greatly on research and development and flexibility in production in this competitive market. In order for Malaysia to become an electronics industry growth centre, the policy to encourage the formation of in-house unions for electronics workers should be a good alternative.[11]

Malaysia has also rejected the previous AFL-CIO accusations, arguing that full employment in the electronics manufacturing sector has maintained better working conditions and wage levels than any trade union could have achieved. The government cited the high wage levels and working conditions in Penang and the Klang Valley as indicative of how full employment guarantees workers' rights.[12]

A survey by the Malaysian American Electronics Industry (MAEI), which represents 16 U.S. firms indicated that in 1994, after six straight years of 8% economic growth or better, wages in Malaysia were higher than in most other Asian countries and were rising at more than 9% a year. The survey revealed that wages of electronics workers rose by more than 100% between 1980 and 1990.[13]

Flexiwages

With increases in incomes and a shortage of skilled workers in Malaysia, substantial interest has been evoked by employer plans to link compensation packages to productivity so that firms can maintain their competitive edge. Malaysian firms also would like to devise payment systems to retain their core unit of skilled employees. In the 1990s Malaysia has been exploring the idea of a flexible wage system, similar to that used in Singapore and modeled after the Japanese arrangement. This has been a reaction to the wage rigidities caused by the traditional three-year collective bargaining agreements which make it difficult for employers to adjust rapidly enough to changing market conditions.

Malaysian employers argue that five features of the collective bargaining process tend to contribute to wage rigidity. First, since each contract matures at a different time, this may contribute to the bunching of wage increases over time so that wage costs will eventually escalate. Second, the minimum three-year validity of contracts tends to delay or prevent wage adjustment, so that the phasing in of wage agreements is often not synchronized with economic reality. Another reason for rigid wages is that some contracts incorporate automatic seniority increments and contractual bonuses that exceed the growth of productivity or the going rate of consumer price inflation. As a result, companies which agreed to give bonuses in good times are forced to continue paying bonuses even when they suffer losses. Wage rigidity can also be caused by wide gaps between the maximum and minimum wage levels in a particular salary scale, which are further widened when rewards are given based on seniority or experience rather than on productivity or performance. Finally, the industrial court, in settling disputes, tends to base its award for wage increases on the cost of living, as derived from the consumer price index (CPI). This is often done with little regard for the financial implications on the industry concerned and possible effect on related or similar industries.[14]

Union Opposition

The National Labor Advisory Council (NLAC) reached a consensus in December 1991, on the need for such a flexible system, but the implementation of wage reform was not resolved and agreed upon by all parties concerned. In fact, strong union opposition was expected and soon developed. The MTUC initially rejected the government's flexi-wage proposals and formed The Technical Committee on Wage Reforms, which announced labor's conditions for acceptance of the wage reforms, including a demand for the new system to retain fixed annual adjustments and increments based on seniority. The Technical Committee proposed its amendments to the wage system to the NLAC, hoping that the new system would be given a three-year trial period.[15]

THE MEF PROPOSALS

In August 1990, bank employees consented to listen to the MEF proposals for a flexi-wage system. The National Union of Bank Employees temporarily relented in its opposition following certain government assurances. The new system entailed salaries being calculated on the basis of individual and company performance. The union still believed that this system disadvantaged the lower income workers and intended to make a strong stand with the backing of the full Malaysian Labor Organization.[16]

In early 1991, predictions were that anticipated large wage increases would be moderated by the adoption in 1992 of a flexible wage system.[17] In February 1992, the hopes for reform brightened at an NLAC meeting. Although what exactly was proposed was far from clear, the Malaysian Employers Federation agreed to give trade unions access to company financial and nonfinancial information which is relevant in determining wages. In return the Malaysian Trade Union Congress dropped its demand for a minimum wage. What was surprising was that, although the MTUC and MLO accepted the principle that wage reform must be based on labor productivity and company performance, they also persuaded the MEF to stop pursuing a flexi-wage system. This seemed odd because flexi-wages were supposed to reflect labor productivity and profitability.[18] Such a system, common among other newly industrialized countries, ties a portion of salaries to a measure of corporate performance such as profits or turnover.

THE BREAKTHROUGH IN MINING

The first flexi-wage system was to be implemented in August 1992, in the mining industry when mining companies and unions were expected to finalize an agreement on a flexible wage system in the near future. It was the first industry to do away with the collective wage system. Under the proposed system, employers would pay additional bonuses to workers once tin prices exceeded $17 per kilogram. While mandatory increments would be abolished, annual increments would be kept to a minimum. The new system would affect 8,000 workers who were represented by the National Mining Workers Union, the All-Malaysian Industry Staff Union and the Mines Security Guards Union.[19]

To extend flexible wages to other industries, unions have to be convinced that the performance-related wage system is an adjusting mechanism used to reduce labor costs without resorting to layoffs unless absolutely necessary. Furthermore, if the performance-related wage program is to succeed, employers need to adopt a participative management style in working out an acceptable formula for wage setting. To initiate the system, firms were expected to opt for the profit-sharing model utilized in Singapore.

The existing wage system would be restructured so as to incorporate several features. One aspect was that an income stability component, which is a basic wage as part of the system, must be sufficient to ensure a decent standard of living and should be above the poverty income line. Also, the basic wage could be revised annually in light of changing economic conditions and a service increment could be offered in recognition of workers' length of service, loyalty, and experience. This annual increment would not exceed 5% of the basic wage or be automatic as it would promote lifetime employment.

A worker who is more productive than the next person will be rewarded in terms of a larger increment or bonuses, or both. In this manner, the employers argued, companies would have a greater chance to survive when times are bad. When times are prosperous, workers would also receive more in terms of increment and bonuses, meaning some element of profit-sharing is feasible.[20]

THE END OF AN IDEA

Although the flexible wage concept was introduced in the tin mining industry, it did not spread. In fact, further implementation of this compensation idea soon stalled. What is baffling is the fact that flexi-wages were discussed by government, employers, and union representatives at the NLAC, the highest tripartite forum on labor issues in the country in early 1992, as previously noted. There, unions led by the MTUC had agreed to wage reform in the private sector. It was the MEF which turned out to be hesitant in the end, since the wage reform would entail sharing all the information in the financial accounts of a company with trade union representatives. The question of trade secrets arose, countered by suspicions of lack of integrity. Several reports were produced and many contentious points agreed to after substantial give-and-take between the employers and the unions. But in the end, it was the Human Resources Ministry which aborted the whole idea.

THE LIM PROPOSAL

The next significant development saw Human Resources Minister Datuk Lim Ah Lek propose wage reform in the private sector to reflect the changing economic scenario, reviving some old, unanswered questions. What happened to those reports and studies which had been painstakingly prepared by the parties involved in the proposed flexi-wage idea? What kind of reform was the ministry thinking of? Until Lim presented a clearer picture of the elements included in the wage reform plan, employers and unions could only speculate on its features. The MTUC and the MLO responded that Malaysia was not ready for the flexi-wage plan. Everyone seemed to be agreed on a more regulated annual wage revision, but for this to become reality, certain basic elements of the existing wage system would have to be eliminated.

Within this context, Lim was required to provide clear guidelines on what the proposed wage reform would comprise if the proposals differed from what had been agreed to by the MEF and the MTUC two years earlier. The minister had the opportunity to examine certain other salary systems around the world, even citing the system practiced by Sweden. What was called for was a comprehensive report on the ideal system for Malaysia.[21] In a flexi-wage system, apart from a basic salary, wages would be combined with variable components. It could either be in the form of profit-sharing, where a quantum or a formula could be worked out based on the workers' employment levels, or the variable productivity payment, which simply means wages are dependent on individual worker productivity.[22]

CONTINUED DISCORD

In July 1994, Prime Minister Mohamed expressed his opinion on a need for a productivity-based wage system and said the government would agree to any wage system as long as it was based on a direct link between salary increases and productivity. The MEP proposed that the government introduce guidelines to prevent wages from rising beyond productivity increases or far in excess of the CPI. Wage increases were more than double the cost-of-living increase and raised fears of inflationary pressures if the situation was allowed to continue.

Responding to these concerns, fresh negotiations for a productivity-based wage system in the private sector began at the NLAC. However, employer and union representatives continued to disagree on key factors for the system. Following the slow start, the subject was referred to the NLAC technical committee for further discussion. Minister Lim remained hopeful that an acceptable formula would eventually be worked out by the tripartite body. Among the disputed areas were the measurement of workers' productivity and the extent employers were prepared to share company and industry secrets, including profits.

The government position was that it was time for employers and unions to re-examine the current wage system, which is based on market forces, with many factors dictating the necessity to adopt a new wage system. But the flexi-wage proposal again encountered strong opposition and was not pursued as employers and union leaders at the NLAC failed to reach a compromise solution.[23]

THE EPU PROPOSAL

In August 1994, prospects were for a tight labor market that would continue indefinitely but that government measures should not be confined to checking the inevitability of wage increases. Malaysia's Economic Planning Unit (EPU) stated that the emphasis should be placed on strategies to promote productivity and labor market flexibility. Also, with wage increases of skilled workers demonstrating greater improvements than among the unskilled, upgrading the quality of labor to raise productivity was considered the better option. The EPU director general said: "The entire discussion of wage reform should focus more importantly on how firms can promote productivity and labor market flexibility rather than merely keeping the lid on wages."[24] He stressed the idea that, with the establishment of more technology and knowledge intensive industries in the future, skills upgrading and human resource development would become increasingly important. Mr. Ali believed that the long overdue implementation of a flexible wage system linking wage increases to productivity and profitability should be initiated by a select group of companies which would serve as models for other firms to emulate. He mentioned that real wages increased by as much as 20% between 1988 and 1993 while labor productivity had gained only 5% during the same period.

THE NEW REMUNERATION SYSTEM

While efforts at wage reform floundered in the private sector, such was not the case in public employment. Unperturbed by the demise of the flexible wage proposal in private employment, the government used its basic features and in January 1992, introduced the New Remuneration System (NRS) in the public and civil services. The NRS was intended to raise productivity and efficiency in the civil service. Under the plan, workers' annual increments were tied to individual productivity, which was decided by their respective superiors and heads of departments. Unions, however, argued that leaving it to heads of departments exposed the system to favoritism and abuse. To the MTUC, MLO, and CUEPACS, the NRS was proof of the failure of the flexi-wage concept. Many civil servants complained of unfair appraisals, with staff working directly with the heads of departments or having close rapport with their superiors receiving large pay increases. Cases of bosses' private secretaries and top officials receiving the diagonal annual increments, which also entitled them to the excellent service award, a one-month bonus, and an additional seven-day annual leave, were prime topics of conversation, and ridicule was directed at a system hailed by the Public Service Department as a "99.9 percent" perfect system.

However, undismayed, top government officials defended the system, arguing that only a small number of government employees, especially those not prepared to change and work hard, were complaining about the NRS. Moreover, analysts contended that the problems encountered in the NRS should not be a basis for opposition to the implementation of the flexi-wage concept in the private sector, since the NRS is a relatively rigid version of the flexi-wage system. Another factor cited was the notion that the civil service sector is unchanged and still operates like a public service. Attitude, red tape, and protocol were things that do not disappear overnight, they reasoned.

Definitely, the NRS, with its shortcomings and abuses, provoked complaints from union leaders who said it should not be extended to the private sector. The MTUC and MLO officials stated their firm belief that the NRS was a flawed idea that was not even feasible for the public sector.[25]

COSTS, ANOMALIES, AND UNION PROTESTS

Estimates were that payments would increase by an average of RM1.4 billion ($520 million) per annum. The total cost to the Malaysian government of the New

Remuneration System was projected to be nearly RM7.2 billion ($2.7 billion) during the 1992–96 period. In addition, the government had to pay arrears of RM1.78 billion ($660 million) following an 8% retroactive salary adjustment for civil servants for the 1989–91 period. The prime minister and cabinet members stood to gain the most from the pay revision, receiving salary increases of 100 and 70%, respectively.[26]

The implementation of the NRS has also led to anomalies in the profile of salary increases for various grades of employment. The system has resulted in top ranked officials receiving increases of more than 10%, largely due to higher allowances, whereas the original increase was to be between 8 and 10%. The CUEPACS, in turn, asked for equivalent across-the-board salary increments for all civil servants. Although the government amended the 1977 Public Services Tribunal Act to enable the tribunal to look into such anomalies, CUEPACS pointed out that the powers of the tribunal have in fact been curtailed. The amended act introduced a number of management prerogatives which are nonnegotiable and against which no appeal can be made. These prerogatives include salary structures and salary scales, promotions, transfers, appointments, termination of services, dismissals and reappointments, granting of responsibility to officers, assessments and recognition of qualifications, performance appraisals, and matters related to pensions. In addition, since all anomalies claims have first to be filed with the Negotiation Division before being referred to the tribunal, there is no recourse to the tribunal if rejected by the division. Furthermore, the statute also bars complainants from making press statements on cases which have already been forwarded to the division or the tribunal.[27]

IMPACT ON GRIEVANCE MACHINERY

In line with the implementation of the NRS for the public sector, the government abolished the five existing National Joint Councils through which government employees air their grievances. The five councils, for statutory bodies, local authorities, the industrial and manual group, education services, and general public services, were replaced by three new councils covering the management and professional group, the science and technological group, and the general services group. While the details of the restructuring were being worked out by the defunct councils, the government terminated meetings with the five councils to discuss employee grievances and instead dealt directly with the 200 or so unions in the public and civil services.

This rush to restructure by the government received a mixed response from council officials, many of whom did not see the necessity for the existing machinery to be dismantled. The restructuring decision also split public sector employees. One group of workers supported the changes while another objected to the new machinery. The former consisted of employees represented on the previous NJCs for general public services, education services, and industrial and manual groups. It went so far as to elect officials to lead the three new NJCs. The latter consisted of employees from the previous NJCs for statutory bodies and local authorities who claimed that the restructuring would lead to their abolition. They demanded specific NJC machinery for statutory bodies and local authorities. In addition, the group announced the establishment of a Malaysian Congress of Employees of Statutory Authorities.[28]

NECESSITY FOR REVIEW

In response to complaints directed against the NRS, the government announced it intended to develop a more satisfactory appraisal system upon review of the NRS in November 1994. Eight hundred, fifty thousand civil servants are covered by the plan. The review was necessitated because of general employee dissatisfaction, especially protests from workers in the lower income categories.

The government would consider their claims for a higher minimum salary for the lower-rated workers, bonus payments for 1994, a housing quota for all civil servants, and bargaining rights for the National Joint Councils. The Mohamed administration, nevertheless, defended the system, claiming the NRS is a good system. It admitted "human shortcomings" in certain areas of implementation which drew criticism, but the Human Resources Ministry chastised workers who resisted change and hard work and complained and criticized others constantly.

In a related development, CUEPACS secretary-general A. H. Ponniah said the congress would seek a major review of the NRS, including abolition of the three-level Matrix Salary Schedule, which was the practice prior to the advent of the NRS. He alleged that: "The Matrix Schedule is a fraud. Those who get to Level Two and Three will enjoy higher increments over the years irrespective of their performance for that particular year. It's very unfair."[29] He said incentives could be awarded in other forms, like the excellent service awards, courses, and promotions.

The CUEPACs also sought a more open assessment system and asked that appraisal officers be held responsible for their reports. The congress, which finalized details for its traditional salary adjustment claims, also requested that the civil service allowance be incorporated into salaries and a new formula for larger pensions be formulated.[30]

THE PLIGHT OF THE PLANTATION WORKERS

Malaysian labor activists who seek causes to support need look no further than one sector which has suffered from continued governmental neglect, the status of plantation workers. Although other sectors such as manufacturing and petroleum have experienced more rapid growth in recent years, the plantation industry and tin mining have been important segments of the Malaysian economy for nearly a century. Their labor force is estimated at 269,000, primarily Indian Tamils rather than Malays. In 1991, the three major plantation crops, rubber, palm oil, and cocoa, contributed RM8.3 million ($3.1 million) in export earnings and plantations regularly contributed

8 to 9% of Malaysia's total tax revenue. The plantations occupy a total cultivated area of 10.5 million acres.[31]

Despite the economic significance of the sector, the welfare of the plantation workers has received scant attention in government planning, with their basic needs and standards of living requirements largely neglected. Conditions remain anachronistic despite considerable structural changes in the industry. For example, the industry for the most part is no longer foreign-owned but is primarily under the control of Malaysian nationals, particularly government-financed Malay companies and the state economic development corporations.[32] This transfer of ownership to local hands has not significantly improved working and living standards on the plantations. Workers still earn meager incomes, live in squalid conditions, and suffer from low levels of health care and personal well-being; entrapped in a life of poverty, they are cut off from mainstream Malaysian society and are generally untouched by the rapid economic development of the country as a whole.[33]

After being neglected in the First and Second Malaysia Plans, which concentrated on strategies to reduce poverty among rural Malays, the condition of plantation workers was finally recognized in the Third Malaysian Plan, where they were classified as a poverty category, along with rice farmers, fishermen, coconut farmers, the urban poor, other agricultural workers, and indigenous people.[34] However, government rural poverty programs excluded the plantation sector in the subsequent fourth and fifth five-year plans and placed the burden for alleviating poverty upon employers: "The Government will pay increasing attention to ensuring that employers improve these facilities, such as housing, water, lighting, medical care and schooling."[35]

THE GUEST WORKER PROGRAM

Another complication which has affected the plantation sector for many years is the influence of foreign workers. Under the 1984 Labour Plan, for example, the government tried to regularize the Indonesian labor force in Malaysia by instituting a guest worker program. For decades, illegal immigrants have swarmed over the Straits of Malacca to work in the Malaysian plantations. The guest worker program was introduced partly to appease the sizable Chinese Malay minority, who feared the growing number of Malay-stock people; Indonesians are of the Malay racial stock and speak the same language and the lesser Indian minority, who in fact make up 50% of the plantation workers. The Indians feared for their job security since Indonesians were prepared to work for less pay.

The program turned out to be a total failure, Workers approved and sent on by the Indonesian government were often unemployed white collar workers, totally unsuited to the rigors of plantation life. Most fled, some without even stopping to pick up their passports, after only a matter of weeks. In the meantime, plantation managers continued to take on illegal Indonesian workers to make up constantly falling workforce figures. One of the urgent problems is, of course, the reluctance of Malays, especially younger ones, to live and work on the land. The exodus from country to city has set in and, probably, is now irreversible. Many believe that rubber and palm oil estate owners do not, however, do as much as they could to make plantation life attractive. Many estates even fail to provide the facilities guaranteed by union contracts.

Thus, the Malaysian government finds itself on the horns of a dilemma. It had been pressured by Chinese and Indian factions to stop the flow of illegal Indonesian workers; yet the plantations depended upon these workers to make up their labor force, as deportation of Indonesian plantation workers would make a severe dent in the country's economy.[36] However, rare good news for plantation workers arrived in November 1993, in the form of a government announcement that the ban on recruitment of unskilled foreign workers would be lifted to resolve the labor shortage in the plantation sector. Employers also asked that work permits of foreign plantation workers be extended to a maximum of five years.[37]

DEFINITIONAL EXCLUSION

An important reason the plantation sector has not been provided with sufficient government support is based on the official classification which places the sector in a definitional "no-man's land." Even though a plantation comes under the rural sector in terms of its economic definition, it falls in neither the rural nor urban zone in geographic area classification for development planning purposes because it is in the category of private property. Consequently, government and policy planners say it is not their responsibility but the duty of employers to provide facilities for workers. To make matters worse, the primary responsibility for plantations does not fall under the Ministry of Rural Development but is shared among various ministries such as Human Resource Development, Health, and Education. This bureaucratic procedure has only served to stifle poverty alleviation efforts on plantations with the result that plantation workers, to a large extent, have been effectively denied access to facilities enjoyed by other rural Malaysians.[38]

The Sixth Malaysian Plan (1991–95) admitted the lack of government action vis-à-vis the plantations and vaguely promised that the government would implement specific strategies to improve housing in the sector to enhance the quality of life of the estate populations. But it stated at the same time that employers were responsible for providing some of these facilities, in those areas where large capital expenditures are involved. While no such initiatives were forthcoming from employers, the Ministry of Human Resource Development and the United Planting Association of Malaysia (UPAM) formulated a five-year plan to improve the quality of basic facilities on plantations; the poverty eradication programs of the Sixth Plan, however, have not been extended to them.

According to the ILO and the United Nations, the concept of basic needs have not been met on the plantations. These include two elements: first, certain minimum private consumption requirements of a family such as adequate food, shelter, and clothing as well as certain household equipment and furniture; and second, essential services provided by and for the community at large, such as safe drinking water, sanitation, transportation, health, and educational and cultural facilities. By and large, all these needs in relation to plantations are covered by the "Rump Labour Code, 1993" and the "Workers Minimum Standards of Housing Act, 1966," which require plantation owners to provide these services to their workforce. However, these laws have never actually been enforced on plantations at any point in the history of the sector. This lack of enforcement of employer obligations in combination with the plantations' exclusion from rural development schemes have left the worker communities economically and socially isolated on the fringes of national life in Malaysia.[39]

WAGE LEVELS

Plantation workers' and especially rubber tappers' wages increased at a lower rate than wages of other workers in Malaysia over the 1974–89 period, according to Table 19-1. In contrast, wages in the high growth electronics industry in the same period registered a 225% increase. Even relatively unskilled transport workers, such as bus conductors and truck attendants, had significant pay increases, and semiskilled workers in the tin industry gained between 127 and 176% in earnings. Furthermore, while plantation workers' wages have remained far below other groups in the nation, productivity in the rubber industry over the past 20 years rose by 225% in current price terms and the profit rate at rubber plantations rose about 100%. Obviously, the fact that the workers' wages did not follow suit has helped push down their average

TABLE 19-1
Wages in Selected Industries, Peninsular Malaysia, 1974–89 (RM)

Industry/occupation	1974	1980	1983	1985	1987	1989	Average annual growth rates (1974–89)
Plantation sector							
Rubber tappers	195	259	279	253	289	339	1.73
Oil palm harvesters	193	308	550	372	427	391	2.02
Transport industry							
Bus drivers	211	313	405	410	422	434	2.05
Truck drivers	211	313	405	410	422	434	2.05
Tin miners							
Dredge crew							
Semiskilled workers	208	229	400	449	460	474	2.27
Gravel pump mines							
Semiskilled workers	199	420	496	530	535	550	2.76
Electronic industry							
Production operators	135	275	444	380	470	480	3.55

Source: Ministry of Labor and Manpower, Human Resources, Kuala Lumpur, Malaysia (RM 2.5 = U.S. $1).

income in comparison to the significant improvements gained by workers in other sectors of the economy.[40]

The National Union of Plantation Workers has tried since 1982 to institute minimum monthly wages for rubber tappers, partially to increase their per capita household income. However, this has not had much success. The matter was referred to the Director General of Industrial Relations in 1984 for conciliation and in 1985 for compulsory arbitration, but the industrial court rejected the monthly wage claim, which was a serious setback for the NUPW and hundreds of thousands of plantation workers. Indeed, it would not be wrong to argue that the industrial court itself may have contributed to the estate workers' wages trailing behind inflation and growth in their productivity. In 1990, after a series of sporadic strikes, the Industrial Consent Award for tappers set the minimum wage at RM7.90 ($2.94) for 10 kilograms of latex, with the onus on employers to provide suitable work for at least 24 days a month. Nevertheless, this minimum wage failed to push up tappers' incomes to bring their per capita monthly household income in line with the national poverty-line household income of RM68 ($25) per person per month.[41]

In frustration with their status, 65,000 plantation workers staged a four-day strike, demanding minimum pay of RM350 ($130) a month instead of the piecerate system they worked under. The NUPW instructed its members to return to work after the Labor Minister agreed to refer their case to the Industrial Court for a binding judgment. The 800 farms affected by the strike also employed 50,000 nonunion workers.[42]

The economic difficulties of plantation workers were dramatized in February 1992, when, after almost two years of haggling, cocoa estate workers received a guaranteed minimum wage. This meant they would receive RM6 ($16) a day during the low-crop season, normally February to June, which was more than twice what they received before. While the collective agreement between the Malaysian Agricultural Producers Association (MAPA) and the NUPW union allowed bonuses to be paid as prices rose, it also limited wage increases to 12% in the event cocoa prices exceeded RM4,500 ($1673) per ton.[43] Additional collective agreements were also signed, including the basic salary structure for workers in palm oil and rubber plantations between the MAPA and the NUPW.[44]

CONTRACT LABOR

Significant numbers of contract workers, including numerous illegal immigrants from Indonesia, work on plantations. Working conditions for these laborers compare poorly with those of direct hire plantation workers, many of whom belong to the NUPW union. Legally ineligible to join a union, contract workers are unprotected by the few existing labor regulations. As a result, there is evidence that employers' hiring of contract labor is increasing. Government investigations into this problem have resulted in a number of steps to eliminate the abuse of contract labor. For example, in addition to expanding programs to regularize the status of immigrant workers, the government investigates the complaints of abuses, endeavors to inform workers of their rights, encourages workers to come forward with their complaints, and warns employers to end abuses. Like other employers, labor contractors may be prosecuted for violating Malaysia's labor laws. The government has taken action against labor contractors who breach the law, and has assessed fines. The minimum fine assessed by law is $4,000. Effective April 1, 1994, the minimum fine increased fivefold. In principle, serious violators can be jailed, but, in practice, such punishments are rare.[45]

Moreover, the government opposed a recommendation of a legislator that Section (A) of the Employment Act of 1955, which permits employers to hire contract workers, be repealed. Instead, the government stated that this employment system should be replaced by direct employment. The legislator asked the Malaysian authorities to conduct a study on the employment of contract workers, which he claimed discriminated against local workers. The government response was that the contract system has been proven in the developed countries and was considered to be effective for Malaysia.[46]

Apparently, instead of looking for ways and means to resolve this problem, the government is preoccupied with efforts to import foreign workers to overcome the purported labor shortage on plantation. The flow of immigrant labor encourages the continuation of cheap labor policies on the estates, which in turn has weakened the bargaining position of resident workers. As a result, a rapidly growing number of young people leave the estates to take advantage of the growing economy outside, leaving behind women and older workers on the plantations.[47]

FOREIGN WORKERS

The Malaysian government has become more flexible in its policies toward foreign workers to cope with growing labor shortages. Indonesia continues to be Malaysia's main source for foreign workers. While most Indonesian workers thus far have been unskilled and employed in the plantation and construction sectors, skilled Indonesians are likely to be important for sustaining the growth of Malaysia's electronics and garment industries.

Many "illegals" work in low-skill jobs in the plantation and construction sectors. Although some illegal workers ultimately are able to regularize their immigration status, others depart voluntarily after a few months, while some are formally deported as illegal migrants. These foreign workers had to be recruited as part of the measures introduced by the government to overcome these labor shortages. As an initial step, these workers were brought in for the plantation sector, this was later extended to cover services and manufacturing. As short-term measures, the government has exempted red identity card holders from having to apply for work permits and has also amended the relevant labor laws to increase the permissible overtime limit from 64 hours to 104 hours a month.[48]

In May 1994, the third Malaysia–Indonesia Joint Commission met in Kuala Lumpur and discussed the issues of illegal immigrants from Aceh and Indonesian migrant workers in Malaysia. Both countries agreed to continue with the existing cooperation efforts and exchanged views on ways and means to prevent illegal entry of workers. Unfortunately, no specific examples were verbally expressed to indicate what exactly were agreed upon. The influx of illegal Indonesian workers to Malaysia was described as an "enormous problem." The question remains, with the general agreement, will new laws and regulations be enacted? Earlier, a memorandum of understanding (MOU) was signed, with Indonesia agreeing to facilitate issuance of permits for Indonesians working abroad so that they do not wind up as illegal workers in Malaysia. How effective the MOU has been since then is still too early to say.[49]

AN EVALUATION

Economic development has been the primary factor influencing the government's policies toward unions in the electronics industry, flexible wages, labor conditions in plantations, and the influx of foreign workers. Unlike Thailand, consistently tight labor market conditions, caused by rapid industrialization, has created shortages of semiskilled and unskilled workers, fueled by a low 3% unemployment rate. This has produced full employment and increasing wage levels.

In electronics, where the majority of firms are multinational corporations, only weak management-controlled, in-house unions have been allowed in order to rein in labor costs. Also, with women making up 90% of the electronics workforce, and in the absence of an equal pay law, lower wage levels have served to placate cost concerns.

The government's attraction toward flexible wage plans in the private sector and the New Remuneration System in public employment, has also been whetted by increased labor costs and the perception that a productivity-linked compensation scheme will lower overall labor costs. However, only the mining industry has adopted the flexi-wage concept as unions in other sectors have opposed the idea until it is fully clarified and they can be certain of the objectivity of measurement criteria and the truthfulness of management's profitability.

Domestic workers, disenchanted by the prospects of jobs in the plantation sector, have departed in large numbers, and the government is relying on the importation of large numbers of foreign workers, mainly Indonesians, to alleviate the resultant labor shortage. The fact that many are illegal and not eligible for union membership weakens the power of the NUPW union and leads to exploitation by owners who pay low wages and force them to endure long hours and substandard working conditions.

Naturally, foreign workers are willing to accept lower wages and difficult employment conditions. However, these propensities undermine existing labor standards, incurring the enmity of Malaysian workers. There is considerable potential for social unrest in this situation, which could be avoided if protective legislation is extended to the foreigners. Existing laws seek only to prevent the illegal hiring of foreign employees and the law that provides for equal pay for both domestic and foreign labor has not been consistently enforced.

Ideally, a country should be willing to accept foreign workers so long as the demand for workers locally exceeds its supply. It is natural for people to migrate from poorer countries to their richer neighbors. There would not be any immigrants if Malaysia had nothing to offer them. However, advising employers not to exploit their foreign laborers because their employment is so convenient and advantageous from a business perspective and treating them humanely may be an unrealistic approach. It would be more realistic for the corporate sector and the government to review and modify policies which impede optimum employment and utilization of human resources.

In the long term, Malaysia may be forced to be selective in its choice of investments, preferring more technology and capital-intensive projects to reduce pressures on its labor supply. Prospective investors should be informed about the labor situation in Malaysia and not be confused by the entirely different scenarios in Indonesia and Thailand, although Thailand is in the preliminary stages of a transition from labor-intensive to capital-intensive industry, despite a surplus of unskilled labor. Malaysia is leaning in the same direction.

Some time ago in London, participants at an investment seminar were astonished when told that labor-intensive industries are no longer welcomed in Malaysia. One investor, who had been keen to relocate in Malaysia commented, "I thought you guys had surplus labor."[50] Malaysia used to. But the employment scenario has drastically changed in the 1990s and if these problems are not addressed seriously, the tight labor market situation in the year 2000 will become even more critical than present projections.

CHAPTER 20

Malaysia and the World Scene

As the world moves toward a global economy, differences in labor standards, worker organization, and labor relations policies among countries at varying levels of development become critical variables in trade and investment decision making. Generalized System of Preferences (GSP) problems plagued Thailand and Indonesia while China had to deal with most favored nation issues. Malaysia also has been subjected to international opprobrium amid allegations it suppresses worker rights while countenancing exploitative labor standards.

These situations have arisen against a background where labor rights have assumed increasing importance on the international agenda as labor movements in many nations emphasize their influential role in trade and development strategies. The International Labor Rights Education and Research Fund (ILREF) has recommended the increased publication of foreign labor rights violations and the consideration of these violations when the United States conducts trade negotiations.[1] These challenges to sovereignty have evolved as the world economy shifts from a nation-based economy to a single, global economy.

In this, the last chapter in Part V, we examine the nature of these challenges and Malaysia's responses, including the reactions of the employer community and labor organizations.

THE GSP PROGRAM

The Generalized System of Preferences (GSP) program is an important one for Malaysia. Since it was introduced in 1964 by the United Nations Conference on Trade and Development (UNCTAD), Malaysian exporters have taken full advantage of the scheme, which gives developing countries tariff-free or concessionary tariff access into three major markets, the United States, Europe, and Japan. Malaysian exports to these three markets under the plan were valued at RM 14.5 billion in 1992, which was 14% of the country's total exports.

To a certain extent, the GSP arrangement has helped Malaysian exporters establish firm footholds in the major markets, contributing in no small way to its rapid rise into the world's top 25 trading nations list. Indeed, Malaysia recorded one of the most impressive climbs up the ladder, from a lowly forty-first ranking in 1973 to nineteenth in 1993. Malaysia's objective is to become the world's fifteenth largest trading nation by the year 2000.

However, as Malaysia takes giant strides forward in international trade and in its industrialization process, it also increasingly faces the danger of losing its GSP privileges. The United States, which joined the GSP program in 1968, has been debating whether to graduate Malaysia from the plan while the European Union is also reviewing its GSP status with the intention of ensuring that the benefits are better spread among the needy countries, with percentage gains by any one country capped at 20%.

In most cases, the loss is justified as the products have reached their competitive need level, which means that a product has captured 50% or more of the market, and is therefore due for phase-out. The United States, for example, has in the past removed several Malaysian products from its GSP scheme, such as rubber gloves and rubber threads. The European Union, in announcing its plans to revamp the program, also gave the assurance that the European Commission will not make brutal or radical changes, and will make the cut less painful by phasing out over two years the products which are no longer eligible for the privilege. In addition, decisions will be based on the level of gross domestic product per capita and the relative importance of manufactured goods in the countries concerned. Malaysia hopes that when the new GSP plan is eventually announced by the European Union, it will not contain "social clauses" linking trade benefits to labor rights, which appear to be increasingly popular weapons used in the developed world against the developing countries.

Malaysia has no quarrel with GSP removal if its products have become competitive. The government has repeatedly warned the private sector that as it sharpens its competitive edge and captures a larger slice of the world market, the GSP status will be withdrawn. After all, the program is not meant to be a permanent crutch for developing countries to gain access to markets. Certainly, if the crutch is removed there will be an initial painful period of adjustment but Malaysian companies have shown that they are capable of moving ahead of the competition, through various measures such as improved productivity and product innovation.

What bothers Malaysia is if the GSP-granting countries start using the program as a bludgeon to ensure that developing nations adhere to their definition of human rights, international labor standards, and environmental concerns. Malaysians believe that Americans are really more concerned about their inability to compete in the international marketplace than for the welfare of workers in developing countries. GSP privileges should, therefore, be granted on the basis of need, which was the primary criterion anyway for eligibility when the program was introduced. Any digression from this objective is unacceptable and defeats the very purpose of helping developing countries compete on a more equal footing with industrialized countries.[2]

CHRONOLOGY OF THE GSP PETITIONS

On June 1, 1988, the AFL-CIO submitted a petition to the U.S. Trade Representative (USTR) urging that Malaysia's tariff preferences under the U.S. Generalized System of Preferences be withdrawn on the grounds that Malaysia did not respect internationally recognized workers rights. In April 1989, the USTR announced that Malaysia had been determined "to be taking, and to have already taken, steps to afford internationally recognized worker rights."[3] As a result, Malaysia retained its GSPs benefits. In April 1990, the International Labor Rights Education and Research Fund, the AFL-CIO, and the International Brotherhood of Electrical Unions filed petitions against Malaysia. The GSP Subcommittee determined that those petitions failed to provide sufficient new information as required by the GSP regulations to warrant another rights review in Malaysia, and so the petitions were rejected for review. In 1991, ILRERF filed another petition against Malaysia which was rejected for review on the same grounds as those in 1990.

The ILRERF claimed that the most significant violation occurred in September 1990 with the dismissal of workers at the Harris electronics factory. The workers were claiming collective bargaining rights, and dismissal followed the ILRERF's unsuccessful petition in 1990. No petitions were filed in 1992. In 1993, the AFL-CIO filed another petition against Malaysia. The AFL-CIO criticized the Malaysian government for threatening to deregister MTUC and MLO. The petition repeated criticisms contained in previous petitions concerning the government's restrictions on unions in the electronics sector and delays in the adjudication of claims in the Industrial Court. The petition also argued that Malaysia's recent economic growth placed it at level of development where they should meet a higher standard than the one they were held to in 1988. A decision was pending in a case characterized as complex.

Malaysia responded that it was prepared to lose its GSP privileges if it had exceeded the "competitive need" level but was not prepared to lose them on issues relating to human rights or the environment. The Malaysian government believes that such issues are best discussed by the ILO, which brings together governments, employers, and unions. In countering U.S. efforts to introduce these issues before the World Trade Organization, Malaysia feels that the WTO should be concerned with liberalizing world trade and ensuring the benefits are spread equitably among member nations, rather than matters involving minimum wage levels, the exploitation of child and slave labor, and collective bargaining.[4]

THE TRADE–LABOR RIGHTS LINKAGE

Malaysia tried to rally developing nations to fight Western moves to link trade with minimum wages in the global trade regime to be governed by the WTO. The proposed linkage was denounced by the Association of Southeast Nations, (ASEAN) and the Group of 15 (G-15) developing countries as an attempt by the economically flagging West to erode the competitiveness of fast-rising Third World nations, particularly those in East Asia. The United States and France, in particular, pushed for the wage–trade link in the WTO, which they hoped would also monitor workers' rights and the use of child or bonded labor to produce cheap exports. The Chinese government agreed that the proposed link would have a serious negative impact on developing countries and that Malaysia could count on China's support, although China was not a GATT member.[5]

THE MTUC POSITION

The Malaysian Trades Union Congress, somewhat surprisingly came out in full support of Prime Minister Mohamed's stand against a global minimum wage. It said it would oppose it during debates at the international level, although some unions from developed countries would like to see the imposition of this standard. A MTUC official maintained that a global minimum wage is an attempt to erode the competitive edge of developing countries, and dictating how workers in developing countries are paid is another protectionist effort to impose conditions on free trade. While it is neither possible nor practical to set a global minimum wage, every country including Malaysia should have its own national minimum wage. He stated that it is in Malaysia's national interest to see that its workers are accorded a minimum standard of housing, food and other benefits. Singapore was cited as an example of a country whose National Wage Council sets wage levels and the parameters for wage increases which in no way makes the republic uncompetitive in the world marketplace.

A separate MTUC statement meanwhile said what was needed was not a global minimum wage but a global regulations for social rights and the right of unions to exist, organize and carry out collective bargaining. The Malaysian government, however, disagreed, saying there should not even be a national minimum wage in Malaysia, let alone a global minimum wage, and there should not be a link between trade and extraneous issues like universally accepted labor standards:

> If it has got to do with issues of wages and labour, this has to be dealt with by the appropriate organization, and we have the ILO that takes care of this.... Each industry is different. We have industries that are labour-capital-and technology-intensive. What is possible is for the particular industry itself to set the norm for wages that should be paid.[6]

A SPLIT IN LABOR RANKS

The MTUC reportedly was working with the ICFTU to establish the linkage while the MLO and CUEPACS were inclined to oppose. An ICFTU spokesperson said the ICFTU wanted the social clause to cover five areas. They are the right of workers for freedom of association, the right for collective bargaining, standards against child labor, polities opposing forced labor, and equality of treatment for men and women.

THE MEF STANCE

The Malaysian Employers Federation (MEF) was also opposed to the imposition of an international minimum wage as a means to put all nations on an equal footing in trading. It said wages should be related to the cost of living. Generally, the cost of living in developing countries is lower than in developed countries. The MEF stated:

> We in MEF have never advocated the concept of a minimum wage even nationally, and of course we oppose any move to introduce it on a world scale.... This should not be globalized on the pretext of providing a better deal for the workers.... There is no need to obtain help for advocates of the international minimum wage or proposers of social clauses.[7]

The MEF believes that although the world has become more interdependent, international trade is still based on the age-old notion of comparative advantage. Relatively lower wage costs, accompanied by relatively lower costs of living in developing countries are very much the cost advantage these countries possess. It is only in well-managed countries and enterprises that workers continue to prosper, and the prosperity itself induces them to bargain for and get the benefits of development, including higher wages and better working conditions. The MEF announced its hope that the various trade unions in Malaysia would support the pronouncement made by the MTUC that it would oppose attempts to introduce a minimum international wage standard.

THE "SOCIAL CLAUSE"

When the 81st International Labor Conference was convened in Geneva on June 8, 1994, government, employer, and worker representatives from some 150 members of the ILO, the oldest United Nations subsidiary, converged on Geneva for the annual ritual. Except that this turned out to be no ordinary ritual. Following close on the heels of the world trade ministers' meeting to ratify the Uruguay Round agreement, which saw developing countries at odds with their industrialized counterparts over a proposed linkage of social clauses with trade, the ILO conference, usually an academic exercise to discuss issues affecting the world of work, came to the verge of a verbal encounter that threatened to explode into a long-standing war on the very issues that threatened to disrupt the Marrakesh meeting in April involving GATT.

The developed countries, led by the United States, were again the proponents of linking the social clause with trade. As in their attempt to include the social clause in the WTO agenda, their participation in the ILO conference was to press the point that labor and trade union rights, wages, and social security have become relevant in the context of international trading practices. The United States and France, together with the Group of Seven (G-7) countries, decided that developing countries, like India and China, are grossly underpaying their overworked workers, making goods made in China or made in India competitive and more affordable in the international markets. Hence, the G-7 countries had decided that there should be a global minimum wage for the developing countries' workforces. Also, in the social clause, there should be a limit to permissible working hours, workers must have the right to unionize, and unions the right to stage industrial strikes.

Such attempts to regulate trade were not new. There were numerous attempts in the past using different pretexts and platforms. Human rights, copyrights, birth rights, even the rights of trees not to be chopped down for firewood have been used. Developing countries were told that their forests should be sustainable, and that they should adopt property rights and should respect the democratic rights of the people to resist economic progress. Now there were demands for the right of the workers in developing countries to be paid as much as their counterparts in developed countries, to work fewer hours, to be able to form unions and down tools when there was a dispute. They have become the champions of workers in the developing world.

In Malaysia's case, as it turned out, there is a clear division between the government and the largest trade union center, the MTUC, on the question of the social clauses. The MTUC supports the imposition of the social clause because its leaders think the clause will help improve the position of Malaysian workers. The government, on the other hand, argues that it is not against the MTUC if they have workers' interest in mind. Prime Minister Mohamed claims that Malaysian workers are where they are now not because of any assistance from the developed countries or their trade union attempts to ensure that Malaysia ratifies international labor standards. He claims that sustained economic growth, political stability, prudent spending and inflation policies, harmonious industrial relations, and the ability of the government to attract foreign investment are the major reasons for the luxuries Malaysian workers now enjoy.

The government claims Malaysian' real per capita income is only $500 ($1 = RM 2.59) less than that of the U.S. Prime Minister Mohamed, known for his virulent anti-Western rhetoric, claims that "Malaysia ratifies more ILO conventions than the U.S., so why is it talking about labour rights and standards?"[8] His position is that developing countries have to resist the attempt to use the ILO and international labor standards to slow down their development. It is fine to talk about earning high salaries and working 40-hour weeks instead of 60 hours. But developing countries need to develop first before they can afford to think about these matters. There are other more pressing concerns, like job creation and easing unemployment, training the workforce, and increasing productivity.

ILO ASSISTANCE

At the same conference, Malaysian employer delegates said that technical assistance from the ILO should not be conditioned upon ratification of its labor standards and conventions. The MEF president, in his address to the plenary session of the conference, said to do so would only result in the assistance being directed to member countries who needed it least. Instead, Datuk Dr. Mokhzani Abdul Rahim said the ILO should reevaluate the relevance of its existing conventions and standards in terms of their effectiveness and suitability in today's world. For that matter, the

record of ratification of conventions by member countries, including developed
countries, which so readily criticized the developing countries has been dismal and
there is no sign that this situation would change in the near future, he alleged.

The ILO provides assistance to its member nations in the form of technical
cooperation programs and research and information. Its membership stands at 169
countries. Malaysia joined soon after its independence in 1957. ILO projects are
funded directly by national development aid agencies of donor countries and trust
fund arrangements with recipient countries. In 1992 the projects amounted to some
$65 million. Its technical cooperation projects are focused on, among other things,
employment and development, alleviation of rural poverty, development of cooperatives, occupational health and safety, and industrial relations. The major share of
technical assistance goes to Africa, followed by the Asia-Pacific, the Americas, West
Asia, and, to a lesser extent, Europe. There is fear, primarily among developing
members, that the ILO's assistance will be made conditional upon ratification of its
conventions and standards, especially in view of the move to link social clauses,
which include international labor standards, with trade and access to markets.

Since its inception in 1919, the ILO has adopted 155 international labor instru-
ments for ratification. Malaysia has ratified 11 of the conventions, but recently
denounced Convention 105 on Abolition of Forced Labor because of the overlapping
definition with earlier conventions. Of interest is the fact that the ratification record of
developed countries is not necessarily better than developing countries. France has
ratified the most conventions, 110 as of 1990, while the United States has ratified less
than 10.[9]

THE MTUC AND THE SOCIAL CLAUSE

The MTUC position regarding the social clause controversy is that some countries have confused the social clauses with a global minimum wage, which the labor
congress is opposed to. It believes that social clauses are aimed at safeguarding
workers' right and will force countries, especially the developing ones, to set their
own national minimum wages, recognize basic worker rights such as striking and
picketing, and banish socioeconomic evils like child and forced labor. In effect, the
social clauses will ensure that Malaysian workers are not manipulated by employers,
and that whatever government is in power will have to guarantee that fundamental
rights of workers are recognized.

The MTUC feels that Malaysia and ASEAN and many other developing countries are wrong about the social clauses; or, rather, confused about their objectives.
Malaysia had been among the first to point out that the social clauses will lead to the
establishment of a global minimum wage. It had also illustrated how the social clauses
were created by the feeling among the leading industrialized nations that they were
disadvantaged by the lower wages and longer working hours, hence greater productivity of the developing countries. If Malaysia, India, and China, for instance, are
forced to adhere to international labor standards, it means their workers will enjoy the

same rights and benefits as workers in the developed countries, which include downing their tools, closing airports, stopping trains, and halting production lines if their demands for higher wages or shorter working hours are not met.

The social clauses do not explicitly propose a global minimum wage, at least not in the sense that there must be only one minimum wage level for all countries. What Malaysia and other governments in developing countries fear is the fact that the industrialized nations had meant to make the minimum wage a global phenomenon, through social clauses. If everyone accepts the social clauses, the minimum wage in Malaysia does not have to be the same as that of India, but both countries will have a national minimum wage. It is understood that the minimum wage of India or Malaysia, sooner rather than later, would have to measure up to the higher minimum wages in the industrialized nations, especially when trade unions are, at the same time, given the strike weapon.

However, the Malaysian government's position is that the most representative labor body in the country, as the MTUC is so fond of calling itself, does not represent the views of developing countries. It heatedly criticized the MTUC position, which it claimed was similar to that of Western trade unions, such as the AFL-CIO and the International Metalworkers Federation. But more disturbing to the Malaysian authorities was the MTUC's failure to question the track records of those who proposed the link between the social clauses and trade. The fact that Malaysia may not have ratified many international labor standards set by the ILO, but has ratified more conventions that the United States, was not mentioned by the labor congress. The Japanese work longer hours than any nation but this too was not questioned. For that matter, the MTUC failed to ask a number of other relevant questions of the proponents of the social clauses and their trade unions at the ILO annual meeting in Geneva. For instance, why is it harder to form a trade union in the United States than in Malaysia? Why are there double-digit unemployment rates in the industrialized countries? Why, with minimum wages, are their workers still staging regular industrial strikes for more wages?[10]

ASEAN OBJECTIONS

Malaysia gained the support of ASEAN at the eighty-first ILO meeting when the regional body also objected to the linking of the social clauses to trade. ASEAN's views were agreed to also by the United Kingdom, China, Sudan, Egypt, India, Bangladesh, and Pakistan. As a result of ASEAN's position, the ILO proposed that the issue be now discussed in a governing body, and a working group was established to provide a more in-depth analysis on the matter.

ASEAN's contention was that social clauses, particularly labor issues, or what Western nations termed as core labor standards, should be dealt with by the ILO, where these matters should be discussed to see how the ILO could play a more effective role to seek greater adherence consistent with its premise that persuasion, dialogue, and cooperation should be the means to assist developing countries to comply with ILO standards The ILO has always held the view that trade restrictions or compulsory equalization of social costs would negate its premise that free trade should be encouraged because of its potential to spur economic development and improve the conditions of life and work. The Malaysian government agrees with this posture, believing that the World Trade Organization should focus on trade promotion and should not impose new conditions that unilaterally inhibit the development efforts of the developing countries.[11]

MALAYSIA AND MINIMUM LABOR STANDARDS

Dr. Mahathir Mohamed, the Malaysian prime minister, is one of the most outspoken critics of the idea of worldwide minimum labor standards. Supporters of minimum standards, especially among trade unions, therefore assume that Malaysia is teeming with sweat shops and child labor. A devil's advocate might argue that there are poor working conditions in some sectors of the Malaysian economy, particularly among immigrant plantation workers, and there are also some restrictions on trade unions. But in most other respects these views are being quickly superseded by Malaysia's rapid economic progress, which is providing its workers with more options.

With unemployment running at less than 3% and annual GDP growth exceeding 8%, Malaysian workers can afford to be selective even if, in sectors such as electronics, they are not allowed to join independent unions. The result is that annual labor turnover is soaring, up to 45% in some areas, and average wages are rising at nearly 7% a year and will converge with U.S. wage rates in about a decade. Mohamed argues that these wage increases are not being won at the expense of decent employment standards since Malaysian workers have some job security and the government regularly encourages employers to adopt high standards of health and safety.

The MTUC secretary general, taking the side of the government, has said that even trade unionism is "semifree" because unions throughout much of the manufacturing sector operate with greater freedom that in most other countries in the region. It is also true that Malaysia's high wages are already causing many assembly operations to relocate to China or Thailand. The government is attempting to emulate neighboring Singapore in shifting to high value-added production. Malaysia's GDP per capita is now nearly $8,000, using purchasing power parity, just above Greece, the poorest European Union nation, so it can no longer compete with the new low-wage Asian competition. Therefore, Malaysia is now too advanced to be affected by most of the minimum labor standards being proposed by Western countries and unions.

The question can be asked why Malaysia's prime minister persists in his attacks on the West and on Malaysia's own trade union leaders. Perhaps his accusations of Western hypocrisy on labor issues have helped to raise his standing in the developing world. He is also worried that the West will try to impose what he believes to be an inappropriate form of trade unionism on countries such as Malaysia through minimum labor standards.

Yet beneath the rhetoric, some flexibility is apparent. Mr Anthony Yeo, the senior official at the Ministry of Human Resources who represents Malaysia at ILO meetings, opposes any link between trade and labor standards but has stated that the ILO should be given more authority to stamp out real abuses, such as child and slave labor. He also says that, while restricted company unions are currently the most appropriate structure for the Malaysian electronics sector, a different approach might be adopted at some future stage. Moreover, if Malaysia is to make the transition to a high value-added economy, it will have to relax the paternalism that pervades the country's culture because modern production methods require an educated workforce capable of making independent decisions. The ICFTU believes also that citizens will have to be trusted to form free trade unions. Developing countries such as Malaysia, which have advanced beyond the first stage of industrialization, have most to gain from minimum standards legislation which will protect it from being undercut by the cheapest labor economies before it is ready to switch to higher value-added production.[12]

CLOSING COMMENTS

Partisan rhetoric aside, certain basis truths exist. Developing countries fear the social clause will be used as means to achieve an end for trade rather than the other way around. For example, ASEAN feels that the U.S. is trying to levy extra duties on products of countries which enjoy the advantage of cheap labor. By making the WTO adopt the social clause, most developing countries fear that it will open the flood gates to link trade with other issues such as minimum wages and labor standards.

The only edge that Malaysia has is its competitive wage levels, which as we have seen, are not low and certainly not as low as they used to be. This appears to be the only competitive advantage the country still enjoys. It does not have the technological nor the latest research and development capabilities. With full employment and the demand for increased personnel there has been an upward pressure on wages. As such, to stay competitive, and especially in the face of rising wages, it is important and essential that productivity be improved.

In this context, Dr. Mohamed's anti-Western outbursts may prove counter-productive because Western countries will view his rhetoric as nothing more than xenophobic verbiage. The truth is that effective unionism does not exist in Malaysia. The MTUC is independent but has not been allowed to progress beyond in-house unions in the electronics industry rather than industry-wide or national forms of representation. Nevertheless, the MTUC has been able to enlist support from international labor organizations and concurrent international condemnation of the government's labor relations policies.

Findings and Reflections

We have examined economic, political, and sociological variables that have influenced the development of worker rights and labor standards in four East Asian countries. Nine propositions were posited to structure our analysis of this topic. Sufficient evidence has been compiled so that we have arrived at the following findings relating to each premise, which will be examined in turn at this point. Each nation has serious problems.

THE ARGUMENTS THE LEADERS OF CHINA, INDONESIA, MALAYSIA, AND THAILAND ARE PRESENTING TO COUNTER WESTERN DEMANDS FOR THE INTRODUCTION OF MINIMUM LABOR STANDARDS IN TRADE AGREEMENTS

Human rights activism is often resented by East Asian leaders as the product of an imported and derogatory Western commentary on their heritage and traditions. Nevertheless, the incorporation of social clause rules into international trade agreements are important because they include such fundamental worker protections as freedom of association, the right to collective bargaining, and the prohibition of forced labor. These rules, however, may not be adopted readily because newly industrializing countries, fearing protectionism, oppose any discussion of worker rights at GATT or the new World Trade Organization (WTO).

Malaysian and Indonesian resentment of Western human rights assertiveness has resulted in these countries systematically and concertedly criticizing the Western approach to this issue in the developing nations. The Malaysian Prime Minister Mohamed Seri Mahathir has been very vocal in attacking the West. He contends that the norms and precepts for the observance of human rights vary from society to society and from one period to another within the same society. He believes that in the developing countries, individual human rights should be balanced with the level of national economic development, otherwise it would damage social stability and economic growth.

The governments of China, Malaysia, and Indonesia, in particular, find it

411

difficult to recognize the legitimacy of Western-style human rights. Instead, they believe that social harmony and control should prevail over individual political freedom. In our opinion, a distinction should be made between trade sanctions aimed at protecting against less than minimal labor standards in the developing nations of East Asia and those directed against serious abuses of worker rights. For example, the argument for leveling working conditions such as hours, sick pay, or even safety standards, as some Western nations want, is driven mainly by fears about competition. On the other hand, concerns about child labor, slavery, and the right to form a labor union seem to be of a different nature. On the surface, at least, there might appear to be a stronger case for using trade restrictions to persuade other countries to guarantee such human rights. The challenge is to find an appropriate balance between the rights and desires of the individual worker and the needs and expectations of the nation in which he or she lives. Enforceable international labor standards are still in their developing stage, needing to catch up with rapid changes in the global economy. What worker rights advocates can bring to the debate is a defense of self-help by workers turning to labor unions as an expression of a human right. Organizing, bargaining, strikes, peaceful picketing, political activity, and other union actions should be treated as basic rights, not variable benefits.

THE INHIBITING EFFECTS OF DIVERGENT NATIONAL VALUES AND CULTURAL CHARACTERISTICS ON IMPROVEMENTS IN THE STATUS OF WORKER RIGHTS AND LABOR STANDARDS

In Indonesia, cultural values apparently serve to inhibit union militancy, especially in foreign joint ventures. Foreign firms have been advised by the manpower minister to keep in mind the strong (government-endorsed) cultural preference for consensus and dislike of confrontation. He noted that workers should have too much "sense of responsibility for anything that happens to the company" to engage in strikes. Rather he indicated that the government favors collective agreements to create and develop harmonious relationships.

The fact of the matter is that Indonesian workers legally have the right to strike but would encounter serious government resistance to such actions. The Suharto regime is eager to keep foreign investors happy, especially those in export-oriented industries, and would oppose any actions that would potentially be politically disruptive.

Many Western observers and scholars have tended to classify "Asians" as a discrete class of people with similar personal characteristics and traits. In reality, however, there are significant differences across and between various Asian cultures. In order to explain such differences an analysis must be made of how culture, and factors that influence cultural variations, affect worker attitudes, perceptions, and values. This requires a four-pronged inquiry into four aspects of cultural influences on the workplace; historical background, current economic and political structure, geographical considerations, and language characteristics. They maintain that the variables influence the general cultural milieu that characterizes the work environment.

The economic success of the last two decades among developing countries in East Asia seems to have involved three key elements. One is the presence of a work force which has a solid basic education. Then there is a government policy oriented toward export-led growth. And finally, there is a cultural respect for authority (although expectations of what authority owes to subordinates varies). For example, in dispute settlement, Malaysian employers, instead of following the Japanese model where every possible attempt is made to resolve disputes through negotiations and discussions with employees, follow the formal dispute settlement procedures prescribed by law and/or by collective agreements, which are not very conducive to harmonious labor relations.

Compared to historical events, the economic–political structure usually affects culture in a relatively gradual, continuous manner. Although the economic–political structure is often imposed upon the people as a result of revolution in a country, over time the values imbedded in that structure may be taken for granted, implying that they gradually become part of the culture. China serves as a good example of this phenomenon. Since 1949 the Peoples' Republic of China has been governed by a socialist government, while Taiwan has had a quasi-capitalistic economic system the past 45 years. Although both countries are populated by Chinese who inherited exactly the same culture, 45 years separation has created a significant difference in their value systems. Egalitarianism is advocated by most people on the mainland, while free competition is the norm in Taiwan. Consequently, in a society dominated by egalitarianism, encouraging workers to compete for productivity-based bonuses may not work. Even if rewards can be equitably dispensed on the basis of productivity, resentment over the inequality of income distribution may generate internal conflicts and hurt the morale of workers in general.

THE MEANS TO PROVIDE COUNTRIES AT ALL STAGES OF DEVELOPMENT WITH OPPORTUNITIES FOR GROWTH THAT DO NOT DEPEND ON ABUSES OF LABOR STANDARDS

From the viewpoint of the North American and European labor movements, the extension of advanced labor standards to developing nations everywhere would be ideal. It is therefore necessary to ask what labor standards can be applied that combine effective protection for the greatest number with the implementation of successful plans for national development. The question already suggests part of the answer, namely the need to fine tune the application of labor standards to local conditions, rather than opt for either their wholesale rejection or acceptance. We can classify items commonly included under labor standards into four categories. The first, basic rights, include standards where a global consensus seems to have been attained and which are thus amenable to international monitoring. They include the rights against the use of child labor, involuntary servitude, and physical coercion. The second classification, which can be termed "survival rights," includes the guarantees of a living wage, accident compensation, and a limited work week. The third grouping, which we will label "security rights," includes protection against arbitrary dismissal, the right to survivors' compensation, and programs of retirement compensation. The final classification, which we shall label "civic rights," provides rights to free association, collective representation, and to free expression of grievances.

The intermediate categories, survival and security rights, depend for their implementation on local conditions and do not lend themselves readily to fixed international standards. They are best left to bargaining between workers, employers, and governments, once basic and civic rights have been fully implemented. Negative consequences associated with premature importation of labor standards have involved primarily these intermediate categories, and not those which could plausibly form part of an internationally accepted package of labor rights. Of the two middle categories, it is the implementation of extensive job security, rather than the existence of minimum wage or other survival rights, which has encountered the greatest resistance. The recent trend in China toward contract labor exemplifies the reluctance of private sector employers to maintain the "iron rice bowl" concept of lifetime employment security.

Therefore, apart from basic and civic rights which may become amenable to internationally enforceable standards, the implementation of others also require fine tuning, lest they act as a brake on economic growth or on the extension of minimal protection to the greatest number of workers. A strong argument can be made against the popular dictum that newly industrializing countries function best when wages are allowed to sink to their "natural" levels. Firms that rely on very cheap labor lack incentives to innovate technologically; their workers lack motivation to remain with a particular firm or collaborate with management in increasing its efficiency; their paltry wages also add insignificantly to domestic demand.

THE REASONS WHY POSITIVE ECONOMIC DEVELOPMENTS IN CHINA, INDONESIA, MALAYSIA, AND THAILAND HAVE NOT PRODUCED CONCOMITANT IMPROVEMENTS IN LABOR STANDARDS

In China, rapid economic growth in large urban centers has caused an influx of an estimated 100 million rural migrant workers and has created serious social problems. Where social services are concerned, the claim of migrant workers is not recognized; only permanent residents have the right to subsidized rations and public welfare. Denial of social entitlements means that temporary residents have to be self-sufficient as possible in obtaining their daily requirements.

Migrants who are able to obtain regular work are more fortunate. Most, however, are engaged as temporary employees and do not enjoy job tenure. Many work under appalling conditions, in unsafe and poor working environments, and with no protection against unreasonable working hours. The failure to address welfare needs of workers is often borne out by frequent and serious outbreaks of industrial accidents. Many enterprises where disasters occur are under joint or foreign ownership. The overseas owners concerned are plainly obsessed with maximizing output and cutting costs, to the complete disregard of work safety. Moreover, employer objection to the formation of labor unions and the lack of organization among migrant workers also mean that they are at the mercy of capitalists and managers.

Up to the present, the central and local governments have been unable or unwilling to manage the migratory labor challenge. Existing policies and practices are haphazard, piecemeal, and uncoordinated. No central agency exists to plan, administer, and supervise work relating to the migrant population. National policies, rather than local ones are imperative in dealing with what is after all a national issue.

In Indonesia, there are also problems with labor conditions, even though, in many ways, this country looks attractive to outsiders. Its per capita annual income has increased from about RP162,610 ($70) in 1970 to RP1,626,100 ($700) recently. About 15% of its population lives in poverty, down from 60%. However, there is a darker side of the picture. Its minimum wage is the lowest among the ASEAN nations at less than RP4646 ($2) per day. It has a single, toothless labor union to channel the grievances of its fast-growing industrial population.

During the past decade, Indonesia has developed a larger and more diversified, export-oriented private sector. In spite of frequent government demands, tens of thousands of employers continue to flout the legal minimum wage, with little effective deterrence due to lax enforcement. In response to these and other difficult circumstances, a second national labor union, SBSI, was founded in 1992. Its 250,000 members and supporters have been the object of intimidation following illegal demonstrations in Jakarta. The union has accused the Suharto regime of failing to guarantee freedom of association and trade union rights and many wildcat strikes have occurred, despite severe strike limitations. Presently, although it has the legal right to organize among enterprises with more than 25 employees, the only officially recognized labor union, the All Indonesian Workers Union (SPSI), has been hindered in its organizing efforts at a large number of firms by employers' resistance, government failure to enforce the law, and its own limitations.

These restrictions on worker rights are simply means to prevent gains in wages and working conditions, which is the main issue that attracts investment to developing countries. The figures are staggering, and certainly cannot be considered in light of the cost of living in the industrialized world. Even by the poverty standards in the developing countries we are discussing, a large portion of workers are severely underpaid. The lure of low labor costs is the primary attraction luring multinational corporations to developing nations. When the wages are kept low because of suppression of worker rights, however, and workers are in some cases barely able to survive, the issue becomes much more complicated than a free market approach to labor costs would suggest.

Malaysia is another of the rapidly emerging East Asian economies, which, in recent years, enjoyed sustained annual rates of real economic growth approaching and sometimes reaching double-digit levels. Malaysia's growth rate has averaged 8% or more for eight consecutive years with inflation running at less than 4% annually during this period but there have been problems. One involves the ability of unions to improve the economic status of their membership. Malaysian unions, especially those in the private sector, engage in collective bargaining. The scope of bargaining is quite limited, however. Matters such as promotion, transfer, dismissal, appointment, and allocation of duties cannot be placed on the bargaining agenda. In addition, "pioneer" industries and others nominated by the Minister of Labor cannot provide employment conditions more favorable than those described in Part XII of the Employment Act of 1955 without approval of the Minister of Labor. Some unions have been critical of government labor policies. For instance, the Electrical Industry Workers Union has been openly against the government's "Look East" policy (that is, emulating Japan and South Korea). The National Union of Plantation Workers, the largest national union, has criticized the government's unwillingness to introduce legislation against low-paying contract labor on plantations and industrial estates.

The Malaysian Trades Union Congress (MTUC) coordinates the various unions in Malaysia, but as its members represent several industries, it is not legally recognized as representing worker interests and thus has no bargaining power. The MTUC has filed cases with the International Labor Organization (ILO) charging the government with violation of ILO Convention No. 98 on the right to organize and collective bargaining, alleging that the Malaysian legal system is biased structurally toward employers and in-house unions and that the labor regulations listed such broad discretion in the Director General of Trade Unions that workers were unable to adequately represent their own interests. Further, the government policy is to only allow in-house unions in the electronics industry, prohibiting the formation of independent unions. There also have been alleged violations of child labor laws, inadequate health and safety laws, gender discrimination, and the lack of a national minimum wage.

Another problem involves foreign migrant workers. Malaysia's rapid growth has resulted in serious labor shortages, producing a surge of immigration from neighboring countries, much of it illegal, to fill the urgent need for workers. The government has usually turned a blind eye to illegal immigrant workers because it knows that they are badly needed if economic growth is to continue. Malaysian labor unions, however, take a different view. Consequently, migrant workers have never been offered the help they need by Malaysian unions to improve their working conditions. There are two reasons for this: they are not potential union members and they are considered a threat to Malaysian workers because of the age-old fear of cheap foreign labor underpricing local labor. This fear is exacerbated by the fact that employers of many of the illegal immigrants do not pay social security contributions for them, nor pay them the same wages as paid to Malaysian workers. Unions also fear that some employers are not trying hard enough to employ domestic workers, as this would increase their total labor costs. Estimates of illegal immigrant workers suggest there are hundreds of thousands of them.

Malaysia's current commitment to export-led growth has been officially interpreted as requiring a low-wage policy, ostensibly in the interest of international competitiveness. Increases in labor productivity are rarely translated into increases in real incomes. Thus, increased productivity mainly benefits employers and consumer abroad. While not dismissing the requirements of international competitiveness, much more could have been done and should be done to improve worker incomes, and hence living standards. Such a policy to improve wages for labor would inevitably price out some industries, leaving the more competitive, better paying industries to employ Malaysian workers. Then there will be little need for or motivation to encourage cheap immigrant labor to depress wages. Unfortunately, however, current labor policy traps Malaysian workers in a relatively low-wage economy, perpetuating the relatively small domestic market. The willingness to pay workers more would certainly deepen the size of the domestic market by improving incomes and economic welfare all around.

In Thailand, rapid economic growth has occurred but to a substantial extent, at the cost of low labor standards. For example, Thailand has had a minimum wage since 1972, but estimates are that 30% of the 300,000 unskilled workers in small and medium-sized industries in the Bangkok area are underpaid despite criminal penalties under labor law. Compliance is even worse in the provinces. Most firms have no operational grievance procedures. Thai management is traditionally paternalistic, especially in small- and medium-sized firms.

The Thai labor movement is not as militant as that of Malaysia. This has been attributed to the fact that Thailand has always been a sovereign, independent nation without a colonial past to overcome, unlike Malaysia and Indonesia. No independence struggle was necessary and the working class has remained politically ineffective, as well as weak in size and organization. Both nonpayment of wages and specially difficult working conditions for Thai women are partly attributable to the fact that the labor force is virtually restricted to company unionism.

Furthermore, harassment and murder of outspoken leaders and the ties between many unions and individual political and military officers has restricted the Thai labor movement at the very time the manufacturing base has been expanding. As well, employers have been harsh in their attitudes: job safety arrangements are generally poor; factories located on the periphery of a designated industrial zone do not have to meet standards. The fact that the great majority of factories around Bangkok are small-scale and using obsolete technology compounds union problems in getting minimum wages actually paid, social insurance for members, etc. Widespread use of subcontracting makes it difficult to contact and organize Bangkok workers.

The share of wage-earners in the increased income produced by industry depends to some extent on the effectiveness of minimum wage legislation and the union defense of labor conditions. These in turn depend on the degree of unionization. Yet, only about 250,000 Thai workers out of nearly 7 million in nonagricultural employment are unionized (3.50%), so it is not surprising that the implementation of the minimum wage has been sporadic at best.

The Status of Protective Labor Legislation and Its Implementation

Each of the four countries has a variety of labor laws, with uneven enforcement and inconsistent implementation being the order of the day, as promanagement policies are often directed against effective representation for workers.

In China, a new National Labor Law went into effectonJanuary1, 1995. It seems to be a positive step but it will be sometime before results will be seen and workers already have questioned the law's effectiveness. China's most renowned labor activist, Han Dongfang, said that the new law is a step in the right direction and has good points, but pointed out that it still did not allow workers to strike.

The law itself is modeled on the conventions of the ILO and covers promotions, labor contracts, working hours, protection for female and juvenile workers' wages, social insurance and welfare, and labor disputes, among other issues. However, the law fails to mention collective bargaining, and decisions of wages and hours are still being reached by discussions between employers and individual workers, where the latter normally have little economic leverage. The most notable changes under the law include a worker's right to choose his or her own job, the development of social insurance, mandatory vocational training, a notice period prior to layoff, and the settlement of labor disputes through arbitration. It has been predicted that it will take three to five years before the sufficient supplementary regulations necessary for proper implementation of these legal changes will be in place.

An example of the difficulties inherent in implementation can be seen by the minimum wage situation. Basic and minimum wage regulations were announced in January 1994, recognizing regional differences in the cost of living. They allowed cities and provinces to set their own minimum wage levels so long as they were at least half the local average wage. These levels were to be published by January 1, 1995. It turned out that many provinces and cities failed to meet this deadline. A major area of concern has been enforcement at the local level. While the efforts of the All China Federation of Trade Unions and the Ministry of Labor have been very strong in Beijing, their ability to ensure that local unions and labor bureaus comply with the new law is limited. Decision-making power in China has been highly centralized and does not reach the local jurisdictions, since there is no chain of command between the Labor Ministry and local labor authorities. This means that rural and township enterprises as well as smaller joint ventures are likely to escape compliance for sometime.

In further efforts to offer Chinese workers better protection, the official work week was changed in March 1994 from six days to five-and-a-half, with hours on the job cut from 48 to 44. The new rules allow for working time to be extended or shortened in cases of "special conditions or urgent tasks." These are not defined further under the new ruling and will presumably be subject to local labor department interpretation.

Indonesia has been coming under increasing domestic and foreign criticism, especially from the United States, for illegal labor abuses. The Suharto regime has been threatened with loss of privileges under the Generalized System of Preferences (GSP) if it does not bring its labor laws into conformity with international standards. The United States has focused on three issues: the use of the military to break strikes, the employment of child labor, and the rights of workers to organize. Consequently, the law allowing the armed forces to intervene in labor disputes has been repealed. A law prohibiting the employment of children has been on the books since 1951. Recognizing that it is widely ignored, the government is reviewing it. A regulation has been issued that permits an independent union to negotiate collective agreements at the factory level, but is largely nullified by other laws barring unions not registered by the government from negotiating on behalf of workers and requiring that for a union to be registered, it must have at least 10,000 members. Also, to establish a union under Indonesian law, a group must form 1,000 local chapters and set up province-level organizations in 20 out of 27 regions before it can apply for registration.

Indonesia, with a 80-million strong labor force and up to 40% underemployment, has drawn criticisms for not protecting workers' rights, including the establishment of free labor unions. The only recognized labor organization is the government-controlled SPSI, which does not function as a proper union. Its funding through workers' dues, is collected by the Ministry of Manpower, and the union appears to have no full-time staff, which raises questions about distributions of the funds. The SPSI is also factionalized because of the civil servant groups within the body which are connected to the Golkar functional group, in effect Indonesia's ruling party.

Additionally, if the government owns any shares in a particular business, it is transformed into a public sector enterprise and unions are banned. In practice, the government applies this prohibition if any member of the government owns a portion of the company in his private capacity. This policy encourages firms to solicit high-ranking government officials to invest in the company for a nominal amount.

For much of the nearly three-decade reign of President Suharto, the government has tried to lure foreign business by keeping wages as low as possible and unions as docile as imaginable. This is accomplished to no small extent by appointing the owner of that nation's fortieth largest conglomerate to be Minister of Manpower. His office sets the minimum wage. Also, an owner of another Indonesian conglomerate is the president of what passes as the country's only legal union, the SPSI. These obvious conflicts of interest have gone unnoticed by the government.

Regarding the Indonesian situation, a human rights activist has aptly summed it up: "A union here is not a union, a minimum wage is not a livable wage, and freedoms are not real freedoms."[1]

The right of unions to bargain collectively with their employers is a basic ingredient of worker rights in the industrialized world. Collective bargaining is effectively denied in many developing countries. The primary preventive device is to engage in measures that ensure that unions are never formed. Other practices are utilized as well. Malaysia is a case in point since its policy is to encourage foreign investment at the expense of worker rights.

Malaysia's main labor laws have been recently amended to increase the power of the Human Resources Ministry officials to suspend unions, forbid strikes, unilaterally intervene in any labor dispute, invalidate strike ballots and regulate relations with international labor bodies, as well as prohibiting high-ranking union leaders and their organizations from engaging in political activity.

Labor legislation tends to ensure union docility. For instance, the Trade Union Act restricts the freedom to organize and gives the Registrar of Trade Unions great discretion in registering new unions or suspending existing ones.

On paper the union recognition provisions appear to be liberal. In practice, however, it is extremely difficult to form a new union and the unions are engaged in a constant game of cat and mouse with the Registrar. Applications are regularly rejected. In one case the textile union wanted to organize the Mattel plant, which makes Barbie dolls, but was told it was a toy and not a textile factory and its application was denied. The Registrar can arbitrarily deregister unions, interfere in the administration and functions of unions, and prevent or "prohibit industrial action in furtherance of a legitimate trade dispute."

A further hindrance to union organization develops in the case of companies labeled as "pioneer enterprises." Here, management is exempt from collective bargaining over any terms and conditions of employment established by the Employment Act of 1955. No collective agreement may contain terms more favorable to workers than those contained in that statute, thus removing a major incentive for workers to unionize. Collective bargaining is further limited because if a bargaining impasse is reached, either party can seek conciliation with the Director General of Labor. If conciliation fails, the Minister of Labor may refer the matter to the Industrial Court for compulsory arbitration. The Industrial Court utilizes fixed formulas to award any wage increases, and the formulas are so conservative that the procedure is stacked against unions and denies them any meaningful right to bargain collectively.

The 1959 Trades Union Act also prescribed a certain type of union structure with a 1987 amendment which attempted to weaken national level unions by favoring in-house or company unions. Public employees could be represented only by the in-house variety of labor organization as well as about half of the country's 400 registered private sector unions.[2] Of course, the practice of arresting union officials is not unique to Malaysia. It is also somewhat reminiscent of early American labor history, when fictitious charges were issued against union organizers who were subsequently imprisoned.

The only true and available weapon that workers have to secure improvements in their working conditions is the strike. However, the right to strike is severely restricted in Malaysia. Presently, a union must obtain the consent of at least two-thirds of its membership via secret ballot before calling a strike. The Registrar of Trade Unions must receive 14 days notice of a vote to strike, and strike action may not be taken until seven days after the notification period. The time lapse is designed to enable the Industrial Relations Department of the Ministry of Human Resources to intervene and encourage an amicable settlement. If this is unsuccessful, and the Minister of Labor refers a labor dispute to the Industrial Court, strikes and lockouts are forbidden. The court can require compulsory arbitration instead of strikes and there is no right of appeal. In practice, that means no strikes. The closest union members get to industrial action is picketing during their lunch breaks.

Thailand's labor law framework, although more permissive than that of Malaysia, is also deficient in the protection of worker rights and the maintenance of acceptable labor standards, although its basic statue, the Labor Relations Act of 1975, resembles the U.S. National Labor Relations Act. The Thai Act is broad in coverage, although it exempts agricultural workers and public employees. State enterprise employees were covered until specifically exempted in 1991. Unions can be organized as in-house organizations or on an industrial basis. They can also organize on a national level. However, there are two important restrictions: (1) the Registrar has the power to register and dissolve unions and (2) outsiders cannot participate or become leaders of unions. Only employees of a given firm can apply for registration and be elected as members of the administrative committee of the union. In practice, this means that unions are generally organized as company unions, i.e., as unions with membership restricted to employees in the same firm.

The Labor Relations Act permits employees to set up a federation as a central organization to improve labor relations and promote education. Collective bargaining, however, is usually undertaken at the company level and the parties involved are the employers and union representatives (or a group of workers not organized as a union). In fact, Thailand requires by law that union representatives must be full-time employees. This was allegedly designed to keep outside agitators away, but has the effect of severely limiting the ability of union representatives to engage in collective bargaining. The law also does not technically protect a union organizer until the union is formed. Thus, workers must organize in secret or risk discharge, blacklisting, or worse. Moreover, even if the law is violated when a union leader is discharged, remedies are inadequate and often do not include reinstatement. These illegalities persist even though the Labor Relations Act of 1975 forbids employers to fire workers for union membership, for participating in legitimate union activities, or to obstruct legitimate union functions.

Workers have the right to strike and may not be discharged or coerced for participating in an authorized walkout. However, Thai courts have ruled that strikers may not picket in large numbers, block entrances, seek a boycott of the employer's products, or publish statements against the employer. They may only withhold labor. Strikes or lockouts are illegal unless there has been an attempt to negotiate, and the union notifies the government mediator of the intent to strike. In many cases the strikers still do not use mediation.

EPILOGUE

Thai employers have grown sophisticated in combatting union activities. They utilize lockouts against strikes and are able to find legal reasons to fire key union personnel. With the growth of the economy and the labor movement, more and more of the larger companies are hiring personnel managers to deal with their workers. Industrial relations in Thailand are slowly become modern. Employers and employees are learning to resolve grievances without resorting to strikes and lockouts. Nevertheless, the restrictions on worker rights we have just discussed are means to prevent gains in wages and improved working conditions, which are the main issues that attract investment to developing nations in East Asia.

THE TYPE OF POLITICAL REGIME AND THE CHOICE OF DEVELOPMENTAL STRATEGY HAVE IMPORTANT ECONOMIC CONSEQUENCES FOR LABOR

In the four countries studied, labor movements have had minimal input into economic development strategies formulated by authoritarian central governments either controlled by the military or strongly influenced by a substantial military presence, either in the legislative branch or behind the scenes.

In China, the Communist Party is still the dominant force. The influence of its economic development policies can clearly be seen following the move to a "socialist market" economy in 1978. With the opening of "free enterprise" zones, joint ventures with foreigners, and generally greater exposure to Western business concepts, the hallowed tradition of lifetime employment was viewed as an obstacle to greater labor productivity. Accordingly, the government in 1986 enacted a system of temporary employment contracts, which no longer provided for lifetime job security. In addition to introducing a labor contract system, the worker recruitment system was to be reformed by replacing the practice of administrative allocation and internal recruitment by open job application and selection with objective standards. Moreover, enterprises were also allowed to dismiss inefficient workers. Therefore, the "iron rice bowl" tradition has ended, at least in the free enterprise zones, where individuals can choose which firms to work for and the companies can select their employees. The result has been that labor mobility has been facilitated, since workers no longer are bound to work in units which guarantee employment, housing, food, medical care, education, etc.

Much of Beijing's legitimacy now comes from its ability to deliver economic gains. With the collapse of communism elsewhere and the demystification of Mao, economic development has become the prime justification for communist rule. Free market reforms on the farms have boosted food production but also liberated from communes millions of peasants who are streaming into cities in search of jobs.

The largest drag on China's economy and drain on Beijing's resources is the huge number of state corporations that are industrial dinosaurs. About half of them, some 50,000 enterprises, are losing money continually. But, rather than close them down, the government continues to lend them funds, fanning inflation and preventing meaningful reforms of the financial system. Chinese leaders talk about letting the losers go bankrupt or cutting off their access to raw materials, but there is little or no sign of action. The senior citizens in charge—the average age of the Politburo is 64— are evidently paralyzed by fears of causing mass unemployment with its potential for explosive social unrest and political instability.

The leading players in the Indonesian government and economy are military men who came up in the Suharto tradition. The Army has never relinquished its aim of becoming a sociopolitical force in the country and it has taken over many functions normally performed by political parties, business, or government itself. It has moved the country into a right-center orientation.

Parliament plays only a supporting role in the political system in any case, as effective power is concentrated in the hand of the president, who delegates some of it to members of his cabinet. Lesser, but nevertheless important, centers of power have been established in the military and the bureaucracy, which have therefore been the traditional areas of political rivalry and policy debate, and will no doubt remain so in the foreseeable future.

Economic growth in Indonesia has averaged around 6.5% annually for the past 20 years, but far from calming political tensions, may actually be contributing to them. Although the living standards of most Indonesians are rising, it is commonly believed that economic growth has brought real wealth only to a relatively small class of people. Factory wages in Indonesia are among the lowest in Asia and, on a day-to-day basis, the average Indonesian still has to endure corrupt and inefficient public services. Labor unrest feeds on such developments and in 1994, for the first time in many years, serious anti-Chinese riots broke out in the city of Medan. Moreover, the U.S. Trade Representative has ordered a review of Indonesia's status under the GSP in order to investigate alleged abuses of workers' rights.

Indonesia has quite a few accomplishments to advertise, among them rapid economic development, a successful birth control program, and the attainment of food self-sufficiency. But, it also has attributes it does not publicize, including the suppression of independent unionism and a closed political climate.

Malaysia's drive to promote foreign investment has created a dependence on foreign-dominated low-cost, labor-intensive manufacturing industries. It has there-fore adopted industrial relations policies geared toward the attraction and retention of foreign capital. In the process of replenishing these probusiness policies, it has moved to contain costs in the export sector by repressing the unionization of the "pioneer industries," as previously noted, refusing to enact minimum wage legislation, reduc-ing overtime pay for working on holidays and rest days, and continuing to refuse to enact equal pay for equal work in the export sector, where approximately 80% of the employees are female. Also, the largest industry, electronics, has been kept virtually union-free due to pressure from foreign investment, and the government's own acceptance of the low-cost, export-oriented strategy.

Another factor working against democratic decision-making is the Malay tradition of strong-man leadership. This has witnessed Prime Minister Mahathir's authoritarian tendencies, where he has moved ruthlessly against all opponents. He has also released almost all restrictions on foreign investments, using Japan as a guide.

Malaysia is currently torn between promoting foreign investment and developing worker rights. Years after the successful implementation of various incentive plans designed to attract foreign investment, Malaysia's labor force has become increasingly restless. Recently, international labor rights organizations have focused international attention on the Malaysian labor policy, accusing the Malaysian government of suppressing the right for workers to bargain collectively. Because the situation in Malaysia is similar to other developing countries hoping to lure foreign capital, the manner in which it addresses the labor situation is likely to set an important precedent. Changes will have to be made in the union regulatory system, which currently removes any bargaining power the labor force may have with management, leaving workers at the mercy of their government and their employers.

In Thailand, in recent years, the processes of government and economic policy are relatively untroubled by recurring coups in which one army Prime Minister generally replaces another. Economic developments include the rise of industrialization with the advent of new types of factories, located in industrial estates throughout the country. Government promotion of these estates resulted from the belief that the workers would enjoy higher wages and better working conditions, as the estates would be characterized by more modern facilities, including water, electricity, telephones and waste treatment plants. One recent case, however, at the Lamphun industrial estate, where 13 workers died suddenly from exposure to as yet unidentified toxic chemicals, demonstrated that the safety standards and working conditions in the factories were not necessarily guaranteed. This occurred despite the official government policy that no amount of export potential or financial backing would stand in the way of the enforcement of standards essential to the welfare of Thai workers.

Although the labor movement has been torn by internal rivalries and factional infighting, it is unified in its general opposition to the privatization of the state enterprise sector. This issue was a particularly troublesome point of contention between labor and the government. It also caused the most serious employment disruptions in recent years, as port workers engaged in strike actions. Unions and army elements also opposed the privatization drive.

Thailand is facing a painful transition from a low-cost manufacturing base to a medium-technology producer. Labor protests over the layoff of workers in the country's flagship textile industry, which is attempting to upgrade its technology, are a sign of things to come. The government, moreover, seems to have no long-term plans to deal with these developments, either for retraining displaced workers or for industrial development.

THE QUESTION AS TO WHETHER PROGRESS TOWARD
DEMOCRATIZATION AND WORKER RIGHTS IS DEPENDENT ON
ECONOMIC DEVELOPMENT IS COMPLEX: IN THE RELATIONSHIP ONE
HAS TO TAKE INTO ACCOUNT INTERVENING VARIABLES, E.G.,
THE SIZE AND CHARACTER OF THE MIDDLE CLASS, THE SET OF
INHERITED VALUES IN A SOCIETY WHICH AFFECT PEOPLES'
ATTITUDES TOWARD GOVERNMENT AND LIBERTY, THE MECHANISMS
FOR THE DISTRIBUTION OF INCOME AND WEALTH

Economic reform in China after 1978 produced rapid economic polarization among the different social sectors and within enterprises, and degenerating labor–management relations in firms as a result of rationalization of the production process and emergence of Tayloristic management practices. Industrial workers were angered by perceived inequitable differences in income distribution in the manufacturing industries by 1989. Factory managers, private entrepreneurs in high-technology industries, self-employed merchants, corrupt officials, and wealthy peasants in suburban agricultural areas—in short, groups whose incomes were several times higher than an ordinary blue or white collar worker—became the targets of jealousy.

The ensuing divisiveness provided the authorities the opportunity to denounce any expressions of dissatisfaction with income distribution, whether well-founded or capricious, as caused by a discredited, Maoist-era egalitarianism. The mass media strongly criticized any claims for equity and social justice during this critical period of a fundamental redistribution of the nation's wealth. Only after the 1989 prodemocracy movement was recognition given to the maldistribution of income and the need for a realization of social justice as a goal of the modernization process. Unlike the revolutions in Eastern Europe and the Soviet Union characterized by grass root uprisings demanding economic and political liberalization, the 1989 upheaval in China largely resulted from a rapid marketization of the economy and, to a more limited extent, political liberalization.

China's rapid economic growth, spurred by market incentives and foreign investment, has reduced party and government control over the economy and permitted ever larger numbers of Chinese to have more control over their lives and livelihood. Despite significant income disparities between coastal regions and the interior, there is now a growing middle class in the cities and rural areas as well as a sharp decline in the number of Chinese at the subsistence level. These economic changes have led to a de facto end to the role of ideology in the economy and an increase in cultural diversity. An example of this is the media, which remains tightly controlled with regard to political questions, although it is now free to report on a wider variety of other issues.

In Indonesia, a burgeoning new rich class finds itself fragmented by complex internal divisions between corporate capital, the petty bourgeoisie, and the middle class, which are further complicated by racial and religious factors. In the context of a highly organized, institutionalized, and pervasive state apparatus, as well as a general belief that there is no alternative system of power to the present regime, cohesive political action by those new social forces is largely immobilized and reduced to palace intrigue. The need for economic restructuring, and the need to organize the political succession to President Suharto, means that the political regime can no longer maintain the existing forms of political and economic control. However, the national legislature simply lacks political will in an environment where the expression "opposition" runs counter to the state ideology of Pancasila and its preoccupation with consensus. One prominent Indonesian stated: "There has not been any develop-ment in ideological thinking from 1965 to now. Because the whole State ideology (Pancasila) was consciously made to support a political power structure, there was no openness in the sense of allowing people to confront issues nationally and interna-tionally. We are not prepared intellectually."

A particularly disturbing feature in Indonesia has been the reemergence of public hostility against the economically powerful ethnic Chinese business community. The protests in North Sumatra in particular have been directed specifically at firms owned by ethnic Chinese entrepreneurs, with one Chinese businessman being killed by the mob in the first wave of rioting in Medan. It is undeniable that there has been an increase in anti-Chinese sentiment at the grass roots. This renewed resentment against the Chinese business community arises to a large extent from the rapid industrializa-tion that Indonesia has experienced in recent years, and has its origins in the enormous disparities in income and wealth between the often enormously wealthy industrialists (the bulk of whom are Chinese despite the recent emergence of a powerful indigenous business class, consisting mainly of relatives and associates of President Suharto), and the growing population of low-paid industrial workers, who are almost all indigenous Indonesians.

There also is a general view that the strength of Indonesia's political stability will be determined largely by the pace of economic growth. By the year 2000, Indonesia's population is projected to reach 216 million, with a labor force of 107 million, compared with 190 million and 81 million, respectively, at present. The disparity between the rich and poor presents another urgent political problem, which President Suharto tried to address, at least symbolically, by persuading 27 of the biggest business conglomerates to divest 1% of their equity to producer and employee cooperatives.

Indonesia's "proper genius," the anthropologist Clifford Geertz wrote in 1961, "has always lain in her ability to work out practicable adjustments among her constituent cultures and to absorb the great host of external influences impinging on her while still somehow maintaining a distinct and overall unique character."[3] It remains to be seen if this prophecy is borne out by future developments in the fourth largest nation in the world.

Malaysia's ethnic composition is almost evenly balanced between Chinese and Indians on the one hand and Malays on the other. The Malays have a slight plurality that becomes a majority through the inclusion of other indigenous groups, particularly in Borneo, under the designation bumiputras (sons of the soil). Differences between the Malays and the Chinese pose the greatest threat to national stability. The unwritten compromise underlying the formation of Malaysia was that the Chinese would retain their economic holdings, while the Malays would have political power and administrative control. However, the Malays have begun demanding greater economic power, while resisting Chinese requests for a greater political voice.

Malay–Chinese tensions were aggravated in 1969 by Chinese electoral success. This produced the country's first serious ethnic riots, which lead to a suspension of the parliamentary government. In the aftermath of the riots the New Economic Policy (NEP) was formulated in an effort to eliminate the connection between ethnic origin and economic function and to eradicate poverty. Under the NEP Malays and other indigenous peoples were to manage and own at least 30% of the total commercial and industrial operations in all categories by 1990. The government conceded that this goal has not been attained. In the Outline Perspective Plan (OPP), the new development plan for the period through the year 2020 outlined by the prime minister in June 1991, the 30% target has been abandoned and replaced by the goal of enhancing national unity.

The gap between the well-off and the economically disadvantaged in Malaysia is complicated by the fact that wealth is largely divided upon racial lines. It will continue to be a particularly divisive political issue because the race that is best-off economically, the Chinese, is not the race that has the most political power. This is wielded by the Malays, who make up just over half of the population. The average Malaysian Chinese household income is 40% greater than the national average, but it is the United Malays National Organization (UMNO) which is the cornerstone of the ruling National Front coalition.

Malaysian workers have been urged to emulate the work ethics of their Japanese counterparts. One of the factors behind the success of Japan has been its high labor productivity, contributed by Japanese workers, who have a positive work attitude toward both their jobs and their employers. Workers are told they must avoid trying to imitate the destructive practices of the West where the philosophy behind industrial relations is based on confrontation. If workers have a confrontational attitude, it is unlikely that Malaysia can achieve the economic prosperity in the manner that the country is presently enjoying. The Malaysian prime minister, Mahathir, has been most vocal in attacking the West, maintaining that the norms and precepts for the observance of human rights varied from society to society and from one period to another within the same society. He also claims that in the developing countries, individual human rights must be balanced with the level of national economic development, otherwise it would damage social stability and economic growth.[4]

On the plus side, industrialization, education, and public sector participation in the economy, together with preferential treatment for Malays in hiring and licensing, have reduced the economic disparity between the Malays and the Chinese. The urban Malay middle class, business class, and work force have grown since the NEP was initiated.

Over the past 20 years, Thai society has changed a great deal. Economic growth has run particularly fast over the past decade at remarkable 8% per annum. The economy has been internationalized. The broad processes of modernization, industrialization, commercialization, and urbanization have fundamentally changed Thailand. Even though 60% of the labor force and as much as 80% of the population remain rural dwellers, it is no longer unusual to see the flicker of television sets even in relatively remote parts of both the northeast and the highlands of the north. People are mobile, aware of changes in the marketplace, and eager to secure a share of the growing wealth they see around them. A glance at the transformation of the labor market, the expansion of employment within the manufacturing and service sectors, which have grown with the economy, signals the extent of the change.

Political events have also changed the landscape. Disgusted with cronyism and corruption in the military, the country's middle class played a key role in preventing the generals from keeping political power in 1992, after the coup. In the case of Thailand the middle class and the business class have grown dramatically, with new institutions expressing and coordinating their new interests. As a consequence, important new contradictions have emerged between these classes and the system of internecine military control of the political system.

Yet, this cannot be assumed to lead to liberal democracy. More sinister political options are presented by the prospect of alliances between elements of the nouveau riche and state officials, and the entry of criminal elements into the political process as a significant force. Undoubtedly the military are well placed to take full advantage of Thailand's booming economy. Members of the elite, including the diplomatic corps, are generally careful about how they refer to the armed forces and do not like to be represented in the media as being at all ill-disposed toward those whom they know may one day be in a position to tell them what to do. As for the military, the bonding that is confirmed within the honor systems of their schools heightens the sense of strategic group membership that works particularly well in Thai society. Whether the middle class will able to hold on to its gains remains in doubt. The same endemic corruption that provided an excuse for the military to intervene in February 1991, has not disappeared. Poor farmers in the northeast have a long-standing record of voting for generals and looking to the military to offset the growing control of the urban middle class. As long as there is an underclass of landless or near landless farmers, undereducated, underprivileged, and neglected people, a way will remain open to the acceptance of authoritarian intervention.

In spite of rapid economic growth political life has retained many of the characteristics of a colony ruled by Bangkok and the barracks. There are still too many poor people who look to the military to put smart, privileged middle-class students in their place. The tradition of elite control through a bureaucracy dominated by the military may be anachronistic but it is still present. There is urgent need for change. The system of government requires a thoroughgoing overhaul. Community representation in local government remains weak and ineffective. The urban, sophisticated, and critically minded middle class have had enough of military generals telling them what to do. The future of Thailand will depend on what these people do but if the past is any indication there is little reason to hope that the lessons of May 1992 will be accepted once and for all time.

The Role Which the ILO Can Play in Improving Worker Rights and Labor Standards in Newly Industrializing Countries

At the 81st ILO conference in Geneva in 1994, China, in comments undoubtedly echoed by representatives from Indonesia, Malaysia, and Thailand, called on the ILO to respect member countries' rights to choose their own path of development and strengthen its cooperation with them. In a world moving toward multipolarity, the ILO should help to resolve the ideological controversies left over the long-time bipolar confrontation and, according to China, show full consideration for the various social systems and values of its members. The organization was urged to step up its cooperation with member states and so promote global prosperity, defend social justice, and protect workers' rights and interests.

With unemployment being the most pressing problem in both the advanced and the developing countries, one could contend that the ILO should make work promotion as its main priority. According to ILO statistics, the number of people registered as jobless in the world now exceeds 120 million, and 700 million are underemployed. Perhaps the ILO should use a more flexible set of labor standards suitable for a broader application internationally and not use them as a condition for technological cooperation with member states, as it would not work if the ILO were to impose standardization on the developing nations.

The ILO, the European Community, and many counties have extensively developed jurisprudence on the right of association, the right to organize and bargain, the right to strike, and other features of trade union activity. Labor rights advocates should consider consolidating these doctrines and determining which are universal, permitting no derogation by a country in the name of economic development or local labor tradition.

Perhaps the greatest challenge here is to define those rights specific to trade union activity that can be asserted as fundamental. Just as there is no debate as to the universality of certain civil and political rights in society at large, like the right to be free of torture or arbitrary arrest and freedom of conscience, workers' right of association and the rights that flow from it—organizing, bargaining and collective action—ought to be unassailable.

In the spectrum from unarguably universal human rights (the right of association, freedom from torture, freedom from slavery, etc.) to arguably "mere" economic benefits (minimum wages, paid leaves, etc.), worker rights to form and join trade unions and to participate in union activity (bargaining, striking, engaging in political and legislative action, etc.) are often placed on the economic and social side of the ledger rather than on the universally recognized rights side. Seen in this light, organizing, bargaining, striking, and other union actions are simply methods of making economic demands that a country or an employer may not be in a position to meet. Their refusal to recognize these union-related rights, therefore, are not human rights violations. The state may impose conditions to channel worker action toward outcomes dictated by development strategy and economic policy making (attracting foreign investment, underselling foreign competitors, or nurturing nascent industries), or simply by the ability or inability to pay for improved salaries and benefits.

The flaw in this view is that rights cannot exist as abstractions. The classic rights of the individual, in fact, cannot be guaranteed in private unless basic economic, social, and cultural needs are fulfilled. Otherwise, desperate actions by impoverished people will provoke repression by governments in a permanent cycle of human rights abuse.

The rich countries will in any case never obtain the necessary consensus within the GATT, or the WTO, to allow trade sanctions to be imposed against countries that fail to observe basic labor standards, because the developing countries will always reject such interference. That is why GATT officials favored keeping the issue of labor standards well away from trade talks, for fear that it could poison other multilateral trade arrangements. It would be more sensible to hand it to the ILO, which was set up with the specific goal of improving international labor standards. Over the years, it has woven a fabric of international law relating to different aspects of working conditions. These laws are admittedly voluntary; the ILO's only tools are moral suasion and, sometimes, public condemnation. But these might well be as effective as trade sanctions, while avoiding any risk of damaging side effects.

POLICIES AND PROGRAMS TO IMPROVE WORKING CONDITIONS FOR WOMEN AND CHILDREN

Despite the fact that nearly all countries have adopted legislation banning the exploitation of children and have ratified international conventions, the ILO has estimates that there are as many as 200 million child laborers worldwide. Perhaps human rights is the area that most clearly demonstrates that a moral issue is at stake that goes beyond simply allowing companies to find the cheapest labor under the most favorable conditions. Multinational corporations that take the most aggressive attitude towards exploiting local practices are able to discriminate freely based on sex and utilize child labor.

The exploitation of child labor is perhaps an even more basic question of morality. While documentation of the problem is difficult because of lack of information, the problem is widespread, particularly in the textile and garment industries. Companies seeking cheap workers are able to find them in many cases because children are performing the tasks.

International standards dictate that the legal age limit of a child laborer should be 14 in developing countries and 15 in developed countries. In the case of Thailand, its law allows children between 13 and 18 to work legally. According to the Thai government, the number of child workers varies greatly, but the ILO puts the number at 4 million with 600,000 between the ages of 13 and 14. Internationally, the Thai government is likely to face unease over child labor, an issue developed countries will raise to pressure Third World governments through the WTO.

In the most recent attempt, the United States and France almost delayed the signing of the Uruguay Round in April 1994, in an effort to put labor standards formally on the agenda of the WTO. They failed, but in a compromise it was agreed labor standards could be discussed in the preparatory committee for the WTO. Although the threat from the WTO is unclear, that from the United States seems clearer. The U.S. Congress has considered the Harkin Bill which might lead to trade sanctions against countries and foreign industries employing children. The bill does not affect only Thailand, but 19 developing countries worldwide.

In Malaysia, parents and employers of children are flouting the law and committing an offense if children are working at night, even in family-run businesses. Under Section 5(1)(a) of the Children and Young Persons Act of 1966, no child is permitted to work between 8:00 P.M. and 7:00 A.M. The Act defines children as any person who has not reached the age of 14. The law is aimed at ensuring the rights of the young children to education and childhood free from excessive workload exploitation. In the longer term, it must be aimed at reducing and eventually eliminating child labor.

Although little documented evidence exists, Malaysia has been charged with de facto violations of child labor laws. The Children and Young Persons Act of 1966 prohibits children under the age of 14 to work except in specified circumstances, such as apprenticeships or public entertainment, but these regulations have been circumvented. It has been reported that 9 out of 10 households on the plantations had children aged between 6 and 15 years out at work, often for long hours, at low wages or perhaps none at all. This evidence exists despite official denials that child labor exists in Malaysia.

In reality, child labor both causes and perpetuates poverty. The worst instances of child labor are found where adult unemployment rates are high in a number of countries. However, developing countries do not have to wait until poverty is eradicated before eliminating the economic exploitation of children. Some countries in Asia—South Korea, Sri Lanka and some parts of India—have successfully concentrated on sending children to school rather than factories. These countries recognize that in the medium and long term, their economies will be competitive only with an educated, skilled and productive work force.

The dangers facing child workers are varied. Carpet weavers toil under conditions that ruin their eyesight and lead to deformed backs and limbs. Those in brick work carry heavy loads that injure and deform. Children working in mines, glass factories, and match factories face multiple hazards. Children toiling in the field can be maimed, killed, and exposed to toxic pesticides. The failure of the General Agreement on Trade and Tariffs to include adequate protection against exploiting children as cheap and servile workers is deplorable.

All is not lost, however. Another international treaty, the Convention on the

Rights of the Child, requires all countries that ratify it to recognize the right of the child to be protected from economic exploitation and from performing any work that is likely to be hazardous or to interfere with the child's education, or to be harmful to the child's health or physical, mental, spiritual, moral, or social development.

More than 100 countries have ratified the treaty. It establishes a committee of 10 experts to oversee compliance, recommend reforms, and denounce violations. The United States could play a leading role in buttressing the treaty and the committee but for one problem; the United States has not ratified the treaty.

Regarding the labor of women, the picture is also not an encouraging one. In Malaysia, the lack of a minimum, statutory wage leaves employers free to discriminate based on gender and to pay women less than men. In September 1991, China's National People's Congress adopted a decision on "strict punishment for criminals who abduct, sell, and kidnap women and children." The language may be strong, but the insidious nature of the crime which too often receives the tacit approval of society requires forceful measures. Such trade in human beings was largely stopped after the Chinese Revolution in 1949, but has started to reappear over the last few years, as has female prostitution.

Additionally, in China, a Bill of Rights enshrining women's equality of treatment with men in all political, cultural, social, economic and family matters was adopted and went into effect in 1992. It was promulgated against a background of continuing discrimination against women, notably in employment and education. At present, women account for around 70% of the urban unemployed and by far the highest proportion of China's illiterates.

Indonesia's current economic policy to promote the growth of its industrial sector aims at creating new businesses and jobs, developing the nation's technological capabilities, producing higher-quality goods, and increasing exports and foreign exchange earnings. Women's participation in this process so far has been limited almost exclusively to low-paid, low-skilled jobs, but as industrial development continues, more jobs will become available for them. If the welfare of women and their families is to be enhanced by expanded employment opportunities, greater attention must be given to their working conditions.

Most developing countries do have a legal framework protecting women's right to equal opportunities. Their constitutions usually provide for equality between the sexes in all spheres of activity, including equal pay for equal work; however, barriers to equal opportunities for women in employment persist. A major obstacle to women's emancipation is the pervasive influence of traditional social attitudes and customs, and the low levels of women's general literacy and professional expertise. These obstacles have been acknowledged in most Asian countries, regardless of their level of development and socioeconomic system.

Enhanced attention to the quality of the working environment of women workers should not be regarded as a threat to the expansion of employment opportunities and industrial development. On the contrary, continued growth in many manufacturing sectors depends on the performance of women workers so that to ignore the very real and special problems faced by them can only be counterproductive. It has been shown the low-cost improvements in workplace facilities and services, and instruction for women about appropriate action to protect their health, are both feasible and effective.

The factors that influence the quality of the working environment of women in developing nations like Indonesia are complex and extend far beyond the factory gates. But the magnitude of the problem should not deter efforts to take constructive action within the factory, however modest in scope. Because the needs of women workers are largely overlooked at present, even small-scale programs can bring them direct and significant benefits. Outside influences can be effective in stimulating improvements in the short term, but long-term changes will require strengthening the ability of workers and employers themselves to introduce and sustain improvements in the working environment.

In summation, during the past two decades China, Indonesia, Malaysia, and Thailand have undergone epochal transformations in their economic, political, and social systems. Throughout the region, patterns of consumption, wage and salary levels, demands for freer information, and greater access to the outside world are increasing. Yet, the consequences for the political and ideological structures of these countries vary considerably. Individual states have different positions in the world economy and there is a varied balance of social and political power within each.

It appears that on the issue of worker rights (within the larger rubric of human rights) capitalist Malaysia and Indonesia, where opposition parties and open elections have at least in appearance become part of the political systems, have spoken with a language apparently similar to that of communist China, where political pluralism still remains an absolute taboo. This is because there exists a lowest common denominator on this issue between China, as an Asian developing country and Malaysia, Indonesia, and Thailand, which are also Asian developing countries. Moreover, China's human rights theory is based on its status as an Asian developing state rather than on traditional communist cliches. As carriers of Asian authoritarian political cultures, the governments of both China, Indonesia, Malaysia, and Thailand to a lesser extent, find it difficult to recognize the legitimacy of Western-style human rights. Instead, they believe that social harmony and control should prevail over individual political freedom. As victims of Western imperialism and colonialism in history, China, Indonesia, and Malaysia are sensitive to a renewal of Western political domination through a human rights crusade, and see a blatant hypocrisy in the former conquerors turning sanctimonious critics. As well, they all consider economic prosperity to have first priority in the task of nation-building and as the major means of maintaining their legitimacy. And, from their perspectives, social and political stability, rather than individual political rights, are a prerequisite for economic growth. In the nations with ethnic, religious, or regional tensions, political stability has rested on a delicate social contract, in which certain groups are implicitly granted economic power as long as they do not compete for political power, or vice versa, such as the situation with ethnic Chinese in Malaysia and Indonesia.

Furthermore, the nature of the political regime, democratic or authoritarian, is only roughly associated with how governments handle worker rights and labor standards, and correspondingly with the options available to unions. More important in shaping unions' behavior are the nature of the political party system and how unions are connected with parties. The conditions needed to gain workers' cooperation are analogous to those which encourage business to invest: political stability, a voice in policy that affects their interests, and, arising from these, the confidence that current sacrifices still ultimately yield a fair share of future benefits.

In the light particularly of its retreat over the issue of most favored nation status for China, but also of unproductive disputes with other Asian countries, including Malaysia, the United States has been rethinking its policy toward the Asian region along less confrontational lines. The fact that President Suharto hosted the APEC meeting in 1994 and the inclusion of Indonesia among the 10 emerging markets that the United States has set its sights on capturing (it estimates that potential sales to Indonesia alone could total $100 billion between now and 2000) are also likely to make its approach to human rights issues in Indonesia less strident. Realistically, however, a tension exists between increased economic growth and protection of workers' rights. Underdeveloped nations seeking to industrialize tend to market the abundance of natural resources in their country, including and often emphasizing the availability of cheap labor. As industrialization benefits these countries, and foreign investors reap profits, workers expect to share proportionately in those gains. The respective governments may thus find themselves caught between the investors they have courted so carefully and the workers they govern. At some point, these countries will be forced to choose between continued governmental favoritism toward foreign investors and government insistence on minimum health, safety, and wage standards for workers. The former risks the exploitation and distrust of constituents, while the latter risks alienating foreign investors who may move their business elsewhere.

The more a country in East Asia industrializes, the larger becomes its number of wage earners who in due course begin to demand certain rights and respect from their employer. The richer a country becomes, the more it has a middle class and develops an intelligentsia, some of whom, for various reasons, tend to support working class demands and lend their organizational and intellectual abilities to groups of workers. In addition, the richer, more educated, more open to the world and dependent on world trade and other international links a country becomes, the harder it is to use direct political repression or explicit prohibitions which belong to the armory of dictators. Countries with growing and ever-richer middle classes, expanding higher education systems, and industrial and service output replacing agriculture cannot so easily opt out of the democratic norms that membership or near-membership of the so-called First World demands, not only as values in themselves but as actual requirements for the efficient functioning of a pluralist, efficient market economy.

It is true, also, that economic development does not necessarily lead to democratic development. However, the lack of economic growth can be an obstacle to creating an open society. It is relatively easier to establish a consensus in a climate of abundance than in societies where there is a terrible struggle about scarce resources. If countries are to aspire to democratic development with better worker rights and labor standards, then economic development is a significant element in this process. All countries must have an interest in an open multilateral trade system and international cooperation.

In many colonized societies the colonial powers aimed at preserving the local culture and social structures. Nowadays these societies are told that their cultures are sometimes an obstacle to democratic development. This relates in particular to societies where family, kinship, and community relations are important in the decision-making process. It is almost unavoidable that certain tensions and cultural clashes will occur within these traditional communities as they evolve towards a modern open society in the same way as tensions occur in modern multicultural democracies.

Cultural differences will prevent a single Asian model of trade unionism emerging, just as the trade union map in Europe is a jigsaw of pieces of different shapes and sizes. It is a challenge for the policymakers in East Asia to help develop effective forms of worker organizations which defend worker rights but also contribute to the efficient and socially just running of society as a whole. The answer to what form of trade unionism takes shape in East Asia, or if any recognizable form emerges at all, will be provided by the workers themselves and the people or groups they chose to work with. The rise of a working class in East Asia and the emergence of the trade union question opens a significant new era in the century-old history of worker organization and trade unionism.

References

Chapter 1

1. The World Book. (1993). *The East Asian Miracle: Economic Growth and Public Policy* (p. 3). New York: Oxford University Press.
2. Lieberthal, K. (1995). A new China policy. *Foreign Affairs, 6*, 47–48.
3. *Far East Economic Review* (1990). *6*, 20.
4. Hossfeld, K.J. (1991). *Common interests: Women organizing in global electronics* (pp. 99–102). New York: Women Working Worldwide.
5. Cooler lumpur. (1995). *The Economist, 11*, 4, 39.

Chapter 2

1. Country Profile. (1993). *Economist Intelligence Unit, 11*, 1.
2. Ibid.
3. A little booing from the audience. (1995). *The Economist, 3*, 25, 38.
4. Wei-Fong, C. (1994). Party cells hit labour unions: Workplaces become focus for control. *South China Morning Post, 11*, 1, 8.
5. Coll, J.H. (1993). The people's republic of China. In M. Rothman, D.R. Briscoe, & R.C.D. Nacamulli (Eds.), *Industrial relations around the world: Labor relations for multinational companies* (p. 97). Berlin: Walter de Gruyter.
6. China: Grim message for the future. (1994). *South China Morning Post, 5*, 29.
7. Chan, A. (1993). Revolution or corporatism? Workers and trade unions in post-Mao China. *The Australian Journal of Chinese Affairs, 29*, 32–35.
8. Chan, A., & Unger, J. (1990). Voices from the protest movement, Chongqing, Sichuan. *The Australian Journal of Chinese Affairs, 24*, 257–279.
9. China's communists: The road from Tiananmen. (1994). *The Economist, 6*, 4, 20.
10. Tyler, P.E. (1995). Chinese leader says mistakes by government fueled inflation. *The New York Times,* 3, 6, A-1.
11. Chen, K. (1995). China's economy appears headed for a soft landing. *The Asian Wall Street Journal Weekly, 5*, 1, 3.
12. An end to the "three irons"? (1992). *Social and Labour Bulletin, 3*, 336–337.
13. Ibid.
14. Employment pattern undergoes major changes. (1994). *Market Daily* (Beijing), 11, 15.; Ministry predicts 268 M unemployed by 2000. (1994). *Reuter Textline,* 8, 24.
15. Population and labour: Unemployment worries. (1994). *Economist Intelligence Unit, 2*, 21.
16. How Chinese workers think of their lives. (1991). *Xinhua Overseas News Service,* 1, 14.
17. Poole, T. (1994). Chinese workers grow restless. *Independent on Sunday,* 5, 11.

18. Yunhe, W. (1994). Cars for all by 2010. *China Daily*, 4, 6.
19. Tyler, P.E. (1995). Daunting challenges for China's leaders. *The New York Times*, 3, C-10.
20. Craig, A.S. (1995). Growing numbers of migrant laborers point up chaos in China's economy. *The Asian Wall Street Journal Weekly*, 2, 6, 7.
21. Chinese worker woes. (1994). *Business Week*, 8, 1, 42–43.
22. Howard, P. (1991). Rice bowls and job security: The urban contract labour system. *The Australian Journal of Chinese Affairs*, *1*, 104–105.
23. China's preliminary statistics for 1993: The good with the bad. (1994). *Business China*, *5*, 16.
24. China's sleeping giants. (1994). *The Economist*, *8*, 27, 53–54.
25. Tong, G.C. (1995). Understand China, and give it some time. *The Asian Wall Street Journal Weekly*, 5, 29, 18.

Chapter 3

1. Deyo, F.C. (1989). *Beneath the miracle: Labor subordination in the new Asian Industrialism* (p.108). Berkeley: University of California Press.
2. Kristof, N.D., & Wudunn, S. (1994). *China wakes: The struggle for the soul of a rising power* (p. 150). New York: Times Books.
3. Lieberthal, K.G. (1994). China—is prosperity creating a free society? *Business Week*, 6, 6, 96.
4. Warner, M. (1993). Chinese trade unions: Structure and function in a decade of economic reform, 1979–1989. In S. Frenkel (Ed.), *Organized labor in the Asia-Pacific region* (p. 59). Ithaca, NY: ILR Press.
5. Hiroyuki, A. (1995). Union leaders says cooperation key-China law targets workers at foreign companies. *Nikkei Weekly*, 2, 6.
6. Coll, J.H. (1993). The people's republic of China. In Rothman, M., Briscoe, D.R., & R.C.D. Nacamulli (Eds.), *Industrial relations around the world: Labor relations for multinational companies* (p. 94). Berlin: Walter de Gruyter.
7. Helburn, I.B., & Shearer, J. C. (1984). Human resources and industrial relations in China: A time of ferment. *Industrial and Labor Relations Review*, 38, 1, 11.
8. Cheng, E. (1995). Getting back to basics. *Far Eastern Economic Review*, 3, 38–40.
9. Barnathan, J. (1995). The next hot spot for m & a: Shanghai. *Business Week*, *3*, 13, 58.
10. Swee, J.K. (1993). Why Deng's new revolution will succeed. *South China Morning Post*, 1, 31, 2.
11. Tyler, P. E. (1995). With Deng's influence waning, privatizing of China's state industries stalls. *The New York Times*, 6, 18, 8.
12. State enterprises reform: management to rest with the enterprise. (1988). *Social and Labour Bulletin*, *3*, 282.
13. Ibid.
14. O'Neill, M. (1995). China bankruptcies seen doubling this year. *Reuter Textline*, 3, 13.
15. Nai, A. (1995). A safety net at what cost? *South China Morning Post*, 2, 12.
16. Sun, L. H. (1994). The dragon within. *The Washington Post*, 10, C-1.
17. Cities trying to handle rural labour influx. (1994). *China Daily*, 7, 20.
18. Leman, E. (1995). Yangtze delta is fertile ground for investors. *The Asian Wall Street Journal Weekly*, 7, 10, 14.
19. Hutchings, G. (1995). Great escape from idiocy of rural life-inside China. *Daily Telegraph*, 2, 25, 6.
20. National conference on floating population opens. (1995). *Xinhau News Agency*, 7, 8.
21. Hunan's growing small towns absorb surplus rural labourers. (1994). *Reuter Textline*, 9, 1.
22. Ginsberg, S. (1995). Small enterprises play a big role in China. *The Asian Wall Street Journal Weekly*, 3, 27, 16.
23. Wong, L. (1994). China's urban migrants-the public policy challenge. *Pacific Affairs*, 67, 3, 353.
24. Coll, op. cit., p. 93.
25. Ibid., p. 91.

26. Helburn and Shearer, op. cit., p. 10.
27. Beijing promotes democratic management among enterprises. (1991). *Xinhua News Agency*, 9, 4.
28. Beijing trade union leader on workers congresses. (1980). *Xinhua News Agency*, 1, 26.
29. Workers congress system must be maintained. (1994). *Xinhau News Agency*, 6, 29.
30. U.S. Department of State. (1994). *China human rights practices*. Washington, DC: USGPO, 1, 3.

Chapter 4

1. Hiroyuki, A. (1995). Union leader says cooperation key-China law targets workers at foreign companies. *Nikkei Weekly*, 2, 6.
2. Henley, J.S., & Nyaw, M.K. (1986). Market forces in Chinese enterprises. *Journal of Management Studies*, 23, 6, 635–656.
3. Zhao Ziyang on trade unions' role. (1988). *Xinhua News Agency*, 10, 22.
4. New trade union act: Towards freedom of association. (1992). *South China Morning Post*, 3, 289–290.
5. U.S. Department of State. (1993). *China human rights practices, 1993*. pp. 12, 27, 17 pages.
6. Nei, G. (1994). City laws on unions and military. *China Daily*, 9, 12.
7. Wai-Fong, C. (1994). Role for unions urged. *South China Morning Post*, 9, 15.
8. Labour. (1994). *Economist Intelligence Unit*, 8, 9.
9. Qian qichen on foreign affairs, Wei Jianxing on labour at CPPCC group discussions. (1995). *BBC Summary of World Broadcasts*, 3, 18.
10. Hiroyuki, op. cit.
11. Zhurun, L. (1993). Unions take to heart problems facing workers. *Xinhua News Agency*, 10, 28.
12. Trade unions prop Tianjin's foreign-funded enterprises. (1995). *Xinhua News Agency*, 3, 7.
13. Overseas-funded firms urged to establish trade unions. (1995). *Xinhua News Agency*, 3, 24.
14. Cited in *China News Analysis*, no. 1460, May 15, 1992, 6.
15. Anti-party trade union organizations are not permitted in China. (1989). *Xinhua News Agency*, 7, 25.
16. O'Neill, M. (1995). China bankruptcies seen doubling this year. *Reuter Textline*, 3, 13.
17. Coll, J.H. (1993). The people's republic of China. In Rothman, R., Briscoe., & Nacamulli, R.C.D. (Eds.), *Industrial relations around the world: Labor relations for multinational companies* (pp. 96–98). Berlin: Walter de Gruyter.

Chapter 5

1. Trade union federation seeks better protection for workers' rights. (1995). *Reuter Textline*, 3, 1.
2. China to spread collective contract system. (1995). *Xinhua News Agency*, 7, 4.
3. Nickerson, D. (1995). Sweeping labor law benefits yet to reach workers. *South China Morning Post*, 1, 12.
4. Naughton, B. (1985). False starts and second wind: Financial reforms in China's industrial system. In E. Perry & C. Wong (Eds.) *The Political economy of reform in post-Mao China* (p. 223). New York: Oxford University Press.
5. White, G. (1987). The politics of economic reform in Chinese industry. *China Quarterly*, 9, 111, 375–376.
6. Provision 860712-Labor Contract Provisions.
7. Zhu, Y. (1995). Major changes under way in China's industrial relations. *International Labour Review*, 134, 1, 41.
8. China's joblessness less than 2.8 percent. (1995). *Xinhua News Agency*, 7, 29.
9. Slow march to unionization in China. (1995). *Business China*, 4, 3.
10. Yuan, Z. (1994). Workers win out in strike at disk factory. *South China Morning Post*, 5, 30.
11. Unwelcome addenda in China. (1995). *Business China*, 4, 3.

12. Ibid.
13. Chenguang, M. (1994). New law approved to protect employees. *China Daily*, 7, 16.
14. China labour minister says strikes inevitable. (1994). *Agence France Presse*, 7, 15.
15. Rising discontent among workers, peasants and urban residents. (1994). *Tangtai* (Chinese) no. 38, 5, 15, 20–22.
16. Fong, C.W. (1995). Backing for strike laws. *South China Morning Post*, 5, 1.
17. Po-Ling, C. (1994). New law curbs right to strike. (1994). *South China Morning Post*, 11, 26, 9.
18. Ibid.
19. China to launch campaign to publicize labor law. (1995). *Xinhua News Agency*, 6, 10.
20. Mediation helps in labor disputes. (1991). *Xinhua News Agency*, 3, 25.
21. Labour rights could be next U.S.-China dispute. (1994). *Reuter Textline*, 3, 27.

Chapter 6

1. Zhu, Y. (1995). Major changes under way in China's industrial relations. *International Labour Review*, 134, 1, 42–43.
2. Chinese trade unions to better protect workers' rights. (1995). *Xinhua News Agency*, 2, 22.
3. Markel, D.C. (1994). Finally, a national labor law. *The China Business Review*, 11–12, 48.
4. Sixteen provinces, municipalities practice minimum wage system. *Reuter Textline*, 2, 18.
5. Labour ministry enforcement of minimum wage standard by end of June. (1995). *Reuter Textline*, 4, 28.
6. Sichuan stipulates minimum wage payment. (1995). *Xinhua News Agency*, 7, 1.
7. Jiangsu protects low-income workers. (1995). *Xinhua News Agency*, 7, 6.
8. Nickerson, D. (1995). Sweeping labour law benefits yet to reach workers. *South China Morning Post*, 1, 12.
9. Wai-Fong, C. (1995). Workers worried by late wage payers. *South China Morning Post*, 2, 13.
10. In the pipeline. (1995). *Business China*, 5, 29.
11. Markel, op. cit., 49.
12. China real urban wages rise six percent in Q 1. (1995). *Reuter Textline*, 5, 7.
13. How not to sell l.2 billion tubes of toothpaste. (1994). *The Economist*, 12, 3.
14. Urbanites' income gaps widen. (1995). *The Asian Wall Street Journal Weekly*, 7, 17, 8.
15. Wong, J. (1995) Reforms in China bring opulence to some, but pain to masses, as state sector withdraws. *The Asian Wall Street Journal Weekly*, 7, 3, 11.
16. Kwan, D. (1995). Cadres fear wealth gap disintegration. *South China Morning Post*, 2, 16.
17. Foreign firms infringing workers' rights and safety. (1994). *Reuter Textline*, 6, 7.
18. Massive survey accuses foreign firms of wantonly abusing workers. (1994). *Reuter Textline*, 3, 2.
19. Wu, J. (1994). Joint venture boss-employee relations: A glimpse of their labor conditions in foreign-funded firms. *China Information*, 3, 13.
20. Kwan, D. (1994). Fujian to police workplace abuse. *South China Morning Post*, 4, 20, 8.
21. Working conditions—look before you leap. (1993). *Business China*, 3, 8.
22. Percival, D. (1994). Report slams Beijing's trade union repression. *Inter Press Service*, 6, 6.
23. Shorter work week. (1994). *Market Reports*, 3, 17.
24. What a five-day workweek means to China.(1995). *Xinhua News Agency*, 5, 1.
25. Hutcheon, S. (1995). Weekend win for China's workers. *Sidney Morning Herald*, 5, 10, 1.
26. Chan, A. (1991). PRC workers under 'capitalism with Chinese characteristics.' *China Information*, 5, 4, 75–82.
27. Wong, L. (1994). China's urban migrants-the public policy challenge. *Pacific Affairs*, 67, 3, 353–354.
28. Ordinary deaths. (1994). *The Economist*, 11, 5, 32.
29. Field, C. (1994). *The Gazette* (Montreal), 3, 3, B-3.
30. Poole, T. (1994). China fire kills 233 as safety standards slip. *Independent*, 11, 30, 31.
31. Wai-Fong, C. (1994). Mining deaths 'soar to l0,000'. *South China Morning Post*, 10, 15.

32. Shang-li, W. (1994). Trade unions founded spontaneously in various localities in Guangdong. *Tangtai* (Hong Kong), 3, 15, 38–39.
33. Girard, G. (1994). Damping labor's fires-can Beijing calm workers and sustain growth? *Business Week*, 8, 1, 40.
34. Yong, C. (1994). *Shanghai Star*, 7, 12.
35. 'Massive survey' accuses foreign firms of 'wantonly' abusing workers. (1994). *Reuter Textline*, 3, 2.
36. Women's rights. (1995). *Business China*, 6, 12.
37. Chinese working women. (1995). *The Washington Post*, 6, 11, A-31.
38. China says foreign firms mistreat women workers. (1995). *Reuter Textline*, 4, 3.
39. *ACFTU Bulletin*. (1988). 6.
40. Women in China: much like others. (1995). *The Economist*, 5, 13, 38.
41. How the other half works. (1995). *Business China*, 6, 12.
42. Mufson, S. (1995). China's raging silver wave. *The Washington Post*, 7, A-2, A-3.
43. China reaffirms stand on export of prison-made goods. (1992). *Social and Labour Bulletin*, 1, 9.
44. China scraps title 'labour reform' for prisons. (1995). *Reuter Textline*, 1, 7.
45. Demographers on population control. (1995). *Reuter Textline*, 2, 28.
46. Walker, T. (1994). China sounds alarm bells on public sector economy. *The Age* (Melbourne), 4, 13, 14.
47. China launches nationwide reemployment project. (1995). *Xinhua News Agency*, 6, 15.
48. Peng, F.C. (1995). Cut in working week to create more jobs. *South China Post*, 5, 1.
49. When the Chinese go on strike. (1993). *The Economist*, 10, 2, 34.
50. The human tidal wave. (1994). *China Information*, 5, 13.
51. Economic policy: Unemployment is likely to go on rising. (1995). *Economist Intelligence Unit*, 6, 6.
52. Nai, A. (1995). A safety net at what cost? *South China Morning Post*, 2, 12.
53. Pension scheme reform. (1992). *Social and Labour Bulletin*, 2, 211.
54. Ibid. p. 212.
55. von Rohland, H.(1994). Social security in China: The shattered rice bowl. In *The World of Work* (pp. 23–25). Geneva: ILO, 7.
56. Goldstein G. & Huus, K. (1994). No workers' paradise. *Far Eastern Economic Review*, 6, 16, 35–36.
57. Ordinary deaths. (1994). *The Economist*, 11, 5, 32.
58. Kwan, D. (1994). Fujian to police workplace abuse. *South China Morning Post*, 4, 20, 8.
59. Wai-Fong, C. (1995). Overseas investors exploiting workers. *South China Morning Post*, 3, 31.
60. Trade unions play important role in foreign-funded companies. (1995). *Xinhua News Agency*, 4, 28.
61. Parker, J. (1994). China eases deadline for unions at foreign firms. *Reuter Textline*, 10, 27.
62. Stevenson, Yang, A. (1994). Labor laments. *The China Business Review*, 5-6, 34.

Part III

1. Indonesia workers risk freedom for their rights. (1994). *Reuter Textline Guardian*, 10, 15.

Chapter 7

1. Country: Indonesia. (1995). *ABC-CLIO, Inc.*, 2, 20.
2. Hooper, N. (1994). Indonesia, the rush is on. *Business Review Weekly*, 7, 11.
3. Bowring, P. (1994). China gets the headlines but Indonesia compares favorably. *International Herald Tribune*, 6, 29.
4. Indonesia: Political Background. (1993). *Country Profile*, 12, 1.
5. Sargent, S. (1990). A political awakening: economic success lifts operations. *Australian Financial Review*, 8, 30.
6. Political climate. (1994). *Business International*, 11, 16.

7. McBeth, J. (1994). Loyal house: but parliament is becoming more animated. *Far Eastern Economic Review*, 9, 8, 32.
8. ABC-CLIO, Inc., op. cit.
9. U.S. Department of State. (1992). *1991 Human Rights Report*, 2, 92.
10. Political scene: the Marsinah case is reopened. (1995). *Country Report*, 7, 17.
11. Djiwandono, S. (1995). Indonesia in 1994. *Asian Survey*, 35, 2, 228.
12. 1991 Human Rights Report, op. cit.
13. Indonesia. (1994). Country Profile, 12, 1.
14. 18-month forecast of labor costs. (1995). *Political Risk Services*, 5, 1.
15. The political scene: political control is tightened. (1995). *Country Report*, 4, 24.
16. Indonesia. (1994). *IBC International Country Risk Guide*, 12.
17. 1991 Human Rights Report, op. cit.
18. That magic name. (1995). *The Economist*, 4, 8, 35.
19. McGuin, W. (1993). Asian dilemmas: can Asia's managed capitalism keep growing if the countries don't open up politically and economically? But if they do open up, will they be inviting western-style welfarism and strife? *National Review*, 45, 23, 12, 29, 32.
20. Political Risk Services, op. cit.
21. Economic forecast: wage and price inflation. (1995). *Country Forecast*, 2, 24.
22. Political Risk Services, op. cit.
23. Country Forecast, op. cit.
24. Wheeler, C. (1994). Indonesia emerging as economic power. *The Financial Post*, 8, 17, 17.
25. Tripathi, S. (1994). Looking ahead: Indonesia. *Asia, Inc.*, 5, 59.
26. Ibid.
27. Demographic and social trends. (1995). *Country Forecast*, 2, 24.
28. Population and society. (1993). *Country Profile*, 12, 1.
29. Indonesia: firm hand. (1995). *Business Asia*, 1, 16, 7.'
30. Wignjowijoto, H. (1995). Indonesia: will the seven headaches go away this year?—the economy. *Business Times* (Singapore), 2, 8.
31. Tripathi, op. cit.

Chapter 8

1. From: Industrial relations and labour studies: The Indonesian case. (1989). *Labour Relations and Development* (pp. 49–50). Bangkok: ILO.
2. Doi, T. (1994). Don't meddle with rights, Jakarta tells Australian trade unions. *The Straits Times* (Singapore), 5, 10, 13.
3. Trade union rights and the growth of new unions. (1991). *Financial Times* (London), 10, 25.
4. 18-month forecast of labor costs. (1995). *Political Risk Services*, 5, 1.
5. Jacob, P. (1994). Rights panel calls on Jakarta to recognize trade union body. *The Straits Times* (Singapore), 6, 19, 16.
6. Seabrook, J. (1994). Indonesian workers risk freedom for their rights. *Guardian*, 10, 14, 15.
7. Ismartono, Y. (1993). Government reluctant to relax grip on labor. *Inter Press Service*, 8, 3.
8. Industrial labour. (1994). *Financing Foreign Operations*, 3, 1.
9. Political Risk Services, op. cit.
10. Kahn, M. (Ed.) (1989). *Labour administration: Profile on Indonesia*. Bangkok: ILO.
11. *World Labour Report*, 1994. (1994). (pp. 61–65). Geneva: ILO.
12. Arasu, K.T. (1994). Indonesian employers eye automation as wages rise. *Reuters World Service*, 10, 4.
13. Indonesian government rejects call for pay rise delay. (1994). *Xinhua News Agency*, 1, 12.
14. Arasu, K. T. (1995). Indonesian bosses slam government on basic wages. *The Reuter-Pacific Business Report*, 3, 8.
15. Ibid.

16. Indonesian firms seek delay on minimum wage. (1995). *Xinhua News Agency*, 7, 7.
17. Seabrook, J. (1994). Indonesian workers risk freedom for their rights. *Guardian*, 10, 14, 15.
18. Indonesia says 50 million workers unproductive. (1994). *Reuter News Service-Far East*, 7, 19.
19. Cohen, M. (1993). Indonesia: Eton of the east. *Far Eastern Economic Review*, 7, 22.
20. Human resources overview. (1994). *Financing Foreign Operations*, 3, 1.
21. Indonesia: upholding the status quo. (1994). *Business Week*, 1, 31.
22. Human resources overview. (1995). *Investing, Licensing & Trading*, 1, 1.
23. Employment of foreigners. (1995). *Investing, Licensing & Trading*, 1, 1.
24. Chua, J. (1994). Human rights should be on agenda in Asia. *The Dallas Morning News*, 10, 15, 17-A.
25. Lopez, L. (1994). Indonesia: hopes of change turn to despair. *Business Times* (Malaysia), 11, 24.

Chapter 9

1. U.S. Department of State (1992). *1991 Human Rights Report*, 2.
2. Economic policy: the government raises minimum wages. (1995). *Country Report*, 2, 14.
3. Indonesia sets minimum wages for workers abroad. (1995). *Xinhua News Agency*, 5, 3.
4. Jacob, P. (1995). Blacklist for firms flouting Indonesian labour laws. (1995). *The Straits Times* (Singapore), 3, 1, 12.
5. Indonesia sets up new team to enforce wage hikes. (1995). *Xinhua News Agency*, 4, 5.
6. 202 companies taken to court for labor law violations in Indonesia. (1995). *Xinhua News Agency*, 5, 29.
7. Indonesian firms seek delay on minimum wage. (1995). *Xinhua News Agency*, 7, 7.
8. Indonesia pay dispute could spark unrest. (1994). *Reuter Textline*, 12, 4.
9. Heng, B. One Singapore worker's salary = Pay of 7 viets, indonesians. (1995). *The Straits Times* (Singapore), 4, 16, 1.
10. Fringe benefits. (1993). *Investing, Licensing & Trading*, 3, 1.
11. Working hours. (1995). *Investing, Licensing & Trading*, 1, 1.
12. Termination of employment. (1994). *Financing Foreign Operations*, 3, 1.
13. Child labor exploited in Indonesia. (1995). *Xinhua News Agency*, 7, 27.
14. Pension funds. (1995). *Financing Foreign Operations*, 4, 1.
15. Social security and labour legislation. (1991). *The Indonesian Times* (Jakarta), 7, 31, 8.
16. U.S. Department of State. (1992). *Indonesia, 1991, Human Rights Report*, 2.
17. Industrial labour. (1995). *Investing, Licensing & Trading*, 1, 1.
18. Human Rights Report, op. cit.
19. Economic forecast: deregulation will continue. (1994). *Country Forecast*, 8, 8.
20. Labour law. (1995). *Investing, Licensing & Trading*, 1, 1.

Chapter 10

1. Way, N. (1994). Indonesian experiment a tricky manoeuvre. *Business Review Weekly*, 7, 18.
2. Indonesia says better labour rights in own interest. (1994). *Reuters World Service*, 1, 20.
3. Wagstaff, J. (1994). Asia watch says Indonesia labour still falls short. *The Reuter Asia-Pacific Business Report*, 1, 24.
4. Murdoch, L. (1994). Activist's death was used to harm Indonesia. *The Age* (Melbourne), 1, 28, 7.
5. Indonesia dissenters say harassed by military. (1994). *Reuter News Service-Far East*, 9, 30.
6. Military says no proof yet in Marsinah case. (1995). *Reuter News Service-Far East*, 5, 19.
7. Sumptuous sumatra. (1994). *The Economist*, 9, 24, 39.
8. Oui, T. (1994). Don't meddle with rights, Jakarta tells Australian trade unions. *The Age* (Melbourne), 5, 10, 13.
9. U.S. Department of State. (1992). *1991 Human Rights Report*, 2.

10. A glut of workers in Indonesia, but few managers. (1991). *Business Asia*, 4, 8.
11. Colebatch, T. (1993). Indonesia's development dilemma. *The Age* (Melbourne), 8, 28.
12. Indonesian textile workers on strike over poor payment. (1992). *Xinhua News Agency*, 11, 4.
13. Sinaga, S. (1993). Indonesian industry suffers worker strikes. *Kyodo News Service*, 1, 2.
14. Ford, M. (1993). US warns Indonesia over worker rights. *Australian Financial Review*, 6, 30, 15.
15. S. Korean firms hit most by strikes in Indonesia. (1993). *Kyodo News Service*, 10, 4.
16. Wagstaff. J. (1994). Indonesia under pressure as strikes widen. *The Reuter Asia-Pacific Business Report*, 2, 3.
17. Nuraheni, E. (1994). Protestors wreck factory as Medan riots widen. *Reuters World Service*, 4, 19.
18. Shari, M. (1994) Jakarta strikers confident of support, government may force HK bank to meet demand. *South China Morning Post*, 2, 2, 14.
19. Seabrook, J. (1994). Indonesian workers risk freedom for their rights. *Guardian*, 10, 14.
20. Indonesia records 1, 130 labour strikes in 1994. (1994). *Reuter News Service-Far East*, 12, 28.
21. Economic liberalization has its limits. (1995). *Crossborder Monitor*, 2, 15.
22. Jacob, P. (1995). Jakarta's tough stance brings industrial peace. *The Straits Times* (Singapore), 3, 19, 8.
23. 6,000 workers launch protest, seek better welfare. (1995). *Kyodo News Service*, 7, 18.
24. Prickly heat. (1995). *Financial Times*, 7, 27, 17.
25. Pisani, E. (1991). Western nations must push Indonesia to allow unions. *The Reuter Library Report*, 5, 17.
26. U.S. Department of Labor, Bureau of International Labor Affairs. (1995). Foreign Labor Trends— Indonesia, 1992, Washington: USGPO.
27. Ford, M. (1995). Pressure on Indonesia to reform labour laws. *Australian Financial Review*, 8, 11, 12.
28. Jacob, P. (1993). Turning point for Indonesia. *The Straits Times*, 9, 12, 7.
29. Indonesia hits U.S. over remarks on labour record. (1995). *Reuter News Service-Far East*, 4, 25.
30. Ibid.
31. U.S. team probes labour situation. (1995). *The Asian Wall Street Journal Weekly*, 6, 26, 8.
32. Wagstaff, J. (1994). World union group protests Indonesian crackdown. *Reuter News Service-Far East*, 4, 28.
33. Indonesia denies pressuring workers. (1994). *Reuter News Service-Far East*, 4, 29.
34. Indonesia seeks to clarify arrest of labour leader. (1994). *Reuter News Service-Far East*, 8, 18.
35. Indonesian union boss hits out at arrest. (1994). *Reuter News Service-Far East*, 8, 19.
36. McHutchin, S. (1994). Australian trade union leader condemns arrest of head of Indonesian banned union. *Reuter Textline*, 8, 17.
37. Wagstaff, J. (1994). World labor body attacks Indonesia worker record. *Reuter News Service-Far East*, 10, 11.
38. Presidency says trade union rights must be respected. (1994). *Agence Europe*, 11, 25.
39. Indonesia trade union claims new harassment. (1995). *Reuter News Service-Far East*, 2, 8.
40. Evans, R. (1995). ILO raps three countries over union killings. *Reuter News Service-Far East*, 4, 6.
41. Yates, D. (1995). Freed indonesian union leader reunited with family. *Reuter News Service-Far East*, 5, 19.
42. Schauble, J. (1991). East Timor tragedy underlines a modern Indonesian dilemma. *Sunday Age* (Melbourne), 11, 17, 13.
43. Keynote address of labor secretary Robert. B. Reich to symposium on international labor standards and global integration. (1994). *Daily Labor Report*, 3, 29.

Part IV

1. Macek, P. (1994). Boom or bust? The heavy price of Thailand's economic development. *Swords & Ploughshares: A Chronicle of International Affairs*, 3, 2.

Chapter 11

1. Richburg, K.B. (1995). Opposition party wins plurality in Thai parliamentary elections. *The Washington Post*, 7, 3, A-16.
2. Shenon, P. (1995). Victors in thailand linked to vote-buying seek coalition. *The New York Times*, 7, 4, 2.
3. Sherer, P.M. (1995). Approval of amendments advances Thailand's move toward democracy. *The Asian Wall Street Journal Weekly*, 1, 9, 12.
4. Cumming-Bruce, N. (1995). Thailand passes democratic reforms. *Guardian*, 1, 5.
5. Political background: history. (1995). *Country Profile*, 8, m.
6. Country: Thailand. (1995). *KCWD Kaleidoscope*, 2, 20.8.
7. Shenon, op. cit.
8. Matthews, R. (1988). Poll will be test for democracy in Thai power system. *The Financial Times*, 5, 21, 3.
9. Shenon, op. cit.
10. Political background: international relations and defense. (1995). *Country Profile*, 1, 1.
11. U.S. Department of Labor, Bureau of International Labor Affairs. (1992). *Foreign Labor Trends Report—Thailand 1990–1991*.
12. Who's nicest? (1994). *The Economist*, 8, 13, 30.
13. Thailand: The poor won't benefit-human resource development plan. (1995). *The Bangkok Post*, 2, 26.
14. Thailand: steady as she goes. (1995). *Business Asia*, 6, 19.
15. Ibid.
16. Human resources—overview. (1995). *Investing, Licensing & Trading*, 1, 1.
17. Great expectations. (1995). *U.S. News & World Report*, 7, 10, IV.
18. Demographic and social trends. (1995). *Business International Forecasting*, 3, 3.
19. Stier, K. (1994). High wages bite workers who rode the boom. *Australian Financial Review*, 5, 12, 16.
20. Demographic and social trends, op. cit.
21. Charles, D. (1995). Weak dollar not seen hurting Thailand's economy. *Reuter News Service-Far East*, 3, 13.
22. Thailand-overseas business report. (1993). *Market Reports*, 1, 15.
23. Vause, W. G. (1992). Labor relations in Thailand. *East Asian Executive Reports*, 14, 11, 9.
24. U.S. Department of Labor, Bureau of International Labor Affairs. (1995). *Foreign Labor Trends—Thailand 1994–1995*, 11–13.
25. Ibid. 13–14.
26. Ibid. 8–9.
27. Ibid. 9–11.
28. Ibid. 10–12.
29. Ibid. 14–15.

Chapter 12

1. U.S. Department of Labor, Bureau of International Labor Affairs. (1995). *Foreign Labor Trends—Thailand 1993–1994*, 6, 7.
2. Ibid. 7, 8.
3. Ibid. 9.
4. Labour law. (1995). *Investing, Licensing & Trading*, 1, 1.
5. Ibid.
6. Ibid.
7. Thailand—overseas business report. (1993). *Market Reports*, 1, 15.
8. Civil and Commercial Code, Book 3, Title VII. *Hire of Services*, 575, 586.

9. Part-time and temporary help. (1995). *Investing, Licensing & Trading*, 1, 1.
10. Wages and fringe benefits. (1995). *Investing, Licensing & Trading*, 1, 1.
11. Working hours. (1995). *Investing, Licensing & Trading*, 1, 1.
12. Labour laws to restrict ordinary working time. (1995). *Bangkok Post*, 1, 1, 3.
13. Charas urges 2-shift working hours. (1994). *Bangkok Post*, 9, 3, 6.
14. Sukpanich, T. (1994). Call for action on labour, health and safety. *Bangkok Post*, 5, 1.
15. Cabinet to get proposals on leave. (1993). *Bangkok Post*, 4, 27, 3.
16. Social and demographic trends. (1989). *Business International Forecasting*, 10, 1.
17. Social security now covers 1.6 million employees. (1990). *Social and Labour Bulletin*, 4, 387.
18. Amended welfare act ups workers' benefits. (1995). *Bangkok Post*, 4, 15, 2.
19. Forsyth, T. (1994). Though not perfect, multinationals are some of Thailand's best employers. *Asia, Inc.*, 4, 34.
20. Muscat, R.J. (1994). *The Fifth Tiger: A Study of Thai Development Policy* (pp. 267–268). Armonk, NY.: M.E. Sharpe, Inc.

Chapter 13

1. Labour and wages. (1990). *Business International Forecasting*, 5, 1.
2. Labor rights to be restored. (1994). *Bangkok Post*, 9, 11.
3. Ibid.
4. Vause, G.W. (1992). Labor relations in Thailand. *East Asian Executive Reports*, 14, 11, 9.
5. Ibid.
6. Industrial labour. (1995). *Investing, Licensing & Trading*, 1, 1.
7. Piriyarongsons, S. & Poonpanich, K. (1994). Labour institutions in an export-oriented country: A case study of Thailand. In G. Rodgers (Ed.), *Workers, Institutions, and Economic Growth in Asia* (p. 230). Geneva: International Institute of Labour Studies.
8. Cabinet approves bill on enterprise labour relations.
9. Soul-searching: issues facing Thai workers. (1994). *Bangkok Post*, 5, 1.
10. Sukpanich, T. (1994). Call for action on labour, health and safety. *Bangkok Post*, 5, 1.
11. Piriyarongsan & Poonpanich, op. cit., 221.
12. Bangkok Post, Sept. 11, 1994, op. cit.
13. Ministry tells company to reinstate workers. (1995). *Bangkok Post*, 1, 21.
14. Minister gets details of labour problems. (1995). *Bangkok Post*, 2, 9.
15. Piriyarongsan & Poonpanich, op. cit., 228.
16. *Bangkok Post*, May 1, 1994, op. cit.
17. Nontarit, W. (1995). Labour leaders ask government not to forget workers. *Bangkok Post*, 1, 3, 3.
18. Vause, op. cit.
19. Infighting blamed for Thai labour movement weakness. (1994). *Bangkok Post*, 11, 28.
20. Piriyarongsan & Poonpanich, op. cit., 233.
21. *Business International Forecasting*, op. cit.
22. Piriyarongsan & Poonpanich, op. cit., 235–236.

Chapter 14

1. U.S. Department of State. (1995). *Market Reports*, 3.
2. U.S. Department of State. (1995). *Market Reports*, 6, 15.
3. Employers want pay reduced in provinces. (1995). *Bangkok Post*, 1, 11, 6.
4. Annual rate for minimum wage favoured. (1995). *Bangkok Post*, 4, 7.
5. Workers call for minimum wage rise. (1995). *Bangkok Post*, 4, 5, 6.

6. Labour experts are for wage increase. (1994). *Bangkok Post*, 1, 5, 3.
7. Tumcharoen, S. (1994). 5-baht rise hinges on "good explanation." *Bangkok Post*, 1, 17, 1.
8. Workers rally for wage rise. (1994). *Bangkok Post*, 5, 7, 2.
9. Time to rethink what minimum wage means—editorial. (1993). *Bangkok Post*, 3, 4, 4.
10. Phoenix workers plan rally to support 27% pay claim. (1995). *Bangkok Post*, 1, 14, 6.
11. Shinada, S. (1995). Thai wages rise on tide of Japanese investment—skilled workers in short supply. *Nikkei Weekly*, 3, 6.
12. Workers urge pm to review pay rise move. (1994). *Bangkok Post*, 9, 27, 3.
13. Fires and explosions; toy factory, Bangkok, Thailand. (1994). *Lloyds List*, 5, 19.
14. Ministry focuses on plight of labourers. (1995). *Bangkok Post*, 2, 24, 6.
15. U.S. Department of State. (1994). *Market Reports*, 4, 20.
16. Buakamsri, T. (1994). The dark side of industrial boom. *Bangkok Post*, 5, 13, 10.
17. Lamphun deaths prompt house review. (1994). *Bangkok Post*, 5, 13, 3.
18. Doctors call for centres to look into workers' illnesses. (1994). *Bangkok Post*, 5, 4, 7.
19. Health official probed after talking to media. (1994). *Bangkok Post*, 6, 8, 3.
20. Call for upgrading of safety standards. (1994). *Bangkok Post*, 9, 6, 6.
21. Government reveals plans to compile work-related health concerns. (1995). *Bangkok Post*, 3, 1, 6.
22. Soul-searching—issues facing Thai workers. (1994). *Bangkok Post*, 5, 1.
23. Child workers: minimum age limit raised. (1988). *The Nation* (Bangkok), 2, 13, 20; 6, 15.
24. Child labor. (1992). *East Asian Executive Reports*, 11, 15.
25. PM orders child labour law review. (1991). *Bangkok Post*, 11, 4, 1.
26. Janchitfah, S. (1995). No labour of love for child workers. *Bangkok Post*, 5, 7.
27. Children's day—labour issues. (1995). *Bangkok Post*, 1, 15.
28. Siengthai, S. & Leelakulthanit, O. (1993). Women in management in Thailand. *Int. Studies of Mgt. & Org.*, 23, 4, 87–102.
29. Piriyaraangsan, S. & Poonpanich, K. (1994). Labour institutions in an export-oriented country: A case study of Thailand. In Rodgers, G. (Ed.), *Workers, Institutions and Economic Growth in Asia* (p. 247). Geneva: International Institute of Labour Studies.
30. Market Reports, op. cit.
31. *Bankok Post.* (1995). 2, 1.
32. Rodgers, op. cit.
33. World Bank. (1989). *Thailand: A country economic memorandum, building on the recent success—a policy framework*. Report No. 7445-TH, vol. 1: The main report. Washington.
34. Telecommunications and power may set privatization trend; part II: privatization experience, TOT power sector. (1993). *East Asian Executive Reports*, 8, 15, 24.
35. State role in the economy. (1993). *Investing, Licensing & Trading*, 12, 1.

Chapter 15

1. Teunissen, H.J.J. (1986). Recommendation on minimum international labor standards. *The American Journal of International Law*, 80, 4, 385.
2. Schlossberg, S. I. (1989). United States participation in the ILO: redefining the role. *Comparative Labor Law Journal*, 11, 48–49, 57–58.
3. Fields, G.S. (1990). Labor standards, economic developments and international trade. In S. Herzenberg & J. F. Perez-Lopez (Eds.), *Labor Standards and Developments in the Global Economy* (pp. 19, 31–32). Washington: U.S. Department of Labor.
4. See *Benz v. Compania Naviera Hidalgo, S.A.*, 353 U.S. 138, 143–44 (1957), (declaring that United States labor law is concerned with industrial strife between American employers and employees.)
5. See Schoenberger, K. (1992). The model here isn't America. *Los Angeles Times*, 1, 30, A-1, quoting Malaysian Prime Minister Mahathir Mohamed's statement to a group of American businessmen that "the hedonistic materialism of present (Western) models (of developments) is not for us." See also

Lewis, P. (1993). Splits may dampen rights conference; some standards don't apply to third world, it says. *New York Times*, 6, 6, at A 1, A 14.

6. International union report places U.S. among violators of basic rights. (1993). *Labor Relations Week*, 7, 5, 5, 441.

7. International unions accuse Food Lion of unfair practices in United States. (1993). *Labor Relations Week*, 7, 6, 16, 577–578.

8. See Bilder, R.B. (1992). (2nd ed.). An overview of international human rights law. In Hannum, H. (Ed.), *Guide to International Human Rights Practices*. New York: The Free Press.

9. Child labour abuse must stop, says government. (1995). *Bangkok Post*, 1, 14.

10. Ministry focuses on plight of labourers. (1995). *Bangkok Post*, 2, 24, 6.

11. Sukpanich, T. (1994). Call for action on labour, health and safety. *Bangkok Post*, 5, 1.

12. ICFTU aims tough blow at Thailand. (1991). *Bangkok Post*, 7, 2, 1.

13. U.S. trade threat targets Thai labour standards. (1993). *Bangkok Post*, 11, 29, 21.

14. Children's day-labour issues. (1995). *Bangkok Post*, 1, 15.

15. Dollah, S. R. ASEAN raps linkage of workers rights with WTO. (1994). *Japan Economic Newswire*, 7, 21.

16. Rights activists get cold reception. (1994). *Bangkok Post*, 7, 26.

17. Thailand slams west for linking workers' rights, trade. (1994). *Japan Economic Newswire*, 7, 22.

18. Soh, F. (1995). ILO dismisses cheap imports lead to losses claim. *The Straits Times* (Singapore), 3, 9, 3.

19. How the GSP system affects Thailand. (1994). *Bangkok Post*, 9, 5, 23.

20. Tougher rules on jobs agencies. (1993). *Bangkok Post*, 8, 5, 21.

21. Thai workers in Japan face hardship. (1994). *Bangkok Post*, 4, 16, 6.

22. Illness, suicide claim lives of 30 Thais in Japan. (1994). *Bangkok Post*, 5, 29, 1.

23. Governments urged to sign rights convention. (1995). *Bangkok Post*, 2, 6, 6.

24. Labour shortage boon for Thai workers. (1990). *Bangkok Post*, 6, 4, 16.

25. Thai government says it is trying to end flood of illegal workers. (1994). *China Economic News Service*, 3, 5.

26. CLA's threat of a freeze puts squeeze on Thai government. (1994). *China Economic News Service*, 3, 10.

27. Top labour official to face probe over "mismanagement." (1994). *Bangkok Post*, 7, 2, 6.

28. Service fees for sending Thais to Taiwan. (1994). *Bangkok Post*, 4, 8, 6.

29. Labour officials accused of graft. (1994). *Bangkok Post*, 5, 25.

30. SUNDS still killing Thais in Singapore. (1994). *Bangkok Post*, 6, 11.

31. Vatona blasts Thai "champagne" envoy. (1990). *Bangkok Post*, 4, 20.

32. Groups seek funds from ministry. (1994). *Bangkok Post*, 5, 8.

33. Foreign workers needed in Thai textile industry. (1995). *Xinhua News Agency*, 6, 5.

Part V

1. Compa L. (1993). International labor rights and the sovereignty question: NAFTA and Guatemala, two case studies. *The American University Journal of International Law & Policy*, 9, 117.

2. Prime minister supports in-house unions. (1983). *New Straits Times* (Malaysia), 3, 17.

Chapter 16

1. Malaysia-only a few worries. (1995). *Business Asia*, 1, 16, 9.

2. U.S. Department of State. (1994). *Malaysia Human Rights Practices, 1993*, 1, 31.

3. Political background: history. (1994). *Economist Intelligence Unit*, 1, 1.

4. Political background: the constitution. (1994). *Economist Intelligence Unit*, 1, 1.

5. Political background: political forces. (1994). *Economist Intelligence Unit*, 1, 1.
6. Business Asia, op. cit.
7. Political forces, op. cit.
8. Yunus, K. (1994). Ah Lek slams union leaders who seek foreigners' help. *Business Times* (Malaysia), 1, 15.
9. PM—be wary of western media control, influence. (1994). *Business Times* (Malaysia), 3, 14.
10. Mills, S. (1994). Progress, but not at any cost—Anwar—human rights. *Australian Financial Review*, 5, 25, 12.
11. Bin Hassan, M.J. (1995). Malaysia in 1994. *Asian Survey*, 35, 2, 186–188.
12. Ibid.
13. Kaur, H. (1993). Malaysia's economic success fostering some unwanted traits? *Business Times* (Malaysia), 6, 3, 20.
14. Yunus, K. (1993). Nation needs 700,000 workers during 1990–98. *Business Times* (Malaysia), 11, 26, 2.
15. Malaysian Human Rights Practices, 1993, op. cit.
16. U.S. Central Intelligence Agency. (1994). *World Factbook: Malaysia 1994*.
17. Malaysia-economic policy & trade practices. (1991). *Market Report*, 2.
18. The new economic policy. (1993). *Pacific Viewpoint*, 3, 93–94.
19. Bosses and workers told to make sacrifices. (1993). *Business Times* (Malaysia), 5, 1, 24.

Chapter 17

1. Labour law. (1994). *Investing, Licensing & Trading*, 5, 1.
2. U.S. Department of State. (1993). *Malaysia Human Rights Practices, 1993*, 12.
3. Yeow, J. (1994). Amendment to give faster recognition to trade unions. *Business Times* (Malaysia), 7, 20.
4. Malaysia Human Rights Practices, 1993, op. cit.
5. Mansor, L. (1994). Trade unions act to be amended—Lim. *Business Times* (Malaysia), 4, 8, 1.
6. Amendments to employment act. (1994). *Business Times* (Malaysia), 11, 25, 2.
7. The Malaysian government is considering legal means of countering the threatened strike by the civil servants and public sector unions (CUEPACS). (1985). *Business Times* (Malaysia), 10, 14.
8. Kuala Lumpur's bid to change labor laws draws mixed review. (1988). *Business Asia*, 20, 51, 12, 19.
9. Malaysian Human Rights Practices, 1993, op. cit.
10. Dispute settlement. (1993). *Business Times* (Malaysia), 5, 5.
11. 18-month forecasts of labor costs. (1992). *Political Risk Services*, 2, 1.
12. Labor in Malaysia; part II; collective bargaining and disputes, strikes, wages and benefits, labor shortage. (1993). *East Asian Executive Reports*, 15, 4, 15, 16.
13. Fringe benefits. (1993). *Investing, Licensing & Trading*, 5, 1.
14. Working hours. (1994). *Financing Foreign Operations*, 3, 1.
15. Investing, Licensing & Trading, op. cit.
16. Fringe benefits. (1994). *Business Times* (Malaysia), 1, 31, 20.
17. East Asian Executive Reports, op. cit.
18. Weng, H.C. (1994). Car loans most common among fringe benefits given to workers-MEF. *Business Times* (Malaysia), 1, 31, 20.
19. Fringe benefits. Investing, Licensing & Trading, op. cit.
20. Sulaiman, S.J. (1994). Sharp rise in number of industrial accidents. *Business Times* (Malaysia), 6, 7, 2.
21. Don't view staff protection as a cost burden. (1994). *Business Times* (Malaysia), 3, 22, 2.
22. East Asian Executive Reports, op. cit.
23. Ibid.
24. U.S. Department of Labor. (1995). *Foreign Labor Trends—Malaysia, 1993–1994*, 7, 8.
25. East Asian Executive Reports, op. cit.
26. Ibid.

27. K'Zamen, B. (1993). Private sector can raise retirement age to 60. *Business Times* (Malaysia), 8, 24, 2.

28. Singh, B. (1994). Vital for employer to take proper steps before firing employee. *Business Times* (Malaysia), 4, 20.

29. Singh, B. (1994). Workers' rights related to termination of employment. *Business Times* (Malaysia), 1, 12.

30. K'Zamen, B. (1994). No case for retrenchment of work continues to exist. *Business Times* (Malaysia), 2, 15, 2.

31. Mansor, L. (1994). Ministry may amend industrial relations act. *Business Times* (Malaysia), 4, 7, 2.

32. Mansor, L. (1994). Labour department probes retrenchment case. *Business Times* (Malaysia), 2, 23. 20.

33. K'Zamen, B. (1994). Can maker on verge of resolving dispute with union. *Business Times* (Malaysia), 5, 26, 18.

34. Sadiq, J. (1993). MEF proposes review of employment laws, strategies. *Business Times* (Malaysia), 10, 15.

35. Tripartite committee to review labor laws. (1994). *Business Times* (Malaysia), 4, 22, 1.

36. Freeman, R.B. (1994). Repressive labor relations and new unionism in East Asia. *Proceedings of the Forty-Sixth annual meeting, Boston, January 3–5, 1994*, Industrial Relations Research Series (Madison, WI: Industrial Relations Research Association), 231–238.

Chapter 18

1. Unions and work stoppages. (1989). *Business International*, 12, 1.

2. U.S. Department of Labor. (1995). *Foreign Labor Trends—Malaysia, 1993—1994*, 8–9.

3. Business International, op. cit.; 10 MTUC members to attend MLO meeting. (1989). *Business Times* (Malaysia), 5, 12, 16.

4. MLO informs ICFTU of its existence. (1990). *Business Times* (Malaysia), 7, 31, 16.

5. Foreign Labor Trends, op. cit.

6. K'Zaman, B. (1994). CUEPACS appointed delegates to world labor meeting. *Business Times* (Malaysia), 5, 24.

7. MTUC wants to be worker delegate. (1994). *Business Times* (Malaysia), 5, 18, 24.

8. Ahmad, B. (1994). ILO panel retains CUEPACS as Malaysia's worker delegate. (1994). *Business Times* (Malaysia), 6, 25, 20.

9. Attan, A. (1994). Don't let bickering drown out our voice in Geneva. *Business Times* (Malaysia), 5, 16.

10. Ibid.

11. Sadiq, J. (1993). MTUC chief-SOCSO appointments unfair. *Business Times* (Malaysia), 8, 11, 2.

12. 18-month forecast of labor costs. (1992). *Political Risk Services*, 12, 1.

13. MTUC hopes to foster close ties with government. (1994). *Business Times* (Malaysia), 1, 1, 24.

14. Attan, A. (1994). MTUC—A change in approach to create more positive image. (1994). *Business Times* (Malaysia), 1, 5, 20.

15. MTUC agrees to accept leaders nominated by government. (1994). *Business Times* (Malaysia), 1, 13, 2.

16. K'Zaman, B. (1993). Government cautions of MTUC's sudden change of stand—Lim. *Business Times* (Malaysia), 4, 20, 2.

17. Malaysian labor costs likely to be lowered by labor law changes. (1987). *Business Asia*, 4, 6, 19, 14.

18. Unions and work stoppages. (1990). *Investing, Licensing & Trading*, 12, 1.

19. Mansor, L. (1993). Tripartite approach vital in handling labor issues—Lim. *Business Times* (Malaysia), 10, 5, 2.

20. K'Zaman, B. (1994). Amend or drop section 9 of safety act-MTUC. *Business Times* (Malaysia), 2, 12.

21. Economic and trade policy. (1992). *Market Reports*, 3.

22. Civil service unions oppose wage freeze proposal. (1987). *Country Report*, 3, 12.

23. Market Reports, op. cit.

24. Unions and work stoppages. (1990). *Investing, Licensing & Trading*, 12, 1.

25. Ebnet, D. (1980). Private sector employees asking for wage hikes. *East Asian Executive Reports*, 2, 10, 11.
26. Ghazali, A. (1994). Bank officers get 13 percent rise in pay under new agreement. *Business Times* (Malaysia), 7, 13, 2.
27. Labor in Malaysia, part II: collective bargaining and disputes, strikes, wages and benefits, labor shortage. (1993). *East Asian Executive Reports*, 4, 15, 15, 4, 16.
28. Four more chairmen for industrial court. (1993). *Business Times* (Malaysia), 9, 3, 3.
29. Maybank officers picket. (1993). *Business Times* (Malaysia), 8, 3.
30. Ghazali, G. (1994). Shell union threatens to seek overseas aid in row. *Business Times* (Malaysia), 1, 15, 2.
31. Yunus, K. (1994). Report on LRC Malaysia's industrial dispute submitted. *Business Times* (Malaysia), 7, 14, 2.
32. ILO to scrutinize Malaysian labour practices. (1994). *Reuter News Service-Far East*, 5, 3.
33. Attan, A. (1994). Too many jobs chasing too few workers. *Business Times* (Malaysia), 1, 6, 4.
34. Haron, S. (1993). Prime Minister—be wary of false sympathy. *Business Times* (Malaysia), 8, 7, 24.

Chapter 19

1. Jones. P.M. (1986). Under fire, unions around the world adapt to change. *Scholastic Update*, 2, 7, 118, 12.
2. Malaysia allows the unionisation of the electronics industry. (1988). *Asian Wall Street Journal Weekly*, 9, 26, 1, 8.
3. Government relaxes union ban in foreign-owned electronics industry. (1988). *Malaysian Business*, 10, 16.
4. Electronics bullish on Malaysian prospects: USA rejects workers' rights. (1989). *Country Report*, 6, 2.
5. Sappani, K. (1990). Malaysia's high-tech workers get low-tech pay. *Japan Economic Newswire*, 6, 29.
6. Duthie, S. (1990). Electronics union in Malaysia stifled by merging of firms. *Asian Wall Street Journal Weekly*, 10, 1, 26.
7. Dennis, W. & Firth, P. (1992). Big firms make working in electronics industry no holiday. *Electronic Times*, 6, 25.
8. Labour and wages. (1992). *Country Report*, 8, 24.
9. Unions and work stoppages. (1993). *Investing, Licensing & Trading*, 5, 1.
10. Lim—MTUC can raise unionisation issue at ILO. (1993). *Business Times* (Malaysia), 5, 25.
11. Yunus, K. (1993). G-7 has no national electronics unions. *Business Times* (Malaysia), 11, 20.
12. Political outlook: foreign relations. (1994). *Country Forecast*, 1, 14.
13. Hamid, A.J. (1994). Malaysia's microchip makers moving up market. *The Reuter European Business Report*, 2, 20.
14. Collective bargaining wage fixing system rigid. (1994). *Business Times* (Malaysia), 4, 1, 17.
15. Union leaders propose flexiwage modifications. (1990). *Business Times* (Malaysia), 7, 17, 1.
16. Bank employees agree to flexiwage deal. (1990). *Business Times* (Malaysia), 7, 28, 2.
17. Union trouble lies ahead in Malaysia. (1991). *Business Asia*, 4, 8.
18. Labour, wage news: civil servants and other workers' wages. (1992). *Country Report*, 2, 25.
19. Labour and wages. (1992). *Country Report*, 8, 24.
20. Study recommends flexible wage policy. (1990). *Business Times* (Malaysia), 5, 4, 26.
21. Reform for growth. (1994). *Business Times* (Malaysia), 7, 14, 4.
22. Ghazali, A. (1994). Flexiwage system issue re-emerges. *Business Times* (Malaysia), 7, 20, 4.
23. Ghazali, A. (1994). MEF urges government to draw up guidelines. *Business Times* (Malaysia), 7, 22, 20.
24. Abdul, T.S.A. (1994). Linking wages with productivity and profitability. Presentation to economic planning unit, director-general, Malaysian employers federation national conference in Langkawi, Malaysia, 8, 29.

25. Ghazali, July 20, 1994, op. cit.
26. Country Report, February 25, 1992, op. cit.
27. Country Report, August 24, 1992, op. cit.
28. Human resources and wages. (1992). *Country Report*, 8, 24.
29. Ghazali, A. (1994). A better appraisal system in the works. *Business Times* (Malaysia), 8, 1, 2.
30. Ghazali, A. (1994). Potential windfall for blue-collar government servants. *Business Times* (Malaysia), 9, 16, 2.
31. Sulaiman, M. (1993). The plantation industry in Malaysia: its importance to the national economy and strategies for continued viability. In K. Ragupathy (Ed.), *Facing 2020: The challenges to the plantation industry* (p. 21). Kuala Lumpur: Institute for Strategic and International Studies.
32. Navamukundan, A. (1985). Structural changes in the Malaysian plantation sector. In *The socio-economic implications of structural changes in plantations in Asian countries* (p. 60). Geneva: International Labour Organization.
33. Ramachondran, S. (1994). *Indian plantation labour in Malaysia*. Kuala Lumpur: Abdul Majid and Co. for The Institute of Social Analysis.
34. *Third Malaysian Plan.* 1976–1980. Kuala Lumpur: Government Printer, 74.
35. Ibid., 174.
36. Labour problems in Malaysia's rubber and oil-palm plantations. (1985). *The Asian Wall Street Journal Weekly*, 5, 11, 1, 7.
37. Yunus, K. (1993). Unskilled aliens—ban may be lifted. *Business Times* (Malaysia), 11, 27, 2.
38. Ramachandran, S., and Shanmugam, B. (1995). Plight of plantation workers in Malaysia: defeated by definitions. *Asian Survey*, 35, 4, 4, 396–397.
39. Ibid. 398.
40. Ibid. 399.
41. Ramachondram & Shanmugam, op. cit., 399–400.
42. Plantation strike ends after four days. (1990). *The Asian Wall Street Journal Weekly*, 2, 5.
43. Country Report, February 25, 1992, op. cit.
44. Mansor, L. (1994). National minimum wage not suitable, says Lim. *Business Times* (Malaysia), 3, 31, 22.
45. U.S. Department of State. (1994). *Malaysian Human Rights Practices, 1993*.
46. Ghazali, A. (1994). No plans to widen contributions to fund, says Mahalingam. *Business Times* (Malaysia), 12, 9.
47. Kulim to increase mechanisation. (1994). *Business Times* (Malaysia), 6, 30.
48. Attan, A. (1994). Too many jobs chasing too few workers. *Business Times* (Malaysia), 1, 6, 4.
49. Hamsawi, R. (1994). Some hiccups in joint commission meeting. *Business Times* (Malaysia), 5, 30.
50. *Business Times* (Malaysia). (1994). 1, 6, 4.

Chapter 20

1. Compa, L. (1993). International labor rights and the sovereignty question: NAFTA and Guatemala, two case studies. *The American University Journal of International Law & Policy*, 117–118.
2. GSP petitions against Kuala Lumpur may fail. (1990). *Business Times* (Singapore), 6, 14, 9.
3. GSP—a crutch or a whip? (1994). *Business Times* (Malaysia), 6, 4, 4.
4. Link of trade to labor defied. (1995). *The Asia Wall Street Journal Weekly*, 4, 10.
5. Malaysia wants third world unity against wage-trade link. (1994). *Japan Economic Newswire*, 4, 7.
6. K'Zaman, B. & Mansor, L. (1994). MTUC backs prime minister's stand against minimum wage bid. *Business Times* (Malaysia), 3, 30, 20.
7. Ismail, R. (1994). MEF against international minimum wage. *Business Times* (Malaysia), 4, 20, 3.
8. Labour of rights. (1994). *Business Times* (Malaysia), 6, 8, P-4.
9. Ahmad, B. (1994). ILO aid should not hinge on ratification of its standards. *Business Times* (Malaysia), 6, 17, 20.

10. No to social clause. (1994). *Business Times* (Malaysia), 6, 24, 4.
11. Ghazali, F. (1994), ASEAN's objection to social clause link gets UK support. *Business Times* (Malaysia), 6, 30, 2.
12. Goodhart, D. (1994). For love of labour: can the debate on minimum labor standards be moved beyond caricature? *Financial Times*, 11, 2, 21.

Chapter 21

1. Indonesian democracy faces many obstacles. (1995). *Bangkok Post*, 3, 28, 4.
2. *Far Eastern Economic Review.* (1987). 8, 13.
3. *Australian Financial Review.* (1990). 8, 30.
4. *Business Times* (Malaysia). (1993). 8, 24.

Index